Business Associations 2021 Statutory Supplement

Douglas Irion
UCLA School of Law

Lynn M. LoPucki
Security Pacific Bank Distinguished Professor of Law
UCLA School of Law

D1412116

Table of Contents

Preface

We designed this Statutory Supplement for use with Lynn M. LoPucki and Andrew Verstein, *Business Associations: A Systems Approach* (Aspen 2020). But it will accomplish its purposes when used with any of the Business Associations or Corporations casebooks typically used in American law schools. Those purposes are first to enable students to read the statutes more carefully than they can electronic copies; second to enable students to mark the statutes with hand-held markers rather than the more cumbersome tools of pdf or other electronic access systems; third, to see each of the statutes as a whole through its table of contents; fourth, to browse the statute by flipping pages; fifth, to compare sections merely by turning pages; and sixth, to provide a copy usable on open book exams when electronic access is not permitted. These methods enable students to use the statutes and become familiar with them.

Electronic copies of statutes provide different advantages. The most important is the ability to conduct word searches. Accordingly, we recommend that students use both hard and electronic copies together. As of this writing, free pdfs of all but two of the documents in this book are available through the links posted on the website for this book at lopucki.com. The Restatement (Third) Agency and Article 8 of the Uniform Commercial Code are available free to students through Westlaw or Lexis.

Both the Uniform Laws Commission and the American Bar Association date their statutes in confusing ways. To give just two examples, the current version of the Model Business Corporation Act is labeled the 2016 version, but it contains amendments made as late as 2019. The current version of the Uniform Partnership Act is labeled the 1997 version, but it contains substantial amendments made in 2013.

When combined with the careless practices of some competing statutory supplements, the poor practices of the promulgators can lead teachers to disaster. One of us learned that the hard way in the fall of 2016. He prepared problems and materials for his class that were linked to the statutes by section numbers. When the statutory supplement arrived in mid-summer, he dutifully checked the years of the statutes to make sure none had changed. Unbeknownst to him, the statutory supplement editors had switched from one version of the "1997" statutes to a later version of the "1997" statute. The latter version had different section numbers. The results were a lot of extra work for the teacher, frustration for the students, and terrible course evaluations.

This book contains the most recent version of each statute or other document. Readers can easily determine the year of each statute because it appears in parentheses after the statute's name. If the promulgators changed their statutes, that fact will be immediately apparent from a glance at the statute's title in this book. Although the most recent version of a model or uniform law may not be the version most widely adopted, we prefer it because it contains the most recent thinking of the experts who revise the statute. The "most widely adopted" version is an elusive quality anyway. Many states make statutory changes piecemeal, resulting in hybrid versions. Nor is teaching the most widely adopted version helpful to students. The most widely adopted version will hold that status for only a brief period of time.

For each of the documents in this book (except the Restatement (Third) Agency and the Securities Exchange Act) we include all of the sections and none of the comments. Some competing statutory supplements include only selected sections and comments. That can be a problem when the user needs a section that has been omitted. Students who need a comment can always find it in their electronic version of the statutes.

This statutory supplement contains several other useful features not found in other statutory supplements. They include a table of contents for each document; running heads that show the document, the document part, and the section number; square paragraphs with bold section numbers that avoid all ambiguity; and full paragraph indentation to clearly communicate their hierarchy. These features are uniform across all the documents.

The feature students may like best about this book is the price. We plan to hold our price at less than half of what the major law-school book publishers are charging.

We provide this book through KDP Publishing. KDP's low cost and flexibility make it possible for us to offer versions of this book that contain different statutes. If you would like to teach the statutes of your state or the LLC law of Delaware, please contact us to discuss the feasibility of our providing exactly what you want.

Douglas Irion
UCLA School of Law

Lynn M. LoPucki
Security Pacific Bank Distinguished Professor of Law
UCLA School of Law

Acknowledgments

We are grateful to Tom Price for solving the difficult word processing issues and to Frank Lopez and Tom Price for the cover design.

The following organizations have granted permission to reproduce the laws indicated:

The American Bar Association

The American Law Institute

The National Conference of Commissioners on Uniform State Laws

The Permanent Editorial Board for the Uniform Commercial Code

The Uniform Law Commission

Restatement (Third) of Agency (2006)

Table of Contents

Chapter 1. Introductory Matters

§ 1.01 Agency Defined

Agency is the fiduciary relationship that arises when one person (a "principal") manifests assent to another person (an "agent") that the agent shall act on the principal's behalf and subject to the principal's control, and the agent manifests assent or otherwise consents so to act.

§ 1.02 Parties' Labeling and Popular Usage Not Controlling

An agency relationship arises only when the elements stated in § 1.01 are present. Whether a relationship is characterized as agency in an agreement between parties or in the context of industry or popular usage is not controlling.

§ 1.03 Manifestation

A person manifests assent or intention through written or spoken words or other conduct.

§ 1.04 Terminology

(1) Coagents. Coagents have agency relationships with the same principal. A coagent may be appointed by the principal or by another agent actually or apparently authorized by the principal to do so.

(2) Disclosed, undisclosed, and unidentified principals.

    (a) Disclosed principal. A principal is disclosed if, when an agent and a third party interact, the third party has notice that the agent is acting for a principal and has notice of the principal's identity.

    (b) Undisclosed principal. A principal is undisclosed if, when an agent and a third party interact, the third party has no notice that the agent is acting for a principal.

    (c) Unidentified principal. A principal is unidentified if, when an agent and a third party interact, the third party has notice that the agent is acting for a principal but does not have notice of the principal's identity.

(3) Gratuitous agent. A gratuitous agent acts without a right to compensation.

(4) Notice. A person has notice of a fact if the person knows the fact, has reason to know the fact, has received an effective notification of the fact, or should know the fact to fulfill a duty owed to another person. Notice of a fact that an agent knows or has reason to know is imputed to the principal as stated in §§ 5.03 and 5.04. A notification given to or by an agent is effective as notice to or by the principal as stated in § 5.02.

(5) Person. A person is

    (a) an individual;

    (b) an organization or association that has legal capacity to possess rights and incur obligations;

    (c) a government, political subdivision, or instrumentality or entity created by government; or

    (d) any other entity that has legal capacity to possess rights and incur obligations.

(6) Power given as security. A power given as security is a power to affect the legal relations of its creator that is created in the form of a manifestation of actual authority and held for the benefit of the holder or a third person. It is given to protect a legal or equitable title or to secure the performance of a duty apart from any duties owed the holder of the power by its creator that are incident to a relationship of agency under § 1.01.

(7) Power of attorney. A power of attorney is an instrument that states an agent's authority.

(8) Subagent. A subagent is a person appointed by an agent to perform functions that the agent has consented to perform on behalf of the agent's principal and for whose conduct the appointing agent is responsible to the principal. The relationship between an appointing agent and a subagent is one of agency, created as stated in § 1.01.

(9) Superior and subordinate coagents. A superior coagent has the right, conferred by the principal, to direct a subordinate coagent.

(10) Trustee and agent-trustee. A trustee is a holder of property who is subject to fiduciary duties to deal with the property for the benefit of charity or for one or more persons, at least one of whom is not the sole trustee. An agent-trustee is a trustee subject to the control of the settlor or of one or more beneficiaries.

Chapter 2. Principles of Attribution

§ 2.01 Actual Authority

An agent acts with actual authority when, at the time of taking action that has legal consequences for the principal, the agent reasonably believes, in accordance with the principal's manifestations to the agent, that the principal wishes the agent so to act.

§ 2.02 Scope of Actual Authority

(1) An agent has actual authority to take action designated or implied in the principal's manifestations to the agent and acts necessary or incidental to achieving the principal's objectives, as the agent reasonably understands the principal's manifestations and objectives when the agent determines how to act.

(2) An agent's interpretation of the principal's manifestations is reasonable if it reflects any meaning known by the agent to be ascribed by the principal and, in the absence of any meaning known to the agent, as a reasonable person in the agent's position would interpret the manifestations in light of the context, including circumstances of which the agent has notice and the agent's fiduciary duty to the principal.

(3) An agent's understanding of the principal's objectives is reasonable if it accords with the principal's manifestations and the inferences that a reasonable person in the agent's position would draw from the circumstances creating the agency.

§ 2.03 Apparent Authority

Apparent authority is the power held by an agent or other actor to affect a principal's legal relations with third parties when a third party reasonably believes the actor has authority to act on behalf of the principal and that belief is traceable to the principal's manifestations.

§ 2.04 Respondeat Superior

An employer is subject to liability for torts committed by employees while acting within the scope of their employment.

§ 2.05 Estoppel to Deny Existence of Agency Relationship

A person who has not made a manifestation that an actor has authority as an agent and who is not otherwise liable as a party to a transaction purportedly done by the actor on that person's account is subject to liability to a third party who justifiably is induced to make a detrimental change in position because the transaction is believed to be on the person's account, if

(1) the person intentionally or carelessly caused such belief, or

(2) having notice of such belief and that it might induce others to change their positions, the person did not take reasonable steps to notify them of the facts.

Chapter 3. Creation and Termination of Authority and Agency Relationships

§ 3.01 Creation of Actual Authority

Actual authority, as defined in § 2.01, is created by a principal's manifestation to an agent that, as reasonably understood by the agent, expresses the principal's assent that the agent take action on the principal's behalf.

§ 3.03 Creation of Apparent Authority

Apparent authority, as defined in § 2.03, is created by a person's manifestation that another has authority to act with legal consequences for the person who makes the manifestation, when a third party reasonably believes the actor to be authorized and the belief is traceable to the manifestation.

§ 3.14 Agents with Multiple Principals

An agent acting in the same transaction or matter on behalf of more than one principal may be one or both of the following:

(a) a subagent, as stated in § 3.15; or

(b) an agent for coprincipals, as stated in § 3.16.

§ 3.15 Subagency

(1) A subagent is a person appointed by an agent to perform functions that the agent has consented to perform on behalf of the agent's principal and for whose conduct the appointing agent is responsible to the principal. The relationships between a subagent and the appointing agent and between the subagent and the appointing agent's principal are relationships of agency as stated in § 1.01.

(2) An agent may appoint a subagent only if the agent has actual or apparent authority to do so.

§ 3.16 Agent for Coprincipals

Two or more persons may as coprincipals appoint an agent to act for them in the same transaction or matter.

Chapter 4. Ratification

§ 4.01 Ratification Defined

(1) Ratification is the affirmance of a prior act done by another, whereby the act is given effect as if done by an agent acting with actual authority.

(2) A person ratifies an act by

(a) manifesting assent that the act shall affect the person's legal relations, or

(b) conduct that justifies a reasonable assumption that the person so consents.

(3) Ratification does not occur unless

(a) the act is ratifiable as stated in § 4.03,

(b) the person ratifying has capacity as stated in § 4.04,

(c) the ratification is timely as stated in § 4.05, and

(d) the ratification encompasses the act in its entirety as stated in § 4.07.

§ 4.03 Acts That May Be Ratified

A person may ratify an act if the actor acted or purported to act as an agent on the person's behalf.

§ 4.05 Timing of Ratification

A ratification of a transaction is not effective unless it precedes the occurrence of circumstances that would cause the ratification to have adverse and inequitable effects on the rights of third parties. These circumstances include:

(1) any manifestation of intention to withdraw from the transaction made by the third party;

(2) any material change in circumstances that would make it inequitable to bind the third party, unless the third party chooses to be bound; and

(3) a specific time that determines whether a third party is deprived of a right or subjected to a liability.

§ 4.06 Knowledge Requisite to Ratification

A person is not bound by a ratification made without knowledge of material facts involved in the original act when the person was unaware of such lack of knowledge.

§ 4.07 No Partial Ratification

A ratification is not effective unless it encompasses the entirety of an act, contract, or other single transaction.

Chapter 5. Notifications and Notice

§ 5.01 Notifications and Notice—In General

(1) A notification is a manifestation that is made in the form required by agreement among parties or by applicable law, or in a reasonable manner in the absence of an agreement or an applicable law, with the intention of affecting the legal rights and duties of the notifier in relation to rights and duties of persons to whom the notification is given.

(2) A notification given to or by an agent is effective as notification to or by the principal as stated in § 5.02.

(3) A person has notice of a fact if the person knows the fact, has reason to know the fact, has received an effective notification of the fact, or should know the fact to fulfill a duty owed to another person.

(4) Notice of a fact that an agent knows or has reason to know is imputed to the principal as stated in §§ 5.03 and 5.04.

§ 5.02 Notification Given by or to an Agent

(1) A notification given to an agent is effective as notice to the principal if the agent has actual or apparent authority to receive the notification, unless the person who gives the notification knows or has reason to know that the agent is acting adversely to the principal as stated in § 5.04.

(2) A notification given by an agent is effective as notification given by the principal if the agent has actual or apparent authority to give the notification, unless the person who receives the notification knows or has reason to know that the agent is acting adversely to the principal as stated in § 5.04.

§ 5.03 Imputation of Notice of Fact to Principal

For purposes of determining a principal's legal relations with a third party, notice of a fact that an agent knows or has reason to know is imputed to the principal if knowledge of the fact is material to the agent's duties to the principal, unless the agent

(a) acts adversely to the principal as stated in § 5.04, or

(b) is subject to a duty to another not to disclose the fact to the principal.

§ 5.04 An Agent Who Acts Adversely to a Principal

For purposes of determining a principal's legal relations with a third party, notice of a fact that an agent knows or has reason to know is not imputed to the principal if the agent acts adversely to the principal in a transaction or matter, intending to act solely for the agent's own purposes or those of another person. Nevertheless, notice is imputed

(a) when necessary to protect the rights of a third party who dealt with the principal in good faith; or

(b) when the principal has ratified or knowingly retained a benefit from the agent's action.

A third party who deals with a principal through an agent, knowing or having reason to know that the agent acts adversely to the principal, does not deal in good faith for this purpose.

Chapter 6. Contracts and Other Transactions with Third Parties

§ 6.01 Agent for Disclosed Principal

When an agent acting with actual or apparent authority makes a contract on behalf of a disclosed principal,

(1) the principal and the third party are parties to the contract; and

(2) the agent is not a party to the contract unless the agent and third party agree otherwise.

§ 6.02 Agent for Unidentified Principal

When an agent acting with actual or apparent authority makes a contract on behalf of an unidentified principal,

(1) the principal and the third party are parties to the contract; and

(2) the agent is a party to the contract unless the agent and the third party agree otherwise.

§ 6.03 Agent for Undisclosed Principal

When an agent acting with actual authority makes a contract on behalf of an undisclosed principal,

(1) unless excluded by the contract, the principal is a party to the contract;

(2) the agent and the third party are parties to the contract; and

(3) the principal, if a party to the contract, and the third party have the same rights, liabilities, and defenses against each other as if the principal made the contract personally, subject to §§ 6.05- 6.09.

§ 6.10 Agent's Implied Warranty of Authority

A person who purports to make a contract, representation, or conveyance to or with a third party on behalf of another person, lacking power to bind that person, gives an implied warranty of authority to the third party and is subject to liability to the third party for damages for loss caused by breach of that warranty, including loss of the benefit expected from performance by the principal, unless

(1) the principal or purported principal ratifies the act as stated in § 4.01; or

(2) the person who purports to make the contract, representation, or conveyance gives notice to the third party that no warranty of authority is given; or

(3) the third party knows that the person who purports to make the contract, representation, or conveyance acts without actual authority.

Chapter 7. Torts—Liability of Agent and Principal

§ 7.06 Failure in Performance of Principal's Duty of Protection

A principal required by contract or otherwise by law to protect another cannot avoid liability by delegating performance of the duty, whether or not the delegate is an agent.

§ 7.07 Employee Acting Within Scope of Employment

(1) An employer is subject to vicarious liability for a tort committed by its employee acting within the scope of employment.

(2) An employee acts within the scope of employment when performing work assigned by the employer or engaging in a course of conduct subject to the employer's control. An employee's act is not within the scope of employment when it occurs within an independent course of conduct not intended by the employee to serve any purpose of the employer.

(3) For purposes of this section,

(a) an employee is an agent whose principal controls or has the right to control the manner and means of the agent's performance of work, and

(b) the fact that work is performed gratuitously does not relieve a principal of liability.

Chapter 8. Duties of Agent and Principal to Each Other

§ 8.01 General Fiduciary Principle

An agent has a fiduciary duty to act loyally for the principal's benefit in all matters connected with the agency relationship.

§ 8.02 Material Benefit Arising Out of Position

An agent has a duty not to acquire a material benefit from a third party in connection with transactions conducted or other actions taken on behalf of the principal or otherwise through the agent's use of the agent's position.

§ 8.03 Acting as or on Behalf of an Adverse Party

An agent has a duty not to deal with the principal as or on behalf of an adverse party in a transaction connected with the agency relationship.

§ 8.04 Competition

Throughout the duration of an agency relationship, an agent has a duty to refrain from competing with the principal and from taking action on behalf of or otherwise assisting the principal's competitors. During that time, an agent may take action, not otherwise wrongful, to prepare for competition following termination of the agency relationship.

§ 8.05 Use of Principal's Property; Use of Confidential Information

An agent has a duty

(1) not to use property of the principal for the agent's own purposes or those of a third party; and

(2) not to use or communicate confidential information of the principal for the agent's own purposes or those of a third party.

§ 8.08 Duties of Care, Competence, and Diligence

Subject to any agreement with the principal, an agent has a duty to the principal to act with the care, competence, and diligence normally exercised by agents in similar circumstances. Special skills or knowledge possessed by an agent are circumstances to be taken into account in determining whether the agent acted with due care and diligence. If an agent claims to possess special skills or knowledge, the agent has a duty to the principal to act with the care, competence, and diligence normally exercised by agents with such skills or knowledge.

§ 8.15 Principal's Duty to Deal Fairly and in Good Faith

A principal has a duty to deal with the agent fairly and in good faith, including a duty to provide the agent with information about risks of physical harm or pecuniary loss that the principal knows, has reason to know, or should know are present in the agent's work but unknown to the agent.

Uniform Partnership Act (2013)

Copyright © 2014 by National Conference of Commissioners
on Uniform State Laws

Table of Contents

Article 1. General Provisions

§ 101. Short Title.

This act may be cited as the Uniform Partnership Act.

§ 102. Definitions.

In this act:

(1) "Business" includes every trade, occupation, and profession.

(2) "Contribution", except in the phrase "right of contribution", means property or a benefit described in § 403 which is provided by a person to a partnership to become a partner or in the person's capacity as a partner.

(3) "Debtor in bankruptcy" means a person that is the subject of:

(A) an order for relief under Title 11 of the United States Code or a comparable order under a successor statute of general application; or

(B) a comparable order under federal, state, or foreign law governing insolvency.

(4) "Distribution" means a transfer of money or other property from a partnership to a person on account of a transferable interest or in a person's capacity as a partner. The term:

(A) includes:

(i) a redemption or other purchase by a partnership of a transferable interest; and

11

(ii) a transfer to a partner in return for the partner's relinquishment of any right to participate as a partner in the management or conduct of the partnership's business or have access to records or other information concerning the partnership's business; and

(B) does not include amounts constituting reasonable compensation for present or past service or payments made in the ordinary course of business under a bona fide retirement plan or other bona fide benefits program.

(5) "Foreign limited liability partnership" means a foreign partnership whose partners have limited liability for the debts, obligations, or other liabilities of the foreign partnership under a provision similar to § 306(c).

(6) "Foreign partnership" means an unincorporated entity formed under the law of a jurisdiction other than this state which would be a partnership if formed under the law of this state. The term includes a foreign limited liability partnership.

(7) "Jurisdiction", used to refer to a political entity, means the United States, a state, a foreign country, or a political subdivision of a foreign country.

(8) "Jurisdiction of formation" means the jurisdiction whose law governs the internal affairs of an entity.

(9) "Limited liability partnership", except in the phrase "foreign limited liability partnership" and in Article 11, means a partnership that has filed a statement of qualification under § 901 and does not have a similar statement in effect in any other jurisdiction.

(10) "Partner" means a person that:

(A) has become a partner in a partnership under § 402 or was a partner in a partnership when the partnership became subject to this act under § 110; and

(B) has not dissociated as a partner under § 601.

(11) "Partnership", except in Article 11, means an association of two or more persons to carry on as co-owners a business for profit formed under this act or that becomes subject to this act under Article 11 or § 110. The term includes a limited liability partnership.

(12) "Partnership agreement" means the agreement, whether or not referred to as a partnership agreement and whether oral, implied, in a record, or in any combination thereof, of all the partners of a partnership concerning the matters described in § 105(a). The term includes the agreement as amended or restated.

(13) "Partnership at will" means a partnership in which the partners have not agreed to remain partners until the expiration of a definite term or the completion of a particular undertaking.

(14) "Person" means an individual, business corporation, nonprofit corporation, partnership, limited partnership, limited liability company, [general cooperative association,] limited cooperative association, unincorporated nonprofit association, statutory trust, business trust, common-law business trust, estate, trust, association, joint venture, public corporation, government or governmental subdivision, agency, or instrumentality, or any other legal or commercial entity.

(15) "Principal office" means the principal executive office of a partnership or a foreign limited liability partnership, whether or not the office is located in this state.

(16) "Property" means all property, whether real, personal, or mixed or tangible or intangible, or any right or interest therein.

(17) "Record", used as a noun, means information that is inscribed on a tangible medium or that is stored in an electronic or other medium and is retrievable in perceivable form.

(18) "Registered agent" means an agent of a limited liability partnership or foreign limited liability partnership which is authorized to receive service of any process, notice, or demand required or permitted by law to be served on the partnership.

(19) "Registered foreign limited liability partnership" means a foreign limited liability partnership that is registered to do business in this state pursuant to a statement of registration filed by the Secretary of State.

(20) "Sign" means, with present intent to authenticate or adopt a record:

(A) to execute or adopt a tangible symbol; or

(B) to attach to or logically associate with the record an electronic symbol, sound, or process.

(21) "State" means a state of the United States, the District of Columbia, Puerto Rico, the United States Virgin Islands, or any territory or insular possession subject to the jurisdiction of the United States.

(22) "Transfer" includes:

(A) an assignment;

(B) a conveyance;

(C) a sale;

(D) a lease;

(E) an encumbrance, including a mortgage or security interest;

(F) a gift; and

(G) a transfer by operation of law.

(23) "Transferable interest" means the right, as initially owned by a person in the person's capacity as a partner, to receive distributions from a partnership, whether or not the person remains a partner or continues to own any part of the right. The term applies to any fraction of the interest, by whomever owned.

(24) "Transferee" means a person to which all or part of a transferable interest has been transferred, whether or not the transferor is a partner.

§ 103. Knowledge; Notice.

(a) A person knows a fact if the person:

(1) has actual knowledge of it; or

(2) is deemed to know it under subsection (d)(1) or law other than this act.

(b) A person has notice of a fact if the person:

(1) has reason to know the fact from all the facts known to the person at the time in question; or

(2) is deemed to have notice of the fact under subsection (d)(2).

(c) Subject to § 117(f), a person notifies another person of a fact by taking steps reasonably required to inform the other person in ordinary course, whether or not those steps cause the other person to know the fact.

(d) A person not a partner is deemed:

(1) to know of a limitation on authority to transfer real property as provided in § 303(g); and

(2) to have notice of:

(A) a person's dissociation as a partner 90 days after a statement of dissociation under § 704 becomes effective; and

(B) a partnership's:

(i) dissolution 90 days after a statement of dissolution under § 802 becomes effective;

(ii) termination 90 days after a statement of termination under § 802 becomes effective; and

(iii) participation in a merger, interest exchange, conversion, or domestication, 90 days after articles of merger, interest exchange, conversion, or domestication under Article 11 become effective.

(e) A partner's knowledge or notice of a fact relating to the partnership is effective immediately as knowledge of or notice to the partnership, except in the case of a fraud on the partnership committed by or with the consent of that partner.

§ 104. Governing Law.

The internal affairs of a partnership and the liability of a partner as a partner for a debt, obligation, or other liability of the partnership are governed by:

(1) in the case of a limited liability partnership, the law of this state; and

13

(2) in the case of a partnership that is not a limited liability partnership, the law of the jurisdiction in which the partnership has its principal office.

§ 105. Partnership Agreement; Scope, Function, and Limitations.

(a) Except as otherwise provided in subsections (c) and (d), the partnership agreement governs:

(1) relations among the partners as partners and between the partners and the partnership;

(2) the business of the partnership and the conduct of that business; and

(3) the means and conditions for amending the partnership agreement.

(b) To the extent the partnership agreement does not provide for a matter described in subsection (a), this act governs the matter.

(c) A partnership agreement may not:

(1) vary the law applicable under § 104(1);

(2) vary the provisions of § 110;

(3) vary the provisions of § 307;

(4) unreasonably restrict the duties and rights under § 408, but the partnership agreement may impose reasonable restrictions on the availability and use of information obtained under that section and may define appropriate remedies, including liquidated damages, for a breach of any reasonable restriction on use;

(5) alter or eliminate the duty of loyalty or the duty of care, except as otherwise provided in subsection (d);

(6) eliminate the contractual obligation of good faith and fair dealing under § 409(d), but the partnership agreement may prescribe the standards, if not manifestly unreasonable, by which the performance of the obligation is to be measured;

(7) unreasonably restrict the right of a person to maintain an action under § 410(b);

(8) relieve or exonerate a person from liability for conduct involving bad faith, willful or intentional misconduct, or knowing violation of law;

(9) vary the power of a person to dissociate as a partner under § 602(a), except to require that the notice under § 601(1) to be in a record;

(10) vary the grounds for expulsion specified in § 601(5);

(11) vary the causes of dissolution specified in § 801(4) or (5);

(12) vary the requirement to wind up the partnership's business as specified in § 802(a), (b)(1), and (d);

(13) vary the right of a partner under § 901(f) to vote on or consent to a cancellation of a statement of qualification;

(14) vary the right of a partner to approve a merger, interest exchange, conversion, or domestication under § 1123(a)(2), 1133(a)(2), 1143(a)(2), or 1153(a)(2);

(15) vary the required contents of a plan of merger under § 1122(a), plan of interest exchange under § 1132(a), plan of conversion under § 1142(a), or plan of domestication under § 1152(a);

(16) vary any requirement, procedure, or other provision of this act pertaining to:

(A) registered agents; or

(B) the Secretary of State, including provisions pertaining to records authorized or required to be delivered to the Secretary of State for filing under this act; or

(17) except as otherwise provided in §§ 106 and 107(b), restrict the rights under this act of a person other than a partner.

(d) Subject to subsection (c)(8), without limiting other terms that may be included in a partnership agreement, the following rules apply:

(1) The partnership agreement may:

(A) specify the method by which a specific act or transaction that would otherwise violate the duty of loyalty may be authorized or ratified by one or more disinterested and independent persons after full disclosure of all material facts; and

(B) alter the prohibition in § 406(a)(2) so that the prohibition requires only that the partnership's total assets not be less than the sum of its total liabilities.

(2) To the extent the partnership agreement expressly relieves a partner of a responsibility that the partner would otherwise have under this act and imposes the responsibility on one or more other partners, the agreement also may eliminate or limit any fiduciary duty of the partner relieved of the responsibility which would have pertained to the responsibility.

(3) If not manifestly unreasonable, the partnership agreement may:

(A) alter or eliminate the aspects of the duty of loyalty stated in § 409(b);

(B) identify specific types or categories of activities that do not violate the duty of loyalty;

(C) alter the duty of care, but may not authorize conduct involving bad faith, willful or intentional misconduct, or knowing violation of law; and

(D) alter or eliminate any other fiduciary duty.

(e) The court shall decide as a matter of law whether a term of a partnership agreement is manifestly unreasonable under subsection (c)(6) or (d)(3). The court:

(1) shall make its determination as of the time the challenged term became part of the partnership agreement and by considering only circumstances existing at that time; and

(2) may invalidate the term only if, in light of the purposes and business of the partnership, it is readily apparent that:

(A) the objective of the term is unreasonable; or

(B) the term is an unreasonable means to achieve the term's objective.

§ 106. Partnership Agreement; Effect on Partnership and Person Becoming Partner; Preformation Agreement.

(a) A partnership is bound by and may enforce the partnership agreement, whether or not the partnership has itself manifested assent to the agreement.

(b) A person that becomes a partner is deemed to assent to the partnership agreement.

(c) Two or more persons intending to become the initial partners of a partnership may make an agreement providing that upon the formation of the partnership the agreement will become the partnership agreement.

§ 107. Partnership Agreement; Effect on Third Parties and Relationship to Records Effective on Behalf of Partnership.

(a) A partnership agreement may specify that its amendment requires the approval of a person that is not a party to the agreement or the satisfaction of a condition. An amendment is ineffective if its adoption does not include the required approval or satisfy the specified condition.

(b) The obligations of a partnership and its partners to a person in the person's capacity as a transferee or person dissociated as a partner are governed by the partnership agreement. Subject only to a court order issued under § 504(b)(2) to effectuate a charging order, an amendment to the partnership agreement made after a person becomes a transferee or is dissociated as a partner:

(1) is effective with regard to any debt, obligation, or other liability of the partnership or its partners to the person in the person's capacity as a transferee or person dissociated as a partner; and

(2) is not effective to the extent the amendment:

(A) imposes a new debt, obligation, or other liability on the transferee or person dissociated as a partner; or

(B) prejudices the rights under § 701 of a person that dissociated as a partner before the amendment was made.

(c) If a record delivered by a partnership to the Secretary of State for filing becomes effective and contains a provision that would be ineffective under § 105(c) or (d)(3) if contained in the partnership agreement, the provision is ineffective in the record.

(d) Subject to subsection (c), if a record delivered by a partnership to the Secretary of State for filing becomes effective and conflicts with a provision of the partnership agreement:

> **(1)** the agreement prevails as to partners, persons dissociated as partners, and transferees; and
>
> **(2)** the record prevails as to other persons to the extent they reasonably rely on the record.

§ 108. Signing of Records to Be Delivered for Filing to Secretary of State.

(a) A record delivered to the Secretary of State for filing pursuant to this act must be signed as follows:

> **(1)** Except as otherwise provided in paragraphs (2) and (3), a record signed by a partnership must be signed by a person authorized by the partnership.
>
> **(2)** A record filed on behalf of a dissolved partnership that has no partner must be signed by the person winding up the partnership's business under § 802(c) or a person appointed under § 802(d) to wind up the business.
>
> **(3)** A statement of denial by a person under § 304 must be signed by that person.
>
> **(4)** Any other record delivered on behalf of a person to the Secretary of State for filing must be signed by that person.

(b) A record filed under this act may be signed by an agent. Whenever this act requires a particular individual to sign a record and the individual is deceased or incompetent, the record may be signed by a legal representative of the individual.

(c) A person that signs a record as an agent or legal representative affirms as a fact that the person is authorized to sign the record.

§ 109. Liability for Inaccurate Information in Filed Record.

(a) If a record delivered to the Secretary of State for filing under this act and filed by the Secretary of State contains inaccurate information, a person that suffers loss by reliance on the information may recover damages for the loss from:

> **(1)** a person that signed the record, or caused another to sign it on the person's behalf, and knew the information to be inaccurate at the time the record was signed; and
>
> **(2)** subject to subsection (b), a partner if:
>
> > **(A)** the record was delivered for filing on behalf of the partnership; and
> >
> > **(B)** the partner knew or had notice of the inaccuracy for a reasonably sufficient time before the information was relied upon so that, before the reliance, the partner reasonably could have:
> >
> > > **(i)** effected an amendment under § 901(f);
> > >
> > > **(ii)** filed a petition under § 112; or
> > >
> > > **(iii)** delivered to the Secretary of State for filing a statement of change under § 909 or a statement of correction under § 116.

(b) To the extent the partnership agreement expressly relieves a partner of responsibility for maintaining the accuracy of information contained in records delivered on behalf of the partnership to the Secretary of State for filing under this act and imposes that responsibility on one or more other partners, the liability stated in subsection (a)(2) applies to those other partners and not to the partner that the partnership agreement relieves of the responsibility.

(c) An individual who signs a record authorized or required to be filed under this act affirms under penalty of perjury that the information stated in the record is accurate.

§ 110. Application to Existing Relationships.

(a) Before [all-inclusive date], this act governs only:

(1) a partnership formed on or after [the effective date of this act]; and

(2) except as otherwise provided in subsection (c), a partnership formed before [the effective date of this act] which elects, in the manner provided in its partnership agreement or by law for amending the partnership agreement, to be subject to this act.

(b) Except as otherwise provided in subsection (c), on and after [all-inclusive date] this act governs all partnerships.

(c) With respect to a partnership that elects pursuant to subsection (a)(2) to be subject to this act, after the election takes effect the provisions of this act relating to the liability of the partnership's partners to third parties apply:

> **(1)** before [all-inclusive date], to:

>> **(A)** a third party that had not done business with the partnership in the year before the election took effect; and

>> **(B)** a third party that had done business with the partnership in the year before the election took effect only if the third party knows or has been notified of the election; and

> **(2)** on and after [all-inclusive date], to all third parties, but those provisions remain inapplicable to any obligation incurred while those provisions were inapplicable under paragraph (1)(B).

Legislative Note: *For states that have previously enacted UPA (1997): For these states this section is unnecessary. There is no need for a delayed effective date, even with regard to pre-existing partnerships. (Presumably, the "linkage" issue [discussed below] was addressed when UPA (1997) was enacted.)*

For states that have not previously enacted UPA (1997): Each enacting jurisdiction should consider whether: (i) this act makes material changes to the "default" (or "gap filler") rules of the predecessor statute; and (ii) if so, whether Subsection (c) should carry forward any of those rules for pre-existing partnerships. In this assessment, the focus is on pre-existing partnerships that have left default rules in place, whether advisedly or not. The central question is whether, for such partnerships, expanding Subsection (c) is necessary to prevent material changes to the partners' "deal."

The "all-inclusive" date should be at least one year after the effective date of this act, § 1206, but no more than two years.

The "linkage" issue—for states that still have ULPA (1976) or ULPA (1976/1985) in effect: These states should enact ULPA (2001) (Last Amended 2013) to take effect in conjunction with this act. If not, a state's current limited partnership act must be amended to link to this act.

§ 111. Delivery of Record.

(a) Except as otherwise provided in this act, permissible means of delivery of a record include delivery by hand, mail, conventional commercial practice, and electronic transmission.

(b) Delivery to the Secretary of State is effective only when a record is received by the Secretary of State.

§ 112. Signing and Filing Pursuant to Judicial Order.

(a) If a person required by this act to sign a record or deliver a record to the Secretary of State for filing under this act does not do so, any other person that is aggrieved may petition [the appropriate court] to order:

> **(1)** the person to sign the record;

> **(2)** the person to deliver the record to the Secretary of State for filing; or

> **(3)** the Secretary of State to file the record unsigned.

(b) If a petitioner under subsection (a) is not the partnership or foreign limited liability partnership to which the record pertains, the petitioner shall make the partnership or foreign partnership a party to the action.

(c) A record filed under subsection (a)(3) is effective without being signed.

§ 113. Filing Requirements.

(a) To be filed by the Secretary of State pursuant to this act, a record must be received by the Secretary of State, comply with this act, and satisfy the following:

(1) The filing of the record must be required or permitted by this act.

(2) The record must be physically delivered in written form unless and to the extent the Secretary of State permits electronic delivery of records.

(3) The words in the record must be in English, and numbers must be in Arabic or Roman numerals, but the name of an entity need not be in English if written in English letters or Arabic or Roman numerals.

(4) The record must be signed by a person authorized or required under this act to sign the record.

(5) The record must state the name and capacity, if any, of each individual who signed it, either on behalf of the individual or the person authorized or required to sign the record, but need not contain a seal, attestation, acknowledgment, or verification.

(b) If law other than this act prohibits the disclosure by the Secretary of State of information contained in a record delivered to the Secretary of State for filing, the Secretary of State shall file the record if the record otherwise complies with this act but may redact the information.

(c) When a record is delivered to the Secretary of State for filing, any fee required under this act and any fee, tax, interest, or penalty required to be paid under this act or law other than this act must be paid in a manner permitted by the Secretary of State or by that law.

(d) The Secretary of State may require that a record delivered in written form be accompanied by an identical or conformed copy.

(e) The Secretary of State may provide forms for filings required or permitted to be made by this act, but, except as otherwise provided in subsection (f), their use is not required.

(f) The Secretary of State may require that a cover sheet for a filing be on a form prescribed by the Secretary of State.

§ 114. Effective Date and Time.

Except as otherwise provided in § 115 and subject to § 116(c), a record filed under this act is effective:

(1) on the date and at the time of its filing by the Secretary of State, as provided in § 117(b);

(2) on the date of filing and at the time specified in the record as its effective time, if later than the time under paragraph (1);

(3) at a specified delayed effective date and time, which may not be more than 90 days after the date of filing; or

(4) if a delayed effective date is specified, but no time is specified, at 12:01 a.m. on the date specified, which may not be more than 90 days after the date of filing.

§ 115. Withdrawal of Filed Record Before Effectiveness.

(a) Except as otherwise provided in §§ 1124, 1134, 1144, and 1154, a record delivered to the Secretary of State for filing may be withdrawn before it takes effect by delivering to the Secretary of State for filing a statement of withdrawal.

(b) A statement of withdrawal must:

(1) be signed by each person that signed the record being withdrawn, except as otherwise agreed by those persons;

(2) identify the record to be withdrawn; and

(3) if signed by fewer than all the persons that signed the record being withdrawn, state that the record is withdrawn in accordance with the agreement of all the persons that signed the record.

(c) On filing by the Secretary of State of a statement of withdrawal, the action or transaction evidenced by the original record does not take effect.

§ 116. Correcting Filed Record.

(a) A person on whose behalf a filed record was delivered to the Secretary of State for filing may correct the record if:

(1) the record at the time of filing was inaccurate;

(2) the record was defectively signed; or

(3) the electronic transmission of the record to the Secretary of State was defective.

(b) To correct a filed record, a person on whose behalf the record was delivered to the Secretary of State must deliver to the Secretary of State for filing a statement of correction.

(c) A statement of correction:

(1) may not state a delayed effective date;

(2) must be signed by the person correcting the filed record;

(3) must identify the filed record to be corrected;

(4) must specify the inaccuracy or defect to be corrected; and

(5) must correct the inaccuracy or defect.

(d) A statement of correction is effective as of the effective date of the filed record that it corrects except for purposes of § 103(d) and as to persons relying on the uncorrected filed record and adversely affected by the correction. For those purposes and as to those persons, the statement of correction is effective when filed.

§ 117. Duty of Secretary of State to File; Review of Refusal to File; Delivery of Record by Secretary of State.

(a) The Secretary of State shall file a record delivered to the Secretary of State for filing which satisfies this act. The duty of the Secretary of State under this section is ministerial.

(b) When the Secretary of State files a record, the Secretary of State shall record it as filed on the date and at the time of its delivery. After filing a record, the Secretary of State shall deliver to the person that submitted the record a copy of the record with an acknowledgment of the date and time

of filing and, in the case of a statement of denial, also to the partnership to which the statement pertains.

(c) If the Secretary of State refuses to file a record, the Secretary of State shall, not later than [15] business days after the record is delivered:

(1) return the record or notify the person that submitted the record of the refusal; and

(2) provide a brief explanation in a record of the reason for the refusal.

(d) If the Secretary of State refuses to file a record, the person that submitted the record may petition [the appropriate court] to compel filing of the record. The record and the explanation of the Secretary of State of the refusal to file must be attached to the petition. The court may decide the matter in a summary proceeding.

(e) The filing of or refusal to file a record does not:

(1) affect the validity or invalidity of the record in whole or in part; or

(2) create a presumption that the information contained in the record is correct or incorrect.

(f) Except as otherwise provided by § 909 or by law other than this act, the Secretary of State may deliver any record to a person by delivering it:

(1) in person to the person that submitted it;

(2) to the address of the person's registered agent;

(3) to the principal office of the person; or

(4) to another address the person provides to the Secretary of State for delivery.

§ 118. Reservation of Power to Amend or Repeal.

The [legislature of this state] has power to amend or repeal all or part of this act at any time, and all limited liability partnerships and foreign limited liability partnerships subject to this act are governed by the amendment or repeal.

§ 119. Supplemental Principles of Law.

Unless displaced by particular provisions of this act, the principles of law and equity supplement this act.

Article 2. Nature of Partnership

§ 201. Partnership as Entity.

(a) A partnership is an entity distinct from its partners.

(b) A partnership is the same entity regardless of whether the partnership has a statement of qualification in effect under § 901.

§ 202. Formation of Partnership.

(a) Except as otherwise provided in subsection (b), the association of two or more persons to carry on as co-owners a business for profit forms a partnership, whether or not the persons intend to form a partnership.

(b) An association formed under a statute other than this act, a predecessor statute, or a comparable statute of another jurisdiction is not a partnership under this act.

(c) In determining whether a partnership is formed, the following rules apply:

(1) Joint tenancy, tenancy in common, tenancy by the entireties, joint property, common property, or part ownership does not by itself establish a partnership, even if the co-owners share profits made by the use of the property.

(2) The sharing of gross returns does not by itself establish a partnership, even if the persons sharing them have a joint or common right or interest in property from which the returns are derived.

(3) A person who receives a share of the profits of a business is presumed to be a partner in the business, unless the profits were received in payment:

(A) of a debt by installments or otherwise;

(B) for services as an independent contractor or of wages or other compensation to an employee;

(C) of rent;

(D) of an annuity or other retirement or health benefit to a deceased or retired partner or a beneficiary, representative, or designee of a deceased or retired partner;

(E) of interest or other charge on a loan, even if the amount of payment varies with the profits of the business, including a direct or indirect present or future ownership of the collateral, or rights to income, proceeds, or increase in value derived from the collateral; or

(F) for the sale of the goodwill of a business or other property by installments or otherwise.

§ 203. Partnership Property.

Property acquired by a partnership is property of the partnership and not of the partners individually.

§ 204. When Property Is Partnership Property.

(a) Property is partnership property if acquired in the name of:

(1) the partnership; or

(2) one or more partners with an indication in the instrument transferring title to the property of the person's capacity as a partner or of the existence of a partnership but without an indication of the name of the partnership.

(b) Property is acquired in the name of the partnership by a transfer to:

(1) the partnership in its name; or

(2) one or more partners in their capacity as partners in the partnership, if the name of the partnership is indicated in the instrument transferring title to the property.

(c) Property is presumed to be partnership property if purchased with partnership assets, even if not acquired in the name of the partnership or of one or more partners with an indication in the instrument transferring title to the property of the person's capacity as a partner or of the existence of a partnership.

(d) Property acquired in the name of one or more of the partners, without an indication in the instrument transferring title to the property of the person's capacity as a partner or of the existence of a partnership and without use of partnership assets, is presumed to be separate property, even if used for partnership purposes.

Article 3. Relations of Partners to Persons Dealing with Partnership

§ 301. Partner Agent of Partnership.

Subject to the effect of a statement of partnership authority under § 303, the following rules apply:

(1) Each partner is an agent of the partnership for the purpose of its business. An act of a partner, including the signing of an instrument in the partnership name, for apparently carrying on in the ordinary course the partnership business or business of the kind carried on by the partnership binds the partnership, unless the partner did not have authority to act for the partnership in the particular matter and the person with which the partner was dealing knew or had notice that the partner lacked authority.

(2) An act of a partner which is not apparently for carrying on in the ordinary course the partnership's business or business of the kind carried on by the partnership binds the partnership only if the act was actually authorized by all the other partners.

§ 302. Transfer of Partnership Property.

(a) Partnership property may be transferred as follows:

(1) Subject to the effect of a statement of partnership authority under § 303, partnership property held in the name of the partnership may be transferred by an instrument of transfer signed by a partner in the partnership name.

(2) Partnership property held in the name of one or more partners with an indication in the instrument transferring the property to them of their capacity as partners or of the existence of a partnership, but without an indication of the name of the partnership, may be transferred by an instrument of transfer signed by the persons in whose name the property is held.

(3) Partnership property held in the name of one or more persons other than the partnership, without an indication in the instrument transferring the property to them of their capacity as partners or of the existence of a partnership, may be transferred by an instrument of transfer signed by the persons in whose name the property is held.

(b) A partnership may recover partnership property from a transferee only if it proves that signing of the instrument of initial transfer did not bind the partnership under § 301 and:

(1) as to a subsequent transferee who gave value for property transferred under subsection (a)(1) and (2), proves that the subsequent transferee knew or had been notified that the person who signed the instrument of initial transfer lacked authority to bind the partnership; or

(2) as to a transferee who gave value for property transferred under subsection (a)(3), proves that the transferee knew or had been notified that the property was partnership property and that the person who signed the instrument of initial transfer lacked authority to bind the partnership.

(c) A partnership may not recover partnership property from a subsequent transferee if the partnership would not have been entitled to recover the property, under subsection (b), from any earlier transferee of the property.

(d) If a person holds all the partners' interests in the partnership, all the partnership property vests in that person. The person may sign a record in the name of the partnership to evidence vesting of the property in that person and may file or record the record.

§ 303. Statement of Partnership Authority.

(a) A partnership may deliver to the Secretary of State for filing a statement of partnership authority. The statement:

(1) must include the name of the partnership and:

(A) if the partnership is not a limited liability partnership, the street and mailing addresses of its principal office; or

(B) if the partnership is a limited liability partnership, the name and street and mailing addresses of its registered agent;

(2) with respect to any position that exists in or with respect to the partnership, may state the authority, or limitations on the authority, of all persons holding the position to:

(A) sign an instrument transferring real property held in the name of the partnership; or

(B) enter into other transactions on behalf of, or otherwise act for or bind, the partnership; and

(3) may state the authority, or limitations on the authority, of a specific person to:

(A) sign an instrument transferring real property held in the name of the partnership; or

(B) enter into other transactions on behalf of, or otherwise act for or bind, the partnership.

(b) To amend or cancel a statement of authority filed by the Secretary of State, a partnership must deliver to the Secretary of State for filing an amendment or cancellation stating:

(1) the name of the partnership;

(2) if the partnership is not a limited liability partnership, the street and mailing addresses of the partnership's principal office;

(3) if the partnership is a limited liability partnership, the name and street and mailing addresses of its registered agent;

(4) the date the statement being affected became effective; and

(5) the contents of the amendment or a declaration that the statement is canceled.

(c) A statement of authority affects only the power of a person to bind a partnership to persons that are not partners.

(d) Subject to subsection (c) and § 103(d)(1), and except as otherwise provided in subsections (f), (g), and (h), a limitation on the authority of a person or a position contained in an effective statement of authority is not by itself evidence of any person's knowledge or notice of the limitation.

(e) Subject to subsection (c), a grant of authority not pertaining to transfers of real property and contained in an effective statement of authority is conclusive in favor of a person that gives value in reliance on the grant, except to the extent that if the person gives value:

(1) the person has knowledge to the contrary;

(2) the statement has been canceled or restrictively amended under subsection (b); or

(3) a limitation on the grant is contained in another statement of authority that became effective after the statement containing the grant became effective.

(f) Subject to subsection (c), an effective statement of authority that grants authority to transfer real property held in the name of the partnership, a certified copy of which statement is recorded in the office for recording transfers of the real property, is conclusive in favor of a person that gives value in reliance on the grant without knowledge to the contrary, except to the extent that when the person gives value:

(1) the statement has been canceled or restrictively amended under subsection (b), and a certified copy of the cancellation or restrictive amendment has been recorded in the office for recording transfers of the real property; or

(2) a limitation on the grant is contained in another statement of authority that became effective after the statement containing the grant became effective, and a certified copy of the later-effective statement is recorded in the office for recording transfers of the real property.

(g) Subject to subsection (c), if a certified copy of an effective statement containing a limitation on the authority to transfer real property held in the name of a partnership is recorded in the office for recording transfers of that real property, all persons are deemed to know of the limitation.

(h) Subject to subsection (i), an effective statement of dissolution is a cancellation of any filed statement of authority for the purposes of subsection (f) and is a limitation on authority for purposes of subsection (g).

(i) After a statement of dissolution becomes effective, a partnership may deliver to the Secretary of State for filing and, if appropriate, may record a statement of authority that is designated as a post-dissolution statement of authority. The statement operates as provided in subsections (f) and (g).

(j) Unless canceled earlier, an effective statement of authority is canceled by operation of law five years after the date on which the statement, or its most recent amendment, becomes effective. The cancellation is effective without recording under subsection (f) or (g).

(k) An effective statement of denial operates as a restrictive amendment under this section and may be recorded by certified copy for purposes of subsection (f)(1).

§ 304. Statement of Denial.

A person named in a filed statement of authority granting that person authority may deliver to the Secretary of State for filing a statement of denial that:

(1) provides the name of the partnership and the caption of the statement of authority to which the statement of denial pertains; and

(2) denies the grant of authority.

§ 305. Partnership Liable for Partner's Actionable Conduct.

(a) A partnership is liable for loss or injury caused to a person, or for a penalty incurred, as a result of a wrongful act or omission, or other actionable conduct, of a partner acting in the ordinary course of business of the partnership or with the actual or apparent authority of the partnership.

(b) If, in the course of the partnership's business or while acting with actual or apparent authority of the partnership, a partner receives or causes the partnership to receive money or property of a person not a partner, and the money or property is misapplied by a partner, the partnership is liable for the loss.

§ 306. Partner's Liability.

(a) Except as otherwise provided in subsections (b) and (c), all partners are liable jointly and severally for all debts, obligations, and other liabilities of the partnership unless otherwise agreed by the claimant or provided by law.

(b) A person that becomes a partner is not personally liable for a debt, obligation, or other liability of the partnership incurred before the person became a partner.

(c) A debt, obligation, or other liability of a partnership incurred while the partnership is a limited liability partnership is solely the debt, obligation, or other liability of the limited liability partnership. A partner is not personally liable, directly or indirectly, by way of contribution or otherwise, for a debt, obligation, or other liability of the limited liability partnership solely by reason of being or acting as a partner. This subsection applies:

(1) despite anything inconsistent in the partnership agreement that existed immediately before the vote or consent required to become a limited liability partnership under § 901(b); and

(2) regardless of the dissolution of the limited liability partnership.

(d) The failure of a limited liability partnership to observe formalities relating to the exercise of its powers or management of its business is not a ground for imposing liability on a partner for a debt, obligation, or other liability of the partnership.

(e) The cancellation or administrative revocation of a limited liability partnership's statement of qualification does not affect the limitation in this section on the liability of a partner for a debt, obligation, or other liability of the partnership incurred while the statement was in effect.

§ 307. Actions by and Against Partnership and Partners.

(a) A partnership may sue and be sued in the name of the partnership.

(b) To the extent not inconsistent with § 306, a partner may be joined in an action against the partnership or named in a separate action.

(c) A judgment against a partnership is not by itself a judgment against a partner. A judgment against a partnership may not be satisfied from a partner's assets unless there is also a judgment against the partner.

(d) A judgment creditor of a partner may not levy execution against the assets of the partner to satisfy a judgment based on a claim against the partnership unless the partner is personally liable for the claim under § 306 and:

> **(1)** a judgment based on the same claim has been obtained against the partnership and a writ of execution on the judgment has been returned unsatisfied in whole or in part;
>
> **(2)** the partnership is a debtor in bankruptcy;
>
> **(3)** the partner has agreed that the creditor need not exhaust partnership assets;
>
> **(4)** a court grants permission to the judgment creditor to levy execution against the assets of a partner based on a finding that partnership assets subject to execution are clearly insufficient to satisfy the judgment, that exhaustion of partnership assets is excessively burdensome, or that the grant of permission is an appropriate exercise of the court's equitable powers; or
>
> **(5)** liability is imposed on the partner by law or contract independent of the existence of the partnership.

(e) This section applies to any debt, liability, or other obligation of a partnership which results from a representation by a partner or purported partner under § 308.

§ 308. Liability of Purported Partner.

(a) If a person, by words or conduct, purports to be a partner, or consents to being represented by another as a partner, in a partnership or with one or more persons not partners, the purported partner is liable to a person to whom the representation is made, if that person, relying on the representation, enters into a transaction with the actual or purported partnership. If the representation, either by the purported partner or by a person with the purported partner's consent, is made in a public manner, the purported partner is liable to a person who relies upon the purported partnership even if the purported partner is not aware of being held out as a partner to the claimant. If partnership liability results, the purported partner is liable with respect to that liability as if the purported partner were a partner. If no partnership liability results, the purported partner is liable with respect to that liability jointly and severally with any other person consenting to the representation.

(b) If a person is thus represented to be a partner in an existing partnership, or with one or more persons not partners, the purported partner is an agent of persons consenting to the representation to bind them to the same extent and in the same manner as if the purported partner were a partner with respect to persons who enter into transactions in reliance upon the representation. If all the partners of the existing partnership consent to the representation, a partnership act or obligation results. If fewer than all the partners of the existing partnership consent to the representation, the person acting and the partners consenting to the representation are jointly and severally liable.

(c) A person is not liable as a partner merely because the person is named by another as a partner in a statement of partnership authority.

(d) A person does not continue to be liable as a partner merely because of a failure to file a statement of dissociation or to amend a statement of partnership authority to indicate the person's dissociation as a partner.

(e) Except as otherwise provided in subsections (a) and (b), persons who are not partners as to each other are not liable as partners to other persons.

Article 4. Relations of Partners to Each Other and to Partnership

§ 401. Partner's Rights and Duties.

(a) Each partner is entitled to an equal share of the partnership distributions and, except in the case of a limited liability partnership, is chargeable with a share of the partnership losses in proportion to the partner's share of the distributions.

(b) A partnership shall reimburse a partner for any payment made by the partner in the course of the partner's activities on behalf of the partnership, if the partner complied with this section and § 409 in making the payment.

(c) A partnership shall indemnify and hold harmless a person with respect to any claim or demand against the person and any debt, obligation, or other liability incurred by the person by reason of the person's former or present capacity as a partner, if the claim, demand, debt, obligation, or other liability does not arise from the person's breach of this section or § 407 or 409.

(d) In the ordinary course of its business, a partnership may advance reasonable expenses, including attorney's fees and costs, incurred by a person in connection with a claim or demand against the person by reason of the person's former or present capacity as a partner, if the person promises to repay the partnership if the person ultimately is determined not to be entitled to be indemnified under subsection (c).

(e) A partnership may purchase and maintain insurance on behalf of a partner against liability asserted against or incurred by the partner in that capacity or arising from that status even if, under § 105(c)(7), the partnership agreement could not eliminate or limit the person's liability to the partnership for the conduct giving rise to the liability.

(f) A partnership shall reimburse a partner for an advance to the partnership beyond the amount of capital the partner agreed to contribute.

(g) A payment or advance made by a partner which gives rise to a partnership obligation under subsection (b) or (f) constitutes a loan to the partnership which accrues interest from the date of the payment or advance.

(h) Each partner has equal rights in the management and conduct of the partnership's business.

(i) A partner may use or possess partnership property only on behalf of the partnership.

(j) A partner is not entitled to remuneration for services performed for the partnership, except for reasonable compensation for services rendered in winding up the business of the partnership.

(k) A difference arising as to a matter in the ordinary course of business of a partnership may be decided by a majority of the partners. An act outside the ordinary course of business of a partnership and an amendment to the partnership agreement may be undertaken only with the affirmative vote or consent of all the partners.

§ 402. Becoming Partner.

(a) Upon formation of a partnership, a person becomes a partner under § 202(a).

(b) After formation of a partnership, a person becomes a partner:

(1) as provided in the partnership agreement;

(2) as a result of a transaction effective under Article 11; or

(3) with the affirmative vote or consent of all the partners.

(c) A person may become a partner without:

(1) acquiring a transferable interest; or

(2) making or being obligated to make a contribution to the partnership.

§ 403. Form of Contribution.

A contribution may consist of property transferred to, services performed for, or another benefit provided to the partnership or an agreement to transfer property to, perform services for, or provide another benefit to the partnership.

§ 404. Liability for Contribution.

(a) A person's obligation to make a contribution to a partnership is not excused by the person's death, disability, termination, or other inability to perform personally.

(b) If a person does not fulfill an obligation to make a contribution other than money, the person is obligated at the option of the partnership to contribute money equal to the value of the part of the contribution which has not been made.

(c) The obligation of a person to make a contribution may be compromised only by the affirmative vote or consent of all the partners. If a creditor of a limited liability partnership extends credit or otherwise acts in reliance on an obligation described in subsection (a) without knowledge or notice of a compromise under this subsection, the creditor may enforce the obligation.

§ 405. Sharing of and Right to Distributions Before Dissolution.

(a) Any distribution made by a partnership before its dissolution and winding up must be in equal shares among partners, except to the extent necessary to comply with a transfer effective under § 503 or charging order in effect under § 504.

(b) Subject to § 701, a person has a right to a distribution before the dissolution and winding up of a partnership only if the partnership decides to make an interim distribution.

(c) A person does not have a right to demand or receive a distribution from a partnership in any form other than money. Except as otherwise provided in § 806, a partnership may distribute an asset in kind only if each part of the asset is fungible with each other part and each person receives a percentage of the asset equal in value to the person's share of distributions.

(d) If a partner or transferee becomes entitled to receive a distribution, the partner or transferee has the status of, and is entitled to all remedies available to, a creditor of the partnership with respect to the distribution. However, the partnership's obligation to make a distribution is subject to offset for any amount owed to the partnership by the partner or a person dissociated as partner on whose account the distribution is made.

§ 406. Limitations on Distributions by Limited Liability Partnership.

(a) A limited liability partnership may not make a distribution, including a distribution under § 806, if after the distribution:

(1) the partnership would not be able to pay its debts as they become due in the ordinary course of the partnership's business; or

(2) the partnership's total assets would be less than the sum of its total liabilities plus the amount that would be needed, if the partnership were to be dissolved and wound up at the time of the distribution, to satisfy the preferential rights upon dissolution and winding up of partners and transferees whose preferential rights are superior to the rights of persons receiving the distribution.

(b) A limited liability partnership may base a determination that a distribution is not prohibited under subsection (a) on:

(1) financial statements prepared on the basis of accounting practices and principles that are reasonable in the circumstances; or

(2) a fair valuation or other method that is reasonable under the circumstances.

(c) Except as otherwise provided in subsection (e), the effect of a distribution under subsection (a) is measured:

(1) in the case of a distribution as defined in § 102(4)(A), as of the earlier of:

(A) the date money or other property is transferred or debt is incurred by the limited liability partnership; or

(B) the date the person entitled to the distribution ceases to own the interest or rights being acquired by the partnership in return for the distribution;

(2) in the case of any other distribution of indebtedness, as of the date the indebtedness is distributed; and

(3) in all other cases, as of the date:

(A) the distribution is authorized, if the payment occurs not later than 120 days after that date; or

(B) the payment is made, if the payment occurs more than 120 days after the distribution is authorized.

(d) A limited liability partnership's indebtedness to a partner or transferee incurred by reason of a distribution made in accordance with this section is at parity with the partnership's indebtedness to its general, unsecured creditors, except to the extent subordinated by agreement.

(e) A limited liability partnership's indebtedness, including indebtedness issued as a distribution, is not a liability for purposes of subsection (a) if the terms of the indebtedness provide that payment of principal and interest is made only if and to the extent that a payment of a distribution could then be made under this section. If the indebtedness is issued as a distribution, each payment of principal or interest is treated as a distribution, the effect of which is measured on the date the payment is made.

(f) In measuring the effect of a distribution under § 806, the liabilities of a dissolved limited liability partnership do not include any claim that has been disposed of under § 807, 808, or 809.

§ 407. Liability for Improper Distributions by Limited Liability Partnership.

(a) Except as otherwise provided in subsection (b), if a partner of a limited liability partnership consents to a distribution made in violation of § 406 and in consenting to the distribution fails to comply with § 409, the partner is personally liable to the partnership for the amount of the distribution which exceeds the amount that could have been distributed without the violation of § 406.

(b) To the extent the partnership agreement of a limited liability partnership expressly relieves a partner of the authority and responsibility to consent to distributions and imposes that authority and responsibility on one or more other partners, the liability stated in subsection (a) applies to the other partners and not to the partner that the partnership agreement relieves of the authority and responsibility.

(c) A person that receives a distribution knowing that the distribution violated § 406 is personally liable to the limited liability partnership but only to the extent that the distribution received by the person exceeded the amount that could have been properly paid under § 406.

(d) A person against which an action is commenced because the person is liable under subsection (a) may:

(1) implead any other person that is liable under subsection (a) and seek to enforce a right of contribution from the person; and

(2) implead any person that received a distribution in violation of subsection (c) and seek to enforce a right of contribution from the person in the amount the person received in violation of subsection (c).

(e) An action under this section is barred unless commenced not later than two years after the distribution.

§ 408. Rights to Information of Partners and Persons Dissociated as Partner.

(a) A partnership shall keep its books and records, if any, at its principal office.

(b) On reasonable notice, a partner may inspect and copy during regular business hours, at a reasonable location specified by the partnership, any record maintained by the partnership regarding the partnership's business, financial condition, and other circumstances, to the extent the information is material to the partner's rights and duties under the partnership agreement or this act.

(c) The partnership shall furnish to each partner:

(1) without demand, any information concerning the partnership's business, financial condition, and other circumstances which the partnership knows and is material to the proper exercise of the partner's rights and duties under the partnership agreement or this act, except to the extent the partnership can establish that it reasonably believes the partner already knows the information; and

(2) on demand, any other information concerning the partnership's business, financial condition, and other circumstances, except to the extent the demand or the information demanded is unreasonable or otherwise improper under the circumstances.

(d) The duty to furnish information under subsection (c) also applies to each partner to the extent the partner knows any of the information described in subsection (c).

(e) Subject to subsection (j), on 10 days' demand made in a record received by a partnership, a person dissociated as a partner may have access to information to which the person was entitled while a partner if:

> **(1)** the information pertains to the period during which the person was a partner;

> **(2)** the person seeks the information in good faith; and

> **(3)** the person satisfies the requirements imposed on a partner by subsection (b).

(f) Not later than 10 days after receiving a demand under subsection (e), the partnership in a record shall inform the person that made the demand of:

> **(1)** the information that the partnership will provide in response to the demand and when and where the partnership will provide the information; and

> **(2)** the partnership's reasons for declining, if the partnership declines to provide any demanded information.

(g) A partnership may charge a person that makes a demand under this section the reasonable costs of copying, limited to the costs of labor and material.

(h) A partner or person dissociated as a partner may exercise the rights under this section through an agent or, in the case of an individual under legal disability, a legal representative. Any restriction or condition imposed by the partnership agreement or under subsection (j) applies both to the agent or legal representative and to the partner or person dissociated as a partner.

(i) Subject to § 505, the rights under this section do not extend to a person as transferee.

(j) In addition to any restriction or condition stated in its partnership agreement, a partnership, as a matter within the ordinary course of its business, may impose reasonable restrictions and conditions on access to and use of information to be furnished under this section, including designating information confidential and imposing nondisclosure and safeguarding obligations on the recipient. In a dispute concerning the reasonableness of a restriction under this subsection, the partnership has the burden of proving reasonableness.

§ 409. Standards of Conduct for Partners.

(a) A partner owes to the partnership and the other partners the duties of loyalty and care stated in subsections (b) and (c).

(b) The fiduciary duty of loyalty of a partner includes the duties:

> **(1)** to account to the partnership and hold as trustee for it any property, profit, or benefit derived by the partner:

> > **(A)** in the conduct or winding up of the partnership's business;

> > **(B)** from a use by the partner of the partnership's property; or

> > **(C)** from the appropriation of a partnership opportunity;

> **(2)** to refrain from dealing with the partnership in the conduct or winding up of the partnership business as or on behalf of a person having an interest adverse to the partnership; and

> **(3)** to refrain from competing with the partnership in the conduct of the partnership's business before the dissolution of the partnership.

(c) The duty of care of a partner in the conduct or winding up of the partnership business is to refrain from engaging in grossly negligent or reckless conduct, willful or intentional misconduct, or a knowing violation of law.

(d) A partner shall discharge the duties and obligations under this act or under the partnership agreement and exercise any rights consistently with the contractual obligation of good faith and fair dealing.

(e) A partner does not violate a duty or obligation under this act or under the partnership agreement solely because the partner's conduct furthers the partner's own interest.

(f) All the partners may authorize or ratify, after full disclosure of all material facts, a specific act or transaction by a partner that otherwise would violate the duty of loyalty.

(g) It is a defense to a claim under subsection (b)(2) and any comparable claim in equity or at common law that the transaction was fair to the partnership.

(h) If, as permitted by subsection (f) or the partnership agreement, a partner enters into a transaction with the partnership which otherwise would be prohibited by subsection (b)(2), the partner's rights and obligations arising from the transaction are the same as those of a person that is not a partner.

§ 410. Actions by Partnership and Partners.

(a) A partnership may maintain an action against a partner for a breach of the partnership agreement, or for the violation of a duty to the partnership, causing harm to the partnership.

(b) A partner may maintain an action against the partnership or another partner, with or without an accounting as to partnership business, to enforce the partner's rights and protect the partner's interests, including rights and interests under the partnership agreement or this act or arising independently of the partnership relationship.

(c) A right to an accounting on dissolution and winding up does not revive a claim barred by law.

§ 411. Continuation of Partnership Beyond Definite Term or Particular Undertaking.

(a) If a partnership for a definite term or particular undertaking is continued, without an express agreement, after the expiration of the term or completion of the undertaking, the rights and duties of the partners remain the same as they were at the expiration or completion, so far as is consistent with a partnership at will.

(b) If the partners, or those of them who habitually acted in the business during the term or undertaking, continue the business without any settlement or liquidation of the partnership, they are presumed to have agreed that the partnership will continue.

Article 5. Transferable Interests and Rights of Transferees and Creditors

§ 501. Partner Not Co-Owner of Partnership Property.

A partner is not a co-owner of partnership property and has no interest in partnership property which can be transferred, either voluntarily or involuntarily.

§ 502. Nature of Transferable Interest.

A transferable interest is personal property.

§ 503. Transfer of Transferable Interest.

(a) A transfer, in whole or in part, of a transferable interest:

(1) is permissible;

(2) does not by itself cause a person's dissociation as a partner or a dissolution and winding up of the partnership business; and

(3) subject to § 505, does not entitle the transferee to:

(A) participate in the management or conduct of the partnership's business; or

(B) except as otherwise provided in subsection (c), have access to records or other information concerning the partnership's business.

(b) A transferee has the r

(1) receive, in accorda
tributions to which th
wise be entitled; and

(2) seek under § 801
tion that it is equitabl
ship business.

30

(c) In a dissolution and winding up of a partnership, a transferee is entitled to an account of the partnership's transactions only from the date of dissolution.

(d) A partnership need not give effect to a transferee's rights under this section until the partnership knows or has notice of the transfer.

(e) A transfer of a transferable interest in violation of a restriction on transfer contained in the partnership agreement is ineffective if the intended transferee has knowledge or notice of the restriction at the time of transfer.

(f) Except as otherwise provided in § 601(4)(B), if a partner transfers a transferable interest, the transferor retains the rights of a partner other than the transferable interest transferred and retains all the duties and obligations of a partner.

(g) If a partner transfers a transferable interest to a person that becomes a partner with respect to the transferred interest, the transferee is liable for the partner's obligations under §§ 404 and 407 known to the transferee when the transferee becomes a partner.

§ 504. Charging Order.

(a) On application by a judgment creditor of a partner or transferee, a court may enter a charging order against the transferable interest of the judgment debtor for the unsatisfied amount of the judgment. A charging order constitutes a lien on a judgment debtor's transferable interest and requires the partnership to pay over to the person to which the charging order was issued any distribution that otherwise would be paid to the judgment debtor.

(b) To the extent necessary to effectuate the collection of distributions pursuant to a charging order in effect under subsection (a), the court may:

    (1) appoint a receiver of the distributions subject to the charging order, with the power to make all inquiries the judgment debtor might have made; and

    (2) make all other orders necessary to give effect to the charging order.

(c) Upon a showing that distributions under a charging order will not pay the judgment debt within a reasonable time, the court may foreclose the lien and order the sale of the transferable interest. The purchaser at the foreclosure sale obtains only the transferable interest, does not thereby become a partner, and is subject to § 503.

(d) At any time before foreclosure under subsection (c), the partner or transferee whose transferable interest is subject to a charging order under subsection (a) may extinguish the charging order by satisfying the judgment and filing a certified copy of the satisfaction with the court that issued the charging order.

(e) At any time before foreclosure under subsection (c), a partnership or one or more partners whose transferable interests are not subject to the charging order may pay to the judgment creditor the full amount due under the judgment and thereby succeed to the rights of the judgment creditor, including the charging order.

(f) This act does not deprive any partner or transferee of the benefit of any exemption law applicable to the transferable interest of the partner or transferee.

(g) This section provides the exclusive remedy by which a person seeking in the capacity of a judgment creditor to enforce a judgment against a partner or transferee may satisfy the judgment from the judgment debtor's transferable interest.

§ 505. Power of Legal Representative of Deceased Partner.

If a partner dies, the deceased partner's legal representative may exercise:

    (1) the rights of a transferee provided in § 503(c); and

    (2) for purposes of settling the estate, the rights the deceased partner had under § 408.

Article 6. Dissociation

§ 601. Events Causing Dissociation.

A person is dissociated as a partner when:

(1) the partnership knows or has notice of the person's express will to withdraw as a partner, but, if the person has specified a withdrawal date later than the date the partnership knew or had notice, on that later date;

(2) an event stated in the partnership agreement as causing the person's dissociation occurs;

(3) the person is expelled as a partner pursuant to the partnership agreement;

(4) the person is expelled as a partner by the affirmative vote or consent of all the other partners if:

(A) it is unlawful to carry on the partnership business with the person as a partner;

(B) there has been a transfer of all of the person's transferable interest in the partnership, other than:

(i) a transfer for security purposes; or

(ii) a charging order in effect under § 504 which has not been foreclosed;

(C) the person is an entity and:

(i) the partnership notifies the person that it will be expelled as a partner because the person has filed a statement of dissolution or the equivalent, the person has been administratively dissolved, the person's charter or the equivalent has been revoked, or the person's right to conduct business has been suspended by the person's jurisdiction of formation; and

(ii) not later than 90 days after the notification, the statement of dissolution or the equivalent has not been withdrawn, rescinded, or revoked, or the person's charter or the equivalent or right to conduct business has not been reinstated; or

(D) the person is an unincorporated entity that has been dissolved and whose activities and affairs are being wound up;

(5) on application by the partnership or another partner, the person is expelled as a partner by judicial order because the person:

(A) has engaged or is engaging in wrongful conduct that has affected adversely and materially, or will affect adversely and materially, the partnership's business;

(B) has committed willfully or persistently, or is committing willfully or persistently, a material breach of the partnership agreement or a duty or obligation under § 409; or

(C) has engaged or is engaging in conduct relating to the partnership's business which makes it not reasonably practicable to carry on the business with the person as a partner;

(6) the person:

(A) becomes a debtor in bankruptcy;

(B) signs an assignment for the benefit of creditors; or

(C) seeks, consents to, or acquiesces in the appointment of a trustee, receiver, or liquidator of the person or of all or substantially all the person's property;

(7) in the case of an individual:

(A) the individual dies;

(B) a guardian or general conservator for the individual is appointed; or

(C) a court orders that the individual has otherwise become incapable of performing the individual's duties as a partner under this act or the partnership agreement;

(8) in the case of a person that is a testamentary or inter vivos trust or is acting as a partner by virtue of being a trustee of such a trust, the trust's entire transferable interest in the partnership is distributed;

(9) in the case of a person that is an estate or is acting as a partner by virtue of being a personal representative of an estate, the estate's entire transferable interest in the partnership is distributed;

(10) in the case of a person that is not an individual, the existence of the person terminates;

(11) the partnership participates in a merger under Article 11 and:

> **(A)** the partnership is not the surviving entity; or

> **(B)** otherwise as a result of the merger, the person ceases to be a partner;

(12) the partnership participates in an interest exchange under Article 11 and, as a result of the interest exchange, the person ceases to be a partner;

(13) the partnership participates in a conversion under Article 11;

(14) the partnership participates in a domestication under Article 11 and, as a result of the domestication, the person ceases to be a partner; or

(15) the partnership dissolves and completes winding up.

§ 602. Power to Dissociate as Partner; Wrongful Dissociation.

(a) A person has the power to dissociate as a partner at any time, rightfully or wrongfully, by withdrawing as a partner by express will under § 601(1).

(b) A person's dissociation as a partner is wrongful only if the dissociation:

> **(1)** is in breach of an express provision of the partnership agreement; or

> **(2)** in the case of a partnership for a definite term or particular undertaking, occurs before the expiration of the term or the completion of the undertaking and:

>> **(A)** the person withdraws as a partner by express will, unless the withdrawal follows not later than 90 days after another person's dissociation by death or otherwise under § 601(6) through (10) or wrongful dissociation under this subsection;

>> **(B)** the person is expelled as a partner by judicial order under § 601(5);

>> **(C)** the person is dissociated under § 601(6); or

>> **(D)** in the case of a person that is not a trust other than a business trust, an estate, or an individual, the person is expelled or otherwise dissociated because it willfully dissolved or terminated.

(c) A person that wrongfully dissociates as a partner is liable to the partnership and to the other partners for damages caused by the dissociation. The liability is in addition to any debt, obligation, or other liability of the partner to the partnership or the other partners.

§ 603. Effect of Dissociation.

(a) If a person's dissociation results in a dissolution and winding up of the partnership business, Article 8 applies; otherwise, Article 7 applies.

(b) If a person is dissociated as a partner:

> **(1)** the person's right to participate in the management and conduct of the partnership's business terminates, except as otherwise provided in § 802(c); and

> **(2)** the person's duties and obligations under § 409 end with regard to matters arising and events occurring after the person's dissociation, except to the extent the partner participates in winding up the partnership's business pursuant to § 802.

(c) A person's dissociation does not of itself discharge the person from any debt, obligation, or other liability to the partnership or the other partners which the person incurred while a partner.

Article 7. Person's Dissociation as a Partner When Business Not Wound Up

§ 701. Purchase of Interest of Person Dissociated as Partner.

(a) If a person is dissociated as a partner without the dissociation resulting in a dissolution and winding up of the partnership business under § 801, the partnership shall cause the person's interest in the partnership to be purchased for a buyout price determined pursuant to subsection (b).

(b) The buyout price of the interest of a person dissociated as a partner is the amount that would have been distributable to the person under § 806(b) if, on the date of dissociation, the assets of the partnership were sold and the partnership were wound up, with the sale price equal to the greater of:

(1) the liquidation value; or

(2) the value based on a sale of the entire business as a going concern without the person.

(c) Interest accrues on the buyout price from the date of dissociation to the date of payment, but damages for wrongful dissociation under § 602(b), and all other amounts owing, whether or not presently due, from the person dissociated as a partner to the partnership, must be offset against the buyout price.

(d) A partnership shall defend, indemnify, and hold harmless a person dissociated as a partner whose interest is being purchased against all partnership liabilities, whether incurred before or after the dissociation, except liabilities incurred by an act of the person under § 702.

(e) If no agreement for the purchase of the interest of a person dissociated as a partner is reached not later than 120 days after a written demand for payment, the partnership shall pay, or cause to be paid, in money to the person the amount the partnership estimates to be the buyout price and accrued interest, reduced by any offsets and accrued interest under subsection (c).

(f) If a deferred payment is authorized under subsection (h), the partnership may tender a written offer to pay the amount it estimates to be the buyout price and accrued interest, reduced by any offsets under subsection (c), stating the time of payment, the amount and type of security for payment, and the other terms and conditions of the obligation.

(g) The payment or tender required by subsection (e) or (f) must be accompanied by the following:

(1) a statement of partnership assets and liabilities as of the date of dissociation;

(2) the latest available partnership balance sheet and income statement, if any;

(3) an explanation of how the estimated amount of the payment was calculated; and

(4) written notice that the payment is in satisfaction of the obligation to purchase unless, not later than 120 days after the written notice, the person dissociated as a partner commences an action to determine the buyout price, any offsets under subsection (c), or other terms of the obligation to purchase.

(h) A person that wrongfully dissociates as a partner before the expiration of a definite term or the completion of a particular undertaking is not entitled to payment of any part of the buyout price until the expiration of the term or completion of the undertaking, unless the person establishes to the satisfaction of the court that earlier payment will not cause undue hardship to the business of the partnership. A deferred payment must be adequately secured and bear interest.

(i) A person dissociated as a partner may maintain an action against the partnership, pursuant to § 410(b)(2), to determine the buyout price of that person's interest, any offsets under subsection (c), or other terms of the obligation to purchase. The action must be commenced not later than 120 days after the partnership has tendered payment or an offer to pay or within one year after written demand for payment if no payment or offer to pay is tendered. The court shall determine the buyout price of the person's interest, any offset due under subsection (c), and accrued interest, and enter judgment for any additional payment or refund. If deferred payment is authorized under subsection (h), the court shall also determine the security for payment and other terms of the obligation to purchase. The court may assess reasonable attorney's fees and the fees and expenses of appraisers or other experts for a party to the action, in amounts the court finds equitable, against a party that the court finds acted arbitrarily, vexatiously, or not in good faith. The finding may be based on the partnership's failure to tender payment or an offer to pay or to comply with subsection (g).

§ 702. Power to Bind and Liability of Person Dissociated as Partner.

(a) After a person is dissociated as a partner without the dissociation resulting in a dissolution and

§ 702

,hip business and before
d out of existence, con-
under Article 11, or dis-
is bound by an act of the

have bound the partnership
e dissociation; and

(2) at the ~ ne other party enters into the transaction:

(A) less than two years has passed since the dissociation; and

(B) the other party does not know or have notice of the dissociation and reasonably believes that the person is a partner.

(b) If a partnership is bound under subsection (a), the person dissociated as a partner which caused the partnership to be bound is liable:

(1) to the partnership for any damage caused to the partnership arising from the obligation incurred under subsection (a); and

(2) if a partner or another person dissociated as a partner is liable for the obligation, to the partner or other person for any damage caused to the partner or other person arising from the liability.

§ 703. Liability of Person Dissociated as Partner to Other Persons.

(a) Except as otherwise provided in subsection (b), a person dissociated as a partner is not liable for a partnership obligation incurred after dissociation.

(b) A person that is dissociated as a partner is liable on a transaction entered into by the partnership after the dissociation only if:

(1) a partner would be liable on the transaction; and

(2) at the time the other party enters into the transaction:

(A) less than two years has passed since the dissociation; and

(B) the other party does not have knowledge or notice of the dissociation and reasonably believes that the person is a partner.

(c) By agreement with a creditor of a partnership and the partnership, a person dissociated as a partner may be released from liability for a debt, obligation, or other liability of the partnership.

(d) A person dissociated as a partner is released from liability for a debt, obligation, or other liability of the partnership if the partnership's creditor, with knowledge or notice of the person's dissociation but without the person's consent, agrees to a material alteration in the nature or time of payment of the debt, obligation, or other liability.

§ 704. Statement of Dissociation.

(a) A person dissociated as a partner or the partnership may deliver to the Secretary of State for filing a statement of dissociation stating the name of the partnership and that the person has dissociated from the partnership.

(b) A statement of dissociation is a limitation on the authority of a person dissociated as a partner for the purposes of § 303.

§ 705. Continued Use of Partnership Name.

Continued use of a partnership name, or the name of a person dissociated as a partner as part of the partnership name, by partners continuing the business does not of itself make the person dissociated as a partner liable for an obligation of the partners or the partnership continuing the business.

Article 8. Dissolution and Winding Up

§ 801. Events Causing Dissolution.

A partnership is dissolved, and its business must be wound up, upon the occurrence of any of the following:

(1) in a partnership at will, the partnership knows or has notice of a person's express will to withdraw as a partner, other than a partner that has dissociated under § 601(2) through (10), but, if the person has specified a withdrawal date later than the date the partnership knew or had notice, on the later date;

(2) in a partnership for a definite term or particular undertaking:

(A) within 90 days after a person's dissociation by death or otherwise under § 601(6) through (10) or wrongful dissociation under § 602(b), the affirmative vote or consent of at least half of the remaining partners to wind up the partnership business, for which purpose a person's rightful dissociation pursuant to § 602(b)(2)(A) constitutes that partner's consent to wind up the partnership business;

(B) the affirmative vote or consent of all the partners to wind up the partnership business; or

(C) the expiration of the term or the completion of the undertaking;

(3) an event or circumstance that the partnership agreement states causes dissolution;

(4) on application by a partner, the entry by [the appropriate court] of an order dissolving the partnership on the grounds that:

(A) the conduct of all or substantially all the partnership's business is unlawful;

(B) the economic purpose of the partnership is likely to be unreasonably frustrated;

(C) another partner has engaged in conduct relating to the partnership business which makes it not reasonably practicable to carry on the business in partnership with that partner; or

(D) it is otherwise not reasonably practicable to carry on the partnership business in conformity with the partnership agreement;

(5) on application by a transferee, the entry by [the appropriate court] of an order dissolving the partnership on the ground that it is equitable to wind up the partnership business:

(A) after the expiration of the term or completion of the undertaking, if the partnership was for a definite term or particular undertaking at the time of the transfer or entry of the charging order that gave rise to the transfer; or

(B) at any time, if the partnership was a partnership at will at the time of the transfer or entry of the charging order that gave rise to the transfer; or

(6) the passage of 90 consecutive days during which the partnership does not have at least two partners.

§ 802. Winding Up.

(a) A dissolved partnership shall wind up its business and, except as otherwise provided in § 803, the partnership continues after dissolution only for the purpose of winding up.

(b) In winding up its business, the partnership:

(1) shall discharge the partnership's debts, obligations, and other liabilities, settle and close the partnership's business, and marshal and distribute the assets of the partnership; and

(2) may:

(A) deliver to the Secretary of State for filing a statement of dissolution stating the name of the partnership and that the partnership is dissolved;

(B) preserve the partnership business and property as a going concern for a reasonable time;

(C) prosecute and defend actions and proceedings, whether civil, criminal, or administrative;

(D) transfer the partnership's property;

(E) settle disputes by mediation or arbitration;

(F) deliver to the Secretary of State for filing a statement of termination stating the name of the partnership and that the partnership is terminated; and

(G) perform other acts necessary or appropriate to the winding up.

(c) A person whose dissociation as a partner resulted in dissolution may participate in winding up as if still a partner, unless the dissociation was wrongful.

(d) If a dissolved partnership does not have a partner and no person has the right to participate in winding up under subsection (c), the personal or legal representative of the last person to have been a partner may wind up the partnership's business. If the representative does not exercise that right, a person to wind up the partnership's business may be appointed by the affirmative vote or consent of transferees owning a majority of the rights to receive distributions at the time the consent is to be effective. A person appointed under this subsection has the powers of a partner under § 804 but is not liable for the debts, obligations, and other liabilities of the partnership solely by reason of having or exercising those powers or otherwise acting to wind up the partnership's business.

(e) On the application of any partner or person entitled under subsection (c) to participate in winding up, the [appropriate court] may order judicial supervision of the winding up of a dissolved partnership, including the appointment of a person to wind up the partnership's business, if:

> **(1)** the partnership does not have a partner and within a reasonable time following the dissolution no person has been appointed under subsection (d); or
>
> **(2)** the applicant establishes other good cause.

§ 803. Rescinding Dissolution.

(a) A partnership may rescind its dissolution, unless a statement of termination applicable to the partnership has become effective or [the appropriate court] has entered an order under § 801(4) or (5) dissolving the partnership.

(b) Rescinding dissolution under this section requires:

> **(1)** the affirmative vote or consent of each partner; and
>
> **(2)** if the partnership has delivered to the Secretary of State for filing a statement of dissolution and:
>
> > **(A)** the statement has not become effective, delivery to the Secretary of State for filing of a statement of withdrawal under § 115 applicable to the statement of dissolution; or
> >
> > **(B)** the statement of dissolution has become effective, delivery to the Secretary of State

for filing of a statement of rescission stating the name of the partnership and that dissolution has been rescinded under this section.

(c) If a partnership rescinds its dissolution:

> **(1)** the partnership resumes carrying on its business as if dissolution had never occurred;
>
> **(2)** subject to paragraph (3), any liability incurred by the partnership after the dissolution and before the rescission has become effective is determined as if dissolution had never occurred; and
>
> **(3)** the rights of a third party arising out of conduct in reliance on the dissolution before the third party knew or had notice of the rescission may not be adversely affected.

§ 804. Power to Bind Partnership After Dissolution.

(a) A partnership is bound by a partner's act after dissolution which:

> **(1)** is appropriate for winding up the partnership business; or
>
> **(2)** would have bound the partnership under § 301 before dissolution if, at the time the other party enters into the transaction, the other party does not know or have notice of the dissolution.

(b) A person dissociated as a partner binds a partnership through an act occurring after dissolution if:

> **(1)** at the time the other party enters into the transaction:
>
> > **(A)** less than two years has passed since the dissociation; and
> >
> > **(B)** the other party does not know or have notice of the dissociation and reasonably believes that the person is a partner; and
>
> **(2)** the act:
>
> > **(A)** is appropriate for winding up the partnership's business; or
> >
> > **(B)** would have bound the partnership under § 301 before dissolution and at the time the other party enters into the transaction the other party does not know or have notice of the dissolution.

§ 805. Liability After Dissolution of Partner and Person Dissociated as Partner.

(a) If a partner having knowledge of the dissolution causes a partnership to incur an obligation under § 804(a) by an act that is not appropriate for winding up the partnership business, the partner is liable:

(1) to the partnership for any damage caused to the partnership arising from the obligation; and

(2) if another partner or person dissociated as a partner is liable for the obligation, to that other partner or person for any damage caused to that other partner or person arising from the liability.

(b) Except as otherwise provided in subsection (c), if a person dissociated as a partner causes a partnership to incur an obligation under § 804(b), the person is liable:

(1) to the partnership for any damage caused to the partnership arising from the obligation; and

(2) if a partner or another person dissociated as a partner is liable for the obligation, to the partner or other person for any damage caused to the partner or other person arising from the obligation.

(c) A person dissociated as a partner is not liable under subsection (b) if:

(1) Section 802(c) permits the person to participate in winding up; and

(2) the act that causes the partnership to be bound under § 804(b) is appropriate for winding up the partnership's business.

§ 806. Disposition of Assets in Winding Up; When Contributions Required.

(a) In winding up its business, a partnership shall apply its assets, including the contributions required by this section, to discharge the partnership's obligations to creditors, including partners that are creditors.

(b) After a partnership complies with subsection (a), any surplus must be distributed in the following order, subject to any charging order in effect under § 504:

(1) to each person owning a transferable interest that reflects contributions made and not previously returned, an amount equal to the value of the unreturned contributions; and

(2) among persons owning transferable interests in proportion to their respective rights to share in distributions immediately before the dissolution of the partnership.

(c) If a partnership's assets are insufficient to satisfy all its obligations under subsection (a), with respect to each unsatisfied obligation incurred when the partnership was not a limited liability partnership, the following rules apply:

(1) Each person that was a partner when the obligation was incurred and that has not been released from the obligation under § 703(c) and (d) shall contribute to the partnership for the purpose of enabling the partnership to satisfy the obligation. The contribution due from each of those persons is in proportion to the right to receive distributions in the capacity of a partner in effect for each of those persons when the obligation was incurred.

(2) If a person does not contribute the full amount required under paragraph (1) with respect to an unsatisfied obligation of the partnership, the other persons required to contribute by paragraph (1) on account of the obligation shall contribute the additional amount necessary to discharge the obligation. The additional contribution due from each of those other persons is in proportion to the right to receive distributions in the capacity of a partner in effect for each of those other persons when the obligation was incurred.

(3) If a person does not make the additional contribution required by paragraph (2), further additional contributions are determined and due in the same manner as provided in that paragraph.

(d) A person that makes an additional contribution under subsection (c)(2) or (3) may recover from any person whose failure to contribute under subsection (c)(1) or (2) necessitated the additional contribution. A person may not recover under this subsection more than the amount additionally contributed. A person's liability under this subsection may not exceed the amount the person failed to contribute.

(e) If a partnership does not have sufficient surplus to comply with subsection (b)(1), any surplus must be distributed among the owners of transferable interests in proportion to the value of the respective unreturned contributions.

(f) All distributions made under subsections (b) and (c) must be paid in money.

§ 807. Known Claims Against Dissolved Limited Liability Partnership.

(a) Except as otherwise provided in subsection (d), a dissolved limited liability partnership may give notice of a known claim under subsection (b), which has the effect provided in subsection (c).

(b) A dissolved limited liability partnership may in a record notify its known claimants of the dissolution. The notice must:

    (1) specify the information required to be included in a claim;

    (2) state that a claim must be in writing and provide a mailing address to which the claim is to be sent;

    (3) state the deadline for receipt of a claim, which may not be less than 120 days after the date the notice is received by the claimant;

    (4) state that the claim will be barred if not received by the deadline; and

    (5) unless the partnership has been throughout its existence a limited liability partnership, state that the barring of a claim against the partnership will also bar any corresponding claim against any partner or person dissociated as a partner which is based on § 306.

(c) A claim against a dissolved limited liability partnership is barred if the requirements of subsection (b) are met and:

    (1) the claim is not received by the specified deadline; or

    (2) if the claim is timely received but rejected by the limited liability partnership:

    (A) the partnership causes the claimant to receive a notice in a record stating that the claim is rejected and will be barred unless the claimant commences an action against the partnership to enforce the claim not later than 90 days after the claimant receives the notice; and

    (B) the claimant does not commence the required action not later than 90 days after the claimant receives the notice.

(d) This section does not apply to a claim based on an event occurring after the date of dissolution or a liability that on that date is contingent.

§ 808. Other Claims Against Dissolved Limited Liability Partnership.

(a) A dissolved limited liability partnership may publish notice of its dissolution and request persons having claims against the partnership to present them in accordance with the notice.

(b) A notice under subsection (a) must:

    (1) be published at least once in a newspaper of general circulation in the [county] in this state in which the dissolved limited liability partnership's principal office is located or, if the principal office is not located in this state, in the [county] in which the office of the partnership's registered agent is or was last located;

    (2) describe the information required to be contained in a claim, state that the claim must be in writing, and provide a mailing address to which the claim is to be sent;

    (3) state that a claim against the partnership is barred unless an action to enforce the claim is commenced not later than three years after publication of the notice; and

    (4) unless the partnership has been throughout its existence a limited liability partnership, state that the barring of a claim against the partnership will also bar any corresponding claim against any partner or person dissociated as a partner which is based on § 306.

(c) If a dissolved limited liability partnership publishes a notice in accordance with subsection (b), the claim of each of the following claimants is barred unless the claimant commences an action to enforce the claim against the partnership not later than three years after the publication date of the notice:

(1) a claimant that did not receive notice in a record under § 807;

(2) a claimant whose claim was timely sent to the partnership but not acted on; and

(3) a claimant whose claim is contingent at, or based on an event occurring after, the date of dissolution.

(d) A claim not barred under this section or § 807 may be enforced:

(1) against a dissolved limited liability partnership, to the extent of its undistributed assets;

(2) except as otherwise provided in § 809, if assets of the partnership have been distributed after dissolution, against a partner or transferee to the extent of that person's proportionate share of the claim or of the partnership's assets distributed to the partner or transferee after dissolution, whichever is less, but a person's total liability for all claims under this paragraph may not exceed the total amount of assets distributed to the person after dissolution; and

(3) against any person liable on the claim under §§ 306, 703, and 805.

§ 809. Court Proceedings.

(a) A dissolved limited liability partnership that has published a notice under § 808 may file an application with [the appropriate court] in the [county] where the partnership's principal office is located or, if the principal office is not located in this state, where the office of its registered agent is or was last located, for a determination of the amount and form of security to be provided for payment of claims that are reasonably expected to arise after the date of dissolution based on facts known to the partnership and:

(1) at the time of the application:

(A) are contingent; or

(B) have not been made known to the partnership; or

(2) are based on an event occurring after the date of dissolution.

(b) Security is not required for any claim that is or is reasonably anticipated to be barred under § 807.

(c) Not later than 10 days after the filing of an application under subsection (a), the dissolved limited liability partnership shall give notice of the proceeding to each claimant holding a contingent claim known to the partnership.

(d) In any proceeding under this section, the court may appoint a guardian ad litem to represent all claimants whose identities are unknown. The reasonable fees and expenses of the guardian, including all reasonable expert witness fees, must be paid by the dissolved limited liability partnership.

(e) A dissolved limited liability partnership that provides security in the amount and form ordered by the court under subsection (a) satisfies the partnership's obligations with respect to claims that are contingent, have not been made known to the partnership, or are based on an event occurring after the date of dissolution, and such claims may not be enforced against a partner or transferee on account of assets received in liquidation.

§ 810. Liability of Partner and Person Dissociated as Partner When Claim Against Partnership Barred.

If a claim against a dissolved partnership is barred under § 807, 808, or 809, any corresponding claim under § 306, 703, or 805 is also barred.

Article 9. Limited Liability Partnership

§ 901. Statement of Qualification.

(a) A partnership may become a limited liability partnership pursuant to this section.

(b) The terms and conditions on which a partnership becomes a limited liability partnership must be approved by the affirmative vote or consent necessary to amend the partnership agreement except, in the case of a partnership agreement that expressly addresses obligations to contribute to the partnership, the affirmative vote or consent necessary to amend those provisions.

(c) After the approval required by subsection (b), a partnership may become a limited liability partnership by delivering to the Secretary of State for filing a statement of qualification. The statement must contain:

> **(1)** the name of the partnership which must comply with § 902;
>
> **(2)** the street and mailing addresses of the partnership's principal office and, if different, the street address of an office in this state, if any;
>
> **(3)** the name and street and mailing addresses in this state of the partnership's registered agent; and
>
> **(4)** a statement that the partnership elects to become a limited liability partnership.

(d) A partnership's status as a limited liability partnership remains effective, regardless of changes in the partnership, until it is canceled pursuant to subsection (f) or administratively revoked pursuant to § 903.

(e) The status of a partnership as a limited liability partnership and the protection against liability of its partners for the debts, obligations, or other liabilities of the partnership while it is a limited liability partnership is not affected by errors or later changes in the information required to be contained in the statement of qualification.

(f) A limited liability partnership may amend or cancel its statement of qualification by delivering to the Secretary of State for filing a statement of amendment or cancellation. The statement must be approved by the affirmative vote or consent of all the partners and state the name of the limited liability partnership and in the case of:

> **(1)** an amendment, state the text of the amendment; and
>
> **(2)** a cancellation, state that the statement of qualification is canceled.

§ 902. Permitted Names.

(a) The name of a partnership that is not a limited liability partnership may not contain the phrase "Registered Limited Liability Partnership" or "Limited Liability Partnership" or the abbreviation "R.L.L.P.", "L.L.P.", "RLLP" , or "LLP".

(b) The name of a limited liability partnership must contain the phrase "Registered Limited Liability Partnership" or "Limited Liability Partnership" or the abbreviation "R.L.L.P.", "L.L.P.", "RLLP", or "LLP".

(c) Except as otherwise provided in subsection (f), the name of a limited liability partnership, and the name under which a foreign limited liability partnership may register to do business in this state, must be distinguishable on the records of the Secretary of State from any:

> **(1)** name of an existing person whose formation required the filing of a record by the Secretary of State and which is not at the time administratively dissolved;
>
> **(2)** name of a limited liability partnership whose statement of qualification is in effect;
>
> **(3)** name under which a person that is registered to do business in this state by the filing of a record by the Secretary of State;
>
> **(4)** name that is reserved under § 903 or other law of this state providing for the reservation of a name by a filing of a record by the Secretary of State;
>
> **(5)** name that is registered under § 904 or other law of this state providing for the registration of a name by a filing of a record by the Secretary of State; and
>
> **(6)** a name registered under [this state's assumed or fictitious name statute].

(d) If a person consents in a record to the use of its name and submits an undertaking in a form satisfactory to the Secretary of State to change its name to a name that is distinguishable on the records of the Secretary of State from any name in any category of names in subsection (c), the name of the consenting person may be used by the person to which the consent was given.

(e) Except as otherwise provided in subsection (f), in determining whether a name is the same as or not distinguishable on the records of the Secretary of State from the name of another person, words, phrases, or abbreviations indicating a type of entity, such as "corporation", "corp.", "incorporated", "Inc.", "professional corporation", "PC", "P.C.", "professional association", "PA", "P.A.", "Limited", "Ltd.", "limited partnership", "LP", "L.P.", "limited liability partnership", "LLP", "L.L.P.", "registered limited liability partnership", "RLLP", "R.L.L.P.", "limited liability limited partnership", "LLLP", "L.L.L.P.", "registered limited liability limited partnership", "RLLLP", "R.L.L.L.P.", "limited liability company", "LLC", or "L.L.C.", "limited cooperative association", "limited cooperative", "LCA", or "L.C.A." may not be taken into account.

(f) A person may consent in a record to the use of a name that is not distinguishable on the records of the Secretary of State from its name except for the addition of a word, phrase, or abbreviation indicating the type of person as provided in subsection (e). In such a case, the person need not change its name pursuant to subsection (d).

(g) The name of a limited liability partnership or foreign limited liability partnership may not contain the words [insert prohibited words or words that may be used only with approval by an appropriate state agency].

(h) A limited liability partnership or foreign limited liability partnership may use a name that is not distinguishable from a name described in subsection (c)(1) through (6) if the partnership delivers to the Secretary of State a certified copy of a final judgment of a court of competent jurisdiction establishing the right of the partnership to use the name in this state.

§ 903. Administrative Revocation of Statement of Qualification.

(a) The Secretary of State may commence a proceeding under subsection (b) to revoke the statement of qualification of a limited liability partnership administratively if the partnership does not:

> **(1)** pay any fee, tax, interest, or penalty required to be paid to the Secretary of State not later than [six months] after it is due;

(2) deliver [an annual] [a biennial] report to the Secretary of State not later than [six months] after it is due; or

(3) have a registered agent in this state for [60] consecutive days.

(b) If the Secretary of State determines that one or more grounds exist for administratively revoking a statement of qualification, the Secretary of State shall serve the partnership with notice in a record of the Secretary of State's determination.

(c) If a limited liability partnership, not later than [60] days after service of the notice under subsection (b), does not cure or demonstrate to the satisfaction of the Secretary of State the nonexistence of each ground determined by the Secretary of State, the Secretary of State shall administratively revoke the statement of qualification by signing a statement of administrative revocation that recites the grounds for revocation and the effective date of the revocation. The Secretary of State shall file the statement and serve a copy on the partnership pursuant to § 116.

(d) An administrative revocation under subsection (c) affects only a partnership's status as a limited liability partnership and is not an event causing dissolution of the partnership.

(e) The administrative revocation of a statement of qualification of a limited liability partnership does not terminate the authority of its registered agent.

§ 904. Reinstatement.

(a) A partnership whose statement of qualification has been revoked administratively under § 903 may apply to the Secretary of State for reinstatement of the statement of qualification [not later than [two] years after the effective date of the revocation]. The application must state:

> **(1)** the name of the partnership at the time of the administrative revocation of its statement of qualification and, if needed, a different name that satisfies § 902;

> **(2)** the address of the principal office of the partnership and the name and street and mailing addresses of its registered agent;

(3) the effective date of administrative revocation of the partnership's statement of qualification; and

(4) that the grounds for revocation did not exist or have been cured.

(b) To have its statement of qualification reinstated, a partnership must pay all fees, taxes, interest, and penalties that were due to the Secretary of State at the time of the administrative revocation and all fees, taxes, interest, and penalties that would have been due to the Secretary of State while the partnership's statement of qualification was revoked administratively.

(c) If the Secretary of State determines that an application under subsection (a) contains the required information, is satisfied that the information is correct, and determines that all payments required to be made to the Secretary of State by subsection (b) have been made, the Secretary of State shall:

(1) cancel the statement of revocation and prepare a statement of reinstatement that states the [Secretary of State's] determination and the effective date of reinstatement; and

(2) file the statement of reinstatement and serve a copy on the partnership.

(d) When reinstatement under this section has become effective, the following rules apply:

(1) The reinstatement relates back to and takes effect as of the effective date of the administrative revocation.

(2) The partnership's status as a limited liability partnership continues as if the revocation had not occurred.

(3) The rights of a person arising out of an act or omission in reliance on the revocation before the person knew or had notice of the reinstatement are not affected.

§ 905. Judicial Review of Denial of Reinstatement.

(a) If the Secretary of State denies a partnership's application for reinstatement following administrative revocation of the partnership's statement of qualification, the Secretary of State shall serve the partnership with a notice in a record that explains the reasons for the denial.

(b) A partnership may seek judicial review of denial of reinstatement in [the appropriate court] not later than [30] days after service of the notice of denial.

§ 906. Reservation of Name.

(a) A person may reserve the exclusive use of a name that complies with § 902 by delivering an application to the Secretary of State for filing. The application must state the name and address of the applicant and the name to be reserved. If the Secretary of State finds that the name is available, the Secretary of State shall reserve the name for the applicant's exclusive use for [120] days.

(b) The owner of a reserved name may transfer the reservation to another person by delivering to the Secretary of State a signed notice in a record of the transfer which states the name and address of the person to which the reservation is being transferred.

§ 907. Registration of Name.

(a) A foreign limited liability partnership not registered to do business in this state under Article 10 may register its name, or an alternate name adopted pursuant to § 902, if the name is distinguishable on the records of the Secretary of State from the names that are not available under § 902.

(b) To register its name or an alternate name adopted pursuant to § 902, a foreign limited liability partnership must deliver to the Secretary of State for filing an application stating the partnership's name, the jurisdiction and date of its formation, and any alternate name adopted pursuant to § 902. If the Secretary of State finds that the name applied for is available, the Secretary of State shall register the name for the applicant's exclusive use.

(c) The registration of a name under this section is effective for [one year] after the date of registration.

(d) A foreign limited liability partnership whose name registration is effective may renew the registration for successive [one-year] periods by delivering, not earlier than [three months] before the expiration of the registration, to the Secretary of State for filing a renewal application that complies with this section. When filed, the renewal application renews the registration for a succeeding [one-year] period.

(e) A foreign limited liability partnership whose name registration is effective may register as a foreign limited liability partnership under the registered name or consent in a signed record to the use of that name by another person that is not an individual.

§ 908. Registered Agent.

(a) Each limited liability partnership and each registered foreign limited liability partnership shall designate and maintain a registered agent in this state. The designation of a registered agent is an affirmation of fact by the partnership or foreign partnership that the agent has consented to serve.

(b) A registered agent for a limited liability partnership or registered foreign limited liability partnership must have a place of business in this state.

(c) The only duties under this act of a registered agent that has complied with this act are:

(1) to forward to the limited liability partnership or registered foreign limited liability partnership at the address most recently supplied to the agent by the partnership or foreign partnership any process, notice, or demand pertaining to the partnership or foreign partnership which is served on or received by the agent;

(2) if the registered agent resigns, to provide the notice required by § 907(c) to the partnership or foreign partnership at the address most recently supplied to the agent by the partnership or foreign partnership; and

(3) to keep current the information with respect to the agent in the statement of qualification or foreign registration statement.

§ 909. Change of Registered Agent or Address for Registered Agent by Limited Liability Partnership.

(a) A limited liability partnership or registered foreign limited liability partnership may change its registered agent or the address of its registered agent by delivering to the Secretary of State for filing a statement of change that states:

(1) the name of the partnership or foreign partnership; and

(2) the information that is to be in effect as a result of the filing of the statement of change.

(b) The partners of a limited liability partnership need not approve the delivery to the Secretary of State for filing of:

(1) a statement of change under this section; or

(2) a similar filing changing the registered agent or registered office, if any, of the partnership in any other jurisdiction.

(c) A statement of change under this section designating a new registered agent is an affirmation of fact by the limited liability partnership or registered foreign limited liability partnership that the agent has consented to serve.

(d) As an alternative to using the procedure in this section, a limited liability partnership may amend its statement of qualification.

§ 910. Resignation of Registered Agent.

(a) A registered agent may resign as an agent for a limited liability partnership or registered foreign limited liability partnership by delivering to the Secretary of State for filing a statement of resignation that states:

(1) the name of the partnership or foreign partnership;

(2) the name of the agent;

(3) that the agent resigns from serving as registered agent for the partnership or foreign partnership; and

(4) the address of the partnership or foreign partnership to which the agent will send the notice required by subsection (c).

(b) A statement of resignation takes effect on the earlier of:

    (1) the 31st day after the day on which it is filed by the Secretary of State; or

    (2) the designation of a new registered agent for the limited liability partnership or registered foreign limited liability partnership.

(c) A registered agent promptly shall furnish to the limited liability partnership or registered foreign limited liability partnership notice in a record of the date on which a statement of resignation was filed.

(d) When a statement of resignation takes effect, the registered agent ceases to have responsibility under this act for any matter thereafter tendered to it as agent for the limited liability partnership or registered foreign limited liability partnership. The resignation does not affect any contractual rights the partnership or foreign partnership has against the agent or that the agent has against the partnership or foreign partnership.

(e) A registered agent may resign with respect to a limited liability partnership or registered foreign limited liability partnership whether or not the partnership or foreign partnership is in good standing.

§ 911. Change of Name or Address by Registered Agent.

(a) If a registered agent changes its name or address, the agent may deliver to the Secretary of State for filing a statement of change that states:

    (1) the name of the limited liability partnership or registered foreign limited liability partnership represented by the registered agent;

    (2) the name of the agent as currently shown in the records of the Secretary of State for the partnership or foreign partnership;

    (3) if the name of the agent has changed, its new name; and

    (4) if the address of the agent has changed, its new address.

(b) A registered agent promptly shall furnish notice to the represented limited liability partnership or registered foreign limited liability partnership of the filing by the Secretary of State of the statement of change and the changes made by the statement.

Legislative Note: *Many registered agents act in that capacity for many entities, and the Model Registered Agents Act (2006) (Last Amended 2013) provides a streamlined method through which a commercial registered agent can make a single filing to change its information for all represented entities. The single filing does not prevent an enacting state from assessing filing fees on the basis of the number of entity records affected. Alternatively the fees can be set on an incremental sliding fee or capitated amount based upon potential economies of costs for a bulk filing.*

§ 912. Service of Process, Notice, or Demand.

(a) A limited liability partnership or registered foreign limited liability partnership may be served with any process, notice, or demand required or permitted by law by serving its registered agent.

(b) If a limited liability partnership or registered foreign limited liability partnership ceases to have a registered agent, or if its registered agent cannot with reasonable diligence be served, the partnership or foreign partnership may be served by registered or certified mail, return receipt requested, or by similar commercial delivery service, addressed to the partnership or foreign partnership at its principal office. The address of the principal office must be as shown in the partnership's or foreign partnership's most recent [annual] [biennial] report filed by the Secretary of State. Service is effected under this subsection on the earliest of:

    (1) the date the partnership or foreign partnership receives the mail or delivery by the commercial delivery service;

    (2) the date shown on the return receipt, if signed by the partnership or foreign partnership; or

    (3) five days after its deposit with the United States Postal Service, or with the commercial delivery service, if correctly addressed and with sufficient postage or payment.

(c) If process, notice, or demand cannot be served on a limited liability partnership or registered foreign limited liability partnership pursuant to subsection (a) or (b), service may be made by handing a copy to the individual in charge of any regular place of business of the partnership or foreign partnership if the individual served is not a plaintiff in the action.

(d) Service of process, notice, or demand on a registered agent must be in a written record.

(e) Service of process, notice, or demand may be made by other means under law other than this act.

§ 913. [Annual] [Biennial] Report for Secretary of State.

(a) A limited liability partnership or registered foreign limited liability partnership shall deliver to the Secretary of State for filing [an annual] [a biennial] report that states:

> **(1)** the name of the partnership or registered foreign partnership;
>
> **(2)** the name and street and mailing addresses of its registered agent in this state;
>
> **(3)** the street and mailing addresses of its principal office;
>
> **(4)** the name of at least one partner; and
>
> **(5)** in the case of a foreign partnership, its jurisdiction of formation and any alternate name adopted under § 1006.

(b) Information in the [annual] [biennial] report must be current as of the date the report is signed by the limited liability partnership or registered foreign limited liability partnership.

(c) The first [annual] [biennial] report must be delivered to the Secretary of State for filing after [January 1] and before [April 1] of the year following the calendar year in which the limited liability partnership's statement of qualification became effective or the registered foreign limited liability partnership registered to do business in this state. Subsequent [annual] [biennial] reports must be delivered to the Secretary of State for filing after [January 1] and before [April 1] of each [second] calendar year thereafter.

(d) If [an annual] [a biennial] report does not contain the information required by this section, the Secretary of State promptly shall notify the reporting limited liability partnership or registered foreign limited liability partnership in a record and return the report for correction.

(e) If [an annual] [a biennial] report contains the name or address of a registered agent which differs from the information shown in the records of the Secretary of State immediately before the report becomes effective, the differing information is considered a statement of change under § 909.

Article 10. Foreign Limited Liability Partnership

§ 1001. Governing Law.

(a) The law of the jurisdiction of formation of a foreign limited liability partnership governs:

> **(1)** the internal affairs of the partnership; and
>
> **(2)** the liability of a partner as partner for a debt, obligation, or other liability of the foreign partnership.

(b) A foreign limited liability partnership is not precluded from registering to do business in this state because of any difference between the law of its jurisdiction of formation and the law of this state.

(c) Registration of a foreign limited liability partnership to do business in this state does not authorize the foreign partnership to engage in any business or exercise any power that a limited liability partnership may not engage in or exercise in this state.

§ 1002. Registration to Do Business in This State.

(a) A foreign limited liability partnership may not do business in this state until it registers with the Secretary of State under this article.

(b) A foreign limited liability partnership doing business in this state may not maintain an action or proceeding in this state unless it has registered to do business in this state.

(c) The failure of a foreign limited liability partnership to register to do business in this state does not impair the validity of a contract or act of the foreign partnership or preclude it from defending an action or proceeding in this state.

(d) A limitation on the liability of a partner of a foreign limited liability partnership is not waived solely because the foreign partnership does business in this state without registering to do business in this state.

(e) Section 1001(a) and (b) applies even if a foreign limited liability partnership fails to register under this article.

§ 1003. Foreign Registration Statement.

To register to do business in this state, a foreign limited liability partnership must deliver a foreign registration statement to the Secretary of State for filing. The statement must state:

(1) the name of the partnership and, if the name does not comply with § 902, an alternate name adopted pursuant to § 1006(a);

(2) that the partnership is a foreign limited liability partnership;

(3) the partnership's jurisdiction of formation;

(4) the street and mailing addresses of the partnership's principal office and, if the law of the partnership's jurisdiction of formation requires the partnership to maintain an office in that jurisdiction, the street and mailing addresses of the required office; and

(5) the name and street and mailing addresses of the partnership's registered agent in this state.

§ 1004. Amendment of Foreign Registration Statement.

A registered foreign limited liability partnership shall deliver to the Secretary of State for filing an amendment to its foreign registration statement if there is a change in:

(1) the name of the partnership;

(2) the partnership's jurisdiction of formation;

(3) an address required by § 1003(4); or

(4) the information required by § 1003(5).

§ 1005. Activities Not Constituting Doing Business.

(a) Activities of a foreign limited liability partnership which do not constitute doing business in this state under this article include:

(1) maintaining, defending, mediating, arbitrating, or settling an action or proceeding;

(2) carrying on any activity concerning its internal affairs, including holding meetings of its partners;

(3) maintaining accounts in financial institutions;

(4) maintaining offices or agencies for the transfer, exchange, and registration of securities of the partnership or maintaining trustees or depositories with respect to those securities;

(5) selling through independent contractors;

(6) soliciting or obtaining orders by any means if the orders require acceptance outside this state before they become contracts;

(7) creating or acquiring indebtedness, mortgages, or security interests in property;

(8) securing or collecting debts or enforcing mortgages or security interests in property securing the debts and holding, protecting, or maintaining property;

(9) conducting an isolated transaction that is not in the course of similar transactions;

(10) owning, without more, property; and

(11) doing business in interstate commerce.

(b) A person does not do business in this state solely by being a partner of a foreign limited liability partnership that does business in this state.

(c) This section does not apply in determining the contacts or activities that may subject a foreign limited liability partnership to service of process, taxation, or regulation under law of this state other than this act.

§ 1006. Noncomplying Name of Foreign Limited Liability Partnership.

(a) A foreign limited liability partnership whose name does not comply with § 902 may not register to do business in this state until it adopts, for the purpose of doing business in this state, an alternate name that complies with § 902. A partnership that registers under an alternate name under this subsection need not comply with [this state's assumed or fictitious name statute]. After registering to do business in this state with an alternate name, a partnership shall do business in this state under:

(1) the alternate name;

(2) the partnership's name, with the addition of its jurisdiction of formation; or

(3) a name the partnership is authorized to use under [this state's assumed or fictitious name statute].

(b) If a registered foreign limited liability partnership changes its name to one that does not comply with § 902, it may not do business in this state until it complies with subsection (a) by amending its registration to adopt an alternate name that complies with § 902.

§ 1007. Withdrawal Deemed on Conversion to Domestic Filing Entity or Domestic Limited Liability Partnership.

A registered foreign limited liability partnership that converts to a domestic limited liability partnership or to a domestic entity whose formation requires the delivery of a record to the Secretary of State for filing is deemed to have withdrawn its registration on the effective date of the conversion.

§ 1008. Withdrawal on Dissolution or Conversion to Nonfiling Entity Other Than Limited Liability Partnership.

(a) A registered foreign limited liability partnership that has dissolved and completed winding up or has converted to a domestic or foreign entity whose formation does not require the public filing of a record, other than a limited liability partnership, shall deliver a statement of withdrawal to the Secretary of State for filing. The statement must state:

(1) in the case of a partnership that has completed winding up:

(A) its name and jurisdiction of formation;

(B) that the partnership surrenders its registration to do business in this state; and

(2) in the case of a partnership that has converted:

(A) the name of the converting partnership and its jurisdiction of formation;

(B) the type of entity to which the partnership has converted and its jurisdiction of formation;

(C) that the converted entity surrenders the converting partnership's registration to do business in this state and revokes the authority of the converting partnership's registered agent to act as registered agent in this state on behalf of the partnership or the converted entity; and

(D) a mailing address to which service of process may be made under subsection (b).

(b) After a withdrawal under this section becomes effective, service of process in any action or proceeding based on a cause of action arising during the time the foreign limited liability partnership was registered to do business in this state may be made pursuant to § 909.

§ 1009. Transfer of Registration.

(a) When a registered foreign limited liability partnership has merged into a foreign entity that is not registered to do business in this state or has converted to a foreign entity required to register with the Secretary of State to do business in this state, the foreign entity shall deliver to the Secretary of State for filing an application for transfer of registration. The application must state:

(1) the name of the registered foreign limited partnership before the merger or conversion;

(2) that before the merger or conversion the registration pertained to a foreign limited liability partnership;

(3) the name of the applicant foreign entity into which the foreign limited liability partnership

has merged or to which it has been converted and, if the name does not comply with § 902, an alternate name adopted pursuant to § 1006(a);

(4) the type of entity of the applicant foreign entity and its jurisdiction of formation;

(5) the street and mailing addresses of the principal office of the applicant foreign entity and, if the law of that entity's jurisdiction of formation requires the entity to maintain an office in that jurisdiction, the street and mailing addresses of that office; and

(6) the name and street and mailing addresses of the applicant foreign entity's registered agent in this state.

(b) When an application for transfer of registration takes effect, the registration of the foreign limited liability limited partnership to do business in this state is transferred without interruption to the foreign entity into which the partnership has merged or to which it has been converted.

§ 1010. Termination of Registration.

(a) The Secretary of State may terminate the registration of a registered foreign limited liability partnership in the manner provided in subsections (b) and (c) if the partnership does not:

(1) pay, not later than [60] days after the due date, any fee, tax, interest, or penalty required to be paid to the Secretary of State under this act or law other than this act;

(2) deliver to the Secretary of State for filing, not later than [60] days after the due date, [an annual] [a biennial] report required under § 913;

(3) have a registered agent as required by § 908; or

(4) deliver to the Secretary of State for filing a statement of a change under § 909 not later than [30] days after a change has occurred in the name or address of the registered agent.

(b) The Secretary of State may terminate the registration of a registered foreign limited liability partnership by:

(1) filing a notice of termination or noting the termination in the records of the Secretary of State; and

(2) delivering a copy of the notice or the information in the notation to the partnership's registered agent or, if the partnership does not have a registered agent, to the partnership's principal office.

(c) A notice or information in a notation under subsection (b) must include:

(1) the effective date of the termination, which must be at least [60] days after the date the Secretary of State delivers the copy; and

(2) the grounds for termination under subsection (a).

(d) The authority of a registered foreign limited liability partnership to do business in this state ceases on the effective date of the notice of termination or notation under subsection (b), unless before that date the partnership cures each ground for termination stated in the notice or notation. If the partnership cures each ground, the Secretary of State shall file a record so stating.

§ 1011. Withdrawal of Registration of Registered Foreign Limited Liability Partnership.

(a) A registered foreign limited liability partnership may withdraw its registration by delivering a statement of withdrawal to the Secretary of State for filing. The statement of withdrawal must state:

(1) the name of the partnership and its jurisdiction of formation;

(2) that the partnership is not doing business in this state and that it withdraws its registration to do business in this state;

(3) that the partnership revokes the authority of its registered agent to accept service on its behalf in this state; and

(4) an address to which service of process may be made under subsection (b).

(b) After the withdrawal of the registration of a foreign limited liability partnership, service of process in any action or proceeding based on a cause of action arising during the time the partnership was registered to do business in this state may be made pursuant to § 909.

§ 1012. Action by [Attorney General].

The [Attorney General] may maintain an action to enjoin a foreign limited liability partnership from doing business in this state in violation of this article.

Article 11. Merger, Interest Exchange, Conversion, and Domestication

Part 1. General Provisions

§ 1101. Definitions.

In this article:

(1) "Acquired entity" means the entity, all of one or more classes or series of interests of which are acquired in an interest exchange.

(2) "Acquiring entity" means the entity that acquires all of one or more classes or series of interests of the acquired entity in an interest exchange.

(3) "Conversion" means a transaction authorized by Part 4.

(4) "Converted entity" means the converting entity as it continues in existence after a conversion.

(5) "Converting entity" means the domestic entity that approves a plan of conversion pursuant to § 1143 or the foreign entity that approves a conversion pursuant to the law of its jurisdiction of formation.

(6) "Distributional interest" means the right under an unincorporated entity's organic law and organic rules to receive distributions from the entity.

(7) "Domestic", with respect to an entity, means governed as to its internal affairs by the law of this state.

(8) "Domesticated limited liability partnership" means a domesticating limited liability partnership as it continues in existence after a domestication.

(9) "Domesticating limited liability partnership" means the domestic limited liability partnership that approves a plan of domestication pursuant to § 1153 or the foreign limited liability partnership that approves a domestication pursuant to the law of its jurisdiction of formation.

(10) "Domestication" means a transaction authorized by Part 5.

(11) "Entity":

(A) means:

(i) a business corporation;

(ii) a nonprofit corporation;

(iii) a general partnership, including a limited liability partnership;

(iv) a limited partnership, including a limited liability limited partnership;

(v) a limited liability company;

[**(vi)** a general cooperative association;]

(vii) a limited cooperative association;

(viii) an unincorporated nonprofit association;

(ix) a statutory trust, business trust, or common-law business trust; or

(x) any other person that has:

(I) a legal existence separate from any interest holder of that person; or

(II) the power to acquire an interest in real property in its own name; and

(B) does not include:

(i) an individual;

(ii) a trust with a predominantly donative purpose or a charitable trust;

(iii) an association or relationship that is not an entity listed in subparagraph (A) and is not a partnership under the rules stated in [§ 202(c) of the Uniform Partnership Act (1997) (Last Amended

2013)] [§ 7 of the Uniform Partnership Act (1914)] or a similar provision of the law of another jurisdiction;

   (iv) a decedent's estate; or

   (v) a government or a governmental subdivision, agency, or instrumentality.

(12) "Filing entity" means an entity whose formation requires the filing of a public organic record. The term does not include a limited liability partnership.

(13) "Foreign", with respect to an entity, means an entity governed as to its internal affairs by the law of a jurisdiction other than this state.

(14) "Governance interest" means a right under the organic law or organic rules of an unincorporated entity, other than as a governor, agent, assignee, or proxy, to:

   (A) receive or demand access to information concerning, or the books and records of, the entity;

   (B) vote for or consent to the election of the governors of the entity; or

   (C) receive notice of or vote on or consent to an issue involving the internal affairs of the entity.

(15) "Governor" means:

   (A) a director of a business corporation;

   (B) a director or trustee of a nonprofit corporation;

   (C) a general partner of a general partnership;

   (D) a general partner of a limited partnership;

   (E) a manager of a manager-managed limited liability company;

   (F) a member of a member-managed limited liability company;

   [(G) a director of a general cooperative association;]

   (H) a director of a limited cooperative association;

   (I) a manager of an unincorporated nonprofit association;

   (J) a trustee of a statutory trust, business trust, or common-law business trust; or

   (K) any other person under whose authority the powers of an entity are exercised and under whose direction the activities and affairs of the entity are managed pursuant to the organic law and organic rules of the entity.

(16) "Interest" means:

   (A) a share in a business corporation;

   (B) a membership in a nonprofit corporation;

   (C) a partnership interest in a general partnership;

   (D) a partnership interest in a limited partnership;

   (E) a membership interest in a limited liability company;

   [(F) a share in a general cooperative association;]

   (G) a member's interest in a limited cooperative association;

   (H) a membership in an unincorporated nonprofit association;

   (I) a beneficial interest in a statutory trust, business trust, or common-law business trust; or

   (J) a governance interest or distributional interest in any other type of unincorporated entity.

(17) "Interest Exchange" means a transaction authorized by Part 3.

(18) "Interest holder" means:

   (A) a shareholder of a business corporation;

   (B) a member of a nonprofit corporation;

   (C) a general partner of a general partnership;

   (D) a general partner of a limited partnership;

   (E) a limited partner of a limited partnership;

   (F) a member of a limited liability company;

   [(G) a shareholder of a general cooperative association;]

   (H) a member of a limited cooperative association;

   (I) a member of an unincorporated nonprofit association;

(J) a beneficiary or beneficial owner of a statutory trust, business trust, or common-law business trust; or

(K) any other direct holder of an interest.

(19) "Interest holder liability" means:

(A) personal liability for a liability of an entity which is imposed on a person:

(i) solely by reason of the status of the person as an interest holder; or

(ii) by the organic rules of the entity which make one or more specified interest holders or categories of interest holders liable in their capacity as interest holders for all or specified liabilities of the entity; or

(B) an obligation of an interest holder under the organic rules of an entity to contribute to the entity.

(20) "Merger" means a transaction authorized by Part 2.

(21) "Merging entity" means an entity that is a party to a merger and exists immediately before the merger becomes effective.

(22) "Organic law" means the law of an entity's jurisdiction of formation governing the internal affairs of the entity.

(23) "Organic rules" means the public organic record and private organic rules of an entity.

(24) "Plan" means a plan of merger, plan of interest exchange, plan of conversion, or plan of domestication.

(25) "Plan of conversion" means a plan under § 1142.

(26) "Plan of domestication" means a plan under § 1152.

(27) "Plan of interest exchange" means a plan under § 1132.

(28) "Plan of merger" means a plan under § 1122.

(29) "Private organic rules" means the rules, whether or not in a record, that govern the internal affairs of an entity, are binding on all its interest holders, and are not part of its public organic record, if any. The term includes:

(A) the bylaws of a business corporation;

(B) the bylaws of a nonprofit corporation;

(C) the partnership agreement of a general partnership;

(D) the partnership agreement of a limited partnership;

(E) the operating agreement of a limited liability company;

[**(F)** the bylaws of a general cooperative association;]

(G) the bylaws of a limited cooperative association;

(H) the governing principles of an unincorporated nonprofit association; and

(I) the trust instrument of a statutory trust or similar rules of a business trust or common-law business trust.

(30) "Protected agreement" means:

(A) a record evidencing indebtedness and any related agreement in effect on [the effective date of this act];

(B) an agreement that is binding on an entity on [the effective date of this act];

(C) the organic rules of an entity in effect on [the effective date of this act]; or

(D) an agreement that is binding on any of the governors or interest holders of an entity on [the effective date of this act].

(31) "Public organic record" means the record the filing of which by the Secretary of State is required to form an entity and any amendment to or restatement of that record. The term includes:

(A) the articles of incorporation of a business corporation;

(B) the articles of incorporation of a nonprofit corporation;

(C) the certificate of limited partnership of a limited partnership;

(D) the certificate of organization of a limited liability company;

[**(E)** the articles of incorporation of a general cooperative association;]

(F) the articles of organization of a limited co-operative association; and

(G) the certificate of trust of a statutory trust or similar record of a business trust.

(32) "Registered foreign entity" means a foreign entity that is registered to do business in this state pursuant to a record filed by the Secretary of State.

(33) "Statement of conversion" means a statement under § 1145.

(34) "Statement of domestication" means a statement under § 1155.

(35) "Statement of interest exchange" means a statement under § 1135.

(36) "Statement of merger" means a statement under § 1125.

(37) "Surviving entity" means the entity that continues in existence after or is created by a merger.

(38) "Type of entity" means a generic form of entity:

(A) recognized at common law; or

(B) formed under an organic law, whether or not some entities formed under that organic law are subject to provisions of that law that create different categories of the form of entity.

§ 1102. Relationship of Article to Other Laws.

(a) This article does not authorize an act prohibited by, and does not affect the application or requirements of, law other than this article.

(b) A transaction effected under this act may not create or impair a right, duty, or obligation of a person under the statutory law of this state relating to a change in control, takeover, business combination, control-share acquisition, or similar transaction involving a domestic merging, acquired, converting, or domesticating business corporation unless:

(1) if the corporation does not survive the transaction, the transaction satisfies any requirements of the law; or

(2) if the corporation survives the transaction, the approval of the plan is by a vote of the shareholders or directors which would be sufficient to create or impair the right, duty, or obligation directly under the law.

§ 1103. Required Notice or Approval.

(a) A domestic or foreign entity that is required to give notice to, or obtain the approval of, a governmental agency or officer of this state to be a party to a merger must give the notice or obtain the approval to be a party to an interest exchange, conversion, or domestication.

(b) Property held for a charitable purpose under the law of this state by a domestic or foreign entity immediately before a transaction under this article becomes effective may not, as a result of the transaction, be diverted from the objects for which it was donated, granted, devised, or otherwise transferred unless, to the extent required by or pursuant to the law of this state concerning cy pres or other law dealing with nondiversion of charitable assets, the entity obtains an appropriate order of [the appropriate court] [the Attorney General] specifying the disposition of the property.

(c) A bequest, devise, gift, grant, or promise contained in a will or other instrument of donation, subscription, or conveyance which is made to a merging entity that is not the surviving entity and which takes effect or remains payable after the merger inures to the surviving entity.

(d) A trust obligation that would govern property if transferred to a nonsurviving entity applies to property that is transferred to the surviving entity under this section.

Legislative Note: As an alternative to enacting Subsection (a), a state may identify each of its regulatory laws that requires prior approval for a merger of a regulated entity, decide whether regulatory approval should be required for an interest exchange, conversion, or domestication, and make amendments as appropriate to those laws.

As with Subsection (a), an adopting state may choose to amend its various laws with respect to the nondiversion of charitable property to cover the various transactions authorized by this act as an alternative to enacting Subsection (b).

§ 1104. Nonexclusivity.

The fact that a transaction under this article produces a certain result does not preclude the same result from being accomplished in any other manner permitted by law other than this article.

§ 1105. Reference to External Facts.

A plan may refer to facts ascertainable outside the plan if the manner in which the facts will operate upon the plan is specified in the plan. The facts may include the occurrence of an event or a determination or action by a person, whether or not the event, determination, or action is within the control of a party to the transaction.

§ 1106. Appraisal Rights.

An interest holder of a domestic merging, acquired, converting, or domesticating partnership is entitled to contractual appraisal rights in connection with a transaction under this article to the extent provided in:

(1) the partnership's organic rules; or

(2) the plan.

[§ 1107. Excluded Entities and Transactions.

(a) The following entities may not participate in a transaction under this article:

(1)

(2).

(b) This article may not be used to effect a transaction that:

(1)

(2).]

Legislative Note: *Subsection (a) may be used by states that have special statutes restricted to the organization of certain types of entities. A common example is banking statutes that prohibit banks from engaging in transactions other than pursuant to those statutes.*

Nonprofit entities may participate in transactions under this act with for-profit entities, subject to compliance with § 1103. If a state desires, however, to exclude entities with a charitable purpose or to exclude other types of entities from the scope of this article, that may be done by referring to those entities in Subsection (a).

Subsection (b) may be used to exclude certain types of transactions governed by more specific statutes. A common example is the conversion of an insurance company from mutual to stock form. There may be other types of transactions that vary greatly among the states.

Part 2. Merger

§ 1121. Merger Authorized.

(a) By complying with this [part]:

(1) one or more domestic partnerships may merge with one or more domestic or foreign entities into a domestic or foreign surviving entity; and

(2) two or more foreign entities may merge into a domestic partnership.

(b) By complying with the provisions of this [part] applicable to foreign entities, a foreign entity may be a party to a merger under this [part] or may be the surviving entity in such a merger if the merger is authorized by the law of the foreign entity's jurisdiction of formation.

§ 1122. Plan of Merger.

(a) A domestic partnership may become a party to a merger under this [part] by approving a plan of merger. The plan must be in a record and contain:

(1) as to each merging entity, its name, jurisdiction of formation, and type of entity;

(2) if the surviving entity is to be created in the merger, a statement to that effect and the entity's name, jurisdiction of formation, and type of entity;

(3) the manner of converting the interests in each party to the merger into interests, securities, obligations, money, other property, rights to acquire interests or securities, or any combination of the foregoing;

(4) if the surviving entity exists before the merger, any proposed amendments to:

(A) its public organic record, if any; or

(B) its private organic rules that are, or are proposed to be, in a record;

(5) if the surviving entity is to be created in the merger:

(A) its proposed public organic record, if any; and

(B) the full text of its private organic rules that are proposed to be in a record;

(6) the other terms and conditions of the merger; and

(7) any other provision required by the law of a merging entity's jurisdiction of formation or the organic rules of a merging entity.

(b) In addition to the requirements of subsection (a), a plan of merger may contain any other provision not prohibited by law.

§ 1123. Approval of Merger.

(a) A plan of merger is not effective unless it has been approved:

(1) by a domestic merging partnership, by all the partners of the partnership entitled to vote on or consent to any matter; and

(2) in a record, by each partner of a domestic merging partnership which will have interest holder liability for debts, obligations, and other liabilities that are incurred after the merger becomes effective, unless:

(A) the partnership agreement of the partnership provides in a record for the approval of a merger in which some or all of its partners become subject to interest holder liability by the affirmative vote or consent of fewer than all the partners; and

(B) the partner consented in a record to or voted for that provision of the partnership agreement or became a partner after the adoption of that provision.

(b) A merger involving a domestic merging entity that is not a partnership is not effective unless the merger is approved by that entity in accordance with its organic law.

(c) A merger involving a foreign merging entity is not effective unless the merger is approved by the

foreign entity in accordance with the law of the foreign entity's jurisdiction of formation.

§ 1124. Amendment or Abandonment of Plan of Merger.

(a) A plan of merger may be amended only with the consent of each party to the plan, except as otherwise provided in the plan.

(b) A domestic merging partnership may approve an amendment of a plan of merger:

(1) in the same manner as the plan was approved, if the plan does not provide for the manner in which it may be amended; or

(2) by its partners in the manner provided in the plan, but a partner that was entitled to vote on or consent to approval of the merger is entitled to vote on or consent to any amendment of the plan that will change:

(A) the amount or kind of interests, securities, obligations, money, other property, rights to acquire interests or securities, or any combination of the foregoing, to be received by the interest holders of any party to the plan;

(B) the public organic record, if any, or private organic rules of the surviving entity that will be in effect immediately after the merger be effective, except for changes that do not require approval of the interest holders of the surviving entity under its organic law or organic rules; or

(C) any other terms or conditions of the plan, if the change would adversely affect the partner in any material respect.

(c) After a plan of merger has been approved and before a statement of merger becomes effective, the plan may be abandoned as provided in the plan. Unless prohibited by the plan, a domestic merging partnership may abandon the plan in the same manner as the plan was approved.

(d) If a plan of merger is abandoned after a statement of merger has been delivered to the Secretary of State for filing and before the statement becomes effective, a statement of abandonment, signed by a party to the plan, must be delivered to the Secretary of State for filing before the statement of merger becomes effective. The statement of abandonment takes effect on filing, and the merger is abandoned and does not become effective. The statement of abandonment must contain:

(1) the name of each party to the plan of merger;

(2) the date on which the statement of merger was filed by the Secretary of State; and

(3) a statement that the merger has been abandoned in accordance with this section.

§ 1125. Statement of Merger; Effective Date of Merger.

(a) A statement of merger must be signed by each merging entity and delivered to the Secretary of State for filing.

(b) A statement of merger must contain:

(1) the name, jurisdiction of formation, and type of entity of each merging entity that is not the surviving entity;

(2) the name, jurisdiction of formation, and type of entity of the surviving entity;

(3) a statement that the merger was approved by each domestic merging entity, if any, in accordance with this [part] and by each foreign merging entity, if any, in accordance with the law of its jurisdiction of formation;

(4) if the surviving entity exists before the merger and is a domestic filing entity, any amendment to its public organic record approved as part of the plan of merger;

(5) if the surviving entity is created by the merger and is a domestic filing entity, its public organic record, as an attachment; and

(6) if the surviving entity is created by the merger and is a domestic limited liability partnership, its statement of qualification, as an attachment.

(c) In addition to the requirements of subsection (b), a statement of merger may contain any other provision not prohibited by law.

(d) If the surviving entity is a domestic entity, its public organic record, if any, must satisfy the requirements of the law of this state, except that the public organic record does not need to be signed.

(e) A plan of merger that is signed by all the merging entities and meets all the requirements of subsection (b) may be delivered to the Secretary of State for filing instead of a statement of merger and on filing has the same effect. If a plan of merger is filed as provided in this subsection, references in this article to a statement of merger refer to the plan of merger filed under this subsection.

(f) If the surviving entity is a domestic partnership, the merger becomes effective when the statement of merger is effective. In all other cases, the merger becomes effective on the later of:

(1) the date and time provided by the organic law of the surviving entity; and

(2) when the statement is effective.

§ 1126. Effect of Merger.

(a) When a merger becomes effective:

(1) the surviving entity continues or comes into existence;

(2) each merging entity that is not the surviving entity ceases to exist;

(3) all property of each merging entity vests in the surviving entity without transfer, reversion, or impairment;

(4) all debts, obligations, and other liabilities of each merging entity are debts, obligations, and other liabilities of the surviving entity;

(5) except as otherwise provided by law or the plan of merger, all the rights, privileges, immunities, powers, and purposes of each merging entity vest in the surviving entity;

(6) if the surviving entity exists before the merger:

(A) all its property continues to be vested in it without transfer, reversion, or impairment;

(B) it remains subject to all its debts, obligations, and other liabilities; and

(C) all its rights, privileges, immunities, powers, and purposes continue to be vested in it;

(7) the name of the surviving entity may be substituted for the name of any merging entity that is a party to any pending action or proceeding;

(8) if the surviving entity exists before the merger:

(A) its public organic record, if any, is amended as provided in the statement of merger; and

(B) its private organic rules that are to be in a record, if any, are amended to the extent provided in the plan of merger;

(9) if the surviving entity is created by the merger, its private organic rules become effective and:

(A) if it is a filing entity, its public organic record becomes effective; and

(B) if it is a limited liability partnership, its statement of qualification becomes effective; and

(10) the interests in each merging entity which are to be converted in the merger are converted, and the interest holders of those interests are entitled only to the rights provided to them under the plan of merger and to any appraisal rights they have under § 1106 and the merging entity's organic law.

(b) Except as otherwise provided in the organic law or organic rules of a merging entity, the merger does not give rise to any rights that an interest holder, governor, or third party would have upon a dissolution, liquidation, or winding up of the merging entity.

(c) When a merger becomes effective, a person that did not have interest holder liability with respect to any of the merging entities and becomes subject to interest holder liability with respect to a domestic entity as a result of the merger has interest holder liability only to the extent provided by the organic law of that entity and only for those debts, obligations, and other liabilities that are incurred after the merger becomes effective.

(d) When a merger becomes effective, the interest holder liability of a person that ceases to hold an interest in a domestic merging partnership with respect to which the person had interest holder liability is subject to the following rules:

(1) The merger does not discharge any interest holder liability under this act to the extent the interest holder liability was incurred before the merger became effective.

(2) The person does not have interest holder liability under this act for any debt, obligation, or other liability that is incurred after the merger becomes effective.

(3) This act continues to apply to the release, collection, or discharge of any interest holder liability preserved under paragraph (1) as if the merger had not occurred and the surviving entity were the domestic merging entity.

(4) The person has whatever rights of contribution from any other person as are provided by this act, law other than this act, or the partnership agreement of the domestic merging partnership with respect to any interest holder liability preserved under paragraph (1) as if the merger had not occurred.

(e) When a merger has become effective, a foreign entity that is the surviving entity may be served with process in this state for the collection and enforcement of any debts, obligations, or other liabilities of a domestic merging partnership as provided in § 119.

(f) When a merger has become effective, the registration to do business in this state of any foreign merging entity that is not the surviving entity is canceled.

Part 3. Interest Exchange

§ 1131. Interest Exchange Authorized.

(a) By complying with this [part]:

(1) a domestic partnership may acquire all of one or more classes or series of interests of another domestic entity or a foreign entity in exchange for interests, securities, obligations, money, other property, rights to acquire interests or securities, or any combination of the foregoing; or

(2) all of one or more classes or series of interests of a domestic partnership may be acquired by another domestic entity or a foreign entity in exchange for interests, securities, obligations, money, other property, rights to acquire interests or securities, or any combination of the foregoing.

(b) By complying with the provisions of this [part] applicable to foreign entities, a foreign entity may be the acquiring or acquired entity in an interest exchange under this [part] if the interest exchange is authorized by the law of the foreign entity's jurisdiction of formation.

(c) If a protected agreement contains a provision that applies to a merger of a domestic partnership but does not refer to an interest exchange, the provision applies to an interest exchange in which the domestic partnership is the acquired entity as if the interest exchange were a merger until the provision is amended after [the effective date of this act].

§ 1132. Plan of Interest Exchange.

(a) A domestic partnership may be the acquired entity in an interest exchange under this [part] by approving a plan of interest exchange. The plan must be in a record and contain:

(1) the name of the acquired entity;

(2) the name, jurisdiction of formation, and type of entity of the acquiring entity;

(3) the manner of converting the interests in the acquired entity into interests, securities, obligations, money, other property, rights to acquire interests or securities, or any combination of the foregoing;

(4) any proposed amendments to the partnership agreement that are, or are proposed to be, in a record of the acquired entity;

(5) the other terms and conditions of the interest exchange; and

(6) any other provision required by the law of this state or the partnership agreement of the acquired entity.

(b) In addition to the requirements of subsection (a), a plan of interest exchange may contain any other provision not prohibited by law.

§ 1133. Approval of Interest Exchange.

(a) A plan of interest exchange is not effective unless it has been approved:

(1) by all the partners of a domestic acquired partnership entitled to vote on or consent to any matter; and

(2) in a record, by each partner of the domestic acquired partnership that will have interest holder liability for debts, obligations, and other liabilities that are incurred after the interest exchange becomes effective, unless:

(A) the partnership agreement of the partnership provides in a record for the approval of an interest exchange or a merger in which some or all its partners become subject to interest holder liability by the affirmative vote or consent of fewer than all the partners; and

(B) the partner consented in a record to or voted for that provision of the partnership agreement or became a partner after the adoption of that provision.

(b) An interest exchange involving a domestic acquired entity that is not a partnership is not effective unless it is approved by the domestic entity in accordance with its organic law.

(c) An interest exchange involving a foreign acquired entity is not effective unless it is approved by the foreign entity in accordance with the law of the foreign entity's jurisdiction of formation.

(d) Except as otherwise provided in its organic law or organic rules, the interest holders of the acquiring entity are not required to approve the interest exchange.

§ 1134. Amendment or Abandonment of Plan of Interest Exchange.

(a) A plan of interest exchange may be amended only with the consent of each party to the plan, except as otherwise provided in the plan.

(b) A domestic acquired partnership may approve an amendment of a plan of interest exchange:

(1) in the same manner as the plan was approved, if the plan does not provide for the manner in which it may be amended; or

(2) by its partners in the manner provided in the plan, but a partner that was entitled to vote on or consent to approval of the interest exchange is entitled to vote on or consent to any amendment of the plan that will change:

(A) the amount or kind of interests, securities, obligations, money, other property, rights to acquire interests or securities, or any combination of the foregoing, to be received by any of the partners of the acquired partnership under the plan;

(B) the partnership agreement of the acquired partnership that will be in effect immediately after the interest exchange becomes effective, except for changes that do not require approval of the partners of the acquired partnership under this act or the partnership agreement; or

(C) any other terms or conditions of the plan, if the change would adversely affect the partner in any material respect.

(c) After a plan of interest exchange has been approved and before a statement of interest exchange becomes effective, the plan may be abandoned as provided in the plan. Unless prohibited by the plan, a domestic acquired partnership may abandon the plan in the same manner as the plan was approved.

(d) If a plan of interest exchange is abandoned after a statement of interest exchange has been delivered to the Secretary of State for filing and before the statement becomes effective, a statement of abandonment, signed by the acquired partnership, must be delivered to the Secretary of State for filing before the statement of interest exchange becomes effective. The statement of abandonment takes effect on filing, and the interest exchange is abandoned and does not become effective. The statement of abandonment must contain:

(1) the name of the acquired partnership;

(2) the date on which the statement of interest exchange was filed by the Secretary of State; and

(3) a statement that the interest exchange has been abandoned in accordance with this section.

§ 1135. Statement of Interest Exchange; Effective Date of Interest Exchange.

(a) A statement of interest exchange must be signed by a domestic acquired partnership and delivered to the Secretary of State for filing.

(b) A statement of interest exchange must contain:

(1) the name of the acquired partnership;

(2) the name, jurisdiction of formation, and type of entity of the acquiring entity; and

(3) a statement that the plan of interest exchange was approved by the acquired partnership in accordance with this [part].

(c) In addition to the requirements of subsection (b), a statement of interest exchange may contain any other provision not prohibited by law.

(d) A plan of interest exchange that is signed by a domestic acquired partnership and meets all the requirements of subsection (b) may be delivered to the Secretary of State for filing instead of a statement of interest exchange and on filing has the same effect. If a plan of interest exchange is filed as provided in this subsection, references in this article to a statement of interest exchange refer to the plan of interest exchange filed under this subsection.

(e) An interest exchange becomes effective when the statement of interest exchange is effective.

§ 1136. Effect of Interest Exchange.

(a) When an interest exchange in which the acquired entity is a domestic partnership becomes effective:

(1) the interests in the acquired partnership which are the subject of the interest exchange are converted, and the partners holding those interests are entitled only to the rights provided to them under the plan of interest exchange and to any appraisal rights they have under § 1106;

(2) the acquiring entity becomes the interest holder of the interests in the acquired partnership stated in the plan of interest exchange to be acquired by the acquiring entity; and

(3) the provisions of the partnership agreement of the acquired partnership that are to be in a record, if any, are amended to the extent provided in the plan of interest exchange.

(b) Except as otherwise provided in the partnership agreement of a domestic acquired partnership, the interest exchange does not give rise to any rights that a partner or third party would have upon a dissolution, liquidation, or winding up of the acquired partnership.

(c) When an interest exchange becomes effective, a person that did not have interest holder liability with respect to a domestic acquired partnership and becomes subject to interest holder liability with respect to a domestic entity as a result of the interest exchange has interest holder liability only to the extent provided by the organic law of the entity and only for those debts, obligations, and other liabilities that are incurred after the interest exchange becomes effective.

(d) When an interest exchange becomes effective, the interest holder liability of a person that ceases to hold an interest in a domestic acquired partnership with respect to which the person had interest holder liability is subject to the following rules:

(1) The interest exchange does not discharge any interest holder liability under this act to the extent the interest holder liability was incurred before the interest exchange became effective.

(2) The person does not have interest holder liability under this act for any debt, obligation, or other liability that is incurred after the interest exchange becomes effective.

(3) This act continues to apply to the release, collection, or discharge of any interest holder liability preserved under paragraph (1) as if the interest exchange had not occurred.

(4) The person has whatever rights of contribution from any other person as are provided by this act, law other than this act, or the partnership agreement of the domestic acquired partnership with respect to any interest holder liability preserved under paragraph (1) as if the interest exchange had not occurred.

Part 4. Conversion

§ 1141. Conversion Authorized.

(a) By complying with this [part], a domestic partnership may become:

(1) a domestic entity that is a different type of entity; or

(2) a foreign entity that is a different type of entity, if the conversion is authorized by the law of the foreign entity's jurisdiction of formation.

(b) By complying with the provisions of this [part] applicable to foreign entities, a foreign entity that is not a foreign partnership may become a domestic partnership if the conversion is authorized by the law of the foreign entity's jurisdiction of formation.

(c) If a protected agreement contains a provision that applies to a merger of a domestic partnership but does not refer to a conversion, the provision applies to a conversion of the partnership as if the conversion were a merger until the provision is amended after [the effective date of this act].

§ 1142. Plan of Conversion.

(a) A domestic partnership may convert to a different type of entity under this [part] by approving a plan of conversion. The plan must be in a record and contain:

(1) the name of the converting partnership;

(2) the name, jurisdiction of formation, and type of entity of the converted entity;

(3) the manner of converting the interests in the converting partnership into interests, securities, obligations, money, other property, rights to acquire interests or securities, or any combination of the foregoing;

(4) the proposed public organic record of the converted entity if it will be a filing entity;

(5) the full text of the private organic rules of the converted entity which are proposed to be in a record;

(6) the other terms and conditions of the conversion; and

(7) any other provision required by the law of this state or the partnership agreement of the converting partnership.

(b) In addition to the requirements of subsection (a), a plan of conversion may contain any other provision not prohibited by law.

§ 1143. Approval of Conversion.

(a) A plan of conversion is not effective unless it has been approved:

(1) by a domestic converting partnership, by all the partners of the partnership entitled to vote on or consent to any matter; and

(2) in a record, by each partner of a domestic converting partnership which will have interest holder liability for debts, obligations, and other liabilities that are incurred after the conversion becomes effective, unless:

(A) the partnership agreement of the partnership provides in a record for the approval of a conversion or a merger in which some or all of its partners become subject to interest holder liability by the affirmative vote or consent of fewer than all the partners; and

(B) the partner voted for or consented in a record to that provision of the partnership agreement or became a partner after the adoption of that provision.

(b) A conversion involving a domestic converting entity that is not a partnership is not effective unless it is approved by the domestic converting entity in accordance with its organic law.

(c) A conversion of a foreign converting entity is not effective unless it is approved by the foreign entity in accordance with the law of the foreign entity's jurisdiction of formation.

§ 1144. Amendment or Abandonment of Plan of Conversion.

(a) A plan of conversion of a domestic converting partnership may be amended:

(1) in the same manner as the plan was approved, if the plan does not provide for the manner in which it may be amended; or

(2) by its partners in the manner provided in the plan, but a partner that was entitled to vote on or consent to approval of the conversion is entitled to vote on or consent to any amendment of the plan that will change:

(A) the amount or kind of interests, securities, obligations, money, other property, rights to acquire interests or securities, or any combination of the foregoing, to be received by any of the partners of the converting partnership under the plan;

(B) the public organic record, if any, or private organic rules of the converted entity which will be in effect immediately after the conversion becomes effective, except for changes that do not require approval of the interest holders of the converted entity under its organic law or organic rules; or

(C) any other terms or conditions of the plan, if the change would adversely affect the partner in any material respect.

(b) After a plan of conversion has been approved by a domestic converting partnership and before a statement of conversion becomes effective, the plan may be abandoned as provided in the plan. Unless prohibited by the plan, a domestic converting partnership may abandon the plan in the same manner as the plan was approved.

(c) If a plan of conversion is abandoned after a statement of conversion has been delivered to the Secretary of State for filing and before the statement becomes effective, a statement of abandonment, signed by the converting entity, must be delivered to the Secretary of State for filing before the statement of conversion becomes effective. The statement of abandonment takes effect on filing, and the conversion is abandoned and does not become effective. The statement of abandonment must contain:

(1) the name of the converting partnership;

(2) the date on which the statement of conversion was filed by the Secretary of State; and

(3) a statement that the conversion has been abandoned in accordance with this section.

§ 1145. Statement of Conversion; Effective Date of Conversion.

(a) A statement of conversion must be signed by the converting entity and delivered to the Secretary of State for filing.

(b) A statement of conversion must contain:

(1) the name, jurisdiction of formation, and type of entity of the converting entity;

(2) the name, jurisdiction of formation, and type of entity of the converted entity;

(3) if the converting entity is a domestic partnership, a statement that the plan of conversion was approved in accordance with this [part] or, if the converting entity is a foreign entity, a statement that the conversion was approved by the foreign entity in accordance with the law of its jurisdiction of formation;

(4) if the converted entity is a domestic filing entity, its public organic record, as an attachment; and

(5) if the converted entity is a domestic limited liability partnership, its statement of qualification, as an attachment.

(c) In addition to the requirements of subsection (b), a statement of conversion may contain any other provision not prohibited by law.

(d) If the converted entity is a domestic entity, its public organic record, if any, must satisfy the requirements of the law of this state, except that the public organic record does not need to be signed.

(e) A plan of conversion that is signed by a domestic converting partnership and meets all the requirements of subsection (b) may be delivered to the Secretary of State for filing instead of a statement of conversion and on filing has the same effect. If a plan of conversion is filed as provided in this subsection, references in this article to a statement of conversion refer to the plan of conversion filed under this subsection.

(f) If the converted entity is a domestic partnership, the conversion becomes effective when the statement of conversion is effective. In all other cases, the conversion becomes effective on the later of:

(1) the date and time provided by the organic law of the converted entity; and

(2) when the statement is effective.

§ 1146. Effect of Conversion.

(a) When a conversion becomes effective:

(1) the converted entity is:

(A) organized under and subject to the organic law of the converted entity; and

(B) the same entity without interruption as the converting entity;

(2) all property of the converting entity continues to be vested in the converted entity without transfer, reversion, or impairment;

(3) all debts, obligations, and other liabilities of the converting entity continue as debts, obligations, and other liabilities of the converted entity;

(4) except as otherwise provided by law or the plan of conversion, all the rights, privileges, immunities, powers, and purposes of the converting entity remain in the converted entity;

(5) the name of the converted entity may be substituted for the name of the converting entity in any pending action or proceeding;

(6) if the converted entity is a limited liability partnership, its statement of qualification becomes effective;

(7) the provisions of the partnership agreement of the converted entity which are to be in a record, if any, approved as part of the plan of conversion become effective; and

(8) the interests in the converting entity are converted, and the interest holders of the converting entity are entitled only to the rights provided to them under the plan of conversion and to any appraisal rights they have under § 1106.

(b) Except as otherwise provided in the partnership agreement of a domestic converting partnership, the conversion does not give rise to any rights that a partner or third party would have upon a dissolution, liquidation, or winding up of the converting entity.

(c) When a conversion becomes effective, a person that did not have interest holder liability with respect to the converting entity and becomes subject to interest holder liability with respect to a domestic entity as a result of the conversion has interest holder liability only to the extent provided by the organic law of the entity and only for those debts, obligations, and other liabilities that are incurred after the conversion becomes effective.

(d) When a conversion becomes effective, the interest holder liability of a person that ceases to hold an interest in a domestic converting partnership with respect to which the person had interest holder liability is subject to the following rules:

(1) The conversion does not discharge any interest holder liability under this act to the extent the interest holder liability was incurred before the conversion became effective.

(2) The person does not have interest holder liability under this act for any debt, obligation, or other liability that is incurred after the conversion becomes effective.

(3) This act continues to apply to the release, collection, or discharge of any interest holder liability preserved under paragraph (1) as if the conversion had not occurred.

(4) The person has whatever rights of contribution from any other person as are provided by this act, law other than this act, or the organic

rules of the converting entity with respect to any interest holder liability preserved under paragraph (1) as if the conversion had not occurred.

(e) When a conversion has become effective, a foreign entity that is the converted entity may be served with process in this state for the collection and enforcement of any of its debts, obligations, and other liabilities as provided in § 119.

(f) If the converting entity is a registered foreign entity, its registration to do business in this state is canceled when the conversion becomes effective.

(g) A conversion does not require the entity to wind up its affairs and does not constitute or cause the dissolution of the entity.

Part 5. Domestication

§ 1151. Domestication Authorized.

(a) By complying with this [part], a domestic limited liability partnership may become a foreign limited liability partnership if the domestication is authorized by the law of the foreign jurisdiction.

(b) By complying with the provisions of this [part] applicable to foreign limited liability partnerships, a foreign limited liability partnership may become a domestic limited liability partnership if the domestication is authorized by the law of the foreign limited liability partnership's jurisdiction of formation.

(c) If a protected agreement contains a provision that applies to a merger of a domestic limited liability partnership but does not refer to a domestication, the provision applies to a domestication of the limited liability partnership as if the domestication were a merger until the provision is amended after [the effective date of this act].

§ 1152. Plan of Domestication.

(a) A domestic limited liability partnership may become a foreign limited liability partnership in a domestication by approving a plan of domestication. The plan must be in a record and contain:

(1) the name of the domesticating limited liability partnership;

(2) the name and jurisdiction of formation of the domesticated limited liability partnership;

(3) the manner of converting the interests in the domesticating limited liability partnership into interests, securities, obligations, money, other property, rights to acquire interests or securities, or any combination of the foregoing;

(4) the proposed statement of qualification of the domesticated limited liability partnership;

(5) the full text of the provisions of the partnership agreement of the domesticated limited liability partnership that are proposed to be in a record;

(6) the other terms and conditions of the domestication; and

(7) any other provision required by the law of this state or the partnership agreement of the domesticating limited liability partnership.

(b) In addition to the requirements of subsection (a), a plan of domestication may contain any other provision not prohibited by law.

§ 1153. Approval of Domestication.

(a) A plan of domestication of a domestic domesticating limited liability partnership is not effective unless it has been approved:

(1) by all the partners entitled to vote on or consent to any matter; and

(2) in a record, by each partner that will have interest holder liability for debts, obligations, and other liabilities that are incurred after the domestication becomes effective, unless:

(A) the partnership agreement of the domesticating partnership in a record provides for the approval of a domestication or merger in which some or all of its partners become subject to interest holder liability by the affirmative vote or consent of fewer than all the partners; and

(B) the partner voted for or consented in a record to that provision of the partnership

agreement or became a partner after the adoption of that provision.

(b) A domestication of a foreign domesticating limited liability partnership is not effective unless it is approved in accordance with the law of the foreign limited liability partnership's jurisdiction of formation.

§ 1154. Amendment or Abandonment of Plan of Domestication.

(a) A plan of domestication of a domestic domesticating limited liability partnership may be amended:

(1) in the same manner as the plan was approved, if the plan does not provide for the manner in which it may be amended; or

(2) by its partners in the manner provided in the plan, but a partner that was entitled to vote on or consent to approval of the domestication is entitled to vote on or consent to any amendment of the plan that will change:

(A) the amount or kind of interests, securities, obligations, money, other property, rights to acquire interests or securities, or any combination of the foregoing, to be received by any of the partners of the domesticating limited liability partnership under the plan;

(B) the partnership agreement of the domesticated limited liability partnership that will be in effect immediately after the domestication becomes effective, except for changes that do not require approval of the partners of the domesticated limited liability partnership under its organic law or partnership agreement; or

(C) any other terms or conditions of the plan, if the change would adversely affect the partner in any material respect.

(b) After a plan of domestication has been approved by a domestic domesticating limited liability partnership and before a statement of domestication becomes effective, the plan may be abandoned as provided in the plan. Unless prohibited by the plan, a domestic domesticating limited liability partnership may abandon the plan in the same manner as the plan was approved.

(c) If a plan of domestication is abandoned after a statement of domestication has been delivered to the Secretary of State for filing and before the statement becomes effective, a statement of abandonment, signed by the domesticating limited liability partnership, must be delivered to the Secretary of State for filing before the statement of domestication becomes effective. The statement of abandonment takes effect on filing, and the domestication is abandoned and does not become effective. The statement of abandonment must contain:

(1) the name of the domesticating limited liability partnership;

(2) the date on which the statement of domestication was filed by the Secretary of State; and

(3) a statement that the domestication has been abandoned in accordance with this section.

§ 1155. Statement of Domestication; Effective Date of Domestication.

(a) A statement of domestication must be signed by the domesticating limited liability partnership and delivered to the Secretary of State for filing.

(b) A statement of domestication must contain:

(1) the name and jurisdiction of formation of the domesticating limited liability partnership;

(2) the name and jurisdiction of formation of the domesticated limited liability partnership;

(3) if the domesticating limited liability partnership is a domestic limited liability partnership, a statement that the plan of domestication was approved in accordance with this [part] or, if the domesticating limited liability partnership is a foreign limited liability partnership, a statement that the domestication was approved in accordance with the law of its jurisdiction of formation; and

(4) the statement of qualification of the domesticated limited liability partnership, as an attachment.

(c) In addition to the requirements of subsection (b), a statement of domestication may contain any other provision not prohibited by law.

(d) The statement of qualification of a domesticated domestic limited liability partnership must satisfy the requirements of this act, but the statement does not need to be signed.

(e) A plan of domestication that is signed by a domesticating domestic limited liability partnership and meets all the requirements of subsection (b) may be delivered to the Secretary of State for filing instead of a statement of domestication and on filing has the same effect. If a plan of domestication is filed as provided in this subsection, references in this article to a statement of domestication refer to the plan of domestication filed under this subsection.

(f) If the domesticated entity is a domestic partnership, the domestication becomes effective when the statement of domestication is effective. If the domesticated entity is a foreign partnership, the domestication becomes effective on the later of:

(1) the date and time provided in the organic law of the domesticated entity; and

(2) when the statement is effective.

§ 1156. Effect of Domestication.

(a) When a domestication becomes effective:

(1) the domesticated entity is:

(A) organized under and subject to the organic law of the domesticated entity; and

(B) the same entity without interruption as the domesticating entity;

(2) all property of the domesticating entity continues to be vested in the domesticated entity without transfer, reversion, or impairment;

(3) all debts, obligations, and other liabilities of the domesticating entity continue as debts, obligations, and other liabilities of the domesticated entity;

(4) except as otherwise provided by law or the plan of domestication, all the rights, privileges,

immunities, powers, and purposes of the domesticating entity remain in the domesticated entity;

(5) the name of the domesticated entity may be substituted for the name of the domesticating entity in any pending action or proceeding;

(6) the statement of qualification of the domesticated entity becomes effective;

(7) the provisions of the partnership agreement of the domesticated entity that are to be in a record, if any, approved as part of the plan of domestication become effective; and

(8) the interests in the domesticating entity are converted to the extent and as approved in connection with the domestication, and the partners of the domesticating entity are entitled only to the rights provided to them under the plan of domestication and to any appraisal rights they have under § 1106.

(b) Except as otherwise provided in the organic law or partnership agreement of the domesticating limited liability partnership, the domestication does not give rise to any rights that a partner or third party would otherwise have upon a dissolution, liquidation, or winding up of the domesticating partnership.

(c) When a domestication becomes effective, a person that did not have interest holder liability with respect to the domesticating limited liability partnership and becomes subject to interest holder liability with respect to a domestic limited liability partnership as a result of the domestication has interest holder liability only to the extent provided by this act and only for those debts, obligations, and other liabilities that are incurred after the domestication becomes effective.

(d) When a domestication becomes effective, the interest holder liability of a person that ceases to hold an interest in a domestic domesticating limited liability partnership with respect to which the person had interest holder liability is subject to the following rules:

(1) The domestication does not discharge any interest holder liability under this act to the extent the interest holder liability was incurred before the domestication became effective.

(2) A person does not have interest holder liability under this act for any debt, obligation, or other liability that is incurred after the domestication becomes effective.

(3) This act continues to apply to the release, collection, or discharge of any interest holder liability preserved under paragraph (1) as if the domestication had not occurred.

(4) A person has whatever rights of contribution from any other person as are provided by this act, law other than this act, or the partnership agreement of the domestic domesticating limited liability partnership with respect to any interest holder liability preserved under paragraph (1) as if the domestication had not occurred.

(e) When a domestication becomes effective, a foreign limited liability partnership that is the domesticated partnership may be served with process in this state for the collection and enforcement of any of its debts, obligations, and other liabilities as provided in § 119.

(f) If the domesticating limited liability partnership is a registered foreign entity, the registration of the partnership is canceled when the domestication becomes effective.

(g) A domestication does not require a domestic domesticating limited liability partnership to wind up its business and does not constitute or cause the dissolution of the partnership.

Article 12. Miscellaneous Provisions

§ 1201. Uniformity of Application and Construction.

In applying and construing this uniform act, consideration must be given to the need to promote lmatter among states that enact it.

§ 1202. Relation to Electronic Signatures in Global and National Commerce Act.

This act modifies, limits, and supersedes the Electronic Signatures in Global and National Commerce Act, 15 U.S.C. § 7001 et seq., but does not modify, limit, or supersede § 101(c) of that act, 15 U.S.C. § 7001(c), or authorize electronic delivery of any of the notices described in § 103(b) of that act, 15 U.S.C. § 7003(b).

§ 1203. Savings Clause.

This act does not affect an action commenced, proceeding brought, or right accrued before [the effective date of this act].

§ 1204. Severability Clause.

If any provision of this act or its application to any person or circumstance is held invalid, the invalidity does not affect other provisions or applications of this act which can be given effect without the invalid provision or application, and to this end the provisions of this act are severable.

Legislative Note: *Include this section only if this state lacks a general severability statute or decision by the highest court of this state stating a general rule of severability.*

§ 1205. Repeals.

The following are repealed:

> **(1)** [the state partnership act as [amended, and as] in effect immediately before [the effective date of this act]].
>
> **(2)** . . . .
>
> **(3)** . . . .

§ 1206. Effective Date.

This act takes effect . . . .

Uniform Limited Liability Company Act (2013)

Copyright © 2014 by National Conference of Commissioners on Uniform State Laws

Table of Contents

[Article] 1. General Provisions

§ 101. Short Title

This [act] may be cited as the Uniform Limited Liability Company Act.

§ 102. Definitions

In this [act]:

(1) "Certificate of organization" means the certificate required by § 201. The term includes the certificate as amended or restated.

(2) "Contribution", except in the phrase "right of contribution", means property or a benefit described in § 402 which is provided by a person to a limited liability company to become a member or in the person's capacity as a member.

(3) "Debtor in bankruptcy" means a person that is the subject of:

(A) an order for relief under Title 11 of the United States Code or a comparable order under a successor statute of general application; or

(B) a comparable order under federal, state, or foreign law governing insolvency.

(4) "Distribution" means a transfer of money or other property from a limited liability company to a person on account of a transferable interest or in the person's capacity as a member. The term:

(A) includes:

(i) a redemption or other purchase by a limited liability company of a transferable interest; and

(ii) a transfer to a member in return for the member's relinquishment of any right to participate as a member in the management or conduct of the company's activities and affairs or to have access to records or other information concerning the company's activities and affairs; and

(B) does not include amounts constituting reasonable compensation for present or past service or payments made in the ordinary course of business under a bona fide retirement plan or other bona fide benefits program.

(5) "Foreign limited liability company" means an unincorporated entity formed under the law of a jurisdiction other than this state which would be a limited liability company if formed under the law of this state.

(6) "Jurisdiction", used to refer to a political entity, means the United States, a state, a foreign county, or a political subdivision of a foreign country.

(7) "Jurisdiction of formation" means the jurisdiction whose law governs the internal affairs of an entity.

(8) "Limited liability company", except in the phrase "foreign limited liability company" and in [Article] 10, means an entity formed under this [act] or which becomes subject to this [act] under [Article] 10 or § 110.

(9) "Manager" means a person that under the operating agreement of a manager- managed limited liability company is responsible, alone or in concert with others, for performing the management functions stated in § 407(c).

(10) "Manager-managed limited liability company" means a limited liability company that qualifies under § 407(a).

(11) "Member" means a person that:

  (A) has become a member of a limited liability company under § 401 or was a member in a company when the company became subject to this [act] under § 110; and

  (B) has not dissociated under § 602.

(12) "Member-managed limited liability company" means a limited liability company that is not a manager-managed limited liability company.

(13) "Operating agreement" means the agreement, whether or not referred to as an operating agreement and whether oral, implied, in a record, or in any combination thereof, of all the members of a limited liability company, including a sole member, concerning the matters described in § 105(a). The term includes the agreement as amended or restated.

(14) "Organizer" means a person that acts under § 201 to form a limited liability company.

(15) "Person" means an individual, business corporation, nonprofit corporation, partnership, limited partnership, limited liability company, [general cooperative association,] limited cooperative association, unincorporated nonprofit association, statutory trust, business trust, common-law business trust, estate, trust, association, joint venture, public corporation, government or governmental subdivision, agency, or instrumentality, or any other legal or commercial entity.

(16) "Principal office" means the principal executive office of a limited liability company or foreign limited liability company, whether or not the office is located in this state.

(17) "Property" means all property, whether real, personal, or mixed or tangible or intangible, or any right or interest therein.

(18) "Record", used as a noun, means information that is inscribed on a tangible medium or that is stored in an electronic or other medium and is retrievable in perceivable form.

(19) "Registered agent" means an agent of a limited liability company or foreign limited liability company which is authorized to receive service of any process, notice, or demand required or permitted by law to be served on the company.

(20) "Registered foreign limited liability company" means a foreign limited liability company that is registered to do business in this state pursuant to a statement of registration filed by the [Secretary of State].

(21) "Sign" means, with present intent to authenticate or adopt a record:

  (A) to execute or adopt a tangible symbol; or

  (B) to attach to or logically associate with the record an electronic symbol, sound, or process.

(22) "State" means a state of the United States, the District of Columbia, Puerto Rico, the United States Virgin Islands, or any territory or insular possession subject to the jurisdiction of the United States.

(23) "Transfer" includes:

    (A) an assignment;

    (B) a conveyance;

    (C) a sale;

    (D) a lease;

    (E) an encumbrance, including a mortgage or security interest;

    (F) a gift; and

    (G) a transfer by operation of law.

(24) "Transferable interest" means the right, as initially owned by a person in the person's capacity as a member, to receive distributions from a limited liability company, whether or not the person remains a member or continues to own any part of the right. The term applies to any fraction of the interest, by whomever owned.

(25) "Transferee" means a person to which all or part of a transferable interest has been transferred, whether or not the transferor is a member. The term includes a person that owns a transferable interest under § 603(a)(3).

§ 103. Knowledge; Notice.

(a) A person knows a fact if the person:

    (1) has actual knowledge of it; or

    (2) is deemed to know it under subsection (d)(1) or law other than this [act].

(b) A person has notice of a fact if the person:

    (1) has reason to know the fact from all the facts known to the person at the time in question; or

    (2) is deemed to have notice of the fact under subsection (d)(2).

(c) Subject to § 210(f), a person notifies another person of a fact by taking steps reasonably required to inform the other person in ordinary course, whether or not those steps cause the other person to know the fact.

(d) A person not a member is deemed:

    (1) to know of a limitation on authority to transfer real property as provided in § 302(g); and

    (2) to have notice of a limited liability company's:

(A) dissolution 90 days after a statement of dissolution under § 702(b)(2)(A) becomes effective;

(B) termination 90 days after a statement of termination under § 702(b)(2)(F) becomes effective; and

(C) participation in a merger, interest exchange, conversion, or domestication, 90 days after articles of merger, interest exchange, conversion, or domestication under [Article] 10 become effective.

§ 104. Governing Law.

The law of this state governs:

(1) the internal affairs of a limited liability company; and

(2) the liability of a member as member and a manager as manager for a debt, obligation, or other liability of a limited liability company.

§ 105. Operating Agreement; Scope, Function, and Limitations.

(a) Except as otherwise provided in subsections (c) and (d), the operating agreement governs:

    (1) relations among the members as members and between the members and the

    limited liability company;

    (2) the rights and duties under this [act] of a person in the capacity of manager;

    (3) the activities and affairs of the company and the conduct of those activities and affairs; and

    (4) the means and conditions for amending the operating agreement.

(b) To the extent the operating agreement does not provide for a matter described in subsection (a), this [act] governs the matter.

(c) An operating agreement may not:

    (1) vary the law applicable under § 104;

    (2) vary a limited liability company's capacity under § 109 to sue and be sued in its own name;

(3) vary any requirement, procedure, or other provision of this [act] pertaining to:

(A) registered agents; or

(B) the [Secretary of State], including provisions pertaining to records authorized or required to be delivered to the [Secretary of State] for filing under this [act];

(4) vary the provisions of § 204;

(5) alter or eliminate the duty of loyalty or the duty of care, except as otherwise provided in subsection (d);

(6) eliminate the contractual obligation of good faith and fair dealing under § 409(d), but the operating agreement may prescribe the standards, if not manifestly unreasonable, by which the performance of the obligation is to be measured;

(7) relieve or exonerate a person from liability for conduct involving bad faith, willful or intentional misconduct, or knowing violation of law;

(8) unreasonably restrict the duties and rights under § 410, but the operating agreement may impose reasonable restrictions on the availability and use of information obtained under that section and may define appropriate remedies, including liquidated damages, for a breach of any reasonable restriction on use;

(9) vary the causes of dissolution specified in § 701(a)(4);

(10) vary the requirement to wind up the company's activities and affairs as specified in § 702(a), (b)(1), and (e);

(11) unreasonably restrict the right of a member to maintain an action under [Article] 8;

(12) vary the provisions of § 805, but the operating agreement may provide that the company may not have a special litigation committee;

(13) vary the right of a member to approve a merger, interest exchange, conversion, or domestication under § 1023(a)(2), 1033(a)(2), 1043(a)(2), or 1053(a)(2);

(14) vary the required contents of a plan of merger under § 1022(a), plan of interest exchange under § 1032(a), plan of conversion under § 1042(a), or plan of domestication under § 1052(a); or

(15) except as otherwise provided in §§ 106 and 107(b), restrict the rights under this [act] of a person other than a member or manager.

(d) Subject to subsection (c)(7), without limiting other terms that may be included in an operating agreement, the following rules apply:

(1) The operating agreement may:

(A) specify the method by which a specific act or transaction that would otherwise violate the duty of loyalty may be authorized or ratified by one or more disinterested and independent persons after full disclosure of all material facts; and

(B) alter the prohibition in § 405(a)(2) so that the prohibition requires only that the company's total assets not be less than the sum of its total liabilities.

(2) To the extent the operating agreement of a member-managed limited liability company expressly relieves a member of a responsibility that the member otherwise would have under this [act] and imposes the responsibility on one or more other members, the agreement also may eliminate or limit any fiduciary duty of the member relieved of the responsibility which would have pertained to the responsibility.

(3) If not manifestly unreasonable, the operating agreement may:

(A) alter or eliminate the aspects of the duty of loyalty stated in § 409(b) and (i);

(B) identify specific types or categories of activities that do not violate the duty of loyalty;

(C) alter the duty of care, but may not authorize conduct involving bad faith, willful or intentional misconduct, or knowing violation of law; and

(D) alter or eliminate any other fiduciary duty.

(e) The court shall decide as a matter of law whether a term of an operating agreement is manifestly unreasonable under subsection (c)(6) or (d)(3). The court:

(1) shall make its determination as of the time the challenged term became part of the operating agreement and by considering only circumstances existing at that time; and

(2) may invalidate the term only if, in light of the purposes, activities, and affairs of the limited liability company, it is readily apparent that:

(A) the objective of the term is unreasonable; or

(B) the term is an unreasonable means to achieve the term's objective.

§ 106. Operating Agreement; Effect on Limited Liability Company and Person Becoming Member; Preformation Agreement.

(a) A limited liability company is bound by and may enforce the operating agreement, whether or not the company has itself manifested assent to the operating agreement.

(b) A person that becomes a member is deemed to assent to the operating agreement.

(c) Two or more persons intending to become the initial members of a limited liability company may make an agreement providing that upon the formation of the company the agreement will become the operating agreement. One person intending to become the initial member of a limited liability company may assent to terms providing that upon the formation of the company the terms will become the operating agreement.

§ 107. Operating Agreement; Effect on Third Parties and Relationship to Records Effective on Behalf of Limited Liability Company.

(a) An operating agreement may specify that its amendment requires the approval of a person that is not a party to the agreement or the satisfaction of a condition. An amendment is ineffective if its adoption does not include the required approval or satisfy the specified condition.

(b) The obligations of a limited liability company and its members to a person in the person's capacity as a transferee or a person dissociated as a member are governed by the operating agreement. Subject only to a court order issued under § 503(b)(2) to effectuate a charging order, an amendment to the operating agreement made after a person becomes a transferee or is dissociated as a member:

(1) is effective with regard to any debt, obligation, or other liability of the limited liability company or its members to the person in the person's capacity as a transferee or person dissociated as a member; and

(2) is not effective to the extent the amendment imposes a new debt, obligation, or other liability on the transferee or person dissociated as a member.

(c) If a record delivered by a limited liability company to the [Secretary of State] for filing becomes effective and contains a provision that would be ineffective under § 105(c) or (d)(3) if contained in the operating agreement, the provision is ineffective in the record.

(d) Subject to subsection (c), if a record delivered by a limited liability company to the [Secretary of State] for filing becomes effective and conflicts with a provision of the operating agreement:

(1) the agreement prevails as to members, persons dissociated as members, transferees, and managers; and

(2) the record prevails as to other persons to the extent they reasonably rely on the record.

§ 108. Nature, Purpose, and Duration of Limited Liability Company.

(a) A limited liability company is an entity distinct from its member or members.

(b) A limited liability company may have any lawful purpose, regardless of whether for profit.

(c) A limited liability company has perpetual duration.

§ 109. Powers.

A limited liability company has the capacity to sue and be sued in its own name and the power to do all things necessary or convenient to carry on its activities and affairs.

§ 110. Application to Existing Relationships.

(a) Before [all-inclusive date], this [act] governs only:

    (1) a limited liability company formed on or after [the effective date of this [act]];

    and

    (2) except as otherwise provided in subsection (c), a limited liability company formed before [the effective date of this [act]] which elects, in the manner provided in its operating agreement or by law for amending the operating agreement, to be subject to this [act].

(b) Except as otherwise provided in subsection (c), on and after [all-inclusive date] this [act] governs all limited liability companies.

(c) For purposes of applying this [act] to a limited liability company formed before [the effective date of this [act]]:

    (1) the company's articles of organization are deemed to be the company's certificate of organization; and

    (2) for purposes of applying § 102(10) and subject to § 107(d),

    language in the company's articles of organization designating the company's management structure operates as if that language were in the operating agreement.

Legislative Note: For states that have previously enacted ULLCA (2006): For these states this section is unnecessary. There is no need for a delayed effective date, even with regard to pre-existing limited liability companies.

For states that have not previously enacted ULLCA (2006):

Each enacting jurisdiction should consider whether: (i) this act makes material changes to the "default" (or "gap filler") rules of a predecessor statute; and (ii) if so, whether Subsection (c)

should carry forward any of those rules for pre-existing limited liability companies. In this assessment, the focus is on pre-existing limited liability companies that have left default rules in place, whether advisedly or not. The central question is whether, for such limited liability companies, expanding Subsection (c) is necessary to prevent material changes to the members' "deal."

Section 301 (de-codifying statutory apparent authority) does not require any special transition provisions, because: (i) applying the law of agency, as explained in the Comments to §§ 301 and 407, will produce appropriate results; and (ii) the notion of "lingering apparent authority" will protect any third party that has previously relied on the statutory apparent authority of a member of a particular member-managed LLC or a manager of a particular manager-managed LLC. Restatement (Third) Of Agency § 3.11, cmt. c (2006).

It is recommended that the "all-inclusive" date should be at least one year after the effective date of this act, § 1106, but no more than two years.

§ 111. Supplemental Principles of Law.

Unless displaced by particular provisions of this [act], the principles of law and equity supplement this [act].

§ 112. Permitted Names.

(a) The name of a limited liability company must contain the phrase "limited liability company" or "limited company" or the abbreviation "L.L.C.", "LLC", "L.C.", or "LC". "Limited" may be abbreviated as "Ltd.", and "company" may be abbreviated as "Co.".

(b) Except as otherwise provided in subsection (d), the name of a limited liability company, and the name under which a foreign limited liability company may register to do business in this state, must be distinguishable on the records of the [Secretary of State] from any:

    (1) name of an existing person whose formation required the filing of a record by the [Secretary of State] and which is not at the time administratively dissolved;

(2) name of a limited liability partnership whose statement of qualification is in effect;

(3) name under which a person is registered to do business in this state by the filing of a record by the [Secretary of State];

(4) name reserved under § 113 or other law of this state providing for the reservation of a name by the filing of a record by the [Secretary of State];

(5) name registered under § 114 or other law of this state providing for the registration of a name by the filing of a record by the [Secretary of State]; and

(6) name registered under [this state's assumed or fictitious name statute].

(c) If a person consents in a record to the use of its name and submits an undertaking in a form satisfactory to the [Secretary of State] to change its name to a name that is distinguishable on the records of the [Secretary of State] from any name in any category of names in subsection (b), the name of the consenting person may be used by the person to which the consent was given.

(d) Except as otherwise provided in subsection (e), in determining whether a name is the same as or not distinguishable on the records of the [Secretary of State] from the name of another person, words, phrases, or abbreviations indicating a type of person, such as "corporation", "corp.", "incorporated", "Inc.", "professional corporation", "P.C.", "PC", "professional association", "P.A.", "PA", "Limited", "Ltd.", "limited partnership", "L.P.", "LP", "limited liability partnership", "L.L.P.", "LLP", "registered limited liability partnership", "R.L.L.P.", "RLLP", "limited liability limited partnership", "L.L.L.P.", "LLLP", "registered limited liability limited partnership", "R.L.L.L.P.", "RLLLP", "limited liability company", "L.L.C.", "LLC", "limited cooperative association", "limited cooperative", or "L.C.A.", or "LCA" may not be taken into account.

(e) A person may consent in a record to the use of a name that is not distinguishable on the records of the [Secretary of State] from its name except for the addition of a word, phrase, or abbreviation indicating the type of person as provided in subsection (d). In such a case, the person need not change its name pursuant to subsection (c).

(f) The name of a limited liability company or foreign limited liability company may not contain the words [insert prohibited word or words that may be used only with approval by an appropriate state agency].

(g) A limited liability company or foreign limited liability company may use a name that is not distinguishable from a name described in subsection (b)(1) through (6) if the company delivers to the [Secretary of State] a certified copy of a final judgment of a court of competent jurisdiction establishing the right of the company to use the name in this state.

§ 113. Reservation of Name.

(a) A person may reserve the exclusive use of a name that complies with § 112 by delivering an application to the [Secretary of State] for filing. The application must state the name and address of the applicant and the name to be reserved. If the [Secretary of State] finds that the name is available, the [Secretary of State] shall reserve the name for the applicant's exclusive use for [120] days.

(b) The owner of a reserved name may transfer the reservation to another person by delivering to the [Secretary of State] a signed notice in a record of the transfer which states the name and address of the person to which the reservation is being transferred.

§ 114. Registration of Name.

(a) A foreign limited liability company not registered to do business in this state under [Article] 9 may register its name, or an alternate name adopted pursuant to § 906, if the name is distinguishable on the records of the [Secretary of State] from the names that are not available under § 112.

(b) To register its name or an alternate name adopted pursuant to § 906, a foreign limited liability company must deliver to the [Secretary of State] for filing an application stating the company's name, the jurisdiction and date of its formation, and any alternate name adopted pursuant to § 906. If the [Secretary of State] finds that the name applied for is available, the [Secretary of State] shall register the name for the applicant's exclusive use.

(c) The registration of a name under this section is effective for [one year] after the date of registration.

(d) A foreign limited liability company whose name registration is effective may renew the registration for successive [one-year] periods by delivering, not earlier than [three months] before the expiration of the registration, to the [Secretary of State] for filing a renewal application that complies with this section. When filed, the renewal application renews the registration for a succeeding [one-year] period.

(e) A foreign limited liability company whose name registration is effective may register as a foreign limited liability company under the registered name or consent in a signed record to the use of that name by another person that is not an individual.

§ 115. Registered Agent.

(a) Each limited liability company and each registered foreign limited liability company shall designate and maintain a registered agent in this state. The designation of a registered agent is an affirmation of fact by the limited liability company or registered foreign limited liability company that the agent has consented to serve.

(b) A registered agent for a limited liability company or registered foreign limited liability company must have a place of business in this state.

(c) The only duties under this [act] of a registered agent that has complied with this [act] are:

    (1) to forward to the limited liability company or registered foreign limited liability company at the address most recently supplied to the agent by the company or foreign company any process, notice, or demand pertaining to the company or foreign company which is served on or received by the agent;

    (2) if the registered agent resigns, to provide the notice required by § 117(c) to the company or foreign company at the address most recently supplied to the agent by the company or foreign company; and

    (3) to keep current the information with respect to the agent in the certificate of organization or foreign registration statement.

§ 116. Change of Registered Agent or Address for Registered Agent by Limited Liability Company.

(a) A limited liability company or registered foreign limited liability company may change its registered agent or the address of its registered agent by delivering to the [Secretary of State] for filing a statement of change that states:

    (1) the name of the company or foreign company; and

    (2) the information that is to be in effect as a result of the filing of the statement of change.

(b) The members or managers of a limited liability company need not approve the delivery to the [Secretary of State] filing of:

    (1) a statement of change under this section; or

    (2) a similar filing changing the registered agent or registered office, if any, of the company in any other jurisdiction.

(c) A statement of change under this section designating a new registered agent is an affirmation of fact by the limited liability company or registered foreign limited liability company that the agent has consented to serve.

(d) As an alternative to using the procedure in this section, a limited liability company may amend its certificate of organization.

§ 117. Resignation of Registered Agent.

(a) A registered agent may resign as an agent for a limited liability company or registered foreign limited liability company by delivering to the [Secretary of State] for filing a statement of resignation that states:

    (1) the name of the company or foreign company;

(2) the name of the agent;

(3) that the agent resigns from serving as registered agent for the company or foreign company; and

(4) the address of the company or foreign company to which the agent will send the notice required by subsection (c).

(b) A statement of resignation takes effect on the earlier of:

(1) the 31st day after the day on which it is filed by the [Secretary of State]; or

(2) the designation of a new registered agent for the limited liability company or registered foreign limited liability company.

(c) A registered agent promptly shall furnish to the limited liability company or registered foreign limited liability company notice in a record of the date on which a statement of resignation was filed.

(d) When a statement of resignation takes effect, the registered agent ceases to have responsibility under this [act] for any matter thereafter tendered to it as agent for the limited liability company or registered foreign limited liability company. The resignation does not affect any contractual rights the company or foreign company has against the agent or that the agent has against the company or foreign company.

(e) A registered agent may resign with respect to a limited liability company or registered foreign limited liability company whether or not the company or foreign company is in good standing.

§ 118. Change of Name or Address by Registered Agent.

(a) If a registered agent changes its name or address, the agent may deliver to the [Secretary of State] for filing a statement of change that states:

(1) the name of the limited liability company or registered foreign limited liability company represented by the registered agent;

(2) the name of the agent as currently shown in the records of the [Secretary of State] for the company or foreign company;

(3) if the name of the agent has changed, its new name; and

(4) if the address of the agent has changed, its new address.

(b) A registered agent promptly shall furnish notice to the represented limited liability company or registered foreign limited liability company of the filing by the [Secretary of State] of the statement of change and the changes made by the statement.

Legislative Note: Many registered agents act in that capacity for many entities, and the Model Registered Agents Act (2006) (Last Amended 2013) provides a streamlined method through which a commercial registered agent can make a single filing to change its information for all represented entities. The single filing does not prevent an enacting state from assessing filing fees on the basis of the number of entity records affected. Alternatively the fees can be set on an incremental sliding fee or capitated amount based upon potential economies of costs for a bulk filing.

§ 119. Service of Process, Notice, or Demand.

(a) A limited liability company or registered foreign limited liability company may be served with any process, notice, or demand required or permitted by law by serving its registered agent.

(b) If a limited liability company or registered foreign limited liability company ceases to have a registered agent, or if its registered agent cannot with reasonable diligence be served, the company or foreign company may be served by registered or certified mail, return receipt requested, or by similar commercial delivery service, addressed to the company or foreign company at its principal office. The address of the principal office must be as shown on the company's or foreign company's most recent [annual] [biennial] report filed by the [Secretary of State]. Service is effected under this subsection on the earliest of:

(1) the date the company or foreign company receives the mail or delivery by the commercial delivery service;

(2) the date shown on the return receipt, if signed by the company or foreign company; or

(3) five days after its deposit with the United States Postal Service, or with the commercial delivery service, if correctly addressed and with sufficient postage or payment.

(c) If process, notice, or demand cannot be served on a limited liability company or registered foreign limited liability company pursuant to subsection (a) or (b), service may be made by handing a copy to the individual in charge of any regular place of business or activity of the company or foreign company if the individual served is not a plaintiff in the action.

(d) Service of process, notice, or demand on a registered agent must be in a written record.

(e) Service of process, notice, or demand may be made by other means under law other than this [act].

§ 120. Delivery of Record.

(a) Except as otherwise provided in this [act], permissible means of delivery of a record include delivery by hand, mail, conventional commercial practice, and electronic transmission.

(b) Delivery to the [Secretary of State] is effective only when a record is received by the [Secretary of State].

§ 121. Reservation of Power to Amend or Repeal.

The [legislature of this state] has power to amend or repeal all or part of this [act] at any time, and all limited liability companies and foreign liability companies subject to this [act] are governed by the amendment or repeal.

[Article] 2. Formation; Certificate of Organization and Other Filings

§ 201. Formation of Limited Liability Company; Certificate of Organization.

(a) One or more persons may act as organizers to form a limited liability company by delivering to the [Secretary of State] for filing a certificate of organization.

(b) A certificate of organization must state:

(1) the name of the limited liability company, which must comply with § 112;

(2) the street and mailing addresses of the company's principal office; and

(3) the name and street and mailing addresses in this state of the company's registered agent.

(c) A certificate of organization may contain statements as to matters other than those required by subsection (b), but may not vary or otherwise affect the provisions specified in § 105(c) and (d) in a manner inconsistent with that section. However, a statement in a certificate of organization is not effective as a statement of authority.

(d) A limited liability company is formed when the certificate of organization becomes effective and at least one person has become a member.

§ 202. Amendment or Restatement of Certificate of Organization.

(a) A certificate of organization may be amended or restated at any time.

(b) To amend its certificate of organization, a limited liability company must deliver to the [Secretary of State] for filing an amendment stating:

(1) the name of the company;

(2) the date of filing of its initial certificate; and

(3) the text of the amendment.

(c) To restate its certificate of organization, a limited liability company must deliver to the [Secretary of State] for filing a restatement, designated as such in its heading.

(d) If a member of a member-managed limited liability company, or a manager of a manager-managed limited liability company, knows that any information in a filed certificate of organization was inaccurate when the certificate was filed or has become inaccurate due to changed circumstances, the member or manager shall promptly:

(1) cause the certificate to be amended; or

(2) if appropriate, deliver to the [Secretary of State] for filing a statement of change under § 116 or a statement of correction under § 209.

§ 203. Signing of Records to Be Delivered for Filing to [Secretary of State].

(a) A record delivered to the [Secretary of State] for filing pursuant to this [act] must be signed as follows:

(1) Except as otherwise provided in paragraphs (2) and (3), a record signed by a limited liability company must be signed by a person authorized by the company.

(2) A company's initial certificate of organization must be signed by at least one person acting as an organizer.

(3) A record delivered on behalf of a dissolved company that has no member must be signed by the person winding up the company's activities and affairs under § 702(c) or a person appointed under § 702(d) to wind up the activities and affairs.

(4) A statement of denial by a person under § 303 must be signed by that person.

(5) Any other record delivered on behalf of a person to the [Secretary of State] for filing must be signed by that person.

(b) A record delivered for filing under this [act] may be signed by an agent. Whenever this [act] requires a particular individual to sign a record and the individual is deceased or incompetent, the record may be signed by a legal representative of the individual.

(c) A person that signs a record as an agent or legal representative affirms as a fact that the person is authorized to sign the record.

§ 204. Signing and Filing Pursuant to Judicial Order.

(a) If a person required by this [act] to sign a record or deliver a record to the [Secretary of State] for filing under this [act] does not do so, any other person that is aggrieved may petition [the appropriate court] to order:

(1) the person to sign the record;

(2) the person to deliver the record to the [Secretary of State] for filing; or

(3) the [Secretary of State] to file the record unsigned.

(b) If a petitioner under subsection (a) is not the limited liability company or foreign limited liability company to which the record pertains, the petitioner shall make the company or foreign company a party to the action.

(c) A record filed under subsection (a)(3) is effective without being signed.

§ 205. Liability for Inaccurate Information in Filed Record.

(a) If a record delivered to the [Secretary of State] for filing under this [act] and filed by the [Secretary of State] contains inaccurate information, a person that suffers loss by reliance on the information may recover damages for the loss from:

(1) a person that signed the record, or caused another to sign it on the person's behalf, and knew the information to be inaccurate at the time the record was signed; and

(2) subject to subsection (b), a member of a member-managed limited liability company or a manager of a manager-managed limited liability company if:

(A) the record was delivered for filing on behalf of the company; and

(B) the member or manager knew or had notice of the inaccuracy for a reasonably sufficient time before the information was relied upon so that, before the reliance, the member or manager reasonably could have:

(i) effected an amendment under § 202;

(ii) filed a petition under § 204; or

(iii) delivered to the [Secretary of State] for filing a statement of change under § 116 or a statement of correction under § 209.

(b) To the extent the operating agreement of a member-managed limited liability company expressly relieves a member of responsibility for maintaining the accuracy of information contained in records delivered on behalf of the company to the [Secretary of State] for filing under this [act] and imposes that responsibility on one or more other members, the liability stated in subsection (a)(2) applies to those other members and not to the member that the operating agreement relieves of the responsibility.

(c) An individual who signs a record authorized or required to be filed under this [act] affirms under penalty of perjury that the information stated in the record is accurate.

§ 206. Filing Requirements.

(a) To be filed by the [Secretary of State] pursuant to this [act], a record must be received by the [Secretary of State], comply with this [act], and satisfy the following:

> **(1)** The filing of the record must be required or permitted by this [act].

> **(2)** The record must be physically delivered in written form unless and to the extent the [Secretary of State] permits electronic delivery of records.

> **(3)** The words in the record must be in English, and numbers must be in Arabic or Roman numerals, but the name of an entity need not be in English if written in English letters or Arabic or Roman numerals.

> **(4)** The record must be signed by a person authorized or required under this [act] to sign the record.

> **(5)** The record must state the name and capacity, if any, of each individual who signed it, either on behalf of the individual or the person authorized or required to sign the record, but need not contain a seal, attestation, acknowledgment, or verification.

(b) If law other than this [act] prohibits the disclosure by the [Secretary of State] of information contained in a record delivered to the [Secretary of State] for filing, the [Secretary of State] shall file the record if the record otherwise complies with this [act] but may redact the information.

(c) When a record is delivered to the [Secretary of State] for filing, any fee required under this [act] and any fee, tax, interest, or penalty required to be paid under this [act] or law other than this [act]

must be paid in a manner permitted by the [Secretary of State] or by that law.

(d) The [Secretary of State] may require that a record delivered in written form be accompanied by an identical or conformed copy.

(e) The [Secretary of State] may provide forms for filings required or permitted to be made by this [act], but, except as otherwise provided in subsection (f), their use is not required.

(f) The [Secretary of State] may require that a cover sheet for a filing be on a form prescribed by the [Secretary of State].

§ 207. Effective Date and Time.

Except as otherwise provided in § 208 and subject to § 209(d), a record filed under this [act] is effective:

(1) on the date and at the time of its filing by the [Secretary of State], as provided in § 210(b);

(2) on the date of filing and at the time specified in the record as its effective time, if later than the time under paragraph (1);

(3) at a specified delayed effective date and time, which may not be more than 90 days after the date of filing; or

(4) if a delayed effective date is specified, but no time is specified, at 12:01 a.m. on the date specified, which may not be more than 90 days after the date of filing.

§ 208. Withdrawal of Filed Record Before Effectiveness.

(a) Except as otherwise provided in §§ 1024, 1034, 1044, and 1054, a record delivered to the [Secretary of State] for filing may be withdrawn before it takes effect by delivering to the [Secretary of State] for filing a statement of withdrawal.

(b) A statement of withdrawal must:

> **(1)** be signed by each person that signed the record being withdrawn, except as otherwise agreed by those persons;

> **(2)** identify the record to be withdrawn; and

> **(3)** if signed by fewer than all the persons that signed the record being withdrawn, state that

the record is withdrawn in accordance with the agreement of all the persons that signed the record.

(c) On filing by the [Secretary of State] of a statement of withdrawal, the action or transaction evidenced by the original record does not take effect.

§ 209. Correcting Filed Record.

(a) A person on whose behalf a filed record was delivered to the [Secretary of State] for filing may correct the record if:

(1) the record at the time of filing was inaccurate;

(2) the record was defectively signed; or

(3) the electronic transmission of the record to the [Secretary of State] was defective.

(b) To correct a filed record, a person on whose behalf the record was delivered to the [Secretary of State] must deliver to the [Secretary of State] for filing a statement of correction.

(c) A statement of correction:

(1) may not state a delayed effective date;

(2) must be signed by the person correcting the filed record;

(3) must identify the filed record to be corrected;

(4) must specify the inaccuracy or defect to be corrected; and

(5) must correct the inaccuracy or defect.

(d) A statement of correction is effective as of the effective date of the filed record that it corrects except for purposes of § 103(d) and as to persons relying on the uncorrected filed record and adversely affected by the correction. For those purposes and as to those persons, the statement of correction is effective when filed.

§ 210. Duty of [Secretary of State] to File; Review of Refusal to File; Delivery of Record by [Secretary of State].

(a) The [Secretary of State] shall file a record delivered to the [Secretary of State] for filing which satisfies this [act]. The duty of the [Secretary of State] under this section is ministerial.

(b) When the [Secretary of State] files a record, the [Secretary of State] shall record it as filed on the date and at the time of its delivery. After filing a record, the [Secretary of State] shall deliver to the person that submitted the record a copy of the record with an acknowledgment of the date and time of filing and, in the case of a statement of denial, also to the limited liability company to which the statement pertains.

(c) If the [Secretary of State] refuses to file a record, the [Secretary of State] shall, not later than [15] business days after the record is delivered:

(1) return the record or notify the person that submitted the record of the refusal; and

(2) provide a brief explanation in a record of the reason for the refusal.

(d) If the [Secretary of State] refuses to file a record, the person that submitted the record may petition [the appropriate court] to compel filing of the record. The record and the explanation of the [Secretary of State] of the refusal to file must be attached to the petition. The court may decide the matter in a summary proceeding.

(e) The filing of or refusal to file a record does not:

(1) affect the validity or invalidity of the record in whole or in part; or

(2) create a presumption that the information contained in the record is correct or incorrect.

(f) Except as otherwise provided by § 119 or by law other than this [act], the [Secretary of State] may deliver any record to a person by delivering it:

(1) in person to the person that submitted it;

(2) to the address of the person's registered agent;

(3) to the principal office of the person; or

(4) to another address the person provides to the [Secretary of State] for delivery.

§ 211. Certificate of Good Standing or Registration.

(a) On request of any person, the [Secretary of State] shall issue a certificate of good standing for a limited liability company or a certificate of registration for a registered foreign limited liability company.

(b) A certificate under subsection (a) must state:

(1) the limited liability company's name or the registered foreign limited liability company's name used in this state;

(2) in the case of a limited liability company:

(A) that a certificate of organization has been filed and has taken effect;

(B) the date the certificate became effective;

(C) the period of the company's duration if the records of the [Secretary of State] reflect that its period of duration is less than perpetual; and

(D) that:

(i) no statement of dissolution, statement of administrative dissolution, or statement of termination has been filed;

(ii) the records of the [Secretary to State] do not otherwise reflect that the company has been dissolved or terminated; and

(iii) a proceeding is not pending under § 708;

(3) in the case of a registered foreign limited liability company, that it is registered to do business in this state;

(4) that all fees, taxes, interest, and penalties owed to this state by the limited liability company or foreign limited liability company and collected through the [Secretary of State] have been paid, if:

(A) payment is reflected in the records of the [Secretary of State]; and

(B) nonpayment affects the good standing or registration of the company or foreign company;

(5) that the most recent [annual] [biennial] report required by § 212 has been delivered to the [Secretary of State] for filing; and

(6) other facts reflected in the records of the [Secretary of State] pertaining to the limited liability company or foreign limited liability company which the person requesting the certificate reasonably requests.

(c) Subject to any qualification stated in the certificate, a certificate issued by the [Secretary of State] under subsection (a) may be relied on as conclusive evidence of the facts stated in the certificate.

§ 212. [Annual] [Biennial] Report for [Secretary of State].

(a) A limited liability company or registered foreign limited liability company shall deliver to the [Secretary of State] for filing [an annual] [a biennial] report that states:

(1) the name of the company or foreign company;

(2) the name and street and mailing addresses of its registered agent in this state;

(3) the street and mailing addresses of its principal office;

(4) if the company is member managed, the name of at least one member;

(5) if the company is manager managed, the name of at least one manager; and

(6) in the case of a foreign company, its jurisdiction of formation and any alternate name adopted under § 906(a).

(b) Information in the [annual] [biennial] report must be current as of the date the report is signed by the limited liability company or registered foreign limited liability company.

(c) The first [annual] [biennial] report must be delivered to the [Secretary of State] for filing after [January 1] and before [April 1] of the year following the calendar year in which the limited liability company's certificate of organization became effective or the registered foreign limited liability company registered to do business in this state. Subsequent [annual] [biennial] reports must be delivered to the [Secretary of State] for filing after

[January 1] and before [April 1] of each [second] calendar year thereafter.

(d) If [an annual] [a biennial] report does not contain the information required by this section, the [Secretary of State] promptly shall notify the reporting limited liability company or registered foreign limited liability company in a record and return the report for correction.

(e) If [an annual] [a biennial] report contains the name or address of a registered agent which differs from the information shown in the records of the [Secretary of State] immediately before the report becomes effective, the differing information in the report is considered a statement of change under § 116.

[Article] 3. Relations of Members and Managers to Persons Dealing with Limited Liability Company

§ 301. No Agency Power of Member as Member.

(a) A member is not an agent of a limited liability company solely by reason of being a member.

(b) A person's status as a member does not prevent or restrict law other than this [act] from imposing liability on a limited liability company because of the person's conduct.

§ 302. Statement of Limited Liability Company Authority.

(a) A limited liability company may deliver to the [Secretary of State] for filing a statement of authority. The statement:

(1) must include the name of the company and the name and street and mailing addresses of its registered agent;

(2) with respect to any position that exists in or with respect to the company, may state the authority, or limitations on the authority, of all persons holding the position to:

(A) sign an instrument transferring real property held in the name of the company; or

(B) enter into other transactions on behalf of, or otherwise act for or bind, the company; and

(3) may state the authority, or limitations on the authority, of a specific person to:

(A) sign an instrument transferring real property held in the name of the company; or

(B) enter into other transactions on behalf of, or otherwise act for or bind, the company.

(b) To amend or cancel a statement of authority filed by the [Secretary of State], a limited liability company must deliver to the [Secretary of State] for filing an amendment or cancellation stating:

(1) the name of the company;

(2) the name and street and mailing addresses of the company's registered agent;

(3) the date the statement being affected became effective; and

(4) the contents of the amendment or a declaration that the statement is canceled.

(c) A statement of authority affects only the power of a person to bind a limited liability company to persons that are not members.

(d) Subject to subsection (c) and § 103(d), and except as otherwise provided in subsections (f), (g), and (h), a limitation on the authority of a person or a position contained in an effective statement of authority is not by itself evidence of any person's knowledge or notice of the limitation.

(e) Subject to subsection (c), a grant of authority not pertaining to transfers of real property and contained in an effective statement of authority is conclusive in favor of a person that gives value in reliance on the grant, except to the extent that when the person gives value:

(1) the person has knowledge to the contrary;

(2) the statement has been canceled or restrictively amended under subsection (b); or

(3) a limitation on the grant is contained in another statement of authority that became effective after the statement containing the grant became effective.

(f) Subject to subsection (c), an effective statement of authority that grants authority to transfer real property held in the name of the limited liability company, a certified copy of which statement is recorded in the office for recording transfers of the real property, is conclusive in favor of a person that gives value in reliance on the grant without knowledge to the contrary, except to the extent that when the person gives value:

> **(1)** the statement has been canceled or restrictively amended under subsection (b), and a certified copy of the cancellation or restrictive amendment has been recorded in the office for recording transfers of the real property; or

> **(2)** a limitation on the grant is contained in another statement of authority that became effective after the statement containing the grant became effective, and a certified copy of the later-effective statement is recorded in the office for recording transfers of the real property.

(g) Subject to subsection (c), if a certified copy of an effective statement containing a limitation on the authority to transfer real property held in the name of a limited liability company is recorded in the office for recording transfers of that real property, all persons are deemed to know of the limitation.

(h) Subject to subsection (i), an effective statement of dissolution or termination is a cancellation of any filed statement of authority for the purposes of subsection (f) and is a limitation on authority for the purposes of subsection (g).

(i) After a statement of dissolution becomes effective, a limited liability company may deliver to the [Secretary of State] for filing and, if appropriate, may record a statement of authority that is designated as a post-dissolution statement of authority. The statement operates as provided in subsections (f) and (g).

(j) Unless earlier canceled, an effective statement of authority is canceled by operation of law five years after the date on which the statement, or its most recent amendment, becomes effective. This cancellation operates without need for any recording under subsection (f) or (g).

(k) An effective statement of denial operates as a restrictive amendment under this section and may be recorded by certified copy for purposes of subsection (f)(1).

§ 303. Statement of Denial.

A person named in a filed statement of authority granting that person authority may deliver to the [Secretary of State] for filing a statement of denial that:

(1) provides the name of the limited liability company and the caption of the statement of authority to which the statement of denial pertains; and

(2) denies the grant of authority.

§ 304. Liability of Members and Managers.

(a) A debt, obligation, or other liability of a limited liability company is solely the debt, obligation, or other liability of the company. A member or manager is not personally liable, directly or indirectly, by way of contribution or otherwise, for a debt, obligation, or other liability of the company solely by reason of being or acting as a member or manager. This subsection applies regardless of the dissolution of the company.

(b) The failure of a limited liability company to observe formalities relating to the exercise of its powers or management of its activities and affairs is not a ground for imposing liability on a member or manager for a debt, obligation, or other liability of the company.

[Article] 4. Relations of Members to Each Other and to Limited Liability Company

§ 401. Becoming Member.

(a) If a limited liability company is to have only one member upon formation, the person becomes a member as agreed by that person and the organizer of the company. That person and the organizer may be, but need not be, different persons. If different, the organizer acts on behalf of the initial member.

(b) If a limited liability company is to have more than one member upon formation, those persons become members as agreed by the persons before the formation of the company. The organizer acts on behalf of the persons in forming the company and may be, but need not be, one of the persons.

(c) After formation of a limited liability company, a person becomes a member:

(1) as provided in the operating agreement;

(2) as the result of a transaction effective under [Article] 10;

(3) with the affirmative vote or consent of all the members; or

(4) as provided in § 701(a)(3).

(d) A person may become a member without:

(1) acquiring a transferable interest; or

(2) making or being obligated to make a contribution to the limited liability company.

§ 402. Form of Contribution.

A contribution may consist of property transferred to, services performed for, or another benefit provided to the limited liability company or an agreement to transfer property to, perform services for, or provide another benefit to the company.

§ 403. Liability for Contributions.

(a) A person's obligation to make a contribution to a limited liability company is not excused by the person's death, disability, termination, or other inability to perform personally.

(b) If a person does not fulfill an obligation to make a contribution other than money, the person is obligated at the option of the limited liability company to contribute money equal to the value of the part of the contribution which has not been made.

(c) The obligation of a person to make a contribution may be compromised only by the affirmative

vote or consent of all the members. If a creditor of a limited liability company extends credit or otherwise acts in reliance on an obligation described in subsection (a) without knowledge or notice of a compromise under this subsection, the creditor may enforce the obligation.

§ 404. Sharing of and Right to Distributions Before Dissolution.

(a) Any distribution made by a limited liability company before its dissolution and winding up must be in equal shares among members and persons dissociated as members, except to the extent necessary to comply with a transfer effective under § 502 or charging order in effect under § 503.

(b) A person has a right to a distribution before the dissolution and winding up of a limited liability company only if the company decides to make an interim distribution. A person's dissociation does not entitle the person to a distribution.

(c) A person does not have a right to demand or receive a distribution from a limited liability company in any form other than money. Except as otherwise provided in § 707(d), a company may distribute an asset in kind only if each part of the asset is fungible with each other part and each person receives a percentage of the asset equal in value to the person's share of distributions.

(d) If a member or transferee becomes entitled to receive a distribution, the member or transferee has the status of, and is entitled to all remedies available to, a creditor of the limited liability company with respect to the distribution. However, the company's obligation to make a distribution is subject to offset for any amount owed to the company by the member or a person dissociated as a member on whose account the distribution is made.

§ 405. Limitations on Distributions.

(a) A limited liability company may not make a distribution, including a distribution under § 707, if after the distribution:

(1) the company would not be able to pay its debts as they become due in the ordinary course of the company's activities and affairs; or

(2) the company's total assets would be less than the sum of its total liabilities plus the amount that would be needed, if the company were to be dissolved and wound up at the time of the distribution, to satisfy the preferential rights upon dissolution and winding up of members and transferees whose preferential rights are superior to the rights of persons receiving the distribution.

(b) A limited liability company may base a determination that a distribution is not prohibited under subsection (a) on:

(1) financial statements prepared on the basis of accounting practices and principles that are reasonable in the circumstances; or

(2) a fair valuation or other method that is reasonable under the circumstances.

(c) Except as otherwise provided in subsection (e), the effect of a distribution under subsection (a) is measured:

(1) in the case of a distribution as defined in § 102(4)(A), as of the earlier of:

(A) the date money or other property is transferred or debt is incurred by the limited liability company; or

(B) the date the person entitled to the distribution ceases to own the interest or right being acquired by the company in return for the distribution;

(2) in the case of any other distribution of indebtedness, as of the date the indebtedness is distributed; and

(3) in all other cases, as of the date:

(A) the distribution is authorized, if the payment occurs not later than 120 days after that date; or

(B) the payment is made, if the payment occurs more than 120 days after the distribution is authorized.

(d) A limited liability company's indebtedness to a member or transferee incurred by reason of a distribution made in accordance with this section is at

parity with the company's indebtedness to its general, unsecured creditors, except to the extent subordinated by agreement.

(e) A limited liability company's indebtedness, including indebtedness issued as a distribution, is not a liability for purposes of subsection (a) if the terms of the indebtedness provide that payment of principal and interest is made only if and to the extent that payment of a distribution could then be made under this section. If the indebtedness is issued as a distribution, each payment of principal or interest is treated as a distribution, the effect of which is measured on the date the payment is made.

(f) In measuring the effect of a distribution under § 707, the liabilities of a dissolved limited liability company do not include any claim that has been disposed of under § 704, 705, or 706.

§ 406. Liability for Improper Distributions.

(a) Except as otherwise provided in subsection (b), if a member of a member-managed limited liability company or manager of a manager-managed limited liability company consents to a distribution made in violation of § 405 and in consenting to the distribution fails to comply with § 409, the member or manager is personally liable to the company for the amount of the distribution which exceeds the amount that could have been distributed without the violation of § 405.

(b) To the extent the operating agreement of a member-managed limited liability company expressly relieves a member of the authority and responsibility to consent to distributions and imposes that authority and responsibility on one or more other members, the liability stated in subsection (a) applies to the other members and not the member that the operating agreement relieves of the authority and responsibility.

(c) A person that receives a distribution knowing that the distribution violated § 405 is personally liable to the limited liability company but only to the extent that the distribution received by the person exceeded the amount that could have been properly paid under § 405.

(d) A person against which an action is commenced because the person is liable under subsection (a) may:

(1) implead any other person that is liable under subsection (a) and seek to enforce a right of contribution from the person; and

(2) implead any person that received a distribution in violation of subsection (c) and seek to enforce a right of contribution from the person in the amount the person received in violation of subsection (c).

(e) An action under this section is barred unless commenced not later than two years after the distribution.

§ 407. Management of Limited Liability Company.

(a) A limited liability company is a member-managed limited liability company unless the operating agreement:

(1) expressly provides that:

(A) the company is or will be "manager-managed";

(B) the company is or will be "managed by managers"; or

(C) management of the company is or will be "vested in managers"; or

(2) includes words of similar import.

(b) In a member-managed limited liability company, the following rules apply:

(1) Except as expressly provided in this [act], the management and conduct of the company are vested in the members.

(2) Each member has equal rights in the management and conduct of the company's activities and affairs.

(3) A difference arising among members as to a matter in the ordinary course of the activities and affairs of the company may be decided by a majority of the members.

(4) The affirmative vote or consent of all the members is required to:

(A) undertake an act outside the ordinary course of the activities and affairs of the company; or

(B) amend the operating agreement.

(c) In a manager-managed limited liability company, the following rules apply:

(1) Except as expressly provided in this [act], any matter relating to the activities and affairs of the company is decided exclusively by the manager, or, if there is more than one manager, by a majority of the managers.

(2) Each manager has equal rights in the management and conduct of the company's activities and affairs.

(3) The affirmative vote or consent of all members is required to:

(A) undertake an act outside the ordinary course of the company's activities and affairs; or

(B) amend the operating agreement.

(4) A manager may be chosen at any time by the affirmative vote or consent of a majority of the members and remains a manager until a successor has been chosen, unless the manager at an earlier time resigns, is removed, or dies, or, in the case of a manager that is not an individual, terminates. A manager may be removed at any time by the affirmative vote or consent of a majority of the members without notice or cause.

(5) A person need not be a member to be a manager, but the dissociation of a member that is also a manager removes the person as a manager. If a person that is both a manager and a member ceases to be a manager, that cessation does not by itself dissociate the person as a member.

(6) A person's ceasing to be a manager does not discharge any debt, obligation, or other liability to the limited liability company or members which the person incurred while a manager.

(d) An action requiring the vote or consent of members under this [act] may be taken without a meeting, and a member may appoint a proxy or other agent to vote, consent, or otherwise act for the member by signing an appointing record, personally or by the member's agent.

(e) The dissolution of a limited liability company does not affect the applicability of this section. However, a person that wrongfully causes dissolution of the company loses the right to participate in management as a member and a manager.

(f) A limited liability company shall reimburse a member for an advance to the company beyond the amount of capital the member agreed to contribute.

(g) A payment or advance made by a member which gives rise to a limited liability company obligation under subsection (f) or § 408(a) constitutes a loan to the company which accrues interest from the date of the payment or advance.

(h) A member is not entitled to remuneration for services performed for a member-managed limited liability company, except for reasonable compensation for services rendered in winding up the activities of the company.

§ 408. Reimbursement; Indemnification; Advancement; and Insurance.

(a) A limited liability company shall reimburse a member of a member-managed company or the manager of a manager-managed company for any payment made by the member or manager in the course of the member's or manager's activities on behalf of the company, if the member or manager complied with §§ 405, 407, and 409 in making the payment.

(b) A limited liability company shall indemnify and hold harmless a person with respect to any claim or demand against the person and any debt, obligation, or other liability incurred by the person by reason of the person's former or present capacity as a member or manager, if the claim, demand, debt, obligation, or other liability does not arise from the person's breach of § 405, 407, or 409.

(c) In the ordinary course of its activities and affairs, a limited liability company may advance reasonable expenses, including attorney's fees and costs, incurred by a person in connection with a claim or demand against the person by reason of the person's former or present capacity as a member or manager, if the person promises to repay the company if the person ultimately is determined not to be entitled to be indemnified under subsection (b).

(d) A limited liability company may purchase and maintain insurance on behalf of a member or manager against liability asserted against or incurred by the member or manager in that capacity or arising from that status even if, under § 105(c)(7), the operating agreement could not eliminate or limit the person's liability to the company for the conduct giving rise to the liability.

§ 409. Standards of Conduct for Members and Managers.

(a) A member of a member-managed limited liability company owes to the company and, subject to § 801, the other members the duties of loyalty and care stated in subsections (b) and (c).

(b) The fiduciary duty of loyalty of a member in a member-managed limited liability company includes the duties:

(1) to account to the company and hold as trustee for it any property, profit, or benefit derived by the member:

(A) in the conduct or winding up of the company's activities and affairs;

(B) from a use by the member of the company's property; or

(C) from the appropriation of a company opportunity;

(2) to refrain from dealing with the company in the conduct or winding up of the company's activities and affairs as or on behalf of a person having an interest adverse to the company; and

(3) to refrain from competing with the company in the conduct of the company's activities and affairs before the dissolution of the company.

(c) The duty of care of a member of a member-managed limited liability company in the conduct or winding up of the company's activities and affairs is to refrain from engaging in grossly negligent or reckless conduct, willful or intentional misconduct, or knowing violation of law.

(d) A member shall discharge the duties and obligations under this [act] or under the operating agreement and exercise any rights consistently with the contractual obligation of good faith and fair dealing.

(e) A member does not violate a duty or obligation under this [act] or under the operating agreement solely because the member's conduct furthers the member's own interest.

(f) All the members of a member-managed limited liability company or a manager-managed limited liability company may authorize or ratify, after full disclosure of all material facts, a specific act or transaction that otherwise would violate the duty of loyalty.

(g) It is a defense to a claim under subsection (b)(2) and any comparable claim in equity or at common law that the transaction was fair to the limited liability company.

(h) If, as permitted by subsection (f) or (i)(6) or the operating agreement, a member enters into a transaction with the limited liability company which otherwise would be prohibited by subsection (b)(2), the member's rights and obligations arising from the transaction are the same as those of a person that is not a member.

(i) In a manager-managed limited liability company, the following rules apply:

(1) Subsections (a), (b), (c), and (g) apply to the manager or managers and not the members.

(2) The duty stated under subsection (b)(3) continues until winding up is completed.

(3) Subsection (d) applies to managers and members.

(4) Subsection (e) applies only to members.

(5) The power to ratify under subsection (f) applies only to the members.

(6) Subject to subsection (d), a member does not have any duty to the company or to any other member solely by reason of being a member.

§ 410. Rights to Information of Member, Manager, and Person Dissociated as Member.

(a) In a member-managed limited liability company, the following rules apply:

(1) On reasonable notice, a member may inspect and copy during regular business hours, at a reasonable location specified by the company, any record maintained by the company regarding the company's activities, affairs, financial condition, and other circumstances, to the extent the information is material to the member's rights and duties under the operating agreement or this [act].

(2) The company shall furnish to each member:

(A) without demand, any information concerning the company's activities, affairs, financial condition, and other circumstances which the company knows and is material to the proper exercise of the member's rights and duties under the operating agreement or this [act], except to the extent the company can establish that it reasonably believes the member already knows the information; and

(B) on demand, any other information concerning the company's activities, affairs, financial condition, and other circumstances, except to the extent the demand for the information demanded is unreasonable or otherwise improper under the circumstances.

(3) The duty to furnish information under paragraph (2) also applies to each member to the extent the member knows any of the information described in paragraph (2).

(b) In a manager-managed limited liability company, the following rules apply:

(1) The informational rights stated in subsection (a) and the duty stated in subsection (a)(3) apply to the managers and not the members.

(2) During regular business hours and at a reasonable location specified by the company, a member may inspect and copy information regarding the activities, affairs, financial condition, and other circumstances of the company as is just and reasonable if:

(A) the member seeks the information for a purpose reasonably related to the member's interest as a member;

(B) the member makes a demand in a record received by the company, describing with reasonable particularity the information sought and the purpose for seeking the information; and

(C) the information sought is directly connected to the member's purpose.

(3) Not later than 10 days after receiving a demand pursuant to paragraph (2)(B), the company shall inform in a record the member that made the demand of:

(A) what information the company will provide in response to the demand and when and where the company will provide the information; and

(B) the company's reasons for declining, if the company declines to provide any demanded information.

(4) Whenever this [act] or an operating agreement provides for a member to vote on or give or withhold consent to a matter, before the vote is cast or consent is given or withheld, the company shall, without demand, provide the member with all information that is known to the company and is material to the member's decision.

(c) Subject to subsection (h), on 10 days' demand made in a record received by a limited liability company, a person dissociated as a member may have access to the information to which the person was entitled while a member if:

(1) the information pertains to the period during which the person was a member;

(2) the person seeks the information in good faith; and

(3) the person satisfies the requirements imposed on a member by subsection (b)(2).

(d) A limited liability company shall respond to a demand made pursuant to subsection (c) in the manner provided in subsection (b)(3).

(e) A limited liability company may charge a person that makes a demand under this section the reasonable costs of copying, limited to the costs of labor and material.

(f) A member or person dissociated as a member may exercise the rights under this section through an agent or, in the case of an individual under legal disability, a legal representative. Any restriction or condition imposed by the operating agreement or under subsection (h) applies both to the agent or legal representative and to the member or person dissociated as a member.

(g) Subject to § 504, the rights under this section do not extend to a person as transferee.

(h) In addition to any restriction or condition stated in its operating agreement, a limited liability company, as a matter within the ordinary course of its activities and affairs, may impose reasonable restrictions and conditions on access to and use of information to be furnished under this section, including designating information confidential and imposing nondisclosure and safeguarding obligations on the recipient. In a dispute concerning the reasonableness of a restriction under this subsection, the company has the burden of proving reasonableness.

[Article] 5. Transferable Interests and Rights of Transferees and Creditors

§ 501. Nature of Transferable Interest.

A transferable interest is personal property.

§ 502. Transfer of Transferable Interest.

(a) Subject to § 503(f), a transfer, in whole or in part, of a transferable interest:

(1) is permissible;

(2) does not by itself cause a person's dissociation as a member or a dissolution and winding

up of the limited liability company's activities and affairs; and

(3) subject to § 504, does not entitle the transferee to:

> **(A)** participate in the management or conduct of the company's activities and affairs; or

> **(B)** except as otherwise provided in subsection (c), have access to records or other information concerning the company's activities and affairs.

(b) A transferee has the right to receive, in accordance with the transfer, distributions to which the transferor would otherwise be entitled.

(c) In a dissolution and winding up of a limited liability company, a transferee is entitled to an account of the company's transactions only from the date of dissolution.

(d) A transferable interest may be evidenced by a certificate of the interest issued by a limited liability company in a record, and, subject to this section, the interest represented by the certificate may be transferred by a transfer of the certificate.

(e) A limited liability company need not give effect to a transferee's rights under this section until the company knows or has notice of the transfer.

(f) A transfer of a transferable interest in violation of a restriction on transfer contained in the operating agreement is ineffective if the intended transferee has knowledge or notice of the restriction at the time of transfer.

(g) Except as otherwise provided in § 602(5)(B), if a member transfers a transferable interest, the transferor retains the rights of a member other than the transferable interest transferred and retains all the duties and obligations of a member.

(h) If a member transfers a transferable interest to a person that becomes a member with respect to the transferred interest, the transferee is liable for the member's obligations under §§ 403 and 406 known to the transferee when the transferee becomes a member.

§ 503. Charging Order.

(a) On application by a judgment creditor of a member or transferee, a court may enter a charging order against the transferable interest of the judgment debtor for the unsatisfied amount of the judgment. Except as otherwise provided in subsection (f), a charging order constitutes a lien on a judgment debtor's transferable interest and requires the limited liability company to pay over to the person to which the charging order was issued any distribution that otherwise would be paid to the judgment debtor.

(b) To the extent necessary to effectuate the collection of distributions pursuant to a charging order in effect under subsection (a), the court may:

> **(1)** appoint a receiver of the distributions subject to the charging order, with the power to make all inquiries the judgment debtor might have made; and

> **(2)** make all other orders necessary to give effect to the charging order.

(c) Upon a showing that distributions under a charging order will not pay the judgment debt within a reasonable time, the court may foreclose the lien and order the sale of the transferable interest. Except as otherwise provided in subsection (f), the purchaser at the foreclosure sale obtains only the transferable interest, does not thereby become a member, and is subject to § 502.

(d) At any time before foreclosure under subsection (c), the member or transferee whose transferable interest is subject to a charging order under subsection (a) may extinguish the charging order by satisfying the judgment and filing a certified copy of the satisfaction with the court that issued the charging order.

(e) At any time before foreclosure under subsection (c), a limited liability company or one or more members whose transferable interests are not subject to the charging order may pay to the judgment creditor the full amount due under the judgment and thereby succeed to the rights of the judgment creditor, including the charging order.

(f) If a court orders foreclosure of a charging order lien against the sole member of a limited liability company:

    (1) the court shall confirm the sale;

    (2) the purchaser at the sale obtains the member's entire interest, not only the member's transferable interest;

    (3) the purchaser thereby becomes a member; and

    (4) the person whose interest was subject to the foreclosed charging order is dissociated as a member.

(g) This [act] does not deprive any member or transferee of the benefit of any exemption law applicable to the transferable interest of the member or transferee.

(h) This section provides the exclusive remedy by which a person seeking in the capacity of judgment creditor to enforce a judgment against a member or transferee may satisfy the judgment from the judgment debtor's transferable interest.

§ 504. Power of Legal Representative of Deceased Member.

If a member dies, the deceased member's legal representative may exercise:

(1) the rights of a transferee provided in § 502(c); and

(2) for the purposes of settling the estate, the rights the deceased member had under § 410.

[Article] 6. Dissociation

§ 601. Power to Dissociate as Member; Wrongful Dissociation.

(a) A person has the power to dissociate as a member at any time, rightfully or wrongfully, by withdrawing as a member by express will under § 602(1).

(b) A person's dissociation as a member is wrongful only if the dissociation:

    (1) is in breach of an express provision of the operating agreement; or

    (2) occurs before the completion of the winding up of the limited liability company and:

        (A) the person withdraws as a member by express will;

        (B) the person is expelled as a member by judicial order under § 602(6);

        (C) the person is dissociated under § 602(8); or

        (D) in the case of a person that is not a trust other than a business trust, an estate, or an individual, the person is expelled or otherwise dissociated as a member because it willfully dissolved or terminated.

(c) A person that wrongfully dissociates as a member is liable to the limited liability company and, subject to § 801, to the other members for damages caused by the dissociation. The liability is in addition to any debt, obligation, or other liability of the member to the company or the other members.

§ 602. Events Causing Dissociation.

A person is dissociated as a member when:

(1) the limited liability company knows or has notice of the person's express will to withdraw as a member, but, if the person has specified a withdrawal date later than the date the company knew or had notice, on that later date;

(2) an event stated in the operating agreement as causing the person's dissociation occurs;

(3) the person's entire interest is transferred in a foreclosure sale under § 503(f);

(4) the person is expelled as a member pursuant to the operating agreement;

(5) the person is expelled as a member by the affirmative vote or consent of all the other members if:

    (A) it is unlawful to carry on the limited liability company's activities and affairs with the person as a member;

    (B) there has been a transfer of all the person's transferable interest in the company, other than:

        (i) a transfer for security purposes; or

(ii) a charging order in effect under § 503 which has not been foreclosed;

(C) the person is an entity and:

(i) the company notifies the person that it will be expelled as a member because the person has filed a statement of dissolution or the equivalent, the person has been administratively dissolved, the person's charter or the equivalent has been revoked, or the person's right to conduct business has been suspended by the person's jurisdiction of formation; and

(ii) not later than 90 days after the notification, the statement of dissolution or the equivalent has not been withdrawn, rescinded, or revoked, the person has not been reinstated, or the person's charter or the equivalent or right to conduct business has not been reinstated; or

(D) the person is an unincorporated entity that has been dissolved and whose activities and affairs are being wound up;

(6) on application by the limited liability company or a member in a direct action under § 801, the person is expelled as a member by judicial order because the person:

(A) has engaged or is engaging in wrongful conduct that has affected adversely and materially, or will affect adversely and materially, the company's activities and affairs;

(B) has committed willfully or persistently, or is committing willfully or persistently, a material breach of the operating agreement or a duty or obligation under § 409; or

(C) has engaged or is engaging in conduct relating to the company's activities and affairs which makes it not reasonably practicable to carry on the activities and affairs with the person as a member;

(7) in the case of an individual:

(A) the individual dies; or

(B) in a member-managed limited liability company:

(i) a guardian or general conservator for the individual is appointed; or

(ii) a court orders that the individual has otherwise become incapable of performing the individual's duties as a member under this [act] or the operating agreement;

(8) in a member-managed limited liability company, the person:

(A) becomes a debtor in bankruptcy;

(B) signs an assignment for the benefit of creditors; or

(C) seeks, consents to, or acquiesces in the appointment of a trustee, receiver, or liquidator of the person or of all or substantially all the person's property;

(9) in the case of a person that is a testamentary or inter vivos trust or is acting as a member by virtue of being a trustee of such a trust, the trust's entire transferable interest in the limited liability company is distributed;

(10) in the case of a person that is an estate or is acting as a member by virtue of being a personal representative of an estate, the estate's entire transferable interest in the limited liability company is distributed;

(11) in the case of a person that is not an individual, the existence of the person terminates;

(12) the limited liability company participates in a merger under [Article] 10 and:

(A) the company is not the surviving entity; or

(B) otherwise as a result of the merger, the person ceases to be a member;

(13) the limited liability company participates in an interest exchange under [Article] 10 and, as a result of the interest exchange, the person ceases to be a member;

(14) the limited liability company participates in a conversion under [Article] 10;

(15) the limited liability company participates in a domestication under [Article] 10 and, as a result of the domestication, the person ceases to be a member; or

(16) the limited liability company dissolves and completes winding up.

§ 603. Effect of Dissociation.

(a) If a person is dissociated as a member:

(1) the person's right to participate as a member in the management and conduct of the limited liability company's activities and affairs terminates;

(2) the person's duties and obligations under § 409 as a member end with regard to matters arising and events occurring after the person's dissociation; and

(3) subject to § 504 and [Article] 10, any transferable interest owned by the person in the person's capacity as a member immediately before dissociation is owned by the person solely as a transferee.

(b) A person's dissociation as a member does not of itself discharge the person from any debt, obligation, or other liability to the limited liability company or the other members which the person incurred while a member.

[Article] 7. Dissolution and Winding Up

§ 701. Events Causing Dissolution.

(a) A limited liability company is dissolved, and its activities and affairs must be wound up, upon the occurrence of any of the following:

(1) an event or circumstance that the operating agreement states causes dissolution;

(2) the affirmative vote or consent of all the members;

(3) the passage of 90 consecutive days during which the company has no members unless before the end of the period:

(A) consent to admit at least one specified person as a member is given by transferees owning the rights to receive a majority of distributions as transferees at the time the consent is to be effective; and

(B) at least one person becomes a member in accordance with the consent;

(4) on application by a member, the entry by [the appropriate court] of an order dissolving the company on the grounds that:

(A) the conduct of all or substantially all the company's activities and affairs is unlawful;

(B) it is not reasonably practicable to carry on the company's activities and affairs in conformity with the certificate of organization and the operating agreement; or

(C) the managers or those members in control of the company:

(i) have acted, are acting, or will act in a manner that is illegal or fraudulent; or

(ii) have acted or are acting in a manner that is oppressive and was, is, or will be directly harmful to the applicant; or

(5) the signing and filing of a statement of administrative dissolution by the [Secretary of State] under § 708.

(b) In a proceeding brought under subsection (a)(4)(C), the court may order a remedy other than dissolution.

§ 702. Winding Up.

(a) A dissolved limited liability company shall wind up its activities and affairs and, except as otherwise provided in § 703, the company continues after dissolution only for the purpose of winding up.

(b) In winding up its activities and affairs, a limited liability company:

(1) shall discharge the company's debts, obligations, and other liabilities, settle and close the company's activities and affairs, and marshal and distribute the assets of the company; and

(2) may:

(A) deliver to the [Secretary of State] for filing a statement of dissolution stating the name of the company and that the company is dissolved;

(B) preserve the company activities, affairs, and property as a going concern for a reasonable time;

(C) prosecute and defend actions and proceedings, whether civil, criminal, or administrative;

(D) transfer the company's property;

(E) settle disputes by mediation or arbitration;

(F) deliver to the [Secretary of State] for filing a statement of termination stating the name of the company and that the company is terminated; and

(G) perform other acts necessary or appropriate to the winding up.

(c) If a dissolved limited liability company has no members, the legal representative of the last person to have been a member may wind up the activities and affairs of the company. If the person does so, the person has the powers of a sole manager under § 407(c) and is deemed to be a manager for the purposes of § 304(a).

(d) If the legal representative under subsection (c) declines or fails to wind up the limited liability company's activities and affairs, a person may be appointed to do so by the consent of transferees owning a majority of the rights to receive distributions as transferees at the time the consent is to be effective. A person appointed under this subsection:

(1) has the powers of a sole manager under § 407(c) and is deemed to be a manager for the purposes of § 304(a); and

(2) shall deliver promptly to the [Secretary of State] for filing an amendment to the company's certificate of organization stating:

(A) that the company has no members;

(B) the name and street and mailing addresses of the person; and

(C) that the person has been appointed pursuant to this subsection to wind up the company.

(e) [The appropriate court] may order judicial supervision of the winding up of a dissolved limited liability company, including the appointment of a person to wind up the company's activities and affairs:

(1) on the application of a member, if the applicant establishes good cause;

(2) on the application of a transferee, if:

(A) the company does not have any members;

(B) the legal representative of the last person to have been a member declines or fails to wind up the company's activities; and

(C) within a reasonable time following the dissolution a person has not been appointed pursuant to subsection (c); or

(3) in connection with a proceeding under § 701(a)(4).

§ 703. Rescinding Dissolution.

(a) A limited liability company may rescind its dissolution, unless a statement of termination applicable to the company has become effective, [the appropriate court] has entered an order under § 701(a)(4) dissolving the company, or the [Secretary of State] has dissolved the company under § 708.

(b) Rescinding dissolution under this section requires:

(1) the affirmative vote or consent of each member; and

(2) if the limited liability company has delivered to the [Secretary of State] for filing a statement of dissolution and:

(A) the statement has not become effective, delivery to the [Secretary of State] for filing of a statement of withdrawal under § 208 applicable to the statement of dissolution; or

(B) if the statement of dissolution has become effective, delivery to the [Secretary of State] for filing of a statement of rescission stating the name of the company and that dissolution has been rescinded under this section.

(c) If a limited liability company rescinds its dissolution:

(1) the company resumes carrying on its activities and affairs as if dissolution had never occurred;

(2) subject to paragraph (3), any liability incurred by the company after the dissolution and before the rescission has becomes effective is determined as if dissolution had never occurred; and

(3) the rights of a third party arising out of conduct in reliance on the dissolution before the third party knew or had notice of the rescission may not be adversely affected.

§ 704. Known Claims Against Dissolved Limited Liability Company.

(a) Except as otherwise provided in subsection (d), a dissolved limited liability company may give notice of a known claim under subsection (b), which has the effect provided in subsection (c).

(b) A dissolved limited liability company may in a record notify its known claimants of the dissolution. The notice must:

(1) specify the information required to be included in a claim;

(2) state that a claim must be in writing and provide a mailing address to which the claim is to be sent;

(3) state the deadline for receipt of a claim, which may not be less than 120 days after the date the notice is received by the claimant; and

(4) state that the claim will be barred if not received by the deadline.

(c) A claim against a dissolved limited liability company is barred if the requirements of subsection (b) are met and:

(1) the claim is not received by the specified deadline; or

(2) if the claim is timely received but rejected by the company:

(A) the company causes the claimant to receive a notice in a record stating that the claim is rejected and will be barred unless the claimant commences an action against the company to enforce the claim not later than 90 days after the claimant receives the notice; and

(B) the claimant does not commence the required action not later than 90 days after the claimant receives the notice.

(d) This section does not apply to a claim based on an event occurring after the date of dissolution or a liability that on that date is contingent.

§ 705. Other Claims Against Dissolved Limited Liability Company.

(a) A dissolved limited liability company may publish notice of its dissolution and request persons having claims against the company to present them in accordance with the notice.

(b) A notice under subsection (a) must:

(1) be published at least once in a newspaper of general circulation in the [county] in this state in which the dissolved limited liability company's principal office is located or, if the principal office is not located in this state, in the [county] in which the office of the company's registered agent is or was last located;

(2) describe the information required to be contained in a claim, state that the claim must be in writing, and provide a mailing address to which the claim is to be sent; and

(3) state that a claim against the company is barred unless an action to enforce the claim is commenced not later than three years after publication of the notice.

(c) If a dissolved limited liability company publishes a notice in accordance with subsection (b), the claim of each of the following claimants is barred unless the claimant commences an action to enforce the claim against the company not later than three years after the publication date of the notice:

(1) a claimant that did not receive notice in a record under § 704;

(2) a claimant whose claim was timely sent to the company but not acted on; and

(3) a claimant whose claim is contingent at, or based on an event occurring after, the date of dissolution.

(d) A claim not barred under this section or § 704 may be enforced:

(1) against a dissolved limited liability company, to the extent of its undistributed assets; and

(2) except as otherwise provided in § 706, if assets of the company have been distributed after dissolution, against a member or transferee to the extent of that person's proportionate share of the claim or of the company's assets distributed to the member or transferee after dissolution, whichever is less, but a person's total liability for all claims under this paragraph may not exceed the total amount of assets distributed to the person after dissolution.

§ 706. Court Proceedings.

(a) A dissolved limited liability company that has published a notice under § 705 may file an application with [the appropriate court] in the [county] where the company's principal office is located or, if the principal office is not located in this state, where the office of its registered agent is or was last located, for a determination of the amount and form of security to be provided for payment of claims that are reasonably expected to arise after the date of dissolution based on facts known to the company and:

(1) at the time of application:

(A) are contingent; or

(B) have not been made known to the company; or

(2) are based on an event occurring after the date of dissolution.

(b) Security is not required for any claim that is or is reasonably anticipated to be barred under § 705.

(c) Not later than 10 days after the filing of an application under subsection (a), the dissolved limited liability company shall give notice of the proceeding to each claimant holding a contingent claim known to the company.

(d) In a proceeding under this section, the court may appoint a guardian ad litem to represent all claimants whose identities are unknown. The reasonable fees and expenses of the guardian, including all reasonable expert witness fees, must be paid by the dissolved limited liability company.

(e) A dissolved limited liability company that provides security in the amount and form ordered by the court under subsection (a) satisfies the company's obligations with respect to claims that are contingent, have not been made known to the company, or are based on an event occurring after the date of dissolution, and such claims may not be enforced against a member or transferee on account of assets received in liquidation.

§ 707. Disposition of Assets in Winding Up.

(a) In winding up its activities and affairs, a limited liability company shall apply its assets to discharge the company's obligations to creditors, including members that are creditors.

(b) After a limited liability company complies with subsection (a), any surplus must be distributed in the following order, subject to any charging order in effect under § 503:

(1) to each person owning a transferable interest that reflects contributions made and not previously returned, an amount equal to the value of the unreturned contributions; and

(2) among persons owning transferable interests in proportion to their respective rights to share in distributions immediately before the dissolution of the company.

(c) If a limited liability company does not have sufficient surplus to comply with subsection (b)(1), any surplus must be distributed among the owners of transferable interests in proportion to the value of the respective unreturned contributions.

(d) All distributions made under subsections (b) and (c) must be paid in money.

§ 708. Administrative Dissolution.

(a) The [Secretary of State] may commence a proceeding under subsection (b) to dissolve a limited liability company administratively if the company does not:

(1) pay any fee, tax, interest, or penalty required to be paid to the [Secretary of State] not later than [six months] after it is due;

(2) deliver [an annual] [a biennial] report to the [Secretary of State] not later than [six months] after it is due; or

(3) have a registered agent in this state for [60] consecutive days.

(b) If the [Secretary of State] determines that one or more grounds exist for administratively dissolving a limited liability company, the [Secretary of State] shall serve the company with notice in a record of the [Secretary of State's] determination.

(c) If a limited liability company, not later than [60] days after service of the notice under subsection (b), does not cure or demonstrate to the satisfaction of the [Secretary of State] the nonexistence of each ground determined by the [Secretary of State], the [Secretary of State] shall administratively dissolve the company by signing a statement of administrative dissolution that recites the grounds for dissolution and the effective date of dissolution. The [Secretary of State] shall file the statement and serve a copy on the company pursuant to § 210.

(d) A limited liability company that is administratively dissolved continues in existence as an entity but may not carry on any activities except as necessary to wind up its activities and affairs and liquidate its assets under §§ 702, 704, 705, 706, and 707, or to apply for reinstatement under § 709.

(e) The administrative dissolution of a limited liability company does not terminate the authority of its registered agent.

§ 709. Reinstatement.

(a) A limited liability company that is administratively dissolved under § 708 may apply to the [Secretary of State] for reinstatement [not later than [two] years after the effective date of dissolution]. The application must state:

(1) the name of the company at the time of its administrative dissolution and, if needed, a different name that satisfies § 112;

(2) the address of the principal office of the company and the name and street and mailing addresses of its registered agent;

(3) the effective date of the company's administrative dissolution; and

(4) that the grounds for dissolution did not exist or have been cured.

(b) To be reinstated, a limited liability company must pay all fees, taxes, interest, and penalties that were due to the [Secretary of State] at the time of the company's administrative dissolution and all fees, taxes, interest, and penalties that would have been due to the [Secretary of State] while the company was administratively dissolved.

(c) If the [Secretary of State] determines that an application under subsection (a) contains the required information, is satisfied that the information is correct, and determines that all payments required to be made to the [Secretary of State] by subsection (b) have been made, the [Secretary of State] shall:

(1) cancel the statement of administrative dissolution and prepare a statement of reinstatement that states the [Secretary of State's] determination and the effective date of reinstatement; and

(2) file the statement of reinstatement and serve a copy on the limited liability company.

(d) When reinstatement under this section has become effective, the following rules apply:

(1) The reinstatement relates back to and takes effect as of the effective date of the administrative dissolution.

(2) The limited liability company resumes carrying on its activities and affairs as if the administrative dissolution had not occurred.

(3) The rights of a person arising out of an act or omission in reliance on the dissolution before the person knew or had notice of the reinstatement are not affected.

§ 710. Judicial Review of Denial of Reinstatement.

(a) If the [Secretary of State] denies a limited liability company's application for reinstatement following administrative dissolution, the [Secretary of State] shall serve the company with a notice in a record that explains the reasons for the denial.

(b) A limited liability company may seek judicial review of denial of reinstatement in [the appropriate court] not later than [30] days after service of the notice of denial.

[Article] 8. Actions by Members

§ 801. Direct Action by Member.

(a) Subject to subsection (b), a member may maintain a direct action against another member, a manager, or the limited liability company to enforce the member's rights and protect the member's interests, including rights and interests under the operating agreement or this [act] or arising independently of the membership relationship.

(b) A member maintaining a direct action under this section must plead and prove an actual or threatened injury that is not solely the result of an injury suffered or threatened to be suffered by the limited liability company.

§ 802. Derivative Action.

A member may maintain a derivative action to enforce a right of a limited liability company if:

(1) the member first makes a demand on the other members in a member-managed limited liability company, or the managers of a manager-managed limited liability company, requesting that they cause the company to bring an action to enforce the right, and the managers or other members do not bring the action within a reasonable time; or

(2) a demand under paragraph (1) would be futile.

§ 803. Proper Plaintiff.

A derivative action to enforce a right of a limited liability company may be maintained only by a person that is a member at the time the action is commenced and:

(1) was a member when the conduct giving rise to the action occurred; or

(2) whose status as a member devolved on the person by operation of law or pursuant to the terms of the operating agreement from a person that was a member at the time of the conduct.

§ 804. Pleading.

In a derivative action, the complaint must state with particularity:

(1) the date and content of plaintiff's demand and the response to the demand by the managers or other members; or

(2) why demand should be excused as futile.

§ 805. Special Litigation Committee.

(a) If a limited liability company is named as or made a party in a derivative proceeding, the company may appoint a special litigation committee to investigate the claims asserted in the proceeding and determine whether pursuing the action is in the best interests of the company. If the company appoints a special litigation committee, on motion by the committee made in the name of the company, except for good cause shown, the court shall stay discovery for the time reasonably necessary to permit the committee to make its investigation. This subsection does not prevent the court from:

   (1) enforcing a person's right to information under § 410; or

   (2) granting extraordinary relief in the form of a temporary restraining order or preliminary injunction.

(b) A special litigation committee must be composed of one or more disinterested and independent individuals, who may be members.

(c) A special litigation committee may be appointed:

   (1) in a member-managed limited liability company:

      (A) by the affirmative vote or consent of a majority of the members not named as parties in the proceeding; or

(B) if all members are named as parties in the proceeding, by a majority of the members named as defendants; or

(2) in a manager-managed limited liability company:

    (A) by a majority of the managers not named as parties in the proceeding; or

    (B) if all managers are named as parties in the proceeding, by a majority of the managers named as defendants.

(d) After appropriate investigation, a special litigation committee may determine that it is in the best interests of the limited liability company that the proceeding:

    (1) continue under the control of the plaintiff;

    (2) continue under the control of the committee;

    (3) be settled on terms approved by the committee; or

    (4) be dismissed.

(e) After making a determination under subsection (d), a special litigation committee shall file with the court a statement of its determination and its report supporting its determination and shall serve each party with a copy of the determination and report. The court shall determine whether the members of the committee were disinterested and independent and whether the committee conducted its investigation and made its recommendation in good faith, independently, and with reasonable care, with the committee having the burden of proof. If the court finds that the members of the committee were disinterested and independent and that the committee acted in good faith, independently, and with reasonable care, the court shall enforce the determination of the committee. Otherwise, the court shall dissolve the stay of discovery entered under subsection (a) and allow the action to continue under the control of the plaintiff.

§ 806. Proceeds and Expenses.

(a) Except as otherwise provided in subsection (b):

    (1) any proceeds or other benefits of a derivative action, whether by judgment, compromise, or settlement, belong to the limited liability company and not to the plaintiff; and

    (2) if the plaintiff receives any proceeds, the plaintiff shall remit them immediately to the company.

(b) If a derivative action is successful in whole or in part, the court may award the plaintiff reasonable expenses, including reasonable attorney's fees and costs, from the recovery of the limited liability company.

(c) A derivative action on behalf of a limited liability company may not be voluntarily dismissed or settled without the court's approval.

[Article] 9. Foreign Limited Liability Companies

§ 901. Governing Law.

(a) The law of the jurisdiction of formation of a foreign limited liability company governs:

    (1) the internal affairs of the company;

    (2) the liability of a member as member and a manager as manager for a debt, obligation, or other liability of the company; and

    (3) the liability of a series of the company.

(b) A foreign limited liability company is not precluded from registering to do business in this state because of any difference between the law of its jurisdiction of formation and the law of this state.

(c) Registration of a foreign limited liability company to do business in this state does not authorize the foreign company to engage in any activities and affairs or exercise any power that a limited liability company may not engage in or exercise in this state.

§ 902. Registration to Do Business in This State.

(a) A foreign limited liability company may not do business in this state until it registers with the [Secretary of State] under this [article].

(b) A foreign limited liability company doing business in this state may not maintain an action or proceeding in this state unless it is registered to do business in this state.

(c) The failure of a foreign limited liability company to register to do business in this state does not impair the validity of a contract or act of the company or preclude it from defending an action or proceeding in this state.

(d) A limitation on the liability of a member or manager of a foreign limited liability company is not waived solely because the company does business in this state without registering to do business in this state.

(e) Section 901(a) and (b) applies even if a foreign limited liability company fails to register under this [article].

§ 903. Foreign Registration Statement.

To register to do business in this state, a foreign limited liability company must deliver a foreign registration statement to the [Secretary of State] for filing. The statement must state:

(1) the name of the company and, if the name does not comply with § 112, an alternate name adopted pursuant to § 906(a);

(2) that the company is a foreign limited liability company;

(3) the company's jurisdiction of formation;

(4) the street and mailing addresses of the company's principal office and, if the law of the company's jurisdiction of formation requires the company to maintain an office in that jurisdiction, the street and mailing addresses of the required office; and

(5) the name and street and mailing addresses of the company's registered agent in this state.

§ 904. Amendment of Foreign Registration Statement.

A registered foreign limited liability company shall deliver to the [Secretary of State] for filing an amendment to its foreign registration statement if there is a change in:

(1) the name of the company;

(2) the company's jurisdiction of formation;

(3) an address required by § 903(4); or

(4) the information required by § 903(5).

§ 905. Activities Not Constituting Doing Business.

(a) Activities of a foreign limited liability company which do not constitute doing business in this state under this [article] include:

(1) maintaining, defending, mediating, arbitrating, or settling an action or proceeding;

(2) carrying on any activity concerning its internal affairs, including holding meetings of its members or managers;

(3) maintaining accounts in financial institutions;

(4) maintaining offices or agencies for the transfer, exchange, and registration of securities of the company or maintaining trustees or depositories with respect to those securities;

(5) selling through independent contractors;

(6) soliciting or obtaining orders by any means if the orders require acceptance outside this state before they become contracts;

(7) creating or acquiring indebtedness, mortgages, or security interests in property;

(8) securing or collecting debts or enforcing mortgages or security interests in property securing the debts and holding, protecting, or maintaining property;

(9) conducting an isolated transaction that is not in the course of similar transactions;

(10) owning, without more, property; and

(11) doing business in interstate commerce.

(b) A person does not do business in this state solely by being a member or manager of a foreign limited liability company that does business in this state.

(c) This section does not apply in determining the contacts or activities that may subject a foreign limited liability company to service of process, taxation, or regulation under law of this state other than this [act].

§ 906. Noncomplying Name of Foreign Limited Liability Company.

(a) A foreign limited liability company whose name does not comply with § 112 may not register to do business in this state until it adopts, for the purpose of doing business in this state, an alternate name that complies with § 112. A company that registers under an alternate name under this subsection need not comply with [this state's assumed or fictitious name statute]. After registering to do business in this state with an alternate name, a company shall do business in this state under:

(1) the alternate name;

(2) the company's name, with the addition of its jurisdiction of formation; or

(3) a name the company is authorized to use under [this state's assumed or fictitious name statute].

(b) If a registered foreign limited liability company changes its name to one that does not comply with § 112, it may not do business in this state until it complies with subsection (a) by amending its registration to adopt an alternate name that complies with § 112.

§ 907. Withdrawal Deemed on Conversion to Domestic Filing Entity or Domestic Limited Liability Partnership.

A registered foreign limited liability company that converts to a domestic limited liability partnership or to a domestic entity whose formation requires delivery of a record to the [Secretary of State] for filing is deemed to have withdrawn its registration on the effective date of the conversion.

§ 908. Withdrawal on Dissolution or Conversion to Nonfiling Entity Other Than Limited Liability Partnership.

(a) A registered foreign limited liability company that has dissolved and completed winding up or has converted to a domestic or foreign entity whose formation does not require the public filing of a record, other than a limited liability partnership, shall deliver a statement of withdrawal to the [Secretary of State] for filing. The statement must state:

(1) in the case of a company that has completed winding up:

(A) its name and jurisdiction of formation;

(B) that the company surrenders its registration to do business in this state; and

(2) in the case of a company that has converted:

(A) the name of the converting company and its jurisdiction of formation;

(B) the type of entity to which the company has converted and its jurisdiction of formation;

(C) that the converted entity surrenders the converting company's registration to do business in this state and revokes the authority of the converting company's registered agent to act as registered agent in this state on behalf of the company or the converted entity; and

(D) a mailing address to which service of process may be made under subsection (b).

(b) After a withdrawal under this section has become effective, service of process in any action or proceeding based on a cause of action arising during the time the foreign limited liability company was registered to do business in this state may be made pursuant to § 119.

§ 909. Transfer of Registration.

(a) When a registered foreign limited liability company has merged into a foreign entity that is not registered to do business in this state or has converted to a foreign entity required to register with the [Secretary of State] to do business in this state, the foreign entity shall deliver to the [Secretary of State] for filing an application for transfer of registration. The application must state:

(1) the name of the registered foreign limited liability company before the merger or conversion;

(2) that before the merger or conversion the registration pertained to a foreign limited liability company;

(3) the name of the applicant foreign entity into which the foreign limited liability company has

merged or to which it has been converted and, if the name does not comply with § 112, an alternate name adopted pursuant to § 906(a);

(4) the type of entity of the applicant foreign entity and its jurisdiction of formation;

(5) the street and mailing addresses of the principal office of the applicant foreign entity and, if the law of the entity's jurisdiction of formation requires the entity to maintain an office in that jurisdiction, the street and mailing addresses of that office; and

(6) the name and street and mailing addresses of the applicant foreign entity's registered agent in this state.

(b) When an application for transfer of registration takes effect, the registration of the foreign limited liability company to do business in this state is transferred without interruption to the foreign entity into which the company has merged or to which it has been converted.

§ 910. Termination of Registration.

(a) The [Secretary of State] may terminate the registration of a registered foreign limited liability company in the manner provided in subsections (b) and (c) if the company does not:

(1) pay, not later than [60] days after the due date, any fee, tax, interest, or penalty required to be paid to the [Secretary of State] under this [act] or law other than this [act];

(2) deliver to the [Secretary of State] for filing, not later than [60] days after the due date, [an annual] [a biennial] report required under § 212;

(3) have a registered agent as required by § 115; or

(4) deliver to the [Secretary of State] for filing a statement of a change under § 116 not later than [30] days after a change has occurred in the name or address of the registered agent.

(b) The [Secretary of State] may terminate the registration of a registered foreign limited liability company by:

(1) filing a notice of termination or noting the termination in the records of the [Secretary of State]; and

(2) delivering a copy of the notice or the information in the notation to the company's registered agent or, if the company does not have a registered agent, to the company's principal office.

(c) The notice must state or the information in the notation must include:

(1) the effective date of the termination, which must be at least [60] days after the date the [Secretary of State] delivers the copy; and

(2) the grounds for termination under subsection (a).

(d) The authority of a registered foreign limited liability company to do business in this state ceases on the effective date of the notice of termination or notation under subsection (b), unless before that date the company cures each ground for termination stated in the notice or notation. If the company cures each ground, the [Secretary of State] shall file a record so stating.

§ 911. Withdrawal of Registration of Registered Foreign Limited Liability Company.

(a) A registered foreign limited liability company may withdraw its registration by delivering a statement of withdrawal to the [Secretary of State] for filing. The statement of withdrawal must state:

(1) the name of the company and its jurisdiction of formation;

(2) that the company is not doing business in this state and that it withdraws its registration to do business in this state;

(3) that the company revokes the authority of its registered agent to accept service on its behalf in this state; and

(4) an address to which service of process may be made under subsection (b).

(b) After the withdrawal of the registration of a foreign limited liability company, service of process in any action or proceeding based on a cause of action arising during the time the company was registered to do business in this state may be made pursuant to § 119.

§ 912. Action by [Attorney General].

The [Attorney General] may maintain an action to enjoin a foreign limited liability company from doing business in this state in violation of this [article].

[Article] 10. Merger, Interest Exchange, Conversion, and Domestication

[Part] 1. General Provisions

§ 1001. Definitions.

In this [article]:

(1) "Acquired entity" means the entity, all of one or more classes or series of interests of which are acquired in an interest exchange.

(2) "Acquiring entity" means the entity that acquires all of one or more classes or series of interests of the acquired entity in an interest exchange.

(3) "Conversion" means a transaction authorized by [Part] 4.

(4) "Converted entity" means the converting entity as it continues in existence after a conversion.

(5) "Converting entity" means the domestic entity that approves a plan of conversion pursuant to § 1043 or the foreign entity that approves a conversion pursuant to the law of its jurisdiction of formation.

(6) "Distributional interest" means the right under an unincorporated entity's organic law and organic rules to receive distributions from the entity.

(7) "Domestic", with respect to an entity, means governed as to its internal affairs by the law of this state.

(8) "Domesticated limited liability company" means the domesticating limited liability company as it continues in existence after a domestication.

(9) "Domesticating limited liability company" means the domestic limited liability company that approves a plan of domestication pursuant to § 1053 or the foreign limited liability company that approves a domestication pursuant to the law of its jurisdiction of formation.

(10) "Domestication" means a transaction authorized by [Part] 5.

(11) "Entity":

(A) means:

(i) a business corporation;

(ii) a nonprofit corporation;

(iii) a general partnership, including a limited liability partnership;

(iv) a limited partnership, including a limited liability limited partnership;

(v) a limited liability company;

[(vi) a general cooperative association;]

(vii) a limited cooperative association;

(viii) an unincorporated nonprofit association;

(ix) a statutory trust, business trust, or common-law business trust; or

(x) any other person that has:

(I) a legal existence separate from any interest holder of that person; or

(II) the power to acquire an interest in real property in its own name; and

(B) does not include:

(i) an individual;

(ii) a trust with a predominantly donative purpose or a charitable trust;

(iii) an association or relationship that is not an entity listed in subparagraph A and is not a partnership under the rules stated in [Section 202(c) of the Uniform Partnership Act (1997) (Last Amended 2013)] [Section 7 of the Uniform Partnership Act (1914)] or a similar provision of the law of another jurisdiction;

(iv) a decedent's estate; or

(v) a government or a governmental subdivision, agency, or instrumentality.

(12) "Filing entity" means an entity whose formation requires the filing of a public organic record. The term does not include a limited liability partnership.

(13) "Foreign", with respect to an entity, means an entity governed as to its internal affairs by the law of a jurisdiction other than this state.

(14) "Governance interest" means a right under the organic law or organic rules of an unincorporated entity, other than as a governor, agent, assignee, or proxy, to:

(A) receive or demand access to information concerning, or the books and records of, the entity;

(B) vote for or consent to the election of the governors of the entity; or

(C) receive notice of or vote on or consent to an issue involving the internal affairs of the entity.

(15) "Governor" means:

(A) a director of a business corporation;

(B) a director or trustee of a nonprofit corporation;

(C) a general partner of a general partnership;

(D) a general partner of a limited partnership;

(E) a manager of a manager-managed limited liability company;

(F) a member of a member-managed limited liability company;

[(G) a director of a general cooperative association;]

(H) a director of a limited cooperative association;

(I) a manager of an unincorporated nonprofit association;

(J) a trustee of a statutory trust, business trust, or common-law business trust; or

(K) any other person under whose authority the powers of an entity are exercised and under whose direction the activities and affairs of the entity are managed pursuant to the organic law and organic rules of the entity.

(16) "Interest" means:

(A) a share in a business corporation;

(B) a membership in a nonprofit corporation;

(C) a partnership interest in a general partnership;

(D) a partnership interest in a limited partnership;

(E) a membership interest in a limited liability company;

[(F) a share in a general cooperative association;]

(G) a member's interest in a limited cooperative association;

(H) a membership in an unincorporated nonprofit association;

(I) a beneficial interest in a statutory trust, business trust, or common-law business trust; or

(J) a governance interest or distributional interest in any other type of unincorporated entity.

(17) "Interest exchange" means a transaction authorized by [Part] 3.

(18) "Interest holder" means:

(A) a shareholder of a business corporation;

(B) a member of a nonprofit corporation;

(C) a general partner of a general partnership;

(D) a general partner of a limited partnership;

(E) a limited partner of a limited partnership;

(F) a member of a limited liability company;

[(G) a shareholder of a general cooperative association;]

(H) a member of a limited cooperative association;

(I) a member of an unincorporated nonprofit association;

(J) a beneficiary or beneficial owner of a statutory trust, business trust, or common-law business trust; or

(K) any other direct holder of an interest.

(19) "Interest holder liability" means:

(A) personal liability for a liability of an entity which is imposed on a person:

(i) solely by reason of the status of the person as an interest holder; or

(ii) by the organic rules of the entity which make one or more specified interest holders or categories of interest holders liable in their capacity as interest holders for all or specified liabilities of the entity; or

(B) an obligation of an interest holder under the organic rules of an entity to contribute to the entity.

(20) "Merger" means a transaction authorized by [Part] 2.

(21) "Merging entity" means an entity that is a party to a merger and exists immediately before the merger becomes effective.

(22) "Organic law" means the law of an entity's jurisdiction of formation governing the internal affairs of the entity.

(23) "Organic rules" means the public organic record and private organic rules of an entity.

(24) "Plan" means a plan of merger, plan of interest exchange, plan of conversion, or plan of domestication.

(25) "Plan of conversion" means a plan under § 1042.

(26) "Plan of domestication" means a plan under § 1052.

(27) "Plan of interest exchange" means a plan under § 1032.

(28) "Plan of merger" means a plan under § 1022.

(29) "Private organic rules" means the rules, whether or not in a record, that govern the internal affairs of an entity, are binding on all its interest holders, and are not part of its public organic record, if any. The term includes:

(A) the bylaws of a business corporation;

(B) the bylaws of a nonprofit corporation;

(C) the partnership agreement of a general partnership;

(D) the partnership agreement of a limited partnership;

(E) the operating agreement of a limited liability company;

[(F) the bylaws of a general cooperative association;]

(G) the bylaws of a limited cooperative association;

(H) the governing principles of an unincorporated nonprofit association; and

(I) the trust instrument of a statutory trust or similar rules of a business trust or common-law business trust.

(30) "Protected agreement" means:

(A) a record evidencing indebtedness and any related agreement in effect on [the effective date of this [act]];

(B) an agreement that is binding on an entity on [the effective date of this [act]];

(C) the organic rules of an entity in effect on [the effective date of this [act]]; or

(D) an agreement that is binding on any of the governors or interest holders of an entity on [the effective date of this [act]].

(31) "Public organic record" means the record the filing of which by the [Secretary of State] is required to form an entity and any amendment to or restatement of that record. The term includes:

(A) the articles of incorporation of a business corporation;

(B) the articles of incorporation of a nonprofit corporation;

(C) the certificate of limited partnership of a limited partnership;

(D) the certificate of organization of a limited liability company;

[(E) the articles of incorporation of a general cooperative association;]

(F) the articles of organization of a limited cooperative association; and

(G) the certificate of trust of a statutory trust or similar record of a business trust.

(32) "Registered foreign entity" means a foreign entity that is registered to do business in this state pursuant to a record filed by the [Secretary of State].

(33) "Statement of conversion" means a statement under § 1045.

(34) "Statement of domestication" means a statement under § 1055.

(35) "Statement of interest exchange" means a statement under § 1035.

(36) "Statement of merger" means a statement under § 1025.

(37) "Surviving entity" means the entity that continues in existence after or is created by a merger.

(38) "Type of entity" means a generic form of entity:

   (A) recognized at common law; or

   (B) formed under an organic law, whether or not some entities formed under that organic law are subject to provisions of that law that create different categories of the form of entity.

§ 1002. Relationship of [Article] to Other Laws.

(a) This [article] does not authorize an act prohibited by, and does not affect the application or requirements of, law other than this [article].

(b) A transaction effected under this [article] may not create or impair a right, duty or obligation of a person under the statutory law of this state other than this [article] relating to a change in control, takeover, business combination, control-share acquisition, or similar transaction involving a domestic merging, acquired, converting, or domesticating business corporation unless:

   (1) if the corporation does not survive the transaction, the transaction satisfies any requirements of the law; or

   (2) if the corporation survives the transaction, the approval of the plan is by a vote of the shareholders or directors which would be sufficient to create or impair the right, duty, or obligation directly under the law.

§ 1003. Required Notice or Approval.

(a) A domestic or foreign entity that is required to give notice to, or obtain the approval of, a governmental agency or officer of this state to be a party to a merger must give the notice or obtain the approval to be a party to an interest exchange, conversion, or domestication.

(b) Property held for a charitable purpose under the law of this state by a domestic or foreign entity immediately before a transaction under this [article] becomes effective may not, as a result of the transaction, be diverted from the objects for which it was donated, granted, devised, or otherwise transferred unless, to the extent required by or pursuant to the law of this state concerning cy pres or other law dealing with nondiversion of charitable assets, the entity obtains an appropriate order of [the appropriate court] [the Attorney General] specifying the disposition of the property.

(c) A bequest, devise, gift, grant, or promise contained in a will or other instrument of donation, subscription, or conveyance which is made to a merging entity that is not the surviving entity and which takes effect or remains payable after the merger inures to the surviving entity.

(d) A trust obligation that would govern property if transferred to a nonsurviving entity applies to property that is transferred to the surviving entity under this section.

Legislative Note: *As an alternative to enacting Subsection (a), a state may identify each of its regulatory laws that requires prior approval for a merger of a regulated entity, decide whether regulatory approval should be required for an interest exchange, conversion, or domestication, and make amendments as appropriate to those laws.*

As with Subsection (a), an adopting state may choose to amend its various laws with respect to the nondiversion of charitable property to cover the various transactions authorized by this act as an alternative to enacting Subsection (b).

§ 1004. Nonexclusivity.

The fact that a transaction under this [article] produces a certain result does not preclude the same result from being accomplished in any other manner permitted by law other than this [article].

§ 1005. Reference to External Facts.

A plan may refer to facts ascertainable outside the plan if the manner in which the facts will operate upon the plan is specified in the plan. The facts may include the occurrence of an event or a determination or action by a person, whether or not the event, determination, or action is within the control of a party to the transaction.

§ 1006. Appraisal Rights.

An interest holder of a domestic merging, acquired, converting, or domesticating limited liability company is entitled to contractual appraisal rights in connection with a transaction under this [article] to the extent provided in:

(1) the operating agreement; or

(2) the plan.

[§ 1007. Excluded Entities and Transactions.

(a) The following entities may not participate in a transaction under this [article]:

(1)

(2).

(b) This [article] may not be used to effect a transaction that:

(1)

(2).]

Legislative Note: Subsection (a) may be used by states that have special statutes restricted to the organization of certain types of entities. A common example is banking statutes that prohibit banks from engaging in transactions other than pursuant to those statutes.

Nonprofit entities may participate in transactions under this act with for-profit entities, subject to compliance with § 1003. If a state desires, however, to exclude entities with a charitable purpose or to exclude other types of entities from the scope of this article, that may be done by referring to those entities in Subsection (a).

Subsection (b) may be used to exclude certain types of transactions governed by more specific

statutes. A common example is the conversion of an insurance company from mutual to stock form. There may be other types of transactions that vary greatly among the states.

[Part] 2. Merger

§ 1021. Merger Authorized.

(a) By complying with this [part]:

(1) one or more domestic limited liability companies may merge with one or more domestic or foreign entities into a domestic or foreign surviving entity; and

(2) two or more foreign entities may merge into a domestic limited liability company.

(b) By complying with the provisions of this [part] applicable to foreign entities, a foreign entity may be a party to a merger under this [part] or may be the surviving entity in such a merger if the merger is authorized by the law of the foreign entity's jurisdiction of formation.

§ 1022. Plan of Merger.

(a) A domestic limited liability company may become a party to a merger under this [part] by approving a plan of merger. The plan must be in a record and contain:

(1) as to each merging entity, its name, jurisdiction of formation, and type of entity;

(2) if the surviving entity is to be created in the merger, a statement to that effect and the entity's name, jurisdiction of formation, and type of entity;

(3) the manner of converting the interests in each party to the merger into interests, securities, obligations, money, other property, rights to acquire interests or securities, or any combination of the foregoing;

(4) if the surviving entity exists before the merger, any proposed amendments to:

(A) its public organic record, if any; and

(B) its private organic rules that are, or are proposed to be, in a record;

(5) if the surviving entity is to be created in the merger:

(A) its proposed public organic record, if any; and

(B) the full text of its private organic rules that are proposed to be in a record;

(6) the other terms and conditions of the merger; and

(7) any other provision required by the law of a merging entity's jurisdiction of formation or the organic rules of a merging entity.

(b) In addition to the requirements of subsection (a), a plan of merger may contain any other provision not prohibited by law.

§ 1023. Approval of Merger.

(a) A plan of merger is not effective unless it has been approved:

(1) by a domestic merging limited liability company, by all the members of the company entitled to vote on or consent to any matter; and

(2) in a record, by each member of a domestic merging limited liability company which will have interest holder liability for debts, obligations, and other liabilities that are incurred after the merger becomes effective, unless:

(A) the operating agreement of the company provides in a record for the approval of a merger in which some or all of its members become subject to interest holder liability by the affirmative vote or consent of fewer than all the members; and

(B) the member consented in a record to or voted for that provision of the operating agreement or became a member after the adoption of that provision.

(b) A merger involving a domestic merging entity that is not a limited liability company is not effective unless the merger is approved by that entity in accordance with its organic law.

(c) A merger involving a foreign merging entity is not effective unless the merger is approved by the foreign entity in accordance with the law of the foreign entity's jurisdiction of formation.

§ 1024. Amendment or Abandonment of Plan of Merger.

(a) A plan of merger may be amended only with the consent of each party to the plan, except as otherwise provided in the plan.

(b) A domestic merging limited liability company may approve an amendment of a plan of merger:

(1) in the same manner as the plan was approved, if the plan does not provide for the manner in which it may be amended; or

(2) by its managers or members in the manner provided in the plan, but a member that was entitled to vote on or consent to approval of the merger is entitled to vote on or consent to any amendment of the plan that will change:

(A) the amount or kind of interests, securities, obligations, money, other property, rights to acquire interests or securities, or any combination of the foregoing, to be received by the interest holders of any party to the plan;

(B) the public organic record, if any, or private organic rules of the surviving entity that will be in effect immediately after the merger becomes effective, except for changes that do not require approval of the interest holders of the surviving entity under its organic law or organic rules; or

(C) any other terms or conditions of the plan, if the change would adversely affect the member in any material respect.

(c) After a plan of merger has been approved and before a statement of merger becomes effective, the plan may be abandoned as provided in the plan. Unless prohibited by the plan, a domestic merging limited liability company may abandon the plan in the same manner as the plan was approved.

(d) If a plan of merger is abandoned after a statement of merger has been delivered to the [Secretary of State] for filing and before the statement becomes effective, a statement of abandonment, signed by a party to the plan, must be delivered to the [Secretary of State] for filing before the statement of merger becomes effective. The statement of abandonment takes effect on filing, and the merger is abandoned and does not become effective. The statement of abandonment must contain:

(1) the name of each party to the plan of merger;

(2) the date on which the statement of merger was filed by the [Secretary of State]; and

(3) a statement that the merger has been abandoned in accordance with this section.

§ 1025. Statement of Merger; Effective Date of Merger.

(a) A statement of merger must be signed by each merging entity and delivered to the [Secretary of State] for filing.

(b) A statement of merger must contain:

(1) the name, jurisdiction of formation, and type of entity of each merging entity that is not the surviving entity;

(2) the name, jurisdiction of formation, and type of entity of the surviving entity;

(3) a statement that the merger was approved by each domestic merging entity, if any, in accordance with this [part] and by each foreign merging entity, if any, in accordance with the law of its jurisdiction of formation;

(4) if the surviving entity exists before the merger and is a domestic filing entity, any amendment to its public organic record approved as part of the plan of merger;

(5) if the surviving entity is created by the merger and is a domestic filing entity, its public organic record, as an attachment; and

(6) if the surviving entity is created by the merger and is a domestic limited liability partnership, its statement of qualification, as an attachment.

(c) In addition to the requirements of subsection (b), a statement of merger may contain any other provision not prohibited by law.

(d) If the surviving entity is a domestic entity, its public organic record, if any, must satisfy the requirements of the law of this state, except that the public organic record does not need to be signed.

(e) A plan of merger that is signed by all the merging entities and meets all the requirements of subsection (b) may be delivered to the [Secretary of State] for filing instead of a statement of merger and on filing has the same effect. If a plan of merger is filed as provided in this subsection, references in this [article] to a statement of merger refer to the plan of merger filed under this subsection.

(f) If the surviving entity is a domestic limited liability company, the merger becomes effective when the statement of merger is effective. In all other cases, the merger becomes effective on the later of:

(1) the date and time provided by the organic law of the surviving entity; and

(2) when the statement is effective.

§ 1026. Effect of Merger.

(a) When a merger becomes effective:

(1) the surviving entity continues or comes into existence;

(2) each merging entity that is not the surviving entity ceases to exist;

(3) all property of each merging entity vests in the surviving entity without transfer, reversion, or impairment;

(4) all debts, obligations, and other liabilities of each merging entity are debts, obligations, and other liabilities of the surviving entity;

(5) except as otherwise provided by law or the plan of merger, all the rights, privileges, immunities, powers, and purposes of each merging entity vest in the surviving entity;

(6) if the surviving entity exists before the merger:

(A) all its property continues to be vested in it without transfer, reversion, or impairment;

(B) it remains subject to all its debts, obligations, and other liabilities; and

(C) all its rights, privileges, immunities, powers, and purposes continue to be vested in it;

(7) the name of the surviving entity may be substituted for the name of any merging entity that is a party to any pending action or proceeding;

(8) if the surviving entity exists before the merger:

(A) its public organic record, if any, is amended to the extent provided in the statement of merger; and

(B) its private organic rules that are to be in a record, if any, are amended to the extent provided in the plan of merger;

(9) if the surviving entity is created by the merger, its private organic rules are effective and:

(A) if it is a filing entity, its public organic record becomes effective; and

(B) if it is a limited liability partnership, its statement of qualification becomes effective; and

(10) the interests in each merging entity which are to be converted in the merger are converted, and the interest holders of those interests are entitled only to the rights provided to them under the plan of merger and to any appraisal rights they have under § 1006 and the merging entity's organic law.

(b) Except as otherwise provided in the organic law or organic rules of a merging entity, the merger does not give rise to any rights that an interest holder, governor, or third party would have upon a dissolution, liquidation, or winding up of the merging entity.

(c) When a merger becomes effective, a person that did not have interest holder liability with respect to any of the merging entities and becomes subject to interest holder liability with respect to a domestic entity as a result of the merger has interest holder liability only to the extent provided by the organic law of that entity and only for those debts, obligations, and other liabilities that are incurred after the merger becomes effective.

(d) When a merger becomes effective, the interest holder liability of a person that ceases to hold an interest in a domestic merging limited liability company with respect to which the person had interest holder liability is subject to the following rules:

(1) The merger does not discharge any interest holder liability under this [act] to the extent the interest holder liability was incurred before the merger became effective.

(2) The person does not have interest holder liability under this [act] for any debt, obligation, or other liability that is incurred after the merger becomes effective.

(3) This [act] continues to apply to the release, collection, or discharge of any interest holder liability preserved under paragraph (1) as if the merger had not occurred.

(4) The person has whatever rights of contribution from any other person as are provided by this [act], law other than this [act], or the operating agreement of the domestic merging limited liability company with respect to any interest holder liability preserved under paragraph (1) as if the merger had not occurred.

(e) When a merger becomes effective, a foreign entity that is the surviving entity may be served with process in this state for the collection and enforcement of any debts, obligations, or other liabilities of a domestic merging limited liability company as provided in § 119.

(f) When a merger becomes effective, the registration to do business in this state of any foreign merging entity that is not the surviving entity is canceled.

[Part] 3. Interest Exchange

§ 1031. Interest Exchange Authorized.

(a) By complying with this [part]:

(1) a domestic limited liability company may acquire all of one or more classes or series of interests of another domestic entity or a foreign entity in exchange for interests, securities, obligations, money, other property, rights to acquire interests or securities, or any combination of the foregoing; or

(2) all of one or more classes or series of interests of a domestic limited liability company may be acquired by another domestic entity or a foreign entity in exchange for interests, securities, obligations, money, other property, rights to acquire interests or securities, or any combination of the foregoing.

(b) By complying with the provisions of this [part] applicable to foreign entities, a foreign entity may be the acquiring or acquired entity in an interest exchange under this [part] if the interest exchange is authorized by the law of the foreign entity's jurisdiction of formation.

(c) If a protected agreement contains a provision that applies to a merger of a domestic limited liability company but does not refer to an interest exchange, the provision applies to an interest exchange in which the domestic limited liability company is the acquired entity as if the interest exchange were a merger until the provision is amended after [the effective date of this [act]].

§ 1032. Plan of Interest Exchange.

(a) A domestic limited liability company may be the acquired entity in an interest exchange under this [part] by approving a plan of interest exchange. The plan must be in a record and contain:

(1) the name of the acquired entity;

(2) the name, jurisdiction of formation, and type of entity of the acquiring entity;

(3) the manner of converting the interests in the acquired entity into interests, securities, obligations, money, other property, rights to acquire interests or securities, or any combination of the foregoing;

(4) any proposed amendments to:

    (A) the certificate of organization of the acquired entity; and

    (B) the operating agreement of the acquired entity that are, or are proposed to be, in a record;

(5) the other terms and conditions of the interest exchange; and

(6) any other provision required by the law of this state or the operating agreement of the acquired entity.

(b) In addition to the requirements of subsection (a), a plan of interest exchange may contain any other provision not prohibited by law.

§ 1033. Approval of Interest Exchange.

(a) A plan of interest exchange is not effective unless it has been approved:

(1) by all the members of a domestic acquired limited liability company entitled to vote on or consent to any matter; and

(2) in a record, by each member of the domestic acquired limited liability company that will have interest holder liability for debts, obligations, and other liabilities that are incurred after the interest exchange becomes effective, unless:

    (A) the operating agreement of the company provides in a record for the approval of an interest exchange or a merger in which some or all of its members become subject to interest holder liability by the affirmative vote or consent of fewer than all the members; and

    (B) the member consented in a record to or voted for that provision of the operating agreement or became a member after the adoption of that provision.

(b) An interest exchange involving a domestic acquired entity that is not a limited liability company is not effective unless it is approved by the domestic entity in accordance with its organic law.

(c) An interest exchange involving a foreign acquired entity is not effective unless it is approved by the foreign entity in accordance with the law of the foreign entity's jurisdiction of formation.

(d) Except as otherwise provided in its organic law or organic rules, the interest holders of the acquiring entity are not required to approve the interest exchange.

§ 1034. Amendment or Abandonment of Plan of Interest Exchange.

(a) A plan of interest exchange may be amended only with the consent of each party to the plan, except as otherwise provided in the plan.

(b) A domestic acquired limited liability company may approve an amendment of a plan of interest exchange:

> **(1)** in the same manner as the plan was approved, if the plan does not provide for the manner in which it may be amended; or

> **(2)** by its managers or members in the manner provided in the plan, but a member that was entitled to vote on or consent to approval of the interest exchange is entitled to vote on or consent to any amendment of the plan that will change:

>> **(A)** the amount or kind of interests, securities, obligations, money, other property, rights to acquire interests or securities, or any combination of the foregoing, to be received by any of the members of the acquired company under the plan;

>> **(B)** the certificate of organization or operating agreement of the acquired company that will be in effect immediately after the interest exchange becomes effective, except for changes that do not require approval of the members of the acquired company under this [act] or the operating agreement; or

>> **(C)** any other terms or conditions of the plan, if the change would adversely affect the member in any material respect.

(c) After a plan of interest exchange has been approved and before a statement of interest exchange becomes effective, the plan may be abandoned as provided in the plan. Unless prohibited by the plan, a domestic acquired limited liability company may abandon the plan in the same manner as the plan was approved.

(d) If a plan of interest exchange is abandoned after a statement of interest exchange has been delivered to the [Secretary of State] for filing and before the statement becomes effective, a statement of abandonment, signed by the acquired limited liability company, must be delivered to the [Secretary of State] for filing before the statement of interest exchange becomes effective. The statement of abandonment takes effect on filing, and the interest exchange is abandoned and does not become effective. The statement of abandonment must contain:

> **(1)** the name of the acquired company;

> **(2)** the date on which the statement of interest exchange was filed by the [Secretary of State]; and

> **(3)** a statement that the interest exchange has been abandoned in accordance with this section.

§ 1035. Statement of Interest Exchange; Effective Date of Interest Exchange.

(a) A statement of interest exchange must be signed by a domestic acquired limited liability company and delivered to the [Secretary of State] for filing.

(b) A statement of interest exchange must contain:

> **(1)** the name of the acquired limited liability company;

> **(2)** the name, jurisdiction of formation, and type of entity of the acquiring entity;

> **(3)** a statement that the plan of interest exchange was approved by the acquired company in accordance with this [part]; and

> **(4)** any amendments to the acquired company's certificate of organization approved as part of the plan of interest exchange.

(c) In addition to the requirements of subsection (b), a statement of interest exchange may contain any other provision not prohibited by law.

(d) A plan of interest exchange that is signed by a domestic acquired limited liability company and meets all the requirements of subsection (b) may be delivered to the [Secretary of State] for filing instead of a statement of interest exchange and on filing has the same effect. If a plan of interest exchange is filed as provided in this subsection, references in this [article] to a statement of interest exchange refer to the plan of interest exchange filed under this subsection.

(e) An interest exchange becomes effective when the statement of interest exchange is effective.

§ 1036. Effect of Interest Exchange.

(a) When an interest exchange in which the acquired entity is a domestic limited liability company becomes effective:

(1) the interests in the acquired company which are the subject of the interest exchange are converted, and the members holding those interests are entitled only to the rights provided to them under the plan of interest exchange and to any appraisal rights they have under § 1006;

(2) the acquiring entity becomes the interest holder of the interests in the acquired company stated in the plan of interest exchange to be acquired by the acquiring entity;

(3) the certificate of organization of the acquired company is amended to the extent provided in the statement of interest exchange; and

(4) the provisions of the operating agreement of the acquired company that are to be in a record, if any, are amended to the extent provided in the plan of interest exchange.

(b) Except as otherwise provided in the operating agreement of a domestic acquired limited liability company, the interest exchange does not give rise to any rights that a member, manager, or third party would have upon a dissolution, liquidation, or winding up of the acquired company.

(c) When an interest exchange becomes effective, a person that did not have interest holder liability with respect to a domestic acquired limited liability company and becomes subject to interest holder liability with respect to a domestic entity as a result of the interest exchange has interest holder liability only to the extent provided by the organic law of the entity and only for those debts, obligations, and other liabilities that are incurred after the interest exchange becomes effective.

(d) When an interest exchange becomes effective, the interest holder liability of a person that ceases to hold an interest in a domestic acquired limited liability company with respect to which the person had interest holder liability is subject to the following rules:

(1) The interest exchange does not discharge any interest holder liability under this [act] to the extent the interest holder liability was incurred before the interest exchange became effective.

(2) The person does not have interest holder liability under this [act] for any debt, obligation, or other liability that is incurred after the interest exchange becomes effective.

(3) This [act] continues to apply to the release, collection, or discharge of any interest holder liability preserved under paragraph (1) as if the interest exchange had not occurred.

(4) The person has whatever rights of contribution from any other person as are provided by this [act], law other than this [act], or the operating agreement of the acquired company with respect to any interest holder liability preserved under paragraph (1) as if the interest exchange had not occurred.

[Part] 4. Conversion

§ 1041. Conversion Authorized.

(a) By complying with this [part], a domestic limited liability company may become:

(1) a domestic entity that is a different type of entity; or

(2) a foreign entity that is a different type of entity, if the conversion is authorized by the law of the foreign entity's jurisdiction of formation.

(b) By complying with the provisions of this [part] applicable to foreign entities, a foreign entity that is not a foreign limited liability company may become a domestic limited liability company if the conversion is authorized by the law of the foreign entity's jurisdiction of formation.

(c) If a protected agreement contains a provision that applies to a merger of a domestic limited liability company but does not refer to a conversion, the provision applies to a conversion of the company as if the conversion were a merger until the provision is amended after [the effective date of this [act]].

§ 1042. Plan of Conversion.

(a) A domestic limited liability company may convert to a different type of entity under this [part] by approving a plan of conversion. The plan must be in a record and contain:

(1) the name of the converting limited liability company;

(2) the name, jurisdiction of formation, and type of entity of the converted entity;

(3) the manner of converting the interests in the converting limited liability company into interests, securities, obligations, money, other property, rights to acquire interests or securities, or any combination of the foregoing;

(4) the proposed public organic record of the converted entity if it will be a filing entity;

(5) the full text of the private organic rules of the converted entity which are proposed to be in a record;

(6) the other terms and conditions of the conversion; and

(7) any other provision required by the law of this state or the operating agreement of the converting limited liability company.

(b) In addition to the requirements of subsection (a), a plan of conversion may contain any other provision not prohibited by law.

§ 1043. Approval of Conversion.

(a) A plan of conversion is not effective unless it has been approved:

(1) by a domestic converting limited liability company, by all the members of the limited liability company entitled to vote on or consent to any matter; and

(2) in a record, by each member of a domestic converting limited liability company which will have interest holder liability for debts, obligations, and other liabilities that are incurred after the conversion becomes effective, unless:

(A) the operating agreement of the company provides in a record for the approval of a conversion or a merger in which some or all of its members become subject to interest holder liability by the affirmative vote or consent of fewer than all the members; and

(B) the member voted for or consented in a record to that provision of the operating agreement or became a member after the adoption of that provision.

(b) A conversion involving a domestic converting entity that is not a limited liability company is not effective unless it is approved by the domestic converting entity in accordance with its organic law.

(c) A conversion of a foreign converting entity is not effective unless it is approved by the foreign entity in accordance with the law of the foreign entity's jurisdiction of formation.

§ 1044. Amendment or Abandonment of Plan of Conversion.

(a) A plan of conversion of a domestic converting limited liability company may be amended:

(1) in the same manner as the plan was approved, if the plan does not provide for the manner in which it may be amended; or

(2) by its managers or members in the manner provided in the plan, but a member that was entitled to vote on or consent to approval of the conversion is entitled to vote on or consent to any amendment of the plan that will change:

(A) the amount or kind of interests, securities, obligations, money, other property, rights to acquire interests or securities, or any combination of the foregoing, to be received by any of the members of the converting company under the plan;

(B) the public organic record, if any, or private organic rules of the converted entity which will be in effect immediately after the conversion becomes effective, except for changes that do not require approval of the interest holders of the converted entity under its organic law or organic rules; or

(C) any other terms or conditions of the plan, if the change would adversely affect the member in any material respect.

(b) After a plan of conversion has been approved by a domestic converting limited liability company and before a statement of conversion becomes effective, the plan may be abandoned as provided in the plan. Unless prohibited by the plan, a domestic converting limited liability company may abandon the plan in the same manner as the plan was approved.

(c) If a plan of conversion is abandoned after a statement of conversion has been delivered to the [Secretary of State] for filing and before the statement becomes effective, a statement of abandonment, signed by the converting entity, must be delivered to the [Secretary of State] for filing before the statement of conversion becomes effective. The statement of abandonment takes effect on filing, and the conversion is abandoned and does not become effective. The statement of abandonment must contain:

    (1) the name of the converting limited liability company;

    (2) the date on which the statement of conversion was filed by the [Secretary of State]; and

    (3) a statement that the conversion has been abandoned in accordance with this section.

§ 1045. Statement of Conversion; Effective Date of Conversion.

(a) A statement of conversion must be signed by the converting entity and delivered to the [Secretary of State] for filing.

(b) A statement of conversion must contain:

    (1) the name, jurisdiction of formation, and type of entity of the converting entity;

    (2) the name, jurisdiction of formation, and type of entity of the converted entity;

    (3) if the converting entity is a domestic limited liability company, a statement that the plan of conversion was approved in accordance with this [part] or, if the converting entity is a foreign entity, a statement that the conversion was

approved by the foreign entity in accordance with the law of its jurisdiction of formation;

    (4) if the converted entity is a domestic filing entity, its public organic record, as an attachment; and

    (5) if the converted entity is a domestic limited liability partnership, its statement of qualification, as an attachment.

(c) In addition to the requirements of subsection (b), a statement of conversion may contain any other provision not prohibited by law.

(d) If the converted entity is a domestic entity, its public organic record, if any, must satisfy the requirements of the law of this state, except that the public organic record does not need to be signed.

(e) A plan of conversion that is signed by a domestic converting limited liability company and meets all the requirements of subsection (b) may be delivered to the [Secretary of State] for filing instead of a statement of conversion and on filing has the same effect. If a plan of conversion is filed as provided in this subsection, references in this [article] to a statement of conversion refer to the plan of conversion filed under this subsection.

(f) If the converted entity is a domestic limited liability company, the conversion becomes effective when the statement of conversion is effective. In all other cases, the conversion becomes effective on the later of:

    (1) the date and time provided by the organic law of the converted entity; and

    (2) when the statement is effective.

§ 1046. Effect of Conversion.

(a) When a conversion becomes effective:

    (1) the converted entity is:

        (A) organized under and subject to the organic law of the converted entity; and

        (B) the same entity without interruption as the converting entity;

    (2) all property of the converting entity continues to be vested in the converted entity without transfer, reversion, or impairment;

(3) all debts, obligations, and other liabilities of the converting entity continue as debts, obligations, and other liabilities of the converted entity;

(4) except as otherwise provided by law or the plan of conversion, all the rights, privileges, immunities, powers, and purposes of the converting entity remain in the converted entity;

(5) the name of the converted entity may be substituted for the name of the converting entity in any pending action or proceeding;

(6) the certificate of organization of the converted entity becomes effective;

(7) the provisions of the operating agreement of the converted entity which are to be in a record, if any, approved as part of the plan of conversion become effective; and

(8) the interests in the converting entity are converted, and the interest holders of the converting entity are entitled only to the rights provided to them under the plan of conversion and to any appraisal rights they have under § 1006.

(b) Except as otherwise provided in the operating agreement of a domestic converting limited liability company, the conversion does not give rise to any rights that a member, manager, or third party would have upon a dissolution, liquidation, or winding up of the converting entity.

(c) When a conversion becomes effective, a person that did not have interest holder liability with respect to the converting entity and becomes subject to interest holder liability with respect to a domestic entity as a result of the conversion has interest holder liability only to the extent provided by the organic law of the entity and only for those debts, obligations, and other liabilities that are incurred after the conversion becomes effective.

(d) When a conversion becomes effective, the interest holder liability of a person that ceases to hold an interest in a domestic converting limited liability company with respect to which the person had interest holder liability is subject to the following rules:

(1) The conversion does not discharge any interest holder liability under this [act] to the extent the interest holder liability was incurred before the conversion became effective;

(2) The person does not have interest holder liability under this [act] for any debt, obligation, or other liability that arises after the conversion becomes effective.

(3) This [act] continues to apply to the release, collection, or discharge of any interest holder liability preserved under paragraph (1) as if the conversion had not occurred.

(4) The person has whatever rights of contribution from any other person as are provided by this [act], law other than this [act], or the organic rules of the converting entity with respect to any interest holder liability preserved under paragraph (1) as if the conversion had not occurred.

(e) When a conversion becomes effective, a foreign entity that is the converted entity may be served with process in this state for the collection and enforcement of any of its debts, obligations, and other liabilities as provided in § 119.

(f) If the converting entity is a registered foreign entity, its registration to do business in this state is canceled when the conversion becomes effective.

(g) A conversion does not require the entity to wind up its affairs and does not constitute or cause the dissolution of the entity.

[Part] 5. Domestication

§ 1051. Domestication Authorized.

(a) By complying with this [part], a domestic limited liability company may become a foreign limited liability company if the domestication is authorized by the law of the foreign jurisdiction.

(b) By complying with the provisions of this [part] applicable to foreign limited liability companies, a foreign limited liability company may become a domestic limited liability company if the domestication is authorized by the law of the foreign limited liability company's jurisdiction of formation.

(c) If a protected agreement contains a provision that applies to a merger of a domestic limited liability company but does not refer to a domestication, the provision applies to a domestication of the limited liability company as if the domestication were a merger until the provision is amended after [the effective date of this [act]].

§ 1052. Plan of Domestication.

(a) A domestic limited liability company may become a foreign limited liability company in a domestication by approving a plan of domestication. The plan must be in a record and contain:

(1) the name of the domesticating limited liability company;

(2) the name and jurisdiction of formation of the domesticated limited liability company;

(3) the manner of converting the interests in the domesticating limited liability company into interests, securities, obligations, money, other property, rights to acquire interests or securities, or any combination of the foregoing;

(4) the proposed certificate of organization of the domesticated limited liability company;

(5) the full text of the provisions of the operating agreement of the domesticated limited liability company that are proposed to be in a record;

(6) the other terms and conditions of the domestication; and

(7) any other provision required by the law of this state or the operating agreement of the domesticating limited liability company.

(b) In addition to the requirements of subsection (a), a plan of domestication may contain any other provision not prohibited by law.

§ 1053. Approval of Domestication.

(a) A plan of domestication of a domestic domesticating limited liability company is not effective unless it has been approved:

(1) by all the members entitled to vote on or consent to any matter; and

(2) in a record, by each member that will have interest holder liability for debts, obligations, and other liabilities that are incurred after the domestication becomes effective, unless:

(A) the operating agreement of the domesticating company in a record provides for the approval of a domestication or merger in which some or all of its members become subject to interest holder liability by the affirmative vote or consent of fewer than all the members; and

(B) the member voted for or consented in a record to that provision of the operating agreement or became a member after the adoption of that provision.

(b) A domestication of a foreign domesticating limited liability company is not effective unless it is approved in accordance with the law of the foreign limited liability company's jurisdiction of formation.

§ 1054. Amendment or Abandonment of Plan of Domestication.

(a) A plan of domestication of a domestic domesticating limited liability company may be amended:

(1) in the same manner as the plan was approved, if the plan does not provide for the manner in which it may be amended; or

(2) by its managers or members in the manner provided in the plan, but a member that was entitled to vote on or consent to approval of the domestication is entitled to vote on or consent to any amendment of the plan that will change:

(A) the amount or kind of interests, securities, obligations, money, other property, rights to acquire interests or securities, or any combination of the foregoing, to be received by any of the members of the domesticating limited liability company under the plan;

(B) the certificate of organization or operating agreement of the domesticated limited liability company that will be in effect immediately after the domestication becomes effective, except for changes that do not require approval of the members of the domesticated limited liability company under its organic law or operating agreement; or

(C) any other terms or conditions of the plan, if the change would adversely affect the member in any material respect.

(b) After a plan of domestication has been approved by a domestic domesticating limited liability company and before a statement of domestication becomes effective, the plan may be abandoned as provided in the plan. Unless prohibited by the plan, a domestic domesticating limited liability company may abandon the plan in the same manner as the plan was approved.

(c) If a plan of domestication is abandoned after a statement of domestication has been delivered to the [Secretary of State] for filing and before the statement becomes effective, a statement of abandonment, signed by the domesticating limited liability company, must be delivered to the [Secretary of State] for filing before the statement of domestication becomes effective. The statement of abandonment takes effect on filing, and the domestication is abandoned and does not become effective. The statement of abandonment must contain:

(1) the name of the domesticating limited liability company;

(2) the date on which the statement of domestication was filed by the [Secretary of State]; and

(3) a statement that the domestication has been abandoned in accordance with this section.

§ 1055. Statement of Domestication; Effective Date of Domestication.

(a) A statement of domestication must be signed by the domesticating limited liability company and delivered to the [Secretary of State] for filing.

(b) A statement of domestication must contain:

(1) the name and jurisdiction of formation of the domesticating limited liability company;

(2) the name and jurisdiction of formation of the domesticated limited liability company;

(3) if the domesticating limited liability company is a domestic limited liability company, a statement that the plan of domestication was approved in accordance with this [part] or, if the domesticating limited liability company is a foreign limited liability company, a statement that the domestication was approved in accordance with the law of its jurisdiction of formation; and

(4) the certificate of organization of the domesticated limited liability company, as an attachment.

(c) In addition to the requirements of subsection (b), a statement of domestication may contain any other provision not prohibited by law.

(d) The certificate of organization of a domestic domesticated limited liability company must satisfy the requirements of this [act], but the certificate does not need to be signed.

(e) A plan of domestication that is signed by a domesticating domestic limited liability company and meets all the requirements of subsection (b) may be delivered to the [Secretary of State] for filing instead of a statement of domestication and on filing has the same effect. If a plan of domestication is filed as provided in this subsection, references in this [article] to a statement of domestication refer to the plan of domestication filed under this subsection.

(f) If the domesticated entity is a domestic limited liability company, the domestication becomes effective when the statement of domestication is effective. If the domesticated entity is a foreign limited liability company, the domestication becomes effective on the later of:

(1) the date and time provided by the organic law of the domesticated entity; and

(2) when the statement is effective.

§ 1056. Effect of Domestication.

(a) When a domestication becomes effective:

(1) the domesticated entity is:

(A) organized under and subject to the organic law of the domesticated entity; and

(B) the same entity without interruption as the domesticating entity;

(2) all property of the domesticating entity continues to be vested in the domesticated entity without transfer, reversion, or impairment;

(3) all debts, obligations, and other liabilities of the domesticating entity continue as debts, obligations, and other liabilities of the domesticated entity;

(4) except as otherwise provided by law or the plan of domestication, all the rights, privileges, immunities, powers, and purposes of the domesticating entity remain in the domesticated entity;

(5) the name of the domesticated entity may be substituted for the name of the domesticating entity in any pending action or proceeding;

(6) the certificate of organization of the domesticated entity becomes effective;

(7) the provisions of the operating agreement of the domesticated entity that are to be in a record, if any, approved as part of the plan of domestication become effective; and

(8) the interests in the domesticating entity are converted to the extent and as approved in connection with the domestication, and the members of the domesticating entity are entitled only to the rights provided to them under the plan of domestication and to any appraisal rights they have under § 1006.

(b) Except as otherwise provided in the organic law or operating agreement of the domesticating limited liability company, the domestication does not give rise to any rights that a member, manager, or third party would otherwise have upon a dissolution, liquidation, or winding up of the domesticating company.

(c) When a domestication becomes effective, a person that did not have interest holder liability with respect to the domesticating limited liability company and becomes subject to interest holder liability with respect to a domestic company as a result of the domestication has interest holder liability only to the extent provided by this [act] and

only for those debts, obligations, and other liabilities that are incurred after the domestication becomes effective.

(d) When a domestication becomes effective, the interest holder liability of a person that ceases to hold an interest in a domestic domesticating limited liability company with respect to which the person had interest holder liability is subject to the following rules:

(1) The domestication does not discharge any interest holder liability under this [act] to the extent the interest holder liability was incurred before the domestication became effective.

(2) A person does not have interest holder liability under this [act] for any debt, obligation, or other liability that is incurred after the domestication becomes effective.

(3) This [act] continues to apply to the release, collection, or discharge of any interest holder liability preserved under paragraph (1) as if the domestication had not occurred.

(4) A person has whatever rights of contribution from any other person as are provided by this [act], law other than this [act], or the operating agreement of the domestic domesticating limited liability company with respect to any interest holder liability preserved under paragraph (1) as if the domestication had not occurred.

(e) When a domestication becomes effective, a foreign limited liability company that is the domesticated company may be served with process in this state for the collection and enforcement of any of its debts, obligations, and other liabilities as provided in § 119.

(f) If the domesticating limited liability company is a registered foreign entity, the registration of the company is canceled when the domestication becomes effective.

(g) A domestication does not require a domestic domesticating limited liability company to wind up its affairs and does not constitute or cause the dissolution of the company.

[Article] 11. Miscellaneous Provisions

§ 1101. Uniformity of Application and Construction.

In applying and construing this uniform act, consideration must be given to the need to promote uniformity of the law with respect to its subject matter among states that enact it.

§ 1102. Relation to Electronic Signatures in Global and National Commerce Act.

This [act] modifies, limits, and supersedes the Electronic Signatures in Global and National Commerce Act, 15 U.S.C. § 7001 et seq., but does not modify, limit, or supersede § 101(c) of that act, 15 U.S.C. § 7001(c), or authorize electronic delivery of any of the notices described in § 103(b) of that act, 15 U.S.C. § 7003(b).

§ 1103. Savings Clause.

This [act] does not affect an action commenced, proceeding brought, or right accrued before [the effective date of this [act]].

[§ 1104. Severability Clause.

If any provision of this [act] or its application to any person or circumstance is held invalid, the invalidity does not affect other provisions or applications of this [act] which can be given effect without the invalid provision or application, and to this end the provisions of this [act] are severable.]

Legislative Note: Include this section only if this state lacks a general severability statute or decision by the highest court of this state stating a general rule of severability.

§ 1105. Repeals.

The following are repealed:

(1) [the state limited liability company act, as [amended, and as] in effect immediately before [the effective date of this [act]];

(2) . . . .

(3) . . . .

§ 1106. Effective Date.

This [act] takes effect . . . .

Uniform Limited Partnership Act (2013)

Copyright © 2014 by National Conference of Commissioners on Uniform State Laws

Table of Contents

[Article] 1. General Provisions

§ 101. Short Title.

This [act] may be cited as the Uniform Limited
Partnership Act.

§ 102. Definitions.

In this [act]:

(1) "Certificate of limited partnership" means the
certificate required by § 201. The term includes
the certificate as amended or restated.

(2) "Contribution", except in the phrase "right of contribution", means property or a benefit described in § 501 which is provided by a person to a limited partnership to become a partner or in the person's capacity as a partner.

(3) "Debtor in bankruptcy" means a person that is the subject of:

(A) an order for relief under Title 11 of the United States Code or a comparable order under a successor statute of general application; or

(B) a comparable order under federal, state, or foreign law governing insolvency.

(4) "Distribution" means a transfer of money or other property from a limited partnership to a person on account of a transferable interest or in the person's capacity as a partner. The term:

(A) includes:

(i) a redemption or other purchase by a limited partnership of a transferable interest; and

(ii) a transfer to a partner in return for the partner's relinquishment of any right to participate as a partner in the management or conduct of the partnership's activities and affairs or to have access to records or other information concerning the partnership's activities and affairs; and

(B) does not include amounts constituting reasonable compensation for present or past service or payments made in the ordinary course of business under a bona fide retirement plan or other bona fide benefits program.

(5) "Foreign limited liability limited partnership" means a foreign limited partnership whose general partners have limited liability for the debts, obligations, or other liabilities of the foreign partnership under a provision similar to § 404(c).

(6) "Foreign limited partnership" means an unincorporated entity formed under the law of a jurisdiction other than this state which would be a limited partnership if formed under the law of this state. The term includes a foreign limited liability limited partnership.

(7) "General partner" means a person that:

(A) has become a general partner under § 401 or was a general partner in a partnership when the partnership became subject to this [act] under § 112; and

(B) has not dissociated as a general partner under § 603.

(8) "Jurisdiction", used to refer to a political entity, means the United States, a state, a foreign country, or a political subdivision of a foreign country.

(9) "Jurisdiction of formation" means the jurisdiction whose law governs the internal affairs of an entity.

(10) "Limited liability limited partnership", except in the phrase "foreign limited liability limited partnership" and in [Article] 11, means a limited partnership whose certificate of limited partnership states that the partnership is a limited liability limited partnership.

(11) "Limited partner" means a person that:

(A) has become a limited partner under § 301 or was a limited partner in a limited partnership when the partnership became subject to this [act] under § 112; and

(B) has not dissociated under § 601.

(12) "Limited partnership", except in the phrase "foreign limited partnership" and in [Article] 11, means an entity formed under this [act] or which becomes subject to this [act] under [Article] 11 or § 112. The term includes a limited liability limited partnership.

(13) "Partner" means a limited partner or general partner.

(14) "Partnership agreement" means the agreement, whether or not referred to as a partnership agreement and whether oral, implied, in a record, or in any combination thereof, of all the partners of a limited partnership concerning the matters described in § 105(a). The term includes the agreement as amended or restated.

(15) "Person" means an individual, business corporation, nonprofit corporation, partnership, limited partnership, limited liability company, [general cooperative association,] limited cooperative association, unincorporated nonprofit association, statutory trust, business trust, common-law business trust, estate, trust, association, joint venture, public corporation, government or governmental subdivision, agency, or instrumentality, or any other legal or commercial entity.

(16) "Principal office" means the principal executive office of a limited partnership or foreign limited partnership, whether or not the office is located in this state.

(17) "Property" means all property, whether real, personal, or mixed or tangible or intangible, or any right or interest therein.

(18) "Record", used as a noun, means information that is inscribed on a tangible medium or that is stored in an electronic or other medium and is retrievable in perceivable form.

(19) "Registered agent" means an agent of a limited partnership or foreign limited partnership which is authorized to receive service of any process, notice, or demand required or permitted by law to be served on the partnership.

(20) "Registered foreign limited partnership" means a foreign limited partnership that is registered to do business in this state pursuant to a statement of registration filed by the [Secretary of State].

(21) "Required information" means the information that a limited partnership is required to maintain under § 108.

(22) "Sign" means, with present intent to authenticate or adopt a record:

    (A) to execute or adopt a tangible symbol; or

    (B) to attach to or logically associate with the record an electronic symbol, sound, or process.

(23) "State" means a state of the United States, the District of Columbia, Puerto Rico, the United States Virgin Islands, or any territory or insular possession subject to the jurisdiction of the United States.

(24) "Transfer" includes:

    (A) an assignment;

    (B) a conveyance;

    (C) a sale;

    (D) a lease;

    (E) an encumbrance, including a mortgage or security interest;

    (F) a gift; and

    (G) a transfer by operation of law.

(25) "Transferable interest" means the right, as initially owned by a person in the person's capacity as a partner, to receive distributions from a limited partnership, whether or not the person remains a partner or continues to own any part of the right. The term applies to any fraction of the interest, by whomever owned.

(26) "Transferee" means a person to which all or part of a transferable interest has been transferred, whether or not the transferor is a partner. The term includes a person that owns a transferable interest under § 602(a)(3) or 605(a)(4).

§ 103. Knowledge; Notice.

(a) A person knows a fact if the person:

    (1) has actual knowledge of it; or

    (2) is deemed to know it under law other than this [act].

(b) A person has notice of a fact if the person:

    (1) has reason to know the fact from all the facts known to the person at the time in question; or

    (2) is deemed to have notice of the fact under subsection (c) or (d).

(c) A certificate of limited partnership on file in the office of the [Secretary of State] is notice that the partnership is a limited partnership and the persons designated in the certificate as general partners are general partners. Except as otherwise provided in subsection (d), the certificate is not notice of any other fact.

(d) A person not a partner is deemed to have notice of:

    (1) a person's dissociation as a general partner 90 days after an amendment to the certificate of limited partnership which states that the other person has dissociated becomes effective or 90 days after a statement of dissociation pertaining to the other person becomes effective, whichever occurs first;

(2) a limited partnership's:

(A) dissolution 90 days after an amendment to the certificate of limited partnership stating that the limited partnership is dissolved becomes effective;

(B) termination 90 days after a statement of termination under § 802(b)(2)(F) becomes effective; and

(C) participation in a merger, interest exchange, conversion, or domestication, 90 days after articles of merger, interest exchange, conversion, or domestication under [Article] 11 become effective.

(e) Subject to § 210(f), a person notifies another person of a fact by taking steps reasonably required to inform the other person in ordinary course, whether or not those steps cause the other person to know the fact.

(f) A general partner's knowledge or notice of a fact relating to the limited partnership is effective immediately as knowledge of or notice to the partnership, except in the case of a fraud on the partnership committed by or with the consent of the general partner. A limited partner's knowledge or notice of a fact relating to the partnership is not effective as knowledge of or notice to the partnership.

§ 104. Governing Law.

The law of this state governs:

(1) the internal affairs of a limited partnership; and

(2) the liability of a partner as partner for a debt, obligation, or other liability of a limited partnership.

§ 105. Partnership Agreement; Scope, Function, and Limitations.

(a) Except as otherwise provided in subsections (c) and (d), the partnership agreement governs:

(1) relations among the partners as partners and between the partners and the limited partnership;

(2) the activities and affairs of the partnership and the conduct of those activities and affairs; and

(3) the means and conditions for amending the partnership agreement.

(b) To the extent the partnership agreement does not provide for a matter described in subsection (a), this [act] governs the matter.

(c) A partnership agreement may not:

(1) vary the law applicable under § 104;

(2) vary a limited partnership's capacity under § 111 to sue and be sued in its own name;

(3) vary any requirement, procedure, or other provision of this [act] pertaining to:

(A) registered agents; or

(B) the [Secretary of State], including provisions pertaining to records authorized or required to be delivered to the [Secretary of State] for filing under this [act];

(4) vary the provisions of § 204;

(5) vary the right of a general partner under § 406(b)(2) to vote on or consent to an amendment to the certificate of limited partnership which deletes a statement that the limited partnership is a limited liability limited partnership;

(6) alter or eliminate the duty of loyalty or the duty of care except as otherwise provided in subsection (d);

(7) eliminate the contractual obligation of good faith and fair dealing under §§ 305(a) and 409(d), but the partnership agreement may prescribe the standards, if not manifestly unreasonable, by which the performance of the obligation is to be measured;

(8) relieve or exonerate a person from liability for conduct involving bad faith, willful or intentional misconduct, or knowing violation of law;

(9) vary the information required under § 108 or unreasonably restrict the duties and rights under § 304 or 407, but the partnership agreement may impose reasonable restrictions on the availability and use of information obtained under those sections and may define appropriate remedies, including liquidated damages, for a breach of any reasonable restriction on use;

(10) vary the grounds for expulsion specified in § 603(5)(B);

(11) vary the power of a person to dissociate as a general partner under § 604(a), except to require that the notice under § 603(1) be in a record;

(12) vary the causes of dissolution specified in § 801(a)(6);

(13) vary the requirement to wind up the partnership's activities and affairs as specified in § 802(a), (b)(1), and (d);

(14) unreasonably restrict the right of a partner to maintain an action under [Article] 9;

(15) vary the provisions of § 905, but the partnership agreement may provide that the partnership may not have a special litigation committee;

(16) vary the right of a partner to approve a merger, interest exchange, conversion, or domestication under § 1123(a)(2), 1133(a)(2), 1143(a)(2), or 1153(a)(2);

(17) vary the required contents of a plan of merger under § 1122(a), plan of interest exchange under § 1132(a), plan of conversion under § 1142(a), or plan of domestication under § 1152(a); or

(18) except as otherwise provided in §§ 106 and 107(b), restrict the rights under this [act] of a person other than a partner.

(d) Subject to subsection (c)(8), without limiting other terms that may be included in a partnership agreement, the following rules apply:

(1) The partnership agreement may:

(A) specify the method by which a specific act or transaction that would otherwise violate the duty of loyalty may be authorized or ratified by one or more disinterested and independent persons after full disclosure of all material facts; and

(B) alter the prohibition in § 504(a)(2) so that the prohibition requires only that the partnership's total assets not be less than the sum of its total liabilities.

(2) If not manifestly unreasonable, the partnership agreement may:

(A) alter or eliminate the aspects of the duty of loyalty stated in § 409(b);

(B) identify specific types or categories of activities that do not violate the duty of loyalty;

(C) alter the duty of care, but may not authorize conduct involving bad faith, willful or intentional misconduct, or knowing violation of law; and

(D) alter or eliminate any other fiduciary duty.

(e) The court shall decide as a matter of law whether a term of a partnership agreement is manifestly unreasonable under subsection (c)(7) or (d)(2). The court:

(1) shall make its determination as of the time the challenged term became part of the partnership agreement and by considering only circumstances existing at that time; and

(2) may invalidate the term only if, in light of the purposes, activities, and affairs of the limited partnership, it is readily apparent that:

(A) the objective of the term is unreasonable; or

(B) the term is an unreasonable means to achieve its objective.

§ 106. Partnership Agreement; Effect on Limited Partnership and Person Becoming Partner; Preformation Agreement.

(a) A limited partnership is bound by and may enforce the partnership agreement, whether or not the partnership has itself manifested assent to the agreement.

(b) A person that becomes a partner is deemed to assent to the partnership agreement.

(c) Two or more persons intending to become the initial partners of a limited partnership may make an agreement providing that upon the formation of the partnership the agreement will become the partnership agreement.

§ 107. Partnership Agreement; Effect on Third Parties and Relationship to Records Effective on Behalf of Limited Partnership.

(a) A partnership agreement may specify that its amendment requires the approval of a person that is not a party to the agreement or the satisfaction of a condition. An amendment is ineffective if its adoption does not include the required approval or satisfy the specified condition.

(b) The obligations of a limited partnership and its partners to a person in the person's capacity as a transferee or person dissociated as a partner are governed by the partnership agreement. Subject only to a court order issued under § 703(b)(2) to effectuate a charging order, an amendment to the partnership agreement made after a person becomes a transferee or is dissociated as a partner:

> **(1)** is effective with regard to any debt, obligation, or other liability of the partnership or its partners to the person in the person's capacity as a transferee or person dissociated as a partner; and

> **(2)** is not effective to the extent the amendment imposes a new debt, obligation, or other liability on the transferee or person dissociated as a partner.

(c) If a record delivered by a limited partnership to the [Secretary of State] for filing becomes effective and contains a provision that would be ineffective under § 105(c) or (d)(2) if contained in the partnership agreement, the provision is ineffective in the record.

(d) Subject to subsection (c), if a record delivered by a limited partnership to the [Secretary of State] for filing becomes effective and conflicts with a provision of the partnership agreement:

(1) the agreement prevails as to partners, persons dissociated as partners, and transferees; and

(2) the record prevails as to other persons to the extent they reasonably rely on the record.

§ 108. Required Information.

A limited partnership shall maintain at its principal office the following information:

(1) a current list showing the full name and last known street and mailing address of each partner, separately identifying the general partners, in alphabetical order, and the limited partners, in alphabetical order;

(2) a copy of the initial certificate of limited partnership and all amendments to and restatements of the certificate, together with signed copies of any powers of attorney under which any certificate, amendment, or restatement has been signed;

(3) a copy of any filed articles of merger, interest exchange, conversion, or domestication;

(4) a copy of the partnership's federal, state, and local income tax returns and reports, if any, for the three most recent years;

(5) a copy of any partnership agreement made in a record and any amendment made in a record to any partnership agreement;

(6) a copy of any financial statement of the partnership for the three most recent years;

(7) a copy of the three most recent [annual] [biennial] reports delivered by the partnership to the [Secretary of State] pursuant to § 212;

(8) a copy of any record made by the partnership during the past three years of any consent given by or vote taken of any partner pursuant to this [act] or the partnership agreement; and

(9) unless contained in a partnership agreement made in a record, a record stating:

> **(A)** a description and statement of the agreed value of contributions other than money made and agreed to be made by each partner;

> **(B)** the times at which, or events on the happening of which, any additional contributions

agreed to be made by each partner are to be made;

(C) for any person that is both a general partner and a limited partner, a specification of what transferable interest the person owns in each capacity; and

(D) any events upon the happening of which the partnership is to be dissolved and its activities and affairs wound up.

§ 109. Dual Capacity.

A person may be both a general partner and a limited partner. A person that is both a general and limited partner has the rights, powers, duties, and obligations provided by this [act] and the partnership agreement in each of those capacities. When the person acts as a general partner, the person is subject to the obligations, duties, and restrictions under this [act] and the partnership agreement for general partners. When the person acts as a limited partner, the person is subject to the obligations, duties, and restrictions under this [act] and the partnership agreement for limited partners.

§ 110. Nature, Purpose, and Duration of Limited Partnership.

(a) A limited partnership is an entity distinct from its partners. A limited partnership is the same entity regardless of whether its certificate states that the limited partnership is a limited liability limited partnership.

(b) A limited partnership may have any lawful purpose, regardless of whether for profit.

(c) A limited partnership has perpetual duration.

§ 111. Powers.

A limited partnership has the capacity to sue and be sued in the name of the partnership and the power to do all things necessary or convenient to carry on the partnership's activities and affairs.

§ 112. Application to Existing Relationships.

(a) Before [all-inclusive date], this [act] governs only:

(1) a limited partnership formed on or after [the effective date of this [act]]; and

(2) except as otherwise provided in subsections (c) and (d), a limited partnership formed before [the effective date of this [act]] which elects, in the manner provided in its partnership agreement or by law for amending the partnership agreement, to be subject to this [act].

(b) Except as otherwise provided in subsections (c) and (d), on and after [all-inclusive date] this [act] governs all limited partnerships.

(c) With respect to a limited partnership formed before [the effective date of this [act]], the following rules apply except as the partners otherwise elect in the manner provided in the partnership agreement or by law for amending the partnership agreement:

(1) Section 110(c) does not apply and the limited partnership has whatever duration it had under the law applicable immediately before [the effective date of this [act]].

(2) the limited partnership is not required to amend its certificate of limited partnership to comply with § 201(b)(5).

(3) Sections 601 and 602 do not apply and a limited partner has the same right and power to dissociate from the limited partnership, with the same consequences, as existed immediately before [the effective date of this [act]].

(4) Section 603(4) does not apply.

(5) Section 603(5) does not apply and a court has the same power to expel a general partner as the court had immediately before [the effective date of this [act]].

(6) Section 801(a)(3) does not apply and the connection between a person's dissociation as a general partner and the dissolution of the limited partnership is the same as existed immediately before [the effective date of this [act]].

(d) With respect to a limited partnership that elects pursuant to subsection (a)(2) to be subject to this [act], after the election takes effect the provisions of this [act] relating to the liability of the limited partnership's general partners to third parties apply:

(1) before [all-inclusive date], to:

(A) a third party that had not done business with the limited partnership in the year before the election took effect; and

(B) a third party that had done business with the limited partnership in the year before the election took effect only if the third party knows or has been notified of the election; and

(2) on and after [all-inclusive date], to all third parties, but those provisions remain inapplicable to any obligation incurred while those provisions were inapplicable under paragraph (1)(B).

Legislative Note: *Subsection 112(c) presupposes that this act is replacing ULPA (1976) (Last Amended 1985). If this act is replacing a substantially different limited partnership act, the enacting jurisdiction should consider whether: (i) this act makes material changes to the "default" (or "gap filler") rules of the predecessor statute; and (ii) if so, whether Subsection (c) should carry forward any of those rules for pre-existing limited partnerships. In this assessment, the focus is on pre-existing limited partnerships that have left default rules in place, whether advisedly or not. The central question is whether, for such limited partnerships, expanding Subsection (c) is necessary to prevent material changes to the partners' "deal."*

In an enacting jurisdiction that has previously amended its existing limited partnership statute to provide for limited liability limited partnerships (LLLPs), this act should include transition provisions specifically applicable to pre-existing limited liability limited partnerships. The precise wording of those provisions must depend on the wording of the State's previously enacted LLLP provisions. However, the following principles apply generally:

1. In §§ 806(b)(5) and 807(b)(4) (notice by dissolved limited partnership to claimants), the phrase "the limited partnership has been throughout its existence a limited liability limited partnership" should be revised to encompass a limited partnership that was a limited liability limited

partnership under the State's previously enacted LLLP provisions.

2. Section 112(d) should provide that, if a pre-existing limited liability limited partnership elects to be subject to this act, this act's provisions relating to the liability of general partners to third parties apply immediately to all third parties, regardless of whether a third party has previously done business with the limited liability limited partnership.

3. A pre-existing limited liability limited partnership that elects to be subject to this act should have to comply with §§ 201(b)(5) (requiring the certificate of limited partnership to state whether the limited partnership is a limited liability limited partnership) and 114(c) (establishing name requirements for a limited liability limited partnership).

4. As for § 112(b) (providing that, after a transition period, this act applies to all preexisting limited partnerships):

a. if a State's previously enacted LLLP provisions have requirements essentially the same as §§ 201(b)(5) and 114(c), pre-existing limited liability limited partnerships should automatically retain LLLP status under this act.

b. if a State's previously enacted LLLP provisions have name requirements essentially the same as § 114(c) and provide that a public filing other than the certificate of limited partnership establishes a limited partnership's status as a limited liability limited partnership:

i. that filing can be deemed to an amendment to the certificate of limited partnership to comply with § 201(b)(5), and

ii. pre-existing limited liability limited partnerships should automatically retain LLLP status under this act.

c. if a State's previously enacted LLLP provisions do not have name requirements essentially the same as § 114(c), it will be impossible both to enforce § 114(c) and provide for automatic transition to LLLP status under this act.

It is recommended that the "all-inclusive" date should be at least one year after the effective date of this act, § 1206, but no more than two years.

§ 113. Supplemental Principles of Law.

Unless displaced by particular provisions of this [act], the principles of law and equity supplement this [act].

§ 114. Permitted Names.

(a) The name of a limited partnership may contain the name of any partner.

(b) The name of a limited partnership that is not a limited liability limited partnership must contain the phrase "limited partnership" or the abbreviation "LP" or "L.P." and may not contain the phrase "limited liability limited partnership" or the abbreviation "LLLP" or "L.L.L.P.".

(c) The name of a limited liability limited partnership must contain the phrase "limited liability limited partnership" or the abbreviation "LLLP" or "L.L.L.P." and must not contain the abbreviation "LP" or "L.P.".

(d) Except as otherwise provided in subsection (g), the name of a limited partnership, and the name under which a foreign limited partnership may register to do business in this state, must be distinguishable on the records of the [Secretary of State] from any:

(1) name of an existing person whose formation required the filing of a record by the [Secretary of State] and which is not at the time administratively dissolved;

(2) name of a limited liability partnership whose statement of qualification is in effect;

(3) name under which a person is registered to do business in this state by the filing of a record by the [Secretary of State];

(4) name reserved under § 115 or other law of this state providing for the reservation of a name by the filing of a record by the [Secretary of State];

(5) name registered under § 116 or other law of this state providing for the registration of a name by the filing of a record by the [Secretary of State]; and

(6) name registered under [this state's assumed or fictitious name statute].

(e) If a person consents in a record to the use of its name and submits an undertaking in a form satisfactory to the [Secretary of State] to change its name to a name that is distinguishable on the records of the [Secretary of State] from any name in any category of names in subsection (d), the name of the consenting person may be used by the person to which the consent was given.

(f) Except as otherwise provided in subsection (g), in determining whether a name is the same as or not distinguishable on the records of the [Secretary of State] from the name of another person, words, phrases, or abbreviations indicating the type of person, such as "corporation", "corp.", "incorporated", "Inc.", "professional corporation", "PC", "P.C.", "professional association", "PA", "P.A.", "Limited", "Ltd.", "limited partnership", "LP", "L.P.", "limited liability partnership", "LLP", "L.L.P.", "registered limited liability partnership", "RLLP", "R.L.L.P.", "limited liability limited partnership", "LLLP", "L.L.L.P.", "registered limited liability limited partnership", "RLLLP", "R.L.L.L.P.", "limited liability company", "LLC", "L.L.C.", "limited cooperative association", "limited cooperative", "LCA", or "L.C.A." may not be taken into account.

(g) A person may consent in a record to the use of a name that is not distinguishable on the records of the [Secretary of State] from its name except for the addition of a word, phrase, or abbreviation indicating the type of person as provided in subsection (f). In such a case, the person need not change its name pursuant to subsection (e).

(h) The name of a limited partnership or foreign limited partnership may not contain the words [insert prohibited words or words that may be used only with approval by an appropriate state agency].

(i) A limited partnership or foreign limited partnership may use a name that is not distinguishable from a name described in subsection (d)(1) through (6) if the partnership delivers to the [Secretary of State] a certified copy of a final judgment of a court of competent jurisdiction establishing the right of the partnership to use the name in this state.

§ 115. Reservation of Name.

(a) A person may reserve the exclusive use of a name that complies with § 114 by delivering an application to the [Secretary of State] for filing. The application must state the name and address of the applicant and the name to be reserved. If the [Secretary of State] finds that the name is available, the [Secretary of State] shall reserve the name for the applicant's exclusive use for [120] days.

(b) The owner of a reserved name may transfer the reservation to another person by delivering to the [Secretary of State] a signed notice in a record of the transfer which states the name and address of the person to which the reservation is being transferred.

§ 116. Registration of Name.

(a) A foreign limited partnership not registered to do business in this state under [Article] 10 may register its name, or an alternate name adopted pursuant to § 1006, if the name is distinguishable on the records of the [Secretary of State] from the names that are not available under § 114.

(b) To register its name or an alternate name adopted pursuant to § 1006, a foreign limited partnership must deliver to the [Secretary of State] for filing an application stating the partnership's name, the jurisdiction and date of its formation, and any alternate name adopted pursuant to § 1006. If the [Secretary of State] finds that the name applied for is available, the [Secretary of State] shall register the name for the applicant's exclusive use.

(c) The registration of a name under this section is effective for [one year] after the date of registration.

(d) A foreign limited partnership whose name registration is effective may renew the registration for successive [one-year] periods by delivering, not earlier than [three months] before the expiration of the registration, to the [Secretary of State] for filing a renewal application that complies with this section. When filed, the renewal application renews the registration for a succeeding [one-year] period.

(e) A foreign limited partnership whose name registration is effective may register as a foreign limited partnership under the registered name or consent in a signed record to the use of that name by another person that is not an individual.

§ 117. Registered Agent.

(a) Each limited partnership and each registered foreign limited partnership shall designate and maintain a registered agent in this state. The designation of a registered agent is an affirmation of fact by the limited partnership or registered foreign limited partnership that the agent has consented to serve.

(b) A registered agent for a limited partnership or registered foreign limited partnership must have a place of business in this state.

(c) The only duties under this [act] of a registered agent that has complied with this [act] are:

    (1) to forward to the limited partnership or registered foreign limited partnership at the address most recently supplied to the agent by the partnership or foreign partnership any process, notice, or demand pertaining to the partnership or foreign partnership which is served on or received by the agent;

    (2) if the registered agent resigns, to provide the notice required by § 119(c) to the partnership or foreign partnership at the address most recently supplied to the agent by the partnership or foreign partnership; and

    (3) to keep current the information with respect to the agent in the certificate of limited partnership.

§ 118. Change of Registered Agent or Address for Registered Agent by Limited Partnership.

(a) A limited partnership or registered foreign limited partnership may change its registered agent or the address of its registered agent by delivering to the [Secretary of State] for filing a statement of change that states:

(1) the name of the partnership or foreign partnership; and

(2) the information that is to be in effect as a result of the filing of the statement of change.

(b) The general or limited partners of a limited partnership need not approve the [delivery to the Secretary of State] for filing of:

(1) a statement of change under this section; or

(2) a similar filing changing the registered agent or registered office, if any, of the partnership in any other jurisdiction.

(c) A statement of change under this section designating a new registered agent is an affirmation of fact by the limited partnership or registered foreign limited partnership that the agent has consented to serve.

(d) As an alternative to using the procedure in this section, a limited partnership may amend its certificate of limited partnership.

§ 119. Resignation of Registered Agent.

(a) A registered agent may resign as an agent for a limited partnership or registered foreign limited partnership by delivering to the [Secretary of State] for filing a statement of resignation that states:

(1) the name of the partnership or foreign partnership;

(2) the name of the agent;

(3) that the agent resigns from serving as registered agent for the partnership or foreign partnership; and

(4) the address of the partnership or foreign partnership to which the agent will send the notice required by subsection (c).

(b) A statement of resignation takes effect on the earlier of:

(1) the 31st day after the day on which it is filed by the [Secretary of State]; or

(2) the designation of a new registered agent for the limited partnership or registered foreign limited partnership.

(c) A registered agent promptly shall furnish to the limited partnership or registered foreign limited partnership notice in a record of the date on which a statement of resignation was filed.

(d) When a statement of resignation takes effect, the registered agent ceases to have responsibility under this [act] for any matter thereafter tendered to it as agent for the limited partnership or registered foreign limited partnership. The resignation does not affect any contractual rights the partnership or foreign partnership has against the agent or that the agent has against the partnership or foreign partnership.

(e) A registered agent may resign with respect to a limited partnership or registered foreign limited partnership whether or not the partnership or foreign partnership is in good standing.

§ 120. Change of Name or Address by Registered Agent.

(a) If a registered agent changes its name or address, the agent may deliver to the [Secretary of State] for filing a statement of change that states:

(1) the name of the limited partnership or registered foreign limited partnership represented by the registered agent;

(2) the name of the agent as currently shown in the records of the [Secretary of State] for the partnership or foreign partnership;

(3) if the name of the agent has changed, its new name; and

(4) if the address of the agent has changed, its new address.

(b) A registered agent promptly shall furnish notice to the represented limited partnership or registered foreign limited partnership of the filing by the [Secretary of State] of the statement of change and the changes made by the statement.

Legislative Note: *Many registered agents act in that capacity for many entities, and the Model Registered Agents Act (2006) (Last Amended*

2013) provides a streamlined method through which a commercial registered agent can make a single filing to change its information for all represented entities. The single filing does not prevent an enacting state from assessing filing fees on the basis of the number of entity records affected. Alternatively the fees can be set on an incremental sliding fee or capitated amount based upon potential economies of costs for a bulk filing.

§ 121. Service of Process, Notice, or Demand.

(a) A limited partnership or registered foreign limited partnership may be served with any process, notice, or demand required or permitted by law by serving its registered agent.

(b) If a limited partnership or registered foreign limited partnership ceases to have a registered agent, or if its registered agent cannot with reasonable diligence be served, the partnership or foreign partnership may be served by registered or certified mail, return receipt requested, or by similar commercial delivery service, addressed to the partnership or foreign partnership at its principal office. The address of the principal office must be as shown in the partnership's or foreign partnership's most recent [annual] [biennial] report filed by the [Secretary of State]. Service is effected under this subsection on the earliest of:

> **(1)** the date the partnership or foreign partnership receives the mail or delivery by the commercial delivery service;

> **(2)** the date shown on the return receipt, if signed by the partnership or foreign partnership; or

> **(3)** five days after its deposit with the United States Postal Service, or with the commercial delivery service, if correctly addressed and with sufficient postage or payment.

(c) If process, notice, or demand cannot be served on a limited partnership or registered foreign limited partnership pursuant to subsection (a) or (b), service may be made by handing a copy to the individual in charge of any regular place of business or activity of the partnership or foreign partnership

if the individual served is not a plaintiff in the action.

(d) Service of process, notice, or demand on a registered agent must be in a written record.

(e) Service of process, notice, or demand may be made by other means under law other than this [act].

§ 122. Delivery of Record.

(a) Except as otherwise provided in this [act], permissible means of delivery of a record include delivery by hand, mail, conventional commercial practice, and electronic transmission.

(b) Delivery to the [Secretary of State] is effective only when a record is received by the [Secretary of State].

§ 123. Reservation of Power to Amend or Repeal.

The [legislature of this state] has power to amend or repeal all or part of this [act] at any time, and all limited partnerships and foreign limited partnerships subject to this [act] are governed by the amendment or repeal.

[Article] 2. Formation; Certificate of Limited Partnership and Other Filings

§ 201. Formation of Limited Partnership; Certificate of Limited Partnership.

(a) To form a limited partnership, a person must deliver a certificate of limited partnership to the [Secretary of State] for filing.

(b) A certificate of limited partnership must state:

> **(1)** the name of the limited partnership, which must comply with § 114;

> **(2)** the street and mailing addresses of the partnership's principal office;

> **(3)** the name and street and mailing addresses in this state of the partnership's registered agent;

> **(4)** the name and street and mailing addresses of each general partner; and

(5) whether the limited partnership is a limited liability limited partnership.

(c) A certificate of limited partnership may contain statements as to matters other than those required by subsection (b), but may not vary or otherwise affect the provisions specified in § 105(c) and (d) in a manner inconsistent with that section.

(d) A limited partnership is formed when:

(1) the certificate of limited partnership becomes effective;

(2) at least two persons have become partners;

(3) at least one person has become a general partner; and

(4) at least one person has become a limited partner.

§ 202. Amendment or Restatement of Certificate of Limited Partnership.

(a) A certificate of limited partnership may be amended or restated at any time.

(b) To amend its certificate of limited partnership, a limited partnership must deliver to the [Secretary of State] for filing an amendment stating:

(1) the name of the partnership;

(2) the date of filing of its initial certificate; and

(3) the text of the amendment.

(c) To restate its certificate of limited partnership, a limited partnership must deliver to the [Secretary of State] for filing a restatement, designated as such in its heading.

(d) A limited partnership shall promptly deliver to the [Secretary of State] for filing an amendment to a certificate of limited partnership to reflect:

(1) the admission of a new general partner;

(2) the dissociation of a person as a general partner; or

(3) the appointment of a person to wind up the limited partnership's activities and affairs under § 802(c) or (d).

(e) If a general partner knows that any information in a filed certificate of limited partnership was in-accurate when the certificate was filed or has become inaccurate due to changed circumstances, the general partner shall promptly:

(1) cause the certificate to be amended; or

(2) if appropriate, deliver to the [Secretary of State] for filing a statement of change under § 118 or a statement of correction under § 209.

§ 203. Signing of Records to Be Delivered for Filing to [Secretary of State].

(a) A record delivered to the [Secretary of State] for filing pursuant to this [act] must be signed as follows:

(1) An initial certificate of limited partnership must be signed by all general partners listed in the certificate.

(2) An amendment to the certificate of limited partnership adding or deleting a statement that the limited partnership is a limited liability limited partnership must be signed by all general partners listed in the certificate.

(3) An amendment to the certificate of limited partnership designating as general partner a person admitted under § 801(a)(3)(B) following the dissociation of a limited partnership's last general partner must be signed by that person.

(4) An amendment to the certificate of limited partnership required by § 802(c) following the appointment of a person to wind up the dissolved limited partnership's activities and affairs must be signed by that person.

(5) Any other amendment to the certificate of limited partnership must be signed by:

(A) at least one general partner listed in the certificate;

(B) each person designated in the amendment as a new general partner; and

(C) each person that the amendment indicates has dissociated as a general partner, unless:

(i) the person is deceased or a guardian or general conservator has been appointed for the person and the amendment so states; or

(ii) the person has previously delivered to the [Secretary of State] for filing a statement of dissociation.

(6) A restated certificate of limited partnership must be signed by at least one general partner listed in the certificate, and, to the extent the restated certificate effects a change under any other paragraph of this subsection, the certificate must be signed in a manner that satisfies that paragraph.

(7) A statement of termination must be signed by all general partners listed in the certificate of limited partnership or, if the certificate of a dissolved limited partnership lists no general partners, by the person appointed pursuant to § 802(c) or (d) to wind up the dissolved limited partnership's activities and affairs.

(8) Any other record delivered by a limited partnership to the [Secretary of State] for filing must be signed by at least one general partner listed in the certificate of limited partnership.

(9) A statement by a person pursuant to § 605(a)(3) stating that the person has dissociated as a general partner must be signed by that person.

(10) A statement of negation by a person pursuant to § 306 must be signed by that person.

(11) Any other record delivered on behalf of a person to the [Secretary of State] for filing must be signed by that person.

(b) Any record delivered for filing under this [act] may be signed by an agent. Whenever this [act] requires a particular individual to sign a record and the individual is deceased or incompetent, the record may be signed by a legal representative of the individual.

(c) A person that signs a record as an agent or legal representative thereby affirms as a fact that the person is authorized to sign the record.

§ 204. Signing and Filing Pursuant to Judicial Order.

(a) If a person required by this [act] to sign a record or deliver a record to the [Secretary of State] for filing under this [act] does not do so, any other person that is aggrieved may petition [the appropriate court] to order:

(1) the person to sign the record;

(2) the person to deliver the record to the [Secretary of State] for filing; or

(3) the [Secretary of State] to file the record unsigned.

(b) If a petitioner under subsection (a) is not the limited partnership or foreign limited partnership to which the record pertains, the petitioner shall make the partnership or foreign partnership a party to the action.

(c) A record filed under subsection (a)(3) is effective without being signed.

§ 205. Liability for Inaccurate Information in Filed Record.

(a) If a record delivered to the [Secretary of State] for filing under this [act] and filed by the [Secretary of State] contains inaccurate information, a person that suffers loss by reliance on the information may recover damages for the loss from:

(1) a person that signed the record, or caused another to sign it on the person's behalf, and knew the information to be inaccurate at the time the record was signed; and

(2) a general partner if:

(A) the record was delivered for filing on behalf of the partnership; and

(B) the general partner knew or had notice of the inaccuracy for a reasonably sufficient time before the information was relied upon so that, before the reliance, the general partner reasonably could have:

(i) effected an amendment under § 202;

(ii) filed a petition under § 204; or

(iii) delivered to the [Secretary of State] for filing a statement of change under

§ 118 or a statement of correction under § 209.

(b) An individual who signs a record authorized or required to be filed under this [act] affirms under penalty of perjury that the information stated in the record is accurate.

§ 206. Filing Requirements.

(a) To be filed by the [Secretary of State] pursuant to this [act], a record must be received by the [Secretary of State], must comply with this [act], and satisfy the following:

   (1) The filing of the record must be required or permitted by this [act].

   (2) The record must be physically delivered in written form unless and to the extent the [Secretary of State] permits electronic delivery of records.

   (3) The words in the record must be in English, and numbers must be in Arabic or Roman numerals, but the name of an entity need not be in English if written in English letters or Arabic or Roman numerals.

   (4) The record must be signed by a person authorized or required under this [act] to sign the record.

   (5) The record must state the name and capacity, if any, of each individual who signed it, either on behalf of the individual or the person authorized or required to sign the record, but need not contain a seal, attestation, acknowledgment, or verification.

(b) If law other than this [act] prohibits the disclosure by the [Secretary of State] of information contained in a record delivered to the [Secretary of State] for filing, the [Secretary of State] shall file the record if the record otherwise complies with this [act] but may redact the information.

(c) When a record is delivered to the [Secretary of State] for filing, any fee required under this [act] and any fee, tax, interest, or penalty required to be paid under this [act] or law other than this [act] must be paid in a manner permitted by the [Secretary of State] or by that law.

(d) The [Secretary of State] may require that a record delivered in written form be accompanied by an identical or conformed copy.

(e) The [Secretary of State] may provide forms for filings required or permitted to be made by this [act], but, except as otherwise provided in subsection (f), their use is not required.

(f) The [Secretary of State] may require that a cover sheet for a filing be on a form prescribed by the [Secretary of State].

§ 207. Effective Date and Time.

Except as otherwise provided in § 208 and subject to § 209(d), a record filed under this [act] is effective:

(1) on the date and at the time of its filing by the [Secretary of State], as provided in § 210(b);

(2) on the date of filing and at the time specified in the record as its effective time, if later than the time under paragraph (1);

(3) at a specified delayed effective date and time, which may not be more than 90 days after the date of filing; or

(4) if a delayed effective date is specified, but no time is specified, at 12:01 a.m. on the date specified, which may not be more than 90 days after the date of filing.

§ 208. Withdrawal of Filed Record Before Effectiveness.

(a) Except as otherwise provided in §§ 1124, 1134, 1144, and 1154, a record delivered to the [Secretary of State] for filing may be withdrawn before it takes effect by delivering to the [Secretary of State] for filing a statement of withdrawal.

(b) A statement of withdrawal must:

   (1) be signed by each person that signed the record being withdrawn, except as otherwise agreed by those persons;

   (2) identify the record to be withdrawn; and

   (3) if signed by fewer than all the persons that signed the record being withdrawn, state that the record is withdrawn in accordance with the agreement of all the persons that signed the record.

(c) On filing by the [Secretary of State] of a statement of withdrawal, the action or transaction evidenced by the original record does not take effect.

§ 209. Correcting Filed Record.

(a) A person on whose behalf a filed record was delivered to the [Secretary of State] for filing may correct the record if:

    (1) the record at the time of filing was inaccurate;

    (2) the record was defectively signed; or

    (3) the electronic transmission of the record to the [Secretary of State] was defective.

(b) To correct a filed record, a person on whose behalf the record was delivered to the [Secretary of State] must deliver to the [Secretary of State] for filing a statement of correction.

(c) A statement of correction:

    (1) may not state a delayed effective date;

    (2) must be signed by the person correcting the filed record;

    (3) must identify the filed record to be corrected;

    (4) must specify the inaccuracy or defect to be corrected; and

    (5) must correct the inaccuracy or defect.

(d) A statement of correction is effective as of the effective date of the filed record that it corrects except for purposes of § 103(d) and as to persons relying on the uncorrected filed record and adversely affected by the correction. For those purposes and as to those persons, the statement of correction is effective when filed.

§ 210. Duty of [Secretary of State] to File; Review of Refusal to File; Delivery of Record by [Secretary of State].

(a) The [Secretary of State] shall file a record delivered to the [Secretary of State] for filing which satisfies this [act]. The duty of the [Secretary of State] under this section is ministerial.

(b) When the [Secretary of State] files a record, the [Secretary of State] shall record it as filed on the date and at the time of its delivery. After filing a record, the [Secretary of State] shall deliver to the person that submitted the record a copy of the record with an acknowledgment of the date and time of filing.

(c) If the [Secretary of State] refuses to file a record, the [Secretary of State] shall, not later than [15] business days after the record is delivered:

    (1) return the record or notify the person that submitted the record of the refusal; and

    (2) provide a brief explanation in a record of the reason for the refusal.

(d) If the [Secretary of State] refuses to file a record, the person that submitted the record may petition [the appropriate court] to compel filing of the record. The record and the explanation of the [Secretary of State] of the refusal to file must be attached to the petition. The court may decide the matter in a summary proceeding.

(e) The filing of or refusal to file a record does not:

    (1) affect the validity or invalidity of the record in whole or in part; or

    (2) create a presumption that the information contained in the record is correct or incorrect.

(f) Except as otherwise provided by § 121 or by law other than this [act], the [Secretary of State] may deliver any record to a person by delivering it:

    (1) in person to the person that submitted it;

    (2) to the address of the person's registered agent;

    (3) to the principal office of the person; or

    (4) to another address the person provides to the [Secretary of State] for delivery.

§ 211. Certificate of Good Standing or Registration.

(a) On request of any person, the [Secretary of State] shall issue a certificate of good standing for a limited partnership or a certificate of registration for a registered foreign limited partnership.

(b) A certificate under subsection (a) must state:

(1) the limited partnership's name or the registered foreign limited partnership's name used in this state;

(2) in the case of a limited partnership:

(A) that a certificate of limited partnership has been filed and has taken effect;

(B) the date the certificate became effective;

(C) the period of the partnership's duration if the records of the [Secretary of State] reflect that its period of duration is less than perpetual; and

(D) that:

(i) no statement of administrative dissolution, or statement of termination has been filed;

(ii) the records of the [Secretary to State] do not otherwise reflect that the partnership has been dissolved or terminated; and

(iii) a proceeding is not pending under § 811;

(3) in the case of a registered foreign limited partnership, that it is registered to do business in this state;

(4) that all fees, taxes, interest, and penalties owed to this state by the limited partnership or the foreign partnership and collected through the [Secretary of State] have been paid, if:

(A) payment is reflected in the records of the [Secretary of State]; and

(B) nonpayment affects the good standing or registration of the partnership or foreign partnership;

(5) that the most recent [annual] [biennial] report required by § 212 has been delivered to the [Secretary of State] for filing; and

(6) other facts reflected in the records of the [Secretary of State] pertaining to the limited partnership or foreign limited partnership which the person requesting the certificate reasonably requests.

(c) Subject to any qualification stated in the certificate, a certificate issued by the [Secretary of State] under subsection (a) may be relied on as conclusive evidence of the facts stated in the certificate.

§ 212. [Annual] [Biennial] Report for [Secretary of State].

(a) A limited partnership or registered foreign limited partnership shall deliver to the [Secretary of State] for filing [an annual] [a biennial] report that states:

(1) the name of the partnership or foreign partnership;

(2) the name and street and mailing addresses of its registered agent in this state;

(3) the street and mailing addresses of its principal office;

(4) the name of at least one general partner; and

(5) in the case of a foreign partnership, its jurisdiction of formation and any alternate name adopted under § 1006(a).

(b) Information in the [annual] [biennial] report must be current as of the date the report is signed by the limited partnership or registered foreign limited partnership.

(c) The first [annual] [biennial] report must be delivered to the [Secretary of State] for filing after [January 1] and before [April 1] of the year following the calendar year in which the limited partnership's certificate of limited partnership became effective or the registered foreign limited partnership registered to do business in this state. Subsequent [annual] [biennial] reports must be delivered to the [Secretary of State] for filing after [January 1] and before [April 1] of each [second] calendar year thereafter.

(d) If [an annual] [a biennial] report does not contain the information required by this section, the [Secretary of State] promptly shall notify the reporting limited partnership or registered foreign limited partnership in a record and return the report for correction.

(e) If [an annual] [a biennial] report contains the name or address of a registered agent which differs from the information shown in the records of the [Secretary of State] immediately before the report becomes effective, the differing information is considered a statement of change under § 118.

[Article] 3. Limited Partners

§ 301. Becoming Limited Partner.

(a) Upon formation of a limited partnership, a person becomes a limited partner as agreed among the persons that are to be the initial partners.

(b) After formation, a person becomes a limited partner:

(1) as provided in the partnership agreement;

(2) as the result of a transaction effective under [Article] 11;

(3) with the affirmative vote or consent of all the partners; or

(4) as provided in § 801(a)(4) or (a)(5).

(c) A person may become a limited partner without:

(1) acquiring a transferable interest; or

(2) making or being obligated to make a contribution to the limited partnership.

§ 302. No Agency Power of Limited Partner as Limited Partner.

(a) A limited partner is not an agent of a limited partnership solely by reason of being a limited partner.

(b) A person's status as a limited partner does not prevent or restrict law other than this [act] from imposing liability on a limited partnership because of the person's conduct.

§ 303. No Liability as Limited Partner for Limited Partnership Obligations.

(a) A debt, obligation, or other liability of a limited partnership is not the debt, obligation, or other liability of a limited partner. A limited partner is not personally liable, directly or indirectly, by way of contribution or otherwise, for a debt, obligation, or other liability of the partnership solely by reason of being or acting as a limited partner, even if the limited partner participates in the management and control of the limited partnership. This subsection applies regardless of the dissolution of the partnership.

(b) The failure of a limited partnership to observe formalities relating to the exercise of its powers or management of its activities and affairs is not a ground for imposing liability on a limited partner for a debt, obligation, or other liability of the partnership.

§ 304. Rights to Information of Limited Partner and Person Dissociated as Limited Partner.

(a) On 10 days' demand, made in a record received by the limited partnership, a limited partner may inspect and copy required information during regular business hours in the limited partnership's principal office. The limited partner need not have any particular purpose for seeking the information.

(b) During regular business hours and at a reasonable location specified by the limited partnership, a limited partner may inspect and copy information regarding the activities, affairs, financial condition, and other circumstances of the limited partnership as is just and reasonable if:

(1) the limited partner seeks the information for a purpose reasonably related to the partner's interest as a limited partner;

(2) the limited partner makes a demand in a record received by the limited partnership, describing with reasonable particularity the information sought and the purpose for seeking the information; and

(3) the information sought is directly connected to the limited partner's purpose.

(c) Not later than 10 days after receiving a demand pursuant to subsection (b), the limited partnership shall inform in a record the limited partner that made the demand of:

(1) what information the partnership will provide in response to the demand and when and

where the partnership will provide the information; and

(2) the partnership's reasons for declining, if the partnership declines to provide any demanded information.

(d) Whenever this [act] or a partnership agreement provides for a limited partner to vote on or give or withhold consent to a matter, before the vote is cast or consent is given or withheld, the limited partnership shall, without demand, provide the limited partner with all information that is known to the partnership and is material to the limited partner's decision.

(e) Subject to subsection (j), on 10 days' demand made in a record received by a limited partnership, a person dissociated as a limited partner may have access to information to which the person was entitled while a limited partner if:

(1) the information pertains to the period during which the person was a limited partner;

(2) the person seeks the information in good faith; and

(3) the person satisfies the requirements imposed on a limited partner by subsection (b).

(f) A limited partnership shall respond to a demand made pursuant to subsection (e) in the manner provided in subsection (c).

(g) A limited partnership may charge a person that makes a demand under this section reasonable costs of copying, limited to the costs of labor and material.

(h) A limited partner or person dissociated as a limited partner may exercise the rights under this section through an agent or, in the case of an individual under legal disability, a legal representative. Any restriction or condition imposed by the partnership agreement or under subsection (j) applies both to the agent or legal representative and to the limited partner or person dissociated as a limited partner.

(i) Subject to § 704, the rights under this section do not extend to a person as transferee.

(j) In addition to any restriction or condition stated in its partnership agreement, a limited partnership, as a matter within the ordinary course of its activities and affairs, may impose reasonable restrictions and conditions on access to and use of information to be furnished under this section, including designating information confidential and imposing nondisclosure and safeguarding obligations on the recipient. In a dispute concerning the reasonableness of a restriction under this subsection, the partnership has the burden of proving reasonableness.

§ 305. Limited Duties of Limited Partners.

(a) A limited partner shall discharge any duties to the partnership and the other partners under the partnership agreement and exercise any rights under this [act] or the partnership agreement consistently with the contractual obligation of good faith and fair dealing.

(b) Except as otherwise provided in subsection (a), a limited partner does not have any duty to the limited partnership or to any other partner solely by reason of acting as a limited partner.

(c) If a limited partner enters into a transaction with a limited partnership, the limited partner's rights and obligations arising from the transaction are the same as those of a person that is not a partner.

§ 306. Person Erroneously Believing Self to Be Limited Partner.

(a) Except as otherwise provided in subsection (b), a person that makes an investment in a business enterprise and erroneously but in good faith believes that the person has become a limited partner in the enterprise is not liable for the enterprise's obligations by reason of making the investment, receiving distributions from the enterprise, or exercising any rights of or appropriate to a limited partner, if, on ascertaining the mistake, the person:

(1) causes an appropriate certificate of limited partnership, amendment, or statement of correction to be signed and delivered to the [Secretary of State] for filing; or

(2) withdraws from future participation as an owner in the enterprise by signing and delivering to the [Secretary of State] for filing a statement of negation under this section.

(b) A person that makes an investment described in subsection (a) is liable to the same extent as a general partner to any third party that enters into a transaction with the enterprise, believing in good faith that the person is a general partner, before the [Secretary of State] files a statement of negation, certificate of limited partnership, amendment, or statement of correction to show that the person is not a general partner.

(c) If a person makes a diligent effort in good faith to comply with subsection (a)(1) and is unable to cause the appropriate certificate of limited partnership, amendment, or statement of correction to be signed and delivered to the [Secretary of State] for filing, the person has the right to withdraw from the enterprise pursuant to subsection (a)(2) even if the withdrawal would otherwise breach an agreement with others that are or have agreed to become co-owners of the enterprise.

[Article] 4. General Partners

§ 401. Becoming General Partner.

(a) Upon formation of a limited partnership, a person becomes a general partner as agreed among the persons that are to be the initial partners.

(b) After formation of a limited partnership, a person becomes a general partner:

(1) as provided in the partnership agreement;

(2) as the result of a transaction effective under [Article] 11;

(3) with the affirmative vote or consent of all the partners; or

(4) as provided in § 801(a)(3)(B).

(c) A person may become a general partner without:

(1) acquiring a transferable interest; or

(2) making or being obligated to make a contribution to the partnership.

§ 402. General Partner Agent of Limited Partnership.

(a) Each general partner is an agent of the limited partnership for the purposes of its activities and affairs. An act of a general partner, including the signing of a record in the partnership's name, for apparently carrying on in the ordinary course the partnership's activities and affairs or activities and affairs of the kind carried on by the partnership binds the partnership, unless the general partner did not have authority to act for the partnership in the particular matter and the person with which the general partner was dealing knew or had notice that the general partner lacked authority.

(b) An act of a general partner which is not apparently for carrying on in the ordinary course the limited partnership's activities and affairs or activities and affairs of the kind carried on by the partnership binds the partnership only if the act was actually authorized by all the other partners.

§ 403. Limited Partnership Liable for General Partner's Actionable Conduct.

(a) A limited partnership is liable for loss or injury caused to a person, or for a penalty incurred, as a result of a wrongful act or omission, or other actionable conduct, of a general partner acting in the ordinary course of activities and affairs of the partnership or with the actual or apparent authority of the partnership.

(b) If, in the course of a limited partnership's activities and affairs or while acting with actual or apparent authority of the partnership, a general partner receives or causes the partnership to receive money or property of a person not a partner, and the money or property is misapplied by a general partner, the partnership is liable for the loss.

§ 404. General Partner's Liability.

(a) Except as otherwise provided in subsections (b) and (c), all general partners are liable jointly and severally for all debts, obligations, and other liabilities of the limited partnership unless otherwise agreed by the claimant or provided by law.

(b) A person that becomes a general partner is not personally liable for a debt, obligation, or other liability of the limited partnership incurred before the person became a general partner.

(c) A debt, obligation, or other liability of a limited partnership incurred while the partnership is a limited liability limited partnership is solely the debt, obligation, or other liability of the limited liability limited partnership. A general partner is not personally liable, directly or indirectly, by way of contribution or otherwise, for a debt, obligation, or other liability of the limited liability limited partnership solely by reason of being or acting as a general partner. This subsection applies:

> **(1)** despite anything inconsistent in the partnership agreement that existed immediately before the vote or consent required to become a limited liability limited partnership under § 406(b)(2); and
>
> **(2)** regardless of the dissolution of the partnership.

(d) The failure of a limited liability limited partnership to observe formalities relating to the exercise of its powers or management of its activities and affairs is not a ground for imposing liability on a general partner for a debt, obligation, or other liability of the partnership.

(e) An amendment of a certificate of limited partnership which deletes a statement that the limited partnership is a limited liability limited partnership does not affect the limitation in this section on the liability of a general partner for a debt, obligation, or other liability of the limited partnership incurred before the amendment became effective.

§ 405. Actions by and Against Partnership and Partners.

(a) To the extent not inconsistent with § 404, a general partner may be joined in an action against the limited partnership or named in a separate action.

(b) A judgment against a limited partnership is not by itself a judgment against a general partner. A judgment against a partnership may not be satisfied from a general partner's assets unless there is also a judgment against the general partner.

(c) A judgment creditor of a general partner may not levy execution against the assets of the general partner to satisfy a judgment based on a claim against the limited partnership, unless the partner is personally liable for the claim under § 404 and:

> **(1)** a judgment based on the same claim has been obtained against the limited partnership and a writ of execution on the judgment has been returned unsatisfied in whole or in part;
>
> **(2)** the partnership is a debtor in bankruptcy;
>
> **(3)** the general partner has agreed that the creditor need not exhaust partnership assets;
>
> **(4)** a court grants permission to the judgment creditor to levy execution against the assets of a general partner based on a finding that partnership assets subject to execution are clearly insufficient to satisfy the judgment, that exhaustion of assets is excessively burdensome, or that the grant of permission is an appropriate exercise of the court's equitable powers; or
>
> **(5)** liability is imposed on the general partner by law or contract independent of the existence of the partnership.

§ 406. Management Rights of General Partner.

(a) Each general partner has equal rights in the management and conduct of the limited partnership's activities and affairs. Except as otherwise provided in this [act], any matter relating to the activities and affairs of the partnership is decided exclusively by the general partner or, if there is more than one general partner, by a majority of the general partners.

(b) The affirmative vote or consent of all the partners is required to:

> **(1)** amend the partnership agreement;
>
> **(2)** amend the certificate of limited partnership to add or delete a statement that the limited partnership is a limited liability limited partnership; and

(3) sell, lease, exchange, or otherwise dispose of all, or substantially all, of the limited partnership's property, with or without the good will, other than in the usual and regular course of the limited partnership's activities and affairs.

(c) A limited partnership shall reimburse a general partner for an advance to the partnership beyond the amount of capital the general partner agreed to contribute.

(d) A payment or advance made by a general partner which gives rise to a limited partnership obligation under subsection (c) or § 408(a) constitutes a loan to the limited partnership which accrues interest from the date of the payment or advance.

(e) A general partner is not entitled to remuneration for services performed for the limited partnership.

§ 407. Rights to Information of General Partner and Person Dissociated as General Partner.

(a) A general partner may inspect and copy required information during regular business hours in the limited partnership's principal office, without having any particular purpose for seeking the information.

(b) On reasonable notice, a general partner may inspect and copy during regular business hours, at a reasonable location specified by the limited partnership, any record maintained by the partnership regarding the partnership's activities, affairs, financial condition, and other circumstances, to the extent the information is material to the general partner's rights and duties under the partnership agreement or this [act].

(c) A limited partnership shall furnish to each general partner:

(1) without demand, any information concerning the partnership's activities, affairs, financial condition, and other circumstances which the partnership knows and is material to the proper exercise of the general partner's rights and duties under the partnership agreement or this [act], except to the extent the partnership

can establish that it reasonably believes the general partner already knows the information; and

(2) on demand, any other information concerning the partnership's activities, affairs, financial condition, and other circumstances, except to the extent the demand or the information demanded is unreasonable or otherwise improper under the circumstances.

(d) The duty to furnish information under subsection (c) also applies to each general partner to the extent the general partner knows any of the information described in subsection (b).

(e) Subject to subsection (j), on 10 days' demand made in a record received by a limited partnership, a person dissociated as a general partner may have access to the information and records described in subsections (a) and (b) at the locations specified in those subsections if:

(1) the information or record pertains to the period during which the person was a general partner;

(2) the person seeks the information or record in good faith; and

(3) the person satisfies the requirements imposed on a limited partner by § 304(b).

(f) A limited partnership shall respond to a demand made pursuant to subsection (e) in the manner provided in § 304(c).

(g) A limited partnership may charge a person that makes a demand under this section the reasonable costs of copying, limited to the costs of labor and material.

(h) A general partner or person dissociated as a general partner may exercise the rights under this section through an agent or, in the case of an individual under legal disability, a legal representative. Any restriction or condition imposed by the partnership agreement or under subsection (j) applies both to the agent or legal representative and to the general partner or person dissociated as a general partner.

(i) The rights under this section do not extend to a person as transferee, but if:

(1) a general partner dies, § 704 applies; and

(2) an individual dissociates as a general partner under § 603(6)(B) or (C), the legal representative of the individual may exercise the rights under subsection (c) of a person dissociated as a general partner.

(j) In addition to any restriction or condition stated in its partnership agreement, a limited partnership, as a matter within the ordinary course of its activities and affairs, may impose reasonable restrictions and conditions on access to and use of information to be furnished under this section, including designating information confidential and imposing nondisclosure and safeguarding obligations on the recipient. In a dispute concerning the reasonableness of a restriction under this subsection, the partnership has the burden of proving reasonableness.

§ 408. Reimbursement; Indemnification; Advancement; and Insurance.

(a) A limited partnership shall reimburse a general partner for any payment made by the general partner in the course of the general partner's activities on behalf of the partnership, if the general partner complied with §§ 406, 409, and 504 in making the payment.

(b) A limited partnership shall indemnify and hold harmless a person with respect to any claim or demand against the person and any debt, obligation, or other liability incurred by the person by reason of the person's former or present capacity as a general partner, if the claim, demand, debt, obligation, or other liability does not arise from the person's breach of § 406, 409, or 504.

(c) In the ordinary course of its activities and affairs, a limited partnership may advance reasonable expenses, including attorney's fees and costs, incurred by a person in connection with a claim or demand against the person by reason of the person's former or present capacity as a general partner, if the person promises to repay the partnership if the person ultimately is determined not to be entitled to be indemnified under subsection (b).

(d) A limited partnership may purchase and maintain insurance on behalf of a general partner against liability asserted against or incurred by the general partner in that capacity or arising from that status even if, under § 105(c)(8), the partnership agreement could not eliminate or limit the person's liability to the partnership for the conduct giving rise to the liability.

§ 409. Standards of Conduct for General Partners.

(a) A general partner owes to the limited partnership and, subject to § 901, the other partners the duties of loyalty and care stated in subsections (b) and (c).

(b) The fiduciary duty of loyalty of a general partner includes the duties:

(1) to account to the limited partnership and hold as trustee for it any property, profit, or benefit derived by the general partner:

(A) in the conduct or winding up of the partnership's activities and affairs;

(B) from a use by the general partner of the partnership's property; or

(C) from the appropriation of a partnership opportunity;

(2) to refrain from dealing with the partnership in the conduct or winding up of the partnership's activities and affairs as or on behalf of a person having an interest adverse to the partnership; and

(3) to refrain from competing with the partnership in the conduct or winding up of the partnership's activities and affairs.

(c) The duty of care of a general partner in the conduct or winding up of the limited partnership's activities and affairs is to refrain from engaging in grossly negligent or reckless conduct, willful or intentional misconduct, or knowing violation of law.

(d) A general partner shall discharge the duties and obligations under this [act] or under the partnership agreement and exercise any rights consistently with the contractual obligation of good faith and fair dealing.

(e) A general partner does not violate a duty or obligation under this [act] or under the partnership agreement solely because the general partner's conduct furthers the general partner's own interest.

(f) All the partners of a limited partnership may authorize or ratify, after full disclosure of all material facts, a specific act or transaction by a general partner that otherwise would violate the duty of loyalty.

(g) It is a defense to a claim under subsection (b)(2) and any comparable claim in equity or at common law that the transaction was fair to the limited partnership.

(h) If, as permitted by subsection (f) or the partnership agreement, a general partner enters into a transaction with the limited partnership which otherwise would be prohibited by subsection (b)(2), the general partner's rights and obligations arising from the transaction are the same as those of a person that is not a general partner.

[Article] 5. Contributions and Distributions

§ 501. Form of Contribution.

A contribution may consist of property transferred to, services performed for, or another benefit provided to the limited partnership or an agreement to transfer property to, perform services for, or provide another benefit to the partnership.

§ 502. Liability for Contribution.

(a) A person's obligation to make a contribution to a limited partnership is not excused by the person's death, disability, termination, or other inability to perform personally.

(b) If a person does not fulfill an obligation to make a contribution other than money, the person is obligated at the option of the limited partnership to contribute money equal to the value, as stated in the required information, of the part of the contribution which has not been made.

(c) The obligation of a person to make a contribution may be compromised only by the affirmative vote or consent of all the partners. If a creditor of a limited partnership extends credit or otherwise acts in reliance on an obligation described in subsection (a) without knowledge or notice of a compromise under this subsection, the creditor may enforce the obligation.

§ 503. Sharing of and Right to Distributions Before Dissolution.

(a) Any distribution made by a limited partnership before its dissolution and winding up must be shared among the partners on the basis of the value, as stated in the required information when the limited partnership decides to make the distribution, of the contributions the limited partnership has received from each partner, except to the extent necessary to comply with a transfer effective under § 702 or charging order in effect under § 703.

(b) A person has a right to a distribution before the dissolution and winding up of a limited partnership only if the partnership decides to make an interim distribution. A person's dissociation does not entitle the person to a distribution.

(c) A person does not have a right to demand or receive a distribution from a limited partnership in any form other than money. Except as otherwise provided in § 810(f), a partnership may distribute an asset in kind only if each part of the asset is fungible with each other part and each person receives a percentage of the asset equal in value to the person's share of distributions.

(d) If a partner or transferee becomes entitled to receive a distribution, the partner or transferee has the status of, and is entitled to all remedies available to, a creditor of the limited partnership with respect to the distribution. However, the partnership's obligation to make a distribution is subject to offset for any amount owed to the partnership by the partner or a person dissociated as a partner on whose account the distribution is made.

§ 504. Limitations on Distributions.

(a) A limited partnership may not make a distribution, including a distribution under § 810, if after the distribution:

(1) the partnership would not be able to pay its debts as they become due in the ordinary course of the partnership's activities and affairs; or

(2) the partnership's total assets would be less than the sum of its total liabilities plus the amount that would be needed, if the partnership were to be dissolved and wound up at the time of the distribution, to satisfy the preferential rights upon dissolution and winding up of partners and transferees whose preferential rights are superior to the rights of persons receiving the distribution.

(b) A limited partnership may base a determination that a distribution is not prohibited under subsection (a) on:

(1) financial statements prepared on the basis of accounting practices and principles that are reasonable in the circumstances; or

(2) a fair valuation or other method that is reasonable under the circumstances.

(c) Except as otherwise provided in subsection (e), the effect of a distribution under subsection (a) is measured:

(1) in the case of a distribution as defined in § 102(4)(A), as of the earlier of:

   (A) the date money or other property is transferred or debt is incurred by the limited partnership; or

   (B) the date the person entitled to the distribution ceases to own the interest or right being acquired by the partnership in return for the distribution;

(2) in the case of any other distribution of indebtedness, as of the date the indebtedness is distributed; and

(3) in all other cases, as of the date:

   (A) the distribution is authorized, if the payment occurs not later than 120 days after that date; or

   (B) the payment is made, if the payment occurs more than 120 days after the distribution is authorized.

(d) A limited partnership's indebtedness to a partner or transferee incurred by reason of a distribution made in accordance with this section is at parity with the partnership's indebtedness to its general, unsecured creditors, except to the extent subordinated by agreement.

(e) A limited partnership's indebtedness, including indebtedness issued as a distribution, is not a liability for purposes of subsection (a) if the terms of the indebtedness provide that payment of principal and interest is made only if and to the extent that payment of a distribution could then be made under this section. If the indebtedness is issued as a distribution, each payment of principal or interest is treated as a distribution, the effect of which is measured on the date the payment is made.

(f) In measuring the effect of a distribution under § 810, the liabilities of a dissolved limited partnership do not include any claim that has been disposed of under § 806, 807, or 808.

§ 505. Liability for Improper Distributions.

(a) If a general partner consents to a distribution made in violation of § 504 and in consenting to the distribution fails to comply with § 409, the general partner is personally liable to the limited partnership for the amount of the distribution which exceeds the amount that could have been distributed without the violation of § 504.

(b) A person that receives a distribution knowing that the distribution violated § 504 is personally liable to the limited partnership but only to the extent that the distribution received by the person exceeded the amount that could have been properly paid under § 504.

(c) A general partner against which an action is commenced because the general partner is liable under subsection (a) may:

(1) implead any other person that is liable under subsection (a) and seek to enforce a right of contribution from the person; and

(2) implead any person that received a distribution in violation of subsection (b) and seek to enforce a right of contribution from the person in the amount the person received in violation of subsection (b).

(d) An action under this section is barred unless commenced not later than two years after the distribution.

[Article] 6. Dissociation

§ 601. Dissociation as Limited Partner.

(a) A person does not have a right to dissociate as a limited partner before the completion of the winding up of the limited partnership.

(b) A person is dissociated as a limited partner when:

(1) the limited partnership knows or has notice of the person's express will to withdraw as a limited partner, but, if the person has specified a withdrawal date later than the date the partnership knew or had notice, on that later date;

(2) an event stated in the partnership agreement as causing the person's dissociation as a limited partner occurs;

(3) the person is expelled as a limited partner pursuant to the partnership agreement;

(4) the person is expelled as a limited partner by the affirmative vote or consent of all the other partners if:

(A) it is unlawful to carry on the limited partnership's activities and affairs with the person as a limited partner;

(B) there has been a transfer of all the person's transferable interest in the partnership, other than:

(i) a transfer for security purposes; or

(ii) a charging order in effect under § 703 which has not been foreclosed;

(C) the person is an entity and:

(i) the partnership notifies the person that it will be expelled as a limited partner because the person has filed a statement of dissolution or the equivalent, the person has been administratively dis-

solved, the person's charter or the equivalent has been revoked, or the person's right to conduct business has been suspended by the person's jurisdiction of formation; and

(ii) not later than 90 days after the notification, the statement of dissolution or the equivalent has not been withdrawn, rescinded, or revoked, the person has not been reinstated, or the person's charter or the equivalent or right to conduct business has not been reinstated; or

(D) the person is an unincorporated entity that has been dissolved and whose activities and affairs are being would up;

(5) on application by the limited partnership or a partner in a direct action under § 901, the person is expelled as a limited partner by judicial order because the person:

(A) has engaged or is engaging in wrongful conduct that has affected adversely and materially, or will affect adversely and materially, the partnership's activities and affairs;

(B) has committed willfully or persistently, or is committing willfully and persistently, a material breach of the partnership agreement or the contractual obligation of good faith and fair dealing under § 305(a); or

(C) has engaged or is engaging in conduct relating to the partnership's activities and affairs which makes it not reasonably practicable to carry on the activities and affairs with the person as a limited partner;

(6) in the case of an individual, the individual dies;

(7) in the case of a person that is a testamentary or inter vivos trust or is acting as a limited partner by virtue of being a trustee of such a trust, the trust's entire transferable interest in the limited partnership is distributed;

(8) in the case of a person that is an estate or is acting as a limited partner by virtue of being a personal representative of an estate, the estate's entire transferable interest in the limited partnership is distributed;

(9) in the case of a person that is not an individual, the existence of the person terminates;

(10) the limited partnership participates in a merger under [Article] 11 and:

> **(A)** the partnership is not the surviving entity; or

> **(B)** otherwise as a result of the merger, the person ceases to be a limited partner;

(11) the limited partnership participates in an interest exchange under [Article] 11 and, as a result of the interest exchange, the person ceases to be a limited partner;

(12) the limited partnership participates in a conversion under [Article] 11;

(13) the limited partnership participates in a domestication under [Article] 11 and, as a result of the domestication, the person ceases to be a limited partner; or

(14) the limited partnership dissolves and completes winding up.

§ 602. Effect of Dissociation as Limited Partner.

(a) If a person is dissociated as a limited partner:

(1) subject to § 704, the person does not have further rights as a limited partner;

(2) the person's contractual obligation of good faith and fair dealing as a limited partner under § 305(a) ends with regard to matters arising and events occurring after the person's dissociation; and

(3) subject to § 704 and [Article] 11, any transferable interest owned by the person in the person's capacity as a limited partner immediately before dissociation is owned by the person solely as a transferee.

(b) A person's dissociation as a limited partner does not of itself discharge the person from any debt, obligation, or other liability to the limited partnership or the other partners which the person incurred while a limited partner.

§ 603. Dissociation as General Partner.

A person is dissociated as a general partner when:

(1) the limited partnership knows or has notice of the person's express will to withdraw as a general partner, but, if the person has specified a withdrawal date later than the date the partnership knew or had notice, on that later date;

(2) an event stated in the partnership agreement as causing the person's dissociation as a general partner occurs;

(3) the person is expelled as a general partner pursuant to the partnership agreement;

(4) the person is expelled as a general partner by the affirmative vote or consent of all the other partners if:

> **(A)** it is unlawful to carry on the limited partnership's activities and affairs with the person as a general partner;

> **(B)** there has been a transfer of all the person's transferable interest in the partnership, other than:

> > **(i)** a transfer for security purposes; or

> > **(ii)** a charging order in effect under § 703 which has not been foreclosed;

> **(C)** the person is an entity and:

> > **(i)** the partnership notifies the person that it will be expelled as a general partner because the person has filed a statement of dissolution or the equivalent, the person has been administratively dissolved, the person's charter or the equivalent has been revoked, or the person's right to conduct business has been suspended by the person's jurisdiction of formation; and

> > **(ii)** not later than 90 days after the notification, the statement of dissolution or the equivalent has not been withdrawn, rescinded, or revoked, the person has not been reinstated, or the person's charter or the equivalent or right to conduct business has not been reinstated; or

(D) the person is an unincorporated entity that has been dissolved and whose activities and affairs are being would up;

(5) on application by the limited partnership or a partner in a direct action under § 901, the person is expelled as a general partner by judicial order because the person:

> **(A)** has engaged or is engaging in wrongful conduct that has affected adversely and materially, or will affect adversely and materially, the partnership's activities and affairs;

> **(B)** has committed willfully or persistently, or is committing willfully or persistently, a material breach of the partnership agreement or a duty or obligation under § 409; or

> **(C)** has engaged or is engaging in conduct relating to the partnership's activities and affairs which makes it not reasonably practicable to carry on the activities and affairs of the limited partnership with the person as a general partner;

(6) in the case of an individual:

> **(A)** the individual dies;

> **(B)** a guardian or general conservator for the individual is appointed; or

> **(C)** a court orders that the individual has otherwise become incapable of performing the individual's duties as a general partner under this [act] or the partnership agreement;

(7) the person:

> **(A)** becomes a debtor in bankruptcy;

> **(B)** executes an assignment for the benefit of creditors; or

> **(C)** seeks, consents to, or acquiesces in the appointment of a trustee, receiver, or liquidator of the person or of all or substantially all the person's property;

(8) in the case of a person that is a testamentary or inter vivos trust or is acting as a general partner by virtue of being a trustee of such a trust, the trust's entire transferable interest in the limited partnership is distributed;

(9) in the case of a person that is an estate or is acting as a general partner by virtue of being a personal representative of an estate, the estate's entire transferable interest in the limited partnership is distributed;

(10) in the case of a person that is not an individual, the existence of the person terminates;

(11) the limited partnership participates in a merger under [Article] 11 and:

> **(A)** the partnership is not the surviving entity; or

> **(B)** otherwise as a result of the merger, the person ceases to be a general partner;

(12) the limited partnership participates in an interest exchange under [Article] 11 and, as a result of the interest exchange, the person ceases to be a general partner;

(13) the limited partnership participates in a conversion under [Article] 11;

(14) the limited partnership participates in a domestication under [Article] 11 and, as a result of the domestication, the person ceases to be a general partner; or

(15) the limited partnership dissolves and completes winding up.

§ 604. Power to Dissociate as General Partner; Wrongful Dissociation.

(a) A person has the power to dissociate as a general partner at any time, rightfully or wrongfully, by withdrawing as a general partner by express will under § 603(1).

(b) A person's dissociation as a general partner is wrongful only if the dissociation:

> **(1)** is in breach of an express provision of the partnership agreement; or

> **(2)** occurs before the completion of the winding up of the limited partnership, and:

>> **(A)** the person withdraws as a general partner by express will;

>> **(B)** the person is expelled as a general partner by judicial order under § 603(5);

(C) the person is dissociated as a general partner under § 603(7); or

(D) in the case of a person that is not a trust other than a business trust, an estate, or an individual, the person is expelled or otherwise dissociated as a general partner because it willfully dissolved or terminated.

(c) A person that wrongfully dissociates as a general partner is liable to the limited partnership and, subject to § 901, to the other partners for damages caused by the dissociation. The liability is in addition to any debt, obligation, or other liability of the general partner to the partnership or the other partners.

§ 605. Effect of Dissociation as General Partner.

(a) If a person is dissociated as a general partner:

(1) the person's right to participate as a general partner in the management and conduct of the limited partnership's activities and affairs terminates;

(2) the person's duties and obligations as a general partner under § 409 end with regard to matters arising and events occurring after the person's dissociation;

(3) the person may sign and deliver to the [Secretary of State] for filing a statement of dissociation pertaining to the person and, at the request of the limited partnership, shall sign an amendment to the certificate of limited partnership which states that the person has dissociated as a general partner; and

(4) subject to § 704 and [Article] 11, any transferable interest owned by the person in the person's capacity as a general partner immediately before dissociation is owned by the person solely as a transferee.

(b) A person's dissociation as a general partner does not of itself discharge the person from any debt, obligation, or other liability to the limited partnership or the other partners which the person incurred while a general partner.

§ 606. Power to Bind and Liability of Person Dissociated as General Partner.

(a) After a person is dissociated as a general partner and before the limited partnership is merged out of existence, converted, or domesticated under [Article] 11, or dissolved, the partnership is bound by an act of the person only if:

(1) the act would have bound the partnership under § 402 before the dissociation; and

(2) at the time the other party enters into the transaction:

(A) less than two years has passed since the dissociation; and

(B) the other party does not know or have notice of the dissociation and reasonably believes that the person is a general partner.

(b) If a limited partnership is bound under subsection (a), the person dissociated as a general partner which caused the partnership to be bound is liable:

(1) to the partnership for any damage caused to the partnership arising from the obligation incurred under subsection (a); and

(2) if a general partner or another person dissociated as a general partner is liable for the obligation, to the general partner or other person for any damage caused to the general partner or other person arising from the liability.

§ 607. Liability of Person Dissociated as General Partner to Other Persons.

(a) A person's dissociation as a general partner does not of itself discharge the person's liability as a general partner for a debt, obligation, or other liability of the limited partnership incurred before dissociation. Except as otherwise provided in subsections (b) and (c), the person is not liable for a partnership obligation incurred after dissociation.

(b) A person whose dissociation as a general partner results in a dissolution and winding up of the limited partnership's activities and affairs is liable on an obligation incurred by the partnership under § 805 to the same extent as a general partner under § 404.

(c) A person that is dissociated as a general partner without the dissociation resulting in a dissolution and winding up of the limited partnership's activities and affairs is liable on a transaction entered into by the partnership after the dissociation only if:

(1) a general partner would be liable on the transaction; and

(2) at the time the other party enters into the transaction:

(A) less than two years has passed since the dissociation; and

(B) the other party does not have knowledge or notice of the dissociation and reasonably believes that the person is a general partner.

(d) By agreement with a creditor of a limited partnership and the partnership, a person dissociated as a general partner may be released from liability for a debt, obligation, or other liability of the partnership.

(e) A person dissociated as a general partner is released from liability for a debt, obligation, or other liability of the limited partnership if the partnership's creditor, with knowledge or notice of the person's dissociation as a general partner but without the person's consent, agrees to a material alteration in the nature or time of payment of the debt, obligation, or other liability.

[Article] 7. Transferable Interests and Rights of Transferees and Creditors

§ 701. Nature of Transferable Interest.

A transferable interest is personal property.

§ 702. Transfer of Transferable Interest.

(a) A transfer, in whole or in part, of a transferable interest:

(1) is permissible;

(2) does not by itself cause a person's dissociation as a partner or a dissolution and winding

up of the limited partnership's activities and affairs; and

(3) subject to § 704, does not entitle the transferee to:

(A) participate in the management or conduct of the partnership's activities and affairs; or

(B) except as otherwise provided in subsection (c), have access to required information, records, or other information concerning the partnership's activities and affairs.

(b) A transferee has the right to receive, in accordance with the transfer, distributions to which the transferor would otherwise be entitled.

(c) In a dissolution and winding up of a limited partnership, a transferee is entitled to an account of the partnership's transactions only from the date of dissolution.

(d) A transferable interest may be evidenced by a certificate of the interest issued by a limited partnership in a record, and, subject to this section, the interest represented by the certificate may be transferred by a transfer of the certificate.

(e) A limited partnership need not give effect to a transferee's rights under this section until the partnership knows or has notice of the transfer.

(f) A transfer of a transferable interest in violation of a restriction on transfer contained in the partnership agreement is ineffective if the intended transferee has knowledge or notice of the restriction at the time of transfer.

(g) Except as otherwise provided in §§ 601(b)(4)(B) and 603(4)(B), if a general or limited partner transfers a transferable interest, the transferor retains the rights of a general or limited partner other than the transferable interest transferred and retains all the duties and obligations of a general or limited partner.

(h) If a general or limited partner transfers a transferable interest to a person that becomes a general or limited partner with respect to the transferred interest, the transferee is liable for the transferor's obligations under §§ 502 and 505 known to the transferee when the transferee becomes a partner.

§ 703. Charging Order.

(a) On application by a judgment creditor of a partner or transferee, a court may enter a charging order against the transferable interest of the judgment debtor for the unsatisfied amount of the judgment. A charging order constitutes a lien on a judgment debtor's transferable interest and requires the limited partnership to pay over to the person to which the charging order was issued any distribution that otherwise would be paid to the judgment debtor.

(b) To the extent necessary to effectuate the collection of distributions pursuant to a charging order in effect under subsection (a), the court may:

> **(1)** appoint a receiver of the distributions subject to the charging order, with the power to make all inquiries the judgment debtor might have made; and

> **(2)** make all other orders necessary to give effect to the charging order.

(c) Upon a showing that distributions under a charging order will not pay the judgment debt within a reasonable time, the court may foreclose the lien and order the sale of the transferable interest. The purchaser at the foreclosure sale obtains only the transferable interest, does not thereby become a partner, and is subject to § 702.

(d) At any time before foreclosure under subsection (c), the partner or transferee whose transferable interest is subject to a charging order under subsection (a) may extinguish the charging order by satisfying the judgment and filing a certified copy of the satisfaction with the court that issued the charging order.

(e) At any time before foreclosure under subsection (c), a limited partnership or one or more partners whose transferable interests are not subject to the charging order may pay to the judgment creditor the full amount due under the judgment and thereby succeed to the rights of the judgment creditor, including the charging order.

(f) This [act] does not deprive any partner or transferee of the benefit of any exemption law applicable to the transferable interest of the partner or transferee.

(g) This section provides the exclusive remedy by which a person seeking in the capacity of a judgment creditor to enforce a judgment against a partner or transferee may satisfy the judgment from the judgment debtor's transferable interest.

§ 704. Power of Legal Representative of Deceased Partner.

If a partner dies, the deceased partner's legal representative may exercise:

(1) the rights of a transferee provided in § 702(c); and

(2) for the purposes of settling the estate, the rights of a current limited partner under § 304.

[Article] 8. Dissolution and Winding Up

§ 801. Events Causing Dissolution.

(a) A limited partnership is dissolved, and its activities and affairs must be wound up, upon the occurrence of any of the following:

> **(1)** an event or circumstance that the partnership agreement states causes dissolution;

> **(2)** the affirmative vote or consent of all general partners and of limited partners owning a majority of the rights to receive distributions as limited partners at the time the vote or consent is to be effective;

> **(3)** after the dissociation of a person as a general partner:

>> **(A)** if the partnership has at least one remaining general partner, the affirmative vote or consent to dissolve the partnership not later than 90 days after the dissociation by partners owning a majority of the rights to receive distributions as partners at the time the vote or consent is to be effective; or

(B) if the partnership does not have a remaining general partner, the passage of 90 days after the dissociation, unless before the end of the period:

    (i) consent to continue the activities and affairs of the partnership and admit at least one general partner is given by limited partners owning a majority of the rights to receive distributions as limited partners at the time the consent is to be effective; and

    (ii) at least one person is admitted as a general partner in accordance with the consent;

(4) the passage of 90 consecutive days after the dissociation of the partnership's last limited partner, unless before the end of the period the partnership admits at least one limited partner;

(5) the passage of 90 consecutive days during which the partnership has only one partner, unless before the end of the period:

    (A) the partnership admits at least one person as a partner;

    (B) if the previously sole remaining partner is only a general partner, the partnership admits the person as a limited partner; and

    (C) if the previously sole remaining partner is only a limited partner, the partnership admits a person as a general partner;

(6) on application by a partner, the entry by [the appropriate court] of an order dissolving the partnership on the grounds that:

    (A) the conduct of all or substantially all the partnership's activities and affairs is unlawful; or

    (B) it is not reasonably practicable to carry on the partnership's activities and affairs in conformity with the certificate of limited partnership and partnership agreement; or

(7) the signing and filing of a statement of administrative dissolution by the [Secretary of State] under § 811.

(b) If an event occurs that imposes a deadline on a limited partnership under subsection (a) and before the partnership has met the requirements of the deadline, another event occurs that imposes a different deadline on the partnership under subsection (a):

    (1) the occurrence of the second event does not affect the deadline caused by the first event; and

    (2) the partnership's meeting of the requirements of the first deadline does not extend the second deadline.

§ 802. Winding Up.

(a) A dissolved limited partnership shall wind up its activities and affairs and, except as otherwise provided in § 803, the partnership continues after dissolution only for the purpose of winding up.

(b) In winding up its activities and affairs, the limited partnership:

    (1) shall discharge the partnership's debts, obligations, and other liabilities, settle and close the partnership's activities and affairs, and marshal and distribute the assets of the partnership; and

    (2) may:

        (A) amend its certificate of limited partnership to state that the partnership is dissolved;

        (B) preserve the partnership activities, affairs, and property as a going concern for a reasonable time;

        (C) prosecute and defend actions and proceedings, whether civil, criminal, or administrative;

        (D) transfer the partnership's property;

        (E) settle disputes by mediation or arbitration;

        (F) deliver to the [Secretary of State] for filing a statement of termination stating the name of the partnership and that the partnership is terminated; and

        (G) perform other acts necessary or appropriate to the winding up.

(c) If a dissolved limited partnership does not have a general partner, a person to wind up the dissolved partnership's activities and affairs may be appointed by the affirmative vote or consent of limited partners owning a majority of the rights to receive distributions as limited partners at the time the vote or consent is to be effective. A person appointed under this subsection:

(1) has the powers of a general partner under § 804 but is not liable for the debts, obligations, and other liabilities of the partnership solely by reason of having or exercising those powers or otherwise acting to wind up the dissolved partnership's activities and affairs; and

(2) shall deliver promptly to the [Secretary of State] for filing an amendment to the partnership's certificate of limited partnership stating:

(A) that the partnership does not have a general partner;

(B) the name and street and mailing addresses of the person; and

(C) that the person has been appointed pursuant to this subsection to wind up the partnership.

(d) On the application of a partner, the [appropriate court] may order judicial supervision of the winding up of a dissolved limited partnership, including the appointment of a person to wind up the partnership's activities and affairs, if:

(1) the partnership does not have a general partner and within a reasonable time following the dissolution no person has been appointed pursuant to subsection (c); or

(2) the applicant establishes other good cause.

§ 803. Rescinding Dissolution.

(a) A limited partnership may rescind its dissolution, unless a statement of termination applicable to the partnership has become effective, [the appropriate court] has entered an order under § 801(a)(6) dissolving the partnership, or the [Secretary of State] has dissolved the partnership under § 811.

(b) Rescinding dissolution under this section requires:

(1) the affirmative vote or consent of each partner; and

(2) if the limited partnership has delivered to the [Secretary of State] for filing an amendment to the certificate of limited partnership stating that the partnership is dissolved and:

(A) the amendment has not become effective, delivery to the [Secretary of State] for filing of a statement of withdrawal under § 208 applicable to the amendment; or

(B) the amendment has become effective, delivery to the [Secretary of State] for filing of an amendment to the certificate of limited partnership stating that dissolution has been rescinded under this section.

(c) If a limited partnership rescinds its dissolution:

(1) the partnership resumes carrying on its activities and affairs as if dissolution had never occurred;

(2) subject to paragraph (3), any liability incurred by the partnership after the dissolution and before the rescission has become effective is determined as if dissolution had never occurred; and

(3) the rights of a third party arising out of conduct in reliance on the dissolution before the third party knew or had notice of the rescission may not be adversely affected.

§ 804. Power to Bind Partnership After Dissolution.

(a) A limited partnership is bound by a general partner's act after dissolution which:

(1) is appropriate for winding up the partnership's activities and affairs; or

(2) would have bound the partnership under § 402 before dissolution if, at the time the other party enters into the transaction, the other party does not know or have notice of the dissolution.

(b) A person dissociated as a general partner binds a limited partnership through an act occurring after dissolution if:

(1) at the time the other party enters into the transaction:

(A) less than two years has passed since the dissociation; and

(B) the other party does not know or have notice of the dissociation and reasonably believes that the person is a general partner; and

(2) the act:

(A) is appropriate for winding up the partnership's activities and affairs; or

(B) would have bound the partnership under § 402 before dissolution and at the time the other party enters into the transaction the other party does not know or have notice of the dissolution.

§ 805. Liability After Dissolution of General Partner and Person Dissociated as General Partner.

(a) If a general partner having knowledge of the dissolution causes a limited partnership to incur an obligation under § 804(a) by an act that is not appropriate for winding up the partnership's activities and affairs, the general partner is liable:

(1) to the partnership for any damage caused to the partnership arising from the obligation; and

(2) if another general partner or a person dissociated as a general partner is liable for the obligation, to that other general partner or person for any damage caused to that other general partner or person arising from the liability.

(b) If a person dissociated as a general partner causes a limited partnership to incur an obligation under § 804(b), the person is liable:

(1) to the partnership for any damage caused to the partnership arising from the obligation; and

(2) if a general partner or another person dissociated as a general partner is liable for the obligation, to the general partner or other person for any damage caused to the general partner or other person arising from the obligation.

§ 806. Known Claims Against Dissolved Limited Partnership.

(a) Except as otherwise provided in subsection (d), a dissolved limited partnership may give notice of a known claim under subsection (b), which has the effect provided in subsection (c).

(b) A dissolved limited partnership may in a record notify its known claimants of the dissolution. The notice must:

(1) specify the information required to be included in a claim;

(2) state that a claim must be in writing and provide a mailing address to which the claim is to be sent;

(3) state the deadline for receipt of a claim, which may not be less than 120 days after the date the notice is received by the claimant;

(4) state that the claim will be barred if not received by the deadline; and

(5) unless the partnership has been throughout its existence a limited liability limited partnership, state that the barring of a claim against the partnership will also bar any corresponding claim against any general partner or person dissociated as a general partner which is based on § 404.

(c) A claim against a dissolved limited partnership is barred if the requirements of subsection (b) are met and:

(1) the claim is not received by the specified deadline; or

(2) if the claim is timely received but rejected by the partnership:

(A) the partnership causes the claimant to receive a notice in a record stating that the claim is rejected and will be barred unless the claimant commences an action against the partnership to enforce the claim not later than 90 days after the claimant receives the notice; and

(B) the claimant does not commence the required action not later than 90 days after the claimant receives the notice.

(d) This section does not apply to a claim based on an event occurring after the date of dissolution or a liability that on that date is contingent.

§ 807. Other Claims Against Dissolved Limited Partnership.

(a) A dissolved limited partnership may publish notice of its dissolution and request persons having claims against the partnership to present them in accordance with the notice.

(b) A notice under subsection (a) must:

(1) be published at least once in a newspaper of general circulation in the [county] in this state in which the dissolved limited partnership's principal office is located or, if the principal office is not located in this state, in the [county] in which the office of the partnership's registered agent is or was last located;

(2) describe the information required to be contained in a claim, state that the claim must be in writing, and provide a mailing address to which the claim is to be sent;

(3) state that a claim against the partnership is barred unless an action to enforce the claim is commenced not later than three years after publication of the notice; and

(4) unless the partnership has been throughout its existence a limited liability limited partnership, state that the barring of a claim against the partnership will also bar any corresponding claim against any general partner or person dissociated as a general partner which is based on § 404.

(c) If a dissolved limited partnership publishes a notice in accordance with subsection (b), the claim of each of the following claimants is barred unless the claimant commences an action to enforce the claim against the partnership not later than three years after the publication date of the notice:

(1) a claimant that did not receive notice in a record under § 806;

(2) a claimant whose claim was timely sent to the partnership but not acted on; and

(3) a claimant whose claim is contingent at, or based on an event occurring after, the date of dissolution.

(d) A claim not barred under this section or § 806 may be enforced:

(1) against the dissolved limited partnership, to the extent of its undistributed assets;

(2) except as otherwise provided in § 808, if assets of the partnership have been distributed after dissolution, against a partner or transferee to the extent of that person's proportionate share of the claim or of the partnership's assets distributed to the partner or transferee after dissolution, whichever is less, but a person's total liability for all claims under this paragraph may not exceed the total amount of assets distributed to the person after dissolution; and

(3) against any person liable on the claim under §§ 404 and 607.

§ 808. Court Proceedings.

(a) A dissolved limited partnership that has published a notice under § 807 may file an application with [the appropriate court] in the [county] where the partnership's principal office is located or, if the principal office is not located in this state, where the office of its registered agent is or was last located, for a determination of the amount and form of security to be provided for payment of claims that are contingent, have not been made known to the partnership, or are based on an event occurring after the date of dissolution but which, based on the facts known to the partnership, are reasonably expected to arise after the date of dissolution. Security is not required for any claim that is or is reasonably anticipated to be barred under § 807.

(b) Not later than 10 days after the filing of an application under subsection (a), the dissolved limited partnership shall give notice of the proceeding to each claimant holding a contingent claim known to the partnership.

(c) In a proceeding brought under this section, the court may appoint a guardian ad litem to represent all claimants whose identities are unknown. The reasonable fees and expenses of the guardian, including all reasonable expert witness fees, must be paid by the dissolved limited partnership.

(d) A dissolved limited partnership that provides security in the amount and form ordered by the court under subsection (a) satisfies the partnership's obligations with respect to claims that are contingent, have not been made known to the partnership, or are based on an event occurring after the date of dissolution, and such claims may not be enforced against a partner or transferee on account of assets received in liquidation.

§ 809. Liability of General Partner and Person Dissociated as General Partner When Claim Against Limited Partnership Barred.

If a claim against a dissolved limited partnership is barred under § 806, 807, or 808, any corresponding claim under § 404 or 607 is also barred.

§ 810. Disposition of Assets in Winding Up; When Contributions Required.

(a) In winding up its activities and affairs, a limited partnership shall apply its assets, including the contributions required by this section, to discharge the partnership's obligations to creditors, including partners that are creditors.

(b) After a limited partnership complies with subsection (a), any surplus must be distributed in the following order, subject to any charging order in effect under § 703:

> **(1)** to each person owning a transferable interest that reflects contributions made and not previously returned, an amount equal to the value of the unreturned contributions; and

> **(2)** among persons owning transferable interests in proportion to their respective rights to share in distributions immediately before the dissolution of the partnership.

(c) If a limited partnership's assets are insufficient to satisfy all of its obligations under subsection (a), with respect to each unsatisfied obligation incurred when the partnership was not a limited liability limited partnership, the following rules apply:

> **(1)** Each person that was a general partner when the obligation was incurred and that has not been released from the obligation under § 607 shall contribute to the partnership for the purpose of enabling the partnership to satisfy the obligation. The contribution due from each

of those persons is in proportion to the right to receive distributions in the capacity of a general partner in effect for each of those persons when the obligation was incurred.

> **(2)** If a person does not contribute the full amount required under paragraph (1) with respect to an unsatisfied obligation of the partnership, the other persons required to contribute by paragraph (1) on account of the obligation shall contribute the additional amount necessary to discharge the obligation. The additional contribution due from each of those other persons is in proportion to the right to receive distributions in the capacity of a general partner in effect for each of those other persons when the obligation was incurred.

> **(3)** If a person does not make the additional contribution required by paragraph (2), further additional contributions are determined and due in the same manner as provided in that paragraph.

(d) A person that makes an additional contribution under subsection (c)(2) or (3) may recover from any person whose failure to contribute under subsection (c)(1) or (2) necessitated the additional contribution. A person may not recover under this subsection more than the amount additionally contributed. A person's liability under this subsection may not exceed the amount the person failed to contribute.

(e) All distributions made under subsections (b) and (c) must be paid in money.

§ 811. Administrative Dissolution.

(a) The [Secretary of State] may commence a proceeding under subsection (b) to dissolve a limited partnership administratively if the partnership does not:

> **(1)** pay any fee, tax, interest, or penalty required to be paid to the [Secretary of State] not later than [six months] after it is due;

> **(2)** deliver [an annual] [a biennial] report to the [Secretary of State] not later than [six months] after it is due; or

(3) have a registered agent in this state for [60] consecutive days.

(b) If the [Secretary of State] determines that one or more grounds exist for administratively dissolving a limited partnership, the [Secretary of State] shall serve the partnership with notice in a record of the [Secretary of State's] determination.

(c) If a limited partnership, not later than [60] days after service of the notice under subsection (b), does not cure or demonstrate to the satisfaction of the [Secretary of State] the nonexistence of each ground determined by the [Secretary of State], the [Secretary of State] shall administratively dissolve the partnership by signing a statement of administrative dissolution that recites the grounds for dissolution and the effective date of dissolution. The [Secretary of State] shall file the statement and serve a copy on the partnership pursuant to § 121.

(d) A limited partnership that is administratively dissolved continues in existence as an entity but may not carry on any activities except as necessary to wind up its activities and affairs and liquidate its assets under §§ 802, 806, 807, 808, and 810, or to apply for reinstatement under § 812.

(e) The administrative dissolution of a limited partnership does not terminate the authority of its registered agent.

§ 812. Reinstatement.

(a) A limited partnership that is administratively dissolved under § 811 may apply to the [Secretary of State] for reinstatement [not later than [two] years after the effective date of dissolution]. The application must state:

(1) the name of the partnership at the time of its administrative dissolution and, if needed, a different name that satisfies § 114;

(2) the address of the principal office of the partnership and the name and street and mailing addresses of its registered agent;

(3) the effective date of the partnership's administrative dissolution; and

(4) that the grounds for dissolution did not exist or have been cured.

(b) To be reinstated, a limited partnership must pay all fees, taxes, interest, and penalties that were due to the [Secretary of State] at the time of the partnership's administrative dissolution and all fees, taxes, interest, and penalties that would have been due to the [Secretary of State] while the partnership was administratively dissolved.

(c) If the [Secretary of State] determines that an application under subsection (a) contains the required information, is satisfied that the information is correct, and determines that all payments required to be made to the [Secretary of State] by subsection (b) have been made, the [Secretary of State] shall:

(1) cancel the statement of administrative dissolution and prepare a statement of reinstatement that states the [Secretary of State's] determination and the effective date of reinstatement; and

(2) file the statement of reinstatement and serve a copy on the limited partnership.

(d) When reinstatement under this section has become effective, the following rules apply:

(1) The reinstatement relates back to and takes effect as of the effective date of the administrative dissolution.

(2) The limited partnership resumes carrying on its activities and affairs as if the administrative dissolution had not occurred.

(3) The rights of a person arising out of an act or omission in reliance on the dissolution before the person knew or had notice of the reinstatement are not affected.

§ 813. Judicial Review of Denial of Reinstatement.

(a) If the [Secretary of State] denies a limited partnership's application for reinstatement following administrative dissolution, the [Secretary of State] shall serve the partnership with a notice in a record that explains the reasons for the denial.

(b) A limited partnership may seek judicial review of denial of reinstatement in [the appropriate court] not later than [30] days after service of the notice of denial.

[Article] 9. Actions by Partners

§ 901. Direct Action by Partner.

(a) Subject to subsection (b), a partner may maintain a direct action against another partner or the limited partnership, with or without an accounting as to the partnership's activities and affairs, to enforce the partner's rights and otherwise protect the partner's interests, including rights and interests under the partnership agreement or this [act] or arising independently of the partnership relationship.

(b) A partner maintaining a direct action under this section must plead and prove an actual or threatened injury that is not solely the result of an injury suffered or threatened to be suffered by the limited partnership.

(c) A right to an accounting on a dissolution and winding up does not revive a claim barred by law.

§ 902. Derivative Action.

A partner may maintain a derivative action to enforce a right of a limited partnership if:

(1) the partner first makes a demand on the general partners, requesting that they cause the partnership to bring an action to enforce the right, and the general partners do not bring the action within a reasonable time; or

(2) a demand under paragraph (1) would be futile.

§ 903. Proper Plaintiff.

A derivative action to enforce a right of a limited partnership may be maintained only by a person that is a partner at the time the action is commenced and:

(1) was a partner when the conduct giving rise to the action occurred; or

(2) whose status as a partner devolved on the person by operation of law or pursuant to the terms of the partnership agreement from a person that was a partner at the time of the conduct.

§ 904. Pleading.

In a derivative action, the complaint must state with particularity:

(1) the date and content of plaintiff's demand and the response to the demand by the general partner; or

(2) why demand should be excused as futile.

§ 905. Special Litigation Committee.

(a) If a limited partnership is named as or made a party in a derivative proceeding, the partnership may appoint a special litigation committee to investigate the claims asserted in the proceeding and determine whether pursuing the action is in the best interests of the partnership. If the partnership appoints a special litigation committee, on motion by the committee made in the name of the partnership, except for good cause shown, the court shall stay discovery for the time reasonably necessary to permit the committee to make its investigation. This subsection does not prevent the court from:

(1) enforcing a person's right to information under § 304 or 407; or

(2) granting extraordinary relief in the form of a temporary restraining order or preliminary injunction.

(b) A special litigation committee must be composed of one or more disinterested and independent individuals, who may be partners.

(c) A special litigation committee may be appointed:

(1) by a majority of the general partners not named as parties in the proceeding; or

(2) if all general partners are named as parties in the proceeding, by a majority of the general partners named as defendants.

(d) After appropriate investigation, a special litigation committee may determine that it is in the best interests of the limited partnership that the proceeding:

(1) continue under the control of the plaintiff;

(2) continue under the control of the committee;

(3) be settled on terms approved by the committee; or

(4) be dismissed.

(e) After making a determination under subsection (d), a special litigation committee shall file with the court a statement of its determination and its report supporting its determination and shall serve each party with a copy of the determination and report. The court shall determine whether the members of the committee were disinterested and independent and whether the committee conducted its investigation and made its recommendation in good faith, independently, and with reasonable care, with the committee having the burden of proof. If the court finds that the members of the committee were disinterested and independent and that the committee acted in good faith, independently, and with reasonable care, the court shall enforce the determination of the committee. Otherwise, the court shall dissolve the stay of discovery entered under subsection (a) and allow the action to continue under the control of the plaintiff.

§ 906. Proceeds and Expenses.

(a) Except as otherwise provided in subsection (b):

(1) any proceeds or other benefits of a derivative action, whether by judgment, compromise, or settlement, belong to the limited partnership and not to the plaintiff; and

(2) if the plaintiff receives any proceeds, the plaintiff shall remit them immediately to the partnership.

(b) If a derivative action is successful in whole or in part, the court may award the plaintiff reasonable expenses, including reasonable attorney's fees and costs, from the recovery of the limited partnership.

(c) A derivative action on behalf of a limited partnership may not be voluntarily dismissed or settled without the court's approval.

[Article] 10. Foreign Limited Partnerships

§ 1001. Governing Law.

(a) The law of the jurisdiction of formation of a foreign limited partnership governs:

(1) the internal affairs of the partnership;

(2) the liability of a partner as partner for a debt, obligation, or other liability of the partnership; and

(3) the liability of a series of the partnership.

(b) A foreign limited partnership is not precluded from registering to do business in this state because of any difference between the law of its jurisdiction of formation and the law of this state.

(c) Registration of a foreign limited partnership to do business in this state does not authorize the foreign partnership to engage in any activities and affairs or exercise any power that a limited partnership may not engage in or exercise in this state.

§ 1002. Registration to Do Business in This State.

(a) A foreign limited partnership may not do business in this state until it registers with the [Secretary of State] under this [article].

(b) A foreign limited partnership doing business in this state may not maintain an action or proceeding in this state unless it is registered to do business in this state.

(c) The failure of a foreign limited partnership to register to do business in this state does not impair the validity of a contract or act of the partnership or preclude it from defending an action or proceeding in this state.

(d) A limitation on the liability of a general partner or limited partner of a foreign limited partnership is not waived solely because the partnership does business in this state without registering to do business in this state.

(e) Section 1001(a) and (b) applies even if the foreign limited partnership fails to register under this [article].

§ 1003. Foreign Registration Statement.

To register to do business in this state, a foreign limited partnership must deliver a foreign registration statement to the [Secretary of State] for filing. The statement must state:

(1) the name of the partnership and, if the name does not comply with § 114, an alternate name adopted pursuant to § 1006(a);

(2) that the partnership is a foreign limited partnership;

(3) the partnership's jurisdiction of formation;

(4) the street and mailing addresses of the partnership's principal office and, if the law of the partnership's jurisdiction of formation requires the partnership to maintain an office in that jurisdiction, the street and mailing addresses of the required office; and

(5) the name and street and mailing addresses of the partnership's registered agent in this state.

§ 1004. Amendment of Foreign Registration Statement.

A registered foreign limited partnership shall deliver to the [Secretary of State] for filing an amendment to its foreign registration statement if there is a change in:

(1) the name of the partnership;

(2) the partnership's jurisdiction of formation;

(3) an address required by § 1003(4); or

(4) the information required by § 1003(5).

§ 1005. Activities Not Constituting Doing Business.

(a) Activities of a foreign limited partnership which do not constitute doing business in this state under this [article] include:

    (1) maintaining, defending, mediating, arbitrating, or settling an action or proceeding;

    (2) carrying on any activity concerning its internal affairs, including holding meetings of its partners;

    (3) maintaining accounts in financial institutions;

    (4) maintaining offices or agencies for the transfer, exchange, and registration of securities of the partnership or maintaining trustees or depositories with respect to those securities;

    (5) selling through independent contractors;

    (6) soliciting or obtaining orders by any means if the orders require acceptance outside this state before they become contracts;

    (7) creating or acquiring indebtedness, mortgages, or security interests in property;

    (8) securing or collecting debts or enforcing mortgages or security interests in property securing the debts and holding, protecting, or maintaining property;

    (9) conducting an isolated transaction that is not in the course of similar transactions;

    (10) owning, without more, property; and

    (11) doing business in interstate commerce.

(b) A person does not do business in this state solely by being a partner of a foreign limited partnership that does business in this state.

(c) This section does not apply in determining the contacts or activities that may subject a foreign limited partnership to service of process, taxation, or regulation under law of this state other than this [act].

§ 1006. Noncomplying Name of Foreign Limited Partnership.

(a) A foreign limited partnership whose name does not comply with § 114 may not register to do business in this state until it adopts, for the purpose of doing business in this state, an alternate name that complies with § 114. A partnership that registers under an alternate name under this subsection need not comply with [this state's assumed or fictitious name statute]. After registering to do business in this state with an alternate name, a partnership shall do business in this state under:

    (1) the alternate name;

    (2) the partnership's name, with the addition of its jurisdiction of formation; or

    (3) a name the partnership is authorized to use under [this state's assumed or fictitious name statute].

(b) If a registered foreign limited partnership changes its name to one that does not comply with § 114, it may not do business in this state until it complies with subsection (a) by amending its registration to adopt an alternate name that complies with § 114.

§ 1007. Withdrawal Deemed on Conversion to Domestic Filing Entity or Domestic Limited Liability Partnership.

A registered foreign limited partnership that converts to a domestic limited liability partnership or to a domestic entity whose formation requires delivery of a record to the [Secretary of State] for filing is deemed to have withdrawn its registration on the effective date of the conversion.

§ 1008. Withdrawal on Dissolution or Conversion to Nonfiling Entity Other Than Limited Liability Partnership.

(a) A registered foreign limited partnership that has dissolved and completed winding up or has converted to a domestic or foreign entity whose formation does not require the public filing of a record, other than a limited liability partnership, shall deliver a statement of withdrawal to the [Secretary of State] for filing. The statement must state:

(1) in the case of a partnership that has completed winding up:

(A) its name and jurisdiction of formation;

(B) that the partnership surrenders its registration to do business in this state; and

(2) in the case of a partnership that has converted:

(A) the name of the converting partnership and its jurisdiction of formation;

(B) the type of entity to which the partnership has converted and its jurisdiction of formation;

(C) that the converted entity surrenders the converting partnership's registration to do business in this state and revokes the authority of the converting partnership's registered agent to act as registered agent in this state on behalf of the partnership or the converted entity; and

(D) a mailing address to which service of process may be made under subsection (b).

(b) After a withdrawal under this section has become effective, service of process in any action or proceeding based on a cause of action arising during the time the foreign limited partnership was registered to do business in this state may be made pursuant to § 121.

§ 1009. Transfer of Registration.

(a) When a registered foreign limited partnership has merged into a foreign entity that is not registered to do business in this state or has converted to a foreign entity required to register with the [Secretary of State] to do business in this state, the foreign entity shall deliver to the [Secretary of State] for filing an application for transfer of registration. The application must state:

(1) the name of the registered foreign limited partnership before the merger or conversion;

(2) that before the merger or conversion the registration pertained to a foreign limited partnership;

(3) the name of the applicant foreign entity into which the foreign limited partnership has merged or to which it has been converted and, if the name does not comply with § 114, an alternate name adopted pursuant to § 1006(a);

(4) the type of entity of the applicant foreign entity and its jurisdiction of formation;

(5) the street and mailing addresses of the principal office of the applicant foreign entity and, if the law of the entity's jurisdiction of formation requires the entity to maintain an office in that jurisdiction, the street and mailing addresses of that office; and

(6) the name and street and mailing addresses of the applicant foreign entity's registered agent in this state.

(b) When an application for transfer of registration takes effect, the registration of the foreign limited partnership to do business in this state is transferred without interruption to the foreign entity into which the partnership has merged or to which it has been converted.

§ 1010. Termination of Registration.

(a) The [Secretary of State] may terminate the registration of a registered foreign limited partnership in the manner provided in subsections (b) and (c) if the partnership does not:

(1) pay, not later than [60] days after the due date, any fee, tax, interest, or penalty required to be paid to the [Secretary of State] under this [act] or law other than this [act];

(2) deliver to the [Secretary of State] for filing, not later than [60] days after the due date, [an annual] [a biennial] report required under § 212;

(3) have a registered agent as required by § 117; or

(4) deliver to the [Secretary of State] for filing a statement of a change under § 118 not later than [30] days after a change has occurred in the name or address of the registered agent.

(b) The [Secretary of State] may terminate the registration of a registered foreign limited partnership by:

(1) filing a notice of termination or noting the termination in the records of the [Secretary of State]; and

(2) delivering a copy of the notice or the information in the notation to the partnership's registered agent or, if the partnership does not have a registered agent, to the partnership's principal office.

(c) The notice must state or the information in the notation must include:

(1) the effective date of the termination, which must be at least [60] days after the date the [Secretary of State] delivers the copy; and

(2) the grounds for termination under subsection (a).

(d) The authority of the registered foreign limited partnership to do business in this state ceases on the effective date of the notice of termination or notation under subsection (b), unless before that date the partnership cures each ground for termi-nation stated in the notice or notation. If the partnership cures each ground, the [Secretary of State] shall file a record so stating.

§ 1011. Withdrawal of Registration of Registered Foreign Limited Partnership.

(a) A registered foreign limited partnership may withdraw its registration by delivering a statement of withdrawal to the [Secretary of State] for filing. The statement of withdrawal must state:

(1) the name of the partnership and its jurisdiction of formation;

(2) that the partnership is not doing business in this state and that it withdraws its registration to do business in this state;

(3) that the partnership revokes the authority of its registered agent to accept service on its behalf in this state; and

(4) an address to which service of process may be made under subsection (b).

(b) After the withdrawal of the registration of a foreign limited partnership, service of process in any action or proceeding based on a cause of action arising during the time the partnership was registered to do business in this state may be made pursuant to § 121.

§ 1012. Action by [Attorney General].

The [Attorney General] may maintain an action to enjoin a foreign limited partnership from doing business in this state in violation of this [article].

[Article] 11. Merger, Interest Exchange, Conversion, and Domestication

[Part] 1. General Provisions

§ 1101. Definitions.

In this [article]:

(1) "Acquired entity" means the entity, all of one or more classes or series of interests of which are acquired in an interest exchange.

(2) "Acquiring entity" means the entity that acquires all of one or more classes or series of interests of the acquired entity in an interest exchange.

(3) "Conversion" means a transaction authorized by [Part] 4.

(4) "Converted entity" means the converting entity as it continues in existence after a conversion.

(5) "Converting entity" means the domestic entity that approves a plan of conversion pursuant to § 1143 or the foreign entity that approves a conversion pursuant to the law of its jurisdiction of formation.

(6) "Distributional interest" means the right under an unincorporated entity's organic law and organic rules to receive distributions from the entity.

(7) "Domestic", with respect to an entity, means governed as to its internal affairs by the law of this state.

(8) "Domesticated limited partnership" means the domesticating limited partnership as it continues in existence after a domestication.

(9) "Domesticating limited partnership" means the domestic limited partnership that approves a plan of domestication pursuant to § 1153 or the foreign limited partnership that approves a domestication pursuant to the law of its jurisdiction of formation.

(10) "Domestication" means a transaction authorized by [Part] 5.

(11) "Entity":

  (A) means:

    (i) a business corporation;

    (ii) a nonprofit corporation;

    (iii) a general partnership, including a limited liability partnership;

    (iv) a limited partnership, including a limited liability limited partnership;

    (v) a limited liability company;

    [**(vi)** a general cooperative association;]

    (vii) a limited cooperative association;

    (viii) an unincorporated nonprofit association;

    (ix) a statutory trust, business trust, or common-law business trust; or

    (x) any other person that has:

      (I) a legal existence separate from any interest holder of that person; or

      (II) the power to acquire an interest in real property in its own name; and

  (B) does not include:

    (i) an individual;

    (ii) a trust with a predominantly donative purpose or a charitable trust;

    (iii) an association or relationship that is not an entity listed in subparagraph A and is not a partnership under the rules stated in [§ 202(c) of the Uniform Partnership Act (1997) (Lasted Amended 2013)] [§ 7 of the Uniform Partnership Act (1914)] or a similar provision of the law of another jurisdiction;

    (iv) a decedent's estate; or

    (v) a government or a governmental subdivision, agency, or instrumentality.

(12) "Filing entity" means an entity whose formation requires the filing of a public organic record. The term does not include a limited liability partnership.

(13) "Foreign", with respect to an entity, means an entity governed as to its internal affairs by the law of a jurisdiction other than this state.

(14) "Governance interest" means a right under the organic law or organic rules of an unincorporated entity, other than as a governor, agent, assignee, or proxy, to:

  (A) receive or demand access to information concerning, or the books and records of, the entity;

  (B) vote for or consent to the election of the governors of the entity; or

  (C) receive notice of or vote on or consent to an issue involving the internal affairs of the entity.

(15) "Governor" means:

(A) a director of a business corporation;

(B) a director or trustee of a nonprofit corporation;

(C) a general partner of a general partnership;

(D) a general partner of a limited partnership;

(E) a manager of a manager-managed limited liability company;

(F) a member of a member-managed limited liability company;

[**(G)** a director of a general cooperative association;]

(H) a director of a limited cooperative association;

(I) a manager of an unincorporated nonprofit association;

(J) a trustee of a statutory trust, business trust, or common-law business trust; or

(K) any other person under whose authority the powers of an entity are exercised and under whose direction the activities and affairs of the entity are managed pursuant to the organic law and organic rules of the entity.

(16) "Interest" means:

(A) a share in a business corporation;

(B) a membership in a nonprofit corporation;

(C) a partnership interest in a general partnership;

(D) a partnership interest in a limited partnership;

(E) a membership interest in a limited liability company;

[**(F)** a share in a general cooperative association;]

(G) a member's interest in a limited cooperative association;

(H) a membership in an unincorporated nonprofit association;

(I) a beneficial interest in a statutory trust, business trust, or common-law business trust; or

(J) a governance interest or distributional interest in any other type of unincorporated entity.

(17) "Interest exchange" means a transaction authorized by [Part] 3.

(18) "Interest holder" means:

(A) a shareholder of a business corporation;

(B) a member of a nonprofit corporation;

(C) a general partner of a general partnership;

(D) a general partner of a limited partnership;

(E) a limited partner of a limited partnership;

(F) a member of a limited liability company;

[**(G)** a shareholder of a general cooperative association;]

(H) a member of a limited cooperative association;

(I) a member of an unincorporated nonprofit association;

(J) a beneficiary or beneficial owner of a statutory trust, business trust, or common-law business trust; or

(K) any other direct holder of an interest.

(19) "Interest holder liability" means:

(A) personal liability for a liability of an entity which is imposed on a person:

(i) solely by reason of the status of the person as an interest holder; or

(ii) by the organic rules of the entity which make one or more specified interest holders or categories of interest holders liable in their capacity as interest holders for all or specified liabilities of the entity; or

(B) an obligation of an interest holder under the organic rules of an entity to contribute to the entity.

(20) "Merger" means a transaction authorized by [Part] 2.

(21) "Merging entity" means an entity that is a party to a merger and exists immediately before the merger becomes effective.

(22) "Organic law" means the law of an entity's jurisdiction of formation governing the internal affairs of the entity.

(23) "Organic rules" means the public organic record and private organic rules of an entity.

(24) "Plan" means a plan of merger, plan of interest exchange, plan of conversion, or plan of domestication.

(25) "Plan of conversion" means a plan under § 1142.

(26) "Plan of domestication" means a plan under § 1152.

(27) "Plan of interest exchange" means a plan under § 1132.

(28) "Plan of merger" means a plan under § 1122.

(29) "Private organic rules" means the rules, whether or not in a record, that govern the internal affairs of an entity, are binding on all its interest holders, and are not part of its public organic record, if any. The term includes:

(A) the bylaws of a business corporation;

(B) the bylaws of a nonprofit corporation;

(C) the partnership agreement of a general partnership;

(D) the partnership agreement of a limited partnership;

(E) the operating agreement of a limited liability company;

[**(F)** the bylaws of a general cooperative association;]

(G) the bylaws of a limited cooperative association;

(H) the governing principles of an unincorporated nonprofit association; and

(I) the trust instrument of a statutory trust or similar rules of a business trust or a common-law business trust.

(30) "Protected agreement" means:

(A) a record evidencing indebtedness and any related agreement in effect on [the effective date of this [act]];

(B) an agreement that is binding on an entity on [the effective date of this [act]];

(C) the organic rules of an entity in effect on [the effective date of this [act]]; or

(D) an agreement that is binding on any of the governors or interest holders of an entity on [the effective date of this [act]].

(31) "Public organic record" means the record the filing of which by the [Secretary of State] is required to form an entity and any amendment to or restatement of that record. The term includes:

(A) the articles of incorporation of a business corporation;

(B) the articles of incorporation of a nonprofit corporation;

(C) the certificate of limited partnership of a limited partnership;

(D) the certificate of organization of a limited liability company;

[**(E)** the articles of incorporation of a general cooperative association;]

(F) the articles of organization of a limited cooperative association; and

(G) the certificate of trust of a statutory trust or similar record of a business trust.

(32) "Registered foreign entity" means a foreign entity that is registered to do business in this state pursuant to a record filed by the [Secretary of State].

(33) "Statement of conversion" means a statement under § 1145.

(34) "Statement of domestication" means a statement under § 1155.

(35) "Statement of interest exchange" means a statement under § 1135.

(36) "Statement of merger" means a statement under § 1125.

(37) "Surviving entity" means the entity that continues in existence after or is created by a merger.

(38) "Type of entity" means a generic form of entity:

(A) recognized at common law; or

(B) formed under an organic law, whether or not some entities formed under that organic law are subject to provisions of that law that create different categories of the form of entity.

§ 1102. Relationship of [Article] to Other Laws.

(a) This [article] does not authorize an act prohibited by, and does not affect the application or requirements of, law other than this [article].

(b) A transaction effected under this [article] may not create or impair a right, duty, or obligation of a person under the statutory law of this state relating to a change in control, takeover, business combination, control-share acquisition, or similar transaction involving a domestic merging, acquired, converting, or domesticating business corporation unless:

> **(1)** if the corporation does not survive the transaction, the transaction satisfies any requirements of the law; or

> **(2)** if the corporation survives the transaction, the approval of the plan is by a vote of the shareholders or directors which would be sufficient to create or impair the right, duty, or obligation directly under the law.

§ 1103. Required Notice or Approval.

(a) A domestic or foreign entity that is required to give notice to, or obtain the approval of, a governmental agency or officer of this state to be a party to a merger must give the notice or obtain the approval to be a party to an interest exchange, conversion, or domestication.

(b) Property held for a charitable purpose under the law of this state by a domestic or foreign entity immediately before a transaction under this [article] becomes effective may not, as a result of the transaction, be diverted from the objects for which it was donated, granted, devised, or otherwise transferred unless, to the extent required by or pursuant to the law of this state concerning cy pres or other law dealing with nondiversion of charitable assets, the entity obtains an appropriate order of [the appropriate court] [the Attorney General] specifying the disposition of the property.

(c) A bequest, devise, gift, grant, or promise contained in a will or other instrument of donation, subscription, or conveyance which is made to a merging entity that is not the surviving entity and which takes effect or remains payable after the merger inures to the surviving entity.

(d) A trust obligation that would govern property if transferred to a nonsurviving entity applies to property that is transferred to the surviving entity under this section.

Legislative Note: *As an alternative to enacting Subsection (a), a state may identify each of its regulatory laws that requires prior approval for a merger of a regulated entity, decide whether regulatory approval should be required for an interest exchange, conversion, or domestication, and make amendments as appropriate to those laws.*

As with Subsection (a), an adopting state may choose to amend its various laws with respect to the nondiversion of charitable property to cover the various transactions authorized by this act as an alternative to enacting Subsection (b).

§ 1104. Nonexclusivity.

The fact that a transaction under this [article] produces a certain result does not preclude the same result from being accomplished in any other manner permitted by law other than this [article].

§ 1105. Reference to External Facts.

A plan may refer to facts ascertainable outside the plan if the manner in which the facts will operate upon the plan is specified in the plan. The facts may include the occurrence of an event or a determination or action by a person, whether or not the event, determination, or action is within the control of a party to the transaction.

§ 1106. Appraisal Rights.

An interest holder of a domestic merging, acquired, converting, or domesticating limited partnership is entitled to contractual appraisal rights in connection with a transaction under this [article] to the extent provided in:

(1) the partnership agreement; or

(2) the plan.

[§ 1107. Excluded Entities and Transactions.

(a) The following entities may not participate in a transaction under this [article]:

(1)

(2).

(b) This [article] may not be used to effect a transaction that:

(1)

(2).]

Legislative Note: *Subsection (a) may be used by states that have special statutes restricted to the organization of certain types of entities. A common example is banking statutes that prohibit banks from engaging in transactions other than pursuant to those statutes.*

Nonprofit entities may participate in transactions under this act with for-profit entities, subject to compliance with § 1103. If a state desires, however, to exclude entities with a charitable purpose or to exclude other types of entities from the scope of this act, that may be done by referring to those entities in Subsection (a).

Subsection (b) may be used to exclude certain types of transactions governed by more specific statutes. A common example is the conversion of an insurance company from mutual to stock form. There may be other types of transactions that vary greatly among the states.

[Part] 2. Merger

§ 1121. Merger Authorized.

(a) By complying with this [part]:

(1) one or more domestic limited partnerships may merge with one or more domestic or foreign entities into a domestic or foreign surviving entity; and

(2) two or more foreign entities may merge into a domestic limited partnership.

(b) By complying with the provisions of this [part] applicable to foreign entities, a foreign entity may be a party to a merger under this [part] or may be

the surviving entity in such a merger if the merger is authorized by the law of the foreign entity's jurisdiction of formation.

§ 1122. Plan of Merger.

(a) A domestic limited partnership may become a party to a merger under this [part] by approving a plan of merger. The plan must be in a record and contain:

(1) as to each merging entity, its name, jurisdiction of formation, and type of entity;

(2) if the surviving entity is to be created in the merger, a statement to that effect and the entity's name, jurisdiction of formation, and type of entity;

(3) the manner of converting the interests in each party to the merger into interests, securities, obligations, money, other property, rights to acquire interests or securities, or any combination of the foregoing;

(4) if the surviving entity exists before the merger, any proposed amendments to:

(A) its public organic record, if any; and

(B) its private organic rules that are, or are proposed to be, in a record;

(5) if the surviving entity is to be created in the merger:

(A) its proposed public organic record, if any; and

(B) the full text of its private organic rules that are proposed to be in a record;

(6) the other terms and conditions of the merger; and

(7) any other provision required by the law of a merging entity's jurisdiction of formation or the organic rules of a merging entity.

(b) In addition to the requirements of subsection (a), a plan of merger may contain any other provision not prohibited by law.

§ 1123. Approval of Merger.

(a) A plan of merger is not effective unless it has been approved:

(1) by a domestic merging limited partnership, by all the partners of the partnership entitled to vote on or consent to any matter; and

(2) in a record, by each partner of a domestic merging limited partnership which will have interest holder liability for debts, obligations, and other liabilities that are incurred after the merger becomes effective, unless:

> **(A)** the partnership agreement of the partnership provides in a record for the approval of a merger in which some or all of its partners become subject to interest holder liability by the affirmative vote or consent of fewer than all the partners; and

> **(B)** the partner consented in a record to or voted for that provision of the partnership agreement or became a partner after the adoption of that provision.

(b) A merger involving a domestic merging entity that is not a limited partnership is not effective unless the merger is approved by that entity in accordance with its organic law.

(c) A merger involving a foreign merging entity is not effective unless the merger is approved by the foreign entity in accordance with the law of the foreign entity's jurisdiction of formation.

§ 1124. Amendment or Abandonment of Plan of Merger.

(a) A plan of merger may be amended only with the consent of each party to the plan, except as otherwise provided in the plan.

(b) A domestic merging limited partnership may approve an amendment of a plan of merger:

> **(1)** in the same manner as the plan was approved, if the plan does not provide for the manner in which it may be amended; or

> **(2)** by its partners in the manner provided in the plan, but a partner that was entitled to vote on or consent to approval of the merger is entitled to vote on or consent to any amendment of the plan that will change:

>> **(A)** the amount or kind of interests, securities, obligations, money, other property,

rights to acquire interests or securities, or any combination of the foregoing, to be received by the interest holders of any party to the plan;

>> **(B)** the public organic record, if any, or private organic rules of the surviving entity that will be in effect immediately after the merger becomes effective, except for changes that do not require approval of the interest holders of the surviving entity under its organic law or organic rules; or

>> **(C)** any other terms or conditions of the plan, if the change would adversely affect the partner in any material respect.

(c) After a plan of merger has been approved and before a statement of merger becomes effective, the plan may be abandoned as provided in the plan. Unless prohibited by the plan, a domestic merging limited partnership may abandon the plan in the same manner as the plan was approved.

(d) If a plan of merger is abandoned after a statement of merger has been delivered to the [Secretary of State] for filing and before the statement becomes effective, a statement of abandonment, signed by a party to the plan, must be delivered to the [Secretary of State] for filing before the statement of merger becomes effective. The statement of abandonment takes effect on filing, and the merger is abandoned and does not become effective. The statement of abandonment must contain:

> **(1)** the name of each party to the plan of merger;

> **(2)** the date on which the statement of merger was filed by the [Secretary of State]; and

> **(3)** a statement that the merger has been abandoned in accordance with this section.

§ 1125. Statement of Merger; Effective Date of Merger.

(a) A statement of merger must be signed by each merging entity and delivered to the [Secretary of State] for filing.

(b) A statement of merger must contain:

(1) the name, jurisdiction of formation, and type of entity of each merging entity that is not the surviving entity;

(2) the name, jurisdiction of formation, and type of entity of the surviving entity;

(3) a statement that the merger was approved by each domestic merging entity, if any, in accordance with this [part] and by each foreign merging entity, if any, in accordance with the law of its jurisdiction of formation;

(4) if the surviving entity exists before the merger and is a domestic filing entity, any amendment to its public organic record approved as part of the plan of merger;

(5) if the surviving entity is created by the merger and is a domestic filing entity, its public organic record, as an attachment; and

(6) if the surviving entity is created by the merger and is a domestic limited liability partnership, its statement of qualification, as an attachment.

(c) In addition to the requirements of subsection (b), a statement of merger may contain any other provision not prohibited by law.

(d) If the surviving entity is a domestic entity, its public organic record, if any, must satisfy the requirements of the law of this state, except that the public organic record does not need to be signed.

(e) A plan of merger that is signed by all the merging entities and meets all the requirements of subsection (b) may be delivered to the [Secretary of State] for filing instead of a statement of merger and on filing has the same effect. If a plan of merger is filed as provided in this subsection, references in this [article] to a statement of merger refer to the plan of merger filed under this subsection.

(f) If the surviving entity is a domestic limited partnership, the merger becomes effective when the statement of merger is effective. In all other cases, the merger becomes effective on the later of:

(1) the date and time provided by the organic law of the surviving entity; and

(2) when the statement is effective.

§ 1126. Effect of Merger.

(a) When a merger becomes effective:

(1) the surviving entity continues or comes into existence;

(2) each merging entity that is not the surviving entity ceases to exist;

(3) all property of each merging entity vests in the surviving entity without transfer, reversion, or impairment;

(4) all debts, obligations, and other liabilities of each merging entity are debts, obligations, and other liabilities of the surviving entity;

(5) except as otherwise provided by law or the plan of merger, all the rights, privileges, immunities, powers, and purposes of each merging entity vest in the surviving entity;

(6) if the surviving entity exists before the merger:

(A) all its property continues to be vested in it without transfer, reversion, or impairment;

(B) it remains subject to all its debts, obligations, and other liabilities; and

(C) all its rights, privileges, immunities, powers, and purposes continue to be vested in it;

(7) the name of the surviving entity may be substituted for the name of any merging entity that is a party to any pending action or proceeding;

(8) if the surviving entity exists before the merger:

(A) its public organic record, if any, is amended to the extent provided in the statement of merger; and

(B) its private organic rules that are to be in a record, if any, are amended to the extent provided in the plan of merger;

(9) if the surviving entity is created by the merger, its private organic rules become effective and:

(A) if it is a filing entity, its public organic record becomes effective; and

(B) if it is a limited liability partnership, its statement of qualification becomes effective; and

(10) the interests in each merging entity which are to be converted in the merger are converted, and the interest holders of those interests are entitled only to the rights provided to them under the plan of merger and to any appraisal rights they have under § 1106 and the merging entity's organic law.

(b) Except as otherwise provided in the organic law or organic rules of a merging entity, the merger does not give rise to any rights that an interest holder, governor, or third party would have upon a dissolution, liquidation, or winding up of the merging entity.

(c) When a merger becomes effective, a person that did not have interest holder liability with respect to any of the merging entities and becomes subject to interest holder liability with respect to a domestic entity as a result of the merger has interest holder liability only to the extent provided by the organic law of that entity and only for those debts, obligations, and other liabilities that are incurred after the merger becomes effective.

(d) When a merger becomes effective, the interest holder liability of a person that ceases to hold an interest in a domestic merging limited partnership with respect to which the person had interest holder liability is subject to the following rules:

(1) The merger does not discharge any interest holder liability under this [act] to the extent the interest holder liability was incurred before the merger became effective.

(2) The person does not have interest holder liability under this [act] for any debt, obligation, or other liability that is incurred after the merger becomes effective.

(3) This [act] continues to apply to the release, collection, or discharge of any interest holder liability preserved under paragraph (1) as if the merger had not occurred.

(4) The person has whatever rights of contribution from any other person as are provided by

this [act], law other than this [act], or the partnership agreement of the domestic merging limited partnership with respect to any interest holder liability preserved under paragraph (1) as if the merger had not occurred.

(e) When a merger becomes effective, a foreign entity that is the surviving entity may be served with process in this state for the collection and enforcement of any debts, obligations, or other liabilities of a domestic merging limited partnership as provided in § 121.

(f) When a merger becomes effective, the registration to do business in this state of any foreign merging entity that is not the surviving entity is canceled.

[Part] 3. Interest Exchange

§ 1131. Interest Exchange Authorized.

(a) By complying with this [part]:

(1) a domestic limited partnership may acquire all of one or more classes or series of interests of another domestic entity or a foreign entity in exchange for interests, securities, obligations, money, other property, rights to acquire interests or securities, or any combination of the foregoing; or

(2) all of one or more classes or series of interests of a domestic limited partnership may be acquired by another domestic entity or a foreign entity in exchange for interests, securities, obligations, money, other property, rights to acquire interests or securities, or any combination of the foregoing.

(b) By complying with the provisions of this [part] applicable to foreign entities, a foreign entity may be the acquiring or acquired entity in an interest exchange under this [part] if the interest exchange is authorized by the law of the foreign entity's jurisdiction of formation.

(c) If a protected agreement contains a provision that applies to a merger of a domestic limited partnership but does not refer to an interest exchange, the provision applies to an interest exchange in which the domestic limited partnership is the acquired entity as if the interest exchange were a merger until the provision is amended after [the effective date of this [act]].

§ 1132. Plan of Interest Exchange.

(a) A domestic limited partnership may be the acquired entity in an interest exchange under this [part] by approving a plan of interest exchange. The plan must be in a record and contain:

(1) the name of the acquired entity;

(2) the name, jurisdiction of formation, and type of entity of the acquiring entity;

(3) the manner of converting the interests in the acquired entity into interests, securities, obligations, money, other property, rights to acquire interests or securities, or any combination of the foregoing;

(4) any proposed amendments to:

(A) the certificate of limited partnership of the acquired entity; and

(B) the partnership agreement of the acquired entity that are, or are proposed to be, in a record;

(5) the other terms and conditions of the interest exchange; and

(6) any other provision required by the law of this state or the partnership agreement of the acquired entity.

(b) In addition to the requirements of subsection (a), a plan of interest exchange may contain any other provision not prohibited by law.

§ 1133. Approval of Interest Exchange.

(a) A plan of interest exchange is not effective unless it has been approved:

(1) by all the partners of a domestic acquired limited partnership entitled to vote on or consent to any matter; and

(2) in a record, by each partner of the domestic acquired limited partnership that will have interest holder liability for debts, obligations, and other liabilities that are incurred after the interest exchange becomes effective, unless:

(A) the partnership agreement of the partnership provides in a record for the approval of an interest exchange or a merger in which some or all its partners become subject to interest holder liability by the affirmative vote or consent of fewer than all of the partners; and

(B) the partner consented in a record to or voted for that provision of the partnership agreement or became a partner after the adoption of that provision.

(b) An interest exchange involving a domestic acquired entity that is not a limited partnership is not effective unless it is approved by the domestic entity in accordance with its organic law.

(c) An interest exchange involving a foreign acquired entity is not effective unless it is approved by the foreign entity in accordance with the law of the foreign entity's jurisdiction of formation.

(d) Except as otherwise provided in its organic law or organic rules, the interest holders of the acquiring entity are not required to approve the interest exchange.

§ 1134. Amendment or Abandonment of Plan of Interest Exchange.

(a) A plan of interest exchange may be amended only with the consent of each party to the plan, except as otherwise provided in the plan.

(b) A domestic acquired limited partnership may approve an amendment of a plan of interest exchange:

(1) in the same manner as the plan was approved, if the plan does not provide for the manner in which it may be amended; or

(2) by its partners in the manner provided in the plan, but a partner that was entitled to vote on or consent to approval of the interest exchange is entitled to vote on or consent to any amendment of the plan that will change:

(A) the amount or kind of interests, securities, obligations, money, other property, rights to acquire interests or securities, or any combination of the foregoing, to be received by any of the partners of the acquired partnership under the plan;

(B) the certificate of limited partnership or partnership agreement of the acquired partnership that will be in effect immediately after the interest exchange becomes effective, except for changes that do not require approval of the partners of the acquired partnership under this [act] or the partnership agreement; or

(C) any other terms or conditions of the plan, if the change would adversely affect the partner in any material respect.

(c) After a plan of interest exchange has been approved and before a statement of interest exchange becomes effective, the plan may be abandoned as provided in the plan. Unless prohibited by the plan, a domestic acquired limited partnership may abandon the plan in the same manner as the plan was approved.

(d) If a plan of interest exchange is abandoned after a statement of interest exchange has been delivered to the [Secretary of State] for filing and before the statement becomes effective, a statement of abandonment, signed by the acquired limited partnership, must be delivered to the [Secretary of State] for filing before the statement of interest exchange becomes effective. The statement of abandonment takes effect on filing, and the interest exchange is abandoned and does not become effective. The statement of abandonment must contain:

(1) the name of the acquired partnership;

(2) the date on which the statement of interest exchange was filed by the [Secretary of State]; and

(3) a statement that the interest exchange has been abandoned in accordance with this section.

§ 1135. Statement of Interest Exchange; Effective Date of Interest Exchange.

(a) A statement of interest exchange must be signed by a domestic acquired limited partnership and delivered to the [Secretary of State] for filing.

(b) A statement of interest exchange must contain:

(1) the name of the acquired limited partnership;

(2) the name, jurisdiction of formation, and type of entity of the acquiring entity;

(3) a statement that the plan of interest exchange was approved by the acquired limited partnership in accordance with this [part]; and

(4) any amendments to the acquired limited partnership's certificate of limited partnership approved as part of the plan of interest exchange.

(c) In addition to the requirements of subsection (b), a statement of interest exchange may contain any other provision not prohibited by law.

(d) A plan of interest exchange that is signed by a domestic acquired limited partnership and meets all the requirements of subsection (b) may be delivered to the [Secretary of State] for filing instead of a statement of interest exchange and on filing has the same effect. If a plan of interest exchange is filed as provided in this subsection, references in this [article] to a statement of interest exchange refer to the plan of interest exchange filed under this subsection.

(e) An interest exchange becomes effective when the statement of interest exchange is effective.

§ 1136. Effect of Interest Exchange.

(a) When an interest exchange in which the acquired entity is a domestic limited partnership becomes effective:

(1) the interests in the acquired partnership which are the subject of the interest exchange are converted, and the partners holding those interests are entitled only to the rights provided to them under the plan of interest exchange and to any appraisal rights they have under § 1106;

(2) the acquiring entity becomes the interest holder of the interests in the acquired partnership stated in the plan of interest exchange to be acquired by the acquiring entity;

(3) the certificate of limited partnership of the acquired partnership is amended to the extent provided in the statement of interest exchange; and

(4) the provisions of the partnership agreement of the acquired partnership that are to be in a record, if any, are amended to the extent provided in the plan of interest exchange.

(b) Except as otherwise provided in the certificate of limited partnership or partnership agreement of a domestic acquired limited partnership, the interest exchange does not give rise to any rights that a partner or third party would have upon a dissolution, liquidation, or winding up of the acquired partnership.

(c) When an interest exchange becomes effective, a person that did not have interest holder liability with respect to a domestic acquired limited partnership and becomes subject to interest holder liability with respect to a domestic entity as a result of the interest exchange has interest holder liability only to the extent provided by the organic law of the entity and only for those debts, obligations, and other liabilities that are incurred after the interest exchange becomes effective.

(d) When an interest exchange becomes effective, the interest holder liability of a person that ceases to hold an interest in a domestic acquired limited partnership with respect to which the person had interest holder liability is subject to the following rules:

(1) The interest exchange does not discharge any interest holder liability under this [act] to the extent the interest holder liability was incurred before the interest exchange became effective.

(2) The person does not have interest holder liability under this [act] for any debt, obligation, or other liability that is incurred after the interest exchange becomes effective.

(3) This [act] continues to apply to the release, collection, or discharge of any interest holder liability preserved under paragraph (1) as if the interest exchange had not occurred.

(4) The person has whatever rights of contribution from any other person as are provided by

this [act], law other than this [act], or the partnership agreement of the domestic acquired partnership with respect to any interest holder liability preserved under paragraph (1) as if the interest exchange had not occurred.

[Part] 4. Conversion

§ 1141. Conversion Authorized.

(a) By complying with this [part], a domestic limited partnership may become:

(1) a domestic entity that is a different type of entity; or

(2) a foreign entity that is a different type of entity, if the conversion is authorized by the law of the foreign entity's jurisdiction of formation.

(b) By complying with the provisions of this [part] applicable to foreign entities, a foreign entity that is not a foreign limited partnership may become a domestic limited partnership if the conversion is authorized by the law of the foreign entity's jurisdiction of formation.

(c) If a protected agreement contains a provision that applies to a merger of a domestic limited partnership but does not refer to a conversion, the provision applies to a conversion of the partnership as if the conversion were a merger until the provision is amended after [the effective date of this [act]].

§ 1142. Plan of Conversion.

(a) A domestic limited partnership may convert to a different type of entity under this [part] by approving a plan of conversion. The plan must be in a record and contain:

(1) the name of the converting limited partnership;

(2) the name, jurisdiction of formation, and type of entity of the converted entity;

(3) the manner of converting the interests in the converting limited partnership into interests, securities, obligations, money, other property, rights to acquire interests or securities, or any combination of the foregoing;

(4) the proposed public organic record of the converted entity if it will be a filing entity;

(5) the full text of the private organic rules of the converted entity which are proposed to be in a record;

(6) the other terms and conditions of the conversion; and

(7) any other provision required by the law of this state or the partnership agreement of the converting limited partnership.

(b) In addition to the requirements of subsection (a), a plan of conversion may contain any other provision not prohibited by law.

§ 1143. Approval of Conversion.

(a) A plan of conversion is not effective unless it has been approved:

(1) by a domestic converting limited partnership, by all the partners of the limited partnership entitled to vote on or consent to any matter; and

(2) in a record, by each partner of a domestic converting limited partnership which will have interest holder liability for debts, obligations, and other liabilities that are incurred after the conversion becomes effective, unless:

(A) the partnership agreement of the partnership provides in a record for the approval of a conversion or a merger in which some or all of its partners become subject to interest holder liability by the affirmative vote or consent of fewer than all the partners; and

(B) the partner voted for or consented in a record to that provision of the partnership agreement or became a partner after the adoption of that provision.

(b) A conversion involving a domestic converting entity that is not a limited partnership is not effective unless it is approved by the domestic converting entity in accordance with its organic law.

(c) A conversion of a foreign converting entity is not effective unless it is approved by the foreign entity in accordance with the law of the foreign entity's jurisdiction of formation.

§ 1144. Amendment or Abandonment of Plan of Conversion.

(a) A plan of conversion of a domestic converting limited partnership may be amended:

(1) in the same manner as the plan was approved, if the plan does not provide for the manner in which it may be amended; or

(2) by its partners in the manner provided in the plan, but a partner that was entitled to vote on or consent to approval of the conversion is entitled to vote on or consent to any amendment of the plan that will change:

(A) the amount or kind of interests, securities, obligations, money, other property, rights to acquire interests or securities, or any combination of the foregoing, to be received by any of the partners of the converting partnership under the plan;

(B) the public organic record, if any, or private organic rules of the converted entity which will be in effect immediately after the conversion becomes effective, except for changes that do not require approval of the interest holders of the converted entity under its organic law or organic rules; or

(C) any other terms or conditions of the plan, if the change would adversely affect the partner in any material respect.

(b) After a plan of conversion has been approved by a domestic converting limited partnership and before a statement of conversion becomes effective, the plan may be abandoned as provided in the plan. Unless prohibited by the plan, a domestic converting limited partnership may abandon the plan in the same manner as the plan was approved.

(c) If a plan of conversion is abandoned after a statement of conversion has been delivered to the [Secretary of State] for filing and before the statement becomes effective, a statement of abandonment, signed by the converting entity, must be delivered to the [Secretary of State] for filing before the statement of conversion becomes effective. The statement of abandonment takes effect on filing, and the conversion is abandoned and does not become effective. The statement of abandonment must contain:

(1) the name of the converting limited partnership;

(2) the date on which the statement of conversion was filed by the [Secretary of State]; and

(3) a statement that the conversion has been abandoned in accordance with this section.

§ 1145. Statement of Conversion; Effective Date of Conversion.

(a) A statement of conversion must be signed by the converting entity and delivered to the [Secretary of State] for filing.

(b) A statement of conversion must contain:

(1) the name, jurisdiction of formation, and type of entity of the converting entity;

(2) the name, jurisdiction of formation, and type of entity of the converted entity;

(3) if the converting entity is a domestic limited partnership, a statement that the plan of conversion was approved in accordance with this [part] or, if the converting entity is a foreign entity, a statement that the conversion was approved by the foreign entity in accordance with the law of its jurisdiction of formation;

(4) if the converted entity is a domestic filing entity, its public organic record, as an attachment; and

(5) if the converted entity is a domestic limited liability partnership, its statement of qualification, as an attachment.

(c) In addition to the requirements of subsection (b), a statement of conversion may contain any other provision not prohibited by law.

(d) If the converted entity is a domestic entity, its public organic record, if any, must satisfy the requirements of the law of this state, except that the public organic record does not need to be signed.

(e) A plan of conversion that is signed by a domestic converting limited partnership and meets all the requirements of subsection (b) may be delivered to the [Secretary of State] for filing instead of a state-

ment of conversion and on filing has the same effect. If a plan of conversion is filed as provided in this subsection, references in this [article] to a statement of conversion refer to the plan of conversion filed under this subsection.

(f) If the converted entity is a domestic limited partnership, the conversion becomes effective when the statement of conversion is effective. In all other cases, the conversion becomes effective on the later of:

(1) the date and time provided by the organic law of the converted entity; and

(2) when the statement is effective.

§ 1146. Effect of Conversion.

(a) When a conversion becomes effective:

(1) the converted entity is:

(A) organized under and subject to the organic law of the converted entity; and

(B) the same entity without interruption as the converting entity;

(2) all property of the converting entity continues to be vested in the converted entity without transfer, reversion, or impairment;

(3) all debts, obligations, and other liabilities of the converting entity continue as debts, obligations, and other liabilities of the converted entity;

(4) except as otherwise provided by law or the plan of conversion, all the rights, privileges, immunities, powers, and purposes of the converting entity remain in the converted entity;

(5) the name of the converted entity may be substituted for the name of the converting entity in any pending action or proceeding;

(6) the certificate of limited partnership of the converted entity becomes effective;

(7) the provisions of the partnership agreement of the converted entity which are to be in a record, if any, approved as part of the plan of conversion become effective; and

(8) the interests in the converting entity are converted, and the interest holders of the con-

verting entity are entitled only to the rights provided to them under the plan of conversion and to any appraisal rights they have under § 1106.

(b) Except as otherwise provided in the partnership agreement of a domestic converting limited partnership, the conversion does not give rise to any rights that a partner or third party would have upon a dissolution, liquidation, or winding up of the converting entity.

(c) When a conversion becomes effective, a person that did not have interest holder liability with respect to the converting entity and becomes subject to interest holder liability with respect to a domestic entity as a result of the conversion has interest holder liability only to the extent provided by the organic law of the entity and only for those debts, obligations, and other liabilities that are incurred after the conversion becomes effective.

(d) When a conversion becomes effective, the interest holder liability of a person that ceases to hold an interest in a domestic converting limited partnership with respect to which the person had interest holder liability is subject to the following rules:

(1) The conversion does not discharge any interest holder liability under this [act] to the extent the interest holder liability was incurred before the conversion became effective.

(2) The person does not have interest holder liability under this [act] for any debt, obligation, or other liability that is incurred after the conversion becomes effective.

(3) This [act] continues to apply to the release, collection, or discharge of any interest holder liability preserved under paragraph (1) as if the conversion had not occurred.

(4) The person has whatever rights of contribution from any other person as are provided by this [act], law other than this [act], or the organic rules of the converting entity with respect to any interest holder liability preserved under paragraph (1) as if the conversion had not occurred.

(e) When a conversion becomes effective, a foreign entity that is the converted entity may be served with process in this state for the collection and enforcement of any of its debts, obligations, and other liabilities as provided in § 121.

(f) If the converting entity is a registered foreign entity, its registration to do business in this state is canceled when the conversion becomes effective.

(g) A conversion does not require the entity to wind up its affairs and does not constitute or cause the dissolution of the entity.

[Part] 5. Domestication

§ 1151. Domestication Authorized.

(a) By complying with this [part], a domestic limited partnership may become a foreign limited partnership if the domestication is authorized by the law of the foreign jurisdiction.

(b) By complying with the provisions of this [part] applicable to foreign limited partnerships, a foreign limited partnership may become a domestic limited partnership if the domestication is authorized by the law of the foreign limited partnership's jurisdiction of formation.

(c) If a protected agreement contains a provision that applies to a merger of a domestic limited partnership but does not refer to a domestication, the provision applies to a domestication of the limited partnership as if the domestication were a merger until the provision is amended after [the effective date of this [act]].

§ 1152. Plan of Domestication.

(a) A domestic limited partnership may become a foreign limited partnership in a domestication by approving a plan of domestication. The plan must be in a record and contain:

(1) the name of the domesticating limited partnership;

(2) the name and jurisdiction of formation of the domesticated limited partnership;

(3) the manner of converting the interests in the domesticating limited partnership into interests, securities, obligations, money, other property, rights to acquire interests or securities, or any combination of the foregoing;

(4) the proposed certificate of limited partnership of the domesticated limited partnership;

(5) the full text of the provisions of the partnership agreement of the domesticated limited partnership, that are proposed to be in a record;

(6) the other terms and conditions of the domestication; and

(7) any other provision required by the law of this state or the partnership agreement of the domesticating limited partnership.

(b) In addition to the requirements of subsection (a), a plan of domestication may contain any other provision not prohibited by law.

§ 1153. Approval of Domestication.

(a) A plan of domestication of a domestic domesticating limited partnership is not effective unless it has been approved:

(1) by all the partners entitled to vote on or consent to any matter; and

(2) in a record, by each partner that will have interest holder liability for debts, obligations, and other liabilities that are incurred after the domestication becomes effective, unless:

(A) the partnership agreement of the domesticating partnership in a record provides for the approval of a domestication or merger in which some or all of its partners become subject to interest holder liability by the affirmative vote or consent of fewer than all the partners; and

(B) the partner voted for or consented in a record to that provision of the partnership agreement or became a partner after the adoption of that provision.

(b) A domestication of a foreign domesticating limited partnership is not effective unless it is approved in accordance with the law of the foreign limited partnership's jurisdiction of formation.

§ 1154. Amendment or Abandonment of Plan of Domestication.

(a) A plan of domestication of a domestic domesticating limited partnership may be amended:

(1) in the same manner as the plan was approved, if the plan does not provide for the manner in which it may be amended; or

(2) by its partners in the manner provided in the plan, but a partner that was entitled to vote on or consent to approval of the domestication is entitled to vote on or consent to any amendment of the plan that will change:

(A) the amount or kind of interests, securities, obligations, money, other property, rights to acquire interests or securities, or any combination of the foregoing, to be received by any of the partners of the domesticating limited partnership under the plan;

(B) the certificate of limited partnership or partnership agreement of the domesticated limited partnership that will be in effect immediately after the domestication becomes effective, except for changes that do not require approval of the partners of the domesticated limited partnership under its organic law or partnership agreement; or

(C) any other terms or conditions of the plan, if the change would adversely affect the partner in any material respect.

(b) After a plan of domestication has been approved by a domestic domesticating limited partnership and before a statement of domestication becomes effective, the plan may be abandoned as provided in the plan. Unless prohibited by the plan, a domestic domesticating limited partnership may abandon the plan in the same manner as the plan was approved.

(c) If a plan of domestication is abandoned after a statement of domestication has been delivered to the [Secretary of State] for filing and before the statement becomes effective, a statement of abandonment, signed by the domesticating limited partnership, must be delivered to the [Secretary of

State] for filing before the statement of domestication becomes effective. The statement of abandonment takes effect on filing, and the domestication is abandoned and does not become effective. The statement of abandonment must contain:

(1) the name of the domesticating limited partnership;

(2) the date on which the statement of domestication was filed by the [Secretary of State]; and

(3) a statement that the domestication has been abandoned in accordance with this section.

§ 1155. Statement of Domestication; Effective Date of Domestication.

(a) A statement of domestication must be signed by the domesticating limited partnership and delivered to the [Secretary of State] for filing.

(b) A statement of domestication must contain:

(1) the name and jurisdiction of formation of the domesticating limited partnership;

(2) the name and jurisdiction of formation of the domesticated limited partnership;

(3) if the domesticating limited partnership is a domestic limited partnership, a statement that the plan of domestication was approved in accordance with this [part] or, if the domesticating limited partnership is a foreign limited partnership, a statement that the domestication was approved in accordance with the law of its jurisdiction of formation; and

(4) the certificate of limited partnership of the domesticated limited partnership, as an attachment.

(c) In addition to the requirements of subsection (b), a statement of domestication may contain any other provision not prohibited by law.

(d) The certificate of limited partnership of a domesticated domestic limited partnership must satisfy the requirements of this [act], but the certificate does not need to be signed.

(e) A plan of domestication that is signed by a domesticating domestic limited partnership and meets all the requirements of subsection (b) may be delivered to the [Secretary of State] for filing instead of a statement of domestication and on filing has the same effect. If a plan of domestication is filed as provided in this subsection, references in this [article] to a statement of domestication refer to the plan of domestication filed under this subsection.

(f) If the domesticated entity is a domestic limited partnership, the domestication becomes effective when the statement of domestication is effective. If the domesticated entity is a foreign limited partnership, the domestication becomes effective on the later of:

(1) the date and time provided by the organic law of the domesticated entity; and

(2) when the statement is effective.

§ 1156. Effect of Domestication.

(a) When a domestication becomes effective:

(1) the domesticated entity is:

(A) organized under and subject to the organic law of the domesticated entity; ; and

(B) the same entity without interruption as the domesticating entity;

(2) all property of the domesticating entity continues to be vested in the domesticated entity without transfer, reversion, or impairment;

(3) all debts, obligations, and other liabilities of the domesticating entity continue as debts, obligations, and other liabilities of the domesticated entity;

(4) except as otherwise provided by law or the plan of domestication, all the rights, privileges, immunities, powers, and purposes of the domesticating entity remain in the domesticated entity;

(5) the name of the domesticated entity may be substituted for the name of the domesticating entity in any pending action or proceeding;

(6) the certificate of limited partnership of the domesticated entity becomes effective;

(7) the provisions of the partnership agreement of the domesticated entity that are to be in a record, if any, approved as part of the plan of domestication become effective; and

(8) the interests in the domesticating entity are converted to the extent and as approved in connection with the domestication, and the partners of the domesticating entity are entitled only to the rights provided to them under the plan of domestication and to any appraisal rights they have under § 1106.

(b) Except as otherwise provided in the organic law or partnership agreement of the domesticating limited partnership, the domestication does not give rise to any rights that an partner or third party would have upon a dissolution, liquidation, or winding up of the domesticating partnership.

(c) When a domestication becomes effective, a person that did not have interest holder liability with respect to the domesticating limited partnership and becomes subject to interest holder liability with respect to a domestic limited partnership as a result of the domestication has interest holder liability only to the extent provided by this [act] and only for those debts, obligations, and other liabilities that are incurred after the domestication becomes effective.

(d) When a domestication becomes effective, the interest holder liability of a person that ceases to hold an interest in a domestic domesticating limited partnership with respect to which the person had interest holder liability is subject to the following rules:

(1) The domestication does not discharge any interest holder liability under this [act] to the extent the interest holder liability was incurred before the domestication became effective.

(2) A person does not have interest holder liability under this [act] for any debt, obligation, or other liability that is incurred after the domestication becomes effective.

(3) This [act] continues to apply to the release, collection, or discharge of any interest holder liability preserved under paragraph (1) as if the domestication had not occurred.

(4) A person has whatever rights of contribution from any other person as are provided by this [act], law other than this [act], or the part-nership agreement of the domestic domesticating limited partnership with respect to any interest holder liability preserved under paragraph (1) as if the domestication had not occurred.

(e) When a domestication becomes effective, a foreign limited partnership that is the domesticated partnership may be served with process in this state for the collection and enforcement of any of its debts, obligations, and other liabilities as provided in § 121.

(f) If the domesticating limited partnership is a registered foreign entity, the registration of the partnership is canceled when the domestication becomes effective.

(g) A domestication does not require a domestic domesticating limited partnership to wind up its affairs and does not constitute or cause the dissolution of the partnership.

[Article] 12. Miscellaneous Provisions

§ 1201. Uniformity of Application and Construction.

In applying and construing this uniform act, consideration must be given to the need to promote uniformity of the law with respect to its subject matter among states that enact it.

§ 1202. Relation to Electronic Signatures in Global and National Commerce Act.

This [act] modifies, limits, and supersedes the Electronic Signatures in Global and National Commerce Act, 15 U.S.C. § 7001 et seq., but does not modify, limit, or supersede § 101(c) of that act, 15 U.S.C. § 7001(c), or authorize electronic delivery of any of the notices described in § 103(b) of that act, 15 U.S.C. § 7003(b).

§ 1203. Savings Clause.

This [act] does not affect an action commenced, proceeding brought, or right accrued before [the effective date of this [act]].

[§ 1204. Severability Clause.

If any provision of this [act] or its application to any person or circumstance is held invalid, the invalidity does not affect other provisions or applications of this [act] which can be given effect without the invalid provision or application, and to this end the provisions of this [act] are severable.]

Legislative Note: Include this section only if this state lacks a general severability statute or decision by the highest court of this state stating a general rule of severability.

§ 1205. Repeals.

The following are repealed:

(1) [the state limited partnership act as [amended, and as] in effect immediately before [the effective date of this [act]].

(2) . . . .

(3) . . . .

§ 1206. Effective Date.

This [act] takes effect ….

Delaware General Corporation Law (2021)

The VisiLaw end of sentence mark has been applied with permission. Patent number US 8,794,972 B2

Table of Contents

Subchapter I. Formation

§ 101. Incorporators; how corporation formed; purposes.

(a) Any person, partnership, association or corporation, singly or jointly with others, and without regard to such person's or entity's residence, domicile or state of incorporation, may incorporate or organize a corporation under this chapter by filing with the Division of Corporations in the Department of State a certificate of incorporation which shall be executed, acknowledged and filed in accordance with § 103 of this title.

(b) A corporation may be incorporated or organized under this chapter to conduct or promote any lawful business or purposes, except as may otherwise be provided by the Constitution or other law of this State.

(c) Corporations for constructing, maintaining and operating public utilities, whether in or outside of this State, may be organized under this chapter, but corporations for constructing, maintaining and operating public utilities within this State shall be subject to, in addition to this chapter, the special provisions and requirements of Title 26 applicable to such corporations.

§ 102. Contents of certificate of incorporation.

(a) The certificate of incorporation shall set forth:

(1) The name of the corporation, which **(i)** shall contain 1 of the words "association," "company," "corporation," "club," "foundation," "fund," "incorporated," "institute," "society," "union," "syndicate," or "limited," (or abbreviations thereof, with or without punctuation), or words (or abbreviations thereof, with or without punctuation) of like import of foreign countries or jurisdictions (provided they are written in roman characters or letters); provided, however, that the Division of Corporations in the Department of State may waive such requirement (unless it determines that such name is, or might otherwise appear to be, that of a natural person) if such corporation executes, acknowledges and files with the Secretary of State in accordance with § 103 of this title a certificate stating that its total assets, as defined in § 503(i) of this title, are not less than $10,000,000, or, in the sole discretion of the Division of Corporations in the Department of State, if the corporation is both a nonprofit nonstock corporation and an association of professionals, **(ii)** shall be such as to distinguish it upon the records in the office of the Division of Corporations in the Department of State from the names that are reserved on such records and from the names on such records of each other corporation, partnership, limited partnership, limited liability company, registered series of a limited liability company, registered series of a limited partnership or statutory trust organized or registered as a domestic or foreign corporation, partnership, limited partnership, limited liability company, registered series of a limited liability company, registered series of a limited partnership or statutory trust under the laws of this State, except with the written consent of the person who has reserved such name or such other foreign corporation or domestic or foreign partnership, limited partnership, limited liability company, registered series of a limited liability company, registered series of a limited partnership or statutory trust, executed, acknowledged and filed with the Secretary of State in accordance with § 103 of this title, or except that, without prejudicing any rights of the person who has reserved such name or such other foreign corporation or domestic or foreign partnership, limited partnership, limited liability company, registered series of a limited liability company, registered series of a limited partnership or statutory trust, the Division of Corporations in the Department of State may waive such requirement if the corporation demonstrates to the satisfaction of the Secretary of State that the corporation or a predecessor entity previously has made substantial use of such name or a substantially similar name, that the corporation has made reasonable efforts to secure such written consent, and that such waiver is in the interest of the State, **(iii)** except as permitted by § 395 of this title, shall not contain the word "trust," and **(iv)** shall not contain the word "bank," or any variation thereof, except for the name of a bank reporting to and under the supervision of the State Bank Commissioner of this State or a subsidiary of a bank or savings association (as those terms are defined in the Federal Deposit Insurance Act, as amended, at 12 U.S.C. § 1813), or a corporation regulated under the Bank Holding Company Act of 1956, as amended, 12 U.S.C. § 1841 et seq., or the Home Owners' Loan Act, as amended, 12 U.S.C. § 1461 et seq.; provided, however, that this section shall not be construed to prevent the use of the word "bank," or any variation thereof, in a context clearly not purporting to refer to a banking business or otherwise likely to mislead the public about the nature of the business of the corporation or to lead to a pattern and practice of abuse that might cause harm to the interests of the public or the State as determined by the Division of Corporations in the Department of State;

(2) The address (which shall be stated in accordance with § 131(c) of this title) of the corporation's registered office in this State, and the name of its registered agent at such address;

(3) The nature of the business or purposes to be conducted or promoted. ■ It shall be sufficient to state, either alone or with other businesses or purposes, that the purpose of the corporation is to engage in any lawful act or activity for which corporations may be organized under the General Corporation Law of Delaware, and by such statement all lawful acts and activities shall be within the purposes of the corporation, except for express limitations, if any;

(4) If the corporation is to be authorized to issue only 1 class of stock, the total number of shares of stock which the corporation shall have authority to issue and the par value of each of such shares, or a statement that all such shares are to be without par value. ■ If the corporation is to be authorized to issue more than 1 class of stock, the certificate of incorporation shall set forth the total number of shares of all classes of stock which the corporation shall have authority to issue and the number of shares of each class and shall specify each class the shares of which are to be without par value and each class the shares of which are to have par value and the par value of the shares of each such class. ■ The certificate of incorporation shall also set forth a statement of the designations and the powers, preferences and rights, and the qualifications, limitations or restrictions thereof, which are permitted by § 151 of this title in respect of any class or classes of stock or any series of any class of stock of the corporation and the fixing of which by the certificate of incorporation is desired, and an express grant of such authority as it may then be desired to grant to the board of directors to fix by resolution or resolutions any thereof that may be desired but which shall not be fixed by the certificate of incorporation. ▪ The foregoing provisions of this paragraph shall not apply to nonstock corporations. ▪ In the case of nonstock corporations, the fact that they are not authorized to issue capital stock shall be stated in the certificate of incorporation. ▪ The conditions of membership, or other criteria for identifying members, of nonstock corporations shall likewise be stated in the certificate of incorporation or the bylaws. ▪ Nonstock corporations shall have members, but failure to have members shall not affect otherwise valid corporate acts or work a forfeiture or dissolution of the corporation. ▪ Nonstock corporations may provide for classes or groups of members having relative rights, powers and duties, and may make provision for the future creation of additional classes or groups of members having such relative rights, powers and duties as may from time to time be established, including rights, powers and duties senior to existing classes and groups of members. ▪ Except as otherwise provided in this chapter, nonstock corporations may also provide that any member or class or group of members shall have full, limited, or no voting rights or powers, including that any member or class or group of members shall have the right to vote on a specified transaction even if that member or class or group of members does not have the right to vote for the election of the members of the governing body of the corporation. ▪ Voting by members of a nonstock corporation may be on a per capita, number, financial interest, class, group, or any other basis set forth. ▪ The provisions referred to in the 3 preceding sentences may be set forth in the certificate of incorporation or the bylaws. ▪ If neither the certificate of incorporation nor the bylaws of a nonstock corporation state the conditions of membership, or other criteria for identifying members, the members of the corporation shall be deemed to be those entitled to vote for the election of the members of the governing body pursuant to the certificate of incorporation or bylaws of such corporation or otherwise until thereafter otherwise provided by the certificate of incorporation or the bylaws;

(5) The name and mailing address of the incorporator or incorporators;

(6) If the powers of the incorporator or incorporators are to terminate upon the filing of the certificate of incorporation, the names and mailing addresses of the persons who are to serve as directors until the first annual meeting of stockholders or until their successors are elected and qualify.

(b) In addition to the matters required to be set forth in the certificate of incorporation by subsection (a) of this section, the certificate of incorporation may also contain any or all of the following matters:

(1) Any provision for the management of the business and for the conduct of the affairs of the corporation, and any provision creating, defining, limiting and regulating the powers of the corporation, the directors, and the stockholders, or any class of the stockholders, or the governing body, members, or any class or group of members of a nonstock corporation; if such provisions are not contrary to the laws of this State. ▪ Any provision which is required or permitted by any section of this chapter to be stated in the bylaws may instead be stated in the certificate of incorporation;

(2) The following provisions, in haec verba,

(i), for a corporation other than a nonstock corporation, viz:

Whenever a compromise or arrangement is proposed between this corporation and its creditors or any class of them and/or between this corporation and its stockholders or any class of them, any court of equitable jurisdiction within the State of Delaware may, on the application in a summary way of this corporation or of any creditor or stockholder thereof or on the application of any receiver or receivers appointed for this corporation under § 291 of Title 8 of the Delaware Code or on the application of trustees in dissolution or of any receiver or receivers appointed for this corporation under § 279 of Title 8 of the Delaware Code order a meeting of the creditors or class of creditors, and/or of the stockholders or class of stockholders of this corporation, as the case may be, to be summoned in such manner as the said court directs. ▪ If a majority in number representing three fourths in value of the creditors or class of creditors, and/or of the stockholders or class of stockholders of this corporation, as the case may be, agree to any compromise or arrangement and to any reorganization of this corporation as consequence of such compromise or arrangement, the said compromise or arrangement and the said reorganization shall, if sanctioned by the court to which the said application has been made, be binding on all the creditors or class of creditors, and/or on all the stockholders or class of stockholders, of this corporation, as the case may be, and also on this corporation; or

(ii), for a nonstock corporation, viz:

Whenever a compromise or arrangement is proposed between this corporation and its creditors or any class of them and/or between this corporation and its members or any class of them, any court of equitable jurisdiction within the State of Delaware may, on the application in a summary way of this corporation or of any creditor or member thereof or on the application of any receiver or receivers appointed for this corporation under § 291 of Title 8 of the Delaware Code or on the application of trustees in dissolution or of any receiver or receivers appointed for this corporation under § 279 of Title 8 of the Delaware Code order a meeting of the creditors or class of creditors, and/or of the members or class of members of this corporation, as the case may be, to be

summoned in such manner as the said court directs. ▪ If a majority in number representing three fourths in value of the creditors or class of creditors, and/or of the members or class of members of this corporation, as the case may be, agree to any compromise or arrangement and to any reorganization of this corporation as consequence of such compromise or arrangement, the said compromise or arrangement and the said reorganization shall, if sanctioned by the court to which the said application has been made, be binding on all the creditors or class of creditors, and/or on all the members or class of members, of this corporation, as the case may be, and also on this corporation;

(3) Such provisions as may be desired granting to the holders of the stock of the corporation, or the holders of any class or series of a class thereof, the preemptive right to subscribe to any or all additional issues of stock of the corporation of any or all classes or series thereof, or to any securities of the corporation convertible into such stock. ▪ No stockholder shall have any preemptive right to subscribe to an additional issue of stock or to any security convertible into such stock unless, and except to the extent that, such right is expressly granted to such stockholder in the certificate of incorporation. ▪ All such rights in existence on July 3, 1967, shall remain in existence unaffected by this paragraph unless and until changed or terminated by appropriate action which expressly provides for the change or termination;

(4) Provisions requiring for any corporate action, the vote of a larger portion of the stock or of any class or series thereof, or of any other securities having voting power, or a larger number of the directors, than is required by this chapter;

(5) A provision limiting the duration of the corporation's existence to a specified date; otherwise, the corporation shall have perpetual existence;

(6) A provision imposing personal liability for the debts of the corporation on its stockholders to a specified extent and upon specified conditions; otherwise, the stockholders of a corporation shall not be personally liable for the payment of the corporation's debts except as they may be liable by reason of their own conduct or acts;

(7) A provision eliminating or limiting the personal liability of a director to the corporation or its stockholders for monetary damages for breach of fiduciary duty as a director, provided that such provision shall not eliminate or limit the liability of a director: **(i)** For any breach of the director's duty of loyalty to the corporation or its stockholders; **(ii)** for acts or omissions not in good faith or which involve intentional misconduct or a knowing violation of law; **(iii)** under § 174 of this title; or **(iv)** for any transaction from which the director derived an improper personal benefit. ▪ No such provision shall eliminate or limit the liability of a director for any act or omission occurring prior to the date when such provision becomes effective. ▪ An amendment, repeal or elimination of such a provision shall not affect its application with respect to an act or omission by a director occurring before such amendment, repeal or elimination unless the provision provides otherwise at the time of such act or omission. ▪ All references in this paragraph to a director shall also be deemed to refer to such other person or persons, if any, who, pursuant to a provision of the certificate of incorporation in accordance with § 141(a) of this title, exercise or perform any of the powers or duties otherwise conferred or imposed upon the board of directors by this title.

(c) It shall not be necessary to set forth in the certificate of incorporation any of the powers conferred on corporations by this chapter.

(d) Except for provisions included pursuant to paragraphs (a)(1), (a)(2), (a)(5), (a)(6), (b)(2), (b)(5), (b)(7) of this section, and provisions included pursuant to paragraph (a)(4) of this section specifying the classes, number of shares, and par value of shares a corporation other than a nonstock corporation is authorized to issue, any provision of the certificate of incorporation may be made dependent upon facts ascertainable outside such instrument, provided that the manner in which such facts shall operate upon the provision is clearly and explicitly set forth therein. ▪ The term "facts," as used in this subsection, includes, but is not limited to, the occurrence of any event, including a determination or action by any person or body, including the corporation.

(e) The exclusive right to the use of a name that is available for use by a domestic or foreign corporation may be reserved by or on behalf of:

(1) Any person intending to incorporate or organize a corporation with that name under this chapter or contemplating such incorporation or organization;

(2) Any domestic corporation or any foreign corporation qualified to do business in the State of Delaware, in either case, intending to change its name or contemplating such a change;

(3) Any foreign corporation intending to qualify to do business in the State of Delaware and adopt that name or contemplating such qualification and adoption; and

(4) Any person intending to organize a foreign corporation and have it qualify to do business in the State of Delaware and adopt that name or contemplating such organization, qualification and adoption.

The reservation of a specified name may be made by filing with the Secretary of State an application, executed by the applicant, certifying that the reservation is made by or on behalf of a domestic corporation, foreign corporation or other person described in paragraphs (e)(1)-(4) of this section above, and specifying the name to be reserved and the name and address of the applicant. ▪ If the Secretary of State finds that the name is available for use by a domestic or foreign corporation, the Secretary shall reserve the name for the use of the applicant for a period of 120 days. ▪ The same applicant may renew for successive 120-day periods a reservation of a specified name by filing with the

Secretary of State, prior to the expiration of such reservation (or renewal thereof), an application for renewal of such reservation, executed by the applicant, certifying that the reservation is renewed by or on behalf of a domestic corporation, foreign corporation or other person described in paragraphs (e)(1)-(4) of this section above and specifying the name reservation to be renewed and the name and address of the applicant. ▪ The right to the exclusive use of a reserved name may be transferred to any other person by filing in the office of the Secretary of State a notice of the transfer, executed by the applicant for whom the name was reserved, specifying the name reservation to be transferred and the name and address of the transferee. ▪ The reservation of a specified name may be cancelled by filing with the Secretary of State a notice of cancellation, executed by the applicant or transferee, specifying the name reservation to be cancelled and the name and address of the applicant or transferee. ▪ Unless the Secretary of State finds that any application, application for renewal, notice of transfer, or notice of cancellation filed with the Secretary of State as required by this subsection does not conform to law, upon receipt of all filing fees required by law the Secretary of State shall prepare and return to the person who filed such instrument a copy of the filed instrument with a notation thereon of the action taken by the Secretary of State. ▪ A fee as set forth in § 391 of this title shall be paid at the time of the reservation of any name, at the time of the renewal of any such reservation and at the time of the filing of a notice of the transfer or cancellation of any such reservation.

(f) The certificate of incorporation may not contain any provision that would impose liability on a stockholder for the attorneys' fees or expenses of the corporation or any other party in connection with an internal corporate claim, as defined in § 115 of this title.

§ 103. Execution, acknowledgment, filing, recording and effective date of original certificate of incorporation and other instruments; exceptions.

(a) Whenever any instrument is to be filed with the Secretary of State or in accordance with this section or chapter, such instrument shall be executed as follows:

(1) The certificate of incorporation, and any other instrument to be filed before the election of the initial board of directors if the initial directors were not named in the certificate of incorporation, shall be signed by the incorporator or incorporators (or, in the case of any such other instrument, such incorporator's or incorporators' successors and assigns). ▪ If any incorporator is not available then any such other instrument may be signed, with the same effect as if such incorporator had signed it, by any person for whom or on whose behalf such incorporator, in executing the certificate of incorporation, was acting directly or indirectly as employee or agent, provided that such other instrument shall state that such incorporator is not available and the reason therefor, that such incorporator in executing the certificate of incorporation was acting directly or indirectly as employee or agent for or on behalf of such person, and that such person's signature on such instrument is otherwise authorized and not wrongful.

(2) All other instruments shall be signed:

a. By any authorized officer of the corporation; or

b. If it shall appear from the instrument that there are no such officers, then by a majority of the directors or by such directors as may be designated by the board; or

c. If it shall appear from the instrument that there are no such officers or directors, then by the holders of record, or such of them as may be designated by the holders of record, of a majority of all outstanding shares of stock; or

d. By the holders of record of all outstanding shares of stock.

(b) Whenever this chapter requires any instrument to be acknowledged, such requirement is satisfied by either:

(1) The formal acknowledgment by the person or 1 of the persons signing the instrument that it is such person's act and deed or the act and deed of the corporation, and that the facts stated therein are true. ▪ Such acknowledgment shall be made before a person who is authorized by the law of the place of execution to take acknowledgments of deeds. ▪ If such person has a seal of office such person shall affix it to the instrument.

(2) The signature, without more, of the person or persons signing the instrument, in which case such signature or signatures shall constitute the affirmation or acknowledgment of the signatory, under penalties of perjury, that the instrument is such person's act and deed or the act and deed of the corporation, and that the facts stated therein are true.

(c) Whenever any instrument is to be filed with the Secretary of State or in accordance with this section or chapter, such requirement means that:

(1) The signed instrument shall be delivered to the office of the Secretary of State;

(2) All taxes and fees authorized by law to be collected by the Secretary of State in connection with the filing of the instrument shall be tendered to the Secretary of State; and

(3) Upon delivery of the instrument, the Secretary of State shall record the date and time of its delivery. ▪ Upon such delivery and tender of the required taxes and fees, the Secretary of State shall certify that the instrument has been filed in the Secretary of State's office by endorsing upon the signed instrument the word "Filed", and the date and time of its filing. ▪ This endorsement is the "filing date" of the instrument, and is conclusive of the date and time of its filing in the absence of actual fraud. ▪ The Secretary of State shall file and index the en-

dorsed instrument. ▪ Except as provided in paragraph (c)(4) of this section and in subsection (i) of this section, such filing date of an instrument shall be the date and time of delivery of the instrument.

(4) Upon request made upon or prior to delivery, the Secretary of State may, to the extent deemed practicable, establish as the filing date of an instrument a date and time after its delivery. ▪ If the Secretary of State refuses to file any instrument due to an error, omission or other imperfection, the Secretary of State may hold such instrument in suspension, and in such event, upon delivery of a replacement instrument in proper form for filing and tender of the required taxes and fees within 5 business days after notice of such suspension is given to the filer, the Secretary of State shall establish as the filing date of such instrument the date and time that would have been the filing date of the rejected instrument had it been accepted for filing. ▪ The Secretary of State shall not issue a certificate of good standing with respect to any corporation with an instrument held in suspension pursuant to this subsection. ▪ The Secretary of State may establish as the filing date of an instrument the date and time at which information from such instrument is entered pursuant to paragraph (c)(8) of this section if such instrument is delivered on the same date and within 4 hours after such information is entered.

(5) The Secretary of State, acting as agent for the recorders of each of the counties, shall collect and deposit in a separate account established exclusively for that purpose a county assessment fee with respect to each filed instrument and shall thereafter weekly remit from such account to the recorder of each of the said counties the amount or amounts of such fees as provided for in paragraph (c)(6) of this section or as elsewhere provided by law. ▪ Said fees shall be for the purposes of defraying certain costs incurred by the counties in merging the information and images of such filed documents with the document information systems of each of the recorder's offices in the counties and in retrieving, maintaining and displaying such information and images in the offices of the recorders and at remote locations in each of such counties. ▪ In consideration for its acting as the agent for the recorders with respect to the collection and payment of the county assessment fees, the Secretary of State shall retain and pay over to the General Fund of the State an administrative charge of 1 percent of the total fees collected.

(6) The assessment fee to the counties shall be $24 for each 1-page instrument filed with the Secretary of State in accordance with this section and $9.00 for each additional page for instruments with more than 1 page. ▪ The recorder's office to receive the assessment fee shall be the recorder's office in the county in which the corporation's registered office in this State is, or is to be, located, except that an assessment fee shall not be charged for either a certificate of dissolution qualifying for treatment under § 391(a)(5)b. of this title or a document filed in accordance with subchapter XVI of this chapter.

(7) The Secretary of State, acting as agent, shall collect and deposit in a separate account established exclusively for that purpose a courthouse municipality fee with respect to each filed instrument and shall thereafter monthly remit funds from such account to the treasuries of the municipalities designated in § 301 of Title 10. ▪ Said fees shall be for the purposes of defraying certain costs incurred by such municipalities in hosting the primary locations for the Delaware courts. ▪ The fee to such municipalities shall be $20 for each instrument filed with the Secretary of State in accordance with this section. ▪ The municipality to receive the fee shall be the municipality designated in § 301 of Title 10 in the county in which the corporation's registered office in this State is, or is to be, located, except that a fee shall not be charged for a certificate of dissolution qualifying for treatment under § 391(a)(5)b. of this title, a resignation of agent without appointment

of a successor under § 136 of this title, or a document filed in accordance with subchapter XVI of this chapter.

(8) The Secretary of State shall cause to be entered such information from each instrument as the Secretary of State deems appropriate into the Delaware Corporation Information System or any system which is a successor thereto in the office of the Secretary of State, and such information and a copy of each such instrument shall be permanently maintained as a public record on a suitable medium. ▪ The Secretary of State is authorized to grant direct access to such system to registered agents subject to the execution of an operating agreement between the Secretary of State and such registered agent. ▪ Any registered agent granted such access shall demonstrate the existence of policies to ensure that information entered into the system accurately reflects the content of instruments in the possession of the registered agent at the time of entry.

(d) Any instrument filed in accordance with subsection (c) of this section shall be effective upon its filing date. ▪ Any instrument may provide that it is not to become effective until a specified time subsequent to the time it is filed, but such time shall not be later than a time on the ninetieth day after the date of its filing. ▪ If any instrument filed in accordance with subsection (c) of this section provides for a future effective date or time and if the transaction is terminated or its terms are amended to change the future effective date or time prior to the future effective date or time, the instrument shall be terminated or amended by the filing, prior to the future effective date or time set forth in such instrument, of a certificate of termination or amendment of the original instrument, executed in accordance with subsection (a) of this section, which shall identify the instrument which has been terminated or amended and shall state that the instrument has been terminated or the manner in which it has been amended.

(e) If another section of this chapter specifically prescribes a manner of executing, acknowledging or filing a specified instrument or a time when such instrument shall become effective which differs from the corresponding provisions of this section, then such other section shall govern.

(f) Whenever any instrument authorized to be filed with the Secretary of State under any provision of this title, has been so filed and is an inaccurate record of the corporate action therein referred to, or was defectively or erroneously executed, sealed or acknowledged, the instrument may be corrected by filing with the Secretary of State a certificate of correction of the instrument which shall be executed, acknowledged and filed in accordance with this section. ▪ The certificate of correction shall specify the inaccuracy or defect to be corrected and shall set forth the portion of the instrument in corrected form. ▪ In lieu of filing a certificate of correction the instrument may be corrected by filing with the Secretary of State a corrected instrument which shall be executed, acknowledged and filed in accordance with this section. ▪ The corrected instrument shall be specifically designated as such in its heading, shall specify the inaccuracy or defect to be corrected, and shall set forth the entire instrument in corrected form. ▪ An instrument corrected in accordance with this section shall be effective as of the date the original instrument was filed, except as to those persons who are substantially and adversely affected by the correction and as to those persons the instrument as corrected shall be effective from the filing date.

(g) Notwithstanding that any instrument authorized to be filed with the Secretary of State under this title is when filed inaccurately, defectively or erroneously executed, sealed or acknowledged, or otherwise defective in any respect, the Secretary of State shall have no liability to any person for the preclearance for filing, the acceptance for filing or the filing and indexing of such instrument by the Secretary of State.

(h) Any signature on any instrument authorized to be filed with the Secretary of State under this title may be a facsimile, a conformed signature or an electronically transmitted signature.

(i) (1) If:

a. Together with the actual delivery of an instrument and tender of the required taxes and fees, there is delivered to the Secretary of State a separate affidavit (which in its heading shall be designated as an "affidavit of extraordinary condition") attesting, on the basis of personal knowledge of the affiant or a reliable source of knowledge identified in the affidavit, that an earlier effort to deliver such instrument and tender such taxes and fees was made in good faith, specifying the nature, date and time of such good faith effort and requesting that the Secretary of State establish such date and time as the filing date of such instrument; or

b. Upon the actual delivery of an instrument and tender of the required taxes and fees, the Secretary of State in the Secretary's discretion provides a written waiver of the requirement for such an affidavit stating that it appears to the Secretary of State that an earlier effort to deliver such instrument and tender such taxes and fees was made in good faith and specifying the date and time of such effort; and

c. The Secretary of State determines that an extraordinary condition existed at such date and time, that such earlier effort was unsuccessful as a result of the existence of such extraordinary condition, and that such actual delivery and tender were made within a reasonable period (not to exceed 2 business days) after the cessation of such extraordinary condition,

then the Secretary of State may establish such date and time as the filing date of such instrument. ▪ No fee shall be paid to the Secretary of State for receiving an affidavit of extraordinary condition.

(2) For purposes of this subsection, an "extraordinary condition" means: any emergency resulting from an attack on, invasion or occupation by foreign military forces of, or disaster, catastrophe, war or other armed conflict, revolution or insurrection, or rioting or civil commotion in, the United States or a locality in which the Secretary of State conducts its business or in which the good faith effort to deliver the instrument and tender the required taxes and fees is made, or the immediate threat of any of the foregoing; or any malfunction or outage of the electrical or telephone service to the Secretary of State's office, or weather or other condition in or about a locality in which the Secretary of State conducts its business, as a result of which the Secretary of State's office is not open for the purpose of the filing of instruments under this chapter or such filing cannot be effected without extraordinary effort. ▪ The Secretary of State may require such proof as it deems necessary to make the determination required under paragraph (i)(1)c. of this section, and any such determination shall be conclusive in the absence of actual fraud.

(3) If the Secretary of State establishes the filing date of an instrument pursuant to this subsection, the date and time of delivery of the affidavit of extraordinary condition or the date and time of the Secretary of State's written waiver of such affidavit shall be endorsed on such affidavit or waiver and such affidavit or waiver, so endorsed, shall be attached to the filed instrument to which it relates. ▪ Such filed instrument shall be effective as of the date and time established as the filing date by the Secretary of State pursuant to this subsection, except as to those persons who are substantially and adversely affected by such establishment and, as to those persons, the instrument shall be effective from the date and time endorsed on the affidavit of extraordinary condition or written waiver attached thereto.

(j) Notwithstanding any other provision of this chapter, it shall not be necessary for any corporation to amend its certificate of incorporation, or any other document, that has been filed prior to August 1, 2011, to comply with § 131(c) of this title, provided that any certificate or other document filed under this chapter on or after August 1, 2011, and changing the address of a registered office shall comply with § 131(c) of this title.

§ 104. Certificate of incorporation; definition.

The term "certificate of incorporation," as used in this chapter, unless the context requires otherwise, includes not only the original certificate of incorporation filed to create a corporation but also all other certificates, agreements of merger or consolidation, plans of reorganization, or other instruments, howsoever designated, which are filed pursuant to § 102, §§ 133-136, § 151, §§ 241-243, § 245, §§ 251-258, §§ 263-264, § 267, § 303, §§ 311-313, or any other section of this title, and which have the effect of amending or supplementing in some respect a corporation's certificate of incorporation.

§ 105. Certificate of incorporation and other certificates; evidence.

A copy of a certificate of incorporation, or a restated certificate of incorporation, or of any other certificate which has been filed in the office of the Secretary of State as required by any provision of this title shall, when duly certified by the Secretary of State, be received in all courts, public offices and official bodies as prima facie evidence of:

(1) Due execution, acknowledgment and filing of the instrument;

(2) Observance and performance of all acts and conditions necessary to have been observed and performed precedent to the instrument becoming effective; and

(3) Any other facts required or permitted by law to be stated in the instrument.

§ 106. Commencement of corporate existence.

Upon the filing with the Secretary of State of the certificate of incorporation, executed and acknowledged in accordance with § 103 of this title, the incorporator or incorporators who signed the certificate, and such incorporator's or incorporators' successors and assigns, shall, from the date of such filing, be and constitute a body corporate, by the name set forth in the certificate, subject to § 103(d) of this title and subject to dissolution or other termination of its existence as provided in this chapter.

§ 107. Powers of incorporators.

If the persons who are to serve as directors until the first annual meeting of stockholders have not been named in the certificate of incorporation, the incorporator or incorporators, until the directors are elected, shall manage the affairs of the corporation and may do whatever is necessary and proper to perfect the organization of the corporation, including the adoption of the original bylaws of the corporation and the election of directors.

§ 108. Organization meeting of incorporators or directors named in certificate of incorporation.

(a) After the filing of the certificate of incorporation an organization meeting of the incorporator or incorporators, or of the board of directors if the initial directors were named in the certificate of incorporation, shall be held, either within or without this State, at the call of a majority of the incorporators or directors, as the case may be, for the purposes of adopting bylaws, electing directors (if the meeting is of the incorporators) to serve or hold office until the first annual meeting of stockholders or until their successors are elected and qualify, electing officers if the meeting is of the directors, doing any other or further acts to perfect the organization of the corporation, and transacting such other business as may come before the meeting.

(b) The persons calling the meeting shall give to each other incorporator or director, as the case may be, at least 2 days' notice thereof in writing or by electronic transmission by any usual means of communication, which notice shall state the time, place and purposes of the meeting as fixed by the persons calling it. ▪ Notice of the meeting need not be given to anyone who attends the meeting or who waives notice either before or after the meeting.

(c) Unless otherwise restricted by the certificate of incorporation, **(1)** any action permitted to be taken at the organization meeting of the incorporators or directors, as the case may be, may be taken without a meeting if each incorporator or director, where there is more than 1, or the sole incorporator or director where there is only 1, consents thereto in writing or by electronic transmission and **(2)** a consent may be documented, signed and delivered in any manner permitted by § 116 of this title. ▪ Any person (whether or not then an incorporator or director) may provide, whether through instruction to an agent or otherwise, that a consent to action will be effective at a future time (including a time determined upon the happening of an event), no later than 60 days after such instruction is given or such provision is made and such consent shall be deemed to have been given for purposes of this subsection at such effective time so long as such person is then an incorporator or director, as the case may be, and did not revoke the consent prior to such time. ▪ Any such consent shall be revocable prior to its becoming effective.

(d) If any incorporator is not available to act, then any person for whom or on whose behalf the incorporator was acting directly or indirectly as employee or agent, may take any action that such incorporator would have been authorized to take under this section or § 107 of this title; provided that any instrument signed by such other person, or any record of the proceedings of a meeting in which such person participated, shall state that such incorporator is not available and the reason therefor, that such incorporator was acting directly or indirectly as employee or agent for or on behalf of such person, and that such person's signature on such instrument or participation in such meeting is otherwise authorized and not wrongful.

§ 109. Bylaws.

(a) The original or other bylaws of a corporation may be adopted, amended or repealed by the incorporators, by the initial directors of a corporation other than a nonstock corporation or initial members of the governing body of a nonstock corporation if they were named in the certificate of incorporation, or, before a corporation other than a nonstock corporation has received any payment for any of its stock, by its board of directors. ▪ After a corporation other than a nonstock corporation has received any payment for any of its stock, the power to adopt, amend or repeal bylaws shall be in the stockholders entitled to vote. ▪ In the case of a nonstock corporation, the power to adopt, amend or repeal bylaws shall be in its members entitled to vote. ■ Notwithstanding the foregoing, any corporation may, in its certificate of incorporation, confer the power to adopt, amend or repeal bylaws upon the directors or, in the case of a nonstock corporation, upon its governing body. ■ The fact that such power has been so conferred upon the directors or governing body, as the case may be, shall not divest the stockholders or members of the power, nor limit their power to adopt, amend or repeal bylaws.

(b) The bylaws may contain any provision, not inconsistent with law or with the certificate of incorporation, relating to the business of the corporation, the conduct of its affairs, and its rights or powers or the rights or powers of its stockholders, directors, officers or employees. The bylaws may not contain any provision that would impose liability on a stockholder for the attorneys' fees or expenses of the corporation or any other party in connection with an internal corporate claim, as defined in § 115 of this title.

§ 110. Emergency bylaws and other powers in emergency.

(a) The board of directors of any corporation may adopt emergency bylaws, subject to repeal or change by action of the stockholders, which, notwithstanding any different provision elsewhere in this chapter or in Chapters 3 [repealed] and 5 [repealed] of Title 26, or in Chapter 7 of Title 5, or in the certificate of incorporation or bylaws, shall be operative during any emergency resulting from an attack on the United States or on a locality in which the corporation conducts its business or customarily holds meetings of its board of directors or its stockholders, or during any nuclear or atomic disaster, or during the existence of any catastrophe, including, but not limited to, an epidemic or pandemic, and a declaration of a national emergency by the United States government, or other similar emergency condition, irrespective of whether a quorum of the board of directors or a standing committee thereof can readily be convened for action. ■ The emergency bylaws contemplated by this section may be adopted by the board of directors or, if a quorum cannot be readily convened for a meeting, by a majority of the directors present. ■ The emergency bylaws may make any provision that may be practical and necessary for the circumstances of the emergency, including provisions that:

> **(1)** A meeting of the board of directors or a committee thereof may be called by any officer or director in such manner and under such conditions as shall be prescribed in the emergency bylaws;
>
> **(2)** The director or directors in attendance at the meeting, or any greater number fixed by the emergency bylaws, shall constitute a quorum; and
>
> **(3)** The officers or other persons designated on a list approved by the board of directors before the emergency, all in such order of priority and subject to such conditions and for such period of time (not longer than reasonably necessary after the termination of the emergency) as may be provided in the emergency bylaws or in the resolution approving the list, shall, to the extent required to provide a quorum at any meeting of the board of directors, be deemed directors for such meeting.

(b) The board of directors, either before or during any such emergency, may provide, and from time to time modify, lines of succession in the event that during such emergency any or all officers or agents of the corporation shall for any reason be rendered incapable of discharging their duties.

(c) The board of directors, either before or during any such emergency, may, effective in the emergency, change the head office or designate several alternative head offices or regional offices, or authorize the officers so to do.

(d) No officer, director or employee acting in accordance with any emergency bylaws shall be liable except for wilful misconduct.

(e) To the extent not inconsistent with any emergency bylaws so adopted, the bylaws of the corporation shall remain in effect during any emergency and upon its termination the emergency bylaws shall cease to be operative.

(f) Unless otherwise provided in emergency by-laws, notice of any meeting of the board of directors during such an emergency may be given only to such of the directors as it may be feasible to reach at the time and by such means as may be feasible at the time, including publication or radio.

(g) To the extent required to constitute a quorum at any meeting of the board of directors during such an emergency, the officers of the corporation who are present shall, unless otherwise provided in emergency bylaws, be deemed, in order of rank and within the same rank in order of seniority, directors for such meeting.

(h) Nothing contained in this section shall be deemed exclusive of any other provisions for emergency powers consistent with other sections of this title which have been or may be adopted by corporations created under this chapter.

(i) During any emergency condition of a type described in subsection (a) of this section, the board of directors (or, if a quorum cannot be readily convened for a meeting, a majority of the directors present) may **(i)** take any action that it determines to be practical and necessary to address the circumstances of such emergency condition with respect to a meeting of stockholders of the corporation notwithstanding anything to the contrary in this chapter or in Chapter 7 of Title 5 or in the certificate of incorporation or bylaws, including, but not limited to, **(1)** to postpone any such meeting to a later time or date (with the record date for determining the stockholders entitled to notice of, and to vote at, such meeting applying to the postponed meeting irrespective of § 213 of this title), and **(2)** with respect to a corporation subject to the reporting requirements of § 13(a) or § 15(d) of the Securities Exchange Act of 1934, as amended, and the rules and regulations promulgated thereunder, to notify stockholders of any postponement or a change of the place of the meeting (or a change to hold the meeting solely by means of remote communication) solely by a document publicly filed by the corporation with the Securities and Exchange Commission pursuant to § 13, § 14 or § 15(d) of such Act and such rules and regulations; and **(ii)** with respect to any dividend that has been

declared as to which the record date has not occurred, change each of the record date and payment date to a later date or dates (provided the payment date as so changed is not more than 60 days after the record date as so changed); provided that, in either case, the corporation gives notice of such change to stockholders as promptly as practicable thereafter (and in any event before the record date theretofore in effect), which notice, in the case of a corporation subject to the reporting requirements of § 13(a) or § 15(d) of the Securities Exchange Act of 1934, as amended, and the rules and regulations promulgated thereunder, may be given solely by a document publicly filed with the Securities and Exchange Commission pursuant to § 13, § 14 or § 15(d) of such Act and such rules and regulations. ▪ No person shall be liable, and no meeting of stockholders shall be postponed or voided, for the failure to make a stocklist available pursuant to § 219 of this title if it was not practicable to allow inspection during any such emergency condition.

§ 111. Jurisdiction to interpret, apply, enforce or determine the validity of corporate instruments and provisions of this title.

(a) Any civil action to interpret, apply, enforce or determine the validity of the provisions of:

(1) The certificate of incorporation or the bylaws of a corporation;

(2) Any instrument, document or agreement **(i)** by which a corporation creates or sells, or offers to create or sell, any of its stock, or any rights or options respecting its stock, or **(ii)** to which a corporation and 1 or more holders of its stock are parties, and pursuant to which any such holder or holders sell or offer to sell any of such stock, or **(iii)** by which a corporation agrees to sell, lease or exchange any of its property or assets, and which by its terms provides that 1 or more holders of its stock approve of or consent to such sale, lease or exchange;

(3) Any written restrictions on the transfer, registration of transfer or ownership of securities under § 202 of this title;

(4) Any proxy under § 212 or § 215 of this title;

(5) Any voting trust or other voting agreement under § 218 of this title;

(6) Any agreement, certificate of merger or consolidation, or certificate of ownership and merger governed by §§ 251-253, §§ 255-258, §§ 263-264, or § 267 of this title;

(7) Any certificate of conversion under § 265 or § 266 of this title;

(8) Any certificate of domestication, transfer or continuance under § 388, § 389 or § 390 of this title; or

(9) Any other instrument, document, agreement, or certificate required by any provision of this title;

may be brought in the Court of Chancery, except to the extent that a statute confers exclusive jurisdiction on a court, agency or tribunal other than the Court of Chancery.

(b) Any civil action to interpret, apply or enforce any provision of this title may be brought in the Court of Chancery.

§ 112. Access to proxy solicitation materials.

The bylaws may provide that if the corporation solicits proxies with respect to an election of directors, it may be required, to the extent and subject to such procedures or conditions as may be provided in the bylaws, to include in its proxy solicitation materials (including any form of proxy it distributes), in addition to individuals nominated by the board of directors, 1 or more individuals nominated by a stockholder. ■ Such procedures or conditions may include any of the following:

(1) A provision requiring a minimum record or beneficial ownership, or duration of ownership, of shares of the corporation's capital stock, by the nominating stockholder, and defining beneficial ownership to take into account options or other rights in respect of or related to such stock;

(2) A provision requiring the nominating stockholder to submit specified information concerning the stockholder and the stockholder's nominees, including information concerning

ownership by such persons of shares of the corporation's capital stock, or options or other rights in respect of or related to such stock;

(3) A provision conditioning eligibility to require inclusion in the corporation's proxy solicitation materials upon the number or proportion of directors nominated by stockholders or whether the stockholder previously sought to require such inclusion;

(4) A provision precluding nominations by any person if such person, any nominee of such person, or any affiliate or associate of such person or nominee, has acquired or publicly proposed to acquire shares constituting a specified percentage of the voting power of the corporation's outstanding voting stock within a specified period before the election of directors;

(5) A provision requiring that the nominating stockholder undertake to indemnify the corporation in respect of any loss arising as a result of any false or misleading information or statement submitted by the nominating stockholder in connection with a nomination; and

(6) Any other lawful condition.

§ 113. Proxy expense reimbursement.

(a) The bylaws may provide for the reimbursement by the corporation of expenses incurred by a stockholder in soliciting proxies in connection with an election of directors, subject to such procedures or conditions as the bylaws may prescribe, including:

(1) Conditioning eligibility for reimbursement upon the number or proportion of persons nominated by the stockholder seeking reimbursement or whether such stockholder previously sought reimbursement for similar expenses;

(2) Limitations on the amount of reimbursement based upon the proportion of votes cast in favor of 1 or more of the persons nominated by the stockholder seeking reimbursement, or upon the amount spent by the corporation in soliciting proxies in connection with the election;

(3) Limitations concerning elections of directors by cumulative voting pursuant to § 214 of this title; or

(4) Any other lawful condition.

(b) No bylaw so adopted shall apply to elections for which any record date precedes its adoption.

§ 114. Application of chapter to nonstock corporations.

(a) Except as otherwise provided in subsections (b) and (c) of this section, the provisions of this chapter and of chapter 5 of this title shall apply to nonstock corporations in the manner specified in the following paragraphs (a)(1)-(4) of this section:

(1) All references to stockholders of the corporation shall be deemed to refer to members of the corporation;

(2) All references to the board of directors of the corporation shall be deemed to refer to the governing body of the corporation;

(3) All references to directors or to members of the board of directors of the corporation shall be deemed to refer to members of the governing body of the corporation; and

(4) All references to stock, capital stock, or shares thereof of a corporation authorized to issue capital stock shall be deemed to refer to memberships of a nonprofit nonstock corporation and to membership interests of any other nonstock corporation.

(b) Subsection (a) of this section shall not apply to:

(1) Sections 102(a)(4), (b)(1) and (2), 109(a), 114, 141, 154, 215, 228, 230(b), 241, 242, 253, 254, 255, 256, 257, 258, 271, 276, 311, 312, 313, 390, and 503 of this title, which apply to nonstock corporations by their terms;

(2) Sections 102(f), 109(b) (last sentence), 151, 152, 153, 155, 156, 157(d), 158, 161, 162, 163, 164, 165, 166, 167, 168, 203, 211, 212, 213, 214, 216, 219, 222, 231, 243, 244, 251, 252, 267, 274, 275, 324, 364, 366(a), 391, and 502(a)(5) of this title; and

(3) Subchapter XIV and subchapter XVI of this chapter.

(c) In the case of a nonprofit nonstock corporation, subsection (a) of this section shall not apply to:

(1) The sections and subchapters listed in subsection (b) of this section;

(2) Sections 102(b)(3), 111(a)(2) and (3), 144(a)(2), 217, 218(a) and (b), and 262 of this title; and

(3) Subchapter V, subchapter VI (other than §§ 204 and 205 of this title) and subchapter XV of this chapter.

(d) For purposes of this chapter:

(1) A "charitable nonstock corporation" is any nonprofit nonstock corporation that is exempt from taxation under § 501(c)(3) of the United States Internal Revenue Code [26 U.S.C. § 501(c)(3)], or any successor provisions.

(2) A "membership interest" is, unless otherwise provided in a nonstock corporation's certificate of incorporation, a member's share of the profits and losses of a nonstock corporation, or a member's right to receive distributions of the nonstock corporation's assets, or both;

(3) A "nonprofit nonstock corporation" is a nonstock corporation that does not have membership interests; and

(4) A "nonstock corporation" is any corporation organized under this chapter that is not authorized to issue capital stock.

§ 115 Forum selection provisions.

The certificate of incorporation or the bylaws may require, consistent with applicable jurisdictional requirements, that any or all internal corporate claims shall be brought solely and exclusively in any or all of the courts in this State, and no provision of the certificate of incorporation or the bylaws may prohibit bringing such claims in the courts of this State. ■ "Internal corporate claims" means claims, including claims in the right of the corporation, **(i)** that are based upon a violation of a duty by a current or former director or officer or stockholder in such capacity, or **(ii)** as to which this title confers jurisdiction upon the Court of Chancery.

§ 116. Document form, signature and delivery.

(a) Except as provided in subsection (b) of this section, without limiting the manner in which any act or transaction may be documented, or the manner in which a document may be signed or delivered:

(1) Any act or transaction contemplated or governed by this chapter or the certificate of incorporation or bylaws may be provided for in a document, and an electronic transmission shall be deemed the equivalent of a written document. ▪ "Document" means:

a. Any tangible medium on which information is inscribed, and includes handwritten, typed, printed or similar instruments, and copies of such instruments; and

b. An electronic transmission.

(2) Whenever this chapter or the certificate of incorporation or bylaws requires or permits a signature, the signature may be a manual, facsimile, conformed or electronic signature. ▪ "Electronic signature" means an electronic symbol or process that is attached to, or logically associated with, a document and executed or adopted by a person with an intent to execute authenticate or adopt the document. ▪ A person may execute a document with such person's signature.

(3) Unless otherwise agreed between the sender and recipient (and in the case of proxies or consents given by or on behalf of a stockholder, subject to the additional requirements set forth in § 212(c)(2) and (3) and § 228(d)(1) of this title, respectively), an electronic transmission shall be deemed delivered to a person for purposes of this chapter and the certificate of incorporation and bylaws when it enters an information processing system that the person has designated for the purpose of receiving electronic transmissions of the type delivered, so long as the electronic transmission is in a form capable of being processed by that system and such person is able to retrieve the electronic transmission. ▪ Whether a person has so designated an information processing system is

determined by the certificate of incorporation, the bylaws or from the context and surrounding circumstances, including the parties' conduct. ▪ An electronic transmission is delivered under this section even if no person is aware of its receipt. ▪ Receipt of an electronic acknowledgement from an information processing system establishes that an electronic transmission was received but, by itself, does not establish that the content sent corresponds to the content received.

This chapter shall not prohibit 1 or more persons from conducting a transaction in accordance with Chapter 12A of Title 6 so long as the part or parts of the transaction that are governed by this chapter are documented, signed and delivered in accordance with this subsection or otherwise in accordance with this chapter. ▪ This subsection shall apply solely for purposes of determining whether an act or transaction has been documented, and the document has been signed and delivered, in accordance with this chapter, the certificate of incorporation and the bylaws.

(b) Subsection (a) of this section shall not apply to:

(1) A document filed with or submitted to the Secretary of State, the Register in Chancery, or a court or other judicial or governmental body of this State;

(2) A document comprising part of the stock ledger;

(3) A certificate representing a security;

(4) Any document expressly referenced as a notice (or waiver of notice) by this chapter, the certificate of incorporation or bylaws;

(5) [Repealed.]

(6) A ballot to vote on actions at a meeting of stockholders; and

(7) An act or transaction effected pursuant to § 280 of this title or subchapters III, XIII or XVI of this chapter. ▪

The foregoing shall not create any presumption about the lawful means to document a matter addressed by this subsection, or the lawful means to sign or deliver a document addressed by this sub-section. ▪ No provision of the certificate of incor-poration or bylaws shall limit the application of subsection (a) of this section except for a provision that expressly restricts or prohibits the use of an electronic transmission or electronic signature (or any form thereof) or expressly restricts or prohib-its the delivery of an electronic transmission to an information processing system.

(c) In the event that any provision of this chapter is deemed to modify, limit or supersede the Elec-tronic Signatures in Global and National Com-merce Act, (15 U.S.C. § 7001 et. seq.), the provi-sions of this chapter shall control to the fullest ex-tent permitted by § 7002(a)(2) of such act [15 U.S.C. § 7002(a)(2)].

Subchapter II. Powers

§ 121. General powers.

(a) In addition to the powers enumerated in § 122 of this title, every corporation, its officers, direc-tors and stockholders shall possess and may exer-cise all the powers and privileges granted by this chapter or by any other law or by its certificate of incorporation, together with any powers incidental thereto, so far as such powers and privileges are necessary or convenient to the conduct, promotion or attainment of the business or purposes set forth in its certificate of incorporation.

(b) Every corporation shall be governed by the provisions and be subject to the restrictions and li-abilities contained in this chapter.

§ 122. Specific powers.

Every corporation created under this chapter shall have power to:

    (1) Have perpetual succession by its corporate name, unless a limited period of duration is stated in its certificate of incorporation;

    (2) Sue and be sued in all courts and participate, as a party or otherwise, in any judicial, admin-istrative, arbitrative or other proceeding, in its corporate name;

    (3) Have a corporate seal, which may be altered at pleasure, and use the same by causing it or a facsimile thereof, to be impressed or affixed or in any other manner reproduced;

    (4) Purchase, receive, take by grant, gift, de-vise, bequest or otherwise, lease, or otherwise acquire, own, hold, improve, employ, use and otherwise deal in and with real or personal property, or any interest therein, wherever situ-ated, and to sell, convey, lease, exchange, trans-fer or otherwise dispose of, or mortgage or pledge, all or any of its property and assets, or any interest therein, wherever situated;

    (5) Appoint such officers and agents as the business of the corporation requires and to pay or otherwise provide for them suitable compen-sation;

    (6) Adopt, amend and repeal bylaws;

    (7) Wind up and dissolve itself in the manner provided in this chapter;

    (8) Conduct its business, carry on its operations and have offices and exercise its powers within or without this State;

    (9) Make donations for the public welfare or for charitable, scientific or educational purposes, and in time of war or other national emergency in aid thereof;

    (10) Be an incorporator, promoter or manager of other corporations of any type or kind;

    (11) Participate with others in any corporation, partnership, limited partnership, joint venture or other association of any kind, or in any trans-action, undertaking or arrangement which the participating corporation would have power to conduct by itself, whether or not such partici-pation involves sharing or delegation of control with or to others;

    (12) Transact any lawful business which the corporation's board of directors shall find to be in aid of governmental authority;

    (13) Make contracts, including contracts of guaranty and suretyship, incur liabilities, bor-row money at such rates of interest as the cor-poration may determine, issue its notes, bonds and other obligations, and secure any of its obligations by mortgage, pledge or other encumbrance of all or any of its property, franchises and income, and make contracts of guaranty and suretyship which are necessary or convenient to the conduct, promotion or attainment of the business of

(a) a corporation all of the outstanding stock of which is owned, directly or indirectly, by the contracting corporation, or

(b) a corporation which owns, directly or indirectly, all of the outstanding stock of the contracting corporation, or

(c) a corporation all of the outstanding stock of which is owned, directly or indirectly, by a corporation which owns, directly or indirectly, all of the outstanding stock of the contracting corporation,

which contracts of guaranty and suretyship shall be deemed to be necessary or convenient to the conduct, promotion or attainment of the business of the contracting corporation, and make other contracts of guaranty and suretyship which are necessary or convenient to the conduct, promotion or attainment of the business of the contracting corporation;

(14) Lend money for its corporate purposes, invest and reinvest its funds, and take, hold and deal with real and personal property as security for the payment of funds so loaned or invested;

(15) Pay pensions and establish and carry out pension, profit sharing, stock option, stock purchase, stock bonus, retirement, benefit, incentive and compensation plans, trusts and provisions for any or all of its directors, officers and employees, and for any or all of the directors, officers and employees of its subsidiaries;

(16) Provide insurance for its benefit on the life of any of its directors, officers or employees, or on the life of any stockholder for the purpose of acquiring at such stockholder's death shares of its stock owned by such stockholder.

(17) Renounce, in its certificate of incorporation or by action of its board of directors, any interest or expectancy of the corporation in, or in being offered an opportunity to participate in, specified business opportunities or specified classes or categories of business opportunities that are presented to the corporation or 1 or more of its officers, directors or stockholders.

§ 123. Powers respecting securities of other corporations or entities.

Any corporation organized under the laws of this State may guarantee, purchase, take, receive, subscribe for or otherwise acquire; own, hold, use or otherwise employ; sell, lease, exchange, transfer or otherwise dispose of; mortgage, lend, pledge or otherwise deal in and with, bonds and other obligations of, or shares or other securities or interests in, or issued by, any other domestic or foreign corporation, partnership, association or individual, or by any government or agency or instrumentality thereof. ▪ A corporation while owner of any such securities may exercise all the rights, powers and privileges of ownership, including the right to vote.

§ 124. Effect of lack of corporate capacity or power; ultra vires.

No act of a corporation and no conveyance or transfer of real or personal property to or by a corporation shall be invalid by reason of the fact that the corporation was without capacity or power to do such act or to make or receive such conveyance or transfer, but such lack of capacity or power may be asserted:

(1) In a proceeding by a stockholder against the corporation to enjoin the doing of any act or acts or the transfer of real or personal property by or to the corporation. ▪ If the unauthorized acts or transfer sought to be enjoined are being, or are to be, performed or made pursuant to any contract to which the corporation is a party, the court may, if all of the parties to the contract are parties to the proceeding and if it deems the same to be equitable, set aside and enjoin the performance of such contract, and in so doing may allow to the corporation or to the other parties to the contract, as the case may be, such compensation as may be equitable for the loss or damage sustained by any of them which may

result from the action of the court in setting aside and enjoining the performance of such contract, but anticipated profits to be derived from the performance of the contract shall not be awarded by the court as a loss or damage sustained;

(2) In a proceeding by the corporation, whether acting directly or through a receiver, trustee or other legal representative, or through stockholders in a representative suit, against an incumbent or former officer or director of the corporation, for loss or damage due to such incumbent or former officer's or director's unauthorized act;

(3) In a proceeding by the Attorney General to dissolve the corporation, or to enjoin the corporation from the transaction of unauthorized business.

§ 125. Conferring academic or honorary degrees.

No corporation organized after April 18, 1945, shall have power to confer academic or honorary degrees unless the certificate of incorporation or an amendment thereof shall so provide and unless the certificate of incorporation or an amendment thereof prior to its being filed in the office of the Secretary of State shall have endorsed thereon the approval of the Department of Education of this State. ▪ No corporation organized before April 18, 1945, any provision in its certificate of incorporation to the contrary notwithstanding, shall possess the power aforesaid without first filing in the office of the Secretary of State a certificate of amendment so providing, the filing of which certificate of amendment in the office of the Secretary of State shall be subject to prior approval of the Department of Education, evidenced as hereinabove provided. ▪ Approval shall be granted only when it appears to the reasonable satisfaction of the Department of Education that the corporation is engaged in conducting a bona fide institution of higher learning, giving instructions in arts and letters, science or the professions, or that the corporation proposes, in good faith, to engage in

that field and has or will have the resources, including personnel, requisite for the conduct of an institution of higher learning. ▪ Upon dissolution, all such corporations shall comply with § 8530 of Title 14. ▪ Notwithstanding any provision herein to the contrary, no corporation shall have the power to conduct a private business or trade school unless the certificate of incorporation or an amendment thereof, prior to its being filed in the office of the Secretary of State, shall have endorsed thereon the approval of the Department of Education pursuant to Chapter 85 of Title 14.

Notwithstanding the foregoing provisions, any corporation conducting a law school, which has its principal place of operation in Delaware, and which intends to meet the standards of approval of the American Bar Association, may, after it has been in actual operation for not less than 1 year, retain at its own expense a dean or dean emeritus of a law school fully approved by the American Bar Association to make an on-site inspection and report concerning the progress of the corporation toward meeting the standards for approval by the American Bar Association. ▪ Such dean or dean emeritus shall be chosen by the Attorney General from a panel of 3 deans whose names are presented to the Attorney General as being willing to serve. ▪ One such dean on this panel shall be nominated by the trustees of said law school corporation; another dean shall be nominated by a committee of the Student Bar Association of said law school; and the other dean shall be nominated by a committee of lawyers who are parents of students attending such law school. ▪ If any of the above-named groups cannot find a dean, it may substitute 2 full professors of accredited law schools for the dean it is entitled to nominate, and in such a case if the Attorney General chooses 1 of such professors, such professor shall serve the function of a dean as herein prescribed. ▪ If the dean so retained shall report in writing that, in such dean's professional judgment, the corporation is attempting, in good faith, to comply with the standards for approval of the American Bar Association and is making reasonable progress toward meeting such standards, the corporation may file a copy of the report with the Secretary of Education and with the Attorney General. ▪ Any corporation which complies with these provisions by filing such report shall be deemed to have temporary approval from the State and shall be entitled to amend its certificate of incorporation to authorize the granting of standard academic law degrees. ▪ Thereafter, until the law school operated by the corporation is approved by the American Bar Association, the corporation shall file once during each academic year a new report, in the same manner as the first report. ▪ If, at any time, the corporation fails to file such a report, or if the dean retained to render such report states that, in such dean's opinion, the corporation is not continuing to make reasonable progress toward accreditation, the Attorney General, at the request of the Secretary of Education, may file a complaint in the Court of Chancery to suspend said temporary approval and degree-granting power until a further report is filed by a dean or dean emeritus of an accredited law school that the school has resumed its progress towards meeting the standards for approval. ▪ Upon approval of the law school by the American Bar Association, temporary approval shall become final, and shall no longer be subject to suspension or vacation under this section.

§ 126. Banking power denied.

(a) No corporation organized under this chapter shall possess the power of issuing bills, notes, or other evidences of debt for circulation as money, or the power of carrying on the business of receiving deposits of money.

(b) Corporations organized under this chapter to buy, sell and otherwise deal in notes, open accounts and other similar evidences of debt, or to loan money and to take notes, open accounts and other similar evidences of debt as collateral security therefor, shall not be deemed to be engaging in the business of banking.

§ 127. Private foundation; powers and duties.

A corporation of this State which is a private foundation under the United States internal revenue laws and whose certificate of incorporation does not expressly provide that this section shall not apply to it is required to act or to refrain from acting so as not to subject itself to the taxes imposed by 26 U.S.C. § 4941 (relating to taxes on self-dealing), § 4942 (relating to taxes on failure to distribute income), § 4943 (relating to taxes on excess business holdings), § 4944 (relating to taxes on investments which jeopardize charitable purpose), or § 4945 (relating to taxable expenditures), or corresponding provisions of any subsequent United States internal revenue law.

Subchapter III. Registered Office and Registered Agent

§ 131. Registered office in State; principal office or place of business in State.

(a) Every corporation shall have and maintain in this State a registered office which may, but need not be, the same as its place of business.

(b) Whenever the term "corporation's principal office or place of business in this State" or "principal office or place of business of the corporation in this State," or other term of like import, is or has been used in a corporation's certificate of incorporation, or in any other document, or in any statute, it shall be deemed to mean and refer to, unless the context indicates otherwise, the corporation's registered office required by this section; and it shall not be necessary for any corporation to amend its certificate of incorporation or any other document to comply with this section.

(c) As contained in any certificate of incorporation or other document filed with the Secretary of State under this chapter, the address of a registered office shall include the street, number, city, county and postal code.

§ 132. Registered agent in State; resident agent.

(a) Every corporation shall have and maintain in this State a registered agent, which agent may be any of:

    (1) The corporation itself;

    (2) An individual resident in this State;

(3) A domestic corporation (other than the corporation itself), a domestic partnership (whether general (including a limited liability partnership) or limited (including a limited liability limited partnership)), a domestic limited liability company or a domestic statutory trust; or

(4) A foreign corporation, a foreign limited liability partnership, a foreign limited partnership, a foreign limited liability limited partnership, a foreign limited liability company or a foreign statutory trust.

(b) Every registered agent for a domestic corporation or a foreign corporation shall:

(1) If an entity, maintain a business office in this State which is generally open, or if an individual, be generally present at a designated location in this State, at sufficiently frequent times to accept service of process and otherwise perform the functions of a registered agent;

(2) If a foreign entity, be authorized to transact business in this State;

(3) Accept service of process and other communications directed to the corporations for which it serves as registered agent and forward same to the corporation to which the service or communication is directed;

(4) Forward to the corporations for which it serves as registered agent the annual report required by § 502 of this title or an electronic notification of same in a form satisfactory to the Secretary of State ("Secretary"); and

(5) Satisfy and adhere to regulations established by the Secretary regarding the verification of both the identity of the entity's contacts and individuals for which the registered agent maintains a record for the reduction of risk of unlawful business purposes.

(c) Any registered agent who at any time serves as registered agent for more than 50 entities (a "commercial registered agent"), whether domestic or foreign, shall satisfy and comply with the following qualifications.

(1) A natural person serving as a commercial registered agent shall:

a. Maintain a principal residence or a principal place of business in this State;

b. Maintain a Delaware business license;

c. Be generally present at a designated location within this State during normal business hours to accept service of process and otherwise perform the functions of a registered agent as specified in subsection (b) of this section;

d. Provide the Secretary upon request with such information identifying and enabling communication with such commercial registered agent as the Secretary shall require; and

e. Satisfy and adhere to regulations established by the Secretary regarding the verification of both the identity of the entity's contacts and individuals for which the natural person maintains a record for the reduction of risk of unlawful business purposes.

(2) A domestic or foreign corporation, a domestic or foreign partnership (whether general (including a limited liability partnership) or limited (including a limited liability limited partnership)), a domestic or foreign limited liability company, or a domestic or foreign statutory trust serving as a commercial registered agent shall:

a. Have a business office within this State which is generally open during normal business hours to accept service of process and otherwise perform the functions of a registered agent as specified in subsection (b) of this section;

b. Maintain a Delaware business license;

c. Have generally present at such office during normal business hours an officer, director or managing agent who is a natural person;

d. Provide the Secretary upon request with such information identifying and enabling communication with such commercial registered agent as the Secretary shall require and

e. Satisfy and adhere to regulations established by the Secretary regarding the verification of both the identity of the entity's contacts and individuals for which it maintains a record for the reduction of risk of unlawful business purposes.

(3) For purposes of this subsection and paragraph (f)(2)a. of this section, a commercial registered agent shall also include any registered agent which has an officer, director or managing agent in common with any other registered agent or agents if such registered agents at any time during such common service as officer, director or managing agent collectively served as registered agents for more than 50 entities, whether domestic or foreign.

(d) Every corporation formed under the laws of this State or qualified to do business in this State shall provide to its registered agent and update from time to time as necessary the name, business address and business telephone number of a natural person who is an officer, director, employee, or designated agent of the corporation, who is then authorized to receive communications from the registered agent. ■ Such person shall be deemed the communications contact for the corporation. ■ Every registered agent shall retain (in paper or electronic form) the above information concerning the current communications contact for each corporation for which he, she or it serves as a registered agent. ■ If the corporation fails to provide the registered agent with a current communications contact, the registered agent may resign as the registered agent for such corporation pursuant to § 136 of this title.

(e) The Secretary is fully authorized to issue such regulations as may be necessary or appropriate to carry out the enforcement of subsections (b), (c) and (d) of this section, and to take actions reasonable and necessary to assure registered agents' compliance with subsections (b), (c) and (d) of this section. ■ Such actions may include refusal to file

documents submitted by a registered agent, including the refusal to file any documents regarding an entity's formation.

(f) Upon application of the Secretary, the Court of Chancery may enjoin any person or entity from serving as a registered agent or as an officer, director or managing agent of a registered agent.

(1) Upon the filing of a complaint by the Secretary pursuant to this section, the Court may make such orders respecting such proceeding as it deems appropriate, and may enter such orders granting interim or final relief as it deems proper under the circumstances.

(2) Any one or more of the following grounds shall be a sufficient basis to grant an injunction pursuant to this section:

a. With respect to any registered agent who at any time within 1 year immediately prior to the filing of the Secretary's complaint is a commercial registered agent, failure after notice and warning to comply with the qualifications set forth in subsection (b) of this section and/or the requirements of subsection (c) or (d) of this section above;

b. The person serving as a registered agent, or any person who is an officer, director or managing agent of an entity registered agent, has been convicted of a felony or any crime which includes an element of dishonesty or fraud or involves moral turpitude;

c. The registered agent has engaged in conduct in connection with acting as a registered agent that is intended to or likely to deceive or defraud the public.

(3) With respect to any order the court enters pursuant to this section with respect to an entity that has acted as a registered agent, the court may also direct such order to any person who has served as an officer, director, or managing agent of such registered agent. ■ Any person who, on or after January 1, 2007, serves as an officer, director, or managing agent of an entity acting as a registered agent in this State shall be deemed thereby to have consented to the appointment of such registered agent as agent upon whom service of process may be made in any action brought pursuant to this section, and service as an officer, director, or managing agent of an entity acting as a registered agent in this State shall be a signification of the consent of such person that any process when so served shall be of the same legal force and validity as if served upon such person within this State, and such appointment of the registered agent shall be irrevocable.

(4) Upon the entry of an order by the Court enjoining any person or entity from acting as a registered agent, the Secretary shall mail or deliver notice of such order to each affected corporation at the address of its principal place of business as specified in its most recent franchise tax report or other record of the Secretary. ■ If such corporation is a domestic corporation and fails to obtain and designate a new registered agent within 30 days after such notice is given, the Secretary shall declare the charter of such corporation forfeited. ■ If such corporation is a foreign corporation, and fails to obtain and designate a new registered agent within 30 days after such notice is given, the Secretary shall forfeit its qualification to do business in this State. ■ If the court enjoins a person or entity from acting as a registered agent as provided in this section and no new registered agent shall have been obtained and designated in the time and manner aforesaid, service of legal process against the corporation for which the registered agent had been acting shall thereafter be upon the Secretary in accordance with § 321 of this title. ■ The Court of Chancery may, upon application of the Secretary on notice to the former registered agent, enter such orders as it deems appropriate to give the Secretary access to information in the former registered agent's possession in order to facilitate communication with the corporations the former registered agent served.

(g) The Secretary is authorized to make a list of registered agents available to the public, and to establish such qualifications and issue such rules and

regulations with respect to such listing as the Secretary deems necessary or appropriate.

(h) Whenever the term "resident agent" or "resident agent in charge of a corporation's principal office or place of business in this State," or other term of like import which refers to a corporation's agent required by statute to be located in this State, is or has been used in a corporation's certificate of incorporation, or in any other document, or in any statute, it shall be deemed to mean and refer to, unless the context indicates otherwise, the corporation's registered agent required by this section; and it shall not be necessary for any corporation to amend its certificate of incorporation or any other document to comply with this section.

§ 133. Change of location of registered office; change of registered agent.

Any corporation may, by resolution of its board of directors, change the location of its registered office in this State to any other place in this State. ■ By like resolution, the registered agent of a corporation may be changed to any other person or corporation including itself. ■ In either such case, the resolution shall be as detailed in its statement as is required by § 102(a)(2) of this title. ■ Upon the adoption of such a resolution, a certificate certifying the change shall be executed, acknowledged, and filed in accordance with § 103 of this title.

§ 134. Change of address or name of registered agent.

(a) A registered agent may change the address of the registered office of the corporation or corporations for which the agent is a registered agent to another address in this State by filing with the Secretary of State a certificate, executed and acknowledged by such registered agent, setting forth the address at which such registered agent has maintained the registered office for each of the corporations for which it is a registered agent, and further certifying to the new address to which each such registered office will be changed on a given day, and at which new address such registered agent will thereafter maintain the registered office for each of the corporations for which it is a registered agent. ■ Thereafter, or until further change of address, as authorized by law, the registered office in this State of each of the corporations for which the agent is a registered agent shall be located at the new address of the registered agent thereof as given in the certificate.

(b) In the event of a change of name of any person or corporation acting as registered agent in this State, such registered agent shall file with the Secretary of State a certificate, executed and acknowledged by such registered agent, setting forth the new name of such registered agent, the name of such registered agent before it was changed, and the address at which such registered agent has maintained the registered office for each of the corporations for which it acts as a registered agent. ▪ A change of name of any person or corporation acting as a registered agent as a result of a merger or consolidation of the registered agent, with or into another person or corporation which succeeds to its assets by operation of law, shall be deemed a change of name for purposes of this section.

§ 135. Resignation of registered agent coupled with appointment of successor.

The registered agent of 1 or more corporations may resign and appoint a successor registered agent by filing a certificate with the Secretary of State, stating the name and address of the successor agent, in accordance with § 102(a)(2) of this title. ▪ There shall be attached to such certificate a statement of each affected corporation ratifying and approving such change of registered agent. ▪ Each such statement shall be executed and acknowledged in accordance with § 103 of this title. ▪ Upon such filing, the successor registered agent shall become the registered agent of such corporations as have ratified and approved such substitution and the successor registered agent's address, as stated in such certificate, shall become the address of each such corporation's registered office in this State.

§ 136. Resignation of registered agent not coupled with appointment of successor.

(a) The registered agent of a corporation, including a corporation which has become void pursuant to § 510 of this title, may resign without appointing a successor by filing a certificate of resignation with the Secretary of State, but such resignation shall not become effective until 30 days after the certificate is filed. ▪ The certificate shall be executed and acknowledged by the registered agent, shall contain a statement that written notice of resignation was given to the corporation at least 30 days prior to the filing of the certificate by mailing or delivering such notice to the corporation at its address last known to the registered agent and shall set forth the date of such notice. ▪ The certificate shall include such information last provided to the registered agent pursuant to § 132(d) of this title for a communications contact for the affected corporation. ▪ Such information regarding the communications contact shall not be deemed public. ▪ A certificate filed pursuant to this section must be on the form prescribed by the Secretary of State.

(b) After receipt of the notice of the resignation of its registered agent, provided for in subsection (a) of this section, the corporation for which such registered agent was acting shall obtain and designate a new registered agent to take the place of the registered agent so resigning in the same manner as provided in § 133 of this title for change of registered agent. ▪ If such corporation, being a corporation of this State, fails to obtain and designate a new registered agent as aforesaid prior to the expiration of the period of 30 days after the filing by the registered agent of the certificate of resignation, the Secretary of State shall declare the charter of such corporation forfeited. ▪ If such corporation, being a foreign corporation, fails to obtain and designate a new registered agent as aforesaid prior to the expiration of the period of 30 days after the filing by the registered agent of the certificate of resignation, the Secretary of State shall forfeit its authority to do business in this State.

(c) After the resignation of the registered agent shall have become effective as provided in this section and if no new registered agent shall have been obtained and designated in the time and manner aforesaid, service of legal process against the corporation for which the resigned registered agent had been acting shall thereafter be upon the Secretary of State in accordance with § 321 of this title. ▪

Subchapter IV. Directors and Officers

§ 141. Board of directors; powers; number, qualifications, terms and quorum; committees; classes of directors; nonstock corporations; reliance upon books; action without meeting; removal.

(a) The business and affairs of every corporation organized under this chapter shall be managed by or under the direction of a board of directors, except as may be otherwise provided in this chapter or in its certificate of incorporation. ▪ If any such provision is made in the certificate of incorporation, the powers and duties conferred or imposed upon the board of directors by this chapter shall be exercised or performed to such extent and by such person or persons as shall be provided in the certificate of incorporation.

(b) The board of directors of a corporation shall consist of 1 or more members, each of whom shall be a natural person. ▪ The number of directors shall be fixed by, or in the manner provided in, the bylaws, unless the certificate of incorporation fixes the number of directors, in which case a change in the number of directors shall be made only by amendment of the certificate. ▪ Directors need not be stockholders unless so required by the certificate of incorporation or the bylaws. ▪ The certificate of incorporation or bylaws may prescribe other qualifications for directors. ▪ Each director shall hold office until such director's successor is elected and qualified or until such director's earlier resignation or removal. ▪ Any director may resign at any time upon notice given in writing or by electronic transmission to the corporation. ▪ A resignation is effective when the resignation is delivered unless the resignation specifies a later effective date or an effective date determined upon the happening of an event or events. ▪ A resignation which is conditioned upon the director

failing to receive a specified vote for reelection as a director may provide that it is irrevocable. ▪ A majority of the total number of directors shall constitute a quorum for the transaction of business unless the certificate of incorporation or the bylaws require a greater number. ▪ Unless the certificate of incorporation provides otherwise, the bylaws may provide that a number less than a majority shall constitute a quorum which in no case shall be less than 1/3 of the total number of directors. ▪ The vote of the majority of the directors present at a meeting at which a quorum is present shall be the act of the board of directors unless the certificate of incorporation or the bylaws shall require a vote of a greater number.

(c)(1) All corporations incorporated prior to July 1, 1996, shall be governed by this paragraph (c)(1) of this section, provided that any such corporation may by a resolution adopted by a majority of the whole board elect to be governed by paragraph (c)(2) of this section, in which case this paragraph (c)(1) of this section shall not apply to such corporation. ▪ All corporations incorporated on or after July 1, 1996, shall be governed by paragraph (c)(2) of this section. ▪ The board of directors may, by resolution passed by a majority of the whole board, designate 1 or more committees, each committee to consist of 1 or more of the directors of the corporation. ▪ The board may designate 1 or more directors as alternate members of any committee, who may replace any absent or disqualified member at any meeting of the committee. ▪ The bylaws may provide that in the absence or disqualification of a member of a committee, the member or members present at any meeting and not disqualified from voting, whether or not the member or members present constitute a quorum, may unanimously appoint another member of the board of directors to act at the meeting in the place of any such absent or disqualified member. ▪ Any such committee, to the extent provided in the resolution of the board of directors, or in the bylaws of the corporation, shall have and may exercise all the powers and authority of the board of directors in the management of the business and affairs of the corporation, and may authorize the seal of the corporation to be affixed to all papers which may require it; but no such committee shall have the power or authority in reference to amending the certificate of incorporation (except that a committee may, to the extent authorized in the resolution or resolutions providing for the issuance of shares of stock adopted by the board of directors as provided in § 151(a) of this title, fix the designations and any of the preferences or rights of such shares relating to dividends, redemption, dissolution, any distribution of assets of the corporation or the conversion into, or the exchange of such shares for, shares of any other class or classes or any other series of the same or any other class or classes of stock of the corporation or fix the number of shares of any series of stock or authorize the increase or decrease of the shares of any series), adopting an agreement of merger or consolidation under § 251, § 252, § 254, § 255, § 256, § 257, § 258, § 263 or § 264 of this title, recommending to the stockholders the sale, lease or exchange of all or substantially all of the corporation's property and assets, recommending to the stockholders a dissolution of the corporation or a revocation of a dissolution, or amending the bylaws of the corporation; and, unless the resolution, bylaws or certificate of incorporation expressly so provides, no such committee shall have the power or authority to declare a dividend, to authorize the issuance of stock or to adopt a certificate of ownership and merger pursuant to § 253 of this title.

(2) The board of directors may designate 1 or more committees, each committee to consist of 1 or more of the directors of the corporation. ▪ The board may designate 1 or more directors as alternate members of any committee, who may replace any absent or disqualified member at any meeting of the committee. ▪ The bylaws may provide that in the absence or disqualification of a member of a committee, the member or members present at any meeting and not disqualified from voting, whether or not such member or members constitute a quorum, may unanimously appoint another member of the board of directors to act at the meeting in the place of any such absent or disqualified member. ▪ Any such committee, to the extent provided in the resolution of the board of directors, or in the bylaws of the corporation, shall have and may exercise all the powers and authority of the board of directors in the management of the business and affairs of the corporation, and may authorize the seal of the corporation to be affixed to all papers which may require it; but no such committee shall have the power or authority in reference to the following matter: **(i)** approving or adopting, or recommending to the stockholders, any action or matter (other than the election or removal of directors) expressly required by this chapter to be submitted to stockholders for approval or **(ii)** adopting, amending or repealing any bylaw of the corporation.

(3) Unless otherwise provided in the certificate of incorporation, the bylaws or the resolution of the board of directors designating the committee, a committee may create 1 or more subcommittees, each subcommittee to consist of 1 or more members of the committee, and delegate to a subcommittee any or all of the powers and authority of the committee. ▪ Except for references to committees and members of committees in subsection (c) of this section, every reference in this chapter to a committee of the board of directors or a member of a committee shall be deemed to include a reference to a subcommittee or member of a subcommittee.

(4) A majority of the directors then serving on a committee of the board of directors or on a subcommittee of a committee shall constitute a quorum for the transaction of business by the committee or subcommittee, unless the certificate of incorporation, the bylaws, a resolution of the board of directors or a resolution of a committee that created the subcommittee requires a greater or lesser number, provided that in no case shall a quorum be less than 1/3 of the directors then serving on the committee or sub-committee. ▪ The vote of the majority of the members of a committee or subcommittee present at a meeting at which a quorum is present shall be the act of the committee or subcommittee, unless the certificate of incorporation, the bylaws, a resolution of the board of directors or a resolution of a committee that created the subcommittee requires a greater number.

(d) The directors of any corporation organized under this chapter may, by the certificate of incorporation or by an initial bylaw, or by a bylaw adopted by a vote of the stockholders, be divided into 1, 2 or 3 classes; the term of office of those of the first class to expire at the first annual meeting held after such classification becomes effective; of the second class 1 year thereafter; of the third class 2 years thereafter; and at each annual election held after such classification becomes effective, directors shall be chosen for a full term, as the case may be, to succeed those whose terms expire. ▪ The certificate of incorporation or bylaw provision dividing the directors into classes may authorize the board of directors to assign members of the board already in office to such classes at the time such classification becomes effective. ▪ The certificate of incorporation may confer upon holders of any class or series of stock the right to elect 1 or more directors who shall serve for such term, and have such voting powers as shall be stated in the certificate of incorporation. ▪ The terms of office and voting powers of the directors elected separately by the holders of any class or series of stock may be greater than or less than those of any other director or class of directors. ▪ In addition, the certificate of incorporation may confer upon 1 or more directors, whether or not elected separately by the holders of any class or series of stock, voting powers greater than or less than those of other directors. ▪ Any such provision conferring greater or lesser voting power shall apply to voting in any committee, unless otherwise provided in the certificate of incorporation or bylaws. ▪ If the certificate of incorporation provides that 1 or more directors shall have more or less than 1 vote per director on any matter, every reference in this chapter to a majority or other proportion of the directors shall refer to a majority or other proportion of the votes of the directors.

(e) A member of the board of directors, or a member of any committee designated by the board of directors, shall, in the performance of such member's duties, be fully protected in relying in good faith upon the records of the corporation and upon such information, opinions, reports or statements presented to the corporation by any of the corporation's officers or employees, or committees of the board of directors, or by any other person as to matters the member reasonably believes are within such other person's professional or expert competence and who has been selected with reasonable care by or on behalf of the corporation.

(f) Unless otherwise restricted by the certificate of incorporation or bylaws, **(1)** any action required or permitted to be taken at any meeting of the board of directors or of any committee thereof may be taken without a meeting if all members of the board or committee, as the case may be, consent thereto in writing, or by electronic transmission, and **(2)** a consent may be documented, signed and delivered in any manner permitted by § 116 of this title. ▪ Any person (whether or not then a director) may provide, whether through instruction to an agent or otherwise, that a consent to action will be effective at a future time (including a time determined upon the happening of an event), no later than 60 days after such instruction is given or such provision is made and such consent shall be deemed to have been given for purposes of this subsection at such effective time so long as such person is then a director and did not revoke the consent prior to such time. ▪ Any such consent shall be revocable prior to its becoming effective. ▪ After an action is taken, the consent or consents relating thereto shall be filed with the minutes of the proceedings of the board of directors, or the committee thereof, in the same paper or electronic form as the minutes are maintained.

(g) Unless otherwise restricted by the certificate of incorporation or bylaws, the board of directors of any corporation organized under this chapter may hold its meetings, and have an office or offices, outside of this State.

(h) Unless otherwise restricted by the certificate of incorporation or bylaws, the board of directors shall have the authority to fix the compensation of directors.

(i) Unless otherwise restricted by the certificate of incorporation or bylaws, members of the board of directors of any corporation, or any committee designated by the board, may participate in a meeting of such board, or committee by means of conference telephone or other communications equipment by means of which all persons participating in the meeting can hear each other, and participation in a meeting pursuant to this subsection shall constitute presence in person at the meeting.

(j) The certificate of incorporation of any nonstock corporation may provide that less than ⅓ of the members of the governing body may constitute a quorum thereof and may otherwise provide that the business and affairs of the corporation shall be managed in a manner different from that provided in this section. ▪ Except as may be otherwise provided by the certificate of incorporation, this section shall apply to such a corporation, and when so applied, all references to the board of directors, to members thereof, and to stockholders shall be deemed to refer to the governing body of the corporation, the members thereof and the members of the corporation, respectively; and all references to stock, capital stock, or shares thereof shall be deemed to refer to memberships of a nonprofit nonstock corporation and to membership interests of any other nonstock corporation.

(k) Any director or the entire board of directors may be removed, with or without cause, by the holders of a majority of the shares then entitled to vote at an election of directors, except as follows:

(1) Unless the certificate of incorporation otherwise provides, in the case of a corporation whose board is classified as provided in subsection (d) of this section, stockholders may effect such removal only for cause; or

(2) In the case of a corporation having cumulative voting, if less than the entire board is to be removed, no director may be removed without cause if the votes cast against such director's removal would be sufficient to elect such director if then cumulatively voted at an election of the entire board of directors, or, if there be classes of directors, at an election of the class of directors of which such director is a part.

Whenever the holders of any class or series are entitled to elect 1 or more directors by the certificate of incorporation, this subsection shall apply, in respect to the removal without cause of a director or directors so elected, to the vote of the holders of the outstanding shares of that class or series and not to the vote of the outstanding shares as a whole.

§ 142. Officers; titles, duties, selection, term; failure to elect; vacancies.

(a) Every corporation organized under this chapter shall have such officers with such titles and duties as shall be stated in the bylaws or in a resolution of the board of directors which is not inconsistent with the bylaws and as may be necessary to enable it to sign instruments and stock certificates which comply with §§ 103(a)(2) and 158 of this title. ▪ One of the officers shall have the duty to record the proceedings of the meetings of the stockholders and directors in a book to be kept for that purpose. ▪ Any number of offices may be held by the same person unless the certificate of incorporation or bylaws otherwise provide.

(b) Officers shall be chosen in such manner and shall hold their offices for such terms as are prescribed by the bylaws or determined by the board of directors or other governing body. Each officer shall hold office until such offi___ ___ssor is elected and qualified or until ___ ___r-lier resignation or removal. ▪ ___ ___ sign at any time upon writt___ ___ration.

(c) The corporation r___ or all of its officer___

(d) A failure t___ otherwise af___

(e) Any vacancy occurring in any office of the corporation by death, resignation, removal or otherwise, shall be filled as the bylaws provide. ▪ In the absence of such provision, the vacancy shall be filled by the board of directors or other governing body.

§ 143. Loans to employees and officers; guaranty of obligations of employees and officers.

Any corporation may lend money to, or guarantee any obligation of, or otherwise assist any officer or other employee of the corporation or of its subsidiary, including any officer or employee who is a director of the corporation or its subsidiary, whenever, in the judgment of the directors, such loan, guaranty or assistance may reasonably be expected to benefit the corporation. ▪ The loan, guaranty or other assistance may be with or without interest, and may be unsecured, or secured in such manner as the board of directors shall approve, including, without limitation, a pledge of shares of stock of the corporation. ▪ Nothing in this section contained shall be deemed to deny, limit or restrict the powers of guaranty or warranty of any corporation at common law or under any statute.

§ 144. Interested directors; quorum.

(a) No contract or transaction between a corporation and 1 or more of its directors or officers, or between a corporation and any other corporation, partnership, association, or other organization in which 1 or more of its directors or officers, are directors or officers, or have a financial interest, shall be void or voidable solely for this reason, or solely because the director or officer is present at or participates in the meeting of the board or committee which authorizes the contract or transaction, or solely because any such director's or officer's votes are counted for such purpose, if:

    (1) The material facts as to the director's or officer's relationship or interest and as to the contract or transaction are disclosed or are known to the board of directors or the committee, and the board or committee in good faith authorizes the contract or transaction by the affirmative

votes of a majority of the disinterested directors, even though the disinterested directors be less than a quorum; or

    (2) The material facts as to the director's or officer's relationship or interest and as to the contract or transaction are disclosed or are known to the stockholders entitled to vote thereon, and the contract or transaction is specifically approved in good faith by vote of the stockholders; or

    (3) The contract or transaction is fair as to the corporation as of the time it is authorized, approved or ratified, by the board of directors, a committee or the stockholders.

(b) Common or interested directors may be counted in determining the presence of a quorum at a meeting of the board of directors or of a committee which authorizes the contract or transaction.

§ 145. Indemnification of officers, directors, employees and agents; insurance.

(a) A corporation shall have power to indemnify any person who was or is a party or is threatened to be made a party to any threatened, pending or completed action, suit or proceeding, whether civil, criminal, administrative or investigative (other than an action by or in the right of the corporation) by reason of the fact that the person is or was a director, officer, employee or agent of the corporation, or is or was serving at the request of the corporation as a director, officer, employee or agent of another corporation, partnership, joint venture, trust or other enterprise, against expenses (including attorneys' fees), judgments, fines and amounts paid in settlement actually and reasonably incurred by the person in connection with such action, suit or proceeding if the person acted in good faith and in a manner the person reasonably believed to be in or not opposed to the best interests of the corporation, and, with respect to any criminal action or proceeding, had no reasonable cause to believe the person's conduct was unlawful. ▪ The termination of any action, suit or proceeding by judgment, order, settlement, conviction, or upon a plea of nolo contendere or its equivalent, shall not, of itself, create a presumption that the person did not act in good faith and in a manner which the person reasonably believed to be in or not opposed to the best interests of the corporation, and, with respect to any criminal action or proceeding, had reasonable cause to believe that the person's conduct was unlawful.

(b) A corporation shall have power to indemnify any person who was or is a party or is threatened to be made a party to any threatened, pending or completed action or suit by or in the right of the corporation to procure a judgment in its favor by reason of the fact that the person is or was a director, officer, employee or agent of the corporation, or is or was serving at the request of the corporation as a director, officer, employee or agent of another corporation, partnership, joint venture, trust or other enterprise against expenses (including attorneys' fees) actually and reasonably incurred by the person in connection with the defense or settlement of such action or suit if the person acted in good faith and in a manner the person reasonably believed to be in or not opposed to the best interests of the corporation and except that no indemnification shall be made in respect of any claim, issue or matter as to which such person shall have been adjudged to be liable to the corporation unless and only to the extent that the Court of Chancery or the court in which such action or suit was brought shall determine upon application that, despite the adjudication of liability but in view of all the circumstances of the case, such person is fairly and reasonably entitled to indemnity for such expenses which the Court of Chancery or such other court shall deem proper.

(c)(1) To the extent that a present or former director or officer of a corporation has been successful on the merits or otherwise in defense of any action, suit or proceeding referred to in subsections (a) and (b) of this section, or in defense of any claim, issue or matter therein, such person shall be indemnified against expenses (including attorneys' fees) actually and reasonably incurred by such person in connection therewith.

■ For indemnification with respect to any act or omission occurring after December 31, 2020, references to "officer" for purposes of this paragraphs (c)(1) and (2) of this section shall mean only a person who at the time of such act or omission is deemed to have consented to service by the delivery of process to the registered agent of the corporation pursuant to § 3114(b) of Title 10 (for purposes of this sentence only, treating residents of this State as if they were nonresidents to apply § 3114(b) of Title 10 to this sentence).

(2) The corporation may indemnify any other person who is not a present or former director or officer of the corporation against expenses (including attorneys' fees) actually and reasonably incurred by such person to the extent he or she has been successful on the merits or otherwise in defense of any action, suit or proceeding referred to in subsections (a) and (b) of this section, or in defense of any claim, issue or matter therein.

(d) Any indemnification under subsections (a) and (b) of this section (unless ordered by a court) shall be made by the corporation only as authorized in the specific case upon a determination that indemnification of the present or former director, officer, employee or agent is proper in the circumstances because the person has met the applicable standard of conduct set forth in subsections (a) and (b) of this section. ■ Such determination shall be made, with respect to a person who is a director or officer of the corporation at the time of such determination:

(1) By a majority vote of the directors who are not parties to such action, suit or proceeding, even though less than a quorum; or

(2) By a committee of such directors designated by majority vote of such directors, even though less than a quorum; or

(3) If there are no such directors, or if such directors so direct, by independent legal counsel in a written opinion; or

(4) By the stockholders.

(e) Expenses (including attorneys' fees) incurred by an officer or director of the corporation in defending any civil, criminal, administrative or investigative action, suit or proceeding may be paid by the corporation in advance of the final disposition of such action, suit or proceeding upon receipt of an undertaking by or on behalf of such director or officer to repay such amount if it shall ultimately be determined that such person is not entitled to be indemnified by the corporation as authorized in this section. ■ Such expenses (including attorneys' fees) incurred by former directors and officers or other employees and agents of the corporation or by persons serving at the request of the corporation as directors, officers, employees or agents of another corporation, partnership, joint venture, trust or other enterprise may be so paid upon such terms and conditions, if any, as the corporation deems appropriate.

(f) The indemnification and advancement of expenses provided by, or granted pursuant to, the other subsections of this section shall not be deemed exclusive of any other rights to which those seeking indemnification or advancement of expenses may be entitled under any bylaw, agreement, vote of stockholders or disinterested directors or otherwise, both as to action in such person's official capacity and as to action in another capacity while holding such office. ■ A right to indemnification or to advancement of expenses arising under a provision of the certificate of incorporation or a bylaw shall not be eliminated or impaired by an amendment to or repeal or elimination of the certificate of incorporation or the bylaws after the occurrence of the act or omission that is the subject of the civil, criminal, administrative or investigative action, suit or proceeding for which indemnification or advancement of expenses is sought, unless the provision in effect at the time of such act or omission explicitly authorizes such elimination or impairment after such action or omission has occurred.

(g) A corporation shall have power to purchase and maintain insurance on behalf of any person who is or was a director, officer, employee or agent of the corporation, or is or was serving at the request of the corporation as a director, officer, employee or agent of another corporation, partnership, joint venture, trust or other enterprise against any liability asserted against such person and incurred by such person in any such capacity, or arising out of such person's status as such, whether or not the corporation would have the power to indemnify such person against such liability under this section.

(h) For purposes of this section, references to "the corporation" shall include, in addition to the resulting corporation, any constituent corporation (including any constituent of a constituent) absorbed in a consolidation or merger which, if its separate existence had continued, would have had power and authority to indemnify its directors, officers, and employees or agents, so that any person who is or was a director, officer, employee or agent of such constituent corporation, or is or was serving at the request of such constituent corporation as a director, officer, employee or agent of another corporation, partnership, joint venture, trust or other enterprise, shall stand in the same position under this section with respect to the resulting or surviving corporation as such person would have with respect to such constituent corporation if its separate existence had continued.

(i) For purposes of this section, references to "other enterprises" shall include employee benefit plans; references to "fines" shall include any excise taxes assessed on a person with respect to any employee benefit plan; and references to "serving at the request of the corporation" shall include any service as a director, officer, employee or agent of the corporation which imposes duties on, or involves services by, such director, officer, employee or agent with respect to an employee benefit plan, its participants or beneficiaries; and a person who acted in good faith and in a manner such person reasonably believed to be in the interest of the participants and beneficiaries of an employee benefit plan shall be deemed to have acted in a manner "not opposed to the best interests of the corporation" as referred to in this section.

(j) The indemnification and advancement of expenses provided by, or granted pursuant to, this section shall, unless otherwise provided when authorized or ratified, continue as to a person who has ceased to be a director, officer, employee or agent and shall inure to the benefit of the heirs, executors and administrators of such a person.

(k) The Court of Chancery is hereby vested with exclusive jurisdiction to hear and determine all actions for advancement of expenses or indemnification brought under this section or under any bylaw, agreement, vote of stockholders or disinterested directors, or otherwise. ▪ The Court of Chancery may summarily determine a corporation's obligation to advance expenses (including attorneys' fees).

§ 146. Submission of matters for stockholder vote.

A corporation may agree to submit a matter to a vote of its stockholders whether or not the board of directors determines at any time subsequent to approving such matter that such matter is no longer advisable and recommends that the stockholders reject or vote against the matter.

Subchapter V. Stock and Dividends

§ 151. Classes and series of stock; redemption; rights.

(a) Every corporation may issue 1 or more classes of stock or 1 or more series of stock within any class thereof, any or all of which classes may be of stock with par value or stock without par value and which classes or series may have such voting powers, full or limited, or no voting powers, and such designations, preferences and relative, participating, optional or other special rights, and qualifications, limitations or restrictions thereof, as shall be stated and expressed in the certificate of incorporation or of any amendment thereto, or in the resolution or resolutions providing for the issue of such stock adopted by the board of directors pursuant to authority expressly vested in it by the provisions of its certificate of incorporation. ▪ Any of the voting powers, designations, preferences, rights and qualifications, limitations or restrictions of any such class or series of stock may be made

dependent upon facts ascertainable outside the certificate of incorporation or of any amendment thereto, or outside the resolution or resolutions providing for the issue of such stock adopted by the board of directors pursuant to authority expressly vested in it by its certificate of incorporation, provided that the manner in which such facts shall operate upon the voting powers, designations, preferences, rights and qualifications, limitations or restrictions of such class or series of stock is clearly and expressly set forth in the certificate of incorporation or in the resolution or resolutions providing for the issue of such stock adopted by the board of directors. ▪ The term "facts," as used in this subsection, includes, but is not limited to, the occurrence of any event, including a determination or action by any person or body, including the corporation. ▪ The power to increase or decrease or otherwise adjust the capital stock as provided in this chapter shall apply to all or any such classes of stock.

(b) Any stock of any class or series may be made subject to redemption by the corporation at its option or at the option of the holders of such stock or upon the happening of a specified event; provided however, that immediately following any such redemption the corporation shall have outstanding 1 or more shares of 1 or more classes or series of stock, which share, or shares together, shall have full voting powers. ▪ Notwithstanding the limitation stated in the foregoing proviso:

(1) Any stock of a regulated investment company registered under the Investment Company Act of 1940 [15 U.S.C. § 80 a-1 et seq.], as heretofore or hereafter amended, may be made subject to redemption by the corporation at its option or at the option of the holders of such stock.

(2) Any stock of a corporation which holds (directly or indirectly) a license or franchise from a governmental agency to conduct its business or is a member of a national securities exchange, which license, franchise or membership is conditioned upon some or all of the holders of its stock possessing prescribed qualifications, may be made subject to redemption by the corporation to the extent necessary to prevent the loss of such license, franchise or membership or to reinstate it.

Any stock which may be made redeemable under this section may be redeemed for cash, property or rights, including securities of the same or another corporation, at such time or times, price or prices, or rate or rates, and with such adjustments, as shall be stated in the certificate of incorporation or in the resolution or resolutions providing for the issue of such stock adopted by the board of directors pursuant to subsection (a) of this section.

(c) The holders of preferred or special stock of any class or of any series thereof shall be entitled to receive dividends at such rates, on such conditions and at such times as shall be stated in the certificate of incorporation or in the resolution or resolutions providing for the issue of such stock adopted by the board of directors as hereinabove provided, payable in preference to, or in such relation to, the dividends payable on any other class or classes or of any other series of stock, and cumulative or noncumulative as shall be so stated and expressed. ▪ When dividends upon the preferred and special stocks, if any, to the extent of the preference to which such stocks are entitled, shall have been paid or declared and set apart for payment, a dividend on the remaining class or classes or series of stock may then be paid out of the remaining assets of the corporation available for dividends as elsewhere in this chapter provided.

(d) The holders of the preferred or special stock of any class or of any series thereof shall be entitled to such rights upon the dissolution of, or upon any distribution of the assets of, the corporation as shall be stated in the certificate of incorporation or in the resolution or resolutions providing for the issue of such stock adopted by the board of directors as hereinabove provided.

(e) Any stock of any class or of any series thereof may be made convertible into, or exchangeable for, at the option of either the holder or the corporation or upon the happening of a specified event, shares of any other class or classes or any other series of the same or any other class or classes of stock of the corporation, at such price or prices or at such rate or rates of exchange and with such adjustments as shall be stated in the certificate of incorporation or in the resolution or resolutions providing for the issue of such stock adopted by the board of directors as hereinabove provided.

(f) If any corporation shall be authorized to issue more than 1 class of stock or more than 1 series of any class, the powers, designations, preferences and relative, participating, optional, or other special rights of each class of stock or series thereof and the qualifications, limitations or restrictions of such preferences and/or rights shall be set forth in full or summarized on the face or back of the certificate which the corporation shall issue to represent such class or series of stock, provided that, except as otherwise provided in § 202 of this title, in lieu of the foregoing requirements, there may be set forth on the face or back of the certificate which the corporation shall issue to represent such class or series of stock, a statement that the corporation will furnish without charge to each stockholder who so requests the powers, designations, preferences and relative, participating, optional, or other special rights of each class of stock or series thereof and the qualifications, limitations or restrictions of such preferences and/or rights. ▪ Within a reasonable time after the issuance or transfer of uncertificated stock, the registered owner thereof shall be given a notice, in writing or by electronic transmission, containing the information required to be set forth or stated on certificates pursuant to this section or § 156, § 202(a), § 218(a) or § 364 of this title or with respect to this section a statement that the corporation will furnish without charge to each stockholder who so requests the powers, designations, preferences and relative participating, optional or other special rights of each class of stock or series thereof and the qualifications, limitations or restrictions of such preferences and/or rights. ▪ Except as otherwise expressly provided by law, the rights and obligations of the holders of uncertificated stock and the rights and obligations of the holders of certificates representing stock of the same class and series shall be identical.

(g) When any corporation desires to issue any shares of stock of any class or of any series of any class of which the powers, designations, preferences and relative, participating, optional or other rights, if any, or the qualifications, limitations or restrictions thereof, if any, shall not have been set forth in the certificate of incorporation or in any amendment thereto but shall be provided for in a resolution or resolutions adopted by the board of directors pursuant to authority expressly vested in it by the certificate of incorporation or any amendment thereto, a certificate of designations setting forth a copy of such resolution or resolutions and the number of shares of stock of such class or series as to which the resolution or resolutions apply shall be executed, acknowledged, filed and shall become effective, in accordance with § 103 of this title. ▪ Unless otherwise provided in any such resolution or resolutions, the number of shares of stock of any such series to which such resolution or resolutions apply may be increased (but not above the total number of authorized shares of the class) or decreased (but not below the number of shares thereof then outstanding) by a certificate likewise executed, acknowledged and filed setting forth a statement that a specified increase or decrease therein had been authorized and directed by a resolution or resolutions likewise adopted by the board of directors. ▪ In case the number of such shares shall be decreased the number of shares so specified in the certificate shall resume the status which they had prior to the adoption of the first resolution or resolutions. ▪ When no shares of any such class or series are outstanding, either because none were issued or because no issued shares of any such class or series remain outstanding, a certificate setting forth a resolution or resolutions adopted by the board of directors that none of the authorized shares of such class or series are outstanding, and that none will be issued subject to the certificate of designations previously filed with respect to such class or series, may be executed, acknowledged and filed in accordance with § 103 of this title and, when such certificate becomes effective, it shall have the effect of eliminating from the certificate of incorporation all matters set forth in the certificate of designations with respect to such class or series of stock. ▪ Unless otherwise provided in the certificate of incorporation, if no shares of stock have been issued of a class or series of stock established by a resolution of the board of directors, the voting powers, designations, preferences and relative, participating, optional or other rights, if any, or the qualifications, limitations or restrictions thereof, may be amended by a resolution or resolutions adopted by the board of directors. ▪ A certificate which:

(1) States that no shares of the class or series have been issued;

(2) Sets forth a copy of the resolution or resolutions; and

(3) If the designation of the class or series is being changed, indicates the original designation and the new designation,

shall be executed, acknowledged and filed and shall become effective, in accordance with § 103 of this title. ▪ When any certificate filed under this subsection becomes effective, it shall have the effect of amending the certificate of incorporation; except that neither the filing of such certificate nor the filing of a restated certificate of incorporation pursuant to § 245 of this title shall prohibit the board of directors from subsequently adopting such resolutions as authorized by this subsection.

§ 152. Issuance of stock; lawful consideration; fully paid stock.

The consideration, as determined pursuant to § 153(a) and (b) of this title, for subscriptions to, or the purchase of, the capital stock to be issued by a corporation shall be paid in such form and in such manner as the board of directors shall determine. ▪ The board of directors may authorize capital stock to be issued for consideration consisting of cash, any tangible or intangible property or any benefit to the corporation, or any combination thereof. ▪ The resolution authorizing the issuance of capital stock may provide that any stock to be issued pursuant to such resolution may be issued in 1 or more transactions in such numbers and at such times as are set forth in or determined by or in the manner set forth in the resolution, which may include a determination or action by any person or body, including the corporation, provided the resolution fixes a maximum number of shares that may be issued pursuant to such resolution, a time period during which such shares may be issued and a minimum amount of consideration for which such shares may be issued. ▪ The board of directors may determine the amount of consideration for which shares may be issued by setting a minimum amount of consideration or approving a formula by which the amount or minimum amount of consideration is determined. ▪ The formula may include or be made dependent upon facts ascertainable outside the formula, provided the manner in which such facts shall operate upon the formula is clearly and expressly set forth in the formula or in the resolution approving the formula. ▪ In the absence of actual fraud in the transaction, the judgment of the directors as to the value of such consideration shall be conclusive. ▪ The capital stock so issued shall be deemed to be fully paid and nonassessable stock upon receipt by the corporation of such consideration; provided, however, nothing contained herein shall prevent the board of directors from issuing partly paid shares under § 156 of this title.

§ 153. Consideration for stock.

(a) Shares of stock with par value may be issued for such consideration, having a value not less than the par value thereof, as determined from time to time by the board of directors, or by the stockholders if the certificate of incorporation so provides.

(b) Shares of stock without par value may be issued for such consideration as is determined from time to time by the board of directors, or by the stockholders if the certificate of incorporation so provides.

(c) Treasury shares may be disposed of by the corporation for such consideration as may be determined from time to time by the board of directors, or by the stockholders if the certificate of incorporation so provides.

(d) If the certificate of incorporation reserves to the stockholders the right to determine the consideration for the issue of any shares, the stockholders

shall, unless the certificate requires a greater vote, do so by a vote of a majority of the outstanding stock entitled to vote thereon.

§ 154. Determination of amount of capital; capital, surplus and net assets defined.

Any corporation may, by resolution of its board of directors, determine that only a part of the consideration which shall be received by the corporation for any of the shares of its capital stock which it shall issue from time to time shall be capital; but, in case any of the shares issued shall be shares having a par value, the amount of the part of such consideration so determined to be capital shall be in excess of the aggregate par value of the shares issued for such consideration having a par value, unless all the shares issued shall be shares having a par value, in which case the amount of the part of such consideration so determined to be capital need be only equal to the aggregate par value of such shares. ▪ In each such case the board of directors shall specify in dollars the part of such consideration which shall be capital. ▪ If the board of directors shall not have determined **(1)** at the time of issue of any shares of the capital stock of the corporation issued for cash or **(2)** within 60 days after the issue of any shares of the capital stock of the corporation issued for consideration other than cash what part of the consideration for such shares shall be capital, the capital of the corporation in respect of such shares shall be an amount equal to the aggregate par value of such shares having a par value, plus the amount of the consideration for such shares without par value. ▪ The amount of the consideration so determined to be capital in respect of any shares without par value shall be the stated capital of such shares. ▪ The capital of the corporation may be increased from time to time by resolution of the board of directors directing that a portion of the net assets of the corporation in excess of the amount so determined to be capital be transferred to the capital account. ▪ The board of directors may direct that the portion of such net assets so transferred shall be treated as capital in respect of any shares of the corporation of any designated class or classes. ▪ The excess, if any, at any given time, of the net assets of the corporation over the amount so determined to be capital shall be surplus. ■ Net assets means the amount by which total assets exceed total liabilities. ■ Capital and surplus are not liabilities for this purpose. ■ Notwithstanding anything in this section to the contrary, for purposes of this section and §§ 160 and 170 of this title, the capital of any nonstock corporation shall be deemed to be zero.

§ 155. Fractions of shares.

A corporation may, but shall not be required to, issue fractions of a share. ■ If it does not issue fractions of a share, it shall **(1)** arrange for the disposition of fractional interests by those entitled thereto, **(2)** pay in cash the fair value of fractions of a share as of the time when those entitled to receive such fractions are determined or **(3)** issue scrip or warrants in registered form (either represented by a certificate or uncertificated) or in bearer form (represented by a certificate) which shall entitle the holder to receive a full share upon the surrender of such scrip or warrants aggregating a full share. ■ A certificate for a fractional share or an uncertificated fractional share shall, but scrip or warrants shall not unless otherwise provided therein, entitle the holder to exercise voting rights, to receive dividends thereon and to participate in any of the assets of the corporation in the event of liquidation. ■ The board of directors may cause scrip or warrants to be issued subject to the conditions that they shall become void if not exchanged for certificates representing the full shares or uncertificated full shares before a specified date, or subject to the conditions that the shares for which scrip or warrants are exchangeable may be sold by the corporation and the proceeds thereof distributed to the holders of scrip or warrants, or subject to any other conditions which the board of directors may impose.

§ 156. Partly paid shares.

Any corporation may issue the whole or any part of its shares as partly paid and subject to call for the remainder of the consideration to be paid therefor. ■ Upon the face or back of each stock certificate issued to represent any such partly paid shares, or upon the books and records of the corporation in the case of uncertificated partly paid shares, the total amount of the consideration to be paid therefor and the amount paid thereon shall be stated. ■ Upon the declaration of any dividend on fully paid shares, the corporation shall declare a dividend upon partly paid shares of the same class, but only upon the basis of the percentage of the consideration actually paid thereon.

§ 157. Rights and options respecting stock.

(a) Subject to any provisions in the certificate of incorporation, every corporation may create and issue, whether or not in connection with the issue and sale of any shares of stock or other securities of the corporation, rights or options entitling the holders thereof to acquire from the corporation any shares of its capital stock of any class or classes, such rights or options to be evidenced by or in such instrument or instruments as shall be approved by the board of directors.

(b) The terms upon which, including the time or times which may be limited or unlimited in duration, at or within which, and the consideration (including a formula by which such consideration may be determined) for which any such shares may be acquired from the corporation upon the exercise of any such right or option, shall be such as shall be stated in the certificate of incorporation, or in a resolution adopted by the board of directors providing for the creation and issue of such rights or options, and, in every case, shall be set forth or incorporated by reference in the instrument or instruments evidencing such rights

formula by which
termin
facts a
the mar
the forn
formula
■ In the
the judg
tion for tl
the suffic

(c) The b
adopted by

226

of the corporation to do 1 or both of the following: **(i)** designate officers and employees of the corporation or of any of its subsidiaries to be recipients of such rights or options created by the corporation, and **(ii)** determine the number of such rights or options to be received by such officers and employees; provided, however, that the resolution so authorizing such officer or officers shall specify the total number of rights or options such officer or officers may so award. ▪ The board of directors may not authorize an officer to designate himself or herself as a recipient of any such rights or options.

(d) In case the shares of stock of the corporation to be issued upon the exercise of such rights or options shall be shares having a par value, the consideration so to be received therefor shall have a value not less than the par value thereof. ▪ In case the shares of stock so to be issued shall be shares of stock without par value, the consideration therefor shall be determined in the manner provided in § 153 of this title.

§ 158. Stock certificates; uncertificated shares.

The shares of a corporation shall be represented by certificates, provided that the board of directors of the corporation may provide by resolution or resolutions that some or all of any or all classes or series of its stock shall be uncertificated shares. ▪ Any such resolution shall not apply to shares represented by a certificate until such certificate is surrendered to the corporation. ▪ Every holder of stock represented by certificates shall be entitled to have a certificate signed by, or in the name of, the corporation by any 2 authorized officers of the corporation representing the number of shares registered in certificate form. ▪ Any or all the signatures on the certificate may be a facsimile. ▪ In any officer, transfer agent or registrar who has or whose facsimile signature has been on a certificate shall have ceased to be transfer agent or registrar before such sued, it may be issued by the corpo- me effect as if such person were agent or registrar at the date ion shall not have power to er form.

§ 159. Shares of stock; personal property, transfer and taxation.

The shares of stock in every corporation shall be deemed personal property and transferable as provided in Article 8 of subtitle I of Title 6. ▪ No stock or bonds issued by any corporation organized under this chapter shall be taxed by this State when the same shall be owned by nonresidents of this State, or by foreign corporations. ▪ Whenever any transfer of shares shall be made for collateral security, and not absolutely, it shall be so expressed in the entry of transfer if, when the certificates are presented to the corporation for transfer or uncertificated shares are requested to be transferred, both the transferor and transferee request the corporation to do so.

§ 160. Corporation's powers respecting ownership, voting, etc., of its own stock; rights of stock called for redemption.

(a) Every corporation may purchase, redeem, receive, take or otherwise acquire, own and hold, sell, lend, exchange, transfer or otherwise dispose of, pledge, use and otherwise deal in and with its own shares; provided, however, that no corporation shall:

(1) Purchase or redeem its own shares of capital stock for cash or other property when the capital of the corporation is impaired or when such purchase or redemption would cause any impairment of the capital of the corporation, except that a corporation other than a nonstock corporation may purchase or redeem out of capital any of its own shares which are entitled upon any distribution of its assets, whether by dividend or in liquidation, to a preference over another class or series of its stock, or, if no shares entitled to such a preference are outstanding, any of its own shares, if such shares will be retired upon their acquisition and the capital of the corporation reduced in accordance with §§ 243 and 244 of this title. ▪ Nothing in this subsection shall invalidate or otherwise affect a note, debenture or other obligation of a corporation given by it as consideration for

its acquisition by purchase, redemption or exchange of its shares of stock if at the time such note, debenture or obligation was delivered by the corporation its capital was not then impaired or did not thereby become impaired;

(2) Purchase, for more than the price at which they may then be redeemed, any of its shares which are redeemable at the option of the corporation; or

(3) **a.** In the case of a corporation other than a nonstock corporation, redeem any of its shares, unless their redemption is authorized by § 151(b) of this title and then only in accordance with such section and the certificate of incorporation, or

b. In the case of a nonstock corporation, redeem any of its membership interests, unless their redemption is authorized by the certificate of incorporation and then only in accordance with the certificate of incorporation.

(b) Nothing in this section limits or affects a corporation's right to resell any of its shares theretofore purchased or redeemed out of surplus and which have not been retired, for such consideration as shall be fixed by the board of directors.

(c) Shares of its own capital stock belonging to the corporation or to another corporation, if a majority of the shares entitled to vote in the election of directors of such other corporation is held, directly or indirectly, by the corporation, shall neither be entitled to vote nor be counted for quorum purposes. ■ Nothing in this section shall be construed as limiting the right of any corporation to vote stock, including but not limited to its own stock, held by it in a fiduciary capacity.

(d) Shares which have been called for redemption shall not be deemed to be outstanding shares for the purpose of voting or determining the total number of shares entitled to vote on any matter on and after the date on which notice of redemption has been sent to holders thereof and a sum sufficient to redeem such shares has been irrevocably deposited or set aside to pay the redemption price

to the holders of the shares upon surrender of certificates therefor.

§ 161. Issuance of additional stock; when and by whom.

The directors may, at any time and from time to time, if all of the shares of capital stock which the corporation is authorized by its certificate of incorporation to issue have not been issued, subscribed for, or otherwise committed to be issued, issue or take subscriptions for additional shares of its capital stock up to the amount authorized in its certificate of incorporation.

§ 162. Liability of stockholder or subscriber for stock not paid in full.

(a) When the whole of the consideration payable for shares of a corporation has not been paid in, and the assets shall be insufficient to satisfy the claims of its creditors, each holder of or subscriber for such shares shall be bound to pay on each share held or subscribed for by such holder or subscriber the sum necessary to complete the amount of the unpaid balance of the consideration for which such shares were issued or are to be issued by the corporation.

(b) The amounts which shall be payable as provided in subsection (a) of this section may be recovered as provided in § 325 of this title, after a writ of execution against the corporation has been returned unsatisfied as provided in said § 325.

(c) Any person becoming an assignee or transferee of shares or of a subscription for shares in good faith and without knowledge or notice that the full consideration therefor has not been paid shall not be personally liable for any unpaid portion of such consideration, but the transferor shall remain liable therefor.

(d) No person holding shares in any corporation as collateral security shall be personally liable as a stockholder but the person pledging such shares shall be considered the holder thereof and shall be so liable. ■ No executor, administrator, guardian, trustee or other fiduciary shall be personally liable as a stockholder, but the estate or funds held by such executor, administrator, guardian, trustee or other fiduciary in such fiduciary capacity shall be liable.

(e) No liability under this section or under § 325 of this title shall be asserted more than 6 years after the issuance of the stock or the date of the subscription upon which the assessment is sought.

(f) In any action by a receiver or trustee of an insolvent corporation or by a judgment creditor to obtain an assessment under this section, any stockholder or subscriber for stock of the insolvent corporation may appear and contest the claim or claims of such receiver or trustee.

§ 163. Payment for stock not paid in full.

The capital stock of a corporation shall be paid for in such amounts and at such times as the directors may require. ▪ The directors may, from time to time, demand payment, in respect of each share of stock not fully paid, of such sum of money as the necessities of the business may, in the judgment of the board of directors, require, not exceeding in the whole the balance remaining unpaid on said stock, and such sum so demanded shall be paid to the corporation at such times and by such installments as the directors shall direct. ▪ The directors shall give notice of the time and place of such payments, which notice shall be given at least 30 days before the time for such payment, to each holder of or subscriber for stock which is not fully paid at such holder's or subscriber's last known address.

§ 164. Failure to pay for stock; remedies.

When any stockholder fails to pay any installment or call upon such stockholder's stock which may have been properly demanded by the directors, at the time when such payment is due, the directors may collect the amount of any such installment or call or any balance thereof remaining unpaid, from the said stockholder by an action at law, or they shall sell at public sale such part of the shares of such delinquent stockholder as will pay all demands then due from such stockholder with interest and all incidental expenses, and shall transfer the shares so sold to the purchaser, who shall be entitled to a certificate therefor.

Notice of the time and place of such sale and of the sum due on each share shall be given by advertisement at least 1 week before the sale, in a newspaper of the county in this State where such corporation's registered office is located, and such notice shall be mailed by the corporation to such delinquent stockholder at such stockholder's last known post-office address, at least 20 days before such sale.

If no bidder can be had to pay the amount due on the stock, and if the amount is not collected by an action at law, which may be brought within the county where the corporation has its registered office, within 1 year from the date of the bringing of such action at law, the said stock and the amount previously paid in by the delinquent stockholder on the stock shall be forfeited to the corporation.

§ 165. Revocability of preincorporation subscriptions.

Unless otherwise provided by the terms of the subscription, a subscription for stock of a corporation to be formed shall be irrevocable, except with the consent of all other subscribers or the corporation, for a period of 6 months from its date.

§ 166. Formalities required of stock subscriptions.

A subscription for stock of a corporation, whether made before or after the formation of a corporation, shall not be enforceable against a subscriber, unless in writing and signed by the subscriber or by such subscriber's agent.

§ 167. Lost, stolen or destroyed stock certificates; issuance of new certificate or uncertificated shares.

A corporation may issue a new certificate of stock or uncertificated shares in place of any certificate theretofore issued by it, alleged to have been lost, stolen or destroyed, and the corporation may require the owner of the lost, stolen or destroyed certificate, or such owner's legal representative to give the corporation a bond sufficient to indemnify it against any claim that may be made against it on account of the alleged loss, theft or destruction of any such certificate or the issuance of such new certificate or uncertificated shares.

§ 168. Judicial proceedings to compel issuance of new certificate or uncertificated shares.

(a) If a corporation refuses to issue new uncertificated shares or a new certificate of stock in place of a certificate theretofore issued by it, or by any corporation of which it is the lawful successor, alleged to have been lost, stolen or destroyed, the owner of the lost, stolen or destroyed certificate or such owner's legal representatives may apply to the Court of Chancery for an order requiring the corporation to show cause why it should not issue new uncertificated shares or a new certificate of stock in place of the certificate so lost, stolen or destroyed. ▪ Such application shall be by a complaint which shall state the name of the corporation, the number and date of the certificate, if known or ascertainable by the plaintiff, the number of shares of stock represented thereby and to whom issued, and a statement of the circumstances attending such loss, theft or destruction. ▪ Thereupon the court shall make an order requiring the corporation to show cause at a time and place therein designated, why it should not issue new uncertificated shares or a new certificate of stock in place of the one described in the complaint. ▪ A copy of the complaint and order shall be served upon the corporation at least 5 days before the time designated in the order.

(b) If, upon hearing, the court is satisfied that the plaintiff is the lawful owner of the number of shares of capital stock, or any part thereof, described in the complaint, and that the certificate therefor has been lost, stolen or destroyed, and no sufficient cause has been shown why new uncertificated shares or a new certificate should not be issued in place thereof, it shall make an order requiring the corporation to issue and deliver to the plaintiff new uncertificated shares or a new certificate for such shares. ▪ In its order the court shall direct that, prior to the issuance and delivery to the plaintiff of such new uncertificated shares or a new certificate, the plaintiff give the corporation a bond in such form and with such security as to the court appears sufficient to indemnify the corporation

against any claim that may be made against it on account of the alleged loss, theft or destruction of any such certificate or the issuance of such new uncertificated shares or new certificate. ▪ No corporation which has issued uncertificated shares or a certificate pursuant to an order of the court entered hereunder shall be liable in an amount in excess of the amount specified in such bond.

§ 169. Situs of ownership of stock.

For all purposes of title, action, attachment, garnishment and jurisdiction of all courts held in this State, but not for the purpose of taxation, the situs of the ownership of the capital stock of all corporations existing under the laws of this State, whether organized under this chapter or otherwise, shall be regarded as in this State.

§ 170. Dividends; payment; wasting asset corporations.

(a) The directors of every corporation, subject to any restrictions contained in its certificate of incorporation, may declare and pay dividends upon the shares of its capital stock either:

   (1) Out of its surplus, as defined in and computed in accordance with §§ 154 and 244 of this title; or

   (2) In case there shall be no such surplus, out of its net profits for the fiscal year in which the dividend is declared and/or the preceding fiscal year.

If the capital of the corporation, computed in accordance with §§ 154 and 244 of this title, shall have been diminished by depreciation in the value of its property, or by losses, or otherwise, to an amount less than the aggregate amount of the capital represented by the issued and outstanding stock of all classes having a preference upon the distribution of assets, the directors of such corporation shall not declare and pay out of such net profits any dividends upon any shares of any classes of its capital stock until the deficiency in the amount of capital represented by the issued and outstanding stock of all classes having a preference upon the distribution of assets shall have been repaired. ▪ Nothing in this subsection shall invalidate or otherwise affect a note, debenture or other obligation of the corporation paid by it as a dividend on shares of its stock, or any payment made thereon, if at the time such note, debenture or obligation was delivered by the corporation, the corporation had either surplus or net profits as provided in (a)(1) or (2) of this section from which the dividend could lawfully have been paid.

(b) Subject to any restrictions contained in its certificate of incorporation, the directors of any corporation engaged in the exploitation of wasting assets (including but not limited to a corporation engaged in the exploitation of natural resources or other wasting assets, including patents, or engaged primarily in the liquidation of specific assets) may determine the net profits derived from the exploitation of such wasting assets or the net proceeds derived from such liquidation without taking into consideration the depletion of such assets resulting from lapse of time, consumption, liquidation or exploitation of such assets.

§ 171. Special purpose reserves.

The directors of a corporation may set apart out of any of the funds of the corporation available for dividends a reserve or reserves for any proper purpose and may abolish any such reserve.

§ 172. Liability of directors and committee members as to dividends or stock redemption.

A member of the board of directors, or a member of any committee designated by the board of directors, shall be fully protected in relying in good faith upon the records of the corporation and upon such information, opinions, reports or statements presented to the corporation by any of its officers or employees, or committees of the board of directors, or by any other person as to matters the director reasonably believes are within such other person's professional or expert competence and who has been selected with reasonable care by or on behalf of the corporation, as to the value and amount of the assets, liabilities and/or net profits of the corporation or any other facts pertinent to the existence and amount of surplus or other funds from which dividends might properly be declared

and paid, or with which the corporation's stock might properly be purchased or redeemed.

§ 173. Declaration and payment of dividends.

No corporation shall pay dividends except in accordance with this chapter. ▪ Dividends may be paid in cash, in property, or in shares of the corporation's capital stock. ▪ If the dividend is to be paid in shares of the corporation's theretofore unissued capital stock the board of directors shall, by resolution, direct that there be designated as capital in respect of such shares an amount which is not less than the aggregate par value of par value shares being declared as a dividend and, in the case of shares without par value being declared as a dividend, such amount as shall be determined by the board of directors. ▪ No such designation as capital shall be necessary if shares are being distributed by a corporation pursuant to a split-up or division of its stock rather than as payment of a dividend declared payable in stock of the corporation.

§ 174. Liability of directors for unlawful payment of dividend or unlawful stock purchase or redemption; exoneration from liability; contribution among directors; subrogation.

(a) In case of any wilful or negligent violation of § 160 or § 173 of this title, the directors under whose administration the same may happen shall be jointly and severally liable, at any time within 6 years after paying such unlawful dividend or after such unlawful stock purchase or redemption, to the corporation, and to its creditors in the event of its dissolution or insolvency, to the full amount of the dividend unlawfully paid, or to the full amount unlawfully paid for the purchase or redemption of the corporation's stock, with interest from the time such liability accrued. ▪ Any director who may have been absent when the same was done, or who may have dissented from the act or resolution by which the same was done, may be exonerated from such liability by causing his or her dissent to be entered on the books containing the minutes of the proceedings of the directors at the time the same was done, or immediately after such director has notice of the same.

(b) Any director against whom a claim is successfully asserted under this section shall be entitled to contribution from the other directors who voted for or concurred in the unlawful dividend, stock purchase or stock redemption.

(c) Any director against whom a claim is successfully asserted under this section shall be entitled, to the extent of the amount paid by such director as a result of such claim, to be subrogated to the rights of the corporation against stockholders who received the dividend on, or assets for the sale or redemption of, their stock with knowledge of facts indicating that such dividend, stock purchase or redemption was unlawful under this chapter, in proportion to the amounts received by such stockholders respectively.

Subchapter VI. Stock Transfers

§ 201. Transfer of stock, stock certificates and uncertificated stock.

Except as otherwise provided in this chapter, the transfer of stock and the certificates of stock which represent the stock or uncertificated stock shall be governed by Article 8 of subtitle I of Title 6. ■ To the extent that any provision of this chapter is inconsistent with any provision of subtitle I of Title 6, this chapter shall be controlling.

§ 202. Restrictions on transfer and ownership of securities.

(a) A written restriction or restrictions on the transfer or registration of transfer of a security of a corporation, or on the amount of the corporation's securities that may be owned by any person or group of persons, if permitted by this section and noted conspicuously on the certificate or certificates representing the security or securities so restricted or, in the case of uncertificated shares, contained in the notice or notices given pursuant to § 151(f) of this title, may be enforced against the holder of the restricted security or securities or any successor or transferee of the holder including an executor, administrator, trustee, guardian or other fiduciary entrusted with like responsibility for the person or estate of the holder. ■ Unless noted conspicuously

on the certificate or certificates representing the security or securities so restricted or, in the case of uncertificated shares, contained in the notice or notices given pursuant to § 151(f) of this title, a restriction, even though permitted by this section, is ineffective except against a person with actual knowledge of the restriction.

(b) A restriction on the transfer or registration of transfer of securities of a corporation, or on the amount of a corporation's securities that may be owned by any person or group of persons, may be imposed by the certificate of incorporation or by the bylaws or by an agreement among any number of security holders or among such holders and the corporation. ■ No restrictions so imposed shall be binding with respect to securities issued prior to the adoption of the restriction unless the holders of the securities are parties to an agreement or voted in favor of the restriction.

(c) A restriction on the transfer or registration of transfer of securities of a corporation or on the amount of such securities that may be owned by any person or group of persons is permitted by this section if it:

> **(1)** Obligates the holder of the restricted securities to offer to the corporation or to any other holders of securities of the corporation or to any other person or to any combination of the foregoing, a prior opportunity, to be exercised within a reasonable time, to acquire the restricted securities; or
>
> **(2)** Obligates the corporation or any holder of securities of the corporation or any other person or any combination of the foregoing, to purchase the securities which are the subject of an agreement respecting the purchase and sale of the restricted securities; or
>
> **(3)** Requires the corporation or the holders of any class or series of securities of the corporation to consent to any proposed transfer of the restricted securities or to approve the proposed transferee of the restricted securities, or to approve the amount of securities of the corporation that may be owned by any person or group of persons; or

(4) Obligates the holder of the restricted securities to sell or transfer an amount of restricted securities to the corporation or to any other holders of securities of the corporation or to any other person or to any combination of the foregoing, or causes or results in the automatic sale or transfer of an amount of restricted securities to the corporation or to any other holders of securities of the corporation or to any other person or to any combination of the foregoing; or

(5) Prohibits or restricts the transfer of the restricted securities to, or the ownership of restricted securities by, designated persons or classes of persons or groups of persons, and such designation is not manifestly unreasonable.

(d) Any restriction on the transfer or the registration of transfer of the securities of a corporation, or on the amount of securities of a corporation that may be owned by a person or group of persons, for any of the following purposes shall be conclusively presumed to be for a reasonable purpose:

(1) Maintaining any local, state, federal or foreign tax advantage to the corporation or its stockholders, including without limitation:

a. Maintaining the corporation's status as an electing small business corporation under subchapter S of the United States Internal Revenue Code [26 U.S.C. § 1371 et seq.], or

b. Maintaining or preserving any tax attribute (including without limitation net operating losses), or

c. Qualifying or maintaining the qualification of the corporation as a real estate investment trust pursuant to the United States Internal Revenue Code or regulations adopted pursuant to the United States Internal Revenue Code, or

(2) Maintaining any statutory or regulatory advantage or complying with any statutory or regulatory requirements under applicable local, state, federal or foreign law.

(e) Any other lawful restriction on transfer or registration of transfer of securities, or on the amount of securities that may be owned by any person or group of persons, is permitted by this section.

§ 203. Business combinations with interested stockholders.

(a) Notwithstanding any other provisions of this chapter, a corporation shall not engage in any business combination with any interested stockholder for a period of 3 years following the time that such stockholder became an interested stockholder, unless:

(1) Prior to such time the board of directors of the corporation approved either the business combination or the transaction which resulted in the stockholder becoming an interested stockholder;

(2) Upon consummation of the transaction which resulted in the stockholder becoming an interested stockholder, the interested stockholder owned at least 85% of the voting stock of the corporation outstanding at the time the transaction commenced, excluding for purposes of determining the voting stock outstanding (but not the outstanding voting stock owned by the interested stockholder) those shares owned **(i)** by persons who are directors and also officers and **(ii)** employee stock plans in which employee participants do not have the right to determine confidentially whether shares held subject to the plan will be tendered in a tender or exchange offer; or

(3) At or subsequent to such time the business combination is approved by the board of directors and authorized at an annual or special meeting of stockholders, and not by written consent, by the affirmative vote of at least 66 2/3% of the outstanding voting stock which is not owned by the interested stockholder.

(b) The restrictions contained in this section shall not apply if:

(1) The corporation's original certificate of incorporation contains a provision expressly electing not to be governed by this section;

(2) The corporation, by action of its board of directors, adopts an amendment to its bylaws within 90 days of February 2, 1988, expressly electing not to be governed by this section, which amendment shall not be further amended by the board of directors;

(3) The corporation, by action of its stockholders, adopts an amendment to its certificate of incorporation or bylaws expressly electing not to be governed by this section; provided that, in addition to any other vote required by law, such amendment to the certificate of incorporation or bylaws must be adopted by the affirmative vote of a majority of the outstanding stock entitled to vote thereon. ▪ In the case of a corporation that both **(i)** has never had a class of voting stock that falls within any of the 2 categories set out in paragraph (b)(4) of this section, and **(ii)** has not elected by a provision in its original certificate of incorporation or any amendment thereto to be governed by this section, such amendment shall become effective upon **(i)** in the case of an amendment to the certificate of incorporation, the date and time at which the certificate filed in accordance with § 103 of this title becomes effective thereunder or **(ii)** in the case of an amendment to the bylaws, the date of the adoption of such amendment. ▪ In all other cases, an amendment adopted pursuant to this paragraph shall become effective **(i)** in the case of an amendment to the certificate of incorporation, 12 months after the date and time at which the certificate filed in accordance with § 103 of this title becomes effective thereunder or **(ii)** in the case of an amendment to the bylaws, 12 months after the date of the adoption of such amendment, and , in either case, the election not to be governed by this section shall not apply to any business combination between such corporation and any person who became an interested stockholder of such corporation on or before **(A)** in the case of an amendment to the certificate of incorporation, the date and time at which the certificate filed in accordance with

§ 103 of this title becomes effective thereunder; or **(B)** in the case of an amendment to the bylaws, the date of the adoption of such amendment. ▪ A bylaw amendment adopted pursuant to this paragraph shall not be further amended by the board of directors;

(4) The corporation does not have a class of voting stock that is: **(i)** Listed on a national securities exchange; or **(ii)** held of record by more than 2,000 stockholders, unless any of the foregoing results from action taken, directly or indirectly, by an interested stockholder or from a transaction in which a person becomes an interested stockholder;

(5) A stockholder becomes an interested stockholder inadvertently and **(i)** as soon as practicable divests itself of ownership of sufficient shares so that the stockholder ceases to be an interested stockholder; and **(ii)** would not, at any time within the 3-year period immediately prior to a business combination between the corporation and such stockholder, have been an interested stockholder but for the inadvertent acquisition of ownership;

(6) The business combination is proposed prior to the consummation or abandonment of and subsequent to the earlier of the public announcement or the notice required hereunder of a proposed transaction which **(i)** constitutes 1 of the transactions described in the second sentence of this paragraph; **(ii)** is with or by a person who either was not an interested stockholder during the previous 3 years or who became an interested stockholder with the approval of the corporation's board of directors or during the period described in paragraph (b)(7) of this section; and **(iii)** is approved or not opposed by a majority of the members of the board of directors then in office (but not less than 1) who were directors prior to any person becoming an interested stockholder during the previous 3 years or were recommended for election or elected to succeed such directors by a majority of such directors. The proposed transactions referred to in the preceding sentence are limited to **(x)** a merger or consolidation of the corporation (except for a merger in respect of which, pursuant to § 251(f) of this title, no vote of the stockholders of the corporation is required); **(y)** a sale, lease, exchange, mortgage, pledge, transfer or other disposition (in 1 transaction or a series of transactions), whether as part of a dissolution or otherwise, of assets of the corporation or of any direct or indirect majority-owned subsidiary of the corporation (other than to any direct or indirect wholly-owned subsidiary or to the corporation) having an aggregate market value equal to 50% or more of either that aggregate market value of all of the assets of the corporation determined on a consolidated basis or the aggregate market value of all the outstanding stock of the corporation; or **(z)** a proposed tender or exchange offer for 50% or more of the outstanding voting stock of the corporation. ▪ The corporation shall give not less than 20 days' notice to all interested stockholders prior to the consummation of any of the transactions described in clause (x) or (y) of the second sentence of this paragraph; or

(7) The business combination is with an interested stockholder who became an interested stockholder at a time when the restrictions contained in this section did not apply by reason of any of paragraphs (b)(1) through (4) of this section, provided, however, that this paragraph (b)(7) shall not apply if, at the time such interested stockholder became an interested stockholder, the corporation's certificate of incorporation contained a provision authorized by the last sentence of this subsection (b).

Notwithstanding paragraphs (b)(1), (2), (3) and (4) of this section, a corporation may elect by a provision of its original certificate of incorporation or any amendment thereto to be governed by this section; provided that any such amendment to the certificate of incorporation shall not apply to restrict a business combination between the corporation and an interested stockholder of the corporation if the interested stockholder became such before the date and time at which the certificate filed in accordance with § 103 of this title becomes effective thereunder.

(c) As used in this section only, the term:

(1) "Affiliate" means a person that directly, or indirectly through 1 or more intermediaries, controls, or is controlled by, or is under common control with, another person.

(2) "Associate," when used to indicate a relationship with any person, means: **(i)** Any corporation, partnership, unincorporated association or other entity of which such person is a director, officer or partner or is, directly or indirectly, the owner of 20% or more of any class of voting stock; **(ii)** any trust or other estate in which such person has at least a 20% beneficial interest or as to which such person serves as trustee or in a similar fiduciary capacity; and **(iii)** any relative or spouse of such person, or any relative of such spouse, who has the same residence as such person.

(3) "Business combination," when used in reference to any corporation and any interested stockholder of such corporation, means:

(i) Any merger or consolidation of the corporation or any direct or indirect majority-owned subsidiary of the corporation with **(A)** the interested stockholder, or **(B)** with any other corporation, partnership, unincorporated association or other entity if the merger or consolidation is caused by the interested stockholder and as a result of such merger or consolidation subsection (a) of this section is not applicable to the surviving entity;

(ii) Any sale, lease, exchange, mortgage, pledge, transfer or other disposition (in 1 transaction or a series of transactions), except proportionately as a stockholder of such corporation, to or with the interested stockholder, whether as part of a dissolution or otherwise, of assets of the corporation or of any direct or indirect majority-owned subsidiary of the corporation which assets have an aggregate market value equal to

10% or more of either the aggregate market value of all the assets of the corporation determined on a consolidated basis or the aggregate market value of all the outstanding stock of the corporation;

(iii) Any transaction which results in the issuance or transfer by the corporation or by any direct or indirect majority-owned subsidiary of the corporation of any stock of the corporation or of such subsidiary to the interested stockholder, except: **(A)** Pursuant to the exercise, exchange or conversion of securities exercisable for, exchangeable for or convertible into stock of such corporation or any such subsidiary which securities were outstanding prior to the time that the interested stockholder became such; **(B)** pursuant to a merger under § 251(g) of this title; **(C)** pursuant to a dividend or distribution paid or made, or the exercise, exchange or conversion of securities exercisable for, exchangeable for or convertible into stock of such corporation or any such subsidiary which security is distributed, pro rata to all holders of a class or series of stock of such corporation subsequent to the time the interested stockholder became such; **(D)** pursuant to an exchange offer by the corporation to purchase stock made on the same terms to all holders of said stock; or **(E)** any issuance or transfer of stock by the corporation; provided however, that in no case under items (C)-(E) of this subparagraph shall there be an increase in the interested stockholder's proportionate share of the stock of any class or series of the corporation or of the voting stock of the corporation;

(iv) Any transaction involving the corporation or any direct or indirect majority-owned subsidiary of the corporation which has the effect, directly or indirectly, of increasing the proportionate share of the stock of any class or series, or securities convertible into the stock of any class or series, of the corporation or of any such subsidiary which is owned by the interested stockholder, except as a result of immaterial changes due to fractional share adjustments or as a result of any purchase or redemption of any shares of stock not caused, directly or indirectly, by the interested stockholder; or

(v) Any receipt by the interested stockholder of the benefit, directly or indirectly (except proportionately as a stockholder of such corporation), of any loans, advances, guarantees, pledges or other financial benefits (other than those expressly permitted in paragraphs (c)(3)(i)-(iv) of this section) provided by or through the corporation or any direct or indirect majority-owned subsidiary.

(4) "Control," including the terms "controlling," "controlled by" and "under common control with," means the possession, directly or indirectly, of the power to direct or cause the direction of the management and policies of a person, whether through the ownership of voting stock, by contract or otherwise. ■ A person who is the owner of 20% or more of the outstanding voting stock of any corporation, partnership, unincorporated association or other entity shall be presumed to have control of such entity, in the absence of proof by a preponderance of the evidence to the contrary; Notwithstanding the foregoing, a presumption of control shall not apply where such person holds voting stock, in good faith and not for the purpose of circumventing this section, as an agent, bank, broker, nominee, custodian or trustee for 1 or more owners who do not individually or as a group have control of such entity.

(5) "Interested stockholder" means any person (other than the corporation and any direct or indirect majority-owned subsidiary of the corporation) that **(i)** is the owner of 15% or more of the outstanding voting stock of the corporation, or **(ii)** is an affiliate or associate of the corporation and was the owner of 15% or more of the outstanding voting stock of the corporation at any time within the 3-year period immediately prior to the date on which it is sought to be determined whether such person is an interested stockholder, and the affiliates and associates of such person; provided, however, that the term "interested stockholder" shall not include **(x)** any person who **(A)** owned shares in excess of the 15% limitation set forth herein as of, or acquired such shares pursuant to a tender offer commenced prior to, December 23, 1987, or pursuant to an exchange offer announced prior to the aforesaid date and commenced within 90 days thereafter and either **(I)** continued to own shares in excess of such 15% limitation or would have but for action by the corporation or **(II)** is an affiliate or associate of the corporation and so continued (or so would have continued but for action by the corporation) to be the owner of 15% or more of the outstanding voting stock of the corporation at any time within the 3-year period immediately prior to the date on which it is sought to be determined whether such a person is an interested stockholder or **(B)** acquired said shares from a person described in item (A) of this paragraph by gift, inheritance or in a transaction in which no consideration was exchanged; or **(y)** any person whose ownership of shares in excess of the 15% limitation set forth herein is the result of action taken solely by the corporation; provided that such person shall be an interested stockholder if thereafter such person acquires additional shares of voting stock of the corporation, except as a result of further corporate action not caused, directly or indirectly, by such person. For the purpose of determining whether a person is an interested stockholder, the voting stock of the corporation deemed to be outstanding shall include stock deemed to be owned by the person through application of paragraph (9) of this subsection but shall not include any other unissued stock of such corporation which may be issuable pursuant to any agreement, arrangement or understanding, or upon exercise of conversion rights, warrants or options, or otherwise.

(6) "Person" means any individual, corporation, partnership, unincorporated association or other entity.

(7) "Stock" means, with respect to any corporation, capital stock and, with respect to any other entity, any equity interest.

(8) "Voting stock" means, with respect to any corporation, stock of any class or series entitled to vote generally in the election of directors and, with respect to any entity that is not a corporation, any equity interest entitled to vote generally in the election of the governing body of such entity. ▪ Every reference to a percentage of voting stock shall refer to such percentage of the votes of such voting stock.

(9) "Owner," including the terms "own" and "owned," when used with respect to any stock, means a person that individually or with or through any of its affiliates or associates:

> **(i)** Beneficially owns such stock, directly or indirectly; or

> **(ii)** Has **(A)** the right to acquire such stock (whether such right is exercisable immediately or only after the passage of time) pursuant to any agreement, arrangement or understanding, or upon the exercise of conversion rights, exchange rights, warrants or options, or otherwise; provided, however, that a person shall not be deemed the owner of stock tendered pursuant to a tender or exchange offer made by such person or any of such person's affiliates or associates until such tendered stock is accepted for purchase or exchange; or **(B)** the right to vote such stock pursuant to any agreement, arrangement or understanding; provided, however, that a person shall not be deemed the owner of any stock because of such person's right to vote such stock if the agreement, arrangement or understanding to vote such stock arises solely from a revocable proxy or consent given in response to a proxy or consent solicitation made to 10 or more persons; or

> **(iii)** Has any agreement, arrangement or understanding for the purpose of acquiring,

holding, voting (except voting pursuant to a revocable proxy or consent as described in item (B) of subparagraph (ii) of this paragraph), or disposing of such stock with any other person that beneficially owns, or whose affiliates or associates beneficially own, directly or indirectly, such stock.

(d) No provision of a certificate of incorporation or bylaw shall require, for any vote of stockholders required by this section, a greater vote of stockholders than that specified in this section.

(e) The Court of Chancery is hereby vested with exclusive jurisdiction to hear and determine all matters with respect to this section.

§ 204. Ratification of defective corporate acts and stock.

(a) Subject to subsection (f) of this section, no defective corporate act or putative stock shall be void or voidable solely as a result of a failure of authorization if ratified as provided in this section or validated by the Court of Chancery in a proceeding brought under § 205 of this title.

(b)(1) In order to ratify 1 or more defective corporate acts pursuant to this section (other than the ratification of an election of the initial board of directors pursuant to paragraph (b)(2) of this section), the board of directors of the corporation shall adopt resolutions stating:

(A) The defective corporate act or acts to be ratified;

(B) The date of each defective corporate act or acts;

(C) If such defective corporate act or acts involved the issuance of shares of putative stock, the number and type of shares of putative stock issued and the date or dates upon which such putative shares were purported to have been issued;

(D) The nature of the failure of authorization in respect of each defective corporate act to be ratified; and

(E) That the board of directors approves the ratification of the defective corporate act or acts. ▪

Such resolutions may also provide that, at any time before the validation effective time in respect of any defective corporate act set forth therein, notwithstanding the approval of the ratification of such defective corporate act by stockholders, the board of directors may abandon the ratification of such defective corporate act without further action of the stockholders. ▪ The quorum and voting requirements applicable to the ratification by the board of directors of any defective corporate act shall be the quorum and voting requirements applicable to the type of defective corporate act proposed to be ratified at the time the board adopts the resolutions ratifying the defective corporate act; provided that if the certificate of incorporation or bylaws of the corporation, any plan or agreement to which the corporation was a party or any provision of this title, in each case as in effect as of the time of the defective corporate act, would have required a larger number or portion of directors or of specified directors for a quorum to be present or to approve the defective corporate act, such larger number or portion of such directors or such specified directors shall be required for a quorum to be present or to adopt the resolutions to ratify the defective corporate act, as applicable, except that the presence or approval of any director elected, appointed or nominated by holders of any class or series of which no shares are then outstanding, or by any person that is no longer a stockholder, shall not be required.

(2) In order to ratify a defective corporate act in respect of the election of the initial board of directors of the corporation pursuant to § 108 of this title, a majority of the persons who, at the time the resolutions required by this paragraph (b)(2) of this section are adopted, are exercising the powers of directors under claim and color of an election or appointment as such may adopt resolutions stating:

(A) The name of the person or persons who first took action in the name of the corporation as the initial board of directors of the corporation;

(B) The earlier of the date on which such persons first took such action or were purported to have been elected as the initial board of directors; and

(C) That the ratification of the election of such person or persons as the initial board of directors is approved.

(c) Each defective corporate act ratified pursuant to paragraph (b)(1) of this section shall be submitted to stockholders for approval as provided in subsection (d) of this section, unless:

(1) (A) No other provision of this title, and no provision of the certificate of incorporation or bylaws of the corporation, or of any plan or agreement to which the corporation is a party, would have required stockholder approval of such defective corporate act to be ratified, either at the time of such defective corporate act or at the time the board of directors adopts the resolutions ratifying such defective corporate act pursuant to paragraph (b)(1) of this section; and (B) such defective corporate act did not result from a failure to comply with § 203 of this title; or

(2) As of the record date for determining the stockholders entitled to vote on the ratification of such defective corporate act, there are no shares of valid stock outstanding and entitled to vote thereon, regardless of whether there then exist any shares of putative stock.

(d) If the ratification of a defective corporate act is required to be submitted to stockholders for approval pursuant to subsection (c) of this section, due notice of the time, place, if any, and purpose of the meeting shall be given at least 20 days before the date of the meeting to each holder of valid stock and putative stock, whether voting or nonvoting, at the address of such holder as it appears or most recently appeared, as appropriate, on the records of the corporation. ■ The notice shall also be given to the holders of record of valid stock and putative stock, whether voting or nonvoting, as of the time of the defective corporate act (or, in the case of any defective corporate act that involved the establishment of a record date for notice of or voting at any meeting of stockholders, for action by written consent of stockholders in lieu of a meeting, or for any other purpose, the record date for notice of or voting at such meeting, the record date for action by written consent, or the record date for such other action, as the case may be), other than holders whose identities or addresses cannot be determined from the records of the corporation. ■ The notice shall contain a copy of the resolutions adopted by the board of directors pursuant to paragraph (b)(1) of this section or the information required by paragraphs (b)(1)(A) through (E) of this section and a statement that any claim that the defective corporate act or putative stock ratified hereunder is void or voidable due to the failure of authorization, or that the Court of Chancery should declare in its discretion that a ratification in accordance with this section not be effective or be effective only on certain conditions must be brought within 120 days from the applicable validation effective time. ■ At such meeting, the quorum and voting requirements applicable to ratification of such defective corporate act shall be the quorum and voting requirements applicable to the type of defective corporate act proposed to be ratified at the time of the approval of the ratification, except that:

(1) If the certificate of incorporation or bylaws of the corporation, any plan or agreement to which the corporation was a party or any provision of this title in effect as of the time of the defective corporate act would have required a larger number or portion of stock or of any class or series thereof or of specified stockholders for a quorum to be present or to approve the defective corporate act, the presence or approval of such larger number or portion of stock or of such class or series thereof or of such specified stockholders shall be required for a quorum to be present or to approve the ratification of the defective corporate act, as applicable, except that the presence or approval of shares of any class or series of which no shares are then outstanding, or of any person that is no longer a stockholder, shall not be required;

(2) The approval by stockholders of the ratification of the election of a director shall require the affirmative vote of the majority of shares present at the meeting and entitled to vote on the election of such director, except that if the certificate of incorporation or bylaws of the corporation then in effect or in effect at the time of the defective election require or required a larger number or portion of stock or of any class or series thereof or of specified stockholders to elect such director, the affirmative vote of such larger number or portion of stock or of any class or series thereof or of such specified stockholders shall be required to ratify the election of such director, except that the presence or approval of shares of any class or series of which no shares are then outstanding, or of any person that is no longer a stockholder, shall not be required; ■ and

(3) In the event of a failure of authorization resulting from failure to comply with the provisions of § 203 of this title, the ratification of the defective corporate act shall require the vote set forth in § 203(a)(3) of this title, regardless of whether such vote would have otherwise been required.

Shares of putative stock on the record date for determining stockholders entitled to vote on any matter submitted to stockholders pursuant to subsection (c) of this section (and without giving effect to any ratification that becomes effective after such record date) shall neither be entitled to vote nor counted for quorum purposes in any vote to ratify any defective corporate act.

(e) If a defective corporate act ratified pursuant to this section would have required under any other section of this title the filing of a certificate in accordance with § 103 of this title, then, whether or not a certificate was previously filed in respect of such defective corporate act and in lieu of filing the certificate otherwise required by this title, the corporation shall file a certificate of validation with respect to such defective corporate act in accordance with § 103 of this title. ■ A separate certificate of validation shall be required for each defective corporate act requiring the filing of a certificate of validation under this section, except that **(i)** 2 or more defective corporate acts may be included in a single certificate of validation if the corporation filed, or to comply with this title would have filed, a single certificate under another provision of this title to effect such acts, and **(ii)** 2 or more overissues of shares of any class, classes or series of stock may be included in a single certificate of validation, provided that the increase in the number of authorized shares of each such class or series set forth in the certificate of validation shall be effective as of the date of the first such overissue. ■ The certificate of validation shall set forth:

(1) Each defective corporate act that is the subject of the certificate of validation (including, in the case of any defective corporate act involving the issuance of shares of putative stock, the number and type of shares of putative stock issued and the date or dates upon which such putative shares were purported to have been issued), the date of such defective corporate act, and the nature of the failure of authorization in respect of such defective corporate act;

(2) A statement that such defective corporate act was ratified in accordance with this section, including the date on which the board of directors ratified such defective corporate act and the date, if any, on which the stockholders approved the ratification of such defective corporate act; and

(3) Information required by 1 of the following paragraphs:

a. If a certificate was previously filed under § 103 of this title in respect of such defective corporate act and no changes to such certificate are required to give effect to such defective corporate act in accordance with this section, the certificate of validation shall set forth **(x)** the name, title and filing date of the certificate previously filed and of any certificate of correction thereto and **(y)** a statement that a copy of the certificate previously filed, together with any certificate of correction thereto, is attached as an exhibit to the certificate of validation;

b. If a certificate was previously filed under § 103 of this title in respect of the defective corporate act and such certificate requires any change to give effect to the defective corporate act in accordance with this section (including a change to the date and time of the effectiveness of such certificate), the certificate of validation shall set forth **(x)** the name, title and filing date of the certificate so previously filed and of any certificate of correction thereto, **(y)** a statement that a certificate containing all of the information required to be included under the applicable section or sections of this title to give effect to the defective corporate act is attached as an exhibit to the certificate of validation, and **(z)** the date and time that such certificate shall be deemed to have become effective pursuant to this section; or

c. If a certificate was not previously filed under § 103 of this title in respect of the defective corporate act and the defective corporate act ratified pursuant to this section would have required under any other section of this title the filing of a certificate in accordance with § 103 of this title, the certificate of validation shall set forth **(x)** a statement that a certificate containing all of the information required to be included under the applicable section or sections of this title to give effect to the defective corporate act is attached as an exhibit to the certificate of validation, and **(y)** the date and time that such certificate shall be deemed to have become effective pursuant to this section.

A certificate attached to a certificate of validation pursuant to paragraph (e)(3)b. or c. of this section need not be separately executed and acknowledged and need not include any statement required by any other section of this title that such instrument has been approved and adopted in accordance with the provisions of such other section.

(f) From and after the validation effective time, unless otherwise determined in an action brought pursuant to § 205 of this title:

(1) Subject to the last sentence of subsection (d) of this section, each defective corporate act ratified in accordance with this section shall no longer be deemed void or voidable as a result of the failure of authorization described in the resolutions adopted pursuant to subsection (b) of this section and such effect shall be retroactive to the time of the defective corporate act; and

(2) Subject to the last sentence of subsection (d) of this section, each share or fraction of a share of putative stock issued or purportedly issued pursuant to any such defective corporate act shall no longer be deemed void or voidable and shall be deemed to be an identical share or fraction of a share of outstanding stock as of the time it was purportedly issued.

(g) In respect of each defective corporate act ratified by the board of directors pursuant to subsection (b) of this section, prompt notice of the ratification shall be given to all holders of valid stock and putative stock, whether voting or nonvoting, as of the date the board of directors adopts the resolutions approving such defective corporate act, or as of a date within 60 days after such date of adoption, as established by the board of directors, at the address of such holder as it appears or most recently appeared, as appropriate, on the records of the corporation. ■ The notice shall also be given to the holders of record of valid stock and putative stock, whether voting or nonvoting, as of the time of the defective corporate act, other than holders whose identities or addresses cannot be determined from the records of the corporation. ■ The notice shall contain a copy of the resolutions adopted pursuant to subsection (b) of this section or the information specified in paragraphs (b)(1)(A) through (E) or paragraphs (b)(2)(A) through (C) of this section, as applicable, and a statement that any claim that the defective corporate act or putative stock ratified hereunder is void or voidable due to the failure of authorization, or that the Court of Chancery should declare in its discretion that a ratification in accordance with this section not be effective or be effective only on certain conditions must be brought within 120 days from the later of the validation effective time or the time at which the notice required by this subsection is given. ▪ Notwithstanding the foregoing, **(i)** no such notice shall be required if notice of the ratification of the defective corporate act is to be given in accordance with subsection (d) of this section, and **(ii)** in the case of a corporation that has a class of stock listed on a national securities exchange, the notice required by this subsection and the second sentence of subsection (d) of this section may be deemed given if disclosed in a document publicly filed by the corporation with the Securities and Exchange Commission pursuant to § 13, § 14 or § 15(d) (15 U.S.C. § 78m, § 77n or § 78o(d)) of the Securities Exchange Act of 1934, as amended, and the rules and regulations promulgated thereunder, or the corresponding provisions of any subsequent United States federal securities laws, rules or regulations. ▪ If any defective corporate act has been approved by stockholders acting pursuant to § 228 of this title, the notice required by this subsection may be included in any notice required to be given pursuant to § 228(e) of this title and, if so given, shall be sent to the stockholders entitled thereto under § 228(e) and to all holders of valid and putative stock to whom notice would be required under this subsection if the defective corporate act had been approved at a meeting other than any stockholder who approved the action by consent in lieu of a meeting pursuant to § 228 of this title or any holder of putative stock who otherwise consented thereto in writing. ▪ Solely for purposes of subsection (d) of this section and this subsection, notice to holders of putative stock, and notice to holders of valid stock and putative stock as of the time of the defective corporate act, shall be treated as notice to holders of valid stock for purposes of §§ 222 and 228, 229, 230, 232 and 233 of this title.

(h) As used in this section and in § 205 of this title only, the term:

(1) "Defective corporate act" means an overissue, an election or appointment of directors that is void or voidable due to a failure of authorization, or any act or transaction purportedly taken by or on behalf of the corporation that is, and at the time such act or transaction was purportedly taken would have been, within the power of a corporation under subchapter II of this chapter (without regard to the failure of authorization identified in § 204(b)(1)(D) of this title), but is void or voidable due to a failure of authorization;

(2) "Failure of authorization" means: **(i)** the failure to authorize or effect an act or transaction in compliance with **(A)** the provisions of this title, **(B)** the certificate of incorporation or bylaws of the corporation, or **(C)** any plan or agreement to which the corporation is a party or the disclosure set forth in any proxy or consent solicitation statement, if and to the extent such failure would render such act or transaction void or voidable; or **(ii)** the failure of the board of directors or any officer of the corporation to authorize or approve any act or transaction taken by or on behalf of the corporation that would have required for its due authorization the approval of the board of directors or such officer;

(3) "Overissue" means the purported issuance of:

a. Shares of capital stock of a class or series in excess of the number of shares of such class or series the corporation has the power to issue under § 161 of this title at the time of such issuance; or

b. Shares of any class or series of capital stock that is not then authorized for issuance by the certificate of incorporation of the corporation;

(4) "Putative stock" means the shares of any class or series of capital stock of the corporation (including shares issued upon exercise of options, rights, warrants or other securities convertible into shares of capital stock of the corporation, or interests with respect thereto that were created or issued pursuant to a defective corporate act) that:

    a. But for any failure of authorization, would constitute valid stock; or

    b. Cannot be determined by the board of directors to be valid stock;

(5) "Time of the defective corporate act" means the date and time the defective corporate act was purported to have been taken;

(6) "Validation effective time" with respect to any defective corporate act ratified pursuant to this section means the latest of:

    a. The time at which the defective corporate act submitted to the stockholders for approval pursuant to subsection (c) of this section is approved by such stockholders or if no such vote of stockholders is required to approve the ratification of the defective corporate act, the time at which the board of directors adopts the resolutions required by paragraph (b)(1) or (b)(2) of this section;

    b. Where no certificate of validation is required to be filed pursuant to subsection (e) of this section, the time, if any, specified by the board of directors in the resolutions adopted pursuant to paragraph (b)(1) or (b)(2) of this section, which time shall not precede the time at which such resolutions are adopted; and

    c. The time at which any certificate of validation filed pursuant to subsection (e) of this section shall become effective in accordance with § 103 of this title.

(7) "Valid stock" means the shares of any class or series of capital stock of the corporation that have been duly authorized and validly issued in accordance with this title.

In the absence of actual fraud in the transaction, the judgment of the board of directors that shares of stock are valid stock or putative stock shall be conclusive, unless otherwise determined by the Court of Chancery in a proceeding brought pursuant to § 205 of this title.

(i) Ratification under this section or validation under § 205 of this title shall not be deemed to be the exclusive means of ratifying or validating any act or transaction taken by or on behalf of the corporation, including any defective corporate act, or any issuance of stock, including any putative stock, or of adopting or endorsing any act or transaction taken by or in the name of the corporation prior to the commencement of its existence, and the absence or failure of ratification in accordance with either this section or validation under § 205 of this title shall not, of itself, affect the validity or effectiveness of any act or transaction or the issuance of any stock properly ratified under common law or otherwise, nor shall it create a presumption that any such act or transaction is or was a defective corporate act or that such stock is void or voidable.

§ 205. Proceedings regarding validity of defective corporate acts and stock.

(a) Subject to subsection (f) of this section, upon application by the corporation, any successor entity to the corporation, any member of the board of directors, any record or beneficial holder of valid stock or putative stock, any record or beneficial holder of valid or putative stock as of the time of a defective corporate act ratified pursuant to § 204 of this title, or any other person claiming to be substantially and adversely affected by a ratification pursuant to § 204 of this title, the Court of Chancery may:

    (1) Determine the validity and effectiveness of any defective corporate act ratified pursuant to § 204 of this title;

    (2) Determine the validity and effectiveness of the ratification of any defective corporate act pursuant to § 204 of this title;

    (3) Determine the validity and effectiveness of any defective corporate act not ratified or not ratified effectively pursuant to § 204 of this title;

(4) Determine the validity of any corporate act or transaction and any stock, rights or options to acquire stock; and

(5) Modify or waive any of the procedures set forth in § 204 of this title to ratify a defective corporate act.

(b) In connection with an action under this section, the Court of Chancery may:

(1) Declare that a ratification in accordance with and pursuant to § 204 of this title is not effective or shall only be effective at a time or upon conditions established by the Court;

(2) Validate and declare effective any defective corporate act or putative stock and impose conditions upon such validation by the Court;

(3) Require measures to remedy or avoid harm to any person substantially and adversely affected by a ratification pursuant to § 204 of this title or from any order of the Court pursuant to this section, excluding any harm that would have resulted if the defective corporate act had been valid when approved or effectuated;

(4) Order the Secretary of State to accept an instrument for filing with an effective time specified by the Court, which effective time may be prior or subsequent to the time of such order, provided that the filing date of such instrument shall be determined in accordance with § 103(c)(3) of this title;

(5) Approve a stock ledger for the corporation that includes any stock ratified or validated in accordance with this section or with § 204 of this title;

(6) Declare that shares of putative stock are shares of valid stock or require a corporation to issue and deliver shares of valid stock in place of any shares of putative stock;

(7) Order that a meeting of holders of valid stock or putative stock be held and exercise the powers provided to the Court under § 227 of this title with respect to such a meeting;

(8) Declare that a defective corporate act validated by the Court shall be effective as of the time of the defective corporate act or at such other time as the Court shall determine;

(9) Declare that putative stock validated by the Court shall be deemed to be an identical share or fraction of a share of valid stock as of the time originally issued or purportedly issued or at such other time as the Court shall determine; and

(10) Make such other orders regarding such matters as it deems proper under the circumstances.

(c) Service of the application under subsection (a) of this section upon the registered agent of the corporation shall be deemed to be service upon the corporation, and no other party need be joined in order for the Court of Chancery to adjudicate the matter. ∎ In an action filed by the corporation, the Court may require notice of the action be provided to other persons specified by the Court and permit such other persons to intervene in the action.

(d) In connection with the resolution of matters pursuant to subsections (a) and (b) of this section, the Court of Chancery may consider the following:

(1) Whether the defective corporate act was originally approved or effectuated with the belief that the approval or effectuation was in compliance with the provisions of this title, the certificate of incorporation or bylaws of the corporation;

(2) Whether the corporation and board of directors has treated the defective corporate act as a valid act or transaction and whether any person has acted in reliance on the public record that such defective corporate act was valid;

(3) Whether any person will be or was harmed by the ratification or validation of the defective corporate act, excluding any harm that would have resulted if the defective corporate act had been valid when approved or effectuated;

(4) Whether any person will be harmed by the failure to ratify or validate the defective corporate act; and

(5) Any other factors or considerations the Court deems just and equitable.

(e) The Court of Chancery is hereby vested with exclusive jurisdiction to hear and determine all actions brought under this section.

(f) Notwithstanding any other provision of this section, no action asserting:

(1) That a defective corporate act or putative stock ratified in accordance with § 204 of this title is void or voidable due to a failure of authorization identified in the resolution adopted in accordance with 204(b) of this title; or

(2) That the Court of Chancery should declare in its discretion that a ratification in accordance with §204 of this title not be effective or be effective only on certain conditions,

may be brought after the expiration of 120 days from the later of the validation effective time and the time notice, if any, that is required to be given pursuant to § 204(g) of this title is given with respect to such ratification, except that this subsection shall not apply to an action asserting that a ratification was not accomplished in accordance with § 204 of this title or to any person to whom notice of the ratification was required to have been given pursuant to § 204(d) or (g) of this title, but to whom such notice was not given.

Subchapter VII. Meetings, Elections, Voting and Notice

§ 211. Meetings of stockholders.

(a)(1) Meetings of stockholders may be held at such place, either within or without this State as may be designated by or in the manner provided in the certificate of incorporation or bylaws, or if not so designated, as determined by the board of directors. ▪ If, pursuant to this paragraph or the certificate of incorporation or the bylaws of the corporation, the board of directors is authorized to determine the place of a meeting of stockholders, the board of directors may, in its sole discretion, determine that the meeting shall not be held at any place, but may instead be held solely by means of remote communication as authorized by paragraph (a)(2) of this section.

(2) If authorized by the board of directors in its sole discretion, and subject to such guidelines and procedures as the board of directors may adopt, stockholders and proxyholders not physically present at a meeting of stockholders may, by means of remote communication:

a. Participate in a meeting of stockholders; and

b. Be deemed present in person and vote at a meeting of stockholders, whether such meeting is to be held at a designated place or solely by means of remote communication, provided that **(i)** the corporation shall implement reasonable measures to verify that each person deemed present and permitted to vote at the meeting by means of remote communication is a stockholder or proxyholder, **(ii)** the corporation shall implement reasonable measures to provide such stockholders and proxyholders a reasonable opportunity to participate in the meeting and to vote on matters submitted to the stockholders, including an opportunity to read or hear the proceedings of the meeting substantially concurrently with such proceedings, and **(iii)** if any stockholder or proxyholder votes or takes other action at the meeting by means of remote communication, a record of such vote or other action shall be maintained by the corporation.

(b) Unless directors are elected by written consent in lieu of an annual meeting as permitted by this subsection, an annual meeting of stockholders shall be held for the election of directors on a date and at a time designated by or in the manner provided in the bylaws. ▪ Stockholders may, unless the certificate of incorporation otherwise provides, act by written consent to elect directors; provided, however, that, if such consent is less than unanimous, such action by written consent may be in lieu of holding an annual meeting only if all of the directorships to which directors could be elected at an annual meeting held at the effective time of such action are vacant and are filled by such action. ■ Any other proper business may be transacted at the annual meeting.

(c) A failure to hold the annual meeting at the designated time or to elect a sufficient number of directors to conduct the business of the corporation shall not affect otherwise valid corporate acts or work a forfeiture or dissolution of the corporation except as may be otherwise specifically provided in this chapter. ■ If the annual meeting for election of directors is not held on the date designated therefor or action by written consent to elect directors in lieu of an annual meeting has not been taken, the directors shall cause the meeting to be held as soon as is convenient. ■ If there be a failure to hold the annual meeting or to take action by written consent to elect directors in lieu of an annual meeting for a period of 30 days after the date designated for the annual meeting, or if no date has been designated, for a period of 13 months after the latest to occur of the organization of the corporation, its last annual meeting or the last action by written consent to elect directors in lieu of an annual meeting, the Court of Chancery may summarily order a meeting to be held upon the application of any stockholder or director. ■ The shares of stock represented at such meeting, either in person or by proxy, and entitled to vote thereat, shall constitute a quorum for the purpose of such meeting, notwithstanding any provision of the certificate of incorporation or bylaws to the contrary. ■ The Court of Chancery may issue such orders as may be appropriate, including, without limitation, orders designating the time and place of such meeting, the record date or dates for determination of stockholders entitled to notice of the meeting and to vote thereat, and the form of notice of such meeting.

(d) Special meetings of the stockholders may be called by the board of directors or by such person or persons as may be authorized by the certificate of incorporation or by the bylaws.

(e) All elections of directors shall be by written ballot unless otherwise provided in the certificate

of incorporation; if authorized by the board of directors, such requirement of a written ballot shall be satisfied by a ballot submitted by electronic transmission, provided that any such electronic transmission must either set forth or be submitted with information from which it can be determined that the electronic transmission was authorized by the stockholder or proxy holder.

§ 212. Voting rights of stockholders; proxies; limitations.

(a) Unless otherwise provided in the certificate of incorporation and subject to § 213 of this title, each stockholder shall be entitled to 1 vote for each share of capital stock held by such stockholder. ■ If the certificate of incorporation provides for more or less than 1 vote for any share, on any matter, every reference in this chapter to a majority or other proportion of stock, voting stock or shares shall refer to such majority or other proportion of the votes of such stock, voting stock or shares.

(b) Each stockholder entitled to vote at a meeting of stockholders or to express consent or dissent to corporate action in writing without a meeting may authorize another person or persons to act for such stockholder by proxy, but no such proxy shall be voted or acted upon after 3 years from its date, unless the proxy provides for a longer period.

(c) Without limiting the manner in which a stockholder may authorize another person or persons to act for such stockholder as proxy pursuant to subsection (b) of this section, the following shall constitute a valid means by which a stockholder may grant such authority:

(1) A stockholder, or such stockholder's authorized officer, director, employee or agent, may execute a document authorizing another person or persons to act for such stockholder as proxy.

(2) A stockholder may authorize another person or persons to act for such stockholder as proxy by transmitting or authorizing the transmission of an electronic transmission to the person who will be the holder of the proxy or to a proxy solicitation firm, proxy support service organization or like agent duly authorized by the person who will be the holder of the proxy to receive such transmission, provided that any such transmission must either set forth or be submitted with information from which it can be determined that the transmission was authorized by the stockholder. ▪ If it is determined that such transmissions are valid, the inspectors or, if there are no inspectors, such other persons making that determination shall specify the information upon which they relied.

(3) The authorization of a person to act as a proxy may be documented, signed and delivered in accordance with § 116 of this title, provided that such authorization shall set forth, or be delivered with information enabling the corporation to determine, the identity of the stockholder granting such authorization.

(d) Any copy, facsimile telecommunication or other reliable reproduction of the document (including any electronic transmission) created pursuant to subsection (c) of this section may be substituted or used in lieu of the original document for any and all purposes for which the original document could be used, provided that such copy, facsimile telecommunication or other reproduction shall be a complete reproduction of the entire original document.

(e) A duly executed proxy shall be irrevocable if it states that it is irrevocable and if, and only as long as, it is coupled with an interest sufficient in law to support an irrevocable power. ▪ A proxy may be made irrevocable regardless of whether the interest with which it is coupled is an interest in the stock itself or an interest in the corporation generally.

§ 213. Fixing date for determination of stockholders of record.

(a) In order that the corporation may determine the stockholders entitled to notice of any meeting of stockholders or any adjournment thereof, the board of directors may fix a record date, which record date shall not precede the date upon which the resolution fixing the record date is adopted by the board of directors, and which record date shall not be more than 60 nor less than 10 days before

the date of such meeting. ▪ If the board of directors so fixes a date, such date shall also be the record date for determining the stockholders entitled to vote at such meeting unless the board of directors determines, at the time it fixes such record date, that a later date on or before the date of the meeting shall be the date for making such determination. ▪ If no record date is fixed by the board of directors, the record date for determining stockholders entitled to notice of and to vote at a meeting of stockholders shall be at the close of business on the day next preceding the day on which notice is given, or, if notice is waived, at the close of business on the day next preceding the day on which the meeting is held. ▪ A determination of stockholders of record entitled to notice of or to vote at a meeting of stockholders shall apply to any adjournment of the meeting; provided, however, that the board of directors may fix a new record date for determination of stockholders entitled to vote at the adjourned meeting, and in such case shall also fix as the record date for stockholders entitled to notice of such adjourned meeting the same or an earlier date as that fixed for determination of stockholders entitled to vote in accordance with the foregoing provisions of this subsection (a) at the adjourned meeting.

(b) In order that the corporation may determine the stockholders entitled to consent to corporate action without a meeting in accordance with § 228 of this title, the board of directors may fix a record date, which record date shall not precede the date upon which the resolution fixing the record date is adopted by the board of directors, and which date shall not be more than 10 days after the date upon which the resolution fixing the record date is adopted by the board of directors. ▪ If no record date has been fixed by the board of directors, the record date for determining stockholders entitled to consent to corporate action without a meeting, when no prior action by the board of directors is required by this chapter, shall be the first date on which a signed consent setting forth the action taken or proposed to be taken is delivered to the corporation in accordance with § 228(d) of this title. ▪ If no record date has been fixed by the board of directors and prior action by the board of directors is required by this chapter, the record date for determining stockholders entitled to consent to corporate action in writing without a meeting shall be at the close of business on the day on which the board of directors adopts the resolution taking such prior action.

(c) In order that the corporation may determine the stockholders entitled to receive payment of any dividend or other distribution or allotment of any rights or the stockholders entitled to exercise any rights in respect of any change, conversion or exchange of stock, or for the purpose of any other lawful action, the board of directors may fix a record date, which record date shall not precede the date upon which the resolution fixing the record date is adopted, and which record date shall be not more than 60 days prior to such action. ■ If no record date is fixed, the record date for determining stockholders for any such purpose shall be at the close of business on the day on which the board of directors adopts the resolution relating thereto.

§ 214. Cumulative voting.

The certificate of incorporation of any corporation may provide that at all elections of directors of the corporation, or at elections held under specified circumstances, each holder of stock or of any class or classes or of a series or series thereof shall be entitled to as many votes as shall equal the number of votes which (except for such provision as to cumulative voting) such holder would be entitled to cast for the election of directors with respect to such holder's shares of stock multiplied by the number of directors to be elected by such holder, and that such holder may cast all of such votes for a single director or may distribute them among the number to be voted for, or for any 2 or more of them as such holder may see fit.

§ 215. Voting rights of members of nonstock corporations; quorum; proxies.

(a) Sections 211 through 214 and 216 of this title shall not apply to nonstock corporations, except that § 211(a) and (d) of this title and § 212(c), (d), and (e) of this title shall apply to such corporations, and, when so applied, all references therein to stockholders and to the board of directors shall be deemed to refer to the members and the governing body of a nonstock corporation, respectively; and all references to stock, capital stock, or shares thereof shall be deemed to refer to memberships of a nonprofit nonstock corporation and to membership interests of any other nonstock corporation.

(b) Unless otherwise provided in the certificate of incorporation or the bylaws of a nonstock corporation, and subject to subsection (f) of this section, each member shall be entitled at every meeting of members to 1 vote on each matter submitted to a vote of members. ■ A member may exercise such voting rights in person or by proxy, but no proxy shall be voted on after 3 years from its date, unless the proxy provides for a longer period.

(c) Unless otherwise provided in this chapter, the certificate of incorporation or bylaws of a nonstock corporation may specify the number of members having voting power who shall be present or represented by proxy at any meeting in order to constitute a quorum for, and the votes that shall be necessary for, the transaction of any business. ■ In the absence of such specification in the certificate of incorporation or bylaws of a nonstock corporation:

(1) One-third of the members of such corporation shall constitute a quorum at a meeting of such members;

(2) In all matters other than the election of the governing body of such corporation, the affirmative vote of a majority of such members present in person or represented by proxy at the meeting and entitled to vote on the subject matter shall be the act of the members, unless the vote of a greater number is required by this chapter;

(3) Members of the governing body shall be elected by a plurality of the votes of the members of the corporation present in person or represented by proxy at the meeting and entitled to vote thereon; and

(4) Where a separate vote by a class or group or classes or groups is required, a majority of the members of such class or group or classes or groups, present in person or represented by proxy, shall constitute a quorum entitled to take action with respect to that vote on that matter and, in all matters other than the election of members of the governing body, the affirmative vote of the majority of the members of such class or group or classes or groups present in person or represented by proxy at the meeting shall be the act of such class or group or classes or groups.

(d) If the election of the governing body of any nonstock corporation shall not be held on the day designated by the bylaws, the governing body shall cause the election to be held as soon thereafter as convenient. ■ The failure to hold such an election at the designated time shall not work any forfeiture or dissolution of the corporation, but the Court of Chancery may summarily order such an election to be held upon the application of any member of the corporation. ■ At any election pursuant to such order the persons entitled to vote in such election who shall be present at such meeting, either in person or by proxy, shall constitute a quorum for such meeting, notwithstanding any provision of the certificate of incorporation or the bylaws of the corporation to the contrary.

(e) If authorized by the governing body, any requirement of a written ballot shall be satisfied by a ballot submitted by electronic transmission, provided that any such electronic transmission must either set forth or be submitted with information from which it can be determined that the electronic transmission was authorized by the member or proxy holder.

(f) Except as otherwise provided in the certificate of incorporation, in the bylaws, or by resolution of the governing body, the record date for any meeting or corporate action shall be deemed to be the date of such meeting or corporate action; provided, however, that no record date may precede any action by the governing body fixing such record date.

§ 216. Quorum and required vote for stock corporations.

Subject to this chapter in respect of the vote that shall be required for a specified action, the certificate of incorporation or bylaws of any corporation authorized to issue stock may specify the number of shares and/or the amount of other securities having voting power the holders of which shall be present or represented by proxy at any meeting in order to constitute a quorum for, and the votes that shall be necessary for, the transaction of any business, but in no event shall a quorum consist of less than 1/3 of the shares entitled to vote at the meeting, except that, where a separate vote by a class or series or classes or series is required, a quorum shall consist of no less than 1/3 of the shares of such class or series or classes or series. ■ In the absence of such specification in the certificate of incorporation or bylaws of the corporation:

(1) A majority of the shares entitled to vote, present in person or represented by proxy, shall constitute a quorum at a meeting of stockholders;

(2) In all matters other than the election of directors, the affirmative vote of the majority of shares present in person or represented by proxy at the meeting and entitled to vote on the subject matter shall be the act of the stockholders;

(3) Directors shall be elected by a plurality of the votes of the shares present in person or represented by proxy at the meeting and entitled to vote on the election of directors; and

(4) Where a separate vote by a class or series or classes or series is required, a majority of the outstanding shares of such class or series or classes or series, present in person or represented by proxy, shall constitute a quorum entitled to take action with respect to that vote on that matter and, in all matters other than the election of directors, the affirmative vote of the majority of shares of such class or series or classes or series present in person or represented by proxy at the meeting shall be the act of such class or series or classes or series.

A bylaw amendment adopted by stockholders which specifies the votes that shall be necessary for the election of directors shall not be further amended or repealed by the board of directors.

§ 217. Voting rights of fiduciaries, pledgors and joint owners of stock.

(a) Persons holding stock in a fiduciary capacity shall be entitled to vote the shares so held. ▪ Persons whose stock is pledged shall be entitled to vote, unless in the transfer by the pledgor on the books of the corporation such person has expressly empowered the pledgee to vote thereon, in which case only the pledgee, or such pledgee's proxy, may represent such stock and vote thereon.

(b) If shares or other securities having voting power stand of record in the names of 2 or more persons, whether fiduciaries, members of a partnership, joint tenants, tenants in common, tenants by the entirety or otherwise, or if 2 or more persons have the same fiduciary relationship respecting the same shares, unless the secretary of the corporation is given written notice to the contrary and is furnished with a copy of the instrument or order appointing them or creating the relationship wherein it is so provided, their acts with respect to voting shall have the following effect:

(1) If only 1 votes, such person's act binds all;

(2) If more than 1 vote, the act of the majority so voting binds all;

(3) If more than 1 vote, but the vote is evenly split on any particular matter, each faction may vote the securities in question proportionally, or any person voting the shares, or a beneficiary, if any, may apply to the Court of Chancery or such other court as may have jurisdiction to appoint an additional person to act with the persons so voting the shares, which shall then be voted as determined by a majority of such persons and the person appointed by the Court. ▪ If the instrument so filed shows that any such tenancy is held in unequal interests, a majority or even split for the purpose of this subsection shall be a majority or even split in interest.

§ 218. Voting trusts and other voting agreements.

(a) One stockholder or 2 or more stockholders may by agreement in writing deposit capital stock of an original issue with or transfer capital stock to any person or persons, or entity or entities authorized to act as trustee, for the purpose of vesting in such person or persons, entity or entities, who may be designated voting trustee, or voting trustees, the right to vote thereon for any period of time determined by such agreement, upon the terms and conditions stated in such agreement. ▪ The agreement may contain any other lawful provisions not inconsistent with such purpose. ▪ After delivery of a copy of the agreement to the registered office of the corporation in this State or the principal place of business of the corporation, which copy shall be open to the inspection of any stockholder of the corporation or any beneficiary of the trust under the agreement daily during business hours, certificates of stock or uncertificated stock shall be issued to the voting trustee or trustees to represent any stock of an original issue so deposited with such voting trustee or trustees, and any certificates of stock or uncertificated stock so transferred to the voting trustee or trustees shall be surrendered and cancelled and new certificates or uncertificated stock shall be issued therefore to the voting trustee or trustees. ▪ In the certificate so issued, if any, it shall be stated that it is issued pursuant to such agreement, and that fact shall also be stated in the stock ledger of the corporation. ▪ The voting trustee or trustees may vote the stock so issued or transferred during the period specified in the agreement. ▪ Stock standing in the name of the voting trustee or trustees may be voted either in person or by proxy, and in voting the stock, the voting trustee or trustees shall incur no responsibility as stockholder, trustee or otherwise, except for their own individual malfeasance. ▪ In any case where 2 or more persons or entities are designated as voting trustees, and the right and method of voting any stock standing in their names at any meeting of the corporation are not fixed by the agreement appointing the trustees, the right to vote the stock and the manner of voting it at the meeting shall be determined by a majority of the trustees, or if they be equally divided as to the right and manner of voting the stock in any particular case, the vote of the stock in such case shall be divided equally among the trustees.

(b) Any amendment to a voting trust agreement shall be made by a written agreement, a copy of which shall be delivered to the registered office of the corporation in this State or principal place of business of the corporation.

(c) An agreement between 2 or more stockholders, if in writing and signed by the parties thereto, may provide that in exercising any voting rights, the shares held by them shall be voted as provided by the agreement, or as the parties may agree, or as determined in accordance with a procedure agreed upon by them.

(d) This section shall not be deemed to invalidate any voting or other agreement among stockholders or any irrevocable proxy which is not otherwise illegal.

§ 219. List of stockholders entitled to vote; penalty for refusal to produce; stock ledger.

(a) The corporation shall prepare, at least 10 days before every meeting of stockholders, a complete list of the stockholders entitled to vote at the meeting; provided, however, if the record date for determining the stockholders entitled to vote is less than 10 days before the meeting date, the list shall reflect the stockholders entitled to vote as of the tenth day before the meeting date, arranged in alphabetical order, and showing the address of each stockholder and the number of shares registered in the name of each stockholder. ■ Nothing contained in this section shall require the corporation to include electronic mail addresses or other electronic contact information on such list. ■ Such list shall be open to the examination of any stockholder for any purpose germane to the meeting for a period of at least 10 days prior to the meeting: **(i)** on a reasonably accessible electronic network, provided that the information required to gain access to such list is provided with the notice of the meeting, or **(ii)** during ordinary business hours, at the principal place of business of the corporation. ■ In

the event that the corporation determines to make the list available on an electronic network, the corporation may take reasonable steps to ensure that such information is available only to stockholders of the corporation. ■ If the meeting is to be held at a place, then a list of stockholders entitled to vote at the meeting shall be produced and kept at the time and place of the meeting during the whole time thereof and may be examined by any stockholder who is present. ■ If the meeting is to be held solely by means of remote communication, then such list shall also be open to the examination of any stockholder during the whole time of the meeting on a reasonably accessible electronic network, and the information required to access such list shall be provided with the notice of the meeting.

(b) If the corporation, or an officer or agent thereof, refuses to permit examination of the list by a stockholder, such stockholder may apply to the Court of Chancery for an order to compel the corporation to permit such examination. ■ The burden of proof shall be on the corporation to establish that the examination such stockholder seeks is for a purpose not germane to the meeting. ■ The Court may summarily order the corporation to permit examination of the list upon such conditions as the Court may deem appropriate, and may make such additional orders as may be appropriate, including, without limitation, postponing the meeting or voiding the results of the meeting.

(c) For purposes of this chapter, "stock ledger" means 1 or more records administered by or on behalf of the corporation in which the names of all of the corporation's stockholders of record, the address and number of shares registered in the name of each such stockholder, and all issuances and transfers of stock of the corporation are recorded in accordance with § 224 of this title. ■ The stock ledger shall be the only evidence as to who are the stockholders entitled by this section to examine the list required by this section or to vote in person or by proxy at any meeting of stockholders.

§ 220. Inspection of books and records.

(a) As used in this section:

(1) "Stockholder" means a holder of record of stock in a stock corporation, or a person who is the beneficial owner of shares of such stock held either in a voting trust or by a nominee on behalf of such person.

(2) "Subsidiary" means any entity directly or indirectly owned, in whole or in part, by the corporation of which the stockholder is a stockholder and over the affairs of which the corporation directly or indirectly exercises control, and includes, without limitation, corporations, partnerships, limited partnerships, limited liability partnerships, limited liability companies, statutory trusts and/or joint ventures.

(3) "Under oath" includes statements the declarant affirms to be true under penalty of perjury under the laws of the United States or any state.

(b) Any stockholder, in person or by attorney or other agent, shall, upon written demand under oath stating the purpose thereof, have the right during the usual hours for business to inspect for any proper purpose, and to make copies and extracts from:

(1) The corporation's stock ledger, a list of its stockholders, and its other books and records; and

(2) A subsidiary's books and records, to the extent that:

a. The corporation has actual possession and control of such records of such subsidiary; or

b. The corporation could obtain such records through the exercise of control over such subsidiary, provided that as of the date of the making of the demand:

1. The stockholder inspection of such books and records of the subsidiary would not constitute a breach of an agreement between the corporation or the subsidiary and a person or persons not affiliated with the corporation; and

2. The subsidiary would not have the right under the law applicable to it to deny the corporation access to such books and records upon demand by the corporation.

In every instance where the stockholder is other than a record holder of stock in a stock corporation, or a member of a nonstock corporation, the demand under oath shall state the person's status as a stockholder, be accompanied by documentary evidence of beneficial ownership of the stock, and state that such documentary evidence is a true and correct copy of what it purports to be. ▪ A proper purpose shall mean a purpose reasonably related to such person's interest as a stockholder. ▪ In every instance where an attorney or other agent shall be the person who seeks the right to inspection, the demand under oath shall be accompanied by a power of attorney or such other writing which authorizes the attorney or other agent to so act on behalf of the stockholder. ▪ The demand under oath shall be directed to the corporation at its registered office in this State or at its principal place of business.

(c) If the corporation, or an officer or agent thereof, refuses to permit an inspection sought by a stockholder or attorney or other agent acting for the stockholder pursuant to subsection (b) of this section or does not reply to the demand within 5 business days after the demand has been made, the stockholder may apply to the Court of Chancery for an order to compel such inspection. ▪ The Court of Chancery is hereby vested with exclusive jurisdiction to determine whether or not the person seeking inspection is entitled to the inspection sought. ▪ The Court may summarily order the corporation to permit the stockholder to inspect the corporation's stock ledger, an existing list of stockholders, and its other books and records, and to make copies or extracts therefrom; or the Court may order the corporation to furnish to the stockholder a list of its stockholders as of a specific date on condition that the stockholder first pay to the corporation the reasonable cost of obtaining and furnishing such list and on such other conditions as the Court deems appropriate. ▪ Where the stockholder seeks to inspect the corporation's books and records, other than its stock ledger or list of stockholders, such stockholder shall first establish that:

(1) Such stockholder is a stockholder;

(2) Such stockholder has complied with this section respecting the form and manner of making demand for inspection of such documents; and

(3) The inspection such stockholder seeks is for a proper purpose.

Where the stockholder seeks to inspect the corporation's stock ledger or list of stockholders and establishes that such stockholder is a stockholder and has complied with this section respecting the form and manner of making demand for inspection of such documents, the burden of proof shall be upon the corporation to establish that the inspection such stockholder seeks is for an improper purpose. ■ The Court may, in its discretion, prescribe any limitations or conditions with reference to the inspection, or award such other or further relief as the Court may deem just and proper. ■ The Court may order books, documents and records, pertinent extracts therefrom, or duly authenticated copies thereof, to be brought within this State and kept in this State upon such terms and conditions as the order may prescribe.

(d) Any director shall have the right to examine the corporation's stock ledger, a list of its stockholders and its other books and records for a purpose reasonably related to the director's position as a director. ■ The Court of Chancery is hereby vested with the exclusive jurisdiction to determine whether a director is entitled to the inspection sought. ■ The Court may summarily order the corporation to permit the director to inspect any and all books and records, the stock ledger and the list of stockholders and to make copies or extracts therefrom. ■ The burden of proof shall be upon the corporation to establish that the inspection such director seeks is for an improper purpose. ■ The Court may, in its discretion, prescribe any limitations or conditions with reference to the inspection, or award such other and further relief as the Court may deem just and proper.

§ 221. Voting, inspection and other rights of bondholders and debenture holders.

Every corporation may in its certificate of incorporation confer upon the holders of any bonds, debentures or other obligations issued or to be issued by the corporation the power to vote in respect to the corporate affairs and management of the corporation to the extent and in the manner provided in the certificate of incorporation and may confer upon such holders of bonds, debentures or other obligations the same right of inspection of its books, accounts and other records, and also any other rights, which the stockholders of the corporation have or may have by reason of this chapter or of its certificate of incorporation. ■ If the certificate of incorporation so provides, such holders of bonds, debentures or other obligations shall be deemed to be stockholders, and their bonds, debentures or other obligations shall be deemed to be shares of stock, for the purpose of any provision of this chapter which requires the vote of stockholders as a prerequisite to any corporate action and the certificate of incorporation may divest the holders of capital stock, in whole or in part, of their right to vote on any corporate matter whatsoever, except as set forth in § 242(b)(2) of this title.

§ 222. Notice of meetings and adjourned meetings.

(a) Whenever stockholders are required or permitted to take any action at a meeting, a notice of the meeting in the form of a writing or electronic transmission shall be given which shall state the place, if any, date and hour of the meeting, the means of remote communications, if any, by which stockholders and proxy holders may be deemed to be present in person and vote at such meeting, the record date for determining the stockholders entitled to vote at the meeting, if such date is different from the record date for determining stockholders entitled to notice of the meeting, and, in the case of a special meeting, the purpose or purposes for which the meeting is called.

(b) Unless otherwise provided in this chapter, the notice of any meeting shall be given not less than 10 nor more than 60 days before the date of the meeting to each stockholder entitled to vote at such meeting as of the record date for determining the stockholders entitled to notice of the meeting.

(c) When a meeting is adjourned to another time or place, unless the bylaws otherwise require, notice need not be given of the adjourned meeting if the time, place, if any, thereof, and the means of remote communications, if any, by which stockholders and proxy holders may be deemed to be present in person and vote at such adjourned meeting are announced at the meeting at which the adjournment is taken. ▪ At the adjourned meeting the corporation may transact any business which might have been transacted at the original meeting. ▪ If the adjournment is for more than 30 days, a notice of the adjourned meeting shall be given to each stockholder of record entitled to vote at the meeting. ▪ If after the adjournment a new record date for stockholders entitled to vote is fixed for the adjourned meeting, the board of directors shall fix a new record date for notice of such adjourned meeting in accordance with § 213(a) of this title, and shall give notice of the adjourned meeting to each stockholder of record entitled to vote at such adjourned meeting as of the record date fixed for notice of such adjourned meeting.

§ 223. Vacancies and newly created directorships.

(a) Unless otherwise provided in the certificate of incorporation or bylaws:

    (1) Vacancies and newly created directorships resulting from any increase in the authorized number of directors elected by all of the stockholders having the right to vote as a single class may be filled by a majority of the directors then in office, although less than a quorum, or by a sole remaining director;

    (2) Whenever the holders of any class or classes of stock or series thereof are entitled to elect 1 or more directors by the certificate of incorporation, vacancies and newly created directorships of such class or classes or series may be filled by a majority of the directors elected by such class or classes or series thereof then in

office, or by a sole remaining director so elected.

If at any time, by reason of death or resignation or other cause, a corporation should have no directors in office, then any officer or any stockholder or an executor, administrator, trustee or guardian of a stockholder, or other fiduciary entrusted with like responsibility for the person or estate of a stockholder, may call a special meeting of stockholders in accordance with the certificate of incorporation or the bylaws, or may apply to the Court of Chancery for a decree summarily ordering an election as provided in § 211 or § 215 of this title.

(b) In the case of a corporation the directors of which are divided into classes, any directors chosen under subsection (a) of this section shall hold office until the next election of the class for which such directors shall have been chosen, and until their successors shall be elected and qualified.

(c) If, at the time of filling any vacancy or any newly created directorship, the directors then in office shall constitute less than a majority of the whole board (as constituted immediately prior to any such increase), the Court of Chancery may, upon application of any stockholder or stockholders holding at least 10 percent of the voting stock at the time outstanding having the right to vote for such directors, summarily order an election to be held to fill any such vacancies or newly created directorships, or to replace the directors chosen by the directors then in office as aforesaid, which election shall be governed by § 211 or § 215 of this title as far as applicable.

(d) Unless otherwise provided in the certificate of incorporation or bylaws, when 1 or more directors shall resign from the board, effective at a future date, a majority of the directors then in office, including those who have so resigned, shall have power to fill such vacancy or vacancies, the vote thereon to take effect when such resignation or resignations shall become effective, and each director so chosen shall hold office as provided in this section in the filling of other vacancies.

§ 224. Form of records.

Any records administered by or on behalf of the corporation in the regular course of its business, including its stock ledger, books of account, and minute books, may be kept on, or by means of, or be in the form of, any information storage device, method, or 1 or more electronic networks or databases (including 1 or more distributed electronic networks or databases), provided that the records so kept can be converted into clearly legible paper form within a reasonable time, and, with respect to the stock ledger, that the records so kept **(i)** can be used to prepare the list of stockholders specified in §§ 219 and 220 of this title, **(ii)** record the information specified in §§ 156, 159, 217(a) and 218 of this title, and **(iii)** record transfers of stock as governed by Article 8 of subtitle I of Title 6. ▪ Any corporation shall convert any records so kept into clearly legible paper form upon the request of any person entitled to inspect such records pursuant to any provision of this chapter. ▪ When records are kept in such manner, a clearly legible paper form prepared from or by means of the information storage device , method, or 1 or more electronic networks or databases (including 1 or more distributed electronic networks or databases) shall be valid and admissible in evidence, and accepted for all other purposes, to the same extent as an original paper record of the same information would have been, provided the paper form accurately portrays the record.

§ 225. Contested election of directors; proceedings to determine validity.

(a) Upon application of any stockholder or director, or any officer whose title to office is contested, the Court of Chancery may hear and determine the validity of any election, appointment, removal or resignation of any director or officer of any corporation, and the right of any person to hold or continue to hold such office, and, in case any such office is claimed by more than 1 person, may determine the person entitled thereto; and to that end make such order or decree in any such case as may be just and proper, with power to enforce the production of any books, papers and records of the corporation relating to the issue. ▪ In case it should

be determined that no valid election has been held, the Court of Chancery may order an election to be held in accordance with § 211 or § 215 of this title. ▪ In any such application, service of copies of the application upon the registered agent of the corporation shall be deemed to be service upon the corporation and upon the person whose title to office is contested and upon the person, if any, claiming such office; and the registered agent shall forward immediately a copy of the application to the corporation and to the person whose title to office is contested and to the person, if any, claiming such office, in a postpaid, sealed, registered letter addressed to such corporation and such person at their post-office addresses last known to the registered agent or furnished to the registered agent by the applicant stockholder. ▪ The Court may make such order respecting further or other notice of such application as it deems proper under the circumstances.

(b) Upon application of any stockholder or upon application of the corporation itself, the Court of Chancery may hear and determine the result of any vote of stockholders upon matters other than the election of directors or officers. ▪ Service of the application upon the registered agent of the corporation shall be deemed to be service upon the corporation, and no other party need be joined in order for the Court to adjudicate the result of the vote. ▪ The Court may make such order respecting notice of the application as it deems proper under the circumstances.

(c) If 1 or more directors has been convicted of a felony in connection with the duties of such director or directors to the corporation, or if there has been a prior judgment on the merits by a court of competent jurisdiction that 1 or more directors has committed a breach of the duty of loyalty in connection with the duties of such director or directors to that corporation, then, upon application by the corporation, or derivatively in the right of the corporation by any stockholder, in a subsequent action brought for such purpose, the Court of Chancery may remove from office such director or directors if the Court determines that the director or directors did not act in good faith in performing the acts resulting in the prior conviction or judgment and judicial removal is necessary to avoid irreparable harm to the corporation. ▪ In connection with such removal, the Court may make such orders as are necessary to effect such removal. ▪ In any such application, service of copies of the application upon the registered agent of the corporation shall be deemed to be service upon the corporation and upon the director or directors whose removal is sought; and the registered agent shall forward immediately a copy of the application to the corporation and to such director or directors, in a postpaid, sealed, registered letter addressed to such corporation and such director or directors at their post office addresses last known to the registered agent or furnished to the registered agent by the applicant. ▪ The Court may make such order respecting further or other notice of such application as it deems proper under the circumstances.

§ 226. Appointment of custodian or receiver of corporation on deadlock or for other cause.

(a) The Court of Chancery, upon application of any stockholder, may appoint 1 or more persons to be custodians, and, if the corporation is insolvent, to be receivers, of and for any corporation when:

(1) At any meeting held for the election of directors the stockholders are so divided that they have failed to elect successors to directors whose terms have expired or would have expired upon qualification of their successors; or

(2) The business of the corporation is suffering or is threatened with irreparable injury because the directors are so divided respecting the management of the affairs of the corporation that the required vote for action by the board of directors cannot be obtained and the stockholders are unable to terminate this division; or

(3) The corporation has abandoned its business and has failed within a reasonable time to take steps to dissolve, liquidate or distribute its assets.

(b) A custodian appointed under this section shall have all the powers and title of a receiver appointed under § 291 of this title, but the authority of the custodian is to continue the business of the corporation and not to liquidate its affairs and distribute its assets, except when the Court shall otherwise order and except in cases arising under paragraph (a)(3) of this section or § 352(a)(2) of this title.

(c) In the case of a charitable nonstock corporation, the applicant shall provide a copy of any application referred to in subsection (a) of this section to the Attorney General of the State of Delaware within 1 week of its filing with the Court of Chancery.

§ 227. Powers of Court in elections of directors.

(a) The Court of Chancery, in any proceeding instituted under § 211, § 215 or § 225 of this title may determine the right and power of persons claiming to own stock to vote at any meeting of the stockholders.

(b) The Court of Chancery may appoint a Master to hold any election provided for in § 211, § 215 or § 225 of this title under such orders and powers as it deems proper; and it may punish any officer or director for contempt in case of disobedience of any order made by the Court; and, in case of disobedience by a corporation of any order made by the Court, may enter a decree against such corporation for a penalty of not more than $5,000.

§ 228. Consent of stockholders or members in lieu of meeting.

(a) Unless otherwise provided in the certificate of incorporation, any action required by this chapter to be taken at any annual or special meeting of stockholders of a corporation, or any action which may be taken at any annual or special meeting of such stockholders, may be taken without a meeting, without prior notice and without a vote, if a consent or consents, setting forth the action so taken, shall be signed by the holders of outstanding stock having not less than the minimum number of votes that would be necessary to authorize or take such action at a meeting at which all shares entitled to vote thereon were present and voted and shall be delivered to the corporation in the manner required by this section.

(b) Unless otherwise provided in the certificate of incorporation, any action required by this chapter to be taken at a meeting of the members of a nonstock corporation, or any action which may be taken at any meeting of the members of a nonstock corporation, may be taken without a meeting, without prior notice and without a vote, if a consent or consents, setting forth the action so taken, shall be signed by members having not less than the minimum number of votes that would be necessary to authorize or take such action at a meeting at which all members having a right to vote thereon were present and voted and shall be delivered to the corporation in the manner required by this section.

(c) A consent must be set forth in writing or in an electronic transmission. ■ No consent shall be effective to take the corporate action referred to therein unless consents signed by a sufficient number of holders or members to take action are delivered to the corporation in the manner required by this section within 60 days of the first date on which a consent is so delivered to the corporation. Any person executing a consent may provide, whether through instruction to an agent or otherwise, that such a consent will be effective at a future time (including a time determined upon the happening of an event), no later than 60 days after such instruction is given or such provision is made, if evidence of such instruction or provision is provided to the corporation. ■ Unless otherwise provided, any such consent shall be revocable prior to its becoming effective. ■ All references to a "consent" in this section means a consent permitted by this section.

(d)(1) A consent permitted by this section shall be delivered: **(i)** to the principal place of business of the corporation; **(ii)** to an officer or agent of the corporation having custody of the book in which proceedings of meetings of stockholders or members are recorded; **(iii)** to the registered office of the corporation in this State by hand or by certified or registered mail, return receipt requested; or **(iv)** subject to the next sentence, in accordance with § 116 of this title to an information processing system, if any, designated by the corporation for receiving such consents. ■ In the case of delivery pursuant to the foregoing clause (iv), such consent must set forth or be delivered with information that enables the corporation to determine the date of delivery of such consent and the identity of the person giving such consent, and, if such consent is given by a person authorized to act for a stockholder or member as proxy, such consent must comply with the applicable provisions of § 212(c)(2) and (3) of this title.

(2) Any copy, facsimile or other reliable reproduction of a consent in writing may be substituted or used in lieu of the original writing for any and all purposes for which the original writing could be used, provided that such copy, facsimile or other reproduction shall be a complete reproduction of the entire original writing. ■ A consent may be documented and signed in accordance with § 116 of this title, and when so documented or signed shall be deemed to be in writing for purposes of this title; provided that if such consent is delivered pursuant to clause (i), (ii) or (iii) of paragraph (d)(1) of this section, such consent must be reproduced and delivered in paper form.

(e) Prompt notice of the taking of the corporate action without a meeting by less than unanimous consent shall be given to those stockholders or members who have not consented and who, if the action had been taken at a meeting, would have been entitled to notice of the meeting if the record date for notice of such meeting had been the date that consents signed by a sufficient number of holders or members to take the action were delivered to the corporation as provided in this section. ■ In the event that the action which is consented to is such as would have required the filing of a certificate under any other section of this title, if such action had been voted on by stockholders or by members at a meeting thereof, the certificate filed under such other section shall state, in lieu of any statement required by such section concerning any vote of stockholders or members, that consent has been given in accordance with this section.

§ 229. Waiver of notice.

Whenever notice is required to be given under any provision of this chapter or the certificate of incorporation or bylaws, a written waiver, signed by the person entitled to notice, or a waiver by electronic transmission by the person entitled to notice, whether before or after the time stated therein, shall be deemed equivalent to notice. ▪ Attendance of a person at a meeting shall constitute a waiver of notice of such meeting, except when the person attends a meeting for the express purpose of objecting at the beginning of the meeting, to the transaction of any business because the meeting is not lawfully called or convened. ▪ Neither the business to be transacted at, nor the purpose of, any regular or special meeting of the stockholders, directors or members of a committee of directors need be specified in any written waiver of notice or any waiver by electronic transmission unless so required by the certificate of incorporation or the bylaws.

§ 230. Exception to requirements of notice.

(a) Whenever notice is required to be given, under any provision of this chapter or of the certificate of incorporation or bylaws of any corporation, to any person with whom communication is unlawful, the giving of such notice to such person shall not be required and there shall be no duty to apply to any governmental authority or agency for a license or permit to give such notice to such person. ▪ Any action or meeting which shall be taken or held without notice to any such person with whom communication is unlawful shall have the same force and effect as if such notice had been duly given. ▪ In the event that the action taken by the corporation is such as to require the filing of a certificate under any of the other sections of this title, the certificate shall state, if such is the fact and if notice is required, that notice was given to all persons entitled to receive notice except such persons with whom communication is unlawful.

(b) Whenever notice is required to be given, under any provision of this title or the certificate of incorporation or bylaws of any corporation, to any stockholder or, if the corporation is a nonstock corporation, to any member, to whom (1) notice of 2 consecutive annual meetings, and all notices of meetings or of the taking of action by written consent without a meeting to such person during the period between such 2 consecutive annual meetings, or (2) all, and at least 2, payments (if sent by first-class mail) of dividends or interest on securities during a 12-month period, have been mailed addressed to such person at such person's address as shown on the records of the corporation and have been returned undeliverable, the giving of such notice to such person shall not be required. ▪ Any action or meeting which shall be taken or held without notice to such person shall have the same force and effect as if such notice had been duly given. ▪ If any such person shall deliver to the corporation a written notice setting forth such person's then current address, the requirement that notice be given to such person shall be reinstated. ▪ In the event that the action taken by the corporation is such as to require the filing of a certificate under any of the other sections of this title, the certificate need not state that notice was not given to persons to whom notice was not required to be given pursuant to this subsection.

(c) The exception in paragraph (b)(1) of this section to the requirement that notice be given shall not be applicable to any notice returned as undeliverable if the notice was given by electronic transmission. ▪ The exception in paragraph (b)(1) of this section to the requirement that notice be given shall not be applicable to any stockholder or member whose electronic mail address appears on the records of the corporation and to whom notice by electronic transmission is not prohibited by § 232 of this title.

§ 231. Voting procedures and inspectors of elections.

(a) The corporation shall, in advance of any meeting of stockholders, appoint 1 or more inspectors to act at the meeting and make a written report thereof. ▪ The corporation may designate 1 or more persons as alternate inspectors to replace any inspector who fails to act. ▪ If no inspector or alternate is able to act at a meeting of stockholders, the person presiding at the meeting shall appoint 1 or more inspectors to act at the meeting. ▪ Each inspector, before entering upon the discharge of the duties of inspector, shall take and sign an oath faithfully to execute the duties of inspector with strict impartiality and according to the best of such inspector's ability.

(b) The inspectors shall:

(1) Ascertain the number of shares outstanding and the voting power of each;

(2) Determine the shares represented at a meeting and the validity of proxies and ballots;

(3) Count all votes and ballots;

(4) Determine and retain for a reasonable period a record of the disposition of any challenges made to any determination by the inspectors; and

(5) Certify their determination of the number of shares represented at the meeting, and their count of all votes and ballots.

The inspectors may appoint or retain other persons or entities to assist the inspectors in the performance of the duties of the inspectors.

(c) The date and time of the opening and the closing of the polls for each matter upon which the stockholders will vote at a meeting shall be announced at the meeting. ▪ No ballot, proxies or votes, nor any revocations thereof or changes thereto, shall be accepted by the inspectors after the closing of the polls unless the Court of Chancery upon application by a stockholder shall determine otherwise.

(d) In determining the validity and counting of proxies and ballots, the inspectors shall be limited to an examination of the proxies, any envelopes submitted with those proxies, any information provided in accordance with § 211(e) or § 212(c)(2) of this title, or any information provided pursuant to § 211(a)(2)b.(i) or (iii) of this title, ballots and the regular books and records of the corporation, except that the inspectors may consider other reliable information for the limited purpose of reconciling proxies and ballots submitted by or on behalf of banks, brokers, their nominees or similar

persons which represent more votes than the holder of a proxy is authorized by the record owner to cast or more votes than the stockholder holds of record. ▪ If the inspectors consider other reliable information for the limited purpose permitted herein, the inspectors at the time they make their certification pursuant to paragraph (b)(5) of this section shall specify the precise information considered by them including the person or persons from whom they obtained the information, when the information was obtained, the means by which the information was obtained and the basis for the inspectors' belief that such information is accurate and reliable.

(e) Unless otherwise provided in the certificate of incorporation or bylaws, this section shall not apply to a corporation that does not have a class of voting stock that is:

(1) Listed on a national securities exchange;

(2) Authorized for quotation on an interdealer quotation system of a registered national securities association; or

(3) Held of record by more than 2,000 stockholders.

§ 232. Delivery of notice; notice by electronic transmission.

(a) Without limiting the manner by which notice otherwise may be given effectively to stockholders, any notice to stockholders given by the corporation under any provision of this chapter, the certificate of incorporation, or the bylaws may be given in writing directed to the stockholder's mailing address (or by electronic transmission directed to the stockholder's electronic mail address, as applicable) as it appears on the records of the corporation and shall be given:

(1) If mailed, when the notice is deposited in the U.S. mail, postage prepaid;

(2) If delivered by courier service, the earlier of when the notice is received or left at such stockholder's address; or

(3) If given by electronic mail, when directed to such stockholder's electronic mail address unless the stockholder has notified the corporation in writing or by electronic transmission of an objection to receiving notice by electronic mail or such notice is prohibited by subsection (e) of this section. ▪

A notice by electronic mail must include a prominent legend that the communication is an important notice regarding the corporation.

(b) Without limiting the manner by which notice otherwise may be given effectively to stockholders, but subject to subsection (e) of this section, any notice to stockholders given by the corporation under any provision of this chapter, the certificate of incorporation, or the bylaws shall be effective if given by a form of electronic transmission consented to by the stockholder to whom the notice is given. ▪ Any such consent shall be revocable by the stockholder by written notice or electronic transmission to the corporation. ▪ A corporation may give a notice by electronic mail in accordance with subsection (a) of this section without obtaining the consent required by this subsection.

(c) Notice given pursuant to subsection (b) of this section shall be deemed given:

(1) If by facsimile telecommunication, when directed to a number at which the stockholder has consented to receive notice;

(2) If by a posting on an electronic network together with separate notice to the stockholder of such specific posting, upon the later of:

a. Such posting; and

b. The giving of such separate notice; and

(3) If by any other form of electronic transmission, when directed to the stockholder.

(d) For purposes of this chapter:

(1) "Electronic transmission" means any form of communication, not directly involving the physical transmission of paper, including the use of, or participation in, 1 or more electronic networks or databases (including 1 or more distributed electronic networks or databases), that creates a record that may be retained, retrieved and reviewed by a recipient thereof, and that

may be directly reproduced in paper form by such a recipient through an automated process;

(2) "Electronic mail" means an electronic transmission directed to a unique electronic mail address (which electronic mail shall be deemed to include any files attached thereto and any information hyperlinked to a website if such electronic mail includes the contact information of an officer or agent of the corporation who is available to assist with accessing such files and information); and

(3) "Electronic mail address" means a destination, commonly expressed as a string of characters, consisting of a unique user name or mailbox (commonly referred to as the "local part" of the address) and a reference to an internet domain (commonly referred to as the "domain part" of the address), whether or not displayed, to which electronic mail can be sent or delivered.

(e) Notwithstanding the foregoing, a notice may not be given by an electronic transmission from and after the time that:

(1) The corporation is unable to deliver by such electronic transmission 2 consecutive notices given by the corporation; and

(2) Such inability becomes known to the secretary or an assistant secretary of the corporation or to the transfer agent, or other person responsible for the giving of notice, provided, however, the inadvertent failure to discover such inability shall not invalidate any meeting or other action.

(f) An affidavit of the secretary or an assistant secretary or of the transfer agent or other agent of the corporation that notice has been given shall, in the absence of fraud, be prima facie evidence of the facts stated therein.

(g) No provision of this section, except for paragraphs (a)(1), (d)(2) and (d)(3) of this section shall apply to § 164, § 296, § 311, § 312, or § 324 of this title.

§ 233. Notice to stockholders sharing an address.

(a) Without limiting the manner by which notice otherwise may be given effectively to stockholders, any notice to stockholders given by the corporation under any provision of this chapter, the certificate of incorporation, or the bylaws shall be effective if given by a single written notice to stockholders who share an address if consented to by the stockholders at that address to whom such notice is given. ■ Any such consent shall be revocable by the stockholder by written notice to the corporation.

(b) Any stockholder who fails to object in writing to the corporation, within 60 days of having been given written notice by the corporation of its intention to send the single notice permitted under subsection (a) of this section, shall be deemed to have consented to receiving such single written notice.

(c) [Repealed.]

(d) This section shall not apply to § 164, § 296, § 311, § 312 or § 324 of this title.

Subchapter VIII. Amendment of Certificate of Incorporation; Changes in Capital and Capital Stock

§ 241. Amendment of certificate of incorporation before receipt of payment for stock.

(a) Before a corporation has received any payment for any of its stock, it may amend its certificate of incorporation at any time or times, in any and as many respects as may be desired, so long as its certificate of incorporation as amended would contain only such provisions as it would be lawful and proper to insert in an original certificate of incorporation filed at the time of filing the amendment.

(b) The amendment of a certificate of incorporation authorized by this section shall be adopted by a majority of the incorporators, if directors were

not named in the original certificate of incorporation or have not yet been elected, or, if directors were named in the original certificate of incorporation or have been elected and have qualified, by a majority of the directors. ■ A certificate setting forth the amendment and certifying that the corporation has not received any payment for any of its stock, or that the corporation has no members, as applicable, and that the amendment has been duly adopted in accordance with this section shall be executed, acknowledged and filed in accordance with § 103 of this title. ■ Upon such filing, the corporation's certificate of incorporation shall be deemed to be amended accordingly as of the date on which the original certificate of incorporation became effective, except as to those persons who are substantially and adversely affected by the amendment and as to those persons the amendment shall be effective from the filing date.

(c) This section will apply to a nonstock corporation before such a corporation has any members; provided, however, that all references to directors shall be deemed to be references to members of the governing body of the corporation.

§ 242. Amendment of certificate of incorporation after receipt of payment for stock; nonstock corporations.

(a) After a corporation has received payment for any of its capital stock, or after a nonstock corporation has members, it may amend its certificate of incorporation, from time to time, in any and as many respects as may be desired, so long as its certificate of incorporation as amended would contain only such provisions as it would be lawful and proper to insert in an original certificate of incorporation filed at the time of the filing of the amendment; and, if a change in stock or the rights of stockholders, or an exchange, reclassification, subdivision, combination or cancellation of stock or rights of stockholders is to be made, such provisions as may be necessary to effect such change, exchange, reclassification, subdivision, combination or cancellation. ■ In particular, and without limitation upon such general power of amendment, a corporation may amend its certificate of incorporation, from time to time, so as:

(1) To change its corporate name; or

(2) To change, substitute, enlarge or diminish the nature of its business or its corporate powers and purposes; or

(3) To increase or decrease its authorized capital stock or to reclassify the same, by changing the number, par value, designations, preferences, or relative, participating, optional, or other special rights of the shares, or the qualifications, limitations or restrictions of such rights, or by changing shares with par value into shares without par value, or shares without par value into shares with par value either with or without increasing or decreasing the number of shares, or by subdividing or combining the outstanding shares of any class or series of a class of shares into a greater or lesser number of outstanding shares; or

(4) To cancel or otherwise affect the right of the holders of the shares of any class to receive dividends which have accrued but have not been declared; or

(5) To create new classes of stock having rights and preferences either prior and superior or subordinate and inferior to the stock of any class then authorized, whether issued or unissued; or

(6) To change the period of its duration; or

(7) To delete:

> **a.** Such provisions of the original certificate of incorporation which named the incorporator or incorporators, the initial board of directors and the original subscribers for shares; and

> **b.** Such provisions contained in any amendment to the certificate of incorporation as were necessary to effect a change, exchange, reclassification, subdivision, combination or cancellation of stock, if such change, exchange, reclassification, subdivision, combination or cancellation has become effective.

Any or all such changes or alterations may be effected by 1 certificate of amendment.

(b) Every amendment authorized by subsection (a) of this section shall be made and effected in the following manner:

(1) If the corporation has capital stock, its board of directors shall adopt a resolution setting forth the amendment proposed, declaring its advisability, and either calling a special meeting of the stockholders entitled to vote in respect thereof for the consideration of such amendment or directing that the amendment proposed be considered at the next annual meeting of the stockholders; provided, however, that unless otherwise expressly required by the certificate of incorporation, no meeting or vote of stockholders shall be required to adopt an amendment that effects only changes described in paragraph (a)(1) or (7) of this section. ■ Such special or annual meeting shall be called and held upon notice in accordance with § 222 of this title. ■ The notice shall set forth such amendment in full or a brief summary of the changes to be effected thereby unless such notice constitutes a notice of internet availability of proxy materials under the rules promulgated under the Securities Exchange Act of 1934 [15 U.S.C. § 78a et seq.]. ■ At the meeting a vote of the stockholders entitled to vote thereon shall be taken for and against any proposed amendment that requires adoption by stockholders. ■ If no vote of stockholders is required to effect such amendment, or if a majority of the outstanding stock entitled to vote thereon, and a majority of the outstanding stock of each class entitled to vote thereon as a class has been voted in favor of the amendment, a certificate se[...]
tifying that [...]
adopted in a [...]
executed, ad [...]
come effect [...]
title.

(2) The hol[...]
class shall [...]
proposed a[...]
to vote the[...]

tion, if the amendment would increase or decrease the aggregate number of authorized shares of such class, increase or decrease the par value of the shares of such class, or alter or change the powers, preferences, or special rights of the shares of such class so as to affect them adversely. ■ If any proposed amendment would alter or change the powers, preferences, or special rights of 1 or more series of any class so as to affect them adversely, but shall not so affect the entire class, then only the shares of the series so affected by the amendment shall be considered a separate class for the purposes of this paragraph. ■ The number of authorized shares of any such class or classes of stock may be increased or decreased (but not below the number of shares thereof then outstanding) by the affirmative vote of the holders of a majority of the stock of the corporation entitled to vote irrespective of this subsection, if so provided in the original certificate of incorporation, in any amendment thereto which created such class or classes of stock or which was adopted prior to the issuance of any shares of such class or classes of stock, or in any amendment thereto which was authorized by a resolution or resolutions adopted by the affirmative vote of the holders of a majority of such class or classes of stock.

(3) If the corporation is a nonstock corporation, then the governing body thereof shall adopt a resolution setting forth the amendment proposed and declaring its advisability. ■ If a majority of all the members of the governing body shall vote in favor of such amendment, a certificate thereof shall be executed, acknowledged and filed and shall become effective in accordance with § 103 of this title. ■ The certificate of incorporation of any nonstock corporation may contain a provision requiring any amendment thereto to be approved by a specified number or percentage of the members or of any such class of members of such corporation in the event such proposed amendment shall to the members or to any specified members of such corporation in the

same manner, so far as applicable, as is provided in this section for an amendment to the certificate of incorporation of a stock corporation; and in the event of the adoption thereof by such members, a certificate evidencing such amendment shall be executed, acknowledged and filed and shall become effective in accordance with § 103 of this title.

(4) Whenever the certificate of incorporation shall require for action by the board of directors of a corporation other than a nonstock corporation or by the governing body of a nonstock corporation, by the holders of any class or series of shares or by the members, or by the holders of any other securities having voting power the vote of a greater number or proportion than is required by any section of this title, the provision of the certificate of incorporation requiring such greater vote shall not be altered, amended or repealed except by such greater vote.

(c) The resolution authorizing a proposed amendment to the certificate of incorporation may provide that at any time prior to the effectiveness of the filing of the amendment with the Secretary of State, notwithstanding authorization of the proposed amendment by the stockholders of the corporation or by the members of a nonstock corporation, the board of directors or governing body may abandon such proposed amendment without further action by the stockholders or members.

§ 243. Retirement of stock.

(a) A corporation, by resolution of its board of directors, may retire any shares of its capital stock that are issued but are not outstanding.

(b) Whenever any shares of the capital stock of a corporation are retired, they shall resume the status of authorized and unissued shares of the class or series to which they belong unless the certificate of incorporation otherwise provides. ■ If the certificate of incorporation prohibits the reissuance of such shares, or prohibits the reissuance of such shares as a part of a specific series only, a certificate stating that reissuance of the shares (as part of the class or series) is prohibited identifying the shares and reciting their retirement shall be executed, acknowledged and filed and shall become effective in accordance with § 103 of this title. ∎ When such certificate becomes effective, it shall have the effect of amending the certificate of incorporation so as to reduce accordingly the number of authorized shares of the class or series to which such shares belong or, if such retired shares constitute all of the authorized shares of the class or series to which they belong, of eliminating from the certificate of incorporation all reference to such class or series of stock.

(c) If the capital of the corporation will be reduced by or in connection with the retirement of shares, the reduction of capital shall be effected pursuant to § 244 of this title.

§ 244. Reduction of capital.

(a) A corporation, by resolution of its board of directors, may reduce its capital in any of the following ways:

(1) By reducing or eliminating the capital represented by shares of capital stock which have been retired;

(2) By applying to an otherwise authorized purchase or redemption of outstanding shares of its capital stock some or all of the capital represented by the shares being purchased or redeemed, or any capital that has not been allocated to any particular class of its capital stock;

(3) By applying to an otherwise authorized conversion or exchange of outstanding shares of its capital stock some or all of the capital represented by the shares being converted or exchanged, or some or all of any capital that has not been allocated to any particular class of its capital stock, or both, to the extent that such capital in the aggregate exceeds the total aggregate par value or the stated capital of any previously unissued shares issuable upon such conversion or exchange; or

(4) By transferring to surplus **(i)** some or all of the capital not represented by any particular class of its capital stock; **(ii)** some or all of the capital represented by issued shares of its par value capital stock, which capital is in excess of the aggregate par value of such shares; or **(iii)** some of the capital represented by issued shares of its capital stock without par value.

(b) Notwithstanding the other provisions of this section, no reduction of capital shall be made or effected unless the assets of the corporation remaining after such reduction shall be sufficient to pay any debts of the corporation for which payment has not been otherwise provided. ∎ No reduction of capital shall release any liability of any stockholder whose shares have not been fully paid.

(c) [Repealed.]

§ 245. Restated certificate of incorporation.

(a) A corporation may, whenever desired, integrate into a single instrument all of the provisions of its certificate of incorporation which are then in effect and operative as a result of there having theretofore been filed with the Secretary of State 1 or more certificates or other instruments pursuant to any of the sections referred to in § 104 of this title, and it may at the same time also further amend its certificate of incorporation by adopting a restated certificate of incorporation.

(b) If the restated certificate of incorporation merely restates and integrates but does not further amend the certificate of incorporation, as theretofore amended or supplemented by any instrument that was filed pursuant to any of the sections mentioned in § 104 of this title, it may be adopted by the board of directors without a vote of the stockholders, or it may be proposed by the directors and submitted by them to the stockholders for adoption, in which case the procedure and vote required, if any, by § 242 of this title for amendment of the certificate of incorporation shall be applicable. ∎ If the restated certificate of incorporation restates and integrates and also further amends in any respect the certificate of incorporation, as theretofore amended or supplemented, it shall be proposed by the directors and adopted by the stockholders in the manner and by the vote prescribed by § 242 of this title or, if the corporation has not received any payment for any of its stock, in the manner and by the vote prescribed by § 241 of this title.

(c) A restated certificate of incorporation shall be specifically designated as such in its heading. ▪ It shall state, either in its heading or in an introductory paragraph, the corporation's present name, and, if it has been changed, the name under which it was originally incorporated, and the date of filing of its original certificate of incorporation with the Secretary of State. ▪ A restated certificate shall also state that it was duly adopted in accordance with this section. ▪ If it was adopted by the board of directors without a vote of the stockholders (unless it was adopted pursuant to § 241 of this title or without a vote of members pursuant to 242(b)(3) of this title), it shall state that it only restates and integrates and does not further amend (except, if applicable, as permitted under § 242(a)(1) and § 242(b)(1) of this title) the provisions of the corporation's certificate of incorporation as theretofore amended or supplemented, and that there is no discrepancy between those provisions and the provisions of the restated certificate. ▪ A restated certificate of incorporation may omit **(a)** such provisions of the original certificate of incorporation which named the incorporator or incorporators, the initial board of directors and the original subscribers for shares, and **(b)** such provisions contained in any amendment to the certificate of incorporation as were necessary to effect a change, exchange, reclassification, subdivision, combination or cancellation of stock, if such change, exchange, reclassification, subdivision, combination or cancellation has become effective. ▪ Any such omissions shall not be deemed a further amendment.

(d) A restated certificate of incorporation shall be executed, acknowledged and filed in accordance with § 103 of this title. ▪ Upon its filing with the Secretary of State, the original certificate of incorporation, as theretofore amended or supplemented, shall be superseded; thenceforth, the restated certificate of incorporation, including any further amendments or changes made thereby, shall be the certificate of incorporation of the corporation, but the original date of incorporation shall remain unchanged.

(e) Any amendment or change effected in connection with the restatement and integration of the certificate of incorporation shall be subject to any other provision of this chapter, not inconsistent with this section, which would apply if a separate certificate of amendment were filed to effect such amendment or change.

§ 246. [Reserved.]

Subchapter IX. Merger, Consolidation or Conversion

§ 251. Merger or consolidation of domestic corporations.

(a) Any 2 or more corporations of this State may merge into a single surviving corporation, which may be any 1 of the constituent corporations or may consolidate into a new resulting corporation formed by the consolidation, pursuant to an agreement of merger or consolidation, as the case may be, complying and approved in accordance with this section.

(b) The board of directors of each corporation which desires to merge or consolidate shall adopt a resolution approving an agreement of merger or consolidation and declaring its advisability. ▪ The agreement shall state:

(1) The terms and conditions of the merger or consolidation;

(2) The mode of carrying the same into effect;

(3) In the case of a merger, such amendments or changes in the certificate of incorporation of the surviving corporation as are desired to be effected by the merger (which amendments or changes may amend and restate the certificate of incorporation of the surviving corporation in its entirety), or, if no such amendments or changes are desired, a statement that the certificate of incorporation of the surviving corporation shall be its certificate of incorporation;

(4) In the case of a consolidation, that the certificate of incorporation of the resulting corporation shall be as is set forth in an attachment to the agreement;

(5) The manner, if any, of converting the shares of each of the constituent corporations into shares or other securities of the corporation surviving or resulting from the merger or consolidation, or of cancelling some or all of such shares, and, if any shares of any of the constituent corporations are not to remain outstanding, to be converted solely into shares or other securities of the surviving or resulting corporation or to be cancelled, the cash, property, rights or securities of any other corporation or entity which the holders of such shares are to receive in exchange for, or upon conversion of such shares and the surrender of any certificates evidencing them, which cash, property, rights or securities of any other corporation or entity may be in addition to or in lieu of shares or other securities of the surviving or resulting corporation; and

(6) Such other details or provisions as are deemed desirable, including, without limiting the generality of the foregoing, a provision for the payment of cash in lieu of the issuance or recognition of fractional shares, rights or other securities of the surviving or resulting corporation or of any other corporation or entity the shares, rights or other securities of which are to be received in the merger or consolidation, or for any other arrangement with respect thereto, consistent with § 155 of this title.

The agreement so adopted shall be executed by an authorized person, provided that if the agreement is filed, it shall be executed and acknowledged in accordance with § 103 of this title. ▪ Any of the terms of the agreement of merger or consolidation may be made dependent upon facts ascertainable outside of such agreement, provided that the manner in which such facts shall operate upon the terms of the agreement is clearly and expressly set forth in the agreement of merger or consolidation. ▪ The term "facts," as used in the preceding sentence, includes, but is not limited to, the occurrence of any event, including a determination or action by any person or body, including the corporation.

(c) The agreement required by subsection (b) of this section shall be submitted to the stockholders of each constituent corporation at an annual or special meeting for the purpose of acting on the agreement. ▪ Due notice of the time, place and purpose of the meeting shall be given to each holder of stock, whether voting or nonvoting, of the corporation at the stockholder's address as it appears on the records of the corporation, at least 20 days prior to the date of the meeting. ▪ The notice shall contain a copy of the agreement or a brief summary thereof. ▪ At the meeting, the agreement shall be considered and a vote taken for its adoption or rejection. ▪ If a majority of the outstanding stock of the corporation entitled to vote thereon shall be voted for the adoption of the agreement, that fact shall be certified on the agreement by the secretary or assistant secretary of the corporation, provided that such certification on the agreement shall not be required if a certificate of merger or consolidation is filed in lieu of filing the agreement. ▪ If the agreement shall be so adopted and certified by each constituent corporation, it shall then be filed and shall become effective, in accordance with § 103 of this title. ▪ In lieu of filing the agreement of merger or consolidation required by this section, the surviving or resulting corporation may file a certificate of merger or consolidation, executed in accordance with § 103 of this title, which states:

(1) The name and state of incorporation of each of the constituent corporations;

(2) That an agreement of merger or consolidation has been approved, adopted, executed and acknowledged by each of the constituent corporations in accordance with this section;

(3) The name of the surviving or resulting corporation;

(4) In the case of a merger, such amendments or changes in the certificate of incorporation of the surviving corporation as are desired to be effected by the merger (which amendments or changes may amend and restate the certificate of incorporation of the surviving corporation in its entirety), or, if no such amendments or changes are desired, a statement that the certificate of incorporation of the surviving corporation shall be its certificate of incorporation;

(5) In the case of a consolidation, that the certificate of incorporation of the resulting corporation shall be as set forth in an attachment to the certificate;

(6) That the executed agreement of consolidation or merger is on file at an office of the surviving or resulting corporation, stating the address thereof; and

(7) That a copy of the agreement of consolidation or merger will be furnished by the surviving or resulting corporation, on request and without cost, to any stockholder of any constituent corporation.

(d) Any agreement of merger or consolidation may contain a provision that at any time prior to the time that the agreement (or a certificate in lieu thereof) filed with the Secretary of State becomes effective in accordance with § 103 of this title, the agreement may be terminated by the board of directors of any constituent corporation notwithstanding approval of the agreement by the stockholders of all or any of the constituent corporations; in the event the agreement of merger or consolidation is terminated after the filing of the agreement (or a certificate in lieu thereof) with the Secretary of State but before the agreement (or a certificate in lieu thereof) has become effective, a certificate of termination or merger or consolidation shall be filed in accordance with § 103 of this title. ■ Any agreement of merger or consolidation may contain a provision that the boards of directors of the constituent corporations may amend the agreement at any time prior to the time that the agreement (or a certificate in lieu thereof) filed with the Secretary of State becomes effective in accordance with § 103 of this title, provided that an amendment made subsequent to the adoption of the agreement by the stockholders of any constituent corporation shall not **(1)** alter or change the amount or kind of shares, securities, cash, property and/or rights to be received in exchange for or on conversion of all or any of the shares of any class

or series thereof of such constituent corporation, **(2)** alter or change any term of the certificate of incorporation of the surviving corporation to be effected by the merger or consolidation, or **(3)** alter or change any of the terms and conditions of the agreement if such alteration or change would adversely affect the holders of any class or series thereof of such constituent corporation; in the event the agreement of merger or consolidation is amended after the filing thereof with the Secretary of State but before the agreement has become effective, a certificate of amendment of merger or consolidation shall be filed in accordance with § 103 of this title.

(e) In the case of a merger, the certificate of incorporation of the surviving corporation shall automatically be amended to the extent, if any, that changes in the certificate of incorporation are set forth in the agreement of merger.

(f) Notwithstanding the requirements of subsection (c) of this section, unless required by its certificate of incorporation, no vote of stockholders of a constituent corporation surviving a merger shall be necessary to authorize a merger if **(1)** the agreement of merger does not amend in any respect the certificate of incorporation of such constituent corporation, **(2)** each share of stock of such constituent corporation outstanding immediately prior to the effective date of the merger is to be an identical outstanding or treasury share of the surviving corporation after the effective date of the merger, and **(3)** either no shares of common stock of the surviving corporation and no shares, securities or obligations convertible into such stock are to be issued or delivered under the plan of merger, or the authorized unissued shares or the treasury shares of common stock of the surviving corporation to be issued or delivered under the plan of merger plus those initially issuable upon conversion of any other shares, securities or obligations to be issued or delivered under such plan do not exceed 20% of the shares of common stock of such constituent corporation outstanding immediately prior to the effective date of the merger. ■ No vote of stockholders of a constituent corporation shall be necessary to authorize a merger or consolidation if no shares of the stock of such corporation shall have been issued prior to the adoption by the board of directors of the resolution approving the agreement of merger or consolidation. ▪ If an agreement of merger is adopted by the constituent corporation surviving the merger, by action of its board of directors and without any vote of its stockholders pursuant to this subsection, the secretary or assistant secretary of that corporation shall certify on the agreement that the agreement has been adopted pursuant to this subsection and, **(1)** if it has been adopted pursuant to the first sentence of this subsection, that the conditions specified in that sentence have been satisfied, or **(2)** if it has been adopted pursuant to the second sentence of this subsection, that no shares of stock of such corporation were issued prior to the adoption by the board of directors of the resolution approving the agreement of merger or consolidation, provided that such certification on the agreement shall not be required if a certificate of merger or consolidation is filed in lieu of filing the agreement. ▪ The agreement so adopted and certified shall then be filed and shall become effective, in accordance with § 103 of this title. ▪ Such filing shall constitute a representation by the person who executes the agreement that the facts stated in the certificate remain true immediately prior to such filing.

(g) Notwithstanding the requirements of subsection (c) of this section, unless expressly required by its certificate of incorporation, no vote of stockholders of a constituent corporation shall be necessary to authorize a merger with or into a single direct or indirect wholly-owned subsidiary of such constituent corporation if:

> **(1)** Such constituent corporation and the direct or indirect wholly-owned subsidiary of such constituent corporation are the only constituent entities to the merger;
>
> **(2)** Each share or fraction of a share of the capital stock of the constituent corporation outstanding immediately prior to the effective time of the merger is converted in the merger into a share or equal fraction of share of capital stock

of a holding company having the same designations, rights, powers and preferences, and the qualifications, limitations and restrictions thereof, as the share of stock of the constituent corporation being converted in the merger;

> **(3)** The holding company and the constituent corporation are corporations of this State and the direct or indirect wholly-owned subsidiary that is the other constituent entity to the merger is a corporation or limited liability company of this State;
>
> **(4)** The certificate of incorporation and bylaws of the holding company immediately following the effective time of the merger contain provisions identical to the certificate of incorporation and bylaws of the constituent corporation immediately prior to the effective time of the merger (other than provisions, if any, regarding the incorporator or incorporators, the corporate name, the registered office and agent, the initial board of directors and the initial subscribers for shares and such provisions contained in any amendment to the certificate of incorporation as were necessary to effect a change, exchange, reclassification, subdivision, combination or cancellation of stock, if such change, exchange, reclassification, subdivision, combination, or cancellation has become effective);
>
> **(5)** As a result of the merger the constituent corporation or its successor becomes or remains a direct or indirect wholly-owned subsidiary of the holding company;
>
> **(6)** The directors of the constituent corporation become or remain the directors of the holding company upon the effective time of the merger;
>
> **(7)** The organizational documents of the surviving entity immediately following the effective time of the merger contain provisions requiring that **(A)** any act or transaction by or involving the surviving entity, other than the election or removal of directors or managers, managing members or other members of the governing body of the surviving entity, that, if taken by the constituent corporation immediately prior to the effective time of the merger,

would require for its adoption under this chapter or under the certificate of incorporation or bylaws of the constituent corporation immediately prior to the effective time of the merger, the approval of the stockholders of the constituent corporation shall, by specific reference to this subsection, require, in addition to approval of the stockholders or members of the surviving entity, the approval of the stockholders of the holding company (or any successor by merger), by the same vote as is required by this chapter and/or by the certificate of incorporation or bylaws of the constituent corporation immediately prior to the effective time of the merger; provided, however, that for purposes of this paragraph (g)(7)(A), any amendment of the organizational documents of a surviving entity that is not a corporation, which amendment would, if adopted by a corporation subject to this chapter, be required to be included in the certificate of incorporation of such corporation, shall, by specific reference to this subsection, require, in addition, the approval of the stockholders of the holding company (or any successor by merger), by the same vote as is required by this chapter and/or by the certificate of incorporation or bylaws of the constituent corporation immediately prior to the effective time of the merger; and **(B)** the business and affairs of a surviving entity that is not a corporation shall be managed by or under the direction of a board of directors, board of managers or other governing body consisting of individuals who are subject to the same fiduciary duties applicable to, and who are liable for breach of such duties to the same extent as, directors of a corporation subject to this chapter; and

(8) The stockholders of the constituent corporation do not recognize gain or loss for United States federal income tax purposes as determined by the board of directors of the constituent corporation. Neither paragraph (g)(7)(A) and (B) of this section nor any provision of a surviving entity's organizational documents required by paragraph (g)(7)(A) and (B) of this section shall be deemed or construed to require

approval of the stockholders of the holding company to elect or remove directors or managers, managing members or other members of the governing body of the surviving entity. ■ The term "organizational documents", as used in paragraph (g)(7) of this section and in the preceding sentence, shall, when used in reference to a corporation, mean the certificate of incorporation of such corporation, and when used in reference to a limited liability company, mean the limited liability company agreement of such limited liability company.

As used in this subsection only, the term "holding company" means a corporation which, from its incorporation until consummation of a merger governed by this subsection, was at all times a direct or indirect wholly-owned subsidiary of the constituent corporation and whose capital stock is issued in such merger. ■ From and after the effective time of a merger adopted by a constituent corporation by action of its board of directors and without any vote of stockholders pursuant to this subsection: **(i)** to the extent the restrictions of § 203 of this title applied to the constituent corporation and its stockholders at the effective time of the merger, such restrictions shall apply to the holding company and its stockholders immediately after the effective time of the merger as though it were the constituent corporation, and all shares of stock of the holding company acquired in the merger shall for purposes of § 203 of this title be deemed to have been acquired at the time that the shares of stock of the constituent corporation converted in the merger were acquired, and provided further that any stockholder who immediately prior to the effective time of the merger was not an interested stockholder within the meaning of § 203 of this title shall not solely by reason of the merger become an interested stockholder of the holding company, **(ii)** if the corporate name of the holding company immediately following the effective time of the merger is the same as the corporate name of the constituent corporation immediately prior to the effective time of the merger, the shares of capital stock of the holding company into which the shares of capital stock of the constituent corporation are converted in the merger shall be represented by the stock certificates that previously represented shares of capital stock of the constituent corporation and **(iii)** to the extent a stockholder of the constituent corporation immediately prior to the merger had standing to institute or maintain derivative litigation on behalf of the constituent corporation, nothing in this section shall be deemed to limit or extinguish such standing. If an agreement of merger is adopted by a constituent corporation by action of its board of directors and without any vote of stockholders pursuant to this subsection, the secretary or assistant secretary of the constituent corporation shall certify on the agreement that the agreement has been adopted pursuant to this subsection and that the conditions specified in the first sentence of this subsection have been satisfied, provided that such certification on the agreement shall not be required if a certificate of merger or consolidation is filed in lieu of filing the agreement. ▪ The agreement so adopted and certified shall then be filed and become effective, in accordance with § 103 of this title. ▪ Such filing shall constitute a representation by the person who executes the agreement that the facts stated in the certificate remain true immediately prior to such filing.

(h) Notwithstanding the requirements of subsection (c) of this section, unless expressly required by its certificate of incorporation, no vote of stockholders of a constituent corporation that has a class or series of stock that is listed on a national securities exchange or held of record by more than 2,000 holders immediately prior to the execution of the agreement of merger by such constituent corporation shall be necessary to authorize a merger if:

(1) The agreement of merger expressly:

a. Permits or requires such merger to be effected under this subsection; and

b. Provides that such merger shall be effected as soon as practicable following the consummation of the offer referred to in paragraph (h)(2) of this section if such merger is effected under this subsection;

(2) A corporation consummates an offer for all of the outstanding stock of such constituent corporation on the terms provided in such agreement of merger that, absent this subsection, would be entitled to vote on the adoption or rejection of the agreement of merger; provided, however, that such offer may be conditioned on the tender of a minimum number or percentage of shares of the stock of such constituent corporation, or of any class or series thereof, and such offer may exclude any excluded stock and provided further that the corporation may consummate separate offers for separate classes or series of the stock of such constituent corporation;

a.–d. [Repealed.]

(3) Immediately following the consummation of the offer referred to in paragraph (h)(2) of this section, the stock irrevocably accepted for purchase or exchange pursuant to such offer and received by the depository prior to expiration of such offer, together with the stock otherwise owned by the consummating corporation or its affiliates and any rollover stock, equals at least such percentage of the shares of stock of such constituent corporation, and of each class or series thereof, that, absent this subsection, would be required to adopt the agreement of merger by this chapter and by the certificate of incorporation of such constituent corporation;

(4) The corporation consummating the offer referred to in paragraph (h)(2) of this section merges with or into such constituent corporation pursuant to such agreement; and

(5) Each outstanding share (other than shares of excluded stock) of each class or series of stock of such constituent corporation that is the subject of and is not irrevocably accepted for purchase or exchange in the offer referred to in paragraph (h)(2) of this section is to be converted in such merger into, or into the right to receive, the same amount and kind of cash, property, rights or securities to be paid for shares of such class or series of stock of such constituent corporation irrevocably accepted for purchase or exchange in such offer. ■

(6) As used in this section only, the term:

a. "Affiliate" means, in respect of the corporation making the offer referred to in paragraph (h)(2) of this section, any person that **(i)** owns, directly or indirectly, all of the outstanding stock of such corporation or **(ii)** is a direct or indirect wholly-owned subsidiary of such corporation or of any person referred to in clause (i) of this definition;

b. "Consummates" (and with correlative meaning, "consummation" and "consummating") means irrevocably accepts for purchase or exchange stock tendered pursuant to an offer;

c. "Depository" means an agent, including a depository, appointed to facilitate consummation of the offer referred to in paragraph (h)(2) of this section;

d. "Excluded stock" means **(i)** stock of such constituent corporation that is owned at the commencement of the offer referred to in paragraph (h)(2) of this section by such constituent corporation, the corporation making the offer referred to in paragraph (h)(2) of this section, any person that owns, directly or indirectly, all of the outstanding stock of the corporation making such offer, or any direct or indirect wholly-owned subsidiary of any of the foregoing and **(ii)** rollover stock;

e. "Person" means any individual, corporation, partnership, limited liability company, unincorporated association or other entity;

f. "Received" (solely for purposes of paragraph (h)(3) of this section) means **(a)** with respect to certificated shares, physical receipt of a stock certificate accompanied by an executed letter of transmittal, **(b)** with respect to uncertificated shares held of record by a clearing corporation as nominee, transfer into the depository's account by means

of an agent's message, and **(c)** with respect to uncertificated shares held of record by a person other than a clearing corporation as nominee, physical receipt of an executed letter of transmittal by the depository; provided, however, that shares shall cease to be "received" **(i)** with respect to certificated shares, if the certificate representing such shares was canceled prior to consummation of the offer referred to in paragraph (h)(2) of this section, or **(ii)** with respect to uncertificated shares, to the extent such uncertificated shares have been reduced or eliminated due to any sale of such shares prior to consummation of the offer referred to in paragraph (h)(2) of this section; and

g. "Rollover stock" means any shares of stock of such constituent corporation that are the subject of a written agreement requiring such shares to be transferred, contributed or delivered to the consummating corporation or any of its affiliates in exchange for stock or other equity interests in such consummating corporation or an affiliate thereof; provided, however, that such shares of stock shall cease to be rollover stock for purposes of paragraph (h)(3) of this section if, immediately prior to the time the merger becomes effective under this chapter, such shares have not been transferred, contributed or delivered to the consummating corporation or any of its affiliates pursuant to such written agreement.

If an agreement of merger is adopted without the vote of stockholders of a corporation pursuant to this subsection, the secretary or assistant secretary of the surviving corporation shall certify on the agreement that the agreement has been adopted pursuant to this subsection and that the conditions specified in this subsection (other than the condition listed in paragraph (h)(4) of this section) have been satisfied; provided that such certification on the agreement shall not be required if a certificate of merger is filed in lieu of filing the agreement. ■ The agreement so adopted and certified shall then be filed and shall become effective, in accordance with § 103 of this title. ▪ Such filing shall constitute a representation by the person who executes the agreement that the facts stated in the certificate remain true immediately prior to such filing.

§ 252. Merger or consolidation of domestic and foreign corporations; service of process upon surviving or resulting corporation.

(a) Any 1 or more corporations of this State may merge or consolidate with 1 or more foreign corporations, unless the laws of the jurisdiction or jurisdictions under which such foreign corporation or corporations are organized prohibit such merger or consolidation. ▪ The constituent corporations may merge into a single surviving corporation, which may be any 1 of the constituent corporations, or they may consolidate into a new resulting corporation formed by the consolidation, which may be a corporation of the jurisdiction of organization of any 1 of the constituent corporations, pursuant to an agreement of merger or consolidation, as the case may be, complying and approved in accordance with this section.

(b) All the constituent corporations shall enter into an agreement of merger or consolidation. ▪ The agreement shall state:

(1) The terms and conditions of the merger or consolidation;

(2) The mode of carrying the same into effect;

(3) In the case of a merger in which the surviving corporation is a corporation of this State, such amendments or changes in the certificate of incorporation of the surviving corporation as are desired to be effected by the merger (which amendments or changes may amend and restate the certificate of incorporation of the surviving corporation in its entirety), or, if no such amendments or changes are desired, a statement that the certificate of incorporation of the surviving corporation shall be its certificate of incorporation;

(4) In the case of a consolidation in which the resulting corporation is a corporation of this State, that the certificate of incorporation of the resulting corporation shall be as is set forth in an attachment to the agreement;

(5) The manner, if any, of converting the shares of each of the constituent corporations into shares or other securities of the corporation surviving or resulting from the merger or consolidation, or of cancelling some or all of such shares, and, if any shares of any of the constituent corporations are not to remain outstanding, to be converted solely into shares or other securities of the surviving or resulting corporation or to be cancelled, the cash, property, rights or securities of any other corporation or entity which the holders of such shares are to receive in exchange for, or upon conversion of, such shares and the surrender of any certificates evidencing them, which cash, property, rights or securities of any other corporation or entity may be in addition to or in lieu of the shares or other securities of the surviving or resulting corporation;

(6) Such other details or provisions as are deemed desirable, including, without limiting the generality of the foregoing, a provision for the payment of cash in lieu of the issuance or recognition of fractional shares, rights or other securities of the surviving or resulting corporation or of any other corporation or entity the shares, rights or other securities of which are to be received in the merger or consolidation, or for some other arrangement with respect thereto, consistent with § 155 of this title; and

(7) Such other provisions or facts as shall be required to be set forth in an agreement of merger or consolidation (including any provision for amendment of the certificate of incorporation (or equivalent document) of a surviving or resulting foreign corporation) by the laws of each jurisdiction under which any of the foreign corporations are organized.

Any of the terms of the agreement of merger or consolidation may be made dependent upon facts ascertainable outside of such agreement, provided that the manner in which such facts shall operate upon the terms of the agreement is clearly and expressly set forth in the agreement of merger or consolidation. ▪ The term "facts," as used in the preceding sentence, includes, but is not limited to, the occurrence of any event, including a determination or action by any person or body, including the corporation.

(c) The agreement shall be adopted, approved, certified, executed and acknowledged by each of the constituent corporations in accordance with the laws under which it is organized, and, in the case of a corporation of this State, in the same manner as is provided in § 251 of this title. ▪ The agreement shall be filed and shall become effective for all purposes of the laws of this State when and as provided in § 251 of this title with respect to the merger or consolidation of corporations of this State. ▪ In lieu of filing the agreement of merger or consolidation, the surviving or resulting corporation may file a certificate of merger or consolidation, executed in accordance with § 103 of this title, which states:

    (1) The name and jurisdiction of organization of each of the constituent corporations;

    (2) That an agreement of merger or consolidation has been approved, adopted, certified, executed and acknowledged by each of the constituent corporations in accordance with this subsection;

    (3) The name of the surviving or resulting corporation;

    (4) In the case of a merger in which the surviving corporation is a corporation of this State such amendments or changes in the certificate of incorporation of the surviving corporation as are desired to be effected by the merger (which amendments or changes may amend and restate the certificate of incorporation of the surviving corporation in its entirety), or, if no such amendments or changes are desired, a statement that the certificate of incorporation of the surviving corporation shall be its certificate of incorporation;

    (5) In the case of a consolidation in which the resulting corporation is a corporation of this State, that the certificate of incorporation of the resulting corporation shall be as is set forth in an attachment to the certificate;

    (6) That the executed agreement of consolidation or merger is on file at an office of the surviving or resulting corporation and the address thereof;

    (7) That a copy of the agreement of consolidation or merger will be furnished by the surviving or resulting corporation, on request and without cost, to any stockholder of any constituent corporation;

    (8) If the corporation surviving or resulting from the merger or consolidation is a corporation of this State, the authorized capital stock of each constituent corporation which is not a corporation of this State; and

    (9) The agreement, if any, required by subsection (d) of this section.

(d) If the corporation surviving or resulting from the merger or consolidation is a foreign corporation, it shall agree that it may be served with process in this State in any proceeding for enforcement of any obligation of any constituent corporation of this State, as well as for enforcement of any obligation of the surviving or resulting corporation arising from the merger or consolidation, including any suit or other proceeding to enforce the right of any stockholders as determined in appraisal proceedings pursuant to § 262 of this title, and shall irrevocably appoint the Secretary of State as its agent to accept service of process in any such suit or other proceedings and shall specify the address to which a copy of such process shall be mailed by the Secretary of State. ▪ Process may be served upon the Secretary of State under this subsection by means of electronic transmission but only as prescribed by the Secretary of State. ▪ The Secretary of State is authorized to issue such rules and regulations with respect to such service as the Secretary of State deems necessary or appropriate. ▪ In the event of such service upon the Secretary of State in accordance with this subsection, the Secretary of State shall forthwith notify such surviving or resulting corporation thereof by letter, directed to such surviving or resulting corporation at its address so specified, unless such surviving or resulting corporation shall have designated in writing to the Secretary of State a different address for such purpose, in which case it shall be mailed to the last address so designated. ▪ Such letter shall be sent by a mail or courier service that includes a record of mailing or deposit with the courier and a record of delivery evidenced by the signature of the recipient. ▪ Such letter shall enclose a copy of the process and any other papers served on the Secretary of State pursuant to this subsection. ▪ It shall be the duty of the plaintiff in the event of such service to serve process and any other papers in duplicate, to notify the Secretary of State that service is being effected pursuant to this subsection and to pay the Secretary of State the sum of $50 for the use of the State, which sum shall be taxed as part of the costs in the proceeding, if the plaintiff shall prevail therein. ▪ The Secretary of State shall maintain an alphabetical record of any such service setting forth the name of the plaintiff and the defendant, the title, docket number and nature of the proceeding in which process has been served, the fact that service has been effected pursuant to this subsection, the return date thereof, and the day and hour service was made. ▪ The Secretary of State shall not be required to retain such information longer than 5 years from receipt of the service of process.

(e) Section 251(d) of this title shall apply to any merger or consolidation under this section; § 251(e) of this title shall apply to a merger under this section in which the surviving corporation is a corporation of this State; and § 251(f) and (h) of this title shall apply to any merger under this section.

§ 253. Merger of parent corporation and subsidiary corporation or corporations.

(a) In any case in which: **(1)** at least 90% of the outstanding shares of each class of the stock of a corporation or corporations (other than a corporation which has in its certificate of incorporation the provision required by § 251(g)(7)(A) and (B) of this title), of which class there are outstanding shares that, absent this subsection, would be entitled to vote on such merger, is owned by a corporation of this State or a foreign corporation, and **(2)** 1 or more of such corporations is a corporation of this State, unless the laws of the jurisdiction or jurisdictions under which the foreign corporation or corporations are organized prohibit such merger, the parent corporation may either merge the subsidiary corporation or corporations into itself and assume all of its or their obligations, or merge itself, or itself and 1 or more of such other subsidiary corporations, into 1 of the subsidiary corporations by executing, acknowledging and filing, in accordance with § 103 of this title, a certificate of such ownership and merger setting forth a copy of the resolution of its board of directors to so merge and the date of the adoption; provided, however, that in case the parent corporation shall not own all the outstanding stock of all the subsidiary corporations, parties to a merger as aforesaid, the resolution of the board of directors of the parent corporation shall state the terms and conditions of the merger, including the securities, cash, property, or rights to be issued, paid, delivered or granted by the surviving corporation upon surrender of each share of the subsidiary corporation or corporations not owned by the parent corporation, or the cancellation of some or all of such shares. ▪ Any of the terms of the resolution of the board of directors to so merge may be made dependent upon facts ascertainable outside of such resolution, provided that the manner in which such facts shall operate upon the terms of the resolution is clearly and expressly set forth in the resolution. ▪ The term "facts," as used in the preceding sentence, includes, but is not limited to, the occurrence of any event, including a determination or action by any person or body, including the corporation. ▪ If the parent corporation be not the surviving corporation, the resolution shall include provision for the pro rata issuance of stock of the surviving corporation to the holders of the stock of the parent corporation on surrender of any certificates therefor, and the certificate of ownership and merger shall state that the proposed merger has been approved by a majority of the outstanding stock of the parent corporation entitled to vote thereon at a meeting duly called and held after 20 days' notice of the purpose of the meeting given to each such stockholder at the stockholder's address as it appears on the records of the corporation if the parent corporation is a corporation of this State or state that the proposed merger has been adopted, approved, certified, executed and acknowledged by the parent corporation in accordance with the laws under which it is organized if the parent corporation is a foreign corporation. ▪ If the surviving corporation is a foreign corporation:

(1) Section 252(d) of this title or § 258(c) of this title, as applicable, shall also apply to a merger under this section; and

(2) The terms and conditions of the merger shall obligate the surviving corporation to provide the agreement, and take the actions, required by § 252(d) of this title or § 258(c) of this title, as applicable.

(b) If the surviving corporation is a Delaware corporation, it may change its corporate name by the inclusion of a provision to that effect in the resolution of merger adopted by the directors of the parent corporation and set forth in the certificate of ownership and merger, and upon the effective date of the merger, the name of the corporation shall be so changed.

(c) Section § 251(d) of this title shall apply to a merger under this section, and § 251(e) of this title shall apply to a merger under this section in which the surviving corporation is the subsidiary corporation and is a corporation of this State. ▪ References to "agreement of merger" in § 251(d) and (e) of this title shall mean for purposes of this subsection the resolution of merger adopted by the board of directors of the parent corporation. ▪ Any merger which effects any changes other than those authorized by this section or made applicable by this subsection shall be accomplished under § 251, § 252, § 257, or § 258 of this title. ▪ Section 262 of this title shall not apply to any merger effected under this section, except as provided in subsection (d) of this section.

(d) In the event all of the stock of a subsidiary Delaware corporation party to a merger effected under this section is not owned by the parent corporation immediately prior to the merger, the stockholders of the subsidiary Delaware corporation party to the merger shall have appraisal rights as set forth in § 262 of this title.

(e) This section shall apply to nonstock corporations if the parent corporation is such a corporation and is the surviving corporation of the merger; provided, however, that references to the directors of the parent corporation shall be deemed to be references to members of the governing body of the parent corporation, and references to the board of directors of the parent corporation shall be deemed to be references to the governing body of the parent corporation.

(f) Nothing in this section shall be deemed to authorize the merger of a corporation with a charitable nonstock corporation, if the charitable status of such charitable nonstock corporation would thereby be lost or impaired.

§ 254. Merger or consolidation of domestic corporations and joint-stock or other associations.

(a) The term "joint-stock association" as used in this section, includes any association of the kind commonly known as a joint-stock association or joint-stock company and any unincorporated association, trust or enterprise having members or having outstanding shares of stock or other evidences of financial or beneficial interest therein, whether formed or organized by agreement or under statutory authority or otherwise and whether formed or organized under the laws of this State or any other jurisdiction, but does not include a corporation, partnership or limited liability company. ▪ The term "stockholder" as used in this section, includes every member of such joint-stock association or holder of a share of stock or other evidence of financial or beneficial interest therein.

(b) Any 1 or more corporations of this State may merge or consolidate with 1 or more joint-stock associations, unless the laws of the jurisdiction or jurisdictions under which such joint-stock association or associations are formed or organized prohibit such merger or consolidation. ▪ Such corporation or corporations and such 1 or more joint-stock associations may merge into a single surviving corporation or joint-stock association, which may be any 1 of such corporations or joint-stock associations, or they may consolidate into a new resulting corporation of this State or a joint-stock association, pursuant to an agreement of merger or consolidation, as the case may be, complying and approved in accordance with this section. ▪ The surviving or resulting entity may be organized for profit or not organized for profit, and if the surviving or resulting entity is a corporation, it may be a stock corporation of this State or a nonstock corporation of this State.

(c) Each such corporation and joint-stock association shall enter into a written agreement of merger or consolidation. ▪ The agreement shall state:

(1) The terms and conditions of the merger or consolidation;

(2) The mode of carrying the same into effect;

(3) In the case of a merger in which the surviving entity is a corporation of this State, such amendments or changes in the certificate of incorporation of the surviving corporation as are desired to be effected by the merger (which amendments or changes may amend and restate the certificate of incorporation of the surviving corporation in its entirety), or, if no such amendments or changes are desired, a statement that the certificate of incorporation of the surviving corporation shall be its certificate of incorporation;

(4) In the case of a consolidation in which the resulting entity is a corporation of this State, that the certificate of incorporation of the resulting corporation shall be as is set forth in an attachment to the agreement;

(5) The manner, if any, of converting the shares of stock of each stock corporation, the interest of members of each nonstock corporation, and the shares, membership or financial or benefi-

cial interests in each of the joint-stock associations into shares or other securities of a stock corporation or membership interests of a nonstock corporation or into shares, memberships or financial or beneficial interests of the joint-stock association surviving or resulting from such merger or consolidation, or of cancelling some or all of such shares, memberships or financial or beneficial interests, and, if any shares of any such stock corporation, any membership interests of any such nonstock corporation or any shares, memberships or financial or beneficial interests in any such joint-stock association are not to remain outstanding, to be converted solely into shares or other securities of the stock corporation or membership interests of the nonstock corporation or into shares, memberships or financial or beneficial interests of the joint-stock association surviving or resulting from such merger or consolidation or to be cancelled, the cash, property, rights or securities of any other corporation or entity which the holders of shares of any such stock corporation, membership interests of any such nonstock corporation, or shares, memberships or financial or beneficial interests of any such joint-stock association are to receive in exchange for, or upon conversion of such shares, membership interests or shares, memberships or financial or beneficial interests, and the surrender of any certificates evidencing them, which cash, property, rights or securities of any other corporation or entity may be in addition to or in lieu of shares or other securities of the stock corporation or membership interests of the nonstock corporation or shares, memberships or financial or beneficial interests of the joint-stock association surviving or resulting from such merger or consolidation;

(6) Such other details or provisions as are deemed desirable, including, without limiting the generality of the foregoing, a provision for the payment of cash in lieu of the issuance or recognition of fractional shares, rights, other securities or interests of the surviving or resulting entity or of fractional shares, rights, other securities or interests of any other corporation or entity the securities of which are to be received in the merger or consolidation, or for some other arrangement with respect thereto, consistent with § 155 of this title; and

(7) Such other provisions or facts as shall be required to be set forth in an agreement of merger or consolidation (including any provision for amendment of the governing documents of a surviving joint-stock association) or required to establish and maintain a joint-stock association by the laws under which the joint-stock association is formed or organized.

Any of the terms of the agreement of merger or consolidation may be made dependent upon facts ascertainable outside of such agreement, provided that the manner in which such facts shall operate upon the terms of the agreement is clearly and expressly set forth in the agreement of merger or consolidation. ▪ The term "facts," as used in the preceding sentence, includes, but is not limited to, the occurrence of any event, including a determination or action by any person or body, including the corporation.

(d) The agreement required by subsection (c) of this section shall be adopted, approved, certified, executed and acknowledged by each of the stock or nonstock corporations in the same manner as is provided in § 251 or § 255 of this title, respectively, and in the case of the joint-stock associations in accordance with the laws of the jurisdiction under which they are formed or organized. ▪ The agreement shall be filed and shall become effective for all purposes of the laws of this State when and as provided in § 251 of this title with respect to the merger or consolidation of corporations of this State. ▪ In lieu of filing the agreement of merger or consolidation, the surviving or resulting entity may file a certificate of merger or consolidation, executed in accordance with § 103 of this title, which states:

(1) The name, jurisdiction of formation or organization and type of entity of each of the constituent entities;

(2) That an agreement of merger or consolidation has been approved, adopted, certified, executed and acknowledged by each of the constituent entities in accordance with this subsection;

(3) The name of the surviving or resulting corporation or joint-stock association;

(4) In the case of a merger in which the surviving entity is a corporation of this State, such amendments or changes in the certificate of incorporation of the surviving corporation as are desired to be effected by the merger (which amendments or changes may amend and restate the certificate of incorporation of the surviving corporation in its entirety), or, if no such amendments or changes are desired, a statement that the certificate of incorporation of the surviving corporation shall be its certificate of incorporation;

(5) In the case of a consolidation in which the resulting entity is a corporation of this State, that the certificate of incorporation of the resulting corporation shall be as is set forth in an attachment to the certificate;

(6) That the executed agreement of consolidation or merger is on file at an office of the surviving or resulting corporation or joint-stock association and the address thereof;

(7) That a copy of the agreement of consolidation or merger will be furnished by the surviving or resulting corporation or joint-stock association, on request and without cost, to any stockholder or member of any constituent entity; and

(8) The agreement, if any, required by § 252(d) of this title.

(e) Sections 251(d), 251(e) to the extent the surviving entity is a corporation of this State, §§ 251(f), 252(d), 259 through 262 and 328 of this title shall, insofar as they are applicable, apply to mergers or consolidations between corporations and joint-stock associations; the word "corporation" where applicable, as used in those sections, being deemed to include joint-stock associations as defined herein. ▪ Where the surviving or resulting entity is a corporation, for purposes of the laws of this State, the personal liability, if any, of any stockholder of a joint-stock association existing at the time of such merger or consolidation shall not thereby be extinguished, shall remain personal to such stockholder and shall not become the liability of any subsequent transferee of any share of stock in such surviving or resulting corporation or of any other stockholder of such surviving or resulting corporation.

(f) Nothing in this section shall be deemed to authorize the merger of a charitable nonstock corporation or charitable joint-stock association into a stock corporation or joint-stock association if the charitable status of such nonstock corporation or joint-stock association would be thereby lost or impaired, but a stock corporation or a joint-stock association may be merged into a charitable nonstock corporation or charitable joint-stock association which shall continue as the surviving corporation or joint-stock association.

§ 255. Merger or consolidation of domestic nonstock corporations.

(a) Any 2 or more nonstock corporations of this State, whether or not organized for profit, may merge into a single surviving corporation, which may be any 1 of the constituent corporations, or they may consolidate into a new resulting nonstock corporation, whether or not organized for profit, formed by the consolidation, pursuant to an agreement of merger or consolidation, as the case may be, complying and approved in accordance with this section.

(b) Subject to subsection (d) of this section, the governing body of each corporation which desires to merge or consolidate shall adopt a resolution approving an agreement of merger or consolidation. ▪ The agreement shall state:

(1) The terms and conditions of the merger or consolidation;

(2) The mode of carrying the same into effect;

(3) In the case of a merger, such amendments or changes in the certificate of incorporation of the surviving corporation as are desired to be effected by the merger (which amendments or changes may amend and restate the certificate of incorporation of the surviving corporation in its entirety), or, if no such amendments or changes are desired, a statement that the certificate of incorporation of the surviving corporation shall be its certificate of incorporation;

(4) In the case of a consolidation, that the certificate of incorporation of the resulting corporation shall be as is set forth in an attachment to the agreement;

(5) The manner, if any, of converting the memberships or membership interests of each of the constituent corporations into memberships or membership interests of the corporation surviving or resulting from the merger or consolidation, or of cancelling some or all of such memberships or membership interests, and, if any memberships or membership interests of any of the constituent corporations are not to remain outstanding, to be converted solely into memberships or membership interests of the surviving or resulting corporation or to be cancelled, the cash, property, rights or securities of any other corporation or entity which the holders of such memberships or membership interests are to receive in exchange for, or upon conversion of, such memberships or membership interests, which cash, property, rights or securities of any other corporation or entity may be in addition to or in lieu of memberships or membership interests of the surviving or resulting corporation; and

(6) Such other details or provisions as are deemed desirable, including, without limiting the generality of the foregoing, a provision for the payment of cash in lieu of the issuance or recognition of fractional shares, rights or other securities of any other corporation or entity the shares, rights or other securities of which are to be received in the merger or consolidation, or for some other arrangement with respect thereto, consistent with § 155 of this title.

The agreement so adopted shall be executed by an authorized person, provided that if the agreement is filed, it shall be executed and acknowledged in accordance with § 103 of this title. ▪ Any of the terms of the agreement of merger or consolidation may be made dependent upon facts ascertainable outside of such agreement, provided that the manner in which such facts shall operate upon the terms of the agreement is clearly and expressly set forth in the agreement of merger or consolidation. ▪ The term "facts," as used in the preceding sentence, includes, but is not limited to, the occurrence of any event, including a determination or action by any person or body, including the corporation.

(c) Subject to subsection (d) of this section, the agreement shall be submitted to the members of each constituent corporation, at an annual or special meeting thereof for the purpose of acting on the agreement. ▪ Due notice of the time, place and purpose of the meeting shall be given to each member of each such corporation who has the right to vote for the election of the members of the governing body of the corporation and to each other member who is entitled to vote on the merger under the certificate of incorporation or the bylaws of such corporation, at the member's address as it appears on the records of the corporation, at least 20 days prior to the date of the meeting. ▪ The notice shall contain a copy of the agreement or a brief summary thereof. ▪ At the meeting the agreement shall be considered and a vote, in person or by proxy, taken for the adoption or rejection of the agreement. ▪ If the agreement is adopted by a majority of the members of each such corporation entitled to vote for the election of the members of the governing body of the corporation and any other members entitled to vote on the merger under the certificate of incorporation or the bylaws of such corporation, then that fact shall be certified on the agreement by the officer of each such corporation performing the duties ordinarily performed by the secretary or assistant secretary of a corporation, provided that such certification on the agreement shall not be required if a certificate of merger or consolidation is filed in lieu of filing the agreement. ▪ If the agreement shall be adopted and certified by each constituent corporation in accordance with this section, it shall be filed and shall become effective in accordance with § 103 of this title. ▪ The provisions set forth in the last sentence of § 251(c) of this title shall apply to a merger under this section, and the reference therein to "stockholder" shall be deemed to include "member" hereunder.

(d) Notwithstanding subsection (b) or (c) of this section, if, under the certificate of incorporation or the bylaws of any 1 or more of the constituent corporations, there shall be no members who have the right to vote for the election of the members of the governing body of the corporation, or for the merger, other than the members of the governing body themselves, no further action by the governing body or the members of such corporation shall be necessary if the resolution approving an agreement of merger or consolidation has been adopted by a majority of all the members of the governing body thereof, and that fact shall be certified on the agreement in the same manner as is provided in the case of the adoption of the agreement by the vote of the members of a corporation, provided that such certification on the agreement shall not be required if a certificate of merger or consolidation is filed in lieu of filing the agreement, and thereafter the same procedure shall be followed to consummate the merger or consolidation.

(e) Section 251(d) of this title shall apply to a merger under this section; provided, however, that references to the board of directors, to stockholders, and to shares of a constituent corporation shall be deemed to be references to the governing body of the corporation, to members of the corporation, and to memberships or membership interests, as applicable, respectively.

(f) Section 251(e) of this title shall apply to a merger under this section.

(g) Nothing in this section shall be deemed to authorize the merger of a charitable nonstock corporation into a nonstock corporation if such charitable nonstock corporation would thereby have its charitable status lost or impaired; but a nonstock corporation may be merged into a charitable nonstock corporation which shall continue as the surviving corporation.

§ 256. Merger or consolidation of domestic and foreign nonstock corporations; service of process upon surviving or resulting corporation.

(a) Any 1 or more nonstock corporations of this State may merge or consolidate with 1 or more foreign nonstock corporations, unless the laws of the jurisdiction or jurisdictions under which such foreign nonstock corporation or corporations are organized prohibit such merger or consolidation.■ The constituent corporations may merge into a single surviving corporation, which may be any 1 of the constituent corporations, or they may consolidate into a new resulting nonstock corporation formed by the consolidation, which may be a corporation of the jurisdiction of organization of any 1 of the constituent corporations, pursuant to an agreement of merger or consolidation, as the case may be, complying and approved in accordance with this section. ■ The term "foreign nonstock corporation" means a nonstock corporation organized under the laws of any jurisdiction other than this State.

(b) All the constituent corporations shall enter into an agreement of merger or consolidation. ■ The agreement shall state:

> **(1)** The terms and conditions of the merger or consolidation;

> **(2)** The mode of carrying the same into effect;

> **(3)** In the case of a merger in which the surviving corporation is a corporation of this State, such amendments or changes in the certificate of incorporation of the surviving corporation as are desired to be effected by the merger (which amendments or changes may amend and restate the certificate of incorporation of the surviving corporation in its entirety), or, if no such amendments or changes are desired, a statement that the certificate of incorporation of the surviving corporation shall be its certificate of incorporation;

> **(4)** In the case of a consolidation in which the resulting corporation is a corporation of this State, that the certificate of incorporation of the resulting corporation shall be as is set forth in an attachment to the agreement;

> **(5)** The manner, if any, of converting the memberships or membership interests of each of the constituent corporations into memberships or membership interests of the corporation surviving or resulting from the merger or consolidation, or of cancelling some or all of such memberships or membership interests, and, if any memberships or membership interests of any of the constituent corporations are not to remain outstanding, to be converted solely into memberships or membership interests of the surviving or resulting corporation or to be cancelled, the cash, property, rights or securities of any other corporation or entity which the holders of such memberships or membership interests are to receive in exchange for, or upon conversion of, such memberships or membership interests, which cash, property, rights or securities of any other corporation or entity may be in addition to or in lieu of memberships or membership interests of the surviving or resulting corporation;

> **(6)** Such other details or provisions as are deemed desirable, including, without limiting the generality of the foregoing, a provision for the payment of cash in lieu of the issuance or recognition of fractional shares, rights or other securities of any other corporation or entity the shares, rights or other securities of which are to be received in the merger or consolidation, or for some other arrangement with respect thereto, consistent with § 155 of this title; and

> **(7)** Such other provisions or facts as shall be required to be set forth in an agreement of merger or consolidation (including any provision for amendment of the certificate of incorporation (or equivalent document) of a surviving foreign nonstock corporation) by the laws of each jurisdiction under which any of the foreign nonstock corporations are organized.

Any of the terms of the agreement of merger or consolidation may be made dependent upon facts ascertainable outside of such agreement, provided that the manner in which such facts shall operate upon the terms of the agreement is clearly and expressly set forth in the agreement of merger or consolidation. ▪ The term "facts," as used in the preceding sentence, includes, but is not limited to, the occurrence of any event, including a determination or action by any person or body, including the corporation.

(c) The agreement shall be adopted, approved, certified, executed and acknowledged by each of the constituent corporations in accordance with the laws under which it is organized and, in the case of a Delaware corporation, in the same manner as is provided in § 255 of this title. ▪ The agreement shall be filed and shall become effective for all purposes of the laws of this State when and as provided in § 255 of this title with respect to the merger of nonstock corporations of this State. ▪ Insofar as they may be applicable, the provisions set forth in the last sentence of § 252(c) of this title shall apply to a merger under this section, and the reference therein to "stockholder" shall be deemed to include "member" hereunder.

(d) If the corporation surviving or resulting from the merger or consolidation is a foreign nonstock corporation, it shall agree that it may be served with process in this State in any proceeding for enforcement of any obligation of any constituent corporation of this State, as well as for enforcement of any obligation of the surviving or resulting corporation arising from the merger or consolidation and shall irrevocably appoint the Secretary of State as its agent to accept service of process in any suit or other proceedings and shall specify the address to which a copy of such process shall be mailed by the Secretary of State. ▪ Process may be served upon the Secretary of State under this subsection by means of electronic transmission but only as prescribed by the Secretary of State. ▪ The Secretary of State is authorized to issue such rules and regulations with respect to such service as the Secretary of State deems necessary or appropriate. ▪ In the event of such service upon the Secretary

of State in accordance with this subsection, the Secretary of State shall forthwith notify such surviving or resulting corporation thereof by letter, directed to such corporation at its address so specified, unless such surviving or resulting corporation shall have designated in writing to the Secretary of State a different address for such purpose, in which case it shall be mailed to the last address so designated. ▪ Such letter shall be sent by a mail or courier service that includes a record of mailing or deposit with the courier and a record of delivery evidenced by the signature of the recipient. ▪ Such letter shall enclose a copy of the process and any other papers served upon the Secretary of State. ▪ It shall be the duty of the plaintiff in the event of such service to serve process and any other papers in duplicate, to notify the Secretary of State that service is being made pursuant to this subsection, and to pay the Secretary of State the sum of $50 for the use of the State, which sum shall be taxed as a part of the costs in the proceeding if the plaintiff shall prevail therein. ▪ The Secretary of State shall maintain an alphabetical record of any such service setting forth the name of the plaintiff and defendant, the title, docket number and nature of the proceeding in which process has been served upon the Secretary of State, the fact that service has been effected pursuant to this subsection, the return date thereof, and the day and hour when the service was made. ▪ The Secretary of State shall not be required to retain such information for a period longer than 5 years from receipt of the service of process.

(e) Section § 251(e) of this title shall apply to a merger under this section if the corporation surviving the merger is a corporation of this State.

(f) Section 251(d) of this title shall apply to a merger under this section; provided, however, that references to the board of directors, to stockholders, and to shares of a constituent corporation shall be deemed to be references to the governing body of the corporation, to members of the corporation, and to memberships or membership interests, as applicable, respectively.

(g) Nothing in this section shall be deemed to authorize the merger of a charitable nonstock corporation into a nonstock corporation, if the charitable status of such charitable nonstock corporation would thereby be lost or impaired; but a nonstock corporation may be merged into a charitable nonstock corporation which shall continue as the surviving corporation.

§ 257. Merger or consolidation of domestic stock and nonstock corporations.

(a) Any 1 or more nonstock corporations of this State, whether or not organized for profit, may merge or consolidate with 1 or more stock corporations of this State, whether or not organized for profit. ∎ The constituent corporations may merge into a single surviving corporation, which may be any 1 of the constituent corporations, or they may consolidate into a new resulting corporation formed by the consolidation, pursuant to an agreement of merger or consolidation, as the case may be, complying and approved in accordance with this section. ∎ The surviving constituent corporation or the resulting corporation may be organized for profit or not organized for profit and may be a stock corporation or a nonstock corporation.

(b) The board of directors of each stock corporation which desires to merge or consolidate and the governing body of each nonstock corporation which desires to merge or consolidate shall adopt a resolution approving an agreement of merger or consolidation. ∎ The agreement shall state:

(1) The terms and conditions of the merger or consolidation;

(2) The mode of carrying the same into effect;

(3) In the case of a merger, such amendments or changes in the certificate of incorporation of the surviving corporation as are desired to be effected by the merger (which amendments or changes may amend and restate the certificate of incorporation of the surviving corporation in its entirety), or, if no such amendments or changes are desired, a statement that the certificate of incorporation of the surviving corporation shall be its certificate of incorporation;

(4) In the case of a consolidation, that the certificate of incorporation of the resulting corporation shall be as is set forth in an attachment to the agreement;

(5) The manner, if any, of converting the shares of stock of a stock corporation and the memberships or membership interests of a nonstock corporation into shares or other securities of a stock corporation or memberships or membership interests of a nonstock corporation surviving or resulting from such merger or consolidation or of cancelling some or all of such shares or memberships or membership interests, and, if any shares of any such stock corporation or memberships or membership interests of any such nonstock corporation are not to remain outstanding, to be converted solely into shares or other securities of the stock corporation or memberships or membership interests of the nonstock corporation surviving or resulting from such merger or consolidation or to be cancelled, the cash, property, rights or securities of any other corporation or entity which the holders of shares of any such stock corporation or memberships or membership interests of any such nonstock corporation are to receive in exchange for, or upon conversion of such shares or memberships or membership interests, and the surrender of any certificates evidencing them, which cash, property, rights or securities of any other corporation or entity may be in addition to or in lieu of shares or other securities of any stock corporation or memberships or membership interests of any nonstock corporation surviving or resulting from such merger or consolidation; and

(6) Such other details or provisions as are deemed desirable, including, without limiting the generality of the foregoing, a provision for the payment of cash in lieu of the issuance or recognition of fractional shares, rights or other securities of the surviving or resulting corporation or of any other corporation or entity the shares, rights or other securities of which are to be received in the merger or consolidation, or for some other arrangement with respect thereto, consistent with § 155 of this title.

Any of the terms of the agreement of merger or consolidation may be made dependent upon facts ascertainable outside of such agreement, provided that the manner in which such facts shall operate upon the terms of the agreement is clearly and expressly set forth in the agreement of merger or consolidation. ▪ The term "facts," as used in the preceding sentence, includes, but is not limited to, the occurrence of any event, including a determination or action by any person or body, including the corporation.

(c) The agreement required by subsection (b) of this section, in the case of each constituent stock corporation, shall be adopted, approved, certified, executed and acknowledged by each constituent corporation in the same manner as is provided in § 251 of this title and, in the case of each constituent nonstock corporation, shall be adopted, approved, certified, executed and acknowledged by each of said constituent corporations in the same manner as is provided in § 255 of this title. ▪ The agreement shall be filed and shall become effective for all purposes of the laws of this State when and as provided in § 251 of this title with respect to the merger of stock corporations of this State. ▪ Insofar as they may be applicable, the provisions set forth in the last sentence of § 251(c) of this title shall apply to a merger under this section, and the reference therein to "stockholder" shall be deemed to include "member" hereunder.

(d) Section 251(e) of this title shall apply to a merger under this section; § 251(d) of this title shall apply to any constituent stock corporation participating in a merger or consolidation under this section; and § 251(f) of this title shall apply to any constituent stock corporation participating in a merger under this section.

(e) Section 251(d) of this title shall apply to a merger under this section; provided, however, that, for purposes of a constituent nonstock corporation, references to the board of directors, to stockholders, and to shares of a constituent corporation shall be deemed to be references to the governing body of the corporation, to members of the corporation, and to memberships or membership interests, as applicable, respectively.

(f) Nothing in this section shall be deemed to authorize the merger of a charitable nonstock corporation into a stock corporation, if the charitable status of such nonstock corporation would thereby be lost or impaired; but a stock corporation may be merged into a charitable nonstock corporation which shall continue as the surviving corporation.

§ 258. Merger or consolidation of domestic and foreign stock and nonstock corporations.

(a) Any 1 or more corporations of this State, whether stock or nonstock corporations and whether or not organized for profit, may merge or consolidate with 1 or more foreign corporations, unless the laws of the jurisdiction or jurisdictions under which such foreign corporation or corporations are organized prohibit such merger or consolidation. ▪ The constituent corporations may merge into a single surviving corporation, which may be any 1 of the constituent corporations, or they may consolidate into a new resulting corporation formed by the consolidation, which may be a corporation of the jurisdiction of organization of any 1 of the constituent corporations, pursuant to an agreement of merger or consolidation, as the case may be, complying and approved in accordance with this section. ▪ The surviving or resulting corporation may be either a domestic or foreign stock corporation or a domestic or foreign nonstock corporation, as shall be specified in the agreement of merger or consolidation required by subsection (b) of this section. ▪ For purposes of this section, the term "foreign corporation" includes a nonstock corporation organized under the laws of any jurisdiction other than this State.

(b) The method and procedure to be followed by the constituent corporations so merging or consolidating shall be as prescribed in § 257 of this title in the case of Delaware corporations. ▪ The agreement of merger or consolidation shall be as provided in § 257 of this title and also set forth such other provisions or facts as shall be required to be set forth in an agreement of merger or consolidation (including any provision for amendment of the certificate of incorporation (or equivalent document) of a surviving foreign corporation) by the laws of the jurisdiction or jurisdictions which are stated in the agreement to be the laws under which the foreign corporation or corporations are organized. ▪ The agreement, in the case of foreign corporations, shall be adopted, approved, certified, executed and acknowledged in accordance with the laws under which each is organized.

(c) The requirements of § 252(d) of this title as to the appointment of the Secretary of State to receive process and the manner of serving the same in the event the surviving or resulting corporation is a foreign corporation shall also apply to mergers or consolidations effected under this section and such appointment, if any, shall be included in the certificate of merger or consolidation, if any, filed pursuant to subsection (b) of this section. ▪ Section 251(e) of this title shall apply to mergers effected under this section if the surviving corporation is a corporation of this State; § 251(d) of this title shall apply to any constituent corporation participating in a merger or consolidation under this section (provided, however, that for purposes of a constituent nonstock corporation, references to the board of directors, to stockholders, and to shares shall be deemed to be references to the governing body of the corporation, to members of the corporation, and to memberships or membership interests of the corporation, as applicable, respectively); and § 251(f) of this title shall apply to any constituent stock corporation of this State participating in a merger under this section.

(d) Nothing in this section shall be deemed to authorize the merger of a charitable nonstock corporation into a stock corporation, if the charitable status of such nonstock corporation would thereby be lost or impaired; but a stock corporation may be merged into a charitable nonstock corporation which shall continue as the surviving corporation.

§ 259. Status, rights, liabilities, of constituent and surviving or resulting corporations following merger or consolidation.

(a) When any merger or consolidation shall have become effective under this chapter, for all purposes of the laws of this State the separate existence of all the constituent corporations, or of all such constituent corporations except the one into which the other or others of such constituent corporations have been merged, as the case may be, shall cease and the constituent corporations shall become a new corporation, or be merged into 1 of such corporations, as the case may be, possessing all the rights, privileges, powers and franchises as well of a public as of a private nature, and being subject to all the restrictions, disabilities and duties of each of such corporations so merged or consolidated; and all and singular, the rights, privileges, powers and franchises of each of said corporations, and all property, real, personal and mixed, and all debts due to any of said constituent corporations on whatever account, as well for stock subscriptions as all other things in action or belonging to each of such corporations shall be vested in the corporation surviving or resulting from such merger or consolidation; and all property, rights, privileges, powers and franchises, and all and every other interest shall be thereafter as effectually the property of the surviving or resulting corporation as they were of the several and respective constituent corporations, and the title to any real estate vested by deed or otherwise, under the laws of this State, in any of such constituent corporations, shall not revert or be in any way impaired by reason of this chapter; but all rights of creditors and all liens upon any property of any of said constituent corporations shall be preserved unimpaired, and all debts, liabilities and duties of the respective constituent corporations shall thenceforth attach to said surviving or resulting corporation, and may be enforced against it to the same extent as if said debts, liabilities and duties had been incurred or contracted by it.

(b) In the case of a merger of banks or trust companies, without any order or action on the part of any court or otherwise, all appointments, designations, and nominations, and all other rights and interests as trustee, executor, administrator, registrar of stocks and bonds, guardian of estates, assignee, receiver, trustee of estates of persons mentally ill and in every other fiduciary capacity, shall be automatically vested in the corporation resulting from or surviving such merger; provided, however, that any party in interest shall have the right to apply to an appropriate court or tribunal for a determination as to whether the surviving corporation shall continue to serve in the same fiduciary capacity as the merged corporation, or whether a new and different fiduciary should be appointed.

§ 260. Powers of corporation surviving or resulting from merger or consolidation; issuance of stock, bonds or other indebtedness.

When 2 or more corporations are merged or consolidated, the corporation surviving or resulting from the merger may issue bonds or other obligations, negotiable or otherwise, and with or without coupons or interest certificates thereto attached, to an amount sufficient with its capital stock to provide for all the payments it will be required to make, or obligations it will be required to assume, in order to effect the merger or consolidation. ▪ For the purpose of securing the payment of any such bonds and obligations, it shall be lawful for the surviving or resulting corporation to mortgage its corporate franchise, rights, privileges and property, real, personal or mixed. ▪ The surviving or resulting corporation may issue certificates of its capital stock or uncertificated stock if authorized to do so and other securities to the stockholders of the constituent corporations in exchange or payment for the original shares, in such amount as shall be necessary in accordance with the terms of the agreement of merger or consolidation in order to effect such merger or consolidation in the manner and on the terms specified in the agreement.

§ 261. Effect of merger upon pending actions.

Any action or proceeding, whether civil, criminal or administrative, pending by or against any corporation which is a party to a merger or consolida-

tion shall be prosecuted as if such merger or consolidation had not taken place, or the corporation surviving or resulting from such merger or consolidation may be substituted in such action or proceeding.

§ 262. Appraisal rights.

(a) Any stockholder of a corporation of this State who holds shares of stock on the date of the making of a demand pursuant to subsection (d) of this section with respect to such shares, who continuously holds such shares through the effective date of the merger or consolidation, who has otherwise complied with subsection (d) of this section and who has neither voted in favor of the merger or consolidation nor consented thereto in writing pursuant to § 228 of this title shall be entitled to an appraisal by the Court of Chancery of the fair value of the stockholder's shares of stock under the circumstances described in subsections (b) and (c) of this section. ▪ As used in this section, the word "stockholder" means a holder of record of stock in a corporation; the words "stock" and "share" mean and include what is ordinarily meant by those words; and the words "depository receipt" mean a receipt or other instrument issued by a depository representing an interest in 1 or more shares, or fractions thereof, solely of stock of a corporation, which stock is deposited with the depository.

(b) Appraisal rights shall be available for the shares of any class or series of stock of a constituent corporation in a merger or consolidation to be effected pursuant to § 251 (other than a merger effected pursuant to § 251(g) of this title), § 252, § 254, § 255, § 256, § 257, § 258, § 263 or § 264 of this title:

> **(1)** Provided, however, that no appraisal rights under this section shall be available for the shares of any class or series of stock, which stock, or depository receipts in respect thereof, at the record date fixed to determine the stockholders entitled to receive notice of the meeting of stockholders to act upon the agreement of merger or consolidation (or, in the case of a merger pursuant to § 251(h), as of immediately

prior to the execution of the agreement of merger), were either: **(i)** listed on a national securities exchange or **(ii)** held of record by more than 2,000 holders; and further provided that no appraisal rights shall be available for any shares of stock of the constituent corporation surviving a merger if the merger did not require for its approval the vote of the stockholders of the surviving corporation as provided in § 251(f) of this title.

(2) Notwithstanding paragraph (b)(1) of this section, appraisal rights under this section shall be available for the shares of any class or series of stock of a constituent corporation if the holders thereof are required by the terms of an agreement of merger or consolidation pursuant to §§ 251, 252, 254, 255, 256, 257, 258, 263 and 264 of this title to accept for such stock anything except:

a. Shares of stock of the corporation surviving or resulting from such merger or consolidation, or depository receipts in respect thereof;

b. Shares of stock of any other corporation, or depository receipts in respect thereof, which shares of stock (or depository receipts in respect thereof) or depository receipts at the effective date of the merger or consolidation will be either listed on a national securities exchange or held of record by more than 2,000 holders;

c. Cash in lieu of fractional shares or fractional depository receipts described in the foregoing paragraphs (b)(2)a. and b. of this section; or

d. Any combination of the shares of stock, depository receipts and cash in lieu of fractional shares or fractional depository receipts described in the foregoing paragraphs (b)(2)a., b. and c. of this section.

(3) In the event all of the stock of a subsidiary Delaware corporation party to a merger effected under § 253 or § 267 of this title is not owned by the parent immediately prior to the merger, appraisal rights shall be available for

the shares of the subsidiary Delaware corporation.

(4) [Repealed.]

(c) Any corporation may provide in its certificate of incorporation that appraisal rights under this section shall be available for the shares of any class or series of its stock as a result of an amendment to its certificate of incorporation, any merger or consolidation in which the corporation is a constituent corporation or the sale of all or substantially all of the assets of the corporation. ▪ If the certificate of incorporation contains such a provision, the provisions of this section, including those set forth in subsections (d), (e), and (g) of this section, shall apply as nearly as is practicable.

(d) Appraisal rights shall be perfected as follows:

(1) If a proposed merger or consolidation for which appraisal rights are provided under this section is to be submitted for approval at a meeting of stockholders, the corporation, not less than 20 days prior to the meeting, shall notify each of its stockholders who was such on the record date for notice of such meeting (or such members who received notice in accordance with § 255(c) of this title) with respect to shares for which appraisal rights are available pursuant to subsection (b) or (c) of this section that appraisal rights are available for any or all of the shares of the constituent corporations, and shall include in such notice a copy of this section and, if 1 of the constituent corporations is a nonstock corporation, a copy of § 114 of this title. ▪ Each stockholder electing to demand the appraisal of such stockholder's shares shall deli...

and that the stockholder intends thereby to demand the appraisal of such stockholder's shares. ▪ A proxy or vote against the merger or consolidation shall not constitute such a demand. ▪ A stockholder electing to take such action must do so by a separate written demand as herein provided. ▪ Within 10 days after the effective date of such merger or consolidation, the surviving or resulting corporation shall notify each stockholder of each constituent corporation who has complied with this subsection and has not voted in favor of or consented to the merger or consolidation of the date that the merger or consolidation has become effective; or

(2) If the merger or consolidation was approved pursuant to § 228, § 251(h), § 253, or § 267 of this title, then either a constituent corporation before the effective date of the merger or consolidation or the surviving or resulting corporation within 10 days thereafter shall notify each of the holders of any class or series of stock of such constituent corporation who are entitled to appraisal rights of the approval of the merger or consolidation and that appraisal rights are available for any or all shares of such class or series of stock of such constituent corporation, and shall include in such notice a copy of this section and, if 1 of the constituent corporations is a nonstock corporation, a copy of § 114 of this title. ▪ Such notice may, and, if given on or after the effective date of the merger or consolidation, shall, also notify such stockholders of the effective date of the merger or consolidation. ▪ Any stockholder entitled to appraisal rights may, within 20 days after the date of giving such notice or, in the case of a merger approved pursuant to § 251(h) of this title, within the later of the consummation of the offer contemplated by § 251(h) of this title and 20 days after the date of giving such notice, demand in writing from the surviving or resulting corporation the appraisal of such holder's shares, provided that a demand may be delivered to the corporation by electronic transmission if directed to an information processing system (if any) expressly designated for that purpose in such notice. ▪ Such demand will be sufficient if it reasonably informs the corporation of the identity of the stockholder and that the stockholder intends thereby to demand the appraisal of such holder's shares. ▪ If such notice did not notify stockholders of the effective date of the merger or consolidation, either **(i)** each such constituent corporation shall send a second notice before the effective date of the merger or consolidation notifying each of the holders of any class or series of stock of such constituent corporation that are entitled to appraisal rights of the effective date of the merger or consolidation or **(ii)** the surviving or resulting corporation shall send such a second notice to all such holders on or within 10 days after such effective date; provided, however, that if such second notice is sent more than 20 days following the sending of the first notice or, in the case of a merger approved pursuant to § 251(h) of this title, later than the later of the consummation of the offer contemplated by § 251(h) of this title and 20 days following the sending of the first notice, such second notice need only be sent to each stockholder who is entitled to appraisal rights and who has demanded appraisal of such holder's shares in accordance with this subsection. ▪ An affidavit of the secretary or assistant secretary or of the transfer agent of the corporation that is required to give either notice that such notice has been given shall, in the absence of fraud, be prima facie evidence of the facts stated therein. ▪ For purposes of determining the stockholders entitled to receive either notice, each constituent corporation may fix, in advance, a record date that shall be not more than 10 days prior to the date the notice is given, provided, that if the notice is given on or after the effective date of the merger or consolidation, the record date shall be such effective date. ▪ If no record date is fixed and the notice is given prior to the effective date, the record date shall be the close of business on the day next preceding the day on which the notice is given.

(e) Within 120 days after the effective date of the merger or consolidation, the surviving or resulting corporation or any stockholder who has complied with subsections (a) and (d) of this section hereof and who is otherwise entitled to appraisal rights, may commence an appraisal proceeding by filing a petition in the Court of Chancery demanding a determination of the value of the stock of all such stockholders. ▪ Notwithstanding the foregoing, at any time within 60 days after the effective date of the merger or consolidation, any stockholder who has not commenced an appraisal proceeding or joined that proceeding as a named party shall have the right to withdraw such stockholder's demand for appraisal and to accept the terms offered upon the merger or consolidation. ▪ Within 120 days after the effective date of the merger or consolidation, any stockholder who has complied with the requirements of subsections (a) and (d) of this section hereof, upon request given in writing (or by electronic transmission directed to an information processing system (if any) expressly designated for that purpose in the notice of appraisal), shall be entitled to receive from the corporation surviving the merger or resulting from the consolidation a statement setting forth the aggregate number of shares not voted in favor of the merger or consolidation (or, in the case of a merger approved pursuant to § 251(h) of this title, the aggregate number of shares (other than any excluded stock (as defined in § 251(h)(6)d. of this title)) that were the subject of, and were not tendered into, and accepted for purchase or exchange in, the offer referred to in § 251(h)(2)), and, in either case, with respect to which demands for appraisal have been received and the aggregate number of holders of such shares. ▪ Such statement shall be given to the stockholder within 10 days after such stockholder's request for such a statement is received by the surviving or resulting corporation or within 10 days after expiration of the period for delivery of demands for appraisal under subsection (d) of this section hereof, whichever is later. ▪ Notwithstanding subsection (a) of this section, a person who is the beneficial owner of shares of such stock held either in a voting trust or by a nominee on behalf of such person may, in such person's own name, file a petition or request from the corporation the statement described in this subsection.

(f) Upon the filing of any such petition by a stockholder, service of a copy thereof shall be made upon the surviving or resulting corporation, which shall within 20 days after such service file in the office of the Register in Chancery in which the petition was filed a duly verified list containing the names and addresses of all stockholders who have demanded payment for their shares and with whom agreements as to the value of their shares have not been reached by the surviving or resulting corporation. ▪ If the petition shall be filed by the surviving or resulting corporation, the petition shall be accompanied by such a duly verified list. ▪ The Register in Chancery, if so ordered by the Court, shall give notice of the time and place fixed for the hearing of such petition by registered or certified mail to the surviving or resulting corporation and to the stockholders shown on the list at the addresses therein stated. ▪ Such notice shall also be given by 1 or more publications at least 1 week before the day of the hearing, in a newspaper of general circulation published in the City of Wilmington, Delaware or such publication as the Court deems advisable. ▪ The forms of the notices by mail and by publication shall be approved by the Court, and the costs thereof shall be borne by the surviving or resulting corporation.

(g) At the hearing on such petition, the Court shall determine the stockholders who have complied with this section and who have become entitled to appraisal rights. ▪ The Court may require the stockholders who have demanded an appraisal for their shares and who hold stock represented by certificates to submit their certificates of stock to the Register in Chancery for notation thereon of the pendency of the appraisal proceedings; and if any stockholder fails to comply with such direction, the Court may dismiss the proceedings as to such stockholder. ▪ If immediately before the merger or consolidation the shares of the class or series of stock of the constituent corporation as to which appraisal rights are available were listed on a national securities exchange, the Court shall dismiss the proceedings as to all holders of such shares who are otherwise entitled to appraisal rights unless **(1)** the total number of shares entitled to appraisal exceeds 1% of the outstanding shares of the class or series eligible for appraisal, **(2)** the value of the consideration provided in the merger or consolidation for such total number of shares exceeds $1 million, or **(3)** the merger was approved pursuant to § 253 or § 267 of this title.

(h) After the Court determines the stockholders entitled to an appraisal, the appraisal proceeding shall be conducted in accordance with the rules of the Court of Chancery, including any rules specifically governing appraisal proceedings. ■ Through such proceeding the Court shall determine the fair value of the shares exclusive of any element of value arising from the accomplishment or expectation of the merger or consolidation, together with interest, if any, to be paid upon the amount determined to be the fair value. ■ In determining such fair value, the Court shall take into account all relevant factors. ■ Unless the Court in its discretion determines otherwise for good cause shown, and except as provided in this subsection, interest from the effective date of the merger through the date of payment of the judgment shall be compounded quarterly and shall accrue at 5% over the Federal Reserve discount rate (including any surcharge) as established from time to time during the period between the effective date of the merger and the date of payment of the judgment. ■ At any time before the entry of judgment in the proceedings, the surviving corporation may pay to each stockholder entitled to appraisal an amount in cash, in which case interest shall accrue thereafter as provided herein only upon the sum of **(1)** the difference, if any, between the amount so paid and the fair value of the shares as determined by the Court, and **(2)** interest theretofore accrued, unless paid at that time. ■ Upon application by the surviving or resulting corporation or by any stockholder entitled to participate in the appraisal proceeding, the Court may, in its discretion, proceed to trial upon the appraisal prior to the final determination of the stockholders entitled to an appraisal. ■ Any stockholder whose name appears on the list filed by the surviving or resulting corporation pursuant to subsection (f) of this section and who has submitted such stockholder's certificates of stock to the Register in Chancery, if such is required, may participate fully in all proceedings until it is finally determined that such stockholder is not entitled to appraisal rights under this section.

(i) The Court shall direct the payment of the fair value of the shares, together with interest, if any, by the surviving or resulting corporation to the stockholders entitled thereto. ■ Payment shall be so made to each such stockholder, in the case of holders of uncertificated stock forthwith, and the case of holders of shares represented by certificates upon the surrender to the corporation of the certificates representing such stock. ■ The Court's decree may be enforced as other decrees in the Court of Chancery may be enforced, whether such surviving or resulting corporation be a corporation of this State or of any state.

(j) The costs of the proceeding may be determined by the Court and taxed upon the parties as the Court deems equitable in the circumstances. ■ Upon application of a stockholder, the Court may order all or a portion of the expenses incurred by any stockholder in connection with the appraisal proceeding, including, without limitation, reasonable attorney's fees and the fees and expenses of experts, to be charged pro rata against the value of all the shares entitled to an appraisal.

(k) From and after the effective date of the merger or consolidation, no stockholder who has demanded appraisal rights as provided in subsection (d) of this section shall be entitled to vote such stock for any purpose or to receive payment of dividends or other distributions on the stock (except dividends or other distributions payable to stockholders of record at a date which is prior to the effective date of the merger or consolidation); provided, however, that if no petition for an appraisal shall be filed within the time provided in subsection (e) of this section, or if such stockholder shall deliver to the surviving or resulting corporation a written withdrawal of such stockholder's demand for an appraisal and an acceptance of the merger or consolidation, either within 60 days after the effective date of the merger or consolidation as provided in subsection (e) of this section or thereafter with the written approval of the corporation, then the right of such stockholder to an appraisal shall cease. ■ Notwithstanding the foregoing, no appraisal proceeding in the Court of Chancery shall be dismissed as to any stockholder without the approval of the Court, and such approval may be conditioned upon such terms as the Court deems just; provided, however that this provision shall not affect the right of any stockholder who has not commenced an appraisal proceeding or joined that proceeding as a named party to withdraw such stockholder's demand for appraisal and to accept the terms offered upon the merger or consolidation within 60 days after the effective date of the merger or consolidation, as set forth in subsection (e) of this section.

(l) The shares of the surviving or resulting corporation to which the shares of such objecting stockholders would have been converted had they assented to the merger or consolidation shall have the status of authorized and unissued shares of the surviving or resulting corporation.

§ 263. Merger or consolidation of domestic corporations and partnerships; service of process upon surviving or resulting corporation or partnership.

(a) Any 1 or more corporations of this State may merge or consolidate with 1 or more partnerships (whether general (including a limited liability partnership) or limited (including a limited liability limited partnership)), unless the laws of the jurisdiction or jurisdictions under which such partnership or partnerships are formed prohibit such merger or consolidation. ■ Such corporation or corporations and such 1 or more partnerships may merge with or into a surviving corporation, which may be any 1 of such corporations, or they may merge with or into a surviving partnership, which may be any 1 of such partnerships, or they may consolidate into a new resulting corporation, which corporation shall be a corporation of this State, or a partnership formed pursuant to an agreement of merger or consolidation, as the case may be, complying and approved in accordance with this section. ■ The term "partnership" as used in this section includes any partnership (whether general (including a limited liability partnership) or limited (including a limited liability limited partnership)) formed under the laws of this State or the laws of any other jurisdiction.

(b) Each such corporation and partnership shall enter into a written agreement of merger or consolidation. ■ The agreement shall state:

(1) The terms and conditions of the merger or consolidation;

(2) The mode of carrying the same into effect;

(3) In the case of a merger in which the surviving entity is a corporation of this State, such amendments or changes in the certificate of incorporation of the surviving corporation as are desired to be effected by the merger (which amendments or changes may amend and restate the certificate of incorporation of the surviving corporation in its entirety), or, if no such amendments or changes are desired, a statement that the certificate of incorporation of the surviving corporation shall be its certificate of incorporation;

(4) In the case of a consolidation in which the resulting entity is a corporation of this State, that the certificate of incorporation of the resulting corporation shall be as is set forth in an attachment to the agreement;

(5) The manner, if any, of converting the shares of stock of each such corporation and the partnership interests of each such partnership into shares, partnership interests or other securities of the entity surviving or resulting from such merger or consolidation or of cancelling some or all of such shares or interests, and if any shares of any such corporation or any partnership interests of any such partnership are not to remain outstanding, to be converted solely into shares, partnership interests or other securities of the entity surviving or resulting from such merger or consolidation or to be cancelled, the cash, property, rights or securities of any other corporation or entity which the holders of such shares or partnership interests are to receive in exchange for, or upon conversion of such shares or partnership interests and the surrender of any certificates evidencing them, which cash, property, rights or securities of any other corporation or entity may be in addition to or in lieu of shares, partnership interests or other securities of the entity surviving or resulting from such merger or consolidation;

(6) Such other details or provisions as are deemed desirable, including, without limiting the generality of the foregoing, a provision for the payment of cash in lieu of the issuance or recognition of fractional shares, rights, other securities or interests of the surviving or resulting corporation or partnership or of any other corporation or entity the shares, rights, other securities or interests of which are to be received in the merger or consolidation, or for some other arrangement with respect thereto, consistent with § 155 of this title; and

(7) Such other provisions or facts as shall be required to be set forth in an agreement of merger or consolidation (including any provision for amendment of the partnership agreement and statement of partnership existence or certificate of limited partnership (or equivalent documents) of the surviving partnership) by the laws of each jurisdiction under which any of the partnerships are formed.

Any of the terms of the agreement of merger or consolidation may be made dependent upon facts ascertainable outside of such agreement, provided that the manner in which such facts shall operate upon the terms of the agreement is clearly and expressly set forth in the agreement of merger or consolidation. ■ The term "facts," as used in the preceding sentence, includes, but is not limited to, the occurrence of any event, including a determination or action by any person or body, including the corporation.

(c) The agreement required by subsection (b) of this section shall be adopted, approved, certified, executed and acknowledged by each of the corporations in the same manner as is provided in § 251 or § 255 of this title and, in the case of the partnerships, in accordance with their partnership agreements and in accordance with the laws of the jurisdiction under which they are formed. ■ If the surviving or resulting entity is a partnership, in addition to any other approvals, each stockholder of a merging corporation who will become a general partner of the surviving or resulting partnership must approve the agreement of merger or consolidation. ■ The agreement shall be filed and shall become effective for all purposes of the laws of this State when and as provided in § 251 or § 255 of this title with respect to the merger or consolidation of corporations of this State. ■ In lieu of filing the agreement of merger or consolidation, the surviving or resulting corporation or partnership may file a certificate of merger or consolidation, executed in accordance with § 103 of this title, if the surviving or resulting entity is a corporation, or by a general partner, if the surviving or resulting entity is a partnership, which states:

(1) The name, jurisdiction of formation or organization and type of entity of each of the constituent entities;

(2) That an agreement of merger or consolidation has been approved, adopted, certified, executed and acknowledged by each of the constituent entities in accordance with this subsection;

(3) The name of the surviving or resulting corporation or partnership;

(4) In the case of a merger in which a corporation is the surviving entity, such amendments or changes in the certificate of incorporation of the surviving corporation as are desired to be effected by the merger (which amendments or changes may amend and restate the certificate of incorporation of the surviving corporation in its entirety), or, if no such amendments or changes are desired, a statement that the certificate of incorporation of the surviving corporation shall be its certificate of incorporation;

(5) In the case of a consolidation in which a corporation is the resulting entity, that the certificate of incorporation of the resulting corporation shall be as is set forth in an attachment to the certificate;

(6) That the executed agreement of consolidation or merger is on file at an office of the surviving or resulting corporation or partnership and the address thereof;

(7) That a copy of the agreement of consolidation or merger will be furnished by the surviving or resulting entity, on request and without cost, to any stockholder of any constituent corporation or any partner of any constituent partnership; and

(8) The agreement, if any, required by subsection (d) of this section.

(d) If the entity surviving or resulting from the merger or consolidation is a partnership formed under the laws of a jurisdiction other than this State, it shall agree that it may be served with process in this State in any proceeding for enforcement of any obligation of any constituent corporation or partnership of this State, as well as for enforcement of any obligation of the surviving or resulting corporation or partnership arising from the merger or consolidation, including any suit or other proceeding to enforce the right of any stockholders as determined in appraisal proceedings pursuant to § 262 of this title, and shall irrevocably appoint the Secretary of State as its agent to accept service of process in any such suit or other proceedings and shall specify the address to which a copy of such process shall be mailed by the Secretary of State. ▪ Process may be served upon the Secretary of State under this subsection by means of electronic transmission but only as prescribed by the Secretary of State. ▪ The Secretary of State is authorized to issue such rules and regulations with respect to such service as the Secretary of State deems necessary or appropriate. ▪ In the event of such service upon the Secretary of State in accordance with this subsection, the Secretary of State shall forthwith notify such surviving or resulting corporation or partnership thereof by letter, directed to such surviving or resulting corporation or partnership at its address so specified, unless such surviving or resulting corporation or partnership shall have designated in writing to the Secretary of State a different address for such purpose, in which case it shall be mailed to the last address so designated. ▪ Such letter shall be sent by a mail or courier service that includes a record of mailing or deposit with the courier and a record of delivery evidenced by the signature of the recipient. ▪ Such letter shall enclose a copy of the process and any other papers served on the Secretary of State pursuant to this subsection. ▪ It shall be the duty of the plaintiff in the event of such service to serve process and any other papers in duplicate, to notify the Secretary of State that service is being effected pursuant to this subsection and to pay the Secretary of State the sum of $50 for the use of the State, which sum shall be taxed as part of the costs in the proceeding, if the plaintiff shall prevail therein. ▪ The Secretary of State shall maintain an alphabetical record of any such service setting forth the name of the plaintiff and the defendant, the title, docket number and nature of the proceeding in which process has been served upon the Secretary of State, the fact that service has been effected pursuant to this subsection, the return date thereof, and the day and hour service was made. ▪ The Secretary of State shall not be required to retain such information longer than 5 years from receipt of the service of process.

(e) Sections 251 (d)-(f), 255(c) (second sentence) and (d)-(f), 259-261 and 328 of this title shall, insofar as they are applicable, apply to mergers or consolidations between corporations and partnerships.

(f) Nothing in this section shall be deemed to authorize the merger of a charitable nonstock corporation into a partnership, if the charitable status of such nonstock corporation would thereby be lost or impaired; but a partnership may be merged into a charitable nonstock corporation which shall continue as the surviving corporation.

§ 264. Merger or consolidation of domestic corporations and limited liability companies; service of process upon surviving or resulting corporation or limited liability company.

(a) Any 1 or more corporations of this State may merge or consolidate with 1 or more limited liability companies, unless the laws of the jurisdiction or jurisdictions under which such limited liability company or limited liability companies are formed prohibit such merger or consolidation. ▪ Such corporation or corporations and such 1 or more limited liability companies may merge with or into a surviving corporation, which may be any 1 of such corporations, or they may merge with or into a surviving limited liability company, which may be any 1 of such limited liability companies, or they may consolidate into a new resulting corporation, which corporation shall be a corporation of this State, or a limited liability company formed pursuant to an agreement of merger or consolidation, as the case may be, complying and approved in accordance with this section. ▪ The term "limited liability company" as used in this section includes any limited liability company formed under the laws of this State or the laws of any other jurisdiction.

(b) Each such corporation and limited liability company shall enter into a written agreement of merger or consolidation. ▪ The agreement shall state:

(1) The terms and conditions of the merger or consolidation;

(2) The mode of carrying the same into effect;

(3) In the case of a merger in which the surviving entity is a corporation of this State, such amendments or changes in the certificate of incorporation of the surviving corporation as are desired to be effected by the merger (which amendments or changes may amend and restate the certificate of incorporation of the surviving corporation in its entirety), or, if no such amendments or changes are desired, a statement that the certificate of incorporation of the surviving corporation shall be its certificate of incorporation;

(4) In the case of a consolidation in which the resulting entity is a corporation of this State, that the certificate of incorporation of the resulting corporation shall be as is set forth in an attachment to the agreement;

(5) The manner, if any, of converting the shares of stock of each such corporation and the limited liability company interests of each such limited liability company into shares, limited liability company interests or other securities of the entity surviving or resulting from such merger or consolidation or of cancelling some or all of such shares or interests, and if any shares of any such corporation or any limited liability company interests of any such limited liability company are not to remain outstanding, to be converted solely into shares, limited liability company interests or other securities of the entity surviving or resulting from such merger or consolidation or to be cancelled, the cash, property, rights or securities of any other corporation or entity which the holders of such shares or limited liability company interests are to receive in exchange for, or upon conversion of such shares or limited liability company interests and the surrender of any certificates evidencing them, which cash, property, rights or securities of any other corporation or entity may be in addition to or in lieu of shares, limited liability company interests or other securities of the entity surviving or resulting from such merger or consolidation;

(6) Such other details or provisions as are deemed desirable, including, without limiting the generality of the foregoing, a provision for the payment of cash in lieu of the issuance or recognition of fractional shares, rights, other securities or interests of the surviving or resulting corporation or limited liability company or of any other corporation or entity the shares, rights, other securities or interests of which are to be received in the merger or consolidation, or for some other arrangement with respect thereto, consistent with § 155 of this title; and

(7) Such other provisions or facts as shall be required to be set forth in an agreement of merger or consolidation (including any provision for amendment of the limited liability company agreement and certificate of formation (or equivalent documents) of the surviving limited liability company) by the laws of each jurisdiction under which any of the limited liability companies are formed.

Any of the terms of the agreement of merger or consolidation may be made dependent upon facts ascertainable outside of such agreement, provided that the manner in which such facts shall operate upon the terms of the agreement is clearly and expressly set forth in the agreement of merger or consolidation. ▪ The term "facts," as used in the preceding sentence, includes, but is not limited to, the occurrence of any event, including a determination or action by any person or body, including the corporation.

(c) The agreement required by subsection (b) of this section shall be adopted, approved, certified, executed and acknowledged by each of the corporations in the same manner as is provided in § 251 or § 255 of this title and, in the case of the limited liability companies, in accordance with their limited liability company agreements and in accordance with the laws of the jurisdiction under which they are formed. ▪ The agreement shall be filed and shall become effective for all purposes of the laws of this State when and as provided in § 251 or § 255 of this title with respect to the merger or consolidation of corporations of this State. ▪ In lieu of filing the agreement of merger or consolidation, the surviving or resulting corporation or limited liability company may file a certificate of merger or consolidation, executed in accordance with § 103 of this title, if the surviving or resulting entity is a corporation, or by an authorized person, if the surviving or resulting entity is a limited liability company, which states:

(1) The name and jurisdiction of formation or organization of each of the constituent entities;

(2) That an agreement of merger or consolidation has been approved, adopted, certified, executed and acknowledged by each of the constituent entities in accordance with this subsection;

(3) The name of the surviving or resulting corporation or limited liability company;

(4) In the case of a merger in which a corporation is the surviving entity, such amendments or changes in the certificate of incorporation of the surviving corporation as are desired to be effected by the merger (which amendments or changes may amend and restate the certificate of incorporation of the surviving corporation in its entirety), or, if no such amendments or changes are desired, a statement that the certificate of incorporation of the surviving corporation shall be its certificate of incorporation;

(5) In the case of a consolidation in which a corporation is the resulting entity, that the certificate of incorporation of the resulting corporation shall be as is set forth in an attachment to the certificate;

(6) That the executed agreement of consolidation or merger is on file at an office of the surviving or resulting corporation or limited liability company and the address thereof;

(7) That a copy of the agreement of consolidation or merger will be furnished by the surviving or resulting entity, on request and without cost, to any stockholder of any constituent corporation or any member of any constituent limited liability company; and

(8) The agreement, if any, required by subsection (d) of this section.

(d) If the entity surviving or resulting from the merger or consolidation is a limited liability company formed under the laws of a jurisdiction other than this State, it shall agree that it may be served with process in this State in any proceeding for enforcement of any obligation of any constituent corporation or limited liability company of this State, as well as for enforcement of any obligation of the surviving or resulting corporation or limited liability company arising from the merger or consolidation, including any suit or other proceeding to enforce the right of any stockholders as determined in appraisal proceedings pursuant to the provisions of § 262 of this title, and shall irrevocably appoint the Secretary of State as its agent to accept service of process in any such suit or other proceedings and shall specify the address to which a copy of such process shall be mailed by the Secretary of State. ■ Process may be served upon the Secretary of State under this subsection by means of electronic transmission but only as prescribed by the Secretary of State. ■ The Secretary of State is authorized to issue such rules and regulations with respect to such service as the Secretary of State deems necessary or appropriate. ■ In the event of such service upon the Secretary of State in accordance with this subsection, the Secretary of State shall forthwith notify such surviving or resulting corporation or limited liability company thereof by letter, directed to such surviving or resulting corporation or limited liability company at its address so specified, unless such surviving or resulting corporation or limited liability company shall have designated in writing to the Secretary of State a different address for such purpose, in which case it shall be mailed to the last address so designated. ■ Such letter shall be sent by a mail or courier service that includes a record of mailing or deposit with the courier and a record of delivery evidenced by the signature of the recipient. ■ Such letter shall enclose a copy of the process and any other papers served on the Secretary of State pursuant to this subsection. ■ It shall be the duty of the plaintiff in the event of such service to serve process and any other papers in duplicate, to notify the Secretary of State that service is being effected pursuant to this subsection and to pay the Secretary of State the sum of $50 for the use of the State, which sum shall be taxed as part of the costs in the proceeding, if the plaintiff shall prevail therein. ■ The Secretary of State shall maintain an alphabetical record of any such service setting forth the name of the plaintiff and the defendant, the title, docket number and nature of the proceeding in which process has been served upon the Secretary of State, the

fact that service has been effected pursuant to this subsection, the return date thereof, and the day and hour service was made. ■ The Secretary of State shall not be required to retain such information longer than 5 years from receipt of the service of process.

(e) Sections 251 (d)-(f), 255(c) (second sentence) and (d)-(f), 259-261 and 328 of this title shall, insofar as they are applicable, apply to mergers or consolidations between corporations and limited liability companies.

(f) Nothing in this section shall be deemed to authorize the merger of a charitable nonstock corporation into a limited liability company, if the charitable status of such nonstock corporation would thereby be lost or impaired; but a limited liability company may be merged into a charitable nonstock corporation which shall continue as the surviving corporation.

§ 265. Conversion of other entities to a domestic corporation.

(a) As used in this section, the term "other entity" means a limited liability company, statutory trust, business trust or association, real estate investment trust, common-law trust or any other unincorporated business including a partnership (whether general (including a limited liability partnership) or limited (including a limited liability limited partnership)), or a foreign corporation.

(b) Any other entity may convert to a corporation of this State by complying with subsection (h) of this section and filing in the office of the Secretary of State:

> **(1)** A certificate of conversion to corporation that has been executed in accordance with subsection (i) of this section and filed in accordance with § 103 of this title; and

> **(2)** A certificate of incorporation that has been executed, acknowledged and filed in accordance with § 103 of this title.

Each of the certificates required by this subsection (b) shall be filed simultaneously in the office of the Secretary of State and, if such certificates are not to become effective upon their filing as permitted by § 103(d) of this title, then each such certificate shall provide for the same effective date or time in accordance with § 103(d) of this title.

(c) The certificate of conversion to corporation shall state:

(1) The date on which and jurisdiction where the other entity was first created, incorporated, formed or otherwise came into being and, if it has changed, its jurisdiction immediately prior to its conversion to a domestic corporation;

(2) The name and type of entity of the other entity immediately prior to the filing of the certificate of conversion to corporation; and

(3) The name of the corporation as set forth in its certificate of incorporation filed in accordance with subsection (b) of this section.

(4) [Repealed.]

(d) Upon the effective time of the certificate of conversion to corporation and the certificate of incorporation, the other entity shall be converted to a corporation of this State and the corporation shall thereafter be subject to all of the provisions of this title, except that notwithstanding § 106 of this title, the existence of the corporation shall be deemed to have commenced on the date the other entity commenced its existence in the jurisdiction in which the other entity was first created, formed, incorporated or otherwise came into being.

(e) The conversion of any other entity to a corporation of this State shall not be deemed to affect any obligations or liabilities of the other entity incurred prior to its conversion to a corporation of this State or the personal liability of any person incurred prior to such conversion.

(f) When an other entity has been converted to a corporation of this State pursuant to this section, the corporation of this State shall, for all purposes of the laws of the State of Delaware, be deemed to be the same entity as the converting other entity. ■ When any conversion shall have become effective under this section, for all purposes of the laws of the State of Delaware, all of the rights, privileges and powers of the other entity that has converted, and all property, real, personal and mixed, and all debts due to such other entity, as well as all other things and causes of action belonging to such other entity, shall remain vested in the domestic corporation to which such other entity has converted and shall be the property of such domestic corporation and the title to any real property vested by deed or otherwise in such other entity shall not revert or be in any way impaired by reason of this chapter; but all rights of creditors and all liens upon any property of such other entity shall be preserved unimpaired, and all debts, liabilities and duties of the other entity that has converted shall remain attached to the corporation of this State to which such other entity has converted, and may be enforced against it to the same extent as if said debts, liabilities and duties had originally been incurred or contracted by it in its capacity as a corporation of this State. ■ The rights, privileges, powers and interests in property of the other entity, as well as the debts, liabilities and duties of the other entity, shall not be deemed, as a consequence of the conversion, to have been transferred to the domestic corporation to which such other entity has converted for any purpose of the laws of the State of Delaware.

(g) Unless otherwise agreed for all purposes of the laws of the State of Delaware or as required under applicable non-Delaware law, the converting other entity shall not be required to wind up its affairs or pay its liabilities and distribute its assets, and the conversion shall not be deemed to constitute a dissolution of such other entity and shall constitute a continuation of the existence of the converting other entity in the form of a corporation of this State.

(h) Prior to filing a certificate of conversion to corporation with the office of the Secretary of State, the conversion shall be approved in the manner provided for by the document, instrument, agreement or other writing, as the case may be, governing the internal affairs of the other entity and the conduct of its business or by applicable law, as appropriate, and a certificate of incorporation shall be approved by the same authorization required to approve the conversion.

(i) The certificate of conversion to corporation shall be signed by any person who is authorized to sign the certificate of conversion to corporation on behalf of the other entity.

(j) In connection with a conversion hereunder, rights or securities of, or interests in, the other entity which is to be converted to a corporation of this State may be exchanged for or converted into cash, property, or shares of stock, rights or securities of such corporation of this State or, in addition to or in lieu thereof, may be exchanged for or converted into cash, property, or shares of stock, rights or securities of or interests in another domestic corporation or other entity or may be cancelled.

§ 266. Conversion of a domestic corporation to other entities.

(a) A corporation of this State may, upon the authorization of such conversion in accordance with this section, convert to a limited liability company, statutory trust, business trust or association, real estate investment trust, common-law trust or any other unincorporated business including a partnership (whether general (including a limited liability partnership) or limited (including a limited liability limited partnership)) or a foreign corporation.

(b) The board of directors of the corporation which desires to convert under this section shall adopt a resolution approving such conversion, specifying the type of entity into which the corporation shall be converted and recommending the approval of such conversion by the stockholders of the corporation. ■ Such resolution shall be submitted to the stockholders of the corporation at an annual or special meeting. ■ Due notice of the time, and purpose of the meeting shall be given to each holder of stock, whether voting or nonvoting, of the corporation at the address of the stockholder as it appears on the records of the corporation, at least 20 days prior to the date of the meeting. ■ At the meeting, the resolution shall be considered and a vote taken for its adoption or rejection. ■ If all outstanding shares of stock of the corporation, whether voting or nonvoting, shall be voted for the adoption of the resolution, the conversion shall be authorized.

(1)-(4) [Repealed.]

(c) If a corporation shall convert in accordance with this section to another entity organized, formed or created under the laws of a jurisdiction other than the State of Delaware, the corporation shall file with the Secretary of State a certificate of conversion executed in accordance with § 103 of this title, which certifies:

(1) The name of the corporation, and if it has been changed, the name under which it was originally incorporated;

(2) The date of filing of its original certificate of incorporation with the Secretary of State;

(3) The name and jurisdiction of the entity to which the corporation shall be converted;

(4) That the conversion has been approved in accordance with the provisions of this section;

(5) The agreement of the corporation that it may be served with process in the State of Delaware in any action, suit or proceeding for enforcement of any obligation of the corporation arising while it was a corporation of this State, and that it irrevocably appoints the Secretary of State as its agent to accept service of process in any such action, suit or proceeding; and

(6) The address to which a copy of the process referred to in paragraph (c)(5) of this section shall be mailed to it by the Secretary of State. ■ Process may be served upon the Secretary of State in accordance with paragraph (c)(5) of this section by means of electronic transmission but only as prescribed by the Secretary of State. ■ The Secretary of State is authorized to issue such rules and regulations with respect to such service as the Secretary of State deems necessary or appropriate. ■ In the event of such service upon the Secretary of State in accordance with paragraph (c)(5) of this section, the Secretary of State shall forthwith notify such corporation that has converted out of the State of Delaware by letter, directed to such corporation that has converted out of the State of Delaware at the address so specified, unless such corporation shall have designated in writing to the Secretary of State a different address for such purpose, in which case it shall be mailed to the last address designated. ▪ Such letter shall be sent by a mail or courier service that includes a record of mailing or deposit with the courier and a record of delivery evidenced by the signature of the recipient. ▪ Such letter shall enclose a copy of the process and any other papers served on the Secretary of State pursuant to this subsection. ▪ It shall be the duty of the plaintiff in the event of such service to serve process and any other papers in duplicate, to notify the Secretary of State that service is being effected pursuant to this subsection and to pay the Secretary of State the sum of $50 for the use of the State, which sum shall be taxed as part of the costs in the proceeding, if the plaintiff shall prevail therein. ▪ The Secretary of State shall maintain an alphabetical record of any such service setting forth the name of the plaintiff and the defendant, the title, docket number and nature of the proceeding in which process has been served, the fact that service has been effected pursuant to this subsection, the return date thereof, and the day and hour service was made. ▪ The Secretary of State shall not be required to retain such information longer than 5 years from receipt of the service of process.

(d) Upon the filing in the Office of the Secretary of State of a certificate of conversion to non-Delaware entity in accordance with subsection (c) of this section or upon the future effective date or time of the certificate of conversion to non-Delaware entity and payment to the Secretary of State of all fees prescribed under this title, the corporation shall cease to exist as a corporation of this State at the time the certificate of conversion becomes effective in accordance with § 103 of this title. ▪ A copy of the certificate of conversion to non-Delaware entity certified by the Secretary of State shall be prima facie evidence of the conversion by such corporation out of the State of Delaware.

(e) The conversion of a corporation out of the State of Delaware in accordance with this section and the resulting cessation of its existence as a corporation of this State pursuant to a certificate of conversion to non-Delaware entity shall not be deemed to affect any obligations or liabilities of the corporation incurred prior to such conversion or the personal liability of any person incurred prior to such conversion, nor shall it be deemed to affect the choice of law applicable to the corporation with respect to matters arising prior to such conversion.

(f) Unless otherwise provided in a resolution of conversion adopted in accordance with this section, the converting corporation shall not be required to wind up its affairs or pay its liabilities and distribute its assets, and the conversion shall not constitute a dissolution of such corporation.

(g) In connection with a conversion of a domestic corporation to another entity pursuant to this section, shares of stock, of the corporation of this State which is to be converted may be exchanged for or converted into cash, property, rights or securities of, or interests in, the entity to which the corporation of this State is being converted or, in addition to or in lieu thereof, may be exchanged for or converted into cash, property, shares of stock, rights or securities of, or interests in, another domestic corporation or other entity or may be cancelled.

(h) When a corporation has been converted to another entity or business form pursuant to this section, the other entity or business form shall, for all purposes of the laws of the State of Delaware, be deemed to be the same entity as the corporation. ▪ When any conversion shall have become effective under this section, for all purposes of the laws of the State of Delaware, all of the rights, privileges and powers of the corporation that has converted, and all property, real, personal and mixed, and all debts due to such corporation, as well as all other things and causes of action belonging to such corporation, shall remain vested in the other entity or business form to which such corporation has converted and shall be the property of such other entity or business form, and the title to any real property vested by deed or otherwise in such corporation shall not revert or be in any way impaired by reason of this chapter; but all rights of creditors and all liens upon any property of such corporation shall be preserved unimpaired, and all debts, liabilities and duties of the corporation that has converted shall remain attached to the other entity or business form to which such corporation has converted, and may be enforced against it to the same extent as if said debts, liabilities and duties had originally been incurred or contracted by it in its capacity as such other entity or business form. ▪ The rights, privileges, powers and interest in property of the corporation that has converted, as well as the debts, liabilities and duties of such corporation, shall not be deemed, as a consequence of the conversion, to have been transferred to the other entity or business form to which such corporation has converted for any purpose of the laws of the State of Delaware.

(i) No vote of stockholders of a corporation shall be necessary to authorize a conversion if no shares of the stock of such corporation shall have been issued prior to the adoption by the board of directors of the resolution approving the conversion.

(j) Nothing in this section shall be deemed to authorize the conversion of a charitable nonstock corporation into another entity, if the charitable status of such charitable nonstock corporation would thereby be lost or impaired.

§ 267. Merger of parent entity and subsidiary corporation or corporations.

(a) In any case in which: **(1)** at least 90% of the outstanding shares of each class of the stock of a corporation or corporations (other than a corporation which has in its certificate of incorporation the provision required by § 251(g)(7)(A) and (B) of this title), of which class there are outstanding shares that, absent this subsection, would be entitled to vote on such merger, is owned by an entity, and **(2)** 1 or more of such corporations is a corporation of this State, unless the laws of the jurisdiction or jurisdictions under which such entity or such foreign corporations are formed or organized prohibit such merger, the entity having such stock ownership may either merge the corporation or corporations into itself and assume all of its or

their obligations, or merge itself, or itself and 1 or more of such corporations, into 1 of the other corporations by **(a)** authorizing such merger in accordance with such entity's governing documents and the laws of the jurisdiction under which such entity is formed or organized and **(b)** acknowledging and filing with the Secretary of State, in accordance with § 103 of this title, a certificate of such ownership and merger certifying **(i)** that such merger was authorized in accordance with such entity's governing documents and the laws of the jurisdiction under which such entity is formed or organized, such certificate executed in accordance with such entity's governing documents and in accordance with the laws of the jurisdiction under which such entity is formed or organized and **(ii)** the type of entity of each constituent entity to the merger; provided, however, that in case the entity shall not own all the outstanding stock of all the corporations, parties to a merger as aforesaid, **(A)** the certificate of ownership and merger shall state the terms and conditions of the merger, including the securities, cash, property, or rights to be issued, paid, delivered or granted by the surviving constituent party upon surrender of each share of the corporation or corporations not owned by the entity, or the cancellation of some or all of such shares and **(B)** such terms and conditions of the merger may not result in a holder of stock in a corporation becoming a general partner in a surviving entity that is a partnership (other than a limited liability partnership or a limited liability limited partnership). ▪ Any of the terms of the merger may be made dependent upon facts ascertainable outside of the certificate of ownership and merger, provided that the manner in which such facts shall operate upon the terms of the merger is clearly and expressly set forth in the certificate of ownership and merger. ▪ The term "facts," as used in the preceding sentence, includes, but is not limited to, the occurrence of any event, including a determination or action by any person or body, including the entity. ▪ If the surviving constituent party is an entity formed or organized under the laws of a jurisdiction other than this State, **(1)** § 252(d) of this title shall also apply to a merger under this section; if the surviving constituent party is the entity, the word "corporation" where applicable, as used in § 252(d) of this title, shall be deemed to include an entity as defined herein; and **(2)** the terms and conditions of the merger shall obligate the surviving constituent party to provide the agreement, and take the actions, required by § 252(d) of this title.

(b) Sections 259, 261, and 328 of this title shall, insofar as they are applicable, apply to a merger under this section, and §§ 260 and 251(e) of this title shall apply to a merger under this section in which the surviving constituent party is a corporation of this State. ■ For purposes of this subsection, references to "agreement of merger" in § 251(e) of this title shall mean the terms and conditions of the merger set forth in the certificate of ownership and merger, and references to "corporation" in §§ 259-261 of this title, and § 328 of this title shall be deemed to include the entity, as applicable. ■ Section 262 of this title shall not apply to any merger effected under this section, except as provided in subsection (c) of this section.

(c) In the event all of the stock of a Delaware corporation party to a merger effected under this section is not owned by the entity immediately prior to the merger, the stockholders of such Delaware corporation party to the merger shall have appraisal rights as set forth in § 262 of this title.

(d) As used in this section only, the term:

(1) "Constituent party" means an entity or corporation to be merged pursuant to this section;

(2) "Entity" means a partnership (whether general (including a limited liability partnership) or limited (including a limited liability limited partnership)), limited liability company, any association of the kind commonly known as a joint-stock association or joint-stock company and any unincorporated association, trust or enterprise having members or having outstanding shares of stock or other evidences of financial or beneficial interest therein, whether formed or organized by agreement or under statutory authority or otherwise and whether formed or organized under the laws of this State or the laws of any other jurisdiction; and

(3) "Governing documents" means a partnership agreement, limited liability company agreement, articles of association or any other instrument containing the provisions by which an entity is formed or organized.

Subchapter X. Sale of Assets, Dissolution and Winding Up

§ 271. Sale, lease or exchange of assets; consideration; procedure.

(a) Every corporation may at any meeting of its board of directors or governing body sell, lease or exchange all or substantially all of its property and assets, including its goodwill and its corporate franchises, upon such terms and conditions and for such consideration, which may consist in whole or in part of money or other property, including shares of stock in, and/or other securities of, any other corporation or corporations, as its board of directors or governing body deems expedient and for the best interests of the corporation, when and as authorized by a resolution adopted by the holders of a majority of the outstanding stock of the corporation entitled to vote thereon or, if the corporation is a nonstock corporation, by a majority of the members having the right to vote for the election of the members of the governing body and any other members entitled to vote thereon under the certificate of incorporation or the bylaws of such corporation, at a meeting duly called upon at least 20 days' notice. ■ The notice of the meeting shall state that such a resolution will be considered.

(b) Notwithstanding authorization or consent to a proposed sale, lease or exchange of a corporation's property and assets by the stockholders or members, the board of directors or governing body may abandon such proposed sale, lease or exchange without further action by the stockholders or members, subject to the rights, if any, of third parties under any contract relating thereto.

(c) For purposes of this section only, the property and assets of the corporation include the property and assets of any subsidiary of the corporation. ■

As used in this subsection, "subsidiary" means any entity wholly-owned and controlled, directly or indirectly, by the corporation and includes, without limitation, corporations, partnerships, limited partnerships, limited liability partnerships, limited liability companies, and/or statutory trusts. ▪ Notwithstanding subsection (a) of this section, except to the extent the certificate of incorporation otherwise provides, no resolution by stockholders or members shall be required for a sale, lease or exchange of property and assets of the corporation to a subsidiary.

§ 272. Mortgage or pledge of assets.

The authorization or consent of stockholders to the mortgage or pledge of a corporation's property and assets shall not be necessary, except to the extent that the certificate of incorporation otherwise provides.

§ 273. Dissolution of joint venture corporation having 2 stockholders.

(a) If the stockholders of a corporation of this State, having only 2 stockholders each of which own 50% of the stock therein, shall be engaged in the prosecution of a joint venture and if such stockholders shall be unable to agree upon the desirability of discontinuing such joint venture and disposing of the assets used in such venture, either stockholder may, unless otherwise provided in the certificate of incorporation of the corporation or in a written agreement between the stockholders, file with the Court of Chancery a petition stating that it desires to discontinue such joint venture and to dispose of the assets used in such venture in accordance with a plan to be agreed upon by both stockholders or that, if no such plan shall be agreed upon by both stockholders, the corporation be dissolved. ▪ Such petition shall have attached thereto a copy of the proposed plan of discontinuance and distribution and a certificate stating that copies of such petition and plan have been transmitted in writing to the other stockholder and to the directors and officers of such corporation. ▪ The petition and certificate shall be executed and acknowledged in accordance with § 103 of this title.

(b) Unless both stockholders file with the Court of Chancery:

(1) Within 3 months of the date of the filing of such petition, a certificate similarly executed and acknowledged stating that they have agreed on such plan, or a modification thereof, and

(2) Within 1 year from the date of the filing of such petition, a certificate similarly executed and acknowledged stating that the distribution provided by such plan had been completed,

the Court of Chancery may dissolve such corporation and may by appointment of 1 or more trustees or receivers with all the powers and title of a trustee or receiver appointed under § 279 of this title, administer and wind up its affairs. ▪ Either or both of the above periods may be extended by agreement of the stockholders, evidenced by a certificate similarly executed, acknowledged and filed with the Court of Chancery prior to the expiration of such period.

(c) In the case of a charitable nonstock corporation, the petitioner shall provide a copy of any petition referred to in subsection (a) of this section to the Attorney General of the State of Delaware within 1 week of its filing with the Court of Chancery.

§ 274. Dissolution before issuance of shares or beginning of business; procedure.

If a corporation has not issued shares or has not commenced the business for which the corporation was organized, a majority of the incorporators, or, if directors were named in the certificate of incorporation or have been elected, a majority of the directors, may surrender all of the corporation's rights and franchises by filing in the office of the Secretary of State a certificate, executed and acknowledged by a majority of the incorporators or directors, stating: that no shares of stock have been issued or that the business or activity for which the corporation was organized has not been begun; the date of filing of the corporation's original certificate of incorporation with the Secretary of State; that no part of the capital of the corporation has been paid, or, if some capital has been paid, that the amount actually paid in for the corporation's shares, less any part thereof disbursed for necessary expenses, has been returned to those entitled thereto; that if the corporation has begun business but it has not issued shares, all debts of the corporation have been paid; that if the corporation has not begun business but has issued stock certificates, all issued stock certificates, if any, have been surrendered and cancelled; and that all rights and franchises of the corporation are surrendered. ■ Upon such certificate becoming effective in accordance with § 103 of this title, the corporation shall be dissolved.

§ 275. Dissolution generally; procedure.

(a) If it should be deemed advisable in the judgment of the board of directors of any corporation that it should be dissolved, the board, after the adoption of a resolution to that effect by a majority of the whole board at any meeting called for that purpose, shall cause notice of the adoption of the resolution and of a meeting of stockholders to take action upon the resolution to be given to each stockholder entitled to vote thereon as of the record date for determining the stockholders entitled to notice of the meeting.

(b) At the meeting a vote shall be taken upon the proposed dissolution. ■ If a majority of the outstanding stock of the corporation entitled to vote thereon shall vote for the proposed dissolution, a certification of dissolution shall be filed with the Secretary of State pursuant to subsection (d) of this section.

(c) Dissolution of a corporation may also be authorized without action of the directors if all the stockholders entitled to vote thereon shall consent in writing and a certificate of dissolution shall be filed with the Secretary of State pursuant to subsection (d) of this section.

(d) If dissolution is authorized in accordance with this section, a certificate of dissolution shall be executed, acknowledged and filed, and shall become effective, in accordance with § 103 of this title. ■ Such certificate of dissolution shall set forth:

(1) The name of the corporation;

(2) The date dissolution was authorized;

(3) That the dissolution has been authorized by the board of directors and stockholders of the corporation, in accordance with subsections (a) and (b) of this section, or that the dissolution has been authorized by all of the stockholders of the corporation entitled to vote on a dissolution, in accordance with subsection (c) of this section;

(4) The names and addresses of the directors and officers of the corporation; and

(5) The date of filing of the corporation's original certificate of incorporation with the Secretary of State.

(e) The resolution authorizing a proposed dissolution may provide that notwithstanding authorization or consent to the proposed dissolution by the stockholders, or the members of a nonstock corporation pursuant to § 276 of this title, the board of directors or governing body may abandon such proposed dissolution without further action by the stockholders or members.

(f) Upon a certificate of dissolution becoming effective in accordance with § 103 of this title, the corporation shall be dissolved.

§ 276. Dissolution of nonstock corporation; procedure.

(a) Whenever it shall be desired to dissolve any nonstock corporation, the governing body shall perform all the acts necessary for dissolution which are required by § 275 of this title to be performed by the board of directors of a corporation having capital stock. ■ If any members of a nonstock corporation are entitled to vote for the election of members of its governing body or are entitled to vote for dissolution under the certificate of incorporation or the bylaws of such corporation, such members shall perform all the acts necessary for dissolution which are contemplated by § 275 of this title to be performed by the stockholders of a corporation having capital stock, including dissolution without action of the members of the governing body if all the members of the corporation entitled to vote thereon shall consent in writing and a certificate of dissolution shall be filed with the Secretary of State pursuant to § 275(d) of this title. ■ If there is no member entitled to vote thereon, the dissolution of the corporation shall be authorized at a meeting of the governing body, upon the adoption of a resolution to dissolve by the vote of a majority of members of its governing body then in office. ■ In all other respects, the method and proceedings for the dissolution of a nonstock corporation shall conform as nearly as may be to the proceedings prescribed by § 275 of this title for the dissolution of corporations having capital stock.

(b) If a nonstock corporation has not commenced the business for which the corporation was organized, a majority of the governing body or, if none, a majority of the incorporators may surrender all of the corporation rights and franchises by filing in the office of the Secretary of State a certificate, executed and acknowledged by a majority of the incorporators or governing body, conforming as nearly as may be to the certificate prescribed by § 274 of this title.

§ 277. Payment of franchise taxes before dissolution, merger, transfer or conversion.

No corporation shall be dissolved, merged, transferred (without continuing its existence as a corporation of this State) or converted under this chapter until:

(1) All franchise taxes due to or assessable by the State including all franchise taxes due or which would be due or assessable for the entire calendar month during which such dissolution, merger, transfer or conversion becomes effective have been paid by the corporation; and

(2) All annual franchise tax reports including a final annual franchise tax report for the year in which such dissolution, merger, transfer or conversion becomes effective have been filed by the corporation;

notwithstanding the foregoing, if the Secretary of State certifies that an instrument to effect a dissolution, merger, transfer or conversion has been filed in the Secretary of State's office, such corporation shall be dissolved, merged, transferred or converted at the effective time of such instrument.

§ 278. Continuation of corporation after dissolution for purposes of suit and winding up affairs.

All corporations, whether they expire by their own limitation or are otherwise dissolved, shall nevertheless be continued, for the term of 3 years from such expiration or dissolution or for such longer period as the Court of Chancery shall in its discretion direct, bodies corporate for the purpose of prosecuting and defending suits, whether civil, criminal or administrative, by or against them, and of enabling them gradually to settle and close their business, to dispose of and convey their property, to discharge their liabilities and to distribute to their stockholders any remaining assets, but not for the purpose of continuing the business for which the corporation was organized. ■ With respect to any action, suit or proceeding begun by or against the corporation either prior to or within 3 years after the date of its expiration or dissolution, the action shall not abate by reason of the dissolution of the corporation; the corporation shall, solely for the purpose of such action, suit or proceeding, be continued as a body corporate beyond the 3-year period and until any judgments, orders or decrees therein shall be fully executed, without the necessity for any special direction to that effect by the Court of Chancery.

Sections 279 through 282 of this title shall apply to any corporation that has expired by its own limitation, and when so applied, all references in those sections to a dissolved corporation or dissolution shall include a corporation that has expired by its own limitation and to such expiration, respectively.

§ 279. Trustees or receivers for dissolved corporations; appointment; powers; duties.

When any corporation organized under this chapter shall be dissolved in any manner whatever, the Court of Chancery, on application of any creditor, stockholder or director of the corporation, or any other person who shows good cause therefor, at any time, may either appoint 1 or more of the directors of the corporation to be trustees, or appoint 1 or more persons to be receivers, of and for the corporation, to take charge of the corporation's property, and to collect the debts and property due and belonging to the corporation, with power to prosecute and defend, in the name of the corporation, or otherwise, all such suits as may be necessary or proper for the purposes aforesaid, and to appoint an agent or agents under them, and to do all other acts which might be done by the corporation, if in being, that may be necessary for the final settlement of the unfinished business of the corporation. ■ The powers of the trustees or receivers may be continued as long as the Court of Chancery shall think necessary for the purposes aforesaid.

§ 280. Notice to claimants; filing of claims.

(a)(1) After a corporation has been dissolved in accordance with the procedures set forth in this chapter, the corporation or any successor entity may give notice of the dissolution, requiring all persons having a claim against the corporation other than a claim against the corporation in a pending action, suit or proceeding to which the corporation is a party to present their claims against the corporation in accordance with such notice. ■ Such notice shall state:

a. That all such claims must be presented in writing and must contain sufficient information reasonably to inform the corporation or successor entity of the identity of the claimant and the substance of the claim;

b. The mailing address to which such a claim must be sent;

c. The date by which such a claim must be received by the corporation or successor entity, which date shall be no earlier than 60 days from the date thereof; and

d. That such claim will be barred if not received by the date referred to in paragraph (a)(1)c. of this section; and

e. That the corporation or a successor entity may make distributions to other claimants and the corporation's stockholders or persons interested as having been such without further notice to the claimant; and

f. The aggregate amount, on an annual basis, of all distributions made by the corporation to its stockholders for each of the 3 years prior to the date the corporation dissolved.

Such notice shall also be published at least once a week for 2 consecutive weeks in a newspaper of general circulation in the county in which the office of the corporation's last registered agent in this State is located and in the corporation's principal place of business and, in the case of a corporation having $10,000,000 or more in total assets at the time of its dissolution, at least once in all editions of a daily newspaper with a national circulation. ■ On or before the date of the first publication of such notice, the corporation or successor entity shall mail a copy of such notice by certified or registered mail, return receipt requested, to each known claimant of the corporation including persons with claims asserted against the corporation in a pending action, suit or proceeding to which the corporation is a party.

(2) Any claim against the corporation required to be presented pursuant to this subsection is barred if a claimant who was given actual notice under this subsection does not present the claim to the dissolved corporation or successor entity by the date referred to in paragraph (a)(1)c. of this section.

(3) A corporation or successor entity may reject, in whole or in part, any claim made by a claimant pursuant to this subsection by mailing notice of such rejection by certified or registered mail, return receipt requested, to the claimant within 90 days after receipt of such claim and, in all events, at least 150 days before the expiration of the period described in § 278 of this title; provided however, that in the case of a claim filed pursuant to § 295 of this title against a corporation or successor entity for which a receiver or trustee has been appointed by the Court of Chancery the time period shall be as provided in § 296 of this title, and the 30-day appeal period provided for in § 296 of this title shall be applicable. ▪ A notice sent by a corporation or successor entity pursuant to this subsection shall state that any claim rejected therein will be barred if an action, suit or proceeding with respect to the claim is not commenced within 120 days of the date thereof, and shall be accompanied by a copy of §§ 278-283 of this title and, in the case of a notice sent by a court-appointed receiver or trustee and as to which a claim has been filed pursuant to § 295 of this title, copies of §§ 295 and 296 of this title.

(4) A claim against a corporation is barred if a claimant whose claim is rejected pursuant to paragraph (a)(3) of this section does not commence an action, suit or proceeding with respect to the claim no later than 120 days after the mailing of the rejection notice.

(b)(1) A corporation or successor entity electing to follow the procedures described in subsection (a) of this section shall also give notice of the dissolution of the corporation to persons with contractual claims contingent upon the occurrence or nonoccurrence of future events or otherwise conditional or unmatured, and request that such persons present such claims in accordance with the terms of such notice. ▪ Provided however, that as used in this section and in § 281 of this title, the term "contractual claims" shall not include any implied warranty as to any product manufactured, sold, distributed or handled by the dissolved corporation. ▪ Such notice shall be in substantially the form, and sent and published in the same manner, as described in paragraph (a)(1) of this section.

(2) The corporation or successor entity shall offer any claimant on a contract whose claim is contingent, conditional or unmatured such security as the corporation or successor entity determines is sufficient to provide compensation to the claimant if the claim matures. ▪ The corporation or successor entity shall mail such offer to the claimant by certified or registered mail, return receipt requested, within 90 days

of receipt of such claim and, in all events, at least 150 days before the expiration of the period described in § 278 of this title. ▪ If the claimant offered such security does not deliver in writing to the corporation or successor entity a notice rejecting the offer within 120 days after receipt of such offer for security, the claimant shall be deemed to have accepted such security as the sole source from which to satisfy the claim against the corporation.

(c)(1) A corporation or successor entity which has given notice in accordance with subsection (a) of this section shall petition the Court of Chancery to determine the amount and form of security that will be reasonably likely to be sufficient to provide compensation for any claim against the corporation which is the subject of a pending action, suit or proceeding to which the corporation is a party other than a claim barred pursuant to subsection (a) of this section.

(2) A corporation or successor entity which has given notice in accordance with subsections (a) and (b) of this section shall petition the Court of Chancery to determine the amount and form of security that will be sufficient to provide compensation to any claimant who has rejected the offer for security made pursuant to paragraph (b)(2) of this section.

(3) A corporation or successor entity which has given notice in accordance with subsection (a) of this section shall petition the Court of Chancery to determine the amount and form of security which will be reasonably likely to be sufficient to provide compensation for claims that have not been made known to the corporation or that have not arisen but that, based on facts known to the corporation or successor entity, are likely to arise or to become known to the corporation or successor entity within 5 years after the date of dissolution or such longer period of time as the Court of Chancery may determine not to exceed 10 years after the date of dissolution. ▪ The Court of Chancery may appoint a guardian ad litem in respect of any such proceeding brought under this subsection. ▪ The reasonable fees and expenses of such guardian, including all reasonable expert witness fees, shall be paid by the petitioner in such proceeding.

(d) The giving of any notice or making of any offer pursuant to this section shall not revive any claim then barred or constitute acknowledgment by the corporation or successor entity that any person to whom such notice is sent is a proper claimant and shall not operate as a waiver of any defense or counterclaim in respect of any claim asserted by any person to whom such notice is sent.

(e) As used in this section, the term "successor entity" shall include any trust, receivership or other legal entity governed by the laws of this State to which the remaining assets and liabilities of a dissolved corporation are transferred and which exists solely for the purposes of prosecuting and defending suits, by or against the dissolved corporation, enabling the dissolved corporation to settle and close the business of the dissolved corporation, to dispose of and convey the property of the dissolved corporation, to discharge the liabilities of the dissolved corporation and to distribute to the dissolved corporation's stockholders any remaining assets, but not for the purpose of continuing the business for which the dissolved corporation was organized.

(f) The time periods and notice requirements of this section shall, in the case of a corporation or successor entity for which a receiver or trustee has been appointed by the Court of Chancery, be subject to variation by, or in the manner provided in, the Rules of the Court of Chancery.

(g) In the case of a nonstock corporation, any notice referred to in the last sentence of paragraph (a)(3) of this section shall include a copy of § 114 of this title. ▪ In the case of a nonprofit nonstock corporation, provisions of this section regarding distributions to members shall not apply to the extent that those provisions conflict with any other applicable law or with that corporation's certificate of incorporation or bylaws.

§ 281. Payment and distribution to claimants and stockholders.

(a) A dissolved corporation or successor entity which has followed the procedures described in § 280 of this title:

(1) Shall pay the claims made and not rejected in accordance with § 280(a) of this title,

(2) Shall post the security offered and not rejected pursuant to § 280(b)(2) of this title,

(3) Shall post any security ordered by the Court of Chancery in any proceeding under § 280(c) of this title, and

(4) Shall pay or make provision for all other claims that are mature, known and uncontested or that have been finally determined to be owing by the corporation or such successor entity.

Such claims or obligations shall be paid in full and any such provision for payment shall be made in full if there are sufficient assets. ▪ If there are insufficient assets, such claims and obligations shall be paid or provided for according to their priority, and, among claims of equal priority, ratably to the extent of assets legally available therefor. ▪ Any remaining assets shall be distributed to the stockholders of the dissolved corporation; provided, however, that such distribution shall not be made before the expiration of 150 days from the date of the last notice of rejections given pursuant to § 280(a)(3) of this title. ▪ In the absence of actual fraud, the judgment of the directors of the dissolved corporation or the governing persons of such successor entity as to the provision made for the payment of all obligations under paragraph (a)(4) of this section shall be conclusive.

(b) A dissolved corporation or successor entity which has not followed the procedures described in § 280 of this title shall, prior to the expiration of the period described in § 278 of this title, adopt a plan of distribution pursuant to which the dissolved corporation or successor entity **(i)** shall pay or make reasonable provision to pay all claims and obligations, including all contingent, conditional or unmatured contractual claims known to the corporation or such successor entity, **(ii)** shall make such provision as will be reasonably likely to be sufficient to provide compensation for any claim against the corporation which is the subject of a pending action, suit or proceeding to which the corporation is a party and **(iii)** shall make such provision as will be reasonably likely to be sufficient to provide compensation for claims that have not been made known to the corporation or that have not arisen but that, based on facts known to the corporation or successor entity, are likely to arise or to become known to the corporation or successor entity within 10 years after the date of dissolution. ▪ The plan of distribution shall provide that such claims shall be paid in full and any such provision for payment made shall be made in full if there are sufficient assets. ▪ If there are insufficient assets, such plan shall provide that such claims and obligations shall be paid or provided for according to their priority and, among claims of equal priority, ratably to the extent of assets legally available therefor. ▪ Any remaining assets shall be distributed to the stockholders of the dissolved corporation.

(c) Directors of a dissolved corporation or governing persons of a successor entity which has complied with subsection (a) or (b) of this section shall not be personally liable to the claimants of the dissolved corporation.

(d) As used in this section, the term "successor entity" has the meaning set forth in § 280(e) of this title.

(e) The term "priority," as used in this section, does not refer either to the order of payments set forth in paragraph (a)(1)-(4) of this section or to the relative times at which any claims mature or are reduced to judgment.

(f) In the case of a nonprofit nonstock corporation, provisions of this section regarding distributions to members shall not apply to the extent that those provisions conflict with any other applicable law or with that corporation's certificate of incorporation or bylaws.

§ 282. Liability of stockholders of dissolved corporations.

(a) A stockholder of a dissolved corporation the assets of which were distributed pursuant to § 281(a) or (b) of this title shall not be liable for any claim against the corporation in an amount in excess of such stockholder's pro rata share of the claim or the amount so distributed to such stockholder, whichever is less.

(b) A stockholder of a dissolved corporation the assets of which were distributed pursuant to § 281(a) of this title shall not be liable for any claim against the corporation on which an action, suit or proceeding is not begun prior to the expiration of the period described in § 278 of this title.

(c) The aggregate liability of any stockholder of a dissolved corporation for claims against the dissolved corporation shall not exceed the amount distributed to such stockholder in dissolution.

§ 283. Jurisdiction.

The Court of Chancery shall have jurisdiction of any application prescribed in this subchapter and of all questions arising in the proceedings thereon, and may make such orders and decrees and issue injunctions therein as justice and equity shall require.

§ 284. Revocation or forfeiture of charter; proceedings.

(a) Upon motion by the Attorney General, the Court of Chancery shall have jurisdiction to revoke or forfeit the charter of any corporation for abuse, misuse or nonuse of its corporate powers, privileges or franchises. ▪ The Attorney General shall proceed for this purpose by complaint in the Court of Chancery.

(b) The Court of Chancery shall have power, by appointment of trustees, receivers or otherwise, to administer and wind up the affairs of any corporation whose charter shall be revoked or forfeited by the Court of Chancery under this section, and to make such orders and decrees with respect thereto as shall be just and equitable respecting its affairs and assets and the rights of its stockholders and creditors.

(c) No proceeding shall be instituted under this section for nonuse of any corporation's powers, privileges or franchises during the first 2 years after its incorporation.

§ 285. Dissolution or forfeiture of charter by decree of court; filing.

Whenever any corporation is dissolved or its charter forfeited by decree or judgment of the Court of Chancery, the decree or judgment shall be forthwith filed by the Register in Chancery of the county in which the decree or judgment was entered, in the office of the Secretary of State, and a note thereof shall be made by the Secretary of State on the corporation's charter or certificate of incorporation and on the index thereof.

Subchapter XI. Insolvency; Receivers and Trustees

§ 291. Receivers for insolvent corporations; appointment and powers.

Whenever a corporation shall be insolvent, the Court of Chancery, on the application of any creditor or stockholder thereof, may, at any time, appoint 1 or more persons to be receivers of and for the corporation, to take charge of its assets, estate, effects, business and affairs, and to collect the outstanding debts, claims, and property due and belonging to the corporation, with power to prosecute and defend, in the name of the corporation or otherwise, all claims or suits, to appoint an agent or agents under them, and to do all other acts which might be done by the corporation and which may be necessary or proper. ▪ The powers of the receivers shall be such and shall continue so long as the Court shall deem necessary.

§ 292. Title to property; filing order of appointment; exception.

(a) Trustees or receivers appointed by the Court of Chancery of and for any corporation, and their respective survivors and successors, shall, upon their appointment and qualification or upon the death, resignation or discharge of any co-trustee or co-receiver, be vested by operation of law and without any act or deed, with the title of the corporation to all of its property, real, personal or mixed of whatsoever nature, kind, class or description, and

wheresoever situate, except real estate situate outside this State.

(b) Trustees or receivers appointed by the Court of Chancery shall, within 20 days from the date of their qualification, file in the office of the recorder in each county in this State, in which any real estate belonging to the corporation may be situated, a certified copy of the order of their appointment and evidence of their qualification.

(c) This section shall not apply to receivers appointed pendente lite.

§ 293. Notices to stockholders and creditors.

All notices required to be given to stockholders and creditors in any action in which a receiver or trustee for a corporation was appointed shall be given by the Register in Chancery, unless otherwise ordered by the Court of Chancery.

§ 294. Receivers or trustees; inventory; list of debts and report.

Trustees or receivers shall, as soon as convenient, file in the office of the Register in Chancery of the county in which the proceeding is pending, a full and complete itemized inventory of all the assets of the corporation which shall show their nature and probable value, and an account of all debts due from and to it, as nearly as the same can be ascertained. ▪ They shall make a report to the Court of their proceedings, whenever and as often as the Court shall direct.

§ 295. Creditors' proofs of claims; when barred; notice.

All creditors shall make proof under oath of their respective claims against the corporation, and cause the same to be filed in the office of the Register in Chancery of the county in which the proceeding is pending within the time fixed by and in accordance with the procedure established by the rules of the Court of Chancery. ▪ All creditors and claimants failing to do so, within the time limited by this section, or the time prescribed by the order of the Court, may, by direction of the Court, be barred from participating in the distribution of the assets of the corporation. ▪ The Court may also prescribe what notice, by publication or otherwise, shall be given to the creditors of the time fixed for the filing and making proof of claims.

§ 296. Adjudication of claims; appeal.

(a) The Register in Chancery, immediately upon the expiration of the time fixed for the filing of claims, in compliance with § 295 of this title, shall notify the trustee or receiver of the filing of the claims, and the trustee or receiver, within 30 days after receiving the notice, shall inspect the claims, and if the trustee or receiver or any creditor shall not be satisfied with the validity or correctness of the same, or any of them, the trustee or receiver shall forthwith notify the creditors whose claims are disputed of such trustee's or receiver's decision. ▪ The trustee or receiver shall require all creditors whose claims are disputed to submit themselves to such examination in relation to their claims as the trustee or receiver shall direct, and the creditors shall produce such books and papers relating to their claims as shall be required. ▪ The trustee or receiver shall have power to examine, under oath or affirmation, all witnesses produced before such trustee or receiver touching the claims, and shall pass upon and allow or disallow the claims, or any part thereof, and notify the claimants of such trustee's or receiver's determination.

(b) Every creditor or claimant who shall have received notice from the receiver or trustee that such creditor's or claimant's claim has been disallowed in whole or in part may appeal to the Court of Chancery within 30 days thereafter. ▪ The Court, after hearing, shall determine the rights of the parties.

§ 297. Sale of perishable or deteriorating property.

Whenever the property of a corporation is at the time of the appointment of a receiver or trustee encumbered with liens of any character, and the validity, extent or legality of any lien is disputed or brought in question, and the property of the corporation is of a character which will deteriorate in value pending the litigation respecting the lien, the Court of Chancery may order the receiver or trustee to sell the property of the corporation, clear of all encumbrances, at public or private sale, for the best price that can be obtained therefor, and pay the net proceeds arising from the sale thereof after deducting the costs of the sale into the Court, there to remain subject to the order of the Court, and to be disposed of as the Court shall direct.

§ 298. Compensation, costs and expenses of receiver or trustee.

The Court of Chancery, before making distribution of the assets of a corporation among the creditors or stockholders thereof, shall allow a reasonable compensation to the receiver or trustee for such receiver's or trustee's services, and the costs and expenses incurred in and about the execution of such receiver's or trustee's trust, and the costs of the proceedings in the Court, to be first paid out of the assets.

§ 299. Substitution of trustee or receiver as party; abatement of actions.

A trustee or receiver, upon application by such receiver or trustee in the court in which any suit is pending, shall be substituted as party plaintiff in the place of the corporation in any suit or proceeding which was so pending at the time of such receiver's or trustee's appointment. ▪ No action against a trustee or receiver of a corporation shall abate by reason of such receiver's or trustee's death, but, upon suggestion of the facts on the record, shall be continued against such receiver's or trustee's successor or against the corporation in case no new trustee or receiver is appointed.

§ 300. Employee's lien for wages when corporation insolvent.

Whenever any corporation of this State, or any foreign corporation doing business in this State, shall become insolvent, the employees doing labor or service of whatever character in the regular employ of the corporation, shall have a lien upon the assets thereof for the amount of the wages due to them, not exceeding 2 months' wages respectively, which shall be paid prior to any other debt or debts of the corporation. ▪ The word "employee" shall not be construed to include any of the officers of the corporation.

§ 301. Discontinuance of liquidation.

The liquidation of the assets and business of an insolvent corporation may be discontinued at any time during the liquidation proceedings when it is established that cause for liquidation no longer exists. ■ In such event the Court of Chancery in its discretion, and subject to such condition as it may deem appropriate, may dismiss the proceedings and direct the receiver or trustee to redeliver to the corporation all of its remaining property and assets.

§ 302. Compromise or arrangement between corporation and creditors or stockholders.

(a) Whenever the provision permitted by § 102(b)(2) of this title is included in the original certificate of incorporation of any corporation, all persons who become creditors or stockholders thereof shall be deemed to have become such creditors or stockholders subject in all respects to that provision and the same shall be absolutely binding upon them. ■ Whenever that provision is inserted in the certificate of incorporation of any such corporation by an amendment of its certificate all persons who become creditors or stockholders of such corporation after such amendment shall be deemed to have become such creditors or stockholders subject in all respects to that provision and the same shall be absolutely binding upon them.

(b) The Court of Chancery may administer and enforce any compromise or arrangement made pursuant to the provision contained in § 102(b)(2) of this title and may restrain, pendente lite, all actions and proceedings against any corporation with respect to which the Court shall have begun the administration and enforcement of that provision and may appoint a temporary receiver for such corporation and may grant the receiver such powers as it deems proper, and may make and enforce such rules as it deems necessary for the exercise of such jurisdiction.

§ 303. Proceeding under the Federal Bankruptcy Code of the United States; effectuation.

(a) Any corporation of this State, an order for relief with respect to which has been entered pursuant to the Federal Bankruptcy Code, 11 U.S.C. § 101 et seq., or any successor statute, may put into effect and carry out any decrees and orders of the court or judge in such bankruptcy proceeding and may take any corporate action provided or directed by such decrees and orders, without further action by its directors or stockholders. ■ Such power and authority may be exercised, and such corporate action may be taken, as may be directed by such decrees or orders, by the trustee or trustees of such corporation appointed or elected in the bankruptcy proceeding (or a majority thereof), or if none be appointed or elected and acting, by designated officers of the corporation, or by a representative appointed by the court or judge, with like effect as if exercised and taken by unanimous action of the directors and stockholders of the corporation.

(b) Such corporation may, in the manner provided in subsection (a) of this section, but without limiting the generality or effect of the foregoing, alter, amend or repeal its bylaws; constitute or reconstitute and classify or reclassify its board of directors, and name, constitute or appoint directors and officers in place of or in addition to all or some of the directors or officers then in office; amend its certificate of incorporation, and make any change in its capital or capital stock, or any other amendment, change, or alteration, or provision, authorized by this chapter; be dissolved, transfer all or part of its assets, merge or consolidate as permitted by this chapter, in which case, however, no stockholder shall have any statutory right of appraisal of such stockholder's stock; change the location of its registered office, change its registered agent, and remove or appoint any agent to receive service of process; authorize and fix the terms, manner and conditions of, the issuance of bonds, debentures or other obligations, whether or not convertible into stock of any class, or bearing warrants or other evidences of optional rights to purchase or subscribe for stock of any class; or lease its property and franchises to any corporation, if permitted by law.

(c) A certificate of any amendment, change or alteration, or of dissolution, or any agreement of merger or consolidation, made by such corporation pursuant to the foregoing provisions, shall be filed with the Secretary of State in accordance with § 103 of this title, and, subject to § 103(d) of this title, shall thereupon become effective in accordance with its terms and the provisions hereof. ■ Such certificate, agreement of merger or other instrument shall be made, executed and acknowledged, as may be directed by such decrees or orders, by the trustee or trustees appointed or elected in the bankruptcy proceeding (or a majority thereof), or, if none be appointed or elected and acting, by the officers of the corporation, or by a representative appointed by the court or judge, and shall certify that provision for the making of such certificate, agreement or instrument is contained in a decree or order of a court or judge having jurisdiction of a proceeding under such Federal Bankruptcy Code or successor statute.

(d) This section shall cease to apply to such corporation upon the entry of a final decree in the bankruptcy proceeding closing the case and discharging the trustee or trustees, if any; provided however, that the closing of a case and discharge of trustee or trustees, if any, will not affect the validity of any act previously performed pursuant to subsections (a) through (c) of this section.

(e) On filing any certificate, agreement, report or other paper made or executed pursuant to this section, there shall be paid to the Secretary of State for the use of the State the same fees as are payable by corporations not in bankruptcy upon the filing of like certificates, agreements, reports or other papers.

Subchapter XII. Renewal, Revival, Extension and Restoration of Certificate of Incorporation or Charter

§ 311. Revocation of voluntary dissolution; restoration of expired certificate of incorporation.

(a) At any time prior to the expiration of 3 years following the dissolution of a corporation pursuant to § 275 of this title or such longer period as the Court of Chancery may have directed pursuant to § 278 of this title, or at any time prior to the expiration of 3 years following the expiration of the time limited for the corporation's existence as provided in its certificate of incorporation or such longer period as the Court of Chancery may have directed pursuant to § 278 of this title, a corporation may revoke the dissolution theretofore effected by it or restore its certificate of incorporation after it has expired by its own limitation in the following manner:

(1) For purposes of this section, the term "stockholders" shall mean the stockholders of record on the date the dissolution became effective or the date of expiration by limitation.

(2) The board of directors shall adopt a resolution recommending that the dissolution be revoked in the case of a dissolution or that the certificate of incorporation be restored in the case of an expiration by limitation and directing that the question of the revocation or restoration be submitted to a vote at a special meeting of stockholders.

(3) Notice of the special meeting of stockholders shall be given in accordance with § 222 of this title to each of the stockholders.

(4) At the meeting a vote of the stockholders shall be taken on a resolution to revoke the dissolution in the case of a dissolution or to restore the certificate of incorporation in the case of an expiration by limitation. ■ If a majority of the stock of the corporation which was outstanding and entitled to vote upon a dissolution at the time of its dissolution , in the case of a revocation of dissolution, or which was outstanding and entitled to vote upon an amendment to the certificate of incorporation to change the period of the corporation's duration at the time of its expiration by limitation, in the case of a restoration, shall be voted for the resolution, a certificate of revocation of dissolution or a certificate of restoration shall be executed, acknowledged and filed in accordance with § 103 of this title, which shall be specifically designated as a certificate of revocation of dissolution or a certificate of restoration in its heading and shall state:

a. The name of the corporation;

b. The address (which shall be stated in accordance with § 131(c) of this title) of the corporation's registered office in this State, and the name of its registered agent at such address;

c. The names and respective addresses of its officers;

d. The names and respective addresses of its directors;

e. That a majority of the stock of the corporation which was outstanding and entitled to vote upon a dissolution at the time of its dissolution have voted in favor of a resolution to revoke the dissolution, in the case of a revocation of dissolution, or that a majority of the stock of the corporation which was outstanding and entitled to vote upon an amendment to the certificate of incorporation to change the period of the corporation's duration at the time of its expiration by limitation, in the case of a restoration, have voted in favor of a resolution to restore the certificate of incorporation; or, if it be the fact, that, in lieu of a meeting and vote of stockholders, the stockholders have given their written consent to the revocation or restoration in accordance with § 228 of this title; and

f. In the case of a restoration, the new specified date limiting the duration of the corporation's existence or that the corporation shall have perpetual existence.

(b) Upon the effective time of the filing in the office of the Secretary of State of the certificate of revocation of dissolution or the certificate of restoration, the revocation of the dissolution or the restoration of the corporation shall become effective and the corporation may again carry on its business.

(c) Upon the effectiveness of the revocation of the dissolution or the restoration of the corporation as provided in subsection (b) of this section, the provisions of § 211(c) of this title shall govern, and the period of time the corporation was in dissolution or was expired by limitation shall be included within the calculation of the 30-day and 13-month periods to which § 211(c) of this title refers. ■ An election of directors, however, may be held at the special meeting of stockholders to which subsection (a) of this section refers, and in that event, that meeting of stockholders shall be deemed an annual meeting of stockholders for purposes of § 211(c) of this title.

(d) If after the dissolution became effective or after the expiration by limitation any other corporation organized under the laws of this State shall have adopted the same name as the corporation, or shall have adopted a name so nearly similar thereto as not to distinguish it from the corporation, or any foreign corporation shall have qualified to do business in this State under the same name as the corporation or under a name so nearly similar thereto as not to distinguish it from the corporation, then, in such case, the corporation shall not be reinstated under the same name which it bore when its dissolution became effective or it expired by limitation, but shall adopt and be reinstated or restored under some other name, and in such case the certificate to be filed under this section shall set forth the name borne by the corporation at the time its dissolution became effective or it expired by limitation and the new name under which the corporation is to be reinstated or restored.

(e) Nothing in this section shall be construed to affect the jurisdiction or power of the Court of Chancery under § 279 or § 280 of this title.

(f) At any time prior to the expiration of 3 years following the dissolution of a nonstock corporation pursuant to § 276 of this title or such longer period as the Court of Chancery may have directed pursuant to § 278 of this title, or at any time prior to the expiration of 3 years following the expiration of the time limited for a nonstock corporation's existence as provided in its certificate of incorporation or such longer period as the Court of Chancery may have directed pursuant to § 278 of this title, a nonstock corporation may revoke the dissolution theretofore effected by it or restore its certificate of incorporation after it has expired by limitation in a manner analogous to that by which the dissolution was authorized or, in the case of a restoration, in the manner in which an amendment to the certificate of incorporation to change the period of the corporation's duration would have been authorized at the time of its expiration by limitation including **(i)** if applicable, a vote of the members entitled to vote, if any, on the dissolution or the amendment and **(ii)** the filing of a certificate of revocation of dissolution or a certificate of restoration containing information comparable to that required by paragraph (a)(4) of this section. ▪ Notwithstanding the foregoing, only subsections (b), (d), and (e) of this section shall apply to nonstock corporations.

(g) Any corporation that revokes its dissolution or restores its certificate of incorporation pursuant to this section shall file all annual franchise tax reports that the corporation would have had to file if it had not dissolved or expired and shall pay all franchise taxes that the corporation would have had to pay if it had not dissolved or expired. ▪ No payment made pursuant to this subsection shall reduce the amount of franchise tax due under Chapter 5 of this title for the year in which such revocation or restoration is effected.

§ 312. Revival of certificate of incorporation.

(a) As used in this section, the term "certificate of incorporation" includes the charter of a corporation organized under any special act or any law of this State.

(b) Any corporation whose certificate of incorporation has become forfeited or void pursuant to this title or whose certificate of incorporation has been revived, but, through failure to comply strictly with the provisions of this chapter, the validity of whose revival has been brought into question, may at any time procure a revival of its certificate of incorporation, together with all the rights, franchises, privileges and immunities and subject to all of its duties, debts and liabilities which had been secured or imposed by its original certificate of in-

corporation and all amendments thereto, by complying with the requirements of this section. ▪ Notwithstanding the foregoing, this section shall not be applicable to a corporation whose certificate of incorporation has been revoked or forfeited pursuant to § 284 of this title.

(c) The revival of the certificate of incorporation may be procured as authorized by the board of directors or members of the governing body of the corporation in accordance with subsection(h) of this section and by executing, acknowledging and filing a certificate of revival in accordance with § 103 of this title.

(d) The certificate required by subsection (c) of this section shall state:

(1) The date of filing of the corporation's original certificate of incorporation; the name under which the corporation was originally incorporated; the name of the corporation at the time its certificate of incorporation became forfeited or void pursuant to this title; and the new name under which the corporation is to be revived to the extent required by subsection (f) of this section;

(2) The address (which shall be stated in accordance with § 131(c) of this title) of the corporation's registered office in this State and the name of its registered agent at such address;

(3) That the corporation desiring to be revived and so reviving its certificate of incorporation was organized under the laws of this State;

(4) The date when the certificate of incorporation became forfeited or void pursuant to this title, or that the validity of any revival has been brought into question; and

(5) That the certificate of revival is filed by authority of the board of directors or members of the governing body of the corporation in accordance with subsection (h) of this section.

(e) Upon the filing of the certificate in accordance with § 103 of this title the corporation shall be revived with the same force and effect as if its certificate of incorporation had not been forfeited or void pursuant to this title. ▪ Such revival shall validate all contracts, acts, matters and things made, done and performed within the scope of its certificate of incorporation by the corporation, its directors or members of its governing body, officers, agents and stockholders or members during the time when its certificate of incorporation was forfeited or void pursuant to this title, with the same force and effect and to all intents and purposes as if the certificate of incorporation had at all times remained in full force and effect. ▪ All real and personal property, rights and credits, which belonged to the corporation at the time its certificate of incorporation became forfeited or void pursuant to this title and which were not disposed of prior to the time of its revival, and all real and personal property, rights and credits acquired by the corporation after its certificate of incorporation became forfeited or void pursuant to this title shall be vested in the corporation, after its revival, as if its certificate of incorporation had at all times remained in full force and effect, and the corporation after its revival shall be as exclusively liable for all contracts, acts, matters and things made, done or performed in its name and on its behalf by its directors or members of its governing body, officers, agents and stockholders or members prior to its revival, as if its certificate of incorporation had at all times remained in full force and effect.

(f) If, since the certificate of incorporation became forfeited or void pursuant to this title, any other corporation organized under the laws of this State shall have adopted the same name as the corporation sought to be revived or shall have adopted a name so nearly similar thereto as not to distinguish it from the corporation to be revived or any foreign corporation qualified in accordance with § 371 of this title shall have adopted the same name as the corporation sought to be revived or shall have adopted a name so nearly similar thereto as not to distinguish it from the corporation to be revived, then in such case the corporation to be revived shall not be revived under the same name which it bore when its certificate of incorporation became forfeited or void pursuant to this title, but shall be revived under some other name as set forth in the certificate to be filed pursuant to subsection (c) of this section.

(g) Any corporation that revives its certificate of incorporation under this chapter shall pay to this State a sum equal to all franchise taxes, penalties and interest thereon due at the time its certificate of incorporation became forfeited or void pursuant to this title; provided, however, that any corporation that revives its certificate of incorporation under this chapter whose certificate of incorporation has been forfeited or void for more than 5 years shall, in lieu of the payment of the franchise taxes and penalties otherwise required by this subsection, pay a sum equal to 3 times the amount of the annual franchise tax that would be due and payable by such corporation for the year in which the revival is effected, computed at the then current rate of taxation. ▪ No payment made pursuant to this subsection shall reduce the amount of franchise tax due under Chapter 5 of this title for the year in which the revival is effected.

(h) For purposes of this section and § 502(a) of this title, the board of directors or governing body of the corporation shall be comprised of the persons, who, but for the certificate of incorporation having become forfeited or void pursuant to this title, would be the duly elected or appointed directors or members of the governing body of the corporation. ▪ The requirement for authorization by the board of directors under subsection (c) of this section shall be satisfied if a majority of the directors or members of the governing body then in office, even though less than a quorum, or the sole director or member of the governing body then in office, authorizes the revival of the certificate of incorporation of the corporation and the filing of the certificate required by subsection (c) of this section. ▪ In any case where there shall be no directors of the corporation available for the purposes aforesaid, the stockholders may elect a full board of directors, as provided by the bylaws of the corporation, and the board so elected may then authorize the revival of the certificate of incorporation of the corporation and the filing of the certificate required by subsection (c) of this section.

■ A special meeting of the stockholders for the purpose of electing directors may be called by any officer or stockholder upon notice given in accordance with § 222 of this title. ■ For purposes of this section, the bylaws shall be the bylaws of the corporation that, but for the certificate of incorporation having become forfeited or void pursuant to this title, would be the duly adopted bylaws of the corporation.

(i) After a revival of the certificate of incorporation of the corporation shall have been effected, the provisions of § 211(c) of this title shall govern and the period of time during which the certificate of incorporation of the corporation was forfeited or void pursuant to this title shall be included within the calculation of the 30-day and 13-month periods to which § 211(c) of this title refers. ■ A special meeting of stockholders held in accordance with subsection (h) of this section shall be deemed an annual meeting of stockholders for purposes of § 211(c) of this title.

(j) Except as otherwise provided in § 313 of this title, whenever it shall be desired to revive the certificate of incorporation of any nonstock corporation, the governing body shall perform all the acts necessary for the revival of the certificate of incorporation of the corporation which are performed by the board of directors in the case of a corporation having capital stock, and the members of any nonstock corporation who are entitled to vote for the election of members of its governing body and any other members entitled to vote for dissolution under the certificate of incorporation or the bylaws of such corporation, shall perform all the acts necessary for the revival of the certificate of incorporation of the corporation which are performed by the stockholders in the case of a corporation having capital stock. ■ Except as otherwise provided in § 313 of this title, in all other respects, the procedure for the revival of the certificate of incorporation of a nonstock corporation shall conform, as nearly as may be applicable, to the procedure prescribed in this section for the revival of the certificate of incorporation of a corporation having capital stock; provided, however, that subsection (i) of

this section shall not apply to nonstock corporations.

§ 313. Revival of certificate of incorporation or charter of exempt corporations.

(a) Every exempt corporation whose certificate of incorporation or charter has become forfeited, pursuant to § 136 (b) of this title for failure to obtain a registered agent, or inoperative and void, by operation of § 510 of this title for failure to file annual franchise tax reports required, and for failure to pay taxes or penalties from which it would have been exempt if the reports had been filed, shall be deemed to have filed all the reports and be relieved of all the taxes and penalties, upon satisfactory proof submitted to the Secretary of State of its right to be classified as an exempt corporation pursuant to § 501(b) of this title, and upon filing with the Secretary of State a certificate of revival in manner and form as required by § 312 of this title.

(b) Upon the filing by the corporation of the proof of classification as required by subsection (a) of this section, the filing of the certificate of revival and payment of the required filing fees, the corporation shall be revived with the same force and effect as provided in § 312(e) of this title for other corporations.

(c) As used in this section, the term "exempt corporation" shall have the meaning given to it in § 501(b) of this title. ■ Nothing contained in this section relieves any exempt corporation from filing the annual report required by § 502 of this title.

§ 314. Status of corporation.

Any corporation desiring to renew, extend and continue its corporate existence shall, upon complying with applicable constitutional provisions of this State, continue as provided in its certificate effecting the foregoing as a corporation and shall, in addition to the rights, privileges and immunities conferred by its charter, possess and enjoy all the benefits of this chapter, which are applicable to the nature of its business, and shall be subject to the restrictions and liabilities by this chapter imposed on such corporations.

Subchapter XIII. Suits Against Corporations, Directors, Officers or Stockholders

§ 321. Service of process on corporations.

(a) Service of legal process upon any corporation of this State shall be made by delivering a copy personally to any officer or director of the corporation in this State, or the registered agent of the corporation in this State, or by leaving it at the dwelling house or usual place of abode in this State of any officer, director or registered agent (if the registered agent be an individual), or at the registered office or other place of business of the corporation in this State. ■ If the registered agent be a corporation, service of process upon it as such agent may be made by serving, in this State, a copy thereof on the president, vice-president, secretary, assistant secretary or any director of the corporate registered agent. ■ Service by copy left at the dwelling house or usual place of abode of any officer, director or registered agent, or at the registered office or other place of business of the corporation in this State, to be effective must be delivered thereat at least 6 days before the return date of the process, and in the presence of an adult person, and the officer serving the process shall distinctly state the manner of service in such person's return thereto. ■ Process returnable forthwith must be delivered personally to the officer, director or registered agent.

(b) In case the officer whose duty it is to serve legal process cannot by due diligence serve the process in any manner provided for by subsection (a) of this section, it shall be lawful to serve the process against the corporation upon the Secretary of State, and such service shall be as effectual for all intents and purposes as if made in any of the ways provided for in subsection (a) of this section. ■ Process may be served upon the Secretary of State under this subsection by means of electronic transmission but only as prescribed by the Secretary of State. ■ The Secretary of State is authorized to issue such rules and regulations with respect to such service as the Secretary of State deems necessary or appropriate. ■ In the event that service is effected through the Secretary of State in accordance with this subsection, the Secretary of State shall forthwith notify the corporation by letter, directed to the corporation at its principal place of business as it appears on the records relating to such corporation on file with the Secretary of State or, if no such address appears, at its last registered office. ■ Such letter shall be sent by a mail or courier service that includes a record of mailing or deposit with the courier and a record of delivery evidenced by the signature of the recipient. ■ Such letter shall enclose a copy of the process and any other papers served on the Secretary of State pursuant to this subsection. ■ It shall be the duty of the plaintiff in the event of such service to serve process and any other papers in duplicate, to notify the Secretary of State that service is being effected pursuant to this subsection, and to pay the Secretary of State the sum of $50 for the use of the State, which sum shall be taxed as part of the costs in the proceeding if the plaintiff shall prevail therein. ■ The Secretary of State shall maintain an alphabetical record of any such service setting forth the name of the plaintiff and defendant, the title, docket number and nature of the proceeding in which process has been served upon the Secretary of State, the fact that service has been effected pursuant to this subsection, the return date thereof, and the day and hour when the service was made. ■ The Secretary of State shall not be required to retain such information for a period longer than 5 years from receipt of the service of process.

(c) Service upon corporations may also be made in accordance with § 3111 of Title 10 or any other statute or rule of court.

§ 322. Failure of corporation to obey order of court; appointment of receiver.

Whenever any corporation shall refuse, fail or neglect to obey any order or decree of any court of this State within the time fixed by the court for its observance, such refusal, failure or neglect shall be a sufficient ground for the appointment of a receiver of the corporation by the Court of Chancery. ■ If the corporation be a foreign corporation, such refusal, failure or neglect shall be a sufficient ground for the appointment of a receiver of the assets of the corporation within this State.

§ 323. Failure of corporation to obey writ of mandamus; quo warranto proceedings for forfeiture of charter.

If any corporation fails to obey the mandate of any peremptory writ of mandamus issued by a court of competent jurisdiction of this State for a period of 30 days after the serving of the writ upon the corporation in any manner as provided by the laws of this State for the service of writs, any party in interest in the proceeding in which the writ of mandamus issued may file a statement of such fact prepared by such party or such party's attorney with the Attorney General of this State, and it shall thereupon be the duty of the Attorney General to forthwith commence proceedings of quo warranto against the corporation in a court of competent jurisdiction, and the court, upon competent proof of such state of facts and proper proceedings had in such proceeding in quo warranto, shall decree the charter of the corporation forfeited.

§ 324. Attachment of shares of stock or any option, right or interest therein; procedure; sale; title upon sale; proceeds.

(a) The shares of any person in any corporation with all the rights thereto belonging, or any person's option to acquire the shares, or such person's right or interest in the shares, may be attached under this section for debt, or other demands, if such person appears on the books of the corporation to hold or own such shares, option, right or interest. ▪ So many of the shares, or so much of the option, right or interest therein may be sold at public sale to the highest bidder, as shall be sufficient to satisfy the debt, or other demand, interest and costs, upon an order issued therefor by the court from which the attachment process issued, and after such notice as is required for sales upon execution process. ▪ Except as to an uncertificated security as defined in § 8-102 of Title 6, the attachment is not laid and no order of sale shall issue unless § 8-112 of Title 6 has been satisfied. ▪ No order of sale shall be issued until after final judgment shall have been rendered in any case. ▪ If the debtor lives out

of the county, a copy of the order shall be sent by registered or certified mail, return receipt requested, to such debtor's last known address, and shall also be published in a newspaper published in the county of such debtor's last known residence, if there be any, 10 days before the sale; and if the debtor be a nonresident of this State shall be mailed as aforesaid and published at least twice for 2 successive weeks, the last publication to be at least 10 days before the sale, in a newspaper published in the county where the attachment process issued. ▪ If the shares of stock or any of them or the option to acquire shares or any such right or interest in shares, or any part of them, be so sold, any assignment, or transfer thereof, by the debtor, after attachment, shall be void.

(b) When attachment process issues for shares of stock, or any option to acquire such or any right or interest in such, a certified copy of the process shall be left in this State with any officer or director, or with the registered agent of the corporation. ▪ Within 20 days after service of the process, the corporation shall serve upon the plaintiff a certificate of the number of shares held or owned by the debtor in the corporation, with the number or other marks distinguishing the same, or in the case the debtor appears on the books of the corporation to have an option to acquire shares of stock or any right or interest in any shares of stock of the corporation, there shall be served upon the plaintiff within 20 days after service of the process a certificate setting forth any such option, right or interest in the shares of the corporation in the language and form in which the option, right or interest appears on the books of the corporation, anything in the certificate of incorporation or bylaws of the corporation to the contrary notwithstanding. ▪ Service upon a corporate registered agent may be made in the manner provided in § 321 of this title.

(c) If, after sale made and confirmed, a certified copy of the order of sale and return and the stock certificate, if any, be left with any officer or director or with the registered agent of the corporation, the purchaser shall be thereby entitled to the shares or any option to acquire shares or any right or interest in shares so purchased, and all income, or dividends which may have been declared, or become payable thereon since the attachment laid. ▪ Such sale, returned and confirmed, shall transfer the shares or the option to acquire shares or any right or interest in shares sold to the purchaser, as fully as if the debtor, or defendant, had transferred the same to such purchaser according to the certificate of incorporation or bylaws of the corporation, anything in the certificate of incorporation or bylaws to the contrary notwithstanding. ▪ The court which issued the levy and confirmed the sale shall have the power to make an order compelling the corporation, the shares of which were sold, to issue new certificates or uncertificated shares to the purchaser at the sale and to cancel the registration of the shares attached on the books of the corporation upon the giving of an open end bond by such purchaser adequate to protect such corporation.

(d) The money arising from the sale of the shares or from the sale of the option or right or interest shall be applied and paid, by the public official receiving the same, as by law is directed as to the sale of personal property in cases of attachment.

§ 325. Actions against officers, directors or stockholders to enforce liability of corporation; unsatisfied judgment against corporation.

(a) When the officers, directors or stockholders of any corporation shall be liable by the provisions of this chapter to pay the debts of the corporation, or any part thereof, any person to whom they are liable may have an action, at law or in equity, against any 1 or more of them, and the complaint shall state the claim against the corporation, and the ground on which the plaintiff expects to charge the defendants personally.

(b) No suit shall be brought against any officer, director or stockholder for any debt of a corporation of which such person is an officer, director or stockholder, until judgment be obtained therefor against the corporation and execution thereon returned unsatisfied.

§ 326. Action by officer, director or stockholder against corporation for corporate debt paid.

When any officer, director or stockholder shall pay any debt of a corporation for which such person is made liable by the provisions of this chapter, such person may recover the amount so paid in an action against the corporation for money paid for its use, and in such action only the property of the corporation shall be liable to be taken, and not the property of any stockholder.

§ 327. Stockholder's derivative action; allegation of stock ownership.

In any derivative suit instituted by a stockholder of a corporation, it shall be averred in the complaint that the plaintiff was a stockholder of the corporation at the time of the transaction of which such stockholder complains or that such stockholder's stock thereafter devolved upon such stockholder by operation of law.

§ 328. Effect of liability of corporation on impairment of certain transactions.

The liability of a corporation of this State, or the stockholders, directors or officers thereof, or the rights or remedies of the creditors thereof, or of persons doing or transacting business with the corporation, shall not in any way be lessened or impaired by the sale of its assets, or by the increase or decrease in the capital stock of the corporation, or by its merger or consolidation with 1 or more corporations or by any change or amendment in its certificate of incorporation.

§ 329. Defective organization of corporation as defense.

(a) No corporation of this State and no person sued by any such corporation shall be permitted to assert the want of legal organization as a defense to any claim.

(b) This section shall not be construed to prevent judicial inquiry into the regularity or validity of the organization of a corporation, or its lawful possession of any corporate power it may assert in any other suit or proceeding where its corporate existence or the power to exercise the corporate rights it asserts is challenged, and evidence tending to sustain the challenge shall be admissible in any such suit or proceeding.

§ 330. Usury; pleading by corporation.

No corporation shall plead any statute against usury in any court of law or equity in any suit instituted to enforce the payment of any bond, note or other evidence of indebtedness issued or assumed by it.

Subchapter XIV. Close Corporations; Special Provisions

§ 341. Law applicable to close corporation.

(a) This subchapter applies to all close corporations, as defined in § 342 of this title. ▪ Unless a corporation elects to become a close corporation under this subchapter in the manner prescribed in this subchapter, it shall be subject in all respects to this chapter, except this subchapter.

(b) This chapter shall be applicable to all close corporations, as defined in § 342 of this title, except insofar as this subchapter otherwise provides.

§ 342. Close corporation defined; contents of certificate of incorporation.

(a) A close corporation is a corporation organized under this chapter whose certificate of incorporation contains the provisions required by § 102 of this title and, in addition, provides that:

(1) All of the corporation's issued stock of all classes, exclusive of treasury shares, shall be represented by certificates and shall be held of record by not more than a specified number of persons, not exceeding 30; and

(2) All of the issued stock of all classes shall be subject to 1 or more of the restrictions on transfer permitted by § 202 of this title; and

(3) The corporation shall make no offering of any of its stock of any class which would constitute a "public offering" within the meaning of the United States Securities Act of 1933 [15 U.S.C. § 77a et seq.] as it may be amended from time to time.

(b) The certificate of incorporation of a close corporation may set forth the qualifications of stockholders, either by specifying classes of persons who shall be entitled to be holders of record of stock of any class, or by specifying classes of persons who shall not be entitled to be holders of stock of any class or both.

(c) For purposes of determining the number of holders of record of the stock of a close corporation, stock which is held in joint or common tenancy or by the entireties shall be treated as held by 1 stockholder.

§ 343. Formation of a close corporation.

A close corporation shall be formed in accordance with §§ 101, 102 and 103 of this title, except that:

(1) Its certificate of incorporation shall contain a heading stating the name of the corporation and that it is a close corporation; and

(2) Its certificate of incorporation shall contain the provisions required by § 342 of this title.

§ 344. Election of existing corporation to become a close corporation.

Any corporation organized under this chapter may become a close corporation under this subchapter by executing, acknowledging and filing, in accordance with § 103 of this title, a certificate of amendment of its certificate of incorporation which shall contain a statement that it elects to become a close corporation, the provisions required by § 342 of this title to appear in the certificate of incorporation of a close corporation, and a heading stating the name of the corporation and that it is a close corporation. ▪ Such amendment shall be adopted in accordance with the requirements of § 241 or 242 of this title, except that it must be approved by a vote of the holders of record of at least 2/3 of the shares of each class of stock of the corporation which are outstanding.

§ 345. Limitations on continuation of close corporation status.

A close corporation continues to be such and to be subject to this subchapter until:

(1) It files with the Secretary of State a certificate of amendment deleting from its certificate of incorporation the provisions required or permitted by § 342 of this title to be stated in the certificate of incorporation to qualify it as a close corporation; or

(2) Any 1 of the provisions or conditions required or permitted by § 342 of this title to be stated in a certificate of incorporation to qualify a corporation as a close corporation has in fact been breached and neither the corporation nor any of its stockholders takes the steps required by § 348 of this title to prevent such loss of status or to remedy such breach.

§ 346. Voluntary termination of close corporation status by amendment of certificate of incorporation; vote required.

(a) A corporation may voluntarily terminate its status as a close corporation and cease to be subject to this subchapter by amending its certificate of incorporation to delete therefrom the additional provisions required or permitted by § 342 of this title to be stated in the certificate of incorporation of a close corporation. ■ Any such amendment shall be adopted and shall become effective in accordance with § 242 of this title, except that it must be approved by a vote of the holders of record of at least 2/3 of the shares of each class of stock of the corporation which are outstanding.

(b) The certificate of incorporation of a close corporation may provide that on any amendment to terminate its status as a close corporation, a vote greater than 2/3 or a vote of all shares of any class shall be required; and if the certificate of incorporation contains such a provision, that provision shall not be amended, repealed or modified by any vote less than that required to terminate the corporation's status as a close corporation.

§ 347. Issuance or transfer of stock of a close corporation in breach of qualifying conditions.

(a) If stock of a close corporation is issued or transferred to any person who is not entitled under any provision of the certificate of incorporation permitted by § 342(b) of this title to be a holder of record of stock of such corporation, and if the certificate for such stock conspicuously notes the qualifications of the persons entitled to be holders of record thereof, such person is conclusively presumed to have notice of the fact of such person's ineligibility to be a stockholder.

(b) If the certificate of incorporation of a close corporation states the number of persons, not in excess of 30, who are entitled to be holders of record of its stock, and if the certificate for such stock conspicuously states such number, and if the issuance or transfer of stock to any person would cause the stock to be held by more than such number of persons, the person to whom such stock is issued or transferred is conclusively presumed to have notice of this fact.

(c) If a stock certificate of any close corporation conspicuously notes the fact of a restriction on transfer of stock of the corporation, and the restriction is one which is permitted by § 202 of this title, the transferee of the stock is conclusively presumed to have notice of the fact that such person has acquired stock in violation of the restriction, if such acquisition violates the restriction.

(d) Whenever any person to whom stock of a close corporation has been issued or transferred has, or is conclusively presumed under this section to have, notice either:

(1) That such person is a person not eligible to be a holder of stock of the corporation, or

(2) That transfer of stock to such person would cause the stock of the corporation to be held by more than the number of persons permitted by its certificate of incorporation to hold stock of the corporation, or

(3) That the transfer of stock is in violation of a restriction on transfer of stock,

the corporation may, at its option, refuse to register transfer of the stock into the name of the transferee.

(e) Subsection (d) of this section shall not be applicable if the transfer of stock, even though otherwise contrary to subsection (a), (b) or (c) of this section has been consented to by all the stockholders of the close corporation, or if the close corporation has amended its certificate of incorporation in accordance with § 346 of this title.

(f) The term "transfer," as used in this section, is not limited to a transfer for value.

(g) The provisions of this section do not in any way impair any rights of a transferee regarding any right to rescind the transaction or to recover under any applicable warranty express or implied.

§ 348. Involuntary termination of close corporation status; proceeding to prevent loss of status.

(a) If any event occurs as a result of which 1 or more of the provisions or conditions included in a close corporation's certificate of incorporation pursuant to § 342 of this title to qualify it as a close corporation has been breached, the corporation's status as a close corporation under this subchapter shall terminate unless:

　(1) Within 30 days after the occurrence of the event, or within 30 days after the event has been discovered, whichever is later, the corporation files with the Secretary of State a certificate, executed and acknowledged in accordance with § 103 of this title, stating that a specified provision or condition included in its certificate of incorporation pursuant to § 342 of this title to qualify it as a close corporation has ceased to be applicable, and furnishes a copy of such certificate to each stockholder; and

　(2) The corporation concurrently with the filing of such certificate takes such steps as are necessary to correct the situation which threatens its status as a close corporation, including, without limitation, the refusal to register the transfer of stock which has been wrongfully transferred as provided by § 347 of this title, or a proceeding under subsection (b) of this section.

(b) The Court of Chancery, upon the suit of the corporation or any stockholder, shall have jurisdiction to issue all orders necessary to prevent the corporation from losing its status as a close corporation, or to restore its status as a close corporation by enjoining or setting aside any act or threatened act on the part of the corporation or a stockholder which would be inconsistent with any of the provisions or conditions required or permitted by § 342 of this title to be stated in the certificate of incorporation of a close corporation, unless it is an act approved in accordance with § 346 of this title. ■ The Court of Chancery may enjoin or set aside any transfer or threatened transfer of stock of a close corporation which is contrary to the terms of its certificate of incorporation or of any transfer restriction permitted by § 202 of this title, and may enjoin any public offering, as defined in § 342 of this title, or threatened public offering of stock of the close corporation.

§ 349. Corporate option where a restriction on transfer of a security is held invalid.

If a restriction on transfer of a security of a close corporation is held not to be authorized by § 202 of this title, the corporation shall nevertheless have an option, for a period of 30 days after the judgment setting aside the restriction becomes final, to acquire the restricted security at a price which is agreed upon by the parties, or if no agreement is reached as to price, then at the fair value as determined by the Court of Chancery. ■ In order to determine fair value, the Court may appoint an appraiser to receive evidence and report to the Court such appraiser's findings and recommendation as to fair value.

§ 350. Agreements restricting discretion of directors.

A written agreement among the stockholders of a close corporation holding a majority of the outstanding stock entitled to vote, whether solely among themselves or with a party not a stockholder, is not invalid, as between the parties to the agreement, on the ground that it so relates to the conduct of the business and affairs of the corporation as to restrict or interfere with the discretion or powers of the board of directors. ■ The effect of any such agreement shall be to relieve the directors and impose upon the stockholders who are parties to the agreement the liability for managerial acts or omissions which is imposed on directors to the extent and so long as the discretion or powers of the board in its management of corporate affairs is controlled by such agreement.

§ 351. Management by stockholders.

The certificate of incorporation of a close corporation may provide that the business of the corporation shall be managed by the stockholders of the corporation rather than by a board of directors. ▪ So long as this provision continues in effect:

(1) No meeting of stockholders need be called to elect directors;

(2) Unless the context clearly requires otherwise, the stockholders of the corporation shall be deemed to be directors for purposes of applying provisions of this chapter; and

(3) The stockholders of the corporation shall be subject to all liabilities of directors.

Such a provision may be inserted in the certificate of incorporation by amendment if all incorporators and subscribers or all holders of record of all of the outstanding stock, whether or not having voting power, authorize such a provision. ▪ An amendment to the certificate of incorporation to delete such a provision shall be adopted by a vote of the holders of a majority of all outstanding stock of the corporation, whether or not otherwise entitled to vote. ▪ If the certificate of incorporation contains a provision authorized by this section, the existence of such provision shall be noted conspicuously on the face or back of every stock certificate issued by such corporation.

§ 352. Appointment of custodian for close corporation.

(a) In addition to § 226 of this title respecting the appointment of a custodian for any corporation, the Court of Chancery, upon application of any stockholder, may appoint 1 or more persons to be custodians, and, if the corporation is insolvent, to be receivers, of any close corporation when:

(1) Pursuant to § 351 of this title the business and affairs of the corporation are managed by the stockholders and they are so divided that the business of the corporation is suffering or is threatened with irreparable injury and any remedy with respect to such deadlock provided in the certificate of incorporation or bylaws or in

any written agreement of the stockholders has failed; or

(2) The petitioning stockholder has the right to the dissolution of the corporation under a provision of the certificate of incorporation permitted by § 355 of this title.

(b) In lieu of appointing a custodian for a close corporation under this section or § 226 of this title the Court of Chancery may appoint a provisional director, whose powers and status shall be as provided in § 353 of this title if the Court determines that it would be in the best interest of the corporation. ▪ Such appointment shall not preclude any subsequent order of the Court appointing a custodian for such corporation.

§ 353. Appointment of a provisional director in certain cases.

(a) Notwithstanding any contrary provision of the certificate of incorporation or the bylaws or agreement of the stockholders, the Court of Chancery may appoint a provisional director for a close corporation if the directors are so divided respecting the management of the corporation's business and affairs that the votes required for action by the board of directors cannot be obtained with the consequence that the business and affairs of the corporation can no longer be conducted to the advantage of the stockholders generally.

(b) An application for relief under this section must be filed (1) by at least one half of the number of directors then in office, (2) by the holders of at least one third of all stock then entitled to elect directors, or, (3) if there be more than 1 class of stock then entitled to elect 1 or more directors, by the holders of two thirds of the stock of any such class; but the certificate of incorporation of a close corporation may provide that a lesser proportion of the directors or of the stockholders or of a class of stockholders may apply for relief under this section.

(c) A provisional director shall be an impartial person who is neither a stockholder nor a creditor of the corporation or of any subsidiary or affiliate of the corporation, and whose further qualifications, if any, may be determined by the Court of Chancery. ■ A provisional director is not a receiver of the corporation and does not have the title and powers of a custodian or receiver appointed under §§ 226 and 291 of this title. ■ A provisional director shall have all the rights and powers of a duly elected director of the corporation, including the right to notice of and to vote at meetings of directors, until such time as such person shall be removed by order of the Court of Chancery or by the holders of a majority of all shares then entitled to vote to elect directors or by the holders of two thirds of the shares of that class of voting shares which filed the application for appointment of a provisional director. ■ A provisional director's compensation shall be determined by agreement between such person and the corporation subject to approval of the Court of Chancery, which may fix such person's compensation in the absence of agreement or in the event of disagreement between the provisional director and the corporation.

(d) Even though the requirements of subsection (b) of this section relating to the number of directors or stockholders who may petition for appointment of a provisional director are not satisfied, the Court of Chancery may nevertheless appoint a provisional director if permitted by § 352(b) of this title.

§ 354. Operating corporation as partnership.

No written agreement among stockholders of a close corporation, nor any provision of the certificate of incorporation or of the bylaws of the corporation, which agreement or provision relates to any phase of the affairs of such corporation, including but not limited to the management of its business or declaration and payment of dividends or other division of profits or the election of directors or officers or the employment of stockholders by the corporation or the arbitration of disputes, shall be invalid on the ground that it is an attempt by the parties to the agreement or by the stockholders of the corporation to treat the corporation as if it were a partnership or to arrange relations among the stockholders or between the stockholders and the corporation in a manner that would be appropriate only among partners.

§ 355. Stockholders' option to dissolve corporation.

(a) The certificate of incorporation of any close corporation may include a provision granting to any stockholder, or to the holders of any specified number or percentage of shares of any class of stock, an option to have the corporation dissolved at will or upon the occurrence of any specified event or contingency. ■ Whenever any such option to dissolve is exercised, the stockholders exercising such option shall give written notice thereof to all other stockholders. ■ After the expiration of 30 days following the sending of such notice, the dissolution of the corporation shall proceed as if the required number of stockholders having voting power had consented in writing to dissolution of the corporation as provided by § 228 of this title.

(b) If the certificate of incorporation as originally filed does not contain a provision authorized by subsection (a) of this section, the certificate may be amended to include such provision if adopted by the affirmative vote of the holders of all the outstanding stock, whether or not entitled to vote, unless the certificate of incorporation specifically authorizes such an amendment by a vote which shall be not less than 2/3 of all the outstanding stock whether or not entitled to vote.

(c) Each stock certificate in any corporation whose certificate of incorporation authorizes dissolution as permitted by this section shall conspicuously note on the face thereof the existence of the provision. ■ Unless noted conspicuously on the face of the stock certificate, the provision is ineffective.

§ 356. Effect of this subchapter on other laws.

This subchapter shall not be deemed to repeal any statute or rule of law which is or would be applicable to any corporation which is organized under this chapter but is not a close corporation.

Subchapter XV. Public Benefit Corporations

§ 361. Law applicable to public benefit corporations; how formed.

This subchapter applies to all public benefit corporations, as defined in §362 of this title. ▪ If a corporation elects to become a public benefit corporation under this subchapter in the manner prescribed in this subchapter, it shall be subject in all respects to the provisions of this chapter, except to the extent this subchapter imposes additional or different requirements, in which case such requirements shall apply.

§ 362. Public benefit corporation defined; contents of certificate of incorporation.

(a) A "public benefit corporation" is a for-profit corporation organized under and subject to the requirements of this chapter that is intended to produce a public benefit or public benefits and to operate in a responsible and sustainable manner. ▪ To that end, a public benefit corporation shall be managed in a manner that balances the stockholders' pecuniary interests, the best interests of those materially affected by the corporation's conduct, and the public benefit or public benefits identified in its certificate of incorporation. ▪ In the certificate of incorporation, a public benefit corporation shall:

> **(1)** Identify within its statement of business or purpose pursuant to §102(a)(3) of this title one or more specific public benefits to be promoted by the corporation; and

> **(2)** State within its heading that it is a public benefit corporation.

(b) "Public benefit" means a positive effect (or reduction of negative effects) on 1 or more categories of persons, entities, communities or interests (other than stockholders in their capacities as stockholders) including, but not limited to, effects of an artistic, charitable, cultural, economic, educational, environmental, literary, medical, religious, scientific or technological nature. ▪ "Public benefit provisions" means the provisions of a certificate of incorporation contemplated by this subchapter.

(c) The name of the public benefit corporation may contain the words "public benefit corporation," or the abbreviation "P.B.C.," or the designation "PBC," which shall be deemed to satisfy the requirements of §102(a)(l)(i) of this title. ▪ If the name does not contain such language, the corporation shall, prior to issuing unissued shares of stock or disposing of treasury shares, provide notice to any person to whom such stock is issued or who acquires such treasury shares that it is a public benefit corporation; provided that such notice need not be provided if the issuance or disposal is pursuant to an offering registered under the Securities Act of 1933 [15 U.S.C. § 77r et seq.] or if, at the time of issuance or disposal, the corporation has a class of securities that is registered under the Securities Exchange Act of 1934 [15 U.S.C. § 78a et seq.].

§ 363. Nonprofit nonstock corporations.

A nonprofit nonstock corporation may not be a constituent corporation to any merger or consolidation with a public benefit corporation or in which the certificate of incorporation of the surviving corporation is amended to include a provision authorized by § 362(a)(1) of this title.

§ 364. Stock certificates; notices regarding uncertificated stock.

Any stock certificate issued by a public benefit corporation shall note conspicuously that the corporation is a public benefit corporation formed pursuant to this subchapter. ▪ Any notice given by a public benefit corporation pursuant to §151(f) of this title shall state conspicuously that the corporation is a public benefit corporation formed pursuant to this subchapter.

§ 365. Duties of directors.

(a) The board of directors shall manage or direct the business and affairs of the public benefit corporation in a manner that balances the pecuniary interests of the stockholders, the best interests of those materially affected by the corporation's conduct, and the specific public benefit or public benefits identified in its certificate of incorporation.

(b) A director of a public benefit corporation shall not, by virtue of the public benefit provisions or §362(a) of this title, have any duty to any person on account of any interest of such person in the public benefit or public benefits identified in the certificate of incorporation or on account of any interest materially affected by the corporation's conduct and, with respect to a decision implicating the balance requirement in subsection (a) of this section, will be deemed to satisfy such director's fiduciary duties to stockholders and the corporation if such director's decision is both informed and disinterested and not such that no person of ordinary, sound judgment would approve.

(c) A director's ownership of or other interest in the stock of the public benefit corporation shall not alone, for the purposes of this section, create a conflict of interest on the part of the director with respect to the director's decision implicating the balancing requirement in subsection (a) of this section, except to the extent that such ownership or interest would create a conflict of interest if the corporation were not a public benefit corporation. ■ In the absence of a conflict of interest, no failure to satisfy that balancing requirement shall, for the purposes of §102(b)(7) or § 145 of this title, constitute an act or omission not in good faith, or a breach of the duty of loyalty, unless the certificate of incorporation so provides.

§ 366. Periodic statements and third-party certification.

(a) A public benefit corporation shall include in every notice of a meeting of stockholders a statement to the effect that it is a public benefit corporation formed pursuant to this subchapter.

(b) A public benefit corporation shall no less than biennially provide its stockholders with a statement as to the corporation's promotion of the public benefit or public benefits identified in the certificate of incorporation and of the best interests of those materially affected by the corporation's conduct. ■ The statement shall include:

(1) The objectives the board of directors has established to promote such public benefit or public benefits and interests;

(2) The standards the board of directors has adopted to measure the corporation's progress in promoting such public benefit or public benefits and interests;

(3) Objective factual information based on those standards regarding the corporation's success in meeting the objectives for promoting such public benefit or public benefits and interests; and

(4) An assessment of the corporation's success in meeting the objectives and promoting such public benefit or public benefits and interests.

(c) The certificate of incorporation or bylaws of a public benefit corporation may require that the corporation:

(1) Provide the statement described in subsection (b) of this section more frequently than biennially;

(2) Make the statement described in subsection (b) of this section available to the public; and/or

(3) Use a third-party standard in connection with and/or attain a periodic third-party certification addressing the corporation's promotion of the public benefit or public benefits identified in the certificate of incorporation and/or the best interests of those materially affected by the corporation's conduct.

§ 367. Suits to enforce the requirements of §365(a) of this title.

Any action to enforce the balancing requirement of § 365(a) of this title, including any individual, derivative or any other type of action, may not be brought unless the plaintiffs in such action own individually or collectively, as of the date of instituting such action, at least 2% of the corporation's outstanding shares or, in the case of a corporation with shares listed on a national securities exchange, the lesser of such percentage or shares of the corporation with a market value of at least $2,000,000 as of the date the action is instituted. ■ This section shall not relieve the plaintiffs from complying with any other conditions applicable to filing a derivative action including § 327 of this title and any rules of the court in which the action is filed.

§ 368. No effect on other corporations.

This subchapter shall not affect a statute or rule of law that is applicable to a corporation that is not a public benefit corporation, except as provided in § 363 of this title.

Subchapter XVI. Foreign Corporations

§ 371. Definition; qualification to do business in State; procedure.

(a) As used in this chapter, the words "foreign corporation" mean a corporation organized under the laws of any jurisdiction other than this State.

(b) No foreign corporation shall do any business in this State, through or by branch offices, agents or representatives located in this State, until it shall have paid to the Secretary of State of this State for the use of this State, $80, and shall have filed in the office of the Secretary of State:

> **(1)** A certificate, as of a date not earlier than 6 months prior to the filing date, issued by an authorized officer of the jurisdiction of its incorporation evidencing its corporate existence. ∎ If such certificate is in a foreign language, a translation thereof, under oath of the translator, shall be attached thereto;

> **(2)** A statement executed by an authorized officer of each corporation setting forth **(i)** the name and address of its registered agent in this State, which agent may be any of the foreign corporation itself, an individual resident in this State, a domestic corporation, a domestic partnership (whether general (including a limited liability partnership) or limited (including a limited liability limited partnership)), a domestic limited liability company, a domestic statutory trust, a foreign corporation (other than the foreign corporation itself), a foreign partner-

ship (whether general (including a limited liability partnership) or limited (including a limited liability limited partnership)), a foreign limited liability company or a foreign statutory trust, **(ii)** a statement, as of a date not earlier than 6 months prior to the filing date, of the assets and liabilities of the corporation, and **(iii)** the business it proposes to do in this State, and a statement that it is authorized to do that business in the jurisdiction of its incorporation. ∎ The statement shall be acknowledged in accordance with § 103 of this title.

(c) The certificate of the Secretary of State, under seal of office, of the filing of the certificates required by subsection (b) of this section, shall be delivered to the registered agent upon the payment to the Secretary of State of the fee prescribed for such certificates, and the certificate shall be prima facie evidence of the right of the corporation to do business in this State; provided, that the Secretary of State shall not issue such certificate unless the name of the corporation is such as to distinguish it upon the records in the office of the Division of Corporations in the Department of State from the names that are reserved on such records and from the names on such records of each other corporation, partnership, limited partnership, limited liability company or statutory trust organized or registered as a domestic or foreign corporation, partnership, limited partnership, limited liability company or statutory trust under the laws of this State, except with the written consent of the person who has reserved such name or such other corporation, partnership, limited partnership, limited liability company or statutory trust, executed, acknowledged and filed with the Secretary of State in accordance with § 103 of this title. ∎ If the name of the foreign corporation conflicts with the name of a corporation, partnership, limited partnership, limited liability company or statutory trust organized under the laws of this State, or a name reserved for a corporation, partnership, limited partnership, limited liability company or statutory trust to be organized under the laws of this State, or a name reserved or registered as that of a foreign corporation, partnership, limited partnership, limited liability company or statutory trust under the laws of this State, the foreign corporation may qualify to do business if it adopts an assumed name which shall be used when doing business in this State as long as the assumed name is authorized for use by this section.

§ 372. Additional requirements in case of change of name, change of business purpose or merger or consolidation.

(a) Every foreign corporation admitted to do business in this State which shall change its corporate name, or enlarge, limit or otherwise change the business which it proposes to do in this State, shall, within 30 days after the time said change becomes effective, file with the Secretary of State a certificate, which shall set forth:

(1) The name of the foreign corporation as it appears on the records of the Secretary of State of this State;

(2) The jurisdiction of its incorporation;

(3) The date it was authorized to do business in this State;

(4) If the name of the foreign corporation has been changed, a statement of the name relinquished, a statement of the new name and a statement that the change of name has been effected under the laws of the jurisdiction of its incorporation and the date the change was effected;

(5) If the business it proposes to do in this State is to be enlarged, limited or otherwise changed, a statement reflecting such change and a statement that it is authorized to do in the jurisdiction of its incorporation the business which it proposes to do in this State.

(b) Whenever a foreign corporation authorized to transact business in this State shall be the survivor of a merger permitted by the laws of the state or country in which it is incorporated, it shall, within 30 days after the merger becomes effective, file a certificate, issued by the proper officer of the state or country of its incorporation, attesting to the occurrence of such event. ▪ If the merger has

changed the corporate name of such foreign corporation or has enlarged, limited or otherwise changed the business it proposes to do in this State, it shall also comply with subsection (a) of this section.

(c) Whenever a foreign corporation authorized to transact business in this State ceases to exist because of a statutory merger or consolidation, it shall comply with § 381 of this title.

(d) The Secretary of State shall be paid, for the use of the State, $50 for filing and indexing each certificate required by subsection (a) or (b) of this section, and in the event of a change of name an additional $50 shall be paid for a certificate to be issued as evidence of filing the change of name.

§ 373. Exceptions to requirements.

(a) No foreign corporation shall be required to comply with §§ 371 and 372 of this title, under any of the following conditions:

(1) If it is in the mail order or a similar business, merely receiving orders by mail or otherwise in pursuance of letters, circulars, catalogs or other forms of advertising, or solicitation, accepting the orders outside this State, and filling them with goods shipped into this State;

(2) If it employs salespersons, either resident or traveling, to solicit orders in this State, either by display of samples or otherwise (whether or not maintaining sales offices in this State), all orders being subject to approval at the offices of the corporation without this State, and all goods applicable to the orders being shipped in pursuance thereof from without this State to the vendee or to the seller or such seller's agent for delivery to the vendee, and if any samples kept within this State are for display or advertising purposes only, and no sales, repairs or replacements are made from stock on hand in this State;

(3) If it sells, by contract consummated outside this State, and agrees, by the contract, to deliver into this State, machinery, plants or equipment, the construction, erection or installation of which within this State requires the supervision

of technical engineers or skilled employees performing services not generally available, and as a part of the contract of sale agrees to furnish such services, and such services only, to the vendee at the time of construction, erection or installation;

(4) If its business operations within this State, although not falling within the terms of paragraphs (a)(1), (2) and (3) of this section or any of them, are nevertheless wholly interstate in character;

(5) If it is an insurance company doing business in this State;

(6) If it creates, as borrower or lender, or acquires, evidences of debt, mortgages or liens on real or personal property;

(7) If it secures or collects debts or enforces any rights in property securing the same.

(b) This section shall have no application to the question of whether any foreign corporation is subject to service of process and suit in this State under § 382 of this title or any other law of this State.

§ 374. Annual report.

Annually on or before June 30, a foreign corporation doing business in this State shall file a report with the Secretary of State. ▪ The report shall be made on a form designated by the Secretary of State and shall be signed by the corporation's president, secretary, treasurer or other proper officer duly authorized so to act, or by any of its directors, or if filing an initial report by any incorporator in the event its board of directors shall not have been elected. ▪ The fact that an individual's name is signed on a certification attached to a corporate report shall be prima facie evidence that such individual is authorized to certify the report on behalf of the corporation; however the official title or position of the individual signing the corporate report shall be designated. ▪ The report shall contain the following information:

(1) The location of its registered office in this State, which shall include the street, number, city and postal code;

(2) The name of the agent upon whom service of process against the corporation may be served;

(3) The location of the principal place of business of the corporation, which shall include the street, number, city, state, or foreign country; and

(4) The names and addresses of all the directors as of the filing date of the report and the name and address of the officer who signs the report.

If any officer or director of a foreign corporation required to file an annual report with the Secretary of State shall knowingly make any false statement in the report, such officer or director shall be guilty of perjury.

§ 375. Failure to file report.

Upon the failure, neglect or refusal of any foreign corporation to file an annual report as required by § 374 of this title, the Secretary of State may, in the Secretary of State's discretion, investigate the reasons therefor and shall terminate the right of the foreign corporation to do business within this State upon failure of the corporation to file an annual report within any 2-year period.

§ 376. Service of process upon qualified foreign corporations.

(a) All process issued out of any court of this State, all orders made by any court of this State, all rules and notices of any kind required to be served on any foreign corporation which has qualified to do business in this State may be served on the registered agent of the corporation designated in accordance with § 371 of this title, or, if there be no such agent, then on any officer, director or other agent of the corporation then in this State.

(b) In case the officer whose duty it is to serve legal process cannot by due diligence serve the process in any manner provided for by subsection (a) of this section, it shall be lawful to serve the process against the corporation upon the Secretary of State, and such service shall be as effectual for all intents and purposes as if made in any of the ways provided for in subsection (a) of this section. ▪ Process may be served upon the Secretary of State under this subsection by means of electronic transmission but only as prescribed by the Secretary of

State. ▪ The Secretary of State is authorized to issue such rules and regulations with respect to such service as the Secretary of State deems necessary or appropriate. ▪ In the event that service is effected through the Secretary of State in accordance with this subsection, the Secretary of State shall forthwith notify the corporation by letter, directed to the corporation at its principal place of business as it appears on the last annual report filed pursuant to § 374 of this title or, if no such address appears, at its last registered office. ▪ Such letter shall be sent by a mail or courier service that includes a record of mailing or deposit with the courier and a record of delivery evidenced by the signature of the recipient. ▪ Such letter shall enclose a copy of the process and any other papers served upon the Secretary of State pursuant to this subsection. ▪ It shall be the duty of the plaintiff in the event of such service to serve process and any other papers in duplicate, to notify the Secretary of State that service is being effected pursuant to this subsection, and to pay the Secretary of State the sum of $50 for the use of the State, which sum shall be taxed as a part of the costs in the proceeding if the plaintiff shall prevail therein. ▪ The Secretary of State shall maintain an alphabetical record of any such service setting forth the name of the plaintiff and the defendant, the title, docket number and nature of the proceeding in which process has been served upon the Secretary of State, the fact that service has been effected pursuant to this subsection, the return date thereof, and the day and hour when the service was made. ▪ The Secretary of State shall not be required to retain such information for a period longer than 5 years from receipt of such service.

§ 377. Change of registered agent

(a) Any foreign corporation, which has qualified to do business in this State, may change its registered agent and substitute another registered agent by filing a certificate with the Secretary of State, acknowledged in accordance with § 103 of this title, setting forth:

> **(1)** The name and address of its registered agent designated in this State upon whom process directed to said corporation may be served; and

> **(2)** A revocation of all previous appointments of agent for such purposes.

Such registered agent shall comply with § 371(b)(2)(i) of this title.

(b) Any individual or entity designated by a foreign corporation as its registered agent for service of process may resign in the same manner as provided in § 136(a) of this title.

(c) If any agent designated and certified as required by § 371 of this title shall die or remove from this State, or resign, then the foreign corporation for which the agent had been so designated and certified shall, within 10 days after the death, removal or resignation of its agent, substitute, designate and certify to the Secretary of State, the name of another registered agent for the purposes of this subchapter, and all process, orders, rules and notices mentioned in § 376 of this title may be served on or given to the substituted agent with like effect as is prescribed in that section.

(d) A foreign corporation whose qualification to do business in this State has been forfeited pursuant to § 132(f)(4) or § 136(b) of this title may be reinstated by filing a certificate of reinstatement with the Secretary of State, acknowledged in accordance with § 103 of this title, setting forth:

> **(1)** The name of the foreign corporation;

> **(2)** The effective date of the forfeiture; and

> **(3)** The name and address of the foreign corporation's registered agent required to be maintained by § 132 of this title.

(e) Upon the filing of a certificate of reinstatement in accordance with subsection (d) of this section, the qualification of the foreign corporation to do business in this State shall be reinstated with the same force and effect as if it had not been forfeited pursuant to this title.

§ 378. Penalties for noncompliance.

Any foreign corporation doing business of any kind in this State without first having complied with any section of this subchapter applicable to it, shall be fined not less than $200 nor more than $500 for each such offense. ▪ Any agent of any foreign corporation that shall do any business in this State for any foreign corporation before the foreign corporation has complied with any section of this subchapter applicable to it, shall be fined not less than $100 nor more than $500 for each such offense.

§ 379. Banking powers denied.

(a) No foreign corporation shall, within the limits of this State, by any implication or construction, be deemed to possess the power of discounting bills, notes or other evidence of debt, of receiving deposits, of buying and selling bills of exchange, or of issuing bills, notes or other evidences of debt upon loan for circulation as money, anything in its charter or articles of incorporation to the contrary notwithstanding, except as otherwise provided in subchapter VII of Chapter 7 or in Chapter 14 of Title 5.

(b) All certificates issued by the Secretary of State under § 371 of this title shall expressly set forth the limitations and restrictions contained in this section.

§ 380. Foreign corporation as fiduciary in this State.

A corporation organized and doing business under the laws of the District of Columbia or of any state of the United States other than Delaware, duly authorized by its certificate of incorporation or by-laws so to act, may be appointed by any last will and testament or other testamentary writing, probated within this State, or by a deed of trust, mortgage or other agreement, as executor, guardian, trustee or other fiduciary, and may act as such within this State, when and to the extent that the laws of the District of Columbia or of the state in which the foreign corporation is organized confer like powers upon corporations organized and doing business under the laws of this State.

§ 381. Withdrawal of foreign corporation from State; procedure; service of process on Secretary of State.

(a) Any foreign corporation which shall have qualified to do business in this State under § 371 of this title, may surrender its authority to do business in

this State and may withdraw therefrom by filing with the Secretary of State:

(1) A certificate executed in accordance with § 103 of this title, stating that it surrenders its authority to transact business in the state and withdraws therefrom; and stating the address to which the Secretary of State may mail any process against the corporation that may be served upon the Secretary of State, or

(2) A copy of an order or decree of dissolution made by any court of competent jurisdiction or other competent authority of the State or other jurisdiction of its incorporation, certified to be a true copy under the hand of the clerk of the court or other official body, and the official seal of the court or official body or clerk thereof, together with a certificate executed in accordance with paragraph (a)(1) of this section, stating the address to which the Secretary of State may mail any process against the corporation that may be served upon the Secretary of State.

(b) The Secretary of State shall, upon payment to the Secretary of State of the fees prescribed in § 391 of this title, issue a sufficient number of certificates, under the Secretary of State's hand and official seal, evidencing the surrender of the authority of the corporation to do business in this State and its withdrawal therefrom. ▪ One of the certificates shall be furnished to the corporation withdrawing and surrendering its right to do business in this State.

(c) Upon the issuance of the certificates by the Secretary of State, the appointment of the registered agent of the corporation in this State, upon whom process against the corporation may be served, shall be revoked, and the corporation shall be deemed to have consented that service of process in any action, suit or proceeding based upon any cause of action arising in this State, during the time the corporation was authorized to transact business in this State, may thereafter be made by service upon the Secretary of State. ▪ Process may be served upon the Secretary of State under this subsection by means of electronic transmission but only as prescribed by the Secretary of State. ▪ The

Secretary of State is authorized to issue such rules and regulations with respect to such service as the Secretary of State deems necessary or appropriate.

(d) In the event of service upon the Secretary of State in accordance with subsection (c) of this section, the Secretary of State shall forthwith notify the corporation by letter, directed to the corporation at the address stated in the certificate which was filed by the corporation with the Secretary of State pursuant to subsection (a) of this section. ▪ Such letter shall be sent by a mail or courier service that includes a record of mailing or deposit with the courier and a record of delivery evidenced by the signature of the recipient. ▪ Such letter shall enclose a copy of the process and any other papers served upon the Secretary of State. ▪ It shall be the duty of the plaintiff in the event of such service to serve process and any other papers in duplicate, to notify the Secretary of State that service is being made pursuant to this subsection, and to pay the Secretary of State the sum of $50 for the use of the State, which sum shall be taxed as part of the cost of the action, suit or proceeding if the plaintiff shall prevail therein. ▪ The Secretary of State shall maintain an alphabetical record of such service setting forth the name of the plaintiff and defendant, the title, docket number and nature of the proceeding in which the process has been served upon the Secretary of State, the fact that service has been effected pursuant to this subsection, the return date thereof, and the day and hour when the service was made. ▪ The Secretary of State shall not be required to retain such information for a period longer than 5 years from receipt of the service of process.

§ 382. Service of process on nonqualifying foreign corporations.

(a) Any foreign corporation which shall transact business in this State without having qualified to do business under § 371 of this title shall be deemed to have thereby appointed and constituted the Secretary of State of this State its agent for the acceptance of legal process in any civil action, suit or proceeding against it in any state or federal court in this State arising or growing out of any business transacted by it within this State. ▪ If any foreign corporation consents in writing to be subject to the jurisdiction of any state or federal court in this State for any civil action, suit or proceeding against it arising or growing out of any business or matter, and if the agreement or instrument setting forth such consent does not otherwise provide a manner of service of legal process in any such civil action, suit or proceeding against it, such foreign corporation shall be deemed to have thereby appointed and constituted the Secretary of State of this State its agent for the acceptance of legal process in any such civil action, suit or proceeding against it. ▪ The transaction of business in this State by such corporation and/or such consent by such corporation to the jurisdiction of any state or federal court in this State without provision for a manner of service of legal process shall be a signification of the agreement of such corporation that any process served upon the Secretary of State when so served shall be of the same legal force and validity as if served upon an authorized officer or agent personally within this State. ▪ Process may be served upon the Secretary of State under this subsection by means of electronic transmission but only as prescribed by the Secretary of State. ▪ The Secretary of State is authorized to issue such rules and regulations with respect to such service as the Secretary of State deems necessary or appropriate.

(b) Section 373 of this title shall not apply in determining whether any foreign corporation is transacting business in this State within the meaning of this section; and "the transaction of business" or "business transacted in this State," by any such foreign corporation, whenever those words are used in this section, shall mean the course or practice of carrying on any business activities in this State, including, without limiting the generality of the foregoing, the solicitation of business or orders in this State. ▪ This section shall not apply to any insurance company doing business in this State.

(c) In the event of service upon the Secretary of State in accordance with subsection (a) of this section, the Secretary of State shall forthwith notify the corporation thereof by letter, directed to the corporation at the address furnished to the Secretary of State by the plaintiff in such action, suit or proceeding. ■ Such letter shall be sent by a mail or courier service that includes a record of mailing or deposit with the courier and a record of delivery evidenced by the signature of the recipient. ■ Such letter shall enclose a copy of the process and any other papers served upon the Secretary of State. ■ It shall be the duty of the plaintiff in the event of such service to serve process and any other papers in duplicate, to notify the Secretary of State that service is being made pursuant to this subsection, and to pay the Secretary of State the sum of $50 for the use of the State, which sum shall be taxed as a part of the costs in the proceeding if the plaintiff shall prevail therein. ■ The Secretary of State shall maintain an alphabetical record of any such process setting forth the name of the plaintiff and defendant, the title, docket number and nature of the proceeding in which process has been served upon the Secretary of State, the fact that service has been effected pursuant to this subsection, the return date thereof, and the day and hour when the service was made. ■ The Secretary of State shall not be required to retain such information for a period longer than 5 years from receipt of the service of process.

§ 383. Actions by and against unqualified foreign corporations.

(a) A foreign corporation which is required to comply with §§ 371 and 372 of this title and which has done business in this State without authority shall not maintain any action or special proceeding in this State unless and until such corporation has been authorized to do business in this State and has paid to the State all fees, penalties and franchise taxes for the years or parts thereof during which it did business in this State without authority. ■ This prohibition shall not apply to any successor in interest of such foreign corporation.

(b) The failure of a foreign corporation to obtain authority to do business in this State shall not impair the validity of any contract or act of the foreign corporation or the right of any other party to the contract to maintain any action or special proceeding thereon, and shall not prevent the foreign corporation from defending any action or special proceeding in this State.

§ 384. Foreign corporations doing business without having qualified; injunctions.

The Court of Chancery shall have jurisdiction to enjoin any foreign corporation, or any agent thereof, from transacting any business in this State if such corporation has failed to comply with any section of this subchapter applicable to it or if such corporation has secured a certificate of the Secretary of State under § 371 of this title on the basis of false or misleading representations. ■ The Attorney General shall, upon the Attorney General's own motion or upon the relation of proper parties, proceed for this purpose by complaint in any county in which such corporation is doing business.

§ 385. Filing of certain instruments with recorder of deeds not required.

No instrument that is required to be filed with the Secretary of State of this State by this subchapter need be filed with the recorder of deeds of any county of this State in order to comply with this subchapter.

Subchapter XVII. Domestication and Transfer

§ 388. Domestication of non-United States entities.

(a) As used in this section, the term:

(1) "Foreign jurisdiction" means any foreign country or other foreign jurisdiction (other than the United States, any state, the District of Columbia, or any possession or territory of the United States); and

(2) "Non-United States entity" means a corporation, a limited liability company, a statutory trust, a business trust or association, a real estate investment trust, a common-law trust, or any other unincorporated business or entity, including a partnership (whether general (including a limited liability partnership) or limited (including a limited liability limited partnership)), formed, incorporated, created or that otherwise came into being under the laws of any foreign jurisdiction.

(b) Any non-United States entity may become domesticated as a corporation in this State by complying with subsection (h) of this section and filing with the Secretary of State:

    (1) A certificate of corporate domestication which shall be executed in accordance with subsection (g) of this section and filed in accordance with § 103 of this title; and

    (2) A certificate of incorporation, which shall be executed, acknowledged and filed in accordance with § 103 of this title.

Each of the certificates required by this subsection (b) shall be filed simultaneously with the Secretary of State and, if such certificates are not to become effective upon their filing as permitted by § 103(d) of this title, then each such certificate shall provide for the same effective date or time in accordance with § 103(d) of this title.

(c) The certificate of corporate domestication shall certify:

    (1) The date on which and jurisdiction where the non-United States entity was first formed, incorporated, created or otherwise came into being;

    (2) The name of the non-United States entity immediately prior to the filing of the certificate of corporate domestication;

    (3) The name of the corporation as set forth in its certificate of incorporation filed in accordance with subsection (b) of this section; and

    (4) The jurisdiction that constituted the seat, siege social, or principal place of business or central administration of the non-United States entity or any other equivalent thereto under applicable law, immediately prior to the filing of the certificate of corporate domestication; and

    (5) That the domestication has been approved in the manner provided for by the document, instrument, agreement or other writing, as the case may be, governing the internal affairs of the non-United States entity and the conduct of its business or by applicable non-Delaware law, as appropriate.

(d) Upon the certificate of corporate domestication and the certificate of incorporation becoming effective in accordance with § 103 of this title, the non-United States entity shall be domesticated as a corporation in this State and the corporation shall thereafter be subject to all of the provisions of this title, except that notwithstanding § 106 of this title, the existence of the corporation shall be deemed to have commenced on the date the non-United States entity commenced its existence in the jurisdiction in which the non-United States entity was first formed, incorporated, created or otherwise came into being.

(e) The domestication of any non-United States entity as a corporation in this State shall not be deemed to affect any obligations or liabilities of the non-United States entity incurred prior to its domestication as a corporation in this State, or the personal liability of any person therefor.

(f) The filing of a certificate of corporate domestication shall not affect the choice of law applicable to the non-United States entity, except that, from the effective time of the domestication, the law of the State of Delaware, including this title, shall apply to the non-United States entity to the same extent as if the non-United States entity had been incorporated as a corporation of this State on that date.

(g) The certificate of corporate domestication shall be signed by any person who is authorized to sign the certificate of corporate domestication on behalf of the non-United States entity.

(h) Prior to the filing of a certificate of corporate domestication with the Secretary of State, the domestication shall be approved in the manner provided for by the document, instrument, agreement or other writing, as the case may be, governing the internal affairs of the non-United States entity and the conduct of its business or by applicable non-Delaware law, as appropriate, and the certificate of incorporation shall be approved by the same authorization required to approve the domestication.

(i) When a non-United States entity has become domesticated as a corporation pursuant to this section, for all purposes of the laws of the State of Delaware, the corporation shall be deemed to be the same entity as the domesticating non-United States entity and the domestication shall constitute a continuation of the existence of the domesticating non-United States entity in the form of a corporation of this State. ■ When any domestication shall have become effective under this section, for all purposes of the laws of the State of Delaware, all of the rights, privileges and powers of the non-United States entity that has been domesticated, and all property, real, personal and mixed, and all debts due to such non-United States entity, as well as all other things and causes of action belonging to such non-United States entity, shall remain vested in the corporation to which such non-United States entity has been domesticated (and also in the non-United States entity, if and for so long as the non-United States entity continues its existence in the foreign jurisdiction in which it was existing immediately prior to the domestication) and shall be the property of such corporation (and also of the non-United States entity, if and for so long as the non-United States entity continues its existence in the foreign jurisdiction in which it was existing immediately prior to the domestication), and the title to any real property vested by deed or otherwise in such non-United States entity shall not revert or be in any way impaired by reason of this title; but all rights of creditors and all liens upon any property of such non-United States entity shall be preserved unimpaired, and all debts, liabilities and duties of the non-United States entity that has been domesticated shall remain attached to the corporation to which such non-United States entity has been domesticated (and also to the non-United States entity, if and for so long as the non-United States entity continues its existence in the foreign jurisdiction in which it was existing immediately prior to the domestication), and may be enforced against it to the same extent as if said debts, liabilities and duties had originally been incurred or contracted by it in its capacity as such corporation. ■ The rights, privileges, powers and interests in property of the non-United States entity, as well as the debts, liabilities and duties of the non-United States entity, shall not be deemed, as a consequence of the domestication, to have been transferred to the corporation to which such non-United States entity has domesticated for any purpose of the laws of the State of Delaware.

(j) Unless otherwise agreed or otherwise required under applicable non-Delaware law, the domesticating non-United States entity shall not be required to wind up its affairs or pay its liabilities and distribute its assets, and the domestication shall not be deemed to constitute a dissolution of such non-United States entity. ■ If, following domestication, a non-United States entity that has become domesticated as a corporation of this State continues its existence in the foreign jurisdiction in which it was existing immediately prior to domestication, the corporation and such non-United States entity shall, for all purposes of the laws of the State of Delaware, constitute a single entity formed, incorporated, created or otherwise having come into being, as applicable, and existing under the laws of the State of Delaware and the laws of such foreign jurisdiction.

(k) In connection with a domestication under this section, shares of stock, rights or securities of, or interests in, the non-United States entity that is to be domesticated as a corporation of this State may be exchanged for or converted into cash, property, or shares of stock, rights or securities of such corporation or, in addition to or in lieu thereof, may be exchanged for or converted into cash, property, or shares of stock, rights or securities of, or interests in, another corporation or other entity or may be cancelled.

§ 389. Temporary transfer of domicile into this State.

(a) As used in this section:

(1) The term "emergency condition" shall be deemed to include but not be limited to any of the following:

a. War or other armed conflict;

b. Revolution or insurrection;

c. Invasion or occupation by foreign military forces;

d. Rioting or civil commotion of an extended nature;

e. Domination by a foreign power;

f. Expropriation, nationalization or confiscation of a material part of the assets or property of the non-United States entity;

g. Impairment of the institution of private property (including private property held abroad);

h. The taking of any action under the laws of the United States whereby persons resident in the jurisdiction, the law of which governs the internal affairs of the non-United States entity, might be treated as "enemies" or otherwise restricted under laws of the United States relating to trading with enemies of the United States;

i. The immediate threat of any of the foregoing; and

j. Such other event which, under the law of the jurisdiction governing the internal affairs of the non-United States entity, permits the non-United States entity to transfer its domicile.

(2) The term "foreign jurisdiction" and the term "non-United States entity" shall have the same meanings as set forth in § 388(a) of this title.

(3) The terms "officers" and "directors" include, in addition to such persons, trustees, managers, partners and all other persons performing functions equivalent to those of officers and directors, however named or described in any relevant instrument.

(b) Any non-United States entity may, subject to and upon compliance with this section, transfer its domicile (which term, as used in this section, shall be deemed to refer in addition to the seat, siege social or principal place of business or central administration of such entity, or any other equivalent thereto under applicable law) into this State, and may perform the acts described in this section, so long as the law by which the internal affairs of such entity are governed does not expressly prohibit such transfer.

(c) Any non-United States entity that shall propose to transfer its domicile into this State shall submit to the Secretary of State for the Secretary of State's review, at least 30 days prior to the proposed transfer of domicile, the following:

(1) A copy of its certificate of incorporation and bylaws (or the equivalent thereof under applicable law), certified as true and correct by the appropriate director, officer or government official;

(2) A certificate issued by an authorized official of the jurisdiction the law of which governs the internal affairs of the non-United States entity evidencing its existence;

(3) A list indicating the person or persons who, in the event of a transfer pursuant to this section, shall be the authorized officers and directors of the non-United States entity, together with evidence of their authority to act and their respective executed agreements in writing regarding service of process as set out in subsection (j) of this section;

(4) A certificate executed by the appropriate officer or director of the non-United States entity, setting forth:

a. The name and address of its registered agent in this State;

b. A general description of the business in which it is engaged;

c. That the filing of such certificate has been duly authorized by any necessary action and does not violate the certificate of incorporation or bylaws (or equivalent thereof under applicable law) or any material agreement or instrument binding on such entity;

d. A list indicating the person or persons authorized to sign the written communications required by subsection (e) of this section;

e. An affirmance that such transfer is not expressly prohibited under the law by which the internal affairs of the non-United States entity are governed; and

f. An undertaking that any transfer of domicile into this State will take place only in the event of an emergency condition in the jurisdiction the law of which governs the internal affairs of the non-United States entity and that such transfer shall continue only so long as such emergency condition, in the judgment of the non-United States entity's management, so requires; and

(5) The examination fee prescribed under § 391 of this title.

If any of the documents referred to in paragraphs (c)(1)-(5) of this section are not in English, a translation thereof, under oath of the translator, shall be attached thereto. ▪ If such documents satisfy the requirements of this section, and if the name of the non-United States entity meets the requirements of § 102(a)(1) of this title, the Secretary of State shall notify the non-United States entity that such documents have been accepted for filing, and the records of the Secretary of State shall reflect such acceptance and such notification. ▪ In addition, the Secretary of State shall enter the name of the non-United States entity on the Secretary of State's reserved list to remain there so long as the non-United States entity is in compliance with this section. ▪ No document submitted under this subsection shall be available for public inspection pursuant to Chapter 100 of Title 29 until, and unless, such entity effects a transfer of its domicile as provided in this section. ▪ The Secretary of State may waive the 30-day period and translation requirement provided for in this subsection upon request by such entity, supported by facts (including, without limitation, the existence of an emergency condition) justifying such waiver.

(d) On or before March 1 in each year, prior to the transfer of its domicile as provided for in subsection (e) of this section, during any such transfer and, in the event that it desires to continue to be subject to a transfer of domicile under this section, after its domicile has ceased to be in this State, the non-United States entity shall file a certificate executed by an appropriate officer or director of the non-United States entity, certifying that the documents submitted pursuant to this section remain in full force and effect or attaching any amendments or supplements thereto and translated as required in subsection (c) of this section, together with the filing fee prescribed under § 391 of this title. ▪ In the event that any non-United States entity fails to file the required certificate on or before March 1 in each year, all certificates and filings made pursuant to this section shall become null and void on March 2 in such year, and any proposed transfer thereafter shall be subject to all of the required submissions and the examination fee set forth in subsection (c) of this section.

(e) If the Secretary of State accepts the documents submitted pursuant to subsection (c) of this section for filing, such entity may transfer its domicile to this State at any time by means of a written communication to such effect addressed to the Secretary of State, signed by 1 of the persons named on the list filed pursuant to paragraph (c)(4)d. of this section, and confirming that the statements made pursuant to paragraph (c)(4) of this section remain true and correct; provided, that if emergency conditions have affected ordinary means of communication, such notification may be made by telegram, telex, telecopy or other form of writing so long as a duly signed duplicate is received by the Secretary of State within 30 days thereafter. ▪ The records of the Secretary of State shall reflect the fact of such transfer. ▪ Upon the payment to the Secretary of State of the fee prescribed under § 391 of this title, the Secretary of State shall certify that the non-United States entity has filed all documents and paid all fees required by this title. ▪ Such certificate of the Secretary of State shall be prima facie evidence of transfer by such non-United States entity of its domicile into this State.

(f) Except to the extent expressly prohibited by the laws of this State, from and after the time that a non-United States entity transfers its domicile to this State pursuant to this section, the non-United States entity shall have all of the powers which it had immediately prior to such transfer under the law of the jurisdiction governing its internal affairs and the directors and officers designated pursuant to paragraph (c)(3) of this section, and their successors, may manage the business and affairs of the non-United States entity in accordance with the laws of such jurisdiction. ▪ Any such activity conducted pursuant to this section shall not be deemed to be doing business within this State for purposes of § 371 of this title. ▪ Any reference in this section to the law of the jurisdiction governing the internal affairs of a non-United States entity which has transferred its domicile into this State shall be deemed to be a reference to such law as in effect immediately prior to the transfer of domicile.

(g) For purposes of any action in the courts of this State, no non-United States entity which has obtained the certificate of the Secretary of State referred to in subsection (e) of this section shall be deemed to be an "enemy" person or entity for any purpose, including, without limitation, in relation to any claim of title to its assets, wherever located, or to its ability to institute suit in said courts.

(h) The transfer by any non-United States entity of its domicile into this State shall not be deemed to affect any obligations or liabilities of such non-United States entity incurred prior to such transfer.

(i) The directors of any non-United States entity which has transferred its domicile into this State may withhold from any holder of equity interests in such entity any amounts payable to such holder on account of dividends or other distributions, if the directors shall determine that such holder will not have the full benefit of such payment, so long as the directors shall make provision for the retention of such withheld payment in escrow or under some similar arrangement for the benefit of such holder.

(j) All process issued out of any court of this State, all orders made by any court of this State and all rules and notices of any kind required to be served on any non-United States entity which has transferred its domicile into this State may be served on the non-United States entity pursuant to § 321 of this title in the same manner as if such entity were a corporation of this State. ▪ The directors of a non-United States entity which has transferred its domicile into this State shall agree in writing that they will be amenable to service of process by the

same means as, and subject to the jurisdiction of the courts of this State to the same extent as are directors of corporations of this State, and such agreements shall be submitted to the Secretary of State for filing before the respective directors take office.

(k) Any non-United States entity which has transferred its domicile into this State may voluntarily return to the jurisdiction the law of which governs its internal affairs by filing with the Secretary of State an application to withdraw from this State. ▪ Such application shall be accompanied by a resolution of the directors of the non-United States entity authorizing such withdrawal and by a certificate of the highest diplomatic or consular official of such jurisdiction accredited to the United States indicating the consent of such jurisdiction to such withdrawal. ▪ The application shall also contain, or be accompanied by, the agreement of the non-United States entity that it may be served with process in this State in any proceeding for enforcement of any obligation of the non-United States entity arising prior to its withdrawal from this State, which agreement shall include the appointment of the Secretary of State as the agent of the non-United States entity to accept service of process in any such proceeding and shall specify the address to which a copy of process served upon the Secretary of State shall be mailed. ▪ Upon the payment of any fees and taxes owed to this State, the Secretary of State shall file the application and the non-United States entity's domicile shall, as of the time of filing, cease to be in this State.

§ 390. Transfer, domestication or continuance of domestic corporations.

(a) Upon compliance with the provisions of this section, any corporation existing under the laws of this State may transfer to or domesticate or continue in any foreign jurisdiction and, in connection therewith, may elect to continue its existence as a corporation of this State. ▪ As used in this section, the term:

> **(1)** "Foreign jurisdiction" means any foreign country, or other foreign jurisdiction (other than the United States, any state, the District of

Columbia, or any possession or territory of the United States); and

(2) "Resulting entity" means the entity formed, incorporated, created or otherwise coming into being as a consequence of the transfer of the corporation to, or its domestication or continuance in, a foreign jurisdiction pursuant to this section.

(b) The board of directors of the corporation which desires to transfer to or domesticate or continue in a foreign jurisdiction shall adopt a resolution approving such transfer, domestication or continuance specifying the foreign jurisdiction to which the corporation shall be transferred or in which the corporation shall be domesticated or continued and, if applicable, that in connection with such transfer, domestication or continuance the corporation's existence as a corporation of this State is to continue and recommending the approval of such transfer or domestication or continuance by the stockholders of the corporation. ■ Such resolution shall be submitted to the stockholders of the corporation at an annual or special meeting. ■ Due notice of the time, place and purpose of the meeting shall be given to each holder of stock, whether voting or nonvoting, of the corporation at the address of the stockholder as it appears on the records of the corporation, at least 20 days prior to the date of the meeting. ■ At the meeting, the resolution shall be considered and a vote taken for its adoption or rejection. ■ If all outstanding shares of stock of the corporation, whether voting or nonvoting, shall be voted for the adoption of the resolution, the corporation shall file with the Secretary of State a certificate of transfer if its existence as a corporation of this State is to cease or a certificate of transfer and domestic continuance if its existence as a corporation of this State is to continue, executed in accordance with § 103 of this title, which certifies:

(1) The name of the corporation, and if it has been changed, the name under which it was originally incorporated.

(2) The date of filing of its original certificate of incorporation with the Secretary of State.

(3) The foreign jurisdiction to which the corporation shall be transferred or in which it shall be domesticated or continued and the name of the resulting entity.

(4) That the transfer, domestication or continuance of the corporation has been approved in accordance with the provisions of this section.

(5) In the case of a certificate of transfer, **(i)** that the existence of the corporation as a corporation of this State shall cease when the certificate of transfer becomes effective, and **(ii)** the agreement of the corporation that it may be served with process in this State in any proceeding for enforcement of any obligation of the corporation arising while it was a corporation of this State which shall also irrevocably appoint the Secretary of State as its agent to accept service of process in any such proceeding and specify the address (which may not be that of the corporation's registered agent without the written consent of the corporation's registered agent, such consent to be filed along with the certificate of transfer) to which a copy of such process shall be mailed by the Secretary of State. ■ Process may be served upon the Secretary of State under this subsection by means of electronic transmission but only as prescribed by the Secretary of State. ■ The Secretary of State is authorized to issue such rules and regulations with respect to such service as the Secretary of State deems necessary or appropriate. ■ In the event of service upon the Secretary of State in accordance with this subsection, the Secretary of State shall forthwith notify such corporation that has transferred out of the State of Delaware by letter, directed to such corporation that has transferred out of the State of Delaware at the address so specified, unless such corporation shall have designated in writing to the Secretary of State a different address for such purpose, in which case it shall be mailed to the last address designated. ■ Such letter shall be sent by a mail or courier service that includes a record of mailing or deposit with the courier and a record of delivery evidenced by the signature of the recipient. ■ Such letter shall enclose a copy of the process and any other papers served on the Secretary of State pursuant to this subsection. ▪ It shall be the duty of the plaintiff in the event of such service to serve process and any other papers in duplicate, to notify the Secretary of State that service is being effected pursuant to this subsection and to pay the Secretary of State the sum of $50 for the use of the State, which sum shall be taxed as part of the costs in the proceeding, if the plaintiff shall prevail therein. ▪ The Secretary of State shall maintain an alphabetical record of any such service setting forth the name of the plaintiff and the defendant, the title, docket number and nature of the proceeding in which process has been served, the fact that service has been effected pursuant to this subsection, the return date thereof, and the day and hour service was made. ▪ The Secretary of State shall not be required to retain such information longer than 5 years from receipt of the service of process.

(6) In the case of a certificate of transfer and domestic continuance, that the corporation will continue to exist as a corporation of this State after the certificate of transfer and domestic continuance becomes effective.

(c) Upon the filing of a certificate of transfer in accordance with subsection (b) of this section and payment to the Secretary of State of all fees prescribed under this title, the Secretary of State shall certify that the corporation has filed all documents and paid all fees required by this title, and thereupon the corporation shall cease to exist as a corporation of this State at the time the certificate of transfer becomes effective in accordance with § 103 of this title. ▪ Such certificate of the Secretary of State shall be prima facie evidence of the transfer, domestication or continuance by such corporation out of this State.

(d) The transfer, domestication or continuance of a corporation out of this State in accordance with this section and the resulting cessation of its existence as a corporation of this State pursuant to a certificate of transfer shall not be deemed to affect any obligations or liabilities of the corporation incurred prior to such transfer, domestication or continuance, the personal liability of any person incurred prior to such transfer, domestication or continuance, or the choice of law applicable to the corporation with respect to matters arising prior to such transfer, domestication or continuance. ▪ Unless otherwise agreed or otherwise provided in the certificate of incorporation, the transfer, domestication or continuance of a corporation out of the State of Delaware in accordance with this section shall not require such corporation to wind up its affairs or pay its liabilities and distribute its assets under this title and shall not be deemed to constitute a dissolution of such corporation.

(e) If a corporation files a certificate of transfer and domestic continuance, after the time the certificate of transfer and domestic continuance becomes effective, the corporation shall continue to exist as a corporation of this State, and the law of the State of Delaware, including this title, shall apply to the corporation to the same extent as prior to such time. ▪ So long as a corporation continues to exist as a corporation of the State of Delaware following the filing of a certificate of transfer and domestic continuance, the continuing corporation and the resulting entity shall, for all purposes of the laws of the State of Delaware, constitute a single entity formed, incorporated, created or otherwise having come into being, as applicable, and existing under the laws of the State of Delaware and the laws of the foreign jurisdiction.

(f) When a corporation has transferred, domesticated or continued pursuant to this section, for all purposes of the laws of the State of Delaware, the resulting entity shall be deemed to be the same entity as the transferring, domesticating or continuing corporation and shall constitute a continuation of the existence of such corporation in the form of the resulting entity. ▪ When any transfer, domestication or continuance shall have become effective under this section, for all purposes of the laws of the State of Delaware, all of the rights, privileges and powers of the corporation that has transferred, domesticated or continued, and all property, real, personal and mixed, and all debts due to such corporation, as well as all other things and causes of action belonging to such corporation, shall remain vested in the resulting entity (and also in the corporation that has transferred, domesticated or continued, if and for so long as such corporation continues its existence as a corporation of this State) and shall be the property of such resulting entity (and also of the corporation that has transferred, domesticated or continued, if and for so long as such corporation continues its existence as a corporation of this State), and the title to any real property vested by deed or otherwise in such corporation shall not revert or be in any way impaired by reason of this title; but all rights of creditors and all liens upon any property of such corporation shall be preserved unimpaired, and all debts, liabilities and duties of such corporation shall remain attached to the resulting entity (and also to the corporation that has transferred, domesticated or continued, if and for so long as such corporation continues its existence as a corporation of this State), and may be enforced against it to the same extent as if said debts, liabilities and duties had originally been incurred or contracted by it in its capacity as such resulting entity. ▪ The rights, privileges, powers and interests in property of the corporation, as well as the debts, liabilities and duties of the corporation, shall not be deemed, as a consequence of the transfer, domestication or continuance, to have been transferred to the resulting entity for any purpose of the laws of the State of Delaware.

(g) In connection with a transfer, domestication or continuance under this section, shares of stock of the transferring, domesticating or continuing corporation may be exchanged for or converted into cash, property, or shares of stock, rights or securities of, or interests in, the resulting entity or, in addition to or in lieu thereof, may be exchanged for or converted into cash, property, or shares of stock, rights or securities of, or interests in, another corporation or other entity or may be cancelled.

(h) No vote of the stockholders of a corporation shall be necessary to authorize a transfer, domestication or continuance if no shares of the stock of such corporation shall have been issued prior to the adoption by the board of directors of the resolution approving the transfer, domestication or continuance.

(i) Whenever it shall be desired to transfer to or domesticate or continue in any foreign jurisdiction any nonstock corporation, the governing body shall perform all the acts necessary to effect a transfer, domestication or continuance which are required by this section to be performed by the board of directors of a corporation having capital stock. ▪ If the members of a nonstock corporation are entitled to vote for the election of members of its governing body or are entitled under the certificate of incorporation or the bylaws of such corporation to vote on such transfer, domestication or continuance or on a merger, consolidation, or dissolution of the corporation, they, and any other holder of any membership interest in the corporation, shall perform all the acts necessary to effect a transfer, domestication or continuance which are required by this section to be performed by the stockholders of a corporation having capital stock. ▪ If there is no member entitled to vote thereon, nor any other holder of any membership interest in the corporation, the transfer, domestication or continuance of the corporation shall be authorized at a meeting of the governing body, upon the adoption of a resolution to transfer or domesticate or continue by the vote of a majority of members of its governing body then in office. ▪ In all other respects, the method and proceedings for the transfer, domestication or continuance of a nonstock corporation shall conform as nearly as may be to the proceedings prescribed by this section for the transfer, domestication or continuance of corporations having capital stock. ▪ In the case of a charitable nonstock corporation, due notice of the corporation's intent to effect a transfer, domestication or continuance shall be mailed to the Attorney General of the State of Delaware 10 days prior to the date of the proposed transfer, domestication or continuance.

Subchapter XVIII. Miscellaneous Provisions

§ 391. Amounts payable to Secretary of State upon filing certificate or other paper.

(a) The following fees and penalties shall be collected by and paid to the Secretary of State, for the use of the State:

(1) Upon the receipt for filing of an original certificate of incorporation, the fee shall be computed on the basis of $0.02 for each share of authorized capital stock having par value up to and including 20,000 shares, $0.01 for each share in excess of 20,000 shares up to and including 200,000 shares, and 2/5 of a $0.01 for each share in excess of 200,000 shares; $0.01 for each share of authorized capital stock without par value up to and including 20,000 shares, 1/2 of $0.01 for each share in excess of 20,000 shares up to and including 2,000,000 shares, and 2/5 of $0.01 for each share in excess of 2,000,000 shares. ▪ In no case shall the amount paid be less than $15. ▪ For the purpose of computing the fee on par value stock each $100 unit of the authorized capital stock shall be counted as 1 assessable share.

(2) Upon the receipt for filing of a certificate of amendment of certificate of incorporation, or a certificate of amendment of certificate of incorporation before payment of capital, or a restated certificate of incorporation, increasing the authorized capital stock of a corporation, the fee shall be an amount equal to the difference between the fee computed at the foregoing rates upon the total authorized capital stock of the corporation including the proposed increase, and the fee computed at the foregoing rates upon the total authorized capital stock excluding the proposed increase. ▪ In no case shall the amount paid be less than $30.

(3) Upon the receipt for filing of a certificate of amendment of certificate of incorporation before payment of capital and not involving an increase of authorized capital stock, or an amendment to the certificate of incorporation not involving an increase of authorized capital stock, or a restated certificate of incorporation not involving an increase of authorized capital stock, or a certificate of retirement of stock, the fee to be paid shall be $30. ▪ For all other certificates relating to corporations, not otherwise provided for, the fee to be paid shall be $5.00. ▪ In the case of exempt corporations no fee shall be paid under this paragraph.

(4) Upon the receipt for filing of a certificate of merger or consolidation of 2 or more corporations, the fee shall be an amount equal to the difference between the fee computed at the foregoing rates upon the total authorized capital stock of the corporation created by the merger or consolidation, and the fee so computed upon the aggregate amount of the total authorized capital stock of the constituent corporations. ▪ In no case shall the amount paid be less than $75. ▪ The foregoing fee shall be in addition to any tax or fee required under any other law of this State to be paid by any constituent entity that is not a corporation in connection with the filing of the certificate of merger or consolidation.

(5) Upon the receipt for filing of a certificate of dissolution, there shall be paid to and collected by the Secretary of State a fee of:

a. Forty dollars; or

b. Ten dollars in the case of a certificate of dissolution which certifies that:

1. The corporation has no assets and has ceased transacting business; and

2. The corporation, for each year since its incorporation in this State, has been required to pay only the minimum franchise tax then prescribed by § 503 of this title; and

3. The corporation has paid all franchise taxes and fees due to or assessable by this State through the end of the year in which said certificate of dissolution is filed.

(6) Upon the receipt for filing of a certificate of reinstatement of a foreign corporation or a certificate of surrender and withdrawal from the State by a foreign corporation, there shall be collected by and paid to the Secretary of State a fee of $10.

(7) For receiving and filing and/or indexing any certificate, affidavit, agreement or any other paper provided for by this chapter, for which no different fee is specifically prescribed, a fee of $115 in each case shall be paid to the Secretary of State. ■ The fee in the case of a certificate of incorporation filed as required by § 102 of this title shall be $25. ■ For entering information from each instrument into the Delaware Corporation Information System in accordance with § 103(c)(8) of this title, the fee shall be $5.00.

a. A certificate of dissolution which meets the criteria stated in paragraph (a)(5)b. of this section shall not be subject to such fee; and

b. A certificate of incorporation filed in accordance with § 102 of this title shall be subject to a fee of $25.

(8) For receiving and filing and/or indexing the annual report of a foreign corporation doing business in this State, a fee of $125 shall be paid. ■ In the event of neglect, refusal or failure on the part of any foreign corporation to file the annual report with the Secretary of State on or before June 30 each year, the corporation shall pay a penalty of $125.

(9) For recording and indexing articles of association and other papers required by this chapter to be recorded by the Secretary of State, a fee computed on the basis of $0.01 a line shall be paid.

(10) For certifying copies of any paper on file provided by this chapter, a fee of $50 shall be paid for each copy certified. ■ In addition, a fee of $2.00 per page shall be paid in each instance where the Secretary of State provides the copies of the document to be certified.

(11) For issuing any certificate of the Secretary of State other than a certification of a copy under paragraph (a)(10) of this section, or a certificate that recites all of a corporation's filings with the Secretary of State, a fee of $50 shall be paid for each certificate. ■ For issuing any certificate of the Secretary of State that recites all of a corporation's filings with the Secretary of State, a fee of $175 shall be paid for each certificate. ■ For issuing any certificate via the Division's online services, a fee of up to $175 shall be paid for each certificate.

(12) For filing in the office of the Secretary of State any certificate of change of location or change of registered agent, as provided in § 133 of this title, there shall be collected by and paid to the Secretary of State a fee of $50, provided that no fee shall be charged pursuant to § 103(c)(6) and (c)(7) of this title.

(13) For filing in the office of the Secretary of State any certificate of change of address or change of name of registered agent, as provided in § 134 of this title, there shall be collected by and paid to the Secretary of State a fee of $50, plus the same fees for receiving, filing, indexing, copying and certifying the same as are charged in the case of filing a certificate of incorporation.

(14) For filing in the office of the Secretary of State any certificate of resignation of a registered agent and appointment of a successor, as provided in § 135 of this title, there shall be collected by and paid to the Secretary of State a fee of $50.

(15) For filing in the office of the Secretary of State, any certificate of resignation of a registered agent without appointment of a successor, as provided in §§ 136 and 377 of this title, there shall be collected by and paid to the Secretary of State a fee of $2.00 for each corporation whose registered agent has resigned by such certificate.

(16) For preparing and providing a written report of a record search, a fee of up to $100 shall be paid.

(17) For preclearance of any document for filing, a fee of $250 shall be paid.

(18) For receiving and filing and/or indexing an annual franchise tax report of a corporation provided for by § 502 of this title, a fee of $25 shall be paid by exempt corporations and a fee of $50 shall be paid by all other corporations.

(19) For receiving and filing and/or indexing by the Secretary of State of a certificate of domestication and certificate of incorporation prescribed in § 388(d) of this title, a fee of $165, plus the fee payable upon the receipt for filing of an original certificate of incorporation, shall be paid.

(20) For receiving, reviewing and filing and/or indexing by the Secretary of State of the documents prescribed in § 389(c) of this title, a fee of $10,000 shall be paid.

(21) For receiving, reviewing and filing and/or indexing by the Secretary of State of the documents prescribed in § 389(d) of this title, an annual fee of $2,500 shall be paid.

(22) Except as provided in this section, the fees of the Secretary of State shall be as provided for in § 2315 of Title 29.

(23) In the case of exempt corporations, the total fees payable to the Secretary of State upon the filing of a Certificate of Change of Registered Agent and/or Registered Office or a Certificate of Revival shall be $5.00 and such filings shall be exempt from any fees or assessments pursuant to the requirements of § 103(c)(6) and (c)(7) of this title.

(24) For accepting a corporate name reservation application, an application for renewal of a corporate name reservation, or a notice of transfer or cancellation of a corporate name reservation, there shall be collected by and paid to the Secretary of State a fee of up to $75.

(25) For receiving and filing and/or indexing by the Secretary of State of a certificate of transfer or a certificate of continuance prescribed in § 390 of this title, a fee of $1,000 shall be paid.

(26) For receiving and filing and/or indexing by the Secretary of State of a certificate of conversion and certificate of incorporation prescribed in § 265 of this title, a fee of $115, plus the fee payable upon the receipt for filing of an original certificate of incorporation, shall be paid.

(27) For receiving and filing and/or indexing by the Secretary of State of a certificate of conversion prescribed in § 266 of this title, a fee of $165 shall be paid.

(28) For receiving and filing and/or indexing by the Secretary of State of a certificate of validation prescribed in § 204 of this title, a fee of $2,500 shall be paid; provided, that if the certificate of validation has the effect of increasing the authorized capital stock of a corporation, an additional fee, calculated in accordance with paragraph (a)(2) of this section, shall also be paid.

(b)(1) For the purpose of computing the fee prescribed in paragraphs (a)(1), (2), (4) and (28) of this section the authorized capital stock of a corporation shall be considered to be the total number of shares which the corporation is authorized to issue, whether or not the total number of shares that may be outstanding at any 1 time be limited to a less number.

(2) For the purpose of computing the fee prescribed in paragraphs (a)(2), (3) and (28) of this section, a certificate of amendment of certificate of incorporation, or an amended certificate of incorporation before payment of capital, or a restated certificate of incorporation, or a certificate of validation, shall be considered as increasing the authorized capital stock of a corporation provided it involves an increase in the number of shares, or an increase in the par value of shares, or a change of shares with par value into shares without par value, or a change of shares without par value into shares with par value, or any combination of 2 or more of the above changes, and provided further that the fee computed at the rates set forth in paragraph (a)(1) of this section upon the total authorized capital stock of the corporation including the proposed change or changes exceeds the fee so computed upon the total authorized stock of the corporation excluding such change or changes.

(c) The Secretary of State may issue photocopies or electronic image copies of instruments on file, as well as instruments, documents and other papers not on file, and for all such photocopies or electronic image copies which are not certified by the Secretary of State, a fee of $10 shall be paid for the first page and $2.00 for each additional page. ■ Notwithstanding Delaware's Freedom of Information Act (Chapter 100 of Title 29) or any other provision of law granting access to public records, the Secretary of State upon request shall issue only photocopies or electronic image copies of public records in exchange for the fees described in this section, and in no case shall the Secretary of State be required to provide copies (or access to copies) of such public records (including without limitation bulk data, digital copies of instruments, documents and other papers, databases or other information) in an electronic medium or in any form other than photocopies or electronic image copies of such public records in exchange, as applicable, for the fees described in this section or § 2318 of Title 29 for each such record associated with a file number.

(d) No fees for the use of the State shall be charged or collected from any corporation incorporated for the drainage and reclamation of lowlands or for the amendment or renewal of the charter of such corporation.

(e) The Secretary of State may in the Secretary of State's discretion permit the extension of credit for the fees required by this section upon such terms as the Secretary of State shall deem to be appropriate.

(f) The Secretary of State shall retain from the revenue collected from the fees required by this section a sum sufficient to provide at all times a fund of at least $500, but not more than $1,500, from which the Secretary of State may refund any payment made pursuant to this section to the extent that it exceeds the fees required by this section. ■

The fund shall be deposited in the financial institution which is the legal depository of state moneys to the credit of the Secretary of State and shall be disbursable on order of the Secretary of State.

(g) The Secretary of State may in the Secretary of State's discretion charge a fee of $60 for each check received for payment of any fee or tax under Chapter 1 or Chapter 6 of this title that is returned due to insufficient funds or as the result of a stop payment order.

(h) In addition to those fees charged under subsections (a) and (c) of this section, there shall be collected by and paid to the Secretary of State the following:

(1) For all services described in subsection (a) of this section that are requested to be completed within 30 minutes on the same day as the day of the request, an additional sum of up to $7,500 and for all services described in subsections (a) and (c) of this section that are requested to be completed within 1 hour on the same day as the day of the request, an additional sum of up to $1,000 and for all services described in subsections (a) and (c) of this section that are requested to be completed within 2 hours on the same day as the day of the request, an additional sum of up to $500; and

(2) For all services described in subsections (a) and (c) of this section that are requested to be completed within the same day as the day of the request, an additional sum of up to $300; and

(3) For all services described in subsections (a) and (c) of this section that are requested to be completed within a 24-hour period from the time of the request, an additional sum of up to $150.

The Secretary of State shall establish (and may from time to time alter or amend) a schedule of specific fees payable pursuant to this subsection.

(i) A domestic corporation or a foreign corporation registered to do business in this State that files with the Secretary of State any instrument or certificate, and in connection therewith, neglects, refuses or fails to pay any fee or tax under Chapter 1 or Chapter 6 of this title shall, after written demand therefor by the Secretary of State by mail addressed to such domestic corporation or foreign corporation in care of its registered agent in this State, cease to be in good standing as a domestic corporation or registered as a foreign corporation in this State on the ninetieth day following the date of mailing of such demand, unless such fee or tax and, if applicable, the fee provided for in subsection (g) of this section are paid in full prior to the ninetieth day following the date of mailing of such demand. ▪ A domestic corporation that has ceased to be in good standing or a foreign corporation that has ceased to be registered by reason of the neglect, refusal or failure to pay any such fee or tax shall be restored to and have the status of a domestic corporation in good standing or a foreign corporation that is registered in this State upon the payment of the fee or tax which such domestic corporation or foreign corporation neglected, refused or failed to pay together with the fee provided for in subsection (g) of this section, if applicable. ▪ The Secretary of State shall not accept for filing any instrument authorized to be filed with the Secretary of State under this title in respect of any domestic corporation that is not in good standing or any foreign corporation that has ceased to be registered by reason of the neglect, refusal or failure to pay any such fee or tax, and shall not issue any certificate of good standing with respect to such domestic corporation or foreign corporation, unless and until such domestic corporation or foreign corporation shall have been restored to and have the status of a domestic corporation in good standing or a foreign corporation duly registered in this State.

(j) As used in this section, the term "exempt corporation" shall have the meaning given to it in § 501(b) of this title.

§ 392. [Reserved.]

§ 393. Rights, liabilities and duties under prior statutes.

All rights, privileges and immunities vested or accrued by and under any laws enacted prior to the adoption or amendment of this chapter, all suits pending, all rights of action conferred, and all duties, restrictions, liabilities and penalties imposed or required by and under laws enacted prior to the adoption or amendment of this chapter, shall not be impaired, diminished or affected by this chapter.

§ 394. Reserved power of State to amend or repeal chapter; chapter part of corporation's charter or certificate of incorporation.

This chapter may be amended or repealed, at the pleasure of the General Assembly, but any amendment or repeal shall not take away or impair any remedy under this chapter against any corporation or its officers for any liability which shall have been previously incurred. ▪ This chapter and all amendments thereof shall be a part of the charter or certificate of incorporation of every corporation except so far as the same are inapplicable and inappropriate to the objects of the corporation.

§ 395. Corporations using "trust" in name, advertisements and otherwise; restrictions; violations and penalties; exceptions.

(a) Except as provided below in subsection (d) of this section, every corporation of this State using the word "trust" as part of its name, except a corporation regulated under the Bank Holding Company Act of 1956, 12 U.S.C. § 1841 et seq., or § 10 of the Home Owners' Loan Act, 12 U.S.C. § 1467a et seq., as those statutes shall from time to time be amended, shall be under the supervision of the State Bank Commissioner of this State and shall make not less than 2 reports during each year to the Commissioner, according to the form which shall be prescribed by the Commissioner, verified by the oaths or affirmations of the president or vice-president, and the treasurer or secretary of the corporation, and attested by the signatures of at least 3 directors.

(b) Except as provided below in subsection (d) of this section, no corporation of this State shall use the word "trust" as part of its name, except a corporation reporting to and under the supervision of the State Bank Commissioner of this State or a corporation regulated under the Bank Holding Company Act of 1956, 12 U.S.C. § 1841 et seq., or § 10 of the Home Owners' Loan Act, 12 U.S.C. § 1467a et seq., as those statutes shall from time to time be amended. ▪ Except as provided below in subsection (d) of this section, the name of any such corporation shall not be amended so as to include the word "trust" unless such corporation shall report to and be under the supervision of the Commissioner, or unless it is regulated under the Bank Holding Company Act of 1956 or the Savings and Loan Holding Company Act.

(c) No corporation of this State, except corporations reporting to and under the supervision of the State Bank Commissioner of this State or corporations regulated under the Bank Holding Company Act of 1956, 12 U.S.C. § 1841 et seq., or § 10 of the Home Owners' Loan Act, 12 U.S.C. § 1467a et seq., as those statutes shall from time to time be amended, shall advertise or put forth any sign as a trust company, or in any way solicit or receive deposits or transact business as a trust company.

(d) The requirements and restrictions set forth above in subsections (a) and (b) of this section shall not apply to, and shall not be construed to prevent the use of the word "trust" as part of the name of, a corporation that is not subject to the supervision of the State Bank Commissioner of this State and that is not regulated under the Bank Holding Company Act of 1956, 12 U.S.C. § 1841 et seq., or § 10 of the Home Owners' Loan Act, 12 U.S.C. § 1467a et seq., where use of the word "trust" as part of such corporation's name clearly:

(1) Does not refer to a trust business;

(2) Is not likely to mislead the public into believing that the nature of the business of the corporation includes activities that fall under the supervision of the State Bank Commissioner of this State or that are regulated under the Bank Holding Company Act of 1956, 12 U.S.C. § 1841 et seq., or § 10 of the Home Owners' Loan Act, 12 U.S.C. § 1467a et seq.; and

(3) Will not otherwise lead to a pattern and practice of abuse that might cause harm to the interests of the public or the State, as determined by the Director of the Division of Corporations and the State Bank Commissioner.

§ 396. Publication of chapter by Secretary of State; distribution.

The Secretary of State may have printed, from time to time as the Secretary of State deems necessary, pamphlet copies of this chapter, and the Secretary of State shall dispose of the copies to persons and corporations desiring the same for a sum not exceeding the cost of printing. ▪ The money received from the sale of the copies shall be disposed of as are other fees of the office of the Secretary of State. ▪ Nothing in this section shall prevent the free distribution of single pamphlet copies of this chapter by the Secretary of State, for the printing of which provision is made from time to time by joint resolution of the General Assembly.

§ 397. Penalty for unauthorized publication of chapter.

Whoever prints or publishes this chapter without the authority of the Secretary of State of this State, shall be fined not more than $500 or imprisoned not more than 3 months, or both.

§ 398. Short title.

This chapter shall be known and may be identified and referred to as the "General Corporation Law of the State of Delaware."

Model Business Corporation Act (2019)

Table of Contents

Chapter 1. General Provisions

Subchapter A. Short Title and Reservation of Power

§ 1.01. Short Title

This Act shall be known and may be cited as the "[name of state] Business Corporation Act."

§ 1.02. Reservation of Power to Amend or Repeal

The [name of state legislature] has power to amend or repeal all or part of this Act at any time and all domestic and foreign corporations subject to this Act are governed by the amendment or repeal.

Subchapter B. Filing Documents

§ 1.20. Requirements for Documents; Extrinsic Facts

(a) A document must satisfy the requirements of this section, and of any other section that adds to or varies these requirements, to be entitled to filing by the secretary of state.

(b) This Act must require or permit filing the document in the office of the secretary of state.

(c) The document must contain the information required by this Act and may contain other information.

(d) The document must be typewritten or printed or, if electronically transmitted, it must be in a format that can be retrieved or reproduced in typewritten or printed form.

(e) The document must be in the English language. A corporate name need not be in English if written in English letters or Arabic or Roman numerals.

(f) The document must be signed:

(1) by the chairman of the board of directors of a domestic or foreign corporation, by its president, or by another of its officers;

(2) if directors have not been selected or the corporation has not been formed, by an incorporator; or

(3) if the corporation is in the hands of a receiver, trustee, or other court-appointed fiduciary, by that fiduciary.

(g) The person executing the document shall sign it and state beneath or opposite the person's signature the person's name and the capacity in which the document is signed. The document may but need not contain a corporate seal, attestation, acknowledgment, or verification.

(h) If the secretary of state has prescribed a mandatory form for the document under § 1.21(a), the document must be in or on the prescribed form.

(i) The document must be delivered to the office of the secretary of state for filing. Delivery may be made by electronic transmission if and to the extent permitted by the secretary of state. If it is filed in typewritten or printed form and not transmitted electronically, the secretary of state may require one exact or conformed copy to be delivered with the document.

(j) When the document is delivered to the office of the secretary of state for filing, the correct filing fee, and any franchise tax, license fee, or penalty required by this Act or other law to be paid at the time of delivery for filing must be paid or provision for payment made in a manner permitted by the secretary of state.

(k) Whenever a provision of this Act permits any of the terms of a plan or a filed document to be dependent on facts objectively ascertainable outside the plan or filed document, the following provisions apply:

(1) The manner in which the facts will operate upon the terms of the plan or filed document must be set forth in the plan or filed document.

(2) The facts may include:

(i) any of the following that is available in a nationally recognized news or information medium either in print or electronically: statistical or market indices, market prices of any security or group of securities, interest rates, currency exchange rates, or similar economic or financial data;

(ii) a determination or action by any person or body, including the corporation or any other party to a plan or filed document; or

(iii) the terms of, or actions taken under, an agreement to which the corporation is a party, or any other agreement or document.

(3) As used in this subsection **(k)**:

(i) "filed document" means a document filed by the secretary of state under any provision of this Act except chapter 15 or § 6.21; and

(ii) "plan" means a plan of domestication, conversion, merger, or share exchange.

(4) The following provisions of a plan or filed document may not be made dependent on facts outside the plan or filed document:

(i) the name and address of any person required in a filed document;

(ii) the registered office of any entity required in a filed document;

(iii) the registered agent of any entity required in a filed document;

(iv) the number of authorized shares and designation of each class or series of shares;

(v) the effective date of a filed document; and

(vi) any required statement in a filed document of the date on which the underlying transaction was approved or the manner in which that approval was given.

(5) If a provision of a filed document is made dependent on a fact ascertainable outside of the filed document, and that fact is neither ascertainable by reference to a source described in subsection (k)(2)(i) or a document that is a matter of public record, nor have the affected shareholders received notice of the fact from the corporation, then the corporation shall file with the secretary of state articles of amendment to the filed document setting forth the fact promptly after the time when the fact referred to is first ascertainable or thereafter changes. Articles of amendment under this subsection (k)(5) are deemed to be authorized by the authorization of the original filed document to which they relate and may be filed by the corporation without further action by the board of directors or the shareholders.

§ 1.21. Forms

(a) The secretary of state may prescribe and furnish on request forms for: (i) an application for a certificate of existence or certificate of registration, (ii) a foreign corporation's registration statement, (iii) a foreign corporation's statement of withdrawal, (iv) a foreign corporation's transfer of registration statement, and (v) the annual report. If the secretary of state so requires, use of these forms is mandatory.

(b) The secretary of state may prescribe and furnish on request forms for other documents required or permitted to be filed by this Act but their use is not mandatory.

§ 1.22. Filing, Service, and Copying Fees

(a) The secretary of state shall collect the following fees when the documents described in this subsection are delivered to the secretary of state for filing:

Document	Fee
Articles of incorporation	$_____.
Application for use of indistinguishable name	$_____.
Application for reserved name	$_____.
Notice of transfer of reserved name	$_____.
Application for registered name	$_____.
Application for renewal of registered name	$_____.
Corporation's statement of change of registered agent or registered office or both	$_____.
Agent's statement of change of registered office for each affected corporation not to exceed a total of $_____	$_____.
Agent's statement of resignation	No fee.
Articles of domestication	$_____.
Articles of conversion	$_____.
Amendment of articles of incorporation	$_____.
Restatement of articles of incorporation with amendment of articles	$_____.
Restatement of articles of incorporation without amendment of articles	$_____.
Articles of merger or share exchange	$_____.
Articles of dissolution	$_____.
Articles of revocation of dissolution	$_____.
Certificate of administrative dissolution	No fee.
Application for reinstatement following administrative dissolution	$_____.
Certificate of reinstatement	No fee
Certificate of judicial dissolution	No fee.
Foreign registration statement	$_____.
Amendment of foreign registration statement	$_____.
Statement of withdrawal	$_____.
Transfer of foreign registration statement	$_____.
Notice of termination of registration	No fee.
Annual report	$_____.
Articles of correction	$_____.
Articles of validation	$_____.

Application for certificate of existence or registration $_____.

Any other document required or permitted to be filed by this Act $_____.

(b) The secretary of state shall collect a fee of $_____ each time process is served on the secretary of state under this Act. The party to a proceeding causing service of process is entitled to recover this fee as costs if such party prevails in the proceeding.

(c) The secretary of state shall collect the following fees for copying and certifying the copy of any filed document relating to a domestic or foreign corporation:

$ _____ a page for copying; and

$ _____ for the certificate.

§ 1.23. Effective Date of Filed Document

(a) Except to the extent otherwise provided in § 1.24(c) and subchapter E of this chapter, a document accepted for filing is effective:

(1) on the date and at the time of filing, as provided in § 1.25(b);

(2) on the date of filing and at the time specified in the document as its effective time if later than the time under subsection (a)(1);

(3) at a specified delayed effective date and time which may not be more than 90 days after filing; or

(4) if a delayed effective date is specified, but no time is specified, at 12:01 a.m. on the date specified, which may not be more than 90 days after the date of filing.

(b) If a filed document does not specify the time zone or place at which a date or time or both is to be determined, the date or time or both at which it becomes effective shall be those prevailing at the place of filing in this state.

§ 1.24. Correcting Filed Document

(a) A document filed by the secretary of state pursuant to this Act may be corrected if (i) the document contains an inaccuracy, (ii) the document was defectively signed, attested, sealed, verified,

or acknowledged, or (iii) the electronic transmission was defective.

(b) A document is corrected:

(1) by preparing articles of correction that

(i) describe the document (including its filing date) or attach a copy of it to the articles of correction,

(ii) specify the inaccuracy or defect to be corrected, and (iii) correct the inaccuracy or defect; and

(2) by delivering the articles of correction to the secretary of state for filing.

(c) Articles of correction are effective on the effective date of the document they correct except as to persons relying on the uncorrected document and adversely affected by the correction. As to those persons, articles of correction are effective when filed.

§ 1.25. Filing Duty of Secretary of State

(a) If a document delivered to the office of the secretary of state for filing satisfies the requirements of § 1.20, the secretary of state shall file it.

(b) The secretary of state files a document by recording it as filed on the date and time of receipt. After filing a document, the secretary of state shall return to the person who delivered the document for filing a copy of the document with an acknowledgement of the date and time of filing.

(c) If the secretary of state refuses to file a document, it shall be returned to the person who delivered the document for filing within five days after the document was delivered, together with a brief, written explanation of the reason for the refusal.

(d) The secretary of state's duty to file documents under this section is ministerial. The secretary of state's filing or refusing to file a document does not create a presumption that: (i) the document does or does not conform to the requirements of the Act; or (ii) the information contained in the document is correct or incorrect.

§ 1.26. Appeal from Secretary of State's Refusal to File Document

(a) If the secretary of state refuses to file a document delivered for filing, the person that delivered the document for filing may petition [name or describe court] to compel its filing. The document and the explanation of the secretary of state of the refusal to file must be attached to the petition. The court may decide the matter in a summary proceeding.

(b) The court may order the secretary of state to file the document or take other action the court considers appropriate.

(c) The court's final decision may be appealed as in other civil proceedings.

§ 1.27. Evidentiary Effect of Certified Copy of Filed Document

A certificate from the secretary of state delivered with a copy of a document filed by the secretary of state is conclusive evidence that the original document is on file with the secretary of state.

§ 1.28. Certificate of Existence or Registration

(a) Any person may apply to the secretary of state to furnish a certificate of existence for a domestic corporation or a certificate of registration for a foreign corporation.

(b) A certificate of existence sets forth:

(1) the domestic corporation's corporate name;

(2) that the domestic corporation is duly incorporated under the law of this state, the date of its incorporation, and the period of its duration if less than perpetual;

(3) that all fees, taxes, and penalties owed to this state have been paid, if

(i) payment is reflected in the records of the secretary of state, and

(ii) nonpayment affects the existence of the domestic corporation;

(4) that its most recent annual report required by § 16.21 has been filed with the secretary of state;

(5) that articles of dissolution have not been filed;

(6) that the corporation is not administratively dissolved and a proceeding is not pending under § 14.21; and

(7) other facts of record in the office of the secretary of state that may be requested by the applicant.

(c) A certificate of registration sets forth:

(1) the foreign corporation's name used in this state;

(2) that the foreign corporation is registered to do business in this state;

(3) that all fees, taxes, and penalties owed to this state have been paid, if

(i) payment is reflected in the records of the secretary of state, and

(ii) nonpayment affects the registration of the foreign corporation;

(4) that its most recent annual report required by § 16.21 has been filed with the secretary of state; and

(5) other facts of record in the office of the secretary of state that may be requested by the applicant.

(d) Subject to any qualification stated in the certificate, a certificate of existence or registration issued by the secretary of state may be relied upon as conclusive evidence of the facts stated in the certificate.

§ 1.29. Penalty for Signing False Document

(a) A person commits an offense by signing a document that the person knows is false in any material respect with intent that the document be delivered to the secretary of state for filing.

(b) An offense under this section is a [_____] misdemeanor [punishable by a fine of not to exceed $ _____].

Subchapter C. Secretary of State

§ 1.30. Powers

The secretary of state has the power reasonably necessary to perform the duties required of the secretary of state by this Act.

Subchapter D. Definitions

§ 1.40. Act Definitions

In this Act, unless otherwise specified:

"Articles of incorporation" means the articles of incorporation described in § 2.02, all amendments to the articles of incorporation, and any other documents permitted or required to be delivered for filing by a domestic business corporation with the secretary of state under any provision of this Act that modify, amend, supplement, restate or replace the articles of incorporation. After an amendment of the articles of incorporation or any other document filed under this Act that restates the articles of incorporation in their entirety, the articles of incorporation shall not include any prior documents. When used with respect to a foreign corporation or a domestic or foreign nonprofit corporation, the "articles of incorporation" of such an entity means the document of such entity that is equivalent to the articles of incorporation of a domestic business corporation.

"Authorized shares" means the shares of all classes a domestic or foreign corporation is authorized to issue.

"Beneficial shareholder" means a person who owns the beneficial interest in shares, which may be a record shareholder or a person on whose behalf shares are registered in the name of an intermediary or nominee.

"Conspicuous" means so written, displayed, or presented that a reasonable person against whom the writing is to operate should have noticed it.

"Corporation," "domestic corporation," "business corporation" or "domestic business corporation" means a corporation for profit, which is not a foreign corporation, incorporated under this Act.

"Deliver" or "delivery" means any method of delivery used in conventional commercial practice, including delivery by hand, mail, commercial delivery, and, if authorized in accordance with § 1.41, by electronic transmission.

"Distribution" means a direct or indirect transfer of cash or other property (except a corporation's own shares) or incurrence of indebtedness by a corporation to or for the benefit of its shareholders in respect of any of its shares. A distribution may be in the form of a payment of a dividend; a purchase, redemption, or other acquisition of shares; a distribution of indebtedness; a distribution in liquidation; or otherwise.

"Document" means (i) any tangible medium on which information is inscribed, and includes handwritten, typed, printed or similar instruments, and copies of such instruments, or (ii) an electronic record.

"Domestic," with respect to an entity, means an entity governed as to its internal affairs by the law of this state.

"Effective date," when referring to a document accepted for filing by the secretary of state, means the time and date determined in accordance with § 1.23.

"Electronic" means relating to technology having electrical, digital, magnetic, wireless, optical, electromagnetic, or similar capabilities.

"Electronic record" means information that is stored in an electronic or other nontangible medium and is retrievable in paper form through an automated process used in conventional commercial practice, unless otherwise authorized in accordance with § 1.41(j).

"Electronic transmission" or "electronically transmitted" means any form or process of communication not directly involving the physical transfer of paper or another tangible medium, which (i) is suitable for the retention, retrieval, and reproduction of information by the recipient, and (ii) is retrievable in paper form by the recipient through an automated process used in conventional commercial practice, unless otherwise authorized in accordance with § 1.41(j).

"Eligible entity" means a domestic or foreign unincorporated entity or a domestic or foreign nonprofit corporation.

"Eligible interests" means interests or memberships.

"Employee" includes an officer but not a director. A director may accept duties that make the director also an employee.

"Entity" includes domestic and foreign business corporation; domestic and foreign nonprofit corporation; estate; trust; domestic and foreign unincorporated entity; and state, United States, and foreign government.

"Expenses" means reasonable expenses of any kind that are incurred in connection with a matter.

"Filing entity" means an unincorporated entity, other than a limited liability partnership, that is of a type that is created by filing a public organic record or is required to file a public organic record that evidences its creation.

"Foreign," with respect to an entity, means an entity governed as to its internal affairs by the organic law of a jurisdiction other than this state.

"Foreign corporation" or "foreign business corporation" means a corporation incorporated under a law other than the law of this state which would be a business corporation if incorporated under the law of this state.

"Foreign nonprofit corporation" means a corporation incorporated under a law other than the law of this state which would be a nonprofit corporation if incorporated under the law of this state.

"Foreign registration statement" means the foreign registration statement described in § 15.03.

"Governmental subdivision" includes authority, county, district, and municipality.

"Governor" means any person under whose authority the powers of an entity are exercised and under whose direction the activities and affairs of the entity are managed pursuant to the organic law governing the entity and its organic rules.

"Includes" and "including" denote a partial definition or a nonexclusive list.

"Individual" means a natural person.

"Interest" means either or both of the following rights under the organic law governing an unincorporated entity:

(i) the right to receive distributions from the entity either in the ordinary course or upon liquidation; or

(ii) the right to receive notice or vote on issues involving its internal affairs, other than as an agent, assignee, proxy or person responsible for managing its business and affairs.

"Interest holder" means a person who holds of record an interest.

"Interest holder liability" means:

(i) personal liability for a debt, obligation, or other liability of a domestic or foreign corporation or eligible entity that is imposed on a person:

(A) solely by reason of the person's status as a shareholder, member or interest holder; or

(B) by the articles of incorporation of the domestic corporation or the organic rules of the eligible entity or foreign corporation that make one or more specified shareholders, members, or interest holders, or categories of shareholders, members, or interest holders, liable in their capacity as shareholders, members, or interest holders for all or specified liabilities of the corporation or eligible entity; or

(ii) an obligation of a shareholder, member, or interest holder under the articles of incorporation of a domestic corporation or the organic rules of an eligible entity or foreign corporation to contribute to the entity.

For purposes of the foregoing, except as otherwise provided in the articles of incorporation of a domestic corporation or the organic law or organic rules of an eligible entity or a foreign corporation, interest holder liability arises under clause (i) when the corporation or eligible entity incurs the liability.

"Jurisdiction of formation" means the state or country the law of which includes the organic law governing a domestic or foreign corporation or eligible entity.

"Means" denotes an exhaustive definition.

"Membership" means the rights of a member in a domestic or foreign nonprofit corporation.

"Merger" means a transaction pursuant to § 11.02.

"Nonfiling entity" means an unincorporated entity that is of a type that is not created by filing a public organic record.

"Nonprofit corporation" or "domestic nonprofit corporation" means a corporation incorporated under the laws of this state and subject to the provisions of the [name of state] Nonprofit Corporation Act.

"Organic law" means the statute governing the internal affairs of a domestic or foreign business or nonprofit corporation or unincorporated entity.

"Organic rules" means the public organic record and private organic rules of a domestic or foreign corporation or eligible entity.

"Person" includes an individual and an entity.

"Principal office" means the office (in or out of this state) so designated in the annual report or foreign registration statement where the principal executive offices of a domestic or foreign corporation are located.

"Private organic rules" means (i) the bylaws of a domestic or foreign business or nonprofit corporation or (ii) the rules, regardless of whether in writing, that govern the internal affairs of an unincorporated entity, are binding on all its interest holders, and are not part of its public organic record, if any. Where private organic rules have been amended or restated, the term means the private organic rules as last amended or restated.

"Proceeding" includes civil suit and criminal, administrative, and investigatory action.

"Public organic record" means (i) the articles of incorporation of a domestic or foreign business or nonprofit corporation or (ii) the document, if any, the filing of which is required to create an unincorporated entity, or which creates the unincorporated entity and is required to be filed. Where a public organic record has been amended or restated, the term means the public organic record as last amended or restated.

"Record date" means the date fixed for determining the identity of the corporation's shareholders and their shareholdings for purposes of this Act. Unless another time is specified when the record date is fixed, the determination shall be made as of the close of business at the principal office of the corporation on the date so fixed.

"Record shareholder" means (i) the person in whose name shares are registered in the records of the corporation or (ii) the person identified as the beneficial owner of shares in a beneficial ownership certificate pursuant to § 7.23 on file with the corporation to the extent of the rights granted by such certificate.

"Registered foreign corporation" means a foreign corporation registered to do business in the state pursuant to chapter 15.

"Secretary" means the corporate officer to whom the board of directors has delegated responsibility under § 8.40(c) to maintain the minutes of the meetings of the board of directors and of the shareholders and for authenticating records of the corporation.

"Share exchange" means a transaction pursuant to § 11.03.

"Shareholder" means a record shareholder.

"Shares" means the units into which the proprietary interests in a domestic or foreign corporation are divided.

"Sign" or "signature" means, with present intent to authenticate or adopt a document:

(i) to execute or adopt a tangible symbol to a document, and includes any manual, facsimile, or conformed signature; or

(ii) to attach to or logically associate with an electronic transmission an electronic sound, symbol, or process, and includes an electronic signature in an electronic transmission.

"State," when referring to a part of the United States, includes a state and commonwealth (and their agencies and governmental subdivisions) and a territory and insular possession (and their agencies and governmental subdivisions) of the United States.

"Subscriber" means a person who subscribes for shares in a corporation, whether before or after incorporation.

"Type of entity" means a generic form of entity:

(i) recognized at common law; or

(ii) formed under an organic law, regardless of whether some entities formed under that law are subject to provisions of that law that create different categories of the form of entity.

"Unincorporated entity" means an organization or artificial legal person that either has a separate legal existence or has the power to acquire an estate in real property in its own name and that is not any of the following: a domestic or foreign business or nonprofit corporation, a series of a limited liability company or of another type of entity, an estate, a trust, a state, United States, or foreign government. The term includes a general partnership, limited liability company, limited partnership, business trust, joint stock association and unincorporated nonprofit association.

"United States" includes district, authority, bureau, commission, department, and any other agency of the United States.

"Unrestricted voting trust beneficial owner" means, with respect to any shareholder rights, a voting trust beneficial owner whose entitlement to exercise the shareholder right in question is not inconsistent with the voting trust agreement.

"Voting group" means all shares of one or more classes or series that under the articles of incorporation or this Act are entitled to vote and be counted together collectively on a matter at a meeting of shareholders. All shares entitled by the articles of incorporation or this Act to vote generally on the matter are for that purpose a single voting group.

"Voting power" means the current power to vote in the election of directors.

"Voting trust beneficial owner" means an owner of a beneficial interest in shares of the corporation held in a voting trust established pursuant to § 7.30(a).

"Writing" or "written" means any information in the form of a document.

§ 1.41. Notices and Other Communications

(a) A notice under this Act must be in writing unless oral notice is reasonable in the circumstances. Unless otherwise agreed between the sender and the recipient, words in a notice or other communication under this Act must be in English.

(b) A notice or other communication may be given by any method of delivery, except that electronic transmissions must be in accordance with this section. If the methods of delivery are impracticable, a notice or other communication may be given by means of a broad nonexclusionary distribution to the public (which may include a newspaper of general circulation in the area where published; radio, television, or other form of public broadcast communication; or other methods of distribution that the corporation has previously identified to its shareholders).

(c) A notice or other communication to a domestic corporation or to a foreign corporation registered to do business in this state may be delivered to the corporation's registered agent at its registered office or to the secretary at the corporation's principal office shown in its most recent annual report or, in the case of a foreign corporation that has not yet delivered an annual report, in its foreign registration statement.

(d) A notice or other communications may be delivered by electronic transmission if consented to by the recipient or if authorized by subsection (j).

(e) Any consent under subsection (d) may be revoked by the person who consented by written or electronic notice to the person to whom the consent was delivered. Any such consent is deemed revoked if (i) the corporation is unable to deliver two consecutive electronic transmissions given by the corporation in accordance with such consent, and (ii) such inability becomes known to the secretary or an assistant secretary or to the transfer agent, or other person responsible for the giving of notice or other communications; provided, however, the inadvertent failure to treat such inability as a revocation shall not invalidate any meeting or other action.

(f) Unless otherwise agreed between the sender and the recipient, an electronic transmission is received when:

(1) it enters an information processing system that the recipient has designated or uses for the purposes of receiving electronic transmissions or information of the type sent, and from which the recipient is able to retrieve the electronic transmission; and

(2) it is in a form capable of being processed by that system.

(g) Receipt of an electronic acknowledgement from an information processing system described in subsection (f)(1) establishes that an electronic transmission was received but, by itself, does not establish that the content sent corresponds to the content received.

(h) An electronic transmission is received under this section even if no person is aware of its receipt.

(i) A notice or other communication, if in a comprehensible form or manner, is effective at the earliest of the following:

(1) if in a physical form, the earliest of when it is actually received, or when it is left at:

(i) a shareholder's address shown on the corporation's record of shareholders maintained by the corporation under § 16.01(d);

(ii) a director's residence or usual place of business; or

(iii) the corporation's principal office;

(2) if mailed postage prepaid and correctly addressed to a shareholder, upon deposit in the United States mail;

(3) if mailed by United States mail postage prepaid and correctly addressed to a recipient other than a shareholder, the earliest of when it is actually received, or:

(i) if sent by registered or certified mail, return receipt requested, the date shown on the return receipt signed by or on behalf of the addressee; or

(ii) five days after it is deposited in the United States mail;

(4) if an electronic transmission, when it is received as provided in subsection (f); and

(5) if oral, when communicated.

(j) A notice or other communication may be in the form of an electronic transmission that cannot be directly reproduced in paper form by the recipient through an automated process used in conventional commercial practice only if (i) the electronic transmission is otherwise retrievable in perceivable form, and (ii) the sender and the recipient have consented in writing to the use of such form of electronic transmission.

(k) If this Act prescribes requirements for notices or other communications in particular circumstances, those requirements govern. If articles of incorporation or bylaws prescribe requirements for notices or other communications, not inconsistent with this section or other provisions of this Act, those requirements govern. The articles of incorporation or bylaws may authorize or require delivery of notices of meetings of directors by electronic transmission.

(l) In the event that any provisions of this Act are deemed to modify, limit, or supersede the federal Electronic Signatures in Global and National Commerce Act, 15 U.S.C. §§ 7001 et seq., the provisions of this Act shall control to the maximum extent permitted by § 102(a)(2) of that federal act.

§ 1.42. Number of Shareholders

(a) For purposes of this Act, the following identified as a shareholder in a corporation's current record of shareholders constitutes one shareholder:

(1) three or fewer co-owners;

(2) a corporation, partnership, trust, estate, or other entity; and

(3) the trustees, guardians, custodians, or other fiduciaries of a single trust, estate, or account.

(b) For purposes of this Act, shareholdings registered in substantially similar names constitute one shareholder if it is reasonable to believe that the names represent the same person.

§ 1.43. Qualified Director

(a) A "qualified director" is a director who, at the time action is to be taken under:

(1) section 2.02(b)(6), is not a director (i) to whom the limitation or elimination of the duty of an officer to offer potential business opportunities to the corporation would apply, or (ii) who has a material relationship with any other person to whom the limitation or elimination would apply;

(2) section 7.44, does not have (i) a material interest in the outcome of the proceeding, or (ii) a material relationship with a person who has such an interest;

(3) section 8.53 or 8.55, (i) is not a party to the proceeding, (ii) is not a director as to whom a transaction is a director's conflicting interest transaction or who sought a disclaimer of the corporation's interest in a business opportunity under § 8.70, which transaction or disclaimer is challenged in the proceeding, and (iii) does not have a material relationship with a director described in either clause (i) or clause (ii) of this subsection (a)(3);

(4) section 8.62, is not a director (i) as to whom the transaction is a director's conflicting interest transaction, or (ii) who has a material relationship with another director as to whom the transaction is a director's conflicting interest transaction; or

(5) section 8.70, is not a director who (i) pursues or takes advantage of the business opportunity, directly, or indirectly through or on behalf of another person, or (ii) has a material relationship with a director or officer who pursues or takes advantage of the business opportunity, directly, or indirectly through or on behalf of another person.

(b) For purposes of this section:

(1) "material relationship" means a familial, financial, professional, employment or other relationship that would reasonably be expected to impair the objectivity of the director's judgment when participating in the action to be taken; and

(2) "material interest" means an actual or potential benefit or detriment (other than one which would devolve on the corporation or the shareholders generally) that would reasonably be expected to impair the objectivity of the director's judgment when participating in the action to be taken.

(c) The presence of one or more of the following circumstances shall not automatically prevent a director from being a qualified director:

(1) nomination or election of the director to the current board by any director who is not a qualified director with respect to the matter (or by any person that has a material relationship with that director), acting alone or participating with others;

(2) service as a director of another corporation of which a director who is not a qualified director with respect to the matter (or any individual who has a material relationship with that director), is or was also a director; or

(3) with respect to action to be taken under § 7.44, status as a named defendant, as a director against whom action is demanded, or as a director who approved the conduct being challenged.

§ 1.44. Householding

(a) A corporation has delivered written notice or any other report or statement under this Act, the articles of incorporation or the bylaws to all share-holders who share a common address if:

    (1) the corporation delivers one copy of the notice, report or statement to the common address;

    (2) the corporation addresses the notice, report or statement to those shareholders either as a group or to each of those shareholders individually or to the shareholders in a form to which each of those shareholders has consented; and

    (3) each of those shareholders consents to delivery of a single copy of such notice, report or statement to the shareholders' common address.

(b) Any such consent described in subsections (a)(2) or (a)(3) shall be revocable by any of such shareholders who deliver written notice of revocation to the corporation. If such written notice of revocation is delivered, the corporation shall begin providing individual notices, reports or other statements to the revoking shareholder no later than 30 days after delivery of the written notice of revocation.

(c) Any shareholder who fails to object by written notice to the corporation, within 60 days of written notice by the corporation of its intention to deliver single copies of notices, reports or statements to shareholders who share a common address as permitted by subsection (a), shall be deemed to have consented to receiving such single copy at the common address; provided that the notice of intention explains that consent may be revoked and the method for revoking.

Subchapter E. Ratification of Defective Corporate Actions

§ 1.45. Definitions

In this subchapter:

"Corporate action" means any action taken by or on behalf of the corporation, including any action taken by the incorporator, the board of directors, a committee of the board of directors, an officer or agent of the corporation or the shareholders.

"Date of the defective corporate action" means the date (or the approximate date, if the exact date is unknown) the defective corporate action was purported to have been taken.

"Defective corporate action" means (i) any corporate action purportedly taken that is, and at the time such corporate action was purportedly taken would have been, within the power of the corporation, but is void or voidable due to a failure of authorization, and (ii) an overissue.

"Failure of authorization" means the failure to authorize, approve or otherwise effect a corporate action in compliance with the provisions of this Act, the articles of incorporation or bylaws, a corporate resolution or any plan or agreement to which the corporation is a party, if and to the extent such failure would render such corporate action void or voidable.

"Overissue" means the purported issuance of:

    (i) shares of a class or series in excess of the number of shares of a class or series the corporation has the power to issue under § 6.01 at the time of such issuance; or

    (ii) shares of any class or series that is not then authorized for issuance by the articles of incorporation.

"Putative shares" means the shares of any class or series (including shares issued upon exercise of rights, options, warrants or other securities convertible into shares of the corporation, or interests with respect to such shares) that were created or issued as a result of a defective corporate action, that (i) but for any failure of authorization would constitute valid shares, or (ii) cannot be determined by the board of directors to be valid shares.

"Valid shares" means the shares of any class or series that have been duly authorized and validly issued in accordance with this Act, including as a result of ratification or validation under this subchapter.

"Validation effective time" with respect to any defective corporate action ratified under this subchapter means the later of:

(i) the time at which the ratification of the defective corporate action is approved by the shareholders, or if approval of shareholders is not required, the time at which the notice required by § 1.49 becomes effective in accordance with § 1.41; and

(ii) the time at which any articles of validation filed in accordance with § 1.51 become effective.

The validation effective time shall not be affected by the filing or pendency of a judicial proceeding under § 1.52 or otherwise, unless otherwise ordered by the court.

§ 1.46 Defective Corporate Actions

(a) A defective corporate action shall not be void or voidable if ratified in accordance with § 1.47 or validated in accordance with § 1.52.

(b) Ratification under § 1.47 or validation under § 1.52 shall not be deemed to be the exclusive means of ratifying or validating any defective corporate action, and the absence or failure of ratification in accordance with this subchapter shall not, of itself, affect the validity or effectiveness of any corporate action properly ratified under common law or otherwise, nor shall it create a presumption that any such corporate action is or was a defective corporate action or void or voidable.

(c) In the case of an overissue, putative shares shall be valid shares effective as of the date originally issued or purportedly issued upon:

(1) the effectiveness under this subchapter and under chapter 10 of an amendment to the articles of incorporation authorizing, designating or creating such shares; or

(2) the effectiveness of any other corporate action under this subchapter ratifying the authorization, designation or creation of such shares.

§ 1.47 Ratification of Defective Corporate Actions

(a) To ratify a defective corporate action under this section (other than the ratification of an election of the initial board of directors under subsection (b)), the board of directors shall take action ratifying the action in accordance with § 1.48, stating:

(1) the defective corporate action to be ratified and, if the defective corporate action involved the issuance of putative shares, the number and type of putative shares purportedly issued;

(2) the date of the defective corporate action;

(3) the nature of the failure of authorization with respect to the defective corporate action to be ratified; and

(4) that the board of directors approves the ratification of the defective corporate action.

(b) In the event that a defective corporate action to be ratified relates to the election of the initial board of directors of the corporation under § 2.05(a)(2), a majority of the persons who, at the time of the ratification, are exercising the powers of directors may take an action stating:

(1) the name of the person or persons who first took action in the name of the corporation as the initial board of directors of the corporation;

(2) the earlier of the date on which such persons first took such action or were purported to have been elected as the initial board of directors; and

(3) that the ratification of the election of such person or persons as the initial board of directors is approved.

(c) If any provision of this Act, the articles of incorporation or bylaws, any corporate resolution or any plan or agreement to which the corporation is a party in effect at the time action under subsection (a) is taken requires shareholder approval or would have required shareholder approval at the date of the occurrence of the defective corporate action, the ratification of the defective corporate action approved in the action taken by the directors under subsection (a) shall be submitted to the shareholders for approval in accordance with § 1.48.

(d) Unless otherwise provided in the action taken by the board of directors under subsection (a), after the action by the board of directors has been taken and, if required, approved by the shareholders, the board of directors may abandon the ratification at any time before the validation effective time without further action of the shareholders.

§ 1.48 Action on Ratification

(a) The quorum and voting requirements applicable to a ratifying action by the board of directors under § 1.47(a) shall be the quorum and voting requirements applicable to the corporate action proposed to be ratified at the time such ratifying action is taken.

(b) If the ratification of the defective corporate action requires approval by the shareholders under § 1.47(c), and if the approval is to be given at a meeting, the corporation shall notify each holder of valid and putative shares, regardless of whether entitled to vote, as of the record date for notice of the meeting and as of the date of the occurrence of defective corporate action, provided that notice shall not be required to be given to holders of valid or putative shares whose identities or addresses for notice cannot be determined from the records of the corporation. The notice must state that the purpose, or one of the purposes, of the meeting, is to consider ratification of a defective corporate action and must be accompanied by (i) either a copy of the action taken by the board of directors in accordance with § 1.47(a) or the information required by sections 1.47(a)(1) through (a)(4), and (ii) a statement that any claim that the ratification of such defective corporate action and any putative shares issued as a result of such defective corporate action should not be effective, or should be effective only on certain conditions, shall be brought within 120 days from the applicable validation effective time.

(c) Except as provided in subsection (d) with respect to the voting requirements to ratify the election of a director, the quorum and voting requirements applicable to the approval by the shareholders required by § 1.47(c) shall be the quorum and voting requirements applicable to the corporate action proposed to be ratified at the time of such shareholder approval.

(d) The approval by shareholders to ratify the election of a director requires that the votes cast within the voting group favoring such ratification exceed the votes cast opposing such ratification of the election at a meeting at which a quorum is present.

(e) Putative shares on the record date for determining the shareholders entitled to vote on any matter submitted to shareholders under § 1.47(c) (and without giving effect to any ratification of putative shares that becomes effective as a result of such vote) shall neither be entitled to vote nor counted for quorum purposes in any vote to approve the ratification of any defective corporate action.

(f) If the approval under this section of putative shares would result in an overissue, in addition to the approval required by § 1.47, approval of an amendment to the articles of incorporation under chapter 10 to increase the number of shares of an authorized class or series or to authorize the creation of a class or series of shares so there would be no overissue shall also be required.

§ 1.49 Notice Requirements

(a) Unless shareholder approval is required under § 1.47(c), prompt notice of an action taken under § 1.47 shall be given to each holder of valid and putative shares, regardless of whether entitled to vote, as of (i) the date of such action by the board of directors and (ii) the date of the defective corporate action ratified, provided that notice shall not be required to be given to holders of valid and putative shares whose identities or addresses for notice cannot be determined from the records of the corporation.

(b) The notice must contain (i) either a copy of the action taken by the board of directors in accordance with § 1.47(a) or (b) or the information required by sections 1.47(a)(1) through (a)(4) or sections 1.47(b)(1) through (b)(3), as applicable, and (ii) a statement that any claim that the ratification of the defective corporate action and any putative shares issued as a result of such defective corporate action should not be effective, or should be effective only on certain conditions, shall be brought within 120 days from the applicable validation effective time.

(c) No notice under this section is required with respect to any action required to be submitted to shareholders for approval under § 1.47(c) if notice is given in accordance with § 1.48(b).

(d) A notice required by this section may be given in any manner permitted by § 1.41 and, for any corporation subject to the reporting requirements of § 13 or 15(d) of the Securities Exchange Act of 1934, may be given by means of a filing or furnishing of such notice with the United States Securities and Exchange Commission.

§ 1.50 Effect of Ratification

From and after the validation effective time, and without regard to the 120-day period during which a claim may be brought under § 1.52:

(a) Each defective corporate action ratified in accordance with § 1.47 shall not be void or voidable as a result of the failure of authorization identified in the action taken under § 1.47(a) or (b) and shall be deemed a valid corporate action effective as of the date of the defective corporate action;

(b) The issuance of each putative share or fraction of a putative share purportedly issued pursuant to a defective corporate action identified in the action taken under § 1.47 shall not be void or voidable, and each such putative share or fraction of a putative share shall be deemed to be an identical share or fraction of a valid share as of the time it was purportedly issued; and

(c) Any corporate action taken subsequent to the defective corporate action ratified in accordance with this subchapter in reliance on such defective corporate action having been validly effected and any subsequent defective corporate action resulting directly or indirectly from such original defective corporate action shall be valid as of the time taken.

§ 1.51 Filings

(a) If the defective corporate action ratified under this subchapter would have required under any other section of this Act a filing in accordance with this Act, then, regardless of whether a filing was previously made in respect of such defective corporate action and in lieu of a filing otherwise required by this Act, the corporation shall file articles of validation in accordance with this section, and such articles of validation shall serve to amend or substitute for any other filing with respect to such defective corporate action required by this Act.

(b) The articles of validation must set forth:

(1) the defective corporate action that is the subject of the articles of validation (including, in the case of any defective corporate action involving the issuance of putative shares, the number and type of putative shares issued and the date or dates upon which such putative shares were purported to have been issued);

(2) the date of the defective corporate action;

(3) the nature of the failure of authorization in respect of the defective corporate action;

(4) a statement that the defective corporate action was ratified in accordance with § 1.47, including the date on which the board of directors ratified such defective corporate action and the date, if any, on which the shareholders approved the ratification of such defective corporate action; and

(5) the information required by subsection (c).

(c) The articles of validation must also contain the following information:

(1) if a filing was previously made in respect of the defective corporate action and no changes to such filing are required to give effect to the ratification of such defective corporate action in accordance with § 1.47, the articles of validation must set forth (i) the name, title and filing date of the filing previously made and any articles of correction to that filing and (ii) a statement that a copy of the filing previously made, together with any articles of correction to that filing, is attached as an exhibit to the articles of validation;

(2) if a filing was previously made in respect of the defective corporate action and such filing requires any change to give effect to the ratification of such defective corporate action in accordance with § 1.47, the articles of validation must set forth (i) the name, title and filing date of the filing previously made and any articles of correction to that filing and (ii) a statement that a filing containing all of the information required to be included under the applicable section or sections of the Act to give effect to such defective corporate action is attached as an exhibit to the articles of validation, and (iii) the date and time that such filing is deemed to have become effective; or

(3) if a filing was not previously made in respect of the defective corporate action and the defective corporate action ratified under § 1.47 would have required a filing under any other section of the Act, the articles of validation must set forth (i) a statement that a filing containing all of the information required to be included under the applicable section or sections of the Act to give effect to such defective corporate action is attached as an exhibit to the articles of validation, and (ii) the date and time that such filing is deemed to have become effective.

§ 1.52 Judicial Proceedings Regarding Validity of Corporate Actions

(a) Upon application by the corporation, any successor entity to the corporation, a director of the corporation, any shareholder, beneficial shareholder or unrestricted voting trust beneficial owner of the corporation, including any such shareholder, beneficial shareholder or unrestricted voting trust beneficial owner as of the date of the defective corporate action ratified under § 1.47, or any other person claiming to be substantially and adversely affected by a ratification under § 1.47, the [name or describe court] may:

    (1) determine the validity and effectiveness of any corporate action or defective corporate action;

    (2) determine the validity and effectiveness of any ratification under § 1.47;

    (3) determine the validity of any putative shares; and

    (4) modify or waive any of the procedures specified in § 1.47 or 1.48 to ratify a defective corporate action.

(b) In connection with an action under this section, the court may make such findings or orders, and take into account any factors or considerations, regarding such matters as it deems proper under the circumstances.

(c) Service of process of the application under subsection (a) on the corporation may be made in any manner provided by statute of this state or by rule of the applicable court for service on the corporation, and no other party need be joined in order for the court to adjudicate the matter. In an action filed by the corporation, the court may require notice of the action be provided to other persons specified by the court and permit such other persons to intervene in the action.

(d) Notwithstanding any other provision of this section or otherwise under applicable law, any action asserting that the ratification of any defective corporate action and any putative shares issued as a result of such defective corporate action should not be effective, or should be effective only on certain conditions, shall be brought within 120 days of the validation effective time.

Chapter 2. Incorporation

§ 2.01. Incorporators

One or more persons may act as the incorporator or incorporators of a corporation by delivering articles of incorporation to the secretary of state for filing.

§ 2.02. Articles of Incorporation

(a) The articles of incorporation must set forth:

    (1) a corporate name for the corporation that satisfies the requirements of § 4.01;

(2) the number of shares the corporation is authorized to issue;

(3) the street and mailing addresses of the corporation's initial registered office and the name of its initial registered agent at that office; and

(4) the name and address of each incorporator.

(b) The articles of incorporation may set forth:

(1) the names and addresses of the individuals who are to serve as the initial directors;

(2) provisions not inconsistent with law regarding:

(i) the purpose or purposes for which the corporation is organized;

(ii) managing the business and regulating the affairs of the corporation;

(iii) defining, limiting, and regulating the powers of the corporation, its board of directors, and shareholders;

(iv) a par value for authorized shares or classes of shares; or

(v) the imposition of interest holder liability on shareholders;

(3) any provision that under this Act is required or permitted to be set forth in the bylaws;

(4) a provision eliminating or limiting the liability of a director to the corporation or its shareholders for money damages for any action taken, or any failure to take any action, as a director, except liability for (i) the amount of a financial benefit received by a director to which the director is not entitled; (ii) an intentional infliction of harm on the corporation or the shareholders; (iii) a violation of § 8.32; or (iv) an intentional violation of criminal law;

(5) a provision permitting or making obligatory indemnification of a director for liability as defined in § 8.50 to any person for any action taken, or any failure to take any action, as a director, except liability for (i) receipt of a financial benefit to which the director is not entitled, (ii) an intentional infliction of harm on the corporation or the shareholders, (iii) a violation of § 8.32, or (iv) an intentional violation of criminal law; and

(6) a provision limiting or eliminating any duty of a director or any other person to offer the corporation the right to have or participate in any, or one or more classes or categories of, business opportunities, before the pursuit or taking of the opportunity by the director or other person; provided that any application of such a provision to an officer or a related person of that officer (i) also requires approval of that application by the board of directors, subsequent to the effective date of the provision, by action of qualified directors taken in compliance with the same procedures as are set forth in § 8.62, and (ii) may be limited by the authorizing action of the board.

(c) The articles of incorporation need not set forth any of the corporate powers enumerated in this Act.

(d) Provisions of the articles of incorporation may be made dependent upon facts objectively ascertainable outside the articles of incorporation in accordance with § 1.20(k).

(e) As used in this section, "related person" has the meaning specified in § 8.60.

§ 2.03. Incorporation

(a) Unless a delayed effective date is specified, the corporate existence begins when the articles of incorporation are filed.

(b) The secretary of state's filing of the articles of incorporation is conclusive proof that the incorporators satisfied all conditions precedent to incorporation except in a proceeding by the state to cancel or revoke the incorporation or involuntarily dissolve the corporation.

§ 2.04. Liability for Preincorporation Transactions

All persons purporting to act as or on behalf of a corporation, knowing there was no incorporation under this Act, are jointly and severally liable for all liabilities created while so acting.

§ 2.05. Organization of Corporation

(a) After incorporation:

(1) if initial directors are named in the articles of incorporation, the initial directors shall hold an organizational meeting, at the call of a majority of the directors, to complete the organization of the corporation by appointing officers, adopting bylaws, and carrying on any other business brought before the meeting; or

(2) if initial directors are not named in the articles of incorporation, the incorporator or incorporators shall hold an organizational meeting at the call of a majority of the incorporators:

(i) to elect initial directors and complete the organization of the corporation; or

(ii) to elect a board of directors who shall complete the organization of the corporation.

(b) Action required or permitted by this Act to be taken by incorporators at an organizational meeting may be taken without a meeting if the action taken is evidenced by one or more written consents describing the action taken and signed by each incorporator.

(c) An organizational meeting may be held in or out of this state.

§ 2.06. Bylaws

(a) The incorporators or board of directors of a corporation shall adopt initial bylaws for the corporation.

(b) The bylaws of a corporation may contain any provision that is not inconsistent with law or the articles of incorporation.

(c) The bylaws may contain one or both of the following provisions:

(1) a requirement that if the corporation solicits proxies or consents with respect to an election of directors, the corporation include in its proxy statement and any form of its proxy or consent, to the extent and subject to such procedures or conditions as are provided in the bylaws, one or more individuals nominated by a shareholder in addition to individuals nominated by the board of directors; and

(2) a requirement that the corporation reimburse the expenses incurred by a shareholder in soliciting proxies or consents in connection with an election of directors, to the extent and subject to such procedures and conditions as are provided in the bylaws, provided that no bylaw so adopted shall apply to elections for which any record date precedes its adoption.

(d) Notwithstanding § 10.20(b)(2), the shareholders in amending, repealing, or adopting a bylaw described in subsection (c) may not limit the authority of the board of directors to amend or repeal any condition or procedure set forth in or to add any procedure or condition to such a bylaw to provide for a reasonable, practical, and orderly process.

§ 2.07. Emergency Bylaws

(a) Unless the articles of incorporation provide otherwise, the board of directors may adopt bylaws to be effective only in an emergency defined in subsection (d). The emergency bylaws, which are subject to amendment or repeal by the shareholders, may make all provisions necessary for managing the corporation during the emergency, including:

(1) procedures for calling a meeting of the board of directors;

(2) quorum requirements for the meeting; and

(3) designation of additional or substitute directors.

(b) All provisions of the regular bylaws not inconsistent with the emergency bylaws remain effective during the emergency. The emergency bylaws are not effective after the emergency ends.

(c) Corporate action taken in good faith in accordance with the emergency bylaws:

(1) binds the corporation; and

(2) may not be used to impose liability on a director, officer, employee, or agent of the corporation.

(d) An emergency exists for purposes of this section if a quorum of the board of directors cannot readily be assembled because of some catastrophic event.

§ 2.08. Forum Selection Provisions

(a) The articles of incorporation or the bylaws may require that any or all internal corporate claims shall be brought exclusively in any specified court or courts of this state and, if so specified, in any additional courts in this state or in any other jurisdictions with which the corporation has a reasonable relationship.

(b) A provision of the articles of incorporation or bylaws adopted under subsection (a) shall not have the effect of conferring jurisdiction on any court or over any person or claim, and shall not apply if none of the courts specified by such provision has the requisite personal and subject matter jurisdiction. If the court or courts of this state specified in a provision adopted under subsection (a) do not have the requisite personal and subject matter jurisdiction and another court of this state does have such jurisdiction, then the internal corporate claim may be brought in such other court of this state, notwithstanding that such other court of this state is not specified in such provision, and in any other court specified in such provision that has the requisite jurisdiction.

(c) No provision of the articles of incorporation or the bylaws may prohibit bringing an internal corporate claim in the courts of this state or require such claims to be determined by arbitration.

(d) "Internal corporate claim" means, for the purposes of this section, (i) any claim that is based upon a violation of a duty under the laws of this state by a current or former director, officer, or shareholder in such capacity, (ii) any derivative action or proceeding brought on behalf of the corporation, (iii) any action asserting a claim arising pursuant to any provision of this Act or the articles of incorporation or bylaws, or (iv) any action asserting a claim governed by the internal affairs doctrine that is not included in (i) through (iii) above.

Chapter 3. Purposes and Powers

§ 3.01. Purposes

(a) Every corporation incorporated under this Act has the purpose of engaging in any lawful business unless a more limited purpose is set forth in the articles of incorporation.

(b) A corporation engaging in a business that is subject to regulation under another statute of this state may incorporate under this Act only if permitted by, and subject to all limitations of, the other statute.

§ 3.02. General Powers

Unless its articles of incorporation provide otherwise, every corporation has perpetual duration and succession in its corporate name and has the same powers as an individual to do all things necessary or convenient to carry out its business and affairs, including power:

> **(a)** to sue and be sued, complain and defend in its corporate name;
>
> **(b)** to have a corporate seal, which may be altered at will, and to use it, or a facsimile of it, by impressing or affixing it or in any other manner reproducing it;
>
> **(c)** to make and amend bylaws, not inconsistent with its articles of incorporation or with the laws of this state, for managing the business and regulating the affairs of the corporation;
>
> **(d)** to purchase, receive, lease, or otherwise acquire, and own, hold, improve, use, and otherwise deal with, real or personal property, or any legal or equitable interest in property, wherever located;
>
> **(e)** to sell, convey, mortgage, pledge, lease, exchange, and otherwise dispose of all or any part of its property;
>
> **(f)** to purchase, receive, subscribe for, or otherwise acquire, own, hold, vote, use, sell, mortgage, lend, pledge, or otherwise dispose of, and deal in and with shares or other interests in, or obligations of, any other entity;

(g) to make contracts and guarantees, incur liabilities, borrow money, issue its notes, bonds, and other securities and obligations (which may be convertible into or include the option to purchase other securities of the corporation), and secure any of its obligations by mortgage or pledge of any of its property, franchises, or income;

(h) to lend money, invest and reinvest its funds, and receive and hold real and personal property as security for repayment;

(i) to be a promoter, partner, member, associate, or manager of any partnership, joint venture, trust, or other entity;

(j) to conduct its business, locate offices, and exercise the powers granted by this Act within or without this state;

(k) to elect directors and appoint officers, employees, and agents of the corporation, define their duties, fix their compensation, and lend them money and credit;

(l) to pay pensions and establish pension plans, pension trusts, profit sharing plans, share bonus plans, share option plans, and benefit or incentive plans for any or all of its current or former directors, officers, employees, and agents;

(m) to make donations for the public welfare or for charitable, scientific, or educational purposes;

(n) to transact any lawful business that will aid governmental policy; and

(o) to make payments or donations, or do any other act, not inconsistent with law, that furthers the business and affairs of the corporation.

§ 3.03. Emergency Powers

(a) In anticipation of or during an emergency defined in subsection (d), the board of directors of a corporation may:

(1) modify lines of succession to accommodate the incapacity of any director, officer, employee, or agent; and

(2) relocate the principal office, designate alternative principal offices or regional offices, or authorize the officers to do so.

(b) During an emergency defined in subsection (d), unless emergency bylaws provide otherwise:

(1) notice of a meeting of the board of directors need be given only to those directors whom it is practicable to reach and may be given in any practicable manner; and

(2) one or more officers of the corporation present at a meeting of the board of directors may be deemed to be directors for the meeting, in order of rank and within the same rank in order of seniority, as necessary to achieve a quorum.

(c) Corporate action taken in good faith during an emergency under this section to further the ordinary business affairs of the corporation:

(1) binds the corporation; and

(2) may not be used to impose liability on a director, officer, employee, or agent.

(d) An emergency exists for purposes of this section if a quorum of the board of directors cannot readily be assembled because of some catastrophic event.

§ 3.04. Lack of Power to Act

(a) Except as provided in subsection (b), the validity of corporate action may not be challenged on the ground that the corporation lacks or lacked power to act.

(b) A corporation's power to act may be challenged:

(1) in a proceeding by a shareholder against the corporation to enjoin the act;

(2) in a proceeding by the corporation, directly, derivatively, or through a receiver, trustee, or other legal representative, against an incumbent or former director, officer, employee, or agent of the corporation; or

(3) in a proceeding by the attorney general under § 14.30.

(c) In a shareholder's proceeding under subsection (b)(1) to enjoin an unauthorized corporate act, the court may enjoin or set aside the act, if equitable and if all affected persons are parties to the proceeding, and may award damages for loss (other than anticipated profits) suffered by the corporation or another party because of enjoining the unauthorized act.

Chapter 4. Name

§ 4.01. Corporate Name

(a) A corporate name:

(1) must contain the word "corporation," "incorporated," "company," or "limited," or the abbreviation "corp.," "inc.," "co.," or "ltd.," or words or abbreviations of like import in another language; and

(2) may not contain language stating or implying that the corporation is organized for a purpose other than that permitted by § 3.01 and its articles of incorporation.

(b) Except as authorized by subsections (c) and (d), a corporate name must be distinguishable upon the records of the secretary of state from:

(1) the corporate name of a corporation incorporated in this state which is not administratively dissolved;

(2) a corporate name reserved or registered under § 4.02 or 4.03 or any similar provision of the law of this state;

(3) the name of a foreign corporation registered to do business in this state or an alternate name adopted by a foreign corporation registered to do business in this state because its corporate name is unavailable;

(4) the corporate name of a nonprofit corporation incorporated in this state which is not administratively dissolved;

(5) the name of a foreign nonprofit corporation registered to do business in this state or an alternate name adopted by a foreign nonprofit corporation registered to conduct activities in this state because its real name is unavailable;

(6) the name of a domestic filing entity or limited liability partnership which is not administratively dissolved;

(7) the name of a foreign unincorporated entity registered to do business in this state or an alternate name adopted by such an entity registered to conduct activities in this state because its real name is unavailable; and

(8) an assumed name registered under [state's assumed name statute].

(c) A corporation may apply to the secretary of state for authorization to use a name that is not distinguishable upon the secretary of state's records from one or more of the names described in subsection (b). The secretary of state shall authorize use of the name applied for if:

(1) the other corporation or unincorporated entity consents to the use in writing and submits an undertaking in form satisfactory to the secretary of state to change its name to a name that is distinguishable upon the records of the secretary of state from the name of the applying corporation; or

(2) the applicant delivers to the secretary of state a certified copy of the final judgment of a court of competent jurisdiction establishing the applicant's right to use the name applied for in this state.

(d) This Act does not control the use of fictitious names.

§ 4.02. Reserved Name

(a) A person may reserve the exclusive use of a corporate name, including a fictitious or alternate name for a foreign corporation whose corporate name is not available, by delivering an application to the secretary of state for filing. The application must set forth the name and address of the applicant and the name proposed to be reserved. If the secretary of state finds that the corporate name applied for is available, the secretary of state shall reserve the name for the applicant's exclusive use for a nonrenewable 120-day period.

(b) The owner of a reserved corporate name may transfer the reservation to another person by delivering to the secretary of state a signed notice of the transfer that states the name and address of the transferee.

§ 4.03. Registered Name

(a) A foreign corporation may register its corporate name (or its corporate name with the addition of any word or abbreviation listed in § 4.01(a)(1) if necessary for the corporate name to comply with § 4.01(a)(1)) if the name is distinguishable upon the records of the secretary of state from the corporate names that are not available under § 4.01(b).

(b) A foreign corporation registers its corporate name (or its corporate name with any addition permitted by subsection (a)) by delivering to the secretary of state for filing an application setting forth that name, the state or country and date of its incorporation, and a brief description of the nature of the business which is to be conducted in this state.

(c) The name is registered for the applicant's exclusive use upon the effective date of the application and for the remainder of the calendar year, unless renewed.

(d) A foreign corporation whose name registration is effective may renew it for successive years by delivering to the secretary of state for filing a renewal application, which complies with the requirements of subsection (b), between October 1 and December 31 of the preceding year. The renewal application when filed renews the registration for the following calendar year.

(e) A foreign corporation whose name registration is effective may thereafter (i) register to do business as a foreign corporation under the registered name (if it complies with § 4.01(a)(2)) or (ii) consent in writing to the use of that name by a domestic corporation thereafter incorporated under this Act or by another foreign corporation. The registration terminates when the domestic corporation is incorporated or the foreign corporation registers to do business under that name.

Chapter 5. Office and Agent

§ 5.01. Registered Office and Agent of Domestic and Registered Foreign Corporations

(a) Each corporation shall continuously maintain in this state:

    (1) a registered office that may be the same as any of its places of business; and

    (2) a registered agent, which may be:

        (i) an individual who resides in this state and whose business office is identical with the registered office; or

        (ii) a domestic or foreign corporation or eligible entity whose business office is identical with the registered office and, in the case of a foreign corporation or foreign eligible entity, is registered to do business in this state.

(b) As used in this chapter, "corporation" means both a domestic corporation and a registered foreign corporation.

§ 5.02. Change of Registered Office or Registered Agent

(a) A corporation may change its registered office or registered agent by delivering to the secretary of state for filing a statement of change that sets forth:

    (1) the name of the corporation;

    (2) the street and mailing addresses of its current registered office;

    (3) if the current registered office is to be changed, the street and mailing addresses of the new registered office;

    (4) the name of its current registered agent;

    (5) if the current registered agent is to be changed, the name of the new registered agent and the new agent's written consent (either on the statement or attached to it) to the appointment; and

(6) that after the change or changes are made, the street and mailing addresses of its registered office and of the business office of its registered agent will be identical.

(b) If the street or mailing address of a registered agent's business office changes, the agent shall change the street or mailing address of the registered office of any corporation for which the agent is the registered agent by delivering a signed written notice of the change to the corporation and delivering to the secretary of state for filing a signed statement that complies with the requirements of subsection (a) and states that the corporation has been notified of the change.

§ 5.03. Resignation of Registered Agent

(a) A registered agent may resign as agent for a corporation by delivering to the secretary of state for filing a statement of resignation signed by the agent which states:

    (1) the name of the corporation;

    (2) the name of the agent;

    (3) that the agent resigns from serving as registered agent for the corporation; and

    (4) the address of the corporation to which the agent will deliver the notice required by subsection (c).

(b) A statement of resignation takes effect on the earlier of:

    (1) 12:01 a.m. on the 31st day after the day on which it is filed by the secretary of state; or

    (2) the designation of a new registered agent for the corporation.

(c) A registered agent promptly shall deliver to the corporation notice of the date on which a statement of resignation was delivered to the secretary of state for filing.

(d) When a statement of resignation takes effect, the person that resigned ceases to have responsibility under this Act for any matter thereafter tendered to it as agent for the corporation. The resignation does not affect any contractual rights the corporation has against the agent or that the agent has against the corporation.

(e) A registered agent may resign with respect to a corporation regardless of whether the corporation is in good standing.

§ 5.04. Service on Corporation

(a) A corporation's registered agent is the corporation's agent for service of process, notice, or demand required or permitted by law to be served on the corporation.

(b) If a corporation has no registered agent, or the agent cannot with reasonable diligence be served, the corporation may be served by registered or certified mail, return receipt requested, addressed to the secretary at the corporation's principal office. Service is perfected under this subsection at the earliest of:

    (1) the date the corporation receives the mail;

    (2) the date shown on the return receipt, if signed on behalf of the corporation; or

    (3) five days after its deposit in the United States mail, as evidenced by the postmark, if mailed postpaid and correctly addressed.

(c) If process, notice, or demand (i) cannot be served on a corporation pursuant to subsection (a) or (b), or (ii) is to be served on a registered foreign corporation that has withdrawn its registration pursuant to § 15.07 or 15.09, or the registration of which has been terminated pursuant to § 15.11, then the secretary of state shall be an agent of the corporation upon whom process, notice, or demand may be served. Service of any process, notice, or demand on the secretary of state as agent for a corporation may be made by delivering to the secretary of state duplicate copies of the process, notice, or demand. If process, notice, or demand is served on the secretary of state, the secretary of state shall forward one of the copies by registered or certified mail, return receipt requested, to the corporation at the last address shown in the records of the secretary of state. Service is effected under this subsection (c) at the earliest of:

    (1) the date the corporation receives the process, notice, or demand;

    (2) the date shown on the return receipt, if signed on behalf of the corporation; or

(3) five days after the process, notice, or demand is deposited with the United States mail by the secretary of state.

(d) This section does not prescribe the only means, or necessarily the required means, of serving a corporation.

Chapter 6. Shares and Distributions

Subchapter A. Shares

§ 6.01. Authorized Shares

(a) The articles of incorporation must set forth any classes of shares and series of shares within a class, and the number of shares of each class and series, that the corporation is authorized to issue. If more than one class or series of shares is authorized, the articles of incorporation must prescribe a distinguishing designation for each class or series and, before the issuance of shares of a class or series, describe the terms, including the preferences, rights, and limitations, of that class or series. Except to the extent varied as permitted by this section, all shares of a class or series must have terms, including preferences, rights, and limitations, that are identical with those of other shares of the same class or series.

(b) The articles of incorporation must authorize:

(1) one or more classes or series of shares that together have full voting rights, and

(2) one or more classes or series of shares (which may be the same class, classes or series as those with voting rights) that together are entitled to receive the net assets of the corporation upon dissolution.

(c) The articles of incorporation may authorize one or more classes or series of shares that:

(1) have special, conditional, or limited voting rights, or no right to vote, except to the extent otherwise provided by this Act;

(2) are redeemable or convertible as specified in the articles of incorporation:

(i) at the option of the corporation, the shareholder, or another person or upon the occurrence of a specified event;

(ii) for cash, indebtedness, securities, or other property; and

(iii) at prices and in amounts specified or determined in accordance with a formula;

(3) entitle the holders to distributions calculated in any manner, including dividends that may be cumulative, noncumulative, or partially cumulative; or

(4) have preference over any other class or series of shares with respect to distributions, including distributions upon the dissolution of the corporation.

(d) Terms of shares may be made dependent upon facts objectively ascertainable outside the articles of incorporation in accordance with § 1.20(k).

(e) Any of the terms of shares may vary among holders of the same class or series so long as such variations are expressly set forth in the articles of incorporation.

(f) The description of the preferences, rights, and limitations of classes or series of shares in subsection (c) is not exhaustive.

§ 6.02. Terms of Class or Series Determined by Board of Directors

(a) If the articles of incorporation so provide, the board of directors is authorized, without shareholder approval, to:

(1) classify any unissued shares into one or more classes or into one or more series within a class;

(2) reclassify any unissued shares of any class into one or more classes or into one or more series within one or more classes; or

(3) reclassify any unissued shares of any series of any class into one or more classes or into one or more series within a class.

(b) If the board of directors acts pursuant to subsection (a), it shall determine the terms, including the preferences, rights, and limitations, to the same extent permitted under § 6.01, of:

(1) any class of shares before the issuance of any shares of that class, or

(2) any series within a class before the issuance of any shares of that series.

(c) Before issuing any shares of a class or series created under this section, the corporation shall deliver to the secretary of state for filing articles of amendment setting forth the terms determined under subsection (a).

§ 6.03. Issued and Outstanding Shares

(a) A corporation may issue the number of shares of each class or series authorized by the articles of incorporation. Shares that are issued are outstanding shares until they are reacquired, redeemed, converted, or cancelled.

(b) The reacquisition, redemption, or conversion of outstanding shares is subject to the limitations of subsection (c) and to § 6.40.

(c) At all times that shares of the corporation are outstanding, one or more shares that together have full voting rights and one or more shares that together are entitled to receive the net assets of the corporation upon dissolution must be outstanding.

§ 6.04. Fractional Shares

(a) A corporation may issue fractions of a share or in lieu of doing so may:

(1) pay in cash the value of fractions of a share;

(2) issue scrip in registered or bearer form entitling the holder to receive a full share upon surrendering enough scrip to equal a full share; or

(3) arrange for disposition of fractional shares by the holders of such shares.

(b) Each certificate representing scrip must be conspicuously labeled "scrip" and must contain the information required by § 6.25(b).

(c) The holder of a fractional share is entitled to exercise the rights of a shareholder, including the rights to vote, to receive dividends and to receive distributions upon dissolution. The holder of scrip is not entitled to any of these rights unless the scrip provides for them.

(d) The board of directors may authorize the issuance of scrip subject to any condition, including that:

(1) the scrip will become void if not exchanged for full shares before a specified date; and

(2) the shares for which the scrip is exchangeable may be sold and the proceeds paid to the scripholders.

Subchapter B. Issuance of Shares

§ 6.20. Subscription for Shares Before Incorporation

(a) A subscription for shares entered into before incorporation is irrevocable for six months unless the subscription agreement provides a longer or shorter period or all the subscribers agree to revocation.

(b) The board of directors may determine the payment terms of subscriptions for shares that were entered into before incorporation, unless the subscription agreement specifies them. A call for payment by the board of directors must be uniform so far as practicable as to all shares of the same class or series, unless the subscription agreement specifies otherwise.

(c) Shares issued pursuant to subscriptions entered into before incorporation are fully paid and nonassessable when the corporation receives the consideration specified in the subscription agreement.

(d) If a subscriber defaults in payment of cash or property under a subscription agreement entered into before incorporation, the corporation may collect the amount owed as any other debt. Alternatively, unless the subscription agreement provides otherwise, the corporation may rescind the agreement and may sell the shares if the debt remains unpaid for more than 20 days after the corporation delivers a written demand for payment to the subscriber.

§ 6.21. Issuance of Shares

(a) The powers granted in this section to the board of directors may be reserved to the shareholders by the articles of incorporation.

(b) The board of directors may authorize shares to be issued for consideration consisting of any tangible or intangible property or benefit to the corporation, including cash, promissory notes, services performed, contracts for services to be performed, or other securities of the corporation.

(c) Before the corporation issues shares, the board of directors shall determine that the consideration received or to be received for shares to be issued is adequate. That determination by the board of directors is conclusive insofar as the adequacy of consideration for the issuance of shares relates to whether the shares are validly issued, fully paid, and nonassessable.

(d) When the corporation receives the consideration for which the board of directors authorized the issuance of shares, the shares issued therefor are fully paid and nonassessable.

(e) The corporation may place in escrow shares issued for a contract for future services or benefits or a promissory note, or make other arrangements to restrict the transfer of the shares, and may credit distributions in respect of the shares against their purchase price, until the services are performed, the benefits are received, or the note is paid. If the services are not performed, the benefits are not received, or the note is not paid, the shares escrowed or restricted and the distributions credited may be cancelled in whole or part.

(f)(1) An issuance of shares or other securities convertible into or rights exercisable for shares in a transaction or a series of integrated transactions requires approval of the shareholders, at a meeting at which a quorum consisting of a majority (or such greater number as the articles of incorporation may prescribe) of the votes entitled to be cast on the matter exists, if:

> **(i)** the shares, other securities, or rights are to be issued for consideration other than cash or cash equivalents, and

> **(ii)** the voting power of shares that are issued and issuable as a result of the transaction or series of integrated transactions will comprise more than 20% of the voting power of the shares of the corporation that

were outstanding immediately before the transaction.

(2) In this subsection:

> **(i)** For purposes of determining the voting power of shares issued and issuable as a result of a transaction or series of integrated transactions, the voting power of shares or other securities convertible into or rights exercisable for shares shall be the greater of (A) the voting power of the shares to be issued, or (B) the voting power of the shares that would be outstanding after giving effect to the conversion of convertible shares and other securities and the exercise of rights to be issued.

> **(ii)** A series of transactions is integrated only if consummation of one transaction is made contingent on consummation of one or more of the other transactions.

§ 6.22. Liability of Shareholders

(a) A purchaser from a corporation of the corporation's own shares is not liable to the corporation or its creditors with respect to the shares except to pay the consideration for which the shares were authorized to be issued or specified in the subscription agreement.

(b) A shareholder of a corporation is not personally liable for any liabilities of the corporation (including liabilities arising from acts of the corporation) except (i) to the extent provided in a provision of the articles of incorporation permitted by § 2.02(b)(2)(v), and (ii) that a shareholder may become personally liable by reason of the shareholder's own acts or conduct.

§ 6.23. Share Dividends

(a) Unless the articles of incorporation provide otherwise, shares may be issued pro rata and without consideration to the corporation's shareholders or to the shareholders of one or more classes or series of shares. An issuance of shares under this subsection is a share dividend.

(b) Shares of one class or series may not be issued as a share dividend in respect of shares of another class or series unless (i) the articles of incorporation so authorize, (ii) a majority of the votes entitled to be cast by the class or series to be issued approve the issue, or (iii) there are no outstanding shares of the class or series to be issued.

(c) The board of directors may fix the record date for determining shareholders entitled to a share dividend, which date may not be retroactive. If the board of directors does not fix the record date for determining shareholders entitled to a share dividend, the record date is the date the board of directors authorizes the share dividend.

§ 6.24. Share Rights, Options, Warrants and Awards

(a) A corporation may issue rights, options, or warrants for the purchase of shares or other securities of the corporation. The board of directors shall determine (i) the terms and conditions upon which the rights, options, or warrants are issued and (ii) the terms, including the consideration for which the shares or other securities are to be issued. The authorization by the board of directors for the corporation to issue such rights, options, or warrants constitutes authorization of the issuance of the shares or other securities for which the rights, options or warrants are exercisable.

(b) The terms and conditions of such rights, options or warrants may include restrictions or conditions that:

> **(1)** preclude or limit the exercise, transfer or receipt of such rights, options or warrants by any person or persons owning or offering to acquire a specified number or percentage of the outstanding shares or other securities of the corporation or by any transferee or transferees of any such person or persons, or

> **(2)** invalidate or void such rights, options, or warrants held by any such person or persons or any such transferee or transferees.

(c) The board of directors may authorize one or more officers to (i) designate the recipients of rights, options, warrants, or other equity compensation awards that involve the issuance of shares and (ii) determine, within an amount and subject to any other limitations established by the board of directors and, if applicable, the shareholders, the number of such rights, options, warrants, or other equity compensation awards and the terms of such rights, options, warrants or awards to be received by the recipients, provided that an officer may not use such authority to designate himself or herself or any other persons as the board of directors may specify as a recipient of such rights, options, warrants, or other equity compensation awards.

§ 6.25. Form and Content of Certificates

(a) Shares may, but need not, be represented by certificates. Unless this Act or another statute expressly provides otherwise, the rights and obligations of shareholders are identical regardless of whether their shares are represented by certificates.

(b) At a minimum each share certificate must state on its face:

> **(1)** the name of the corporation and that it is organized under the law of this state;

> **(2)** the name of the person to whom issued; and

> **(3)** the number and class of shares and the designation of the series, if any, the certificate represents.

(c) If the corporation is authorized to issue different classes of shares or series of shares within a class, the front or back of each certificate must summarize (i) the preferences, rights, and limitations applicable to each class and series, (ii) any variations in preferences, rights, and limitations among the holders of the same class or series, and (iii) the authority of the board of directors to determine the terms of future classes or series. Alternatively, each certificate may state conspicuously on its front or back that the corporation will furnish the shareholder this information on request in writing and without charge.

(d) Each share certificate must be signed by two officers designated in the bylaws.

(e) If the person who signed a share certificate no longer holds office when the certificate is issued, the certificate is nevertheless valid.

§ 6.26. Shares Without Certificates

(a) Unless the articles of incorporation or bylaws provide otherwise, the board of directors of a corporation may authorize the issuance of some or all of the shares of any or all of its classes or series without certificates. The authorization does not affect shares already represented by certificates until they are surrendered to the corporation.

(b) Within a reasonable time after the issuance or transfer of shares without certificates, the corporation shall deliver to the shareholder a written statement of the information required on certificates by sections 6.25(b) and (c), and, if applicable, § 6.27.

§ 6.27. Restriction on Transfer of Shares

(a) The articles of incorporation, the bylaws, an agreement among shareholders, or an agreement between shareholders and the corporation may impose restrictions on the transfer or registration of transfer of shares of the corporation. A restriction does not affect shares issued before the restriction was adopted unless the holders of the shares are parties to the restriction agreement or voted in favor of the restriction.

(b) A restriction on the transfer or registration of transfer of shares is valid and enforceable against the holder or a transferee of the holder if the restriction is authorized by this section and its existence is noted conspicuously on the front or back of the certificate or is contained in the information statement required by § 6.26(b). Unless so noted or contained, a restriction is not enforceable against a person without knowledge of the restriction.

(c) A restriction on the transfer or registration of transfer of shares is authorized:

> **(1)** to maintain the corporation's status when it is dependent on the number or identity of its shareholders;

> **(2)** to preserve exemptions under federal or state securities law; or

> **(3)** for any other reasonable purpose.

(d) A restriction on the transfer or registration of transfer of shares may:

(1) obligate the shareholder first to offer the corporation or other persons (separately, consecutively, or simultaneously) an opportunity to acquire the restricted shares;

(2) obligate the corporation or other persons (separately, consecutively, or simultaneously) to acquire the restricted shares;

(3) require the corporation, the holders of any class or series of its shares, or other persons to approve the transfer of the restricted shares, if the requirement is not manifestly unreasonable; or

(4) prohibit the transfer of the restricted shares to designated persons or classes of persons, if the prohibition is not manifestly unreasonable.

(e) For purposes of this section, "shares" includes a security convertible into or carrying a right to subscribe for or acquire shares.

Subchapter C. Subsequent Acquisition of Shares by Shareholders and Corporation

§ 6.30. Shareholders' Preemptive Rights

(a) The shareholders of a corporation do not have a preemptive right to acquire the corporation's unissued shares except to the extent the articles of incorporation so provide.

(b) A statement included in the articles of incorporation that "the corporation elects to have preemptive rights" (or words of similar effect) means that the following principles apply except to the extent the articles of incorporation expressly provide otherwise:

(1) The shareholders of the corporation have a preemptive right, granted on uniform terms and conditions prescribed by the board of directors to provide a fair and reasonable opportunity to exercise the right, to acquire proportional amounts of the corporation's unisssued shares upon the decision of the board of directors to issue them.

(2) A preemptive right may be waived by a shareholder. A waiver evidenced by a writing is irrevocable even though it is not supported by consideration.

(3) There is no preemptive right with respect to:

(i) shares issued as compensation to directors, officers, employees or agents of the corporation, its subsidiaries or affiliates;

(ii) shares issued to satisfy conversion or option rights created to provide compensation to directors, officers, employees or agents of the corporation, its subsidiaries or affiliates;

(iii) shares authorized in the articles of incorporation that are issued within six months from the effective date of incorporation; or (iv) shares sold otherwise than for cash.

(4) Holders of shares of any class or series without voting power but with preferential rights to distributions have no preemptive rights with respect to shares of any class or series.

(5) Holders of shares of any class or series with voting power but without preferential rights to distributions have no preemptive rights with respect to shares of any class or series with preferential rights to distributions unless the shares with preferential rights are convertible into or carry a right to subscribe for or acquire the shares without preferential rights.

(6) Shares subject to preemptive rights that are not acquired by shareholders may be issued to any person for a period of one year after being offered to shareholders at a consideration set by the board of directors that is not lower than the consideration set for the exercise of preemptive rights. An offer at a lower consideration or after the expiration of one year is subject to the shareholders' preemptive rights.

(c) For purposes of this section, "shares" includes a security convertible into or carrying a right to subscribe for or acquire shares.

§ 6.31. Corporation's Acquisition of Its Own Shares

(a) A corporation may acquire its own shares, and shares so acquired constitute authorized but unissued shares.

(b) If the articles of incorporation prohibit the reissue of the acquired shares, the number of authorized shares is reduced by the number of shares acquired.

Subchapter D. Distributions

§ 6.40. Distributions to Shareholders

(a) A board of directors may authorize and the corporation may make distributions to its shareholders subject to restriction by the articles of incorporation and the limitation in subsection (c).

(b) The board of directors may fix the record date for determining shareholders entitled to a distribution, which date may not be retroactive. If the board of directors does not fix a record date for determining shareholders entitled to a distribution (other than one involving a purchase, redemption, or other acquisition of the corporation's shares), the record date is the date the board of directors authorizes the distribution.

(c) No distribution may be made if, after giving it effect:

(1) the corporation would not be able to pay its debts as they become due in the usual course of business; or

(2) the corporation's total assets would be less than the sum of its total liabilities plus (unless the articles of incorporation permit otherwise) the amount that would be needed, if the corporation were to be dissolved at the time of the distribution, to satisfy the preferential rights upon dissolution of shareholders whose preferential rights are superior

to those receiving the distribution.

(d) The board of directors may base a determination that a distribution is not prohibited under subsection (c) either on financial statements prepared on the basis of accounting practices and principles that are reasonable in the circumstances or on a fair valuation or other method that is reasonable in the circumstances.

(e) Except as provided in subsection (g), the effect of a distribution under subsection (c) is measured:

> **(1)** in the case of distribution by purchase, redemption, or other acquisition of the corporation's shares, as of the earlier of (i) the date cash or other property is transferred or debt to a shareholder is incurred by the corporation or (ii) the date the shareholder ceases to be a shareholder with respect to the acquired shares;
>
> **(2)** in the case of any other distribution of indebtedness, as of the date the indebtedness is distributed; and
>
> **(3)** in all other cases, as of (i) the date the distribution is authorized if the payment occurs within 120 days after the date of authorization or (ii) the date the payment is made if it occurs more than 120 days after the date of authorization.

(f) A corporation's indebtedness to a shareholder incurred by reason of a distribution made in accordance with this section is at parity with the corporation's indebtedness to its general, unsecured creditors except to the extent subordinated by agreement.

(g) Indebtedness of a corporation, including indebtedness issued as a distribution, is not considered a liability for purposes of determinations under subsection (c) if its terms provide that payment of principal and interest are made only if and to the extent that payment of a distribution to shareholders could then be made under this section. If such indebtedness is issued as a distribution, each payment of principal or interest is treated as a distribution, the effect of which is measured on the date the payment is actually made.

(h) This section shall not apply to distributions in liquidation under chapter 14.

Chapter 7. Shareholders

Subchapter A. Meetings

§ 7.01. Annual Meeting

(a) Unless directors are elected by written consent in lieu of an annual meeting as permitted by § 7.04, a corporation shall hold a meeting of shareholders annually at a time stated in or fixed in accordance with the bylaws at which directors shall be elected.

(b) Unless the board of directors determines to hold the meeting solely by means of remote communication in accordance with § 7.09(c), annual meetings may be held (i) in or out of this state at the place stated in or fixed in accordance with the bylaws, or (ii) if no place is stated or fixed in accordance with the bylaws, at the corporation's principal office.

(c) The failure to hold an annual meeting at the time stated in or fixed in accordance with a corporation's bylaws does not affect the validity of any corporate action.

§ 7.02. Special Meeting

(a) A corporation shall hold a special meeting of shareholders:

> **(1)** on call of its board of directors or the person or persons authorized to do so by the articles of incorporation or bylaws; or
>
> **(2)** if shareholders holding at least 10% of all the votes entitled to be cast on an issue proposed to be considered at the proposed special meeting sign, date, and deliver to the corporation one or more written demands for the meeting describing the purpose or purposes for which it is to be held, provided that the articles of incorporation may fix a lower percentage or a higher percentage not exceeding 25% of all the votes entitled to be cast on any issue proposed to be considered. Unless otherwise provided in the articles of incorporation, a written demand for a special meeting may be revoked by a writing to that effect received by the corporation before the receipt by the corporation

of demands sufficient in number to require the holding of a special meeting.

(b) If not otherwise fixed under § 7.03 or 7.07, the record date for determining shareholders entitled to demand a special meeting shall be the first date on which a signed shareholder demand is delivered to the corporation. No written demand for a special meeting shall be effective unless, within 60 days of the earliest date on which such a demand delivered to the corporation as required by this section was signed, written demands signed by shareholders holding at least the percentage of votes specified in or fixed in accordance with subsection (a)(2) have been delivered to the corporation.

(c) Unless he board of directors determines to hold the meeting solely by remote participation in accordance with § 7.09(c), special meetings of shareholders may be held (i) in or out of this state at the place stated in or fixed in accordance with the bylaws, or (ii) if no place is stated in or fixed in accordance with the bylaws, at the corporation's principal office.

(d) Only business within the purpose or purposes described in the meeting notice required by § 7.05(c) may be conducted at a special meeting of shareholders.

§ 7.03. Court-Ordered Meeting

(a) The [name or describe court] may summarily order a meeting to be held:

(1) on application of any shareholder of the corporation if an annual meeting was not held or action by written consent in lieu of an annual meeting did not become effective within the earlier of six months after the end of the corporation's fiscal year or 15 months after its last annual meeting; or

(2) on application of one or more shareholders who signed a demand for a special meeting valid under § 7.02, if:

(i) notice of the special meeting was not given within 30 days after the first day on

which the requisite number of such demands have been delivered to the corporation; or

(ii) the special meeting was not held in accordance with the notice.

(b) The court may fix the time and place of the meeting, determine the shares entitled to participate in the meeting, specify a record date or dates for determining shareholders entitled to notice of and to vote at the meeting, prescribe the form and content of the meeting notice, fix the quorum required for specific matters to be considered at the meeting (or direct that the shares represented at the meeting constitute a quorum for action on those matters), and enter other orders necessary to accomplish the purpose or purposes of the meeting.

(c) For purposes of subsection (a)(1), "shareholder" means a record shareholder, a beneficial shareholder, and an unrestricted voting trust beneficial owner.

§ 7.04. Action Without Meeting

(a) Action required or permitted by this Act to be taken at a shareholders' meeting may be taken without a meeting if the action is taken by all the shareholders entitled to vote on the action. The action must be evidenced by one or more written consents bearing the date of signature and describing the action taken, signed by all the shareholders entitled to vote on the action and delivered to the corporation for filing by the corporation with the minutes or corporate records.

(b) The articles of incorporation may provide that any action required or permitted by this Act to be taken at a shareholders' meeting may be taken without a meeting, and without prior notice, if consents in writing setting forth the action so taken are signed by the holders of outstanding shares having not less than the minimum number of votes that would be required to authorize or take the action at a meeting at which all shares entitled to vote on the action were present and voted; provided, however, that if a corporation's articles of incorporation authorize shareholders to cumulate their votes when electing directors pursuant to § 7.28, directors may not be elected by less than unanimous written consent. A written consent must bear the date of signature of the shareholder who signs the consent and be delivered to the corporation for filing by the corporation with the minutes or corporate records.

(c) If not otherwise fixed under § 7.07 and if prior action by the board of directors is not required respecting the action to be taken without a meeting, the record date for determining the shareholders entitled to take action without a meeting shall be the first date on which a signed written consent is delivered to the corporation. If not otherwise fixed under § 7.07 and if prior action by the board of directors is required respecting the action to be taken without a meeting, the record date shall be the close of business on the day the resolution of the board of directors taking such prior action is adopted. No written consent shall be effective to take the corporate action referred to therein unless, within 60 days of the earliest date on which a consent delivered to the corporation as required by this section was signed, written consents signed by sufficient shareholders to take the action have been delivered to the corporation. A written consent may be revoked by a writing to that effect delivered to the corporation before unrevoked written consents sufficient in number to take the corporate action have been delivered to the corporation.

(d) A consent signed pursuant to the provisions of this section has the effect of a vote taken at a meeting and may be described as such in any document. Unless the articles of incorporation, bylaws or a resolution of the board of directors provides for a reasonable delay to permit tabulation of written consents, the action taken by written consent shall be effective when written consents signed by sufficient shareholders to take the action have been delivered to the corporation.

(e) If this Act requires that notice of a proposed action be given to nonvoting shareholders and the action is to be taken by written consent of the voting shareholders, the corporation shall give its nonvoting shareholders written notice of the action not more than 10 days after (i) written consents sufficient to take the action have been delivered to

the corporation, or (ii) such later date that tabulation of consents is completed pursuant to an authorization under subsection (d). The notice must reasonably describe the action taken and contain or be accompanied by the same material that, under any provision of this Act, would have been required to be sent to nonvoting shareholders in a notice of a meeting at which the proposed action would have been submitted to the shareholders for action.

(f) If action is taken by less than unanimous written consent of the voting shareholders, the corporation shall give its nonconsenting voting shareholders written notice of the action not more than 10 days after (i) written consents sufficient to take the action have been delivered to the corporation, or (ii) such later date that tabulation of consents is completed pursuant to an authorization under subsection (d). The notice must reasonably describe the action taken and contain or be accompanied by the same material that, under any provision of this Act, would have been required to be sent to voting shareholders in a notice of a meeting at which the action would have been submitted to the shareholders for action.

(g) The notice requirements in subsections (e) and (f) shall not delay the effectiveness of actions taken by written consent, and a failure to comply with such notice requirements shall not invalidate actions taken by written consent, provided that this subsection shall not be deemed to limit judicial power to fashion any appropriate remedy in favor of a shareholder adversely affected by a failure to give such notice within the required time period.

§ 7.05. Notice of Meeting

(a) A corporation shall notify shareholders of the date, time, and place, if any, of each annual and special shareholders' meeting no fewer than 10 nor more than 60 days before the meeting date. If the board of directors has authorized participation by means of remote communication pursuant to § 7.09 for holders of any class or series of shares, the notice to the holders of such class or series of shares must describe the means of remote communication to be used. The notice must include the record date for determining the shareholders entitled to vote at the meeting, if such date is different from the record date for determining shareholders entitled to notice of the meeting. Unless this Act or the articles of incorporation require otherwise, the corporation is required to give notice only to shareholders entitled to vote at the meeting as of the record date for determining the shareholders entitled to notice of the meeting.

(b) Unless this Act or the articles of incorporation require otherwise, the notice of an annual meeting of shareholders need not include a description of the purpose or purposes for which

the meeting is called.

(c) Notice of a special meeting of shareholders must include a description of the purpose or purposes for which the meeting is called.

(d) If not otherwise fixed under § 7.03 or 7.07, the record date for determining shareholders entitled to notice of and to vote at an annual or special shareholders' meeting is the day before the first notice is delivered to shareholders.

(e) Unless the bylaws require otherwise, if an annual or special shareholders' meeting is adjourned to a different date, time, or place, if any, notice need not be given of the new date, time, or place, if any, if the new date, time, or place, if any, is announced at the meeting before adjournment. If a new record date for the adjourned meeting is or must be fixed under § 7.07, however, notice of the adjourned meeting shall be given under this section to shareholders entitled to vote at such adjourned meeting as of the record date fixed for notice of such adjourned meeting.

§ 7.06. Waiver of Notice

(a) A shareholder may waive any notice required by this Act or the articles of incorporation or bylaws, before or after the date and time stated in the notice. The waiver must be in writing, be signed by the shareholder entitled to the notice, and be delivered to the corporation for filing by the corporation with the minutes or corporate records.

(b) A shareholder's attendance at a meeting:

(1) waives objection to lack of notice or defective notice of the meeting, unless the shareholder at the beginning of the meeting objects to holding the meeting or transacting business at the meeting; and

(2) waives objection to consideration of a particular matter at the meeting that is not within the purpose or purposes described in the meeting notice, unless the shareholder objects to considering the matter when it is presented.

§ 7.07. Record Date for Meeting

(a) The bylaws may fix or provide the manner of fixing the record date or dates for one or more voting groups to determine the shareholders entitled to notice of a shareholders' meeting, to demand a special meeting, to vote, or to take any other action. If the bylaws do not fix or provide for fixing a record date, the board of directors may fix the record date.

(b) A record date fixed under this section may not be more than 70 days before the meeting or action requiring a determination of shareholders and may not be retroactive.

(c) A determination of shareholders entitled to notice of or to vote at a shareholders' meeting is effective for any adjournment of the meeting unless the board of directors fixes a new record date or dates, which it shall do if the meeting is adjourned to a date more than 120 days after the date fixed for the original meeting.

(d) If a court orders a meeting adjourned to a date more than 120 days after the date fixed for the original meeting, it may provide that the original record date or dates continues in effect or it may fix a new record date or dates.

(e) The record dates for a shareholders' meeting fixed by or in the manner provided in the bylaws or by the board of directors shall be the record date for determining shareholders entitled both to notice of and to vote at the shareholders' meeting, unless in the case of a record date fixed by the board of directors and to the extent not prohibited by the bylaws, the board, at the time it fixes the record date for shareholders entitled to notice of the meeting, fixes a later record date on or before the date of the meeting to determine the shareholders entitled to vote at the meeting.

§ 7.08. Conduct of Meeting

(a) At each meeting of shareholders, a chair shall preside. The chair shall be appointed as provided in the bylaws or, in the absence of such provision, by the board of directors.

(b) The chair, unless the articles of incorporation or bylaws provide otherwise, shall determine the order of business and shall have the authority to establish rules for the conduct of the meeting.

(c) Any rules adopted for, and the conduct of, the meeting shall be fair to shareholders.

(d) The chair of the meeting shall announce at the meeting when the polls close for each matter voted upon. If no announcement is made, the polls shall be deemed to have closed upon the final adjournment of the meeting. After the polls close, no ballots, proxies or votes nor any revocations or changes to such ballots, proxies or votes may be accepted.

§ 7.09. Remote Participation in Shareholders' Meetings; Meetings Held Solely by Remote Participation

(a) Shareholders of any class or series of shares may participate in any meeting of shareholders by means of remote communication to the extent the board of directors authorizes such participation for such class or series. Participation as a shareholder by means of remote communication shall be subject to such guidelines and procedures as the board of directors adopts, and shall be in conformity with subsection (b).

(b) Shareholders participating in a shareholders' meeting by means of remote communication shall be deemed present and may vote at such a meeting if the corporation has implemented reasonable measures:

    (1) to verify that each person participating remotely as a shareholder is a shareholder; and

(2) to provide such shareholders a reasonable opportunity to participate in the meeting and to vote on matters submitted to the shareholders, including an opportunity to communicate, and to read or hear the proceedings of the meeting, substantially concurrently with such proceedings.

(c) Unless the bylaws require the meeting of shareholders to be held at a place, the board of directors may determine that any meeting of shareholders shall not be held at any place and shall instead be held solely by means of remote communication, but only if the corporation implements the measures specified in subsection (b).

Subchapter B. Voting

§ 7.20. Shareholders' List for Meeting

(a) After fixing a record date for a meeting, a corporation shall prepare an alphabetical list of the names of all its shareholders who are entitled to notice of a shareholders' meeting. If the board of directors fixes a different record date under § 7.07(e) to determine the shareholders entitled to vote at the meeting, a corporation also shall prepare an alphabetical list of the names of all its shareholders who are entitled to vote at the meeting. A list must be arranged by voting group (and within each voting group by class or series of shares) and show the address of and number of shares held by each shareholder. Nothing contained in this subsection shall require the corporation to include on such list the electronic mail address or other electronic contact information of a shareholder.

(b) The shareholders' list for notice shall be available for inspection by any shareholder, beginning two business days after notice of the meeting is given for which the list was prepared and continuing through the meeting, (i) at the corporation's principal office or at a place identified in the meeting notice in the city where the meeting will be held or (ii) on a reasonable accessible electronic network, provided that the information required to gain access to such list is provided with the notice of the meeting. In the event that the corporation determines to make the list available on an electronic network, the corporation may take reasonable steps to ensure that such information is available only to shareholders of the corporation. A shareholders' list for voting shall be similarly available for inspection promptly after the record date for voting. A shareholder, or the shareholder's agent or attorney, is entitled on written demand to inspect and, subject to the requirements of § 16.02(c), to copy a list, during regular business hours and at the shareholder's expense, during the period it is available for inspection.

(c) If the meeting is to be held at a place, the corporation shall make the list of shareholders entitled to vote available at the meeting, and any shareholder, or the shareholder's agent or attorney, is entitled to inspect the list at any time during the meeting or any adjournment. If the meeting is to be held solely by means of remote communication, then such list shall also be open to such inspection during the meeting on a reasonably accessible electronic network, and the information required to access such list shall be provided with the notice of the meeting.

(d) If the corporation refuses to allow a shareholder, or the shareholder's agent or attorney, to inspect a shareholders' list before or at the meeting (or copy a list as permitted by subsection (b)), the [name or describe court], on application of the shareholder, may summarily order the inspection or copying at the corporation's expense and may postpone the meeting for which the list was prepared until the inspection or copying is complete.

(e) Refusal or failure to prepare or make available the shareholders' list does not affect the validity of action taken at the meeting.

§ 7.21. Voting Entitlement of Shares

(a) Except as provided in subsections (b) and (d) or unless the articles of incorporation provide otherwise, each outstanding share, regardless of class or series, is entitled to one vote on each matter voted on at a shareholders' meeting. Only shares are entitled to vote.

(b) Shares of a corporation are not entitled to vote if they are owned by or otherwise belong to the corporation directly, or indirectly through an entity of which a majority of the voting power is held directly or indirectly by the corporation or which is otherwise controlled by the corporation.

(c) Shares held by the corporation in a fiduciary capacity for the benefit of any person are entitled to vote unless they are held for the benefit of, or otherwise belong to, the corporation directly, or indirectly through an entity of which a majority of the voting power is held directly or indirectly by the corporation or which is otherwise controlled by the corporation.

(d) Redeemable shares are not entitled to vote after delivery of written notice of redemption is effective and a sum sufficient to redeem the shares has been deposited with a bank, trust company, or other financial institution under an irrevocable obligation to pay the holders the redemption price on surrender of the shares.

(e) For purposes of this section, "voting power" means the current power to vote in the election of directors of a corporation or to elect, select or appoint governors of another entity.

§ 7.22. Proxies

(a) A shareholder may vote the shareholder's shares in person or by proxy.

(b) A shareholder, or the shareholder's agent or attorney-in-fact, may appoint a proxy to vote or otherwise act for the shareholder by signing an appointment form, or by an electronic transmission. An electronic transmission must contain or be accompanied by information from which the recipient can determine the date of the transmission and that the transmission was authorized by the sender or the sender's agent or attorney-in-fact.

(c) An appointment of a proxy is effective when a signed appointment form or an electronic transmission of the appointment is received by the inspector of election or the officer or agent of the corporation authorized to count votes. An appointment is valid for the term provided in the appointment form, and, if no term is provided, is valid for

11 months unless the appointment is irrevocable under subsection (d).

(d) An appointment of a proxy is revocable unless the appointment form or electronic transmission states that it is irrevocable and the appointment is coupled with an interest. Appointments coupled with an interest include the appointment of:

  (1) a pledgee;

  (2) a person who purchased or agreed to purchase the shares;

  (3) a creditor of the corporation who extended it credit under terms requiring the appointment;

  (4) an employee of the corporation whose employment contract requires the appointment; or

  (5) a party to a voting agreement created under § 7.31.

(e) The death or incapacity of the shareholder appointing a proxy does not affect the right of the corporation to accept the proxy's authority unless notice of the death or incapacity is received by the secretary or other officer or agent authorized to tabulate votes before the proxy exercises authority under the appointment.

(f) An appointment made irrevocable under subsection (d) is revoked when the interest with which it is coupled is extinguished.

(g) Unless it otherwise provides, an appointment made irrevocable under subsection (d) continues in effect after a transfer of the shares and a transferee takes subject to the appointment, except that a transferee for value of shares subject to an irrevocable appointment may revoke the appointment if the transferee did not know of its existence when acquiring the shares and the existence of the irrevocable appointment was not noted conspicuously on the certificate representing the shares or on the information statement for shares without certificates.

(h) Subject to § 7.24 and to any express limitation on the proxy's authority stated in the appointment form or electronic transmission, a corporation is entitled to accept the proxy's vote or other action as that of the shareholder making the appointment.

§ 7.23. Shares Held by Intermediaries and Nominees

(a) A corporation's board of directors may establish a procedure under which a person on whose behalf shares are registered in the name of an intermediary or nominee may elect to be treated by the corporation as the record shareholder by filing with the corporation a beneficial ownership certificate. The terms, conditions, and limitations of this treatment shall be specified in the procedure. To the extent such person is treated under such procedure as having rights or privileges that the record shareholder otherwise would have, the record shareholder shall not have those rights or privileges.

(b) The procedure must specify:

  (1) the types of intermediaries or nominees to which it applies;

  (2) the rights or privileges that the corporation recognizes in a person with respect to whom a beneficial ownership certificate is filed;

  (3) the manner in which the procedure is selected which must include that the beneficial ownership certificate be signed or assented to by or on behalf of the record shareholder and the person on whose behalf the shares are held;

  (4) the information that must be provided when the procedure is selected;

  (5) the period for which selection of the procedure is effective;

  (6) requirements for notice to the corporation with respect to the arrangement; and

  (7) the form and contents of the beneficial ownership certificate.

(c) The procedure may specify any other aspects of the rights and duties created by the filing of a beneficial ownership certificate.

§ 7.24. Acceptance of Votes and Other Instruments

(a) If the name signed on a vote, ballot, consent, waiver, shareholder demand, or proxy appointment corresponds to the name of a shareholder, the corporation, if acting in good faith, is entitled to accept the vote, ballot, consent, waiver, shareholder demand, or proxy appointment and give it effect as the act of the shareholder.

(b) If the name signed on a vote, ballot, consent, waiver, shareholder demand, or proxy appointment does not correspond to the name of its shareholder, the corporation, if acting in good faith, is nevertheless entitled to accept the vote, ballot, consent, waiver, shareholder demand, or proxy appointment and give it effect as the act of the shareholder if:

(1) the shareholder is an entity and the name signed purports to be that of an officer or agent of the entity;

(2) the name signed purports to be that of an administrator, executor, guardian, or conservator representing the shareholder and, if the corporation requests, evidence of fiduciary status acceptable to the corporation has been presented with respect to the vote, ballot, consent, waiver, shareholder demand, or proxy appointment;

(3) the name signed purports to be that of a receiver or trustee in bankruptcy of the shareholder and, if the corporation requests, evidence of this status acceptable to the corporation has been presented with respect to the vote, ballot, consent, waiver, shareholder demand, or proxy appointment;

(4) the name signed purports to be that of a pledgee, beneficial owner, or attorney-in-fact of the shareholder and, if the corporation requests, evidence acceptable to the corporation of the signatory's authority to sign for the shareholder has been presented with respect to the vote, ballot, consent, waiver, shareholder demand, or proxy appointment; or

(5) two or more persons are the shareholder as co-tenants or fiduciaries and the name signed purports to be the name of at least one of the co-owners and the person signing appears to be acting on behalf of all the co-owners.

(c) The corporation is entitled to reject a vote, ballot, consent, waiver, shareholder demand, or proxy appointment if the person authorized to accept or reject such instrument, acting in good faith, has reasonable basis for doubt about the validity of the signature on it or about the signatory's authority to sign for the shareholder.

(d) Neither the corporation or any person authorized by it, nor an inspector of election appointed under § 7.29, that accepts or rejects a vote, ballot, consent, waiver, shareholder demand, or proxy appointment in good faith and in accordance with the standards of this § 7.24 or § 7.22(b) is liable in damages to the shareholder for the consequences of the acceptance or rejection.

(e) Corporate action based on the acceptance or rejection of a vote, ballot, consent, waiver, shareholder demand, or proxy appointment under this section is valid unless a court of competent jurisdiction determines otherwise.

(f) If an inspector of election has been appointed under § 7.29, the inspector of election also has the authority to request information and make determinations under subsections (a), (b), and (c). Any determination made by the inspector of election under those subsections is controlling.

§ 7.25. Quorum and Voting Requirements for Voting Groups

(a) Shares entitled to vote as a separate voting group may take action on a matter at a meeting only if a quorum of those shares exists with respect to that matter. Unless the articles of incorporation provide otherwise, shares representing a majority of the votes entitled to be cast on the matter by the voting group constitutes a quorum of that voting group for action on that matter. Whenever this Act requires a particular quorum for a specified action, the articles of incorporation may not provide for a lower quorum.

(b) Once a share is represented for any purpose at a meeting, it is deemed present for quorum purposes for the remainder of the meeting and for any adjournment of that meeting unless a new record date is or must be fixed for that adjourned meeting.

(c) If a quorum exists, action on a matter (other than the election of directors) by a voting group is approved if the votes cast within the voting group favoring the action exceed the votes cast opposing the action, unless the articles of incorporation require a greater number of affirmative votes.

(d) An amendment of the articles of incorporation adding, changing, or deleting a quorum or voting requirement for a voting group greater than specified in subsection (a) or (c) is governed by § 7.27.

(e) The election of directors is governed by § 7.28.

(f) Whenever a provision of this Act provides for voting of classes or series as separate voting groups, the rules provided in § 10.04(c) for amendments of the articles of incorporation apply to that provision.

§ 7.26. Action by Single and Multiple Voting Groups

(a) If the articles of incorporation or this Act provide for voting by a single voting group on a matter, action on that matter is taken when voted upon by that voting group as provided in § 7.25.

(b) If the articles of incorporation or this Act provide for voting by two or more voting groups on a matter, action on that matter is taken only when voted upon by each of those voting groups counted separately as provided in § 7.25. Action may be taken by different voting groups on a matter at different times.

§ 7.27. Modifying Quorum or Voting Requirements

An amendment to the articles of incorporation that adds, changes, or deletes a quorum or voting requirement shall meet the same quorum requirement and be adopted by the same vote and voting groups required to take action under the quorum and voting requirements then in effect or proposed to be adopted, whichever is greater.

§ 7.28. Voting for Directors; Cumulative Voting

(a) Unless otherwise provided in the articles of incorporation, directors are elected by a plurality of the votes cast by the shares entitled to vote in the election at a meeting at which a quorum is present.

(b) Shareholders do not have a right to cumulate their votes for directors unless the articles of incorporation so provide.

(c) A statement included in the articles of incorporation that "[all] [a designated voting group of] shareholders are entitled to cumulate their votes for directors" (or words of similar import) means that the shareholders designated are entitled to multiply the number of votes they are entitled to cast by the number of directors for whom they are entitled to vote and cast the product for a single candidate or distribute the product among two or more candidates.

(d) Shares otherwise entitled to vote cumulatively may not be voted cumulatively at a particular meeting unless:

> **(1)** the meeting notice or proxy statement accompanying the notice states conspicuously that cumulative voting is authorized; or

> **(2)** a shareholder who has the right to cumulate the shareholder's votes gives notice to the corporation not less than 48 hours before the time set for the meeting of the shareholder's intent to cumulate votes during the meeting, and if one shareholder gives this notice all other shareholders in the same voting group participating in the election are entitled to cumulate their votes without giving further notice.

§ 7.29. Inspectors of Election

(a) A corporation that has a class of equity securities registered pursuant to § 12 of the Securities Exchange Act of 1934 shall, and any other corporation may, appoint one or more inspectors to act at a meeting of shareholders in connection with determining voting results. Each inspector shall verify in writing that the inspector will faithfully execute the duties of inspector with strict impartiality and according to the best of the inspector's ability. An inspector may be an officer or employee of the corporation. The inspectors may appoint or retain other persons to assist the inspectors in the performance of the duties of inspector under subsection (b), and may rely on information provided by such persons and other persons, including those appointed to tabulate votes, unless the inspectors believe reliance is unwarranted.

(b) The inspectors shall:

(1) ascertain the number of shares outstanding and the voting power of each;

(2) determine the shares represented at a meeting;

(3) determine the validity of proxy appointments and ballots;

(4) count the votes; and

(5) make a written report of the results.

(c) In performing their duties, the inspectors may examine (i) the proxy appointment forms and any other information provided in accordance with § 7.22(b), (ii) any envelope or related writing submitted with those appointment forms, (iii) any ballots, (iv) any evidence or other information specified in § 7.24 and (v) the relevant books and records of the corporation relating to its shareholders and their entitlement to vote, including any securities position list provided by a depository clearing agency.

(d) The inspectors also may consider other information that they believe is relevant and reliable for the purpose of performing any of the duties assigned to them pursuant to subsection (b), including for the purpose of evaluating inconsistent, incomplete or erroneous information and reconciling information submitted on behalf of banks, brokers, their nominees or similar persons that indicates more votes being cast than a proxy authorized by the record shareholder is entitled to cast. If the inspectors consider other information allowed by this subsection, they shall in their report under subsection (b) specify the information considered by them, including the purpose or purposes for which the information was considered, the person or persons from whom they obtained the information, when the information was obtained, the means by which the information was obtained, and the basis for the inspectors' belief that such information is relevant and reliable.

(e) Determinations of law by the inspectors of election are subject to de novo review by a court in a proceeding under § 7.49 or other judicial proceeding.

Subchapter C. Voting Trusts and Agreements

§ 7.30. Voting Trusts

(a) One or more shareholders may create a voting trust, conferring on a trustee the right to vote or otherwise act for them, by signing an agreement setting out the provisions of the trust (which may include anything consistent with its purpose) and transferring their shares to the trustee. When a voting trust agreement is signed, the trustee shall prepare a list of the names and addresses of all voting trust beneficial owners, together with the number and class of shares each transferred to the trust, and deliver copies of the list and agreement to the corporation at its principal office.

(b) A voting trust becomes effective on the date the first shares subject to the trust are registered in the trustee's name.

(c) Limits, if any, on the duration of a voting trust shall be as set forth in the voting trust. A voting trust that became effective when this Act provided a 10-year limit on its duration remains governed by the provisions of this section concerning duration then in effect, unless the voting trust is amended to provide otherwise by unanimous agreement of the parties to the voting trust.

§ 7.31. Voting Agreements

(a) Two or more shareholders may provide for the manner in which they will vote their shares by signing an agreement for that purpose. A voting agreement created under this section is not subject to the provisions of § 7.30.

(b) A voting agreement created under this section is specifically enforceable.

§ 7.32. Shareholder Agreements

(a) An agreement among the shareholders of a corporation that complies with this section is effective among the shareholders and the corporation even though it is inconsistent with one or more other provisions of this Act in that it:

(1) eliminates the board of directors or restricts the discretion or powers of the board of directors;

(2) governs the authorization or making of distributions, regardless of whether they are in proportion to ownership of shares, subject to the limitations in § 6.40;

(3) establishes who shall be directors or officers of the corporation, or their terms of office or manner of selection or removal;

(4) governs, in general or in regard to specific matters, the exercise or division of voting power by or between the shareholders and directors or by or among any of them, including use of weighted voting rights or director proxies;

(5) establishes the terms and conditions of any agreement for the transfer or use of property or the provision of services between the corporation and any shareholder, director, officer or employee of the corporation or among any of them;

(6) transfers to one or more shareholders or other persons all or part of the authority to exercise the corporate powers or to manage the business and affairs of the corporation, including the resolution of any issue about which there exists a deadlock among directors or shareholders;

(7) requires dissolution of the corporation at the request of one or more of the shareholders or upon the occurrence of a specified event or contingency; or

(8) otherwise governs the exercise of the corporate powers or the management of the business and affairs of the corporation or the relationship among the shareholders, the directors and the corporation, or among any of them, and is not contrary to public policy.

(b) An agreement authorized by this section shall be:

(1) as set forth (i) in the articles of incorporation or bylaws and approved by all persons who are shareholders at the time of the agreement, or (ii) in a written agreement that is signed by all persons who are shareholders at the time of the agreement and is made known to the corporation; and

(2) subject to amendment only by all persons who are shareholders at the time of the amendment, unless the agreement provides otherwise.

(c) The existence of an agreement authorized by this section shall be noted conspicuously on the front or back of each certificate for outstanding shares or on the information statement required by § 6.26(b). If at the time of the agreement the corporation has shares outstanding represented by certificates, the corporation shall recall the outstanding certificates and issue substitute certificates that comply with this subsection. The failure to note the existence of the agreement on the certificate or information statement shall not affect the validity of the agreement or any action taken pursuant to it. Any purchaser of shares who, at the time of purchase, did not have knowledge of the existence of the agreement shall be entitled to rescission of the purchase. A purchaser shall be deemed to have knowledge of the existence of the agreement if its existence is noted on the certificate or information statement for the shares in compliance with this subsection and, if the shares are not represented by a certificate, the information statement is delivered to the purchaser at or before the time of purchase of the shares. An action to enforce the right of rescission authorized by this subsection shall be commenced within the earlier of 90 days after discovery of the existence of the agreement or two years after the time of purchase of the shares.

(d) If the agreement ceases to be effective for any reason, the board of directors may, if the agreement is contained or referred to in the corporation's articles of incorporation or bylaws, adopt an amendment to the articles of incorporation or bylaws, without shareholder action, to delete the agreement and any references to it.

(e) An agreement authorized by this section that limits the discretion or powers of the board of directors shall relieve the directors of, and impose upon the person or persons in whom such discretion or powers are vested, liability for acts or omissions imposed by law on directors to the extent that the discretion or powers of the directors are limited by the agreement.

(f) The existence or performance of an agreement authorized by this section shall not be a ground for imposing personal liability on any shareholder for the acts or debts of the corporation even if the agreement or its performance treats the corporation as if it were a partnership or results in failure to observe the corporate formalities otherwise applicable to the matters governed by the agreement.

(g) Incorporators or subscribers for shares may act as shareholders with respect to an agreement authorized by this section if no shares have been issued when the agreement is made.

(h) Limits, if any, on the duration of an agreement authorized by this section must be set forth in the agreement. An agreement that became effective when this Act provided for a 10-year limit on duration of shareholder agreements, unless the agreement provided otherwise, remains governed by the provisions of this section concerning duration then in effect.

Subchapter D. Derivative Proceedings

§ 7.40. Subchapter Definitions

In this subchapter:

"Derivative proceeding" means a civil suit in the right of a domestic corporation or, to the extent provided in § 7.47, in the right of a foreign corporation.

"Shareholder" means a record shareholder, a beneficial shareholder, and an unrestricted voting trust beneficial owner.

§ 7.41. Standing

A shareholder may not commence or maintain a derivative proceeding unless the shareholder (i) was a shareholder of the corporation at the time of the act or omission complained of or became a shareholder through transfer by operation of law from one who was a shareholder at that time and (ii) fairly and adequately represents the interests of the corporation in enforcing the right of the corporation.

§ 7.42. Demand

No shareholder may commence a derivative proceeding until (i) a written demand has been made upon the corporation to take suitable action and (ii) 90 days have expired from the date delivery of the demand was made unless the shareholder has earlier been notified that the demand has been rejected by the corporation or unless irreparable injury to the corporation would result by waiting for the expiration of the 90-day period.

§ 7.43. Stay of Proceedings

If the corporation commences an inquiry into the allegations made in the demand or complaint, the court may stay any derivative proceeding for such period as the court deems appropriate.

§ 7.44. Dismissal

(a) A derivative proceeding shall be dismissed by the court on motion by the corporation if one of the groups specified in subsection (b) or subsection (e) has determined in good faith, after conducting a reasonable inquiry upon which its conclusions are based, that the maintenance of the derivative proceeding is not in the best interests of the corporation.

(b) Unless a panel is appointed pursuant to subsection (e), the determination in subsection (a) shall be made by:

(1) a majority vote of qualified directors present at a meeting of the board of directors if the qualified directors constitute a quorum; or

(2) a majority vote of a committee consisting of two or more qualified directors appointed by majority vote of qualified directors present at a meeting of the board of directors, regardless of whether such qualified directors constitute a quorum.

(c) If a derivative proceeding is commenced after a determination has been made rejecting a demand by a shareholder, the complaint shall allege with particularity facts establishing either (1) that a majority of the board of directors did not consist of qualified directors at the time the determination was made or (2) that the requirements of subsection (a) have not been met.

(d) If a majority of the board of directors consisted of qualified directors at the time the determination was made, the plaintiff shall have the burden of proving that the requirements of subsection (a) have not been met; if not, the corporation shall have the burden of proving that the requirements of subsection (a) have been met.

(e) Upon motion by the corporation, the court may appoint a panel of one or more individuals to make a determination whether the maintenance of the derivative proceeding is in the best interests of the corporation. In such case, the plaintiff shall have the burden of proving that the requirements of subsection (a) have not been met.

§ 7.45. Discontinuance or Settlement

A derivative proceeding may not be discontinued or settled without the court's approval. If the court determines that a proposed discontinuance or settlement will substantially affect the interests of the corporation's shareholders or a class or series of shareholders, the court shall direct that notice be given to the shareholders affected.

§ 7.46. Payment of Expenses

On termination of the derivative proceeding the court may:

    (1) order the corporation to pay the plaintiff's expenses incurred in the proceeding if it finds that the proceeding has resulted in a substantial benefit to the corporation;

    (2) order the plaintiff to pay any defendant's expenses incurred in defending the proceeding if it finds that the proceeding was commenced or maintained without reasonable cause or for an improper purpose; or

    (3) order a party to pay an opposing party's expenses incurred because of the filing of a pleading, motion or other paper, if it finds that the pleading, motion or other paper (i) was not well grounded in fact, after reasonable inquiry, or warranted by existing law or a good faith argument for the extension, modification or reversal of existing law or (ii) was interposed for an improper purpose, such as to harass or cause unnecessary delay or needless increase in the cost of litigation.

§ 7.47. Applicability to Foreign Corporations

In any derivative proceeding in the right of a foreign corporation, the matters covered by this subchapter shall be governed by the laws of the jurisdiction of incorporation of the foreign corporation except for sections 7.43, 7.45, and 7.46.

Subchapter E. Judicial Proceedings

§ 7.48. Shareholder Action to Appoint a Custodian or Receiver

(a) The [name or describe court] may appoint one or more persons to be custodians, or, if the corporation is insolvent, to be receivers, of and for a corporation in a proceeding by a shareholder where it is established that:

    (1) the directors are deadlocked in the management of the corporate affairs, the shareholders are unable to break the deadlock, and irreparable injury to the corporation is threatened or being suffered; or

    (2) the directors or those in control of the corporation are acting fraudulently and irreparable injury to the corporation is threatened or being suffered.

(b) The court:

    (1) may issue injunctions, appoint a temporary custodian or temporary receiver with all the powers and duties the court directs, take other action to preserve the corporate assets wherever located, and carry on the business of the corporation until a full hearing is held;

(2) shall hold a full hearing, after notifying all parties to the proceeding and any interested persons designated by the court, before appointing a custodian or receiver; and

(3) has jurisdiction over the corporation and all of its property, wherever located.

(c) The court may appoint an individual or domestic or foreign corporation (registered to do business in this state) as a custodian or receiver and may require the custodian or receiver to post bond, with or without sureties, in an amount the court directs.

(d) The court shall describe the powers and duties of the custodian or receiver in its appointing order, which may be amended from time to time. Among other powers:

(1) a custodian may exercise all of the powers of the corporation, through or in place of its board of directors, to the extent necessary to manage the business and affairs of the corporation; and

(2) a receiver (i) may dispose of all or any part of the assets of the corporation wherever located, at a public or private sale, if authorized by the court; and (ii) may sue and defend in the receiver's own name as receiver in all courts of this state.

(e) The court during a custodianship may redesignate the custodian a receiver, and during a receivership may redesignate the receiver a custodian, if doing so is in the best interests of the corporation.

(f) The court from time to time during the custodianship or receivership may order compensation paid and expense disbursements or reimbursements made to the custodian or receiver from the assets of the corporation or proceeds from the sale of its assets.

(g) In this section, "shareholder" means a record shareholder, a beneficial shareholder, and an unrestricted voting trust beneficial owner.

§ 7.49. Judicial Determination of Corporate Offices and Review of Elections and Shareholder Votes

(a) Upon application of or in a proceeding commenced by a person specified in subsection (b), the [name or describe court] may determine:

(1) the result or validity of the election, appointment, removal or resignation of a director or officer of the corporation;

(2) the right of an individual to hold the office of director or officer of the corporation;

(3) the result or validity of any vote by the shareholders of the corporation;

(4) the right of a director to membership on a committee of the board of directors; and

(5) the right of a person to nominate or an individual to be nominated as a candidate for election or appointment as a director of the corporation, and any right under a bylaw adopted pursuant to § 2.06(c) or any comparable right under any provision of the articles of incorporation, contract, or applicable law.

(b) An application or proceeding pursuant to subsection (a) of this section may be filed or commenced by any of the following persons:

(1) the corporation;

(2) any record shareholder, beneficial shareholder or unrestricted voting trust beneficial owner of the corporation;

(3) a director of the corporation, an individual claiming the office of director, or a director whose membership on a committee of the board of directors is contested, in each case who is seeking a determination of his or her right to such office or membership;

(4) an officer of the corporation or an individual claiming to be an officer of the corporation, in each case who is seeking a determination of his or her right to such office; and

(5) a person claiming a right covered by subsection (a)(5) and who is seeking a determination of such right.

(c) In connection with any application or proceeding under subsection (a), the following shall be named as defendants, unless such person made the application or commenced the proceeding:

(1) the corporation;

(2) any individual whose right to office or membership on a committee of the board of directors is contested;

(3) any individual claiming the office or membership at issue; and

(4) any person claiming a right covered by subsection (a)(5) that is at issue.

(d) In connection with any application or proceeding under subsection (a), service of process may be made upon each of the persons specified in subsection (c) either by:

(1) service of process on the corporation addressed to such person in any manner provided by statute of this state or by rule of the applicable court for service on the corporation; or

(2) service of process on the person in any manner provided by statute of this state or by rule of the applicable court.

(e) When service of process is made upon a person other than the corporation by service upon the corporation pursuant to subsection (d)(1), the plaintiff and the corporation or its registered agent shall promptly provide written notice of such service, together with copies of all process and the application or complaint, to the person at the person's last known residence or business address, or as permitted by statute of this state or by rule of the applicable court.

(f) In connection with any application or proceeding under subsection (a), the court shall dispose of the application or proceeding on an expedited basis and also may:

(1) order such additional or further notice as the court deems proper under the circumstances;

(2) order that additional persons be joined as parties to the proceeding if the court determines that such joinder is necessary for a just adjudication of matters before the court;

(3) order an election or meeting be held in accordance with the provisions of § 7.03(b) or otherwise;

(4) appoint a master to conduct an election or meeting;

(5) enter temporary, preliminary or permanent injunctive relief;

(6) resolve solely for the purpose of this proceeding any legal or factual issues necessary for the resolution of any of the matters specified in subsection (a), including the right and power of persons claiming to own shares to vote at any meeting of the shareholders; and

(7) order such other relief as the court determines is equitable, just and proper.

(g) It is not necessary to make shareholders a party to a proceeding or application pursuant to this section unless the shareholder is a required defendant under subsection (c)(4), relief is sought against the shareholder individually, or the court orders joinder pursuant to subsection (f)(2).

(h) Nothing in this section limits, restricts, or abolishes the subject matter jurisdiction or powers of the court as existed before the enactment of this section, and an application or proceeding pursuant to this section is not the exclusive remedy or proceeding available with respect to the matters specified in subsection (a).

Chapter 8. Directors and Officers

Subchapter A. Board of Directors

§ 8.01. Requirement for and Functions of Board of Directors

(a) Except as may be provided in an agreement authorized under § 7.32, each corporation shall have a board of directors.

(b) Except as may be provided in an agreement authorized under § 7.32, and subject to any limitation in the articles of incorporation permitted by § 2.02(b), all corporate powers shall be exercised by or under the authority of the board of directors, and the business and affairs of the corporation shall be managed by or under the direction, and subject to the oversight, of the board of directors.

§ 8.02. Qualifications of Directors

(a) The articles of incorporation or bylaws may prescribe qualifications for directors or for nominees for directors. Qualifications must be reasonable as applied to the corporation and be lawful.

(b) A requirement that is based on a past, prospective, or current action, or expression of opinion, by a nominee or director that could limit the ability of a nominee or director to discharge his or her duties as a director is not a permissible qualification under this section. Notwithstanding the foregoing, qualifications may include not being or having been subject to specified criminal, civil, or regulatory sanctions or not having been removed as a director by judicial action or for cause.

(c) A director need not be a resident of this state or a shareholder unless the articles of incorporation or bylaws so prescribe.

(d) A qualification for nomination for director prescribed before a person's nomination shall apply to such person at the time of nomination. A qualification for nomination for director prescribed after a person's nomination shall not apply to such person with respect to such nomination.

(e) A qualification for director prescribed before a director has been elected or appointed may apply only at the time an individual becomes a director or may apply during a director's term. A qualification prescribed after a director has been elected or appointed shall not apply to that director before the end of that director's term.

§ 8.03. Number and Election of Directors

(a) A board of directors shall consist of one or more individuals, with the number specified in or fixed in accordance with the articles of incorporation or bylaws.

(b) The number of directors may be increased or decreased from time to time by amendment to, or in the manner provided in, the articles of incorporation or bylaws.

(c) Directors are elected at the first annual shareholders' meeting and at each annual shareholders' meeting thereafter unless elected by written consent in lieu of an annual meeting as permitted by § 7.04 or unless their terms are staggered under § 8.06.

§ 8.04. Election of Directors by Certain Classes or Series of Shares

If the articles of incorporation or action by the board of directors pursuant to § 6.02 authorize dividing the shares into classes or series, the articles of incorporation may also authorize the election of all or a specified number of directors by the holders of one or more authorized classes or series of shares. A class or series (or multiple classes or series) of shares entitled to elect one or more directors is a separate voting group for purposes of the election of directors.

§ 8.05. Terms of Directors Generally

(a) The terms of the initial directors of a corporation expire at the first shareholders' meeting at which directors are elected.

(b) The terms of all other directors expire at the next, or if their terms are staggered in accordance with § 8.06, at the applicable second or third, annual shareholders' meeting following their election, except to the extent (i) provided in § 10.22 if a bylaw electing to be governed by that section is in effect, or (ii) a shorter term is specified in the articles of incorporation in the event of a director nominee failing to receive a specified vote for election.

(c) A decrease in the number of directors does not shorten an incumbent director's term.

(d) The term of a director elected to fill a vacancy expires at the next shareholders' meeting at which directors are elected.

(e) Except to the extent otherwise provided in the articles of incorporation or under § 10.22 if a bylaw electing to be governed by that section is in effect, despite the expiration of a director's term, the director continues to serve until the director's successor is elected and qualifies or there is a decrease in the number of directors.

§ 8.06. Staggered Terms for Directors

The articles of incorporation may provide for staggering the terms of directors by dividing the total number of directors into two or three groups, with each group containing half or one-third of the total, as near as may be practicable. In that event, the terms of directors in the first group expire at the first annual shareholders' meeting after their election, the terms of the second group expire at the second annual shareholders' meeting after their election, and the terms of the third group, if any, expire at the third annual shareholders' meeting after their election. At each annual shareholders' meeting held thereafter, directors shall be elected for a term of two years or three years, as the case may be, to succeed those whose terms expire.

§ 8.07. Resignation of Directors

(a) A director may resign at any time by delivering a written notice of resignation to the board of directors or its chair, or to the secretary.

(b) A resignation is effective as provided in § 1.41(i) unless the resignation provides for a delayed effectiveness, including effectiveness determined upon a future event or events. A resignation that is conditioned upon failing to receive a specified vote for election as a director may provide that it is irrevocable.

§ 8.08. Removal of Directors by Shareholders

(a) The shareholders may remove one or more directors with or without cause unless the articles of incorporation provide that directors may be removed only for cause.

(b) If a director is elected by a voting group of shareholders, only the shareholders of that voting group may participate in the vote to remove that director.

(c) A director may be removed if the number of votes cast to remove exceeds the number of votes cast not to remove the director, except to the extent the articles of incorporation or bylaws require a greater number; provided that if cumulative voting is authorized, a director may not be removed if, in the case of a meeting, the number of votes sufficient to elect the director under cumulative voting

is voted against removal and, if action is taken by less than unanimous written consent, voting shareholders entitled to the number of votes sufficient to elect the director under cumulative voting do not consent to the removal.

(d) A director may be removed by the shareholders only at a meeting called for the purpose of removing the director and the meeting notice must state that removal of the director is a purpose of the meeting.

§ 8.09. Removal of Directors by Judicial Proceeding

(a) The [name or describe court] may remove a director from office or may order other relief, including barring the director from reelection for a period prescribed by the court, in a proceeding commenced by or in the right of the corporation if the court finds that (i) the director engaged in fraudulent conduct with respect to the corporation or its shareholders, grossly abused the position of director, or intentionally inflicted harm on the corporation; and (ii) considering the director's course of conduct and the inadequacy of other available remedies, removal or such other relief would be in the best interest of the corporation.

(b) A shareholder proceeding on behalf of the corporation under subsection (a) shall comply with all of the requirements of subchapter 7D, except clause (i) of § 7.41.

§ 8.10. Vacancy on Board of Directors

(a) Unless the articles of incorporation provide otherwise, if a vacancy occurs on a board of directors, including a vacancy resulting from an increase in the number of directors:

> **(1)** the shareholders may fill the vacancy;

> **(2)** the board of directors may fill the vacancy; or

> **(3)** if the directors remaining in office are less than a quorum, they may fill the vacancy by the affirmative vote of a majority of all the directors remaining in office.

(b) If the vacant office was held by a director elected by a voting group of shareholders, only the holders of shares of that voting group are entitled to vote to fill the vacancy if it is filled by the share-holders, and only the remaining directors elected by that voting group, even if less than a quorum, are entitled to fill the vacancy if it is filled by the directors.

(c) A vacancy that will occur at a specific later date (by reason of a resignation effective at a later date under § 8.07(b) or otherwise) may be filled before the vacancy occurs but the new director may not take office until the vacancy occurs.

§ 8.11. Compensation of Directors

Unless the articles of incorporation or bylaws provide otherwise, the board of directors may fix the compensation of directors.

Subchapter B. Meetings and Action of the Board

§ 8.20. Meetings

(a) The board of directors may hold regular or special meetings in or out of this state.

(b) Unless restricted by the articles of incorporation or bylaws, any or all directors may participate in any meeting of the board of directors through the use of any means of communication by which all directors participating may simultaneously hear each other during the meeting. A director participating in a meeting by this means is deemed to be present in person at the meeting.

§ 8.21. Action Without Meeting

(a) Except to the extent that the articles of incorporation or bylaws require that action by the board of directors be taken at a meeting, action required or permitted by this Act to be taken by the board of directors may be taken without a meeting if each director signs a consent describing the action to be taken and delivers it to the corporation.

(b) Action taken under this section is the act of the board of directors when one or more consents signed by all the directors are delivered to the corporation. The consent may specify a later time as the time at which the action taken is to be effective.

A director's consent may be withdrawn by a revocation signed by the director and delivered to the corporation before delivery to the corporation of unrevoked written consents signed by all the directors.

(c) A consent signed under this section has the effect of action taken at a meeting of the board of directors and may be described as such in any document.

§ 8.22. Notice of Meeting

(a) Unless the articles of incorporation or bylaws provide otherwise, regular meetings of the board of directors may be held without notice of the date, time, place, or purpose of the meeting.

(b) Unless the articles of incorporation or bylaws provide for a longer or shorter period, special meetings of the board of directors shall be preceded by at least two days' notice of the date, time, and place of the meeting. The notice need not describe the purpose of the special meeting unless required by the articles of incorporation or bylaws.

§ 8.23. Waiver of Notice

(a) A director may waive any notice required by this Act, the articles of incorporation or the bylaws before or after the date and time stated in the notice. Except as provided by subsection (b), the waiver must be in writing, signed by the director entitled to the notice and delivered to the corporation for filing by the corporation with the minutes or corporate records.

(b) A director's attendance at or participation in a meeting waives any required notice to the director of the meeting unless the director at the beginning of the meeting (or promptly upon arrival) objects to holding the meeting or transacting business at the meeting and does not after objecting vote for or assent to action taken at the meeting.

§ 8.24. Quorum and Voting

(a) Unless the articles of incorporation or bylaws provide for a greater or lesser number or unless otherwise expressly provided in this Act, a quorum of a board of directors consists of a majority of the number of directors specified in or fixed in accordance with the articles of incorporation or bylaws.

(b) The quorum of the board of directors specified in or fixed in accordance with the articles of incorporation or bylaws may not consist of less than one-third of the specified or fixed number of directors.

(c) If a quorum is present when a vote is taken, the affirmative vote of a majority of directors present is the act of the board of directors unless the articles of incorporation or bylaws require the vote of a greater number of directors or unless otherwise expressly provided in this Act.

(d) A director who is present at a meeting of the board of directors or a committee when corporate action is taken is deemed to have assented to the action taken unless: (i) the director objects at the beginning of the meeting (or promptly upon arrival) to holding it or transacting business at the meeting; (ii) the dissent or abstention from the action taken is entered in the minutes of the meeting; or (iii) the director delivers written notice of the director's dissent or abstention to the presiding officer of the meeting before its adjournment or to the corporation immediately after adjournment of the meeting. The right of dissent or abstention is not available to a director who votes in favor of the action taken.

§ 8.25. Committees of the Board

(a) Unless this Act, the articles of incorporation or the bylaws provide otherwise, a board of directors may establish one or more board committees composed exclusively of one or more directors to perform functions of the board of directors.

(b) The establishment of a board committee and appointment of members to it shall be approved by the greater of (i) a majority of all the directors in office when the action is taken or (ii) the number of directors required by the articles of incorporation or bylaws to take action under § 8.24, unless, in either case, this Act or the articles of incorporation provide otherwise.

(c) Sections 8.20 through 8.24 apply to board committees and their members.

(d) A board committee may exercise the powers of the board of directors under § 8.01, to the extent specified by the board of directors or in the articles of incorporation or bylaws, except that a board committee may not:

(1) authorize or approve distributions, except according to a formula or method, or within limits, prescribed by the board of directors;

(2) approve or propose to shareholders action that this Act requires be approved by shareholders;

(3) fill vacancies on the board of directors or, subject to subsection (e), on any board committees; or

(4) adopt, amend, or repeal bylaws.

(e) The board of directors may appoint one or more directors as alternate members of any board committee to replace any absent or disqualified member during the member's absence or disqualification. If the articles of incorporation, the bylaws, or the resolution creating the board committee so provide, the member or members present at any board committee meeting and not disqualified from voting may, by unanimous action, appoint another director to act in place of an absent or disqualified member during that member's absence or disqualification.

§ 8.26. Submission of Matters for Shareholder Vote

A corporation may agree to submit a matter to a vote of its shareholders even if, after approving the matter, the board of directors determines it no longer recommends the matter.

Subchapter C. Directors

§ 8.30. Standards of Conduct for Directors

(a) Each member of the board of directors, when discharging the duties of a director, shall act: (i) in good faith, and (ii) in a manner the director reasonably believes to be in the best interests of the corporation.

(b) The members of the board of directors or a board committee, when becoming informed in connection with their decision-making function or devoting attention to their oversight function, shall discharge their duties with the care that a person in a like position would reasonably believe appropriate under similar circumstances.

(c) In discharging board or board committee duties, a director shall disclose, or cause to be disclosed, to the other board or committee members information not already known by them but known by the director to be material to the discharge of their decision-making or oversight functions, except that disclosure is not required to the extent that the director reasonably believes that doing so would violate a duty imposed under law, a legally enforceable obligation of confidentiality, or a professional ethics rule.

(d) In discharging board or board committee duties, a director who does not have knowledge that makes reliance unwarranted is entitled to rely on the performance by any of the persons specified in subsection (f)(1) or subsection (f)(3) to whom the board may have delegated, formally or informally by course of conduct, the authority or duty to perform one or more of the board's functions that are delegable under applicable law.

(e) In discharging board or board committee duties, a director who does not have knowledge that makes reliance unwarranted is entitled to rely on information, opinions, reports, or statements, including financial statements and other financial data, prepared or presented by any of the persons specified in subsection (f).

(f) A director is entitled to rely, in accordance with subsection (d) or (e), on:

(1) one or more officers or employees of the corporation whom the director reasonably believes to be reliable and competent in the functions performed or the information, opinions, reports or statements provided;

(2) legal counsel, public accountants, or other persons retained by the corporation as to matters involving skills or expertise the director reasonably believes are matters (i) within the

particular person's professional or expert competence, or (ii) as to which the particular person merits confidence; or

(3) a board committee of which the director is not a member if the director reasonably believes the committee merits confidence.

§ 8.31. Standards of Liability for Directors

(a) A director shall not be liable to the corporation or its shareholders for any decision to take or not to take action, or any failure to take any action, as a director, unless the party asserting liability in a proceeding establishes that:

(1) no defense interposed by the director based on (i) any provision in the articles of incorporation authorized by § 2.02(b)(4) or by § 2.02(b)(6), (ii) the protection afforded by § 8.61 (for action taken in compliance with § 8.62 or § 8.63), or (iii) the protection afforded by § 8.70, precludes liability; and

(2) the challenged conduct consisted or was the result of:

(i) action not in good faith; or

(ii) a decision

(A) which the director did not reasonably believe to be in the best interests of the corporation, or

(B) as to which the director was not informed to an extent the director reasonably believed appropriate in the circumstances; or

(iii) a lack of objectivity due to the director's familial, financial or business relationship with, or a lack of independence due to the director's domination or control by, another person having a material interest in the challenged conduct,

(A) which relationship or which domination or control could reasonably be

expected to have affected the director's judgment respecting the challenged conduct in a manner adverse to the corporation, and

(B) after a reasonable expectation to such effect has been established, the director shall not have established that the challenged conduct was reasonably believed by the director to be in the best interests of the corporation; or

(iv) a sustained failure of the director to devote attention to ongoing oversight of the business and affairs of the corporation, or a failure to devote timely attention, by making (or causing to be made) appropriate inquiry, when particular facts and circumstances of significant concern materialize that would alert a reasonably attentive director to the need for such inquiry; or

(v) receipt of a financial benefit to which the director was not entitled or any other breach of the director's duties to deal fairly with the corporation and its shareholders that is actionable under applicable law.

(b) The party seeking to hold the director liable:

(1) for money damages, shall also have the burden of establishing that:

(i) harm to the corporation or its shareholders has been suffered, and

(ii) the harm suffered was proximately caused by the director's challenged conduct; or

(2) for other money payment under a legal remedy, such as compensation for the unauthorized use of corporate assets, shall also have whatever persuasion burden may be called for to establish that the payment sought is appropriate in the circumstances; or

(3) for other money payment under an equitable remedy, such as profit recovery by or disgorgement to the corporation, shall also have whatever persuasion burden may be called for to establish that the equitable remedy sought is appropriate in the circumstances.

(c) Nothing contained in this section shall (i) in any instance where fairness is at issue, such as consideration of the fairness of a transaction to the corporation under § 8.61(b)(3), alter the burden of proving the fact or lack of fairness otherwise applicable, (ii) alter the fact or lack of liability of a director under another section of this Act, such as the provisions governing the consequences of an unlawful distribution under § 8.32 or a transactional interest under § 8.61, or (iii) affect any rights to which the corporation or a shareholder may be entitled under another statute of this state or the United States.

§ 8.32. Directors' Liability for Unlawful Distributions

(a) A director who votes for or assents to a distribution in excess of what may be authorized and made pursuant to § 6.40(a) or 14.09(a) is personally liable to the corporation for the amount of the distribution that exceeds what could have been distributed without violating § 6.40(a) or 14.09(a) if the party asserting liability establishes that when taking the action the director did not comply with § 8.30.

(b) A director held liable under subsection (a) for an unlawful distribution is entitled to:

(1) contribution from every other director who could be held liable under subsection (a) for the unlawful distribution; and

(2) recoupment from each shareholder of the pro-rata portion of the amount of the unlawful distribution the shareholder accepted, knowing the distribution was made in violation of § 6.40(a) or 14.09(a).

(c) A proceeding to enforce:

(1) the liability of a director under subsection (a) is barred unless it is commenced within two years after the date (i) on which the effect of the distribution was measured under § 6.40(e) or (g), (ii) as of which the violation of § 6.40(a) occurred as the consequence of disregard of a restriction in the articles of incorporation, or (iii) on which the distribution of assets to shareholders under § 14.09(a) was made; or

(2) contribution or recoupment under subsection (b) is barred unless it is commenced within one year after the liability of the claimant has been finally adjudicated under subsection (a).

Subchapter D. Officers

§ 8.40. Officers

(a) A corporation has the officers described in its bylaws or appointed by the board of directors in accordance with the bylaws.

(b) The board of directors may elect individuals to fill one or more offices of the corporation. An officer may appoint one or more officers if authorized by the bylaws or the board of directors.

(c) The bylaws or the board of directors shall assign to an officer responsibility for maintaining and authenticating the records of the corporation required to be kept under § 16.01(a).

(d) The same individual may simultaneously hold more than one office in a corporation.

§ 8.41. Functions of Officers

Each officer has the authority and shall perform the functions set forth in the bylaws or, to the extent consistent with the bylaws, the functions prescribed by the board of directors or by direction of an officer authorized by the board of directors to prescribe the functions of other officers.

§ 8.42. Standards of Conduct for Officers

(a) An officer, when performing in such capacity, has the duty to act:

(1) in good faith;

(2) with the care that a person in a like position would reasonably exercise under similar circumstances; and

(3) in a manner the officer reasonably believes to be in the best interests of the corporation.

(b) The duty of an officer includes the obligation:

(1) to inform the superior officer to whom, or the board of directors or the board committee to which, the officer reports of information about the affairs of the corporation known to the officer, within the scope of the officer's functions, and known to the officer to be material to such superior officer, board or committee; and

(2) to inform his or her superior officer, or another appropriate person within the corporation, or the board of directors, or a board committee, of any actual or probable material violation of law involving the corporation or material breach of duty to the corporation by an officer, employee, or agent of the corporation, that the officer believes has occurred or is likely to occur.

(c) In discharging his or her duties, an officer who does not have knowledge that makes reliance unwarranted is entitled to rely on:

(1) the performance of properly delegated responsibilities by one or more employees of the corporation whom the officer reasonably believes to be reliable and competent in performing the responsibilities delegated; or

(2) information, opinions, reports or statements, including financial statements and other financial data, prepared or presented by one or more employees of the corporation whom the officer reasonably believes to be reliable and competent in the matters presented or by legal counsel, public accountants, or other persons retained by the corporation as to matters involving skills or expertise the officer reasonably believes are matters (i) within the particular person's professional or expert competence or (ii) as to which the particular person merits confidence.

(d) An officer shall not be liable to the corporation or its shareholders for any decision to take or not to take action, or any failure to take any action, as an officer, if the duties of the office are performed in compliance with this section. Whether an officer who does not comply with this section shall have liability will depend in such instance on applicable law, including those principles of § 8.31 that have relevance.

§ 8.43. Resignation and Removal of Officers

(a) An officer may resign at any time by delivering a written notice to the board of directors, or its chair, or to the appointing officer or the secretary. A resignation is effective as provided in § 1.41(i) unless the notice provides for a delayed effectiveness, including effectiveness determined upon a future event or events. If effectiveness of a resignation is stated to be delayed and the board of directors or the appointing officer accepts the delay, the board of directors or the appointing officer may fill the pending vacancy before the delayed effectiveness but the new officer may not take office until the vacancy occurs.

(b) An officer may be removed at any time with or without cause by (i) the board of directors; (ii) the appointing officer, unless the bylaws or the board of directors provide otherwise; or (iii) any other officer if authorized by the bylaws or the board of directors.

(c) In this section, "appointing officer" means the officer (including any successor to that officer) who appointed the officer resigning or being removed.

§ 8.44. Contract Rights of Officers

(a) The election or appointment of an officer does not itself create contract rights.

(b) An officer's removal does not affect the officer's contract rights, if any, with the corporation. An officer's resignation does not affect the corporation's contract rights, if any, with the officer.

Subchapter E. Indemnification and Advance for Expenses

§ 8.50. Subchapter Definitions

In this subchapter:

"Corporation" includes any domestic or foreign predecessor entity of a corporation in a merger.

"Director" or "officer" means an individual who is or was a director or officer, respectively, of a corporation or who, while a director or officer of the corporation, is or was serving at the corporation's request as a director, officer, manager, partner, trustee, employee, or agent of another entity or employee benefit plan. A director or officer is considered to be serving an employee benefit plan at the corporation's request if the individual's duties to the corporation also impose duties on, or otherwise involve services by, the individual to the plan or to participants in or beneficiaries of the plan. "Director" or "officer" includes, unless the context requires otherwise, the estate or personal representative of a director or officer.

"Liability" means the obligation to pay a judgment, settlement, penalty, fine (including an excise tax assessed with respect to an employee benefit plan), or expenses incurred with respect to a proceeding.

"Official capacity" means: (i) when used with respect to a director, the office of director in a corporation; and (ii) when used with respect to an officer, as contemplated in § 8.56, the office in a corporation held by the officer. "Official capacity" does not include service for any other domestic or foreign corporation or any joint venture, trust, employee benefit plan, or other entity.

"Party" means an individual who was, is, or is threatened to be made, a defendant or respondent in a proceeding.

"Proceeding" means any threatened, pending, or completed action, suit, or proceeding, whether civil, criminal, administrative, arbitrative, or investigative and whether formal or informal.

§ 8.51. Permissible Indemnification

(a) Except as otherwise provided in this section, a corporation may indemnify an individual who is a party to a proceeding because the individual is a director against liability incurred in the proceeding if:

> **(1)(i)** the director conducted himself or herself in good faith; and
>
> > **(ii)** the director reasonably believed:
> >
> > > **(A)** in the case of conduct in an official capacity, that his or her conduct was in the best interests of the corporation; and
> > >
> > > **(B)** in all other cases, that his or her conduct was at least not opposed to the best interests of the corporation; and

(iii) in the case of any criminal proceeding, the director had no reasonable cause to believe his or her conduct was unlawful; or

(2) the director engaged in conduct for which broader indemnification has been made permissible or obligatory under a provision of the articles of incorporation (as authorized by § 2.02(b)(5)).

(b) A director's conduct with respect to an employee benefit plan for a purpose the director reasonably believed to be in the interests of the participants in, and the beneficiaries of, the plan is conduct that satisfies the requirement of subsection (a)(1)(ii)(B).

(c) The termination of a proceeding by judgment, order, settlement, or conviction, or upon a plea of nolo contendere or its equivalent, is not, of itself, determinative that the director did not meet the relevant standard of conduct described in this section.

(d) Unless ordered by a court under § 8.54(a)(3), a corporation may not indemnify a director:

(1) in connection with a proceeding by or in the right of the corporation, except for expenses incurred in connection with the proceeding if it is determined that the director has met the relevant standard of conduct under subsection **(a)**; or

(2) in connection with any proceeding with respect to conduct for which the director was adjudged liable on the basis of receiving a financial benefit to which he or she was not entitled, regardless of whether it involved action in the director's official capacity.

§ 8.52. Mandatory Indemnification

A corporation shall indemnify a director who was wholly successful, on the merits or otherwise, in the defense of any proceeding to which the director was a party because he or she was a director of the corporation against expenses incurred by the director in connection with the proceeding.

§ 8.53. Advance for Expenses

(a) A corporation may, before final disposition of a proceeding, advance funds to pay for or reimburse expenses incurred in connection with the proceeding by an individual who is a party to the proceeding because that individual is a director if the director delivers to the corporation a signed written undertaking of the director to repay any funds advanced if (i) the director is not entitled to mandatory indemnification under § 8.52 and (ii) it is ultimately determined under § 8.54 or § 8.55 that the director is not entitled to indemnification.

(b) The undertaking required by subsection (a) must be an unlimited general obligation of the director but need not be secured and may be accepted without reference to the financial ability of the director to make repayment.

(c) Authorizations under this section shall be made:

(1) by the board of directors:

(i) if there are two or more qualified directors, by a majority vote of all the qualified directors (a majority of whom shall for such purpose constitute a quorum) or by a majority of the members of a committee consisting solely of two or more qualified directors appointed by such a vote; or

(ii) if there are fewer than two qualified directors, by the vote necessary for action by the board of directors in accordance with § 8.24(c), in which authorization directors who are not qualified directors may participate; or

(2) by the shareholders, but shares owned by or voted under the control of a director who at the time is not a qualified director may not be voted on the authorization.

§ 8.54. Court-Ordered Indemnification and Advance for Expenses

(a) A director who is a party to a proceeding because he or she is a director may apply for indemnification or an advance for expenses to the court conducting the proceeding or to another court of competent jurisdiction. After receipt of an application and after giving any notice it considers necessary, the court shall:

(1) order indemnification if the court determines that the director is entitled to mandatory indemnification under § 8.52;

(2) order indemnification or advance for expenses if the court determines that the director is entitled to indemnification or advance for expenses pursuant to a provision authorized by § 8.58(a); or

(3) order indemnification or advance for expenses if the court determines, in view of all the relevant circumstances, that it is fair and reasonable (i) to indemnify the director, or (ii) to advance expenses to the director, even if, in the case of (i) or (ii), he or she has not met the relevant standard of conduct set forth in § 8.51(a), failed to comply with § 8.53 or was adjudged liable in a proceeding referred to in § 8.51(d)(1) or (d)(2), but if the director was adjudged so liable indemnification shall be limited to expenses incurred in connection with the proceeding.

(b) If the court determines that the director is entitled to indemnification under subsection (a)(1) or to indemnification or advance for expenses under subsection (a)(2), it shall also order the corporation to pay the director's expenses incurred in connection with obtaining courtordered indemnification or advance for expenses. If the court determines that the director is entitled to indemnification or advance for expenses under subsection (a)(3), it may also order the corporation to pay the director's expenses to obtain court-ordered indemnification or advance for expenses.

§ 8.55. Determination and Authorization of Indemnification

(a) A corporation may not indemnify a director under § 8.51 unless authorized for a specific proceeding after a determination has been made that indemnification is permissible because the director has met the relevant standard of conduct set forth in § 8.51.

(b) The determination shall be made:

(1) if there are two or more qualified directors, by the board of directors by a majority vote of all the qualified directors (a majority of whom shall for such purpose constitute a quorum), or by a majority of the members of a committee of two or more qualified directors appointed by such a vote;

(2) by special legal counsel:

(i) selected in the manner prescribed in subsection (b)(1); or

(ii) if there are fewer than two qualified directors, selected by the board of directors (in which selection directors who are not qualified directors may participate); or

(3) by the shareholders, but shares owned by or voted under the control of a director who at the time is not a qualified director may not be voted on the determination.

(c) Authorization of indemnification shall be made in the same manner as the determination that indemnification is permissible except that if there are fewer than two qualified directors, or if the determination is made by special legal counsel, authorization of indemnification shall be made by those entitled to select special legal counsel under subsection (b)(2)(ii).

§ 8.56. Indemnification of Officers

(a) A corporation may indemnify and advance expenses under this subchapter to an officer who is a party to a proceeding because he or she is an officer

(1) to the same extent as a director; and

(2) if he or she is an officer but not a director, to such further extent as may be provided by the articles of incorporation or the bylaws, or by a resolution adopted or a contract approved by the board of directors or shareholders, except for

(i) liability in connection with a proceeding by or in the right of the corporation other than for expenses incurred in connection with the proceeding, or

(ii) liability arising out of conduct that constitutes

(A) receipt by the officer of a financial benefit to which he or she is not entitled,

(B) an intentional infliction of harm on the corporation or the shareholders, or

(C) an intentional violation of criminal law.

(b) Subsection (a)(2) shall apply to an officer who is also a director if he or she is made a party to the proceeding based on an act or omission solely as an officer.

(c) An officer who is not a director is entitled to mandatory indemnification under § 8.52, and may apply to a court under § 8.54 for indemnification or an advance for expenses, in each case to the same extent to which a director may be entitled to indemnification or advance for expenses under those sections.

§ 8.57. Insurance

A corporation may purchase and maintain insurance on behalf of an individual who is a director or officer of the corporation, or who, while a director or officer of the corporation, serves at the corporation's request as a director, officer, partner, trustee, employee, or agent of another domestic or foreign corporation or a joint venture, trust, employee benefit plan, or other entity, against liability asserted against or incurred by the individual in that capacity or arising from the individual's status as a director or officer, regardless of whether the corporation would have power to indemnify or advance expenses to the individual against the same liability under this subchapter.

§ 8.58. Variation by Corporate Action; Application of Subchapter

(a) A corporation may, by a provision in its articles of incorporation or bylaws or in a resolution adopted or a contract approved by the board of directors or shareholders, obligate itself in advance of the act or omission giving rise to a proceeding to provide indemnification in accordance with § 8.51 or advance funds to pay for or reimburse expenses in accordance with § 8.53. Any such obligatory provision shall be deemed to satisfy the requirements for authorization referred to in § 8.53(c) and in § 8.55(c). Any such provision that obligates the corporation to provide indemnification to the fullest extent permitted by law shall be deemed to obligate the corporation to advance funds to pay for or reimburse expenses in accordance with § 8.53 to the fullest extent permitted by law, unless the provision expressly provides otherwise.

(b) A right of indemnification or to advances for expenses created by this subchapter or under subsection (a) and in effect at the time of an act or omission shall not be eliminated or impaired with respect to such act or omission by an amendment of the articles of incorporation or bylaws or a resolution of the board of directors or shareholders, adopted after the occurrence of such act or omission, unless, in the case of a right created under subsection (a), the provision creating such right and in effect at the time of such act or omission explicitly authorizes such elimination or impairment after such act or omission has occurred.

(c) Any provision pursuant to subsection (a) shall not obligate the corporation to indemnify or advance expenses to a director of a predecessor of the corporation, pertaining to conduct with respect to the predecessor, unless otherwise expressly provided. Any provision for indemnification or advance for expenses in the articles of incorporation or bylaws, or a resolution of the board of directors or shareholders of a predecessor of the corporation in a merger or in a contract to which the predecessor is a party, existing at the time the merger takes effect, shall be governed by § 11.07(a)(4).

(d) Subject to subsection (b), a corporation may, by a provision in its articles of incorporation, limit any of the rights to indemnification or advance for expenses created by or pursuant to this subchapter.

(e) This subchapter does not limit a corporation's power to pay or reimburse expenses incurred by a director or an officer in connection with appearing as a witness in a proceeding at a time when he or she is not a party.

(f) This subchapter does not limit a corporation's power to indemnify, advance expenses to or provide or maintain insurance on behalf of an employee or agent.

§ 8.59. Exclusivity of Subchapter

A corporation may provide indemnification or advance expenses to a director or an officer only as permitted by this subchapter.

Subchapter F. Director's Conflicting Interest Transactions

§ 8.60. Subchapter Definitions

In this subchapter:

"Control" (including the term "controlled by") means (i) having the power, directly or indirectly, to elect or remove a majority of the members of the board of directors or other governing body of an entity, whether through the ownership of voting shares or interests, by contract, or otherwise, or (ii) being subject to a majority of the risk of loss from the entity's activities or entitled to receive a majority of the entity's residual returns.

"Director's conflicting interest transaction" means a transaction effected or proposed to be effected by the corporation (or by an entity controlled by the corporation)

    (i) to which, at the relevant time, the director is a party;

    (ii) respecting which, at the relevant time, the director had knowledge and a material financial interest known to the director; or

    (iii) respecting which, at the relevant time, the director knew that a related person was a party or had a material financial interest.

"Fair to the corporation" means, for purposes of § 8.61(b)(3), that the transaction as a whole was beneficial to the corporation, taking into appropriate account whether it was (i) fair in terms of the director's dealings with the corporation, and (ii) comparable to what might have been obtainable in an arm's length transaction, given the consideration paid or received by the corporation.

"Material financial interest" means a financial interest in a transaction that would reasonably be expected to impair the objectivity of the director's judgment when participating in action on the authorization of the transaction.

"Related person" means:

    (i) the individual's spouse;

    (ii) a child, stepchild, grandchild, parent, step parent, grandparent, sibling, step sibling, half sibling, aunt, uncle, niece or nephew (or spouse of any such person) of the individual or of the individual's spouse;

    (iii) a natural person living in the same home as the individual;

    (iv) an entity (other than the corporation or an entity controlled by the corporation) controlled by the individual or any person specified above in this definition;

    (v) a domestic or foreign (A) business or non-profit corporation (other than the corporation or an entity controlled by the corporation) of which the individual is a director, (B) unincorporated entity of which the individual is a general partner or a member of the governing body, or (C) individual, trust or estate for whom or of which the individual is a trustee, guardian, personal representative or like fiduciary; or

    (vi) a person that is, or an entity that is controlled by, an employer of the individual.

"Relevant time" means (i) the time at which directors' action respecting the transaction is taken in compliance with § 8.62, or (ii) if the transaction is not brought before the board of directors (or a committee) for action under § 8.62, at the time the corporation (or an entity controlled by the corporation) becomes legally obligated to consummate the transaction.

"Required disclosure" means disclosure of (i) the existence and nature of the director's conflicting interest, and (ii) all facts known to the director respecting the subject matter of the transaction that a director free of such conflicting interest would reasonably believe to be material in deciding whether to proceed with the transaction.

§ 8.61. Judicial Action

(a) A transaction effected or proposed to be effected by the corporation (or by an entity controlled by the corporation) may not be the subject of equitable relief, or give rise to an award of damages or other sanctions against a director of the corporation, in a proceeding by a shareholder or by or in the right of the corporation, on the ground that the director has an interest respecting the transaction, if it is not a director's conflicting interest transaction.

(b) A director's conflicting interest transaction may not be the subject of equitable relief, or give rise to an award of damages or other sanctions against a director of the corporation, in a proceeding by a shareholder or by or in the right of the corporation, on the ground that the director has an interest respecting the transaction, if:

(1) directors' action respecting the transaction was taken in compliance with § 8.62 at any time; or

(2) shareholders' action respecting the transaction was taken in compliance with § 8.63 at any time; or

(3) the transaction, judged according to the circumstances at the relevant time, is established to have been fair to the corporation.

§ 8.62. Directors' Action

(a) Directors' action respecting a director's conflicting interest transaction is effective for purposes of § 8.61(b)(1) if the transaction has been authorized by the affirmative vote of a majority (but no fewer than two) of the qualified directors who voted on the transaction, after required disclosure by the conflicted director of information not already known by such qualified directors, or after modified disclosure in compliance with subsection (b), provided that:

(1) the qualified directors have deliberated and voted outside the presence of and without the participation by any other director; and

(2) where the action has been taken by a board committee, all members of the committee were qualified directors, and either (i) the committee

was composed of all the qualified directors on the board of directors or (ii) the members of the committee were appointed by the affirmative vote of a majority of the qualified directors on the board of directors.

(b) Notwithstanding subsection (a), when a transaction is a director's conflicting interest transaction only because a related person described in clause (v) or (vi) of the definition of "related person" in § 8.60 is a party to or has a material financial interest in the transaction, the conflicted director is not obligated to make required disclosure to the extent that the director reasonably believes that doing so would violate a duty imposed under law, a legally enforceable obligation of confidentiality, or a professional ethics rule, provided that the conflicted director discloses to the qualified directors voting on the transaction:

(1) all information required to be disclosed that is not so violative,

(2) the existence and nature of the director's conflicting interest, and

(3) the nature of the conflicted director's duty not to disclose the confidential information.

(c) A majority (but no fewer than two) of all the qualified directors on the board of directors, or on the board committee, constitutes a quorum for purposes of action that complies with this section.

(d) Where directors' action under this section does not satisfy a quorum or voting requirement applicable to the authorization of the transaction by reason of the articles of incorporation or bylaws or a provision of law, independent action to satisfy those authorization requirements shall be taken by the board of directors or a board committee, in which action directors who are not qualified directors may participate.

§ 8.63. Shareholders' Action

(a) Shareholders' action respecting a director's conflicting interest transaction is effective for purposes of § 8.61(b)(2) if a majority of the votes cast by the holders of all qualified shares are in favor of the transaction after (i) notice to shareholders describing the action to be taken respecting the transaction, (ii) provision to the corporation of the information referred to in subsection (b), and (iii) communication to the shareholders entitled to vote on the transaction of the information that is the subject of required disclosure, to the extent the information is not known by them. In the case of shareholders' action at a meeting, the shareholders entitled to vote shall be determined as of the record date for notice of the meeting.

(b) A director who has a conflicting interest respecting the transaction shall, before the shareholders' vote, inform the secretary or other officer or agent of the corporation authorized to tabulate votes, in writing, of the number of shares that the director knows are not qualified shares under subsection (c), and the identity of the holders of those shares.

(c) For purposes of this section: (i) "holder" means and "held by" refers to shares held by a record shareholder, a beneficial shareholder, and an unrestricted voting trust beneficial owner; and (ii) "qualified shares" means all shares entitled to be voted with respect to the transaction except for shares that the secretary or other officer or agent of the corporation authorized to tabulate votes either knows, or under subsection (b) is notified, are held by (A) a director who has a conflicting interest respecting the transaction or (B) a related person of the director (excluding a person described in clause (vi) of the definition of "related person" in § 8.60).

(d) A majority of the votes entitled to be cast by the holders of all qualified shares constitutes a quorum for purposes of compliance with this section. Subject to the provisions of subsection (e), shareholders' action that otherwise complies with this section is not affected by the presence of holders, or by the voting, of shares that are not qualified shares.

(e) If a shareholders' vote does not comply with subsection (a) solely because of a director's failure to comply with subsection (b), and if the director establishes that the failure was not intended to influence and did not in fact determine the outcome

of the vote, the court may take such action respecting the transaction and the director, and may give such effect, if any, to the shareholders' vote, as the court considers appropriate in the circumstances.

(f) Where shareholders' action under this section does not satisfy a quorum or voting requirement applicable to the authorization of the transaction by reason of the articles of incorporation or the by-laws or a provision of law, independent action to satisfy those authorization requirements shall be taken by the shareholders, in which action shares that are not qualified shares may participate.

Subchapter G. Business Opportunities

§ 8.70. Business Opportunities

(a) If a director or officer pursues or takes advantage of a business opportunity directly, or indirectly through or on behalf of another person, that action may not be the subject of equitable relief, or give rise to an award of damages or other sanctions against the director, officer or other person, in a proceeding by or in the right of the corporation on the ground that the opportunity should have first been offered to the corporation, if

(1) before the director, officer or other person becomes legally obligated respecting the opportunity the director or officer brings it to the attention of the corporation and either:

(i) action by qualified directors disclaiming the corporation's interest in the opportunity is taken in compliance with the same procedures as are set forth in § 8.62, or

(ii) shareholders' action disclaiming the corporation's interest in the opportunity is taken in compliance with the procedures set forth in § 8.63, in either case as if the decision being made concerned a director's conflicting interest transaction, except that, rather than making "required disclosure" as defined in § 8.60, the director or officer shall have made prior disclosure to those acting on behalf of the corporation of all material facts concerning the business opportunity known to the director or officer; or

(2) the duty to offer the corporation the business opportunity has been limited or eliminated pursuant to a provision of the articles of incorporation adopted (and where required, made effective by action of qualified directors) in accordance with § 2.02(b)(6).

(b) In any proceeding seeking equitable relief or other remedies based upon an alleged improper pursuit or taking advantage of a business opportunity by a director or officer, directly, or indirectly through or on behalf of another person, the fact that the director or officer did not employ the procedure described in subsection (a)(1)(i) or (ii) before pursuing or taking advantage of the opportunity shall not create an implication that the opportunity should have been first presented to the corporation or alter the burden of proof otherwise applicable to establish that the director or officer breached a duty to the corporation in the circumstances.

Chapter 9. Domestication and Conversion

Note on Adoption: Some states may wish to generalize the provisions of this chapter so that they are not limited to transactions involving a domestic business corporation. For example, a state may wish to permit a domestic limited partnership to become a domestic limited liability company. The Model Entity Transactions Act prepared by the Uniform Law Commission is such a generalized statute. Some states have elected to include transactions that are described in chapter 9 as domestications in their definition of conversions and not to refer to domestication separately.

Subchapter A. Preliminary Provisions

§ 9.01. Definitions

As used in this chapter:

"Conversion" means a transaction pursuant to subchapter C.

"Converted entity" means the converting entity as it continues in existence after a conversion.

"Converting entity" means the domestic corporation or eligible entity that approves a plan of conversion pursuant to § 9.32 or the foreign eligible entity that approves a conversion pursuant to the organic law of the eligible entity.

"Domesticated corporation" means the domesticating corporation as it continues in existence after a domestication.

"Domesticating corporation" means the domestic corporation that approves a plan of domestication pursuant to § 9.21 or the foreign corporation that approves a domestication pursuant to the organic law of the foreign corporation.

"Domestication" means a transaction pursuant to subchapter B.

"Protected agreement" means:

(i) a document evidencing indebtedness of a domestic corporation or eligible entity and any related agreement in effect immediately before the enactment date;

(ii) an agreement that is binding on a domestic corporation or eligible entity immediately before the enactment date;

(iii) the articles of incorporation or bylaws of a domestic corporation or the organic rules of a domestic eligible entity, in each case in effect immediately before the enactment date; or

(iv) an agreement that is binding on any of the shareholders, members, interest holders, directors or other governors of a domestic corporation or eligible entity, in their capacities as such, immediately before the enactment date.

For purposes of this definition and sections 9.20 and 9.30, "enactment date" means the first date on which the law of this state authorized a transaction having the effect of a domestication or a conversion, as applicable.

Note on adoption: When adopting the definition of "protected agreement," a state could consider setting out in the last sentence of the definition the actual dates when domestication and conversion statutes were first enacted in the state so those dates would be apparent on the face of the statute.

§ 9.02. Excluded Transactions [Optional]

This chapter may not be used to effect a transaction that:

(a) [converts a company organized on the mutual principle to one organized on the basis of share ownership]; or

(b) [other examples]

Note on adoption: A state should use this section to list those situations in which the state has enacted specific legislation governing the domestication or conversion of domestic corporations that engage in particular types of activities or that do business in a regulated industry. Mutual to share conversions (for instance, of an insurance company, bank, savings institution or credit union) are examples of such transactions.

§ 9.03. Required Approvals [Optional]

If a domestic or foreign corporation or eligible entity may not be a party to a merger without the approval of the [attorney general], the [department of banking], the [department of insurance] or the [public utility commission], and the applicable statutes or regulations do not specifically deal with transactions under this chapter but do require such approval for mergers, a corporation or eligible entity shall not be a party to a transaction under this chapter without the prior approval of that agency or official.

Note on adoption: Section 9.03 is an optional provision that should be considered in states where corporations or other entities that conduct regulated activities, such as banking, insurance or the

provision of public utility services, are incorporated or organized under general laws instead of under special laws applicable only to entities conducting the regulated activity. If this section is used, the list of officials and agencies should be conformed to the laws of the enacting state.

§ 9.04. Relationship of Chapter to Other Laws [Optional]

A transaction effected under this chapter may not create or impair a right, duty or obligation of a person under the statutory law of this state other than this chapter relating to a change in control, business combination, control-share acquisition, or similar transaction involving a domesticating or converting domestic corporation, unless the approval of the plan of domestication or conversion is by a vote of the shareholders or the board of directors which would be sufficient to create or impair the right, duty or obligation directly under that law.

Subchapter B. Domestication

§ 9.20. Domestication

(a) By complying with the provisions of this subchapter applicable to foreign corporations, a foreign corporation may become a domestic corporation if the domestication is permitted by the organic law of the foreign corporation.

(b) By complying with the provisions of this subchapter, a domestic corporation may become a foreign corporation pursuant to a plan of domestication if the domestication is permitted by the organic law of the foreign corporation.

(c) The plan of domestication must include:

(1) the name of the domesticating corporation;

(2) the name and jurisdiction of formation of the domesticated corporation;

(3) the manner and basis of reclassifying the shares of the domesticating corporation into shares or other securities, obligations, rights to acquire shares or other securities, cash, other property, or any combination of the foregoing;

(4) the proposed articles of incorporation and bylaws of the domesticated corporation; and

(5) the other terms and conditions of the domestication.

(d) In addition to the requirements of subsection (c), a plan of domestication may contain any other provision not prohibited by law.

(e) The terms of a plan of domestication may be made dependent upon facts objectively ascertainable outside the plan in accordance with § 1.20(k).

(f) If a protected agreement of a domestic domesticating corporation in effect immediately before the domestication becomes effective contains a provision applying to a merger of the corporation and the agreement does not refer to a domestication of the corporation, the provision applies to a domestication of the corporation as if the domestication were a merger until such time as the provision is first amended after the enactment date.

§ 9.21. Action on a Plan of Domestication

In the case of a domestication of a domestic corporation into a foreign jurisdiction, the plan of domestication shall be adopted in the following manner:

(a) The plan of domestication shall first be adopted by the board of directors.

(b) The plan of domestication shall then be approved by the shareholders. In submitting the plan of domestication to the shareholders for approval, the board of directors shall recommend that the shareholders approve the plan, unless (i) the board of directors makes a determination that because of conflicts of interest or other special circumstances it should not make such a recommendation or (ii) § 8.26 applies. If either (i) or (ii) applies, the board shall inform the shareholders of the basis for its so proceeding.

(c) The board of directors may set conditions for approval of the plan of domestication by the shareholders or the effectiveness of the plan of domestication.

(d) If the approval of the shareholders is to be given at a meeting, the corporation shall notify each shareholder, regardless of whether entitled to vote, of the meeting of shareholders at which the plan of domestication is to be submitted for approval. The notice must state that the purpose, or one of the purposes, of the meeting is to consider the plan of domestication and must contain or be accompanied by a copy or summary of the plan. The notice must include or be accompanied by a copy of the articles of incorporation and the bylaws as they will be in effect immediately after the domestication.

(e) Unless the articles of incorporation, or the board of directors acting pursuant to subsection (c), require a greater vote or a greater quorum, approval of the plan of domestication requires (i) the approval of the shareholders at a meeting at which a quorum exists consisting of a majority of the votes entitled to be cast on the plan, and, (ii) except as provided in subsection (f), the approval of each class or series of shares voting as a separate voting group at a meeting at which a quorum of the voting group exists consisting of a majority of the votes entitled to be cast on the plan by that voting group.

(f) The articles of incorporation may expressly limit or eliminate the separate voting rights provided in subsection (e)(ii) as to any class or series of shares, except when the articles of incorporation of the foreign corporation resulting from the domestication include what would be in effect an amendment that would entitle the class or series to vote as a separate group under § 10.04 if it were a proposed amendment of the articles of incorporation of the domestic domesticating corporation.

(g) If as a result of a domestication one or more shareholders of a domestic domesticating corporation would become subject to interest holder liability, approval of the plan of domestication shall require the signing in connection with the domestication, by each such shareholder, of a separate written consent to become subject to such interest holder liability, unless in the case of a shareholder that already has interest holder liability with respect to the domesticating corporation, the terms and conditions of the interest holder liability with respect to the domesticated corporation are substantially identical to those of the existing interest holder liability (other than for changes that eliminate or reduce such interest holder liability).

§ 9.22. Articles of Domestication; Effectiveness

(a) After (i) a plan of domestication of a domestic corporation has been adopted and approved as required by this Act, or (ii) a foreign corporation that is the domesticating corporation has approved a domestication as required under its organic law, articles of domestication shall be signed by the domesticating corporation. The articles must set forth:

> **(1)** the name of the domesticating corporation and its jurisdiction of formation;
>
> **(2)** the name and jurisdiction of formation of the domesticated corporation; and
>
> **(3)** if the domesticating corporation is a domestic corporation, a statement that the plan of domestication was approved in accordance with this chapter or, if the domesticating corporation is a foreign corporation, a statement that the domestication was approved in accordance with its organic law.

(b) If the domesticated corporation is a domestic corporation, the articles of domestication must attach articles of incorporation of the domesticated corporation that satisfy the requirements of § 2.02. Provisions that would not be required to be included in restated articles of incorporation may be omitted from the articles of incorporation attached to the articles of domestication.

(c) The articles of domestication shall be delivered to the secretary of state for filing, and shall take effect at the effective date determined in accordance with § 1.23.

(d) If the domesticated corporation is a domestic corporation, the domestication becomes effective when the articles of domestication are effective. If the domesticated corporation is a foreign corporation, the domestication becomes effective on the later of (i) the date and time provided by the organic law of the domesticated corporation, and (ii) when the articles of domestication are effective.

(e) If the domesticating corporation is a foreign corporation that is registered to do business in this state under chapter 15, its registration statement shall be cancelled automatically when the domestication becomes effective.

§ 9.23. Amendment of Plan of Domestication; Abandonment

(a) A plan of domestication of a domestic corporation may be amended:

> **(1)** in the same manner as the plan was approved, if the plan does not provide for the manner in which it may be amended; or
>
> **(2)** in the manner provided in the plan, except that a shareholder that was entitled to vote on or consent to approval of the plan is entitled to vote on or consent to any amendment of the plan that will change:
>
>> **(i)** the amount or kind of shares or other securities, obligations, rights to acquire shares or other securities, cash, other property, or any combination of the foregoing, to be received by any of the shareholders of the domesticating corporation under the plan;
>>
>> **(ii)** the articles of incorporation or bylaws of the domesticated corporation that will be in effect immediately after the domestication becomes effective, except for changes that do not require approval of the shareholders of the domesticated corporation under its organic law or its proposed articles of incorporation or bylaws as set forth in the plan; or
>>
>> **(iii)** any of the other terms or conditions of the plan, if the change would adversely affect the shareholder in any material respect.

(b) After a plan of domestication has been adopted and approved by a domestic corporation as required by this subchapter, and before the articles of domestication have become effective, the plan may be abandoned by the corporation without action by its shareholders in accordance with any procedures set forth in the plan or, if no such procedures are set forth in the plan, in the manner determined by the board of directors.

(c) If a domestication is abandoned after the articles of domestication have been delivered to the secretary of state for filing but before the articles of domestication have become effective, articles of abandonment, signed by the domesticating corporation, must be delivered to the secretary of state for filing before the articles of domestication become effective. The articles of abandonment take effect upon filing, and the domestication shall be deemed abandoned and shall not become effective. The articles of abandonment must contain:

(1) the name of the domesticating corporation;

(2) the date on which the articles of domestication were filed by the secretary of state; and (3) a statement that the domestication has been abandoned in accordance with this section.

§ 9.24. Effect of Domestication

(a) When a domestication becomes effective:

(1) all property owned by, and every contract right possessed by, the domesticating corporation are the property and contract rights of the domesticated corporation without transfer, reversion or impairment;

(2) all debts, obligations and other liabilities of the domesticating corporation are the debts, obligations and other liabilities of the domesticated corporation;

(3) the name of the domesticated corporation may but need not be substituted for the name of the domesticating corporation in any pending proceeding;

(4) the articles of incorporation and bylaws of the domesticated corporation become effective;

(5) the shares of the domesticating corporation are reclassified into shares or other securities, obligations, rights to acquire shares or other securities, cash or other property in accordance with the terms of the domestication, and the shareholders of the domesticating corporation are entitled only to the rights provided to them by those terms and to any appraisal rights they may have under the organic law of the domesticating corporation; and

(6) the domesticated corporation is:

(i) incorporated under and subject to the organic law of the domesticated corporation;

(ii) the same corporation without interruption as the domesticating corporation; and

(iii) deemed to have been incorporated on the date the domesticating corporation was originally incorporated.

(b) When a domestication of a domestic corporation into a foreign jurisdiction becomes effective, the domesticated corporation is deemed to:

(1) appoint the secretary of state as its agent for service of process in a proceeding to enforce the rights of shareholders who exercise appraisal rights in connection with the domestication; and

(2) agree that it will promptly pay the amount, if any, to which such shareholders are entitled under chapter 13.

(c) Except as otherwise provided in the organic law or organic rules of a domesticating foreign corporation, the interest holder liability of a shareholder in a foreign corporation that is domesticated into this state who had interest holder liability in respect of such domesticating corporation before the domestication becomes effective shall be as follows:

(1) The domestication does not discharge that prior interest holder liability with respect to any interest holder liabilities that arose before the domestication becomes effective.

(2) The provisions of the organic law of the domesticating corporation shall continue to apply to the collection or discharge of any interest holder liabilities preserved by subsection (c)(1), as if the domestication had not occurred.

(3) The shareholder shall have such rights of contribution from other persons as are provided by the organic law of the domesticating corporation with respect to any interest holder liabilities preserved by subsection (c)(1), as if the domestication had not occurred.

(4) The shareholder shall not, by reason of such prior interest holder liability, have interest holder liability with respect to any interest

holder liabilities that are incurred after the domestication becomes effective.

(d) A shareholder who becomes subject to interest holder liability in respect of the domesticated corporation as a result of the domestication shall have such interest holder liability only in respect of interest holder liabilities that arise after the domestication becomes effective.

(e) A domestication does not constitute or cause the dissolution of the domesticating corporation.

(f) Property held for charitable purposes under the laws of this state by a domestic or foreign corporation immediately before a domestication shall not, as a result of the transaction, be diverted from the objects for which it was donated, granted, devised, or otherwise transferred except and to the extent permitted by or pursuant to the laws of this state addressing cy près or dealing with nondiversion of charitable assets.

(g) A bequest, devise, gift, grant, or promise contained in a will or other instrument of donation, subscription, or conveyance which is made to the domesticating corporation and which takes effect or remains payable after the domestication inures to the domesticated corporation.

(h) A trust obligation that would govern property if transferred to the domesticating corporation applies to property that is transferred to the domesticated corporation after the domestication takes effect.

Subchapter C. Conversion

§ 9.30. Conversion

(a) By complying with this chapter, a domestic corporation may become (i) a domestic eligible entity or (ii) a foreign eligible entity if the conversion is permitted by the organic law of the foreign entity.

(b) By complying with this subchapter and applicable provisions of its organic law, a domestic eligible entity may become a domestic corporation. If procedures for the approval of a conversion are not provided by the organic law or organic rules of a domestic eligible entity, the conversion shall be adopted and approved in the same manner as a merger of that eligible entity. If the organic law or organic rules of a domestic eligible entity do not provide procedures for the approval of either a conversion or a merger, a plan of conversion may nonetheless be adopted and approved by the unanimous consent of all the interest holders of such eligible entity. In either such case, the conversion thereafter may be effected as provided in the other provisions of this subchapter; and for purposes of applying this chapter in such a case:

> **(1)** the eligible entity, its members or interest holders, eligible interests and organic rules taken together, shall be deemed to be a domestic business corporation, shareholders, shares and articles of incorporation, respectively and vice versa, as the context may require; and

> **(2)** if the business and affairs of the eligible entity are managed by a person or persons that are not identical to the members or interest holders, that person or persons shall be deemed to be the board of directors.

(c) By complying with the provisions of this subchapter applicable to foreign entities, a foreign eligible entity may become a domestic corporation if the organic law of the foreign eligible entity permits it to become a business corporation in another jurisdiction.

(d) If a protected agreement of a domestic converting corporation in effect immediately before the conversion becomes effective contains a provision applying to a merger of the corporation that is a converting entity and the agreement does not refer to a conversion of the corporation, the provision applies to a conversion of the corporation as if the conversion were a merger, until such time as the provision is first amended after the enactment date.

§ 9.31. Plan of Conversion

(a) A domestic corporation may convert to a domestic or foreign eligible entity under this subchapter by approving a plan of conversion. The plan of conversion must include:

(1) the name of the converting corporation;

(2) the name, jurisdiction of formation and type of entity of the converted entity;

(3) the manner and basis of converting the shares of the domestic corporation into eligible interests or other securities, obligations, rights to acquire eligible interests or other securities, cash, other property, or any combination of the foregoing;

(4) the other terms and conditions of the conversion; and

(5) the full text, as it will be in effect immediately after the conversion becomes effective, of the organic rules of the converted entity which are to be in writing.

(b) In addition to the requirements of subsection (a), a plan of conversion may contain any other provision not prohibited by law.

(c) The terms of a plan of conversion may be made dependent upon facts objectively ascertainable outside the plan in accordance with § 1.20(k).

§ 9.32. Action on a Plan of Conversion

In the case of a conversion of a domestic corporation to a domestic or foreign eligible entity, the plan of conversion shall be adopted in the following manner:

(a) The plan of conversion shall first be adopted by the board of directors.

(b) The plan of conversion shall then be approved by the shareholders. In submitting the plan of conversion to the shareholders for their approval, the board of directors must recommend that the shareholders approve the plan, unless (i) the board of directors makes a determination that because of conflicts of interest or other special circumstances it should not make such a recommendation, or (ii) § .26 applies. If either (i) or (ii) applies, the board of directors shall inform the shareholders of the basis for its so proceeding.

(c) The board of directors may set conditions for approval of the plan of conversion by the shareholders or the effectiveness of the plan of conversion.

(d) If the approval of the shareholders is to be given at a meeting, the corporation shall notify each shareholder, regardless of whether entitled to vote, of the meeting of shareholders at which the plan of conversion is to be submitted for approval. The notice must state that the purpose, or one of the purposes, of the meeting is to consider the plan of conversion and must contain or be accompanied by a copy or summary of the plan. The notice must include or be accompanied by a copy of the organic rules of the converted entity which are to be in writing as they will be in effect immediately after the conversion.

(e) Unless the articles of incorporation, or the board of directors acting pursuant to subsection (c), require a greater vote or a greater quorum, approval of the plan of conversion requires (i) the approval of the shareholders at a meeting at which a quorum exists consisting of a majority of the votes entitled to be cast on the plan, and (ii) the approval of each class or series of shares voting as a separate voting group at a meeting at which a quorum of the voting group exists consisting of a majority of the votes entitled to be cast on the plan by that voting group.

(f) If as a result of the conversion one or more shareholders of the converting domestic corporation would become subject to interest holder liability, approval of the plan of conversion shall require the signing in connection with the transaction, by each such shareholder, of a separate written consent to become subject to such interest holder liability.

§ 9.33. Articles of Conversion; Effectiveness

(a) After (i) a plan of conversion of a domestic corporation has been adopted and approved as required by this Act, or (ii) a domestic or foreign eligible entity that is the converting entity has approved a conversion as required under its organic law, articles of conversion shall be signed by the converting entity and must:

(1) state the name, jurisdiction of formation, and type of entity of the converting entity;

(2) state the name, jurisdiction of formation, and type of entity of the converted entity;

(3) if the converting entity is (i) a domestic corporation, state that the plan of conversion was approved in accordance with this subchapter; or (ii) an eligible entity, (A) state that the conversion was approved by the eligible entity in accordance with its organic law or (B) if the converting entity is a domestic eligible entity the organic law of which does not provide for approval of the conversion, state that the conversion was approved by the domestic eligible entity in accordance with this subchapter; and

(4) if the converted entity is (i) a domestic business corporation, or a domestic nonprofit corporation or filing entity, have attached the public organic record of the converted entity, except that provisions that would not be required to be included in a restated public organic record may be omitted; or (ii) a domestic limited liability partnership, have attached the filing required to become a limited liability partnership.

(b) If the converted entity is a domestic corporation, its articles of incorporation must satisfy the requirements of § 2.02, except that provisions that would not be required to be included in restated articles of incorporation may be omitted from the articles of incorporation. If the converted entity is a domestic eligible entity, its public organic record, if any, must satisfy the requirements of the organic law of this state, except that the public organic record does not need to be signed.

(c) The articles of conversion shall be delivered to the secretary of state for filing, and shall take effect at the effective date determined in accordance with § 1.23.

(d) If a converted entity is a domestic entity, the conversion becomes effective when the articles of conversion are effective. With respect to a conversion in which the converted entity is a foreign eligible entity, the conversion itself shall become effective at the later of (i) the date and time provided by the organic law of that eligible entity, and (ii) when the articles of conversion become effective.

(e) Articles of conversion under this section may be combined with any required conversion filing under the organic law of a domestic eligible entity

that is the converting entity or converted entity if the combined filing satisfies the requirements of both this section and the other organic law.

(f) If the converting entity is a foreign eligible entity that is registered to do business in this state under a provision of law similar to chapter 15, its registration statement or other type of foreign qualification shall be cancelled automatically on the effective date of its conversion.

§ 9.34. Amendment of Plan of Conversion; Abandonment

(a) A plan of conversion of a converting entity that is a domestic corporation may be amended:

(1) in the same manner as the plan was approved, if the plan does not provide for the manner in which it may be amended; or

(2) in the manner provided in the plan, except that shareholders that were entitled to vote on or consent to approval of the plan are entitled to vote on or consent to any amendment of the plan that will change:

(i) the amount or kind of eligible interests or other securities, obligations, rights to acquire eligible interests or other securities, cash, other property, or any combination of the foregoing, to be received by any of the shareholders of the converting corporation under the plan;

(ii) the organic rules of the converted entity that will be in effect immediately after the conversion becomes effective, except for changes that do not require approval of the eligible interest holders of the converted entity under its organic law or organic rules; or

(iii) any other terms or conditions of the plan, if the change would adversely affect such shareholders in any material respect.

(b) After a plan of conversion has been approved by a converting entity that is a domestic corporation in the manner required by this subchapter and before the articles of conversion become effective, the plan may be abandoned by the corporation without action by its shareholders in accordance with any procedures set forth in the plan or, if no such procedures are set forth in the plan, in the manner determined by the board of directors.

(c) If a conversion is abandoned after the articles of conversion have been delivered to the secretary of state for filing and before the articles of conversion become effective, articles of abandonment, signed by the converting entity, must be delivered to the secretary of state for filing before the articles of conversion become effective. The articles of abandonment take effect on filing, and the conversion is abandoned and does not become effective. The articles of abandonment must contain:

> **(1)** the name of the converting entity;

> **(2)** the date on which the articles of conversion were filed by the secretary of state; and (3) a statement that the conversion has been abandoned in accordance with this section.

§ 9.35. Effect of Conversion

(a) When a conversion becomes effective:

> **(1)** all property owned by, and every contract right possessed by, the converting entity remain the property and contract rights of the converted entity without transfer, reversion or impairment;

> **(2)** all debts, obligations and other liabilities of the converting entity remain the debts, obligations and other liabilities of the converted entity;

> **(3)** the name of the converted entity may but need not be substituted for the name of the converting entity in any pending action or proceeding;

> **(4)** if the converted entity is a filing entity or a domestic business corporation or a domestic or foreign nonprofit corporation, its public organic record and its private organic rules become effective;

> **(5)** if the converted entity is a nonfiling entity, its private organic rules become effective;

> **(6)** if the converted entity is a limited liability partnership, the filing required to become a limited liability partnership and its private organic rules become effective;

> **(7)** the shares or eligible interests of the converting entity are reclassified into shares, eligible interests or other securities, obligations, rights to acquire shares, eligible interests or other securities, cash, or other property in accordance with the terms of the conversion, and the shareholders or interest holders of the converting entity are entitled only to the rights provided to them by those terms and to any appraisal rights they may have under the organic law of the converting entity; and

> **(8)** the converted entity is:

>> **(i)** incorporated or organized under and subject to the organic law of the converted entity;

>> **(ii)** the same entity without interruption as the converting entity; and

>> **(iii)** deemed to have been incorporated or otherwise organized on the date that the converting entity was originally incorporated or organized.

(b) When a conversion of a domestic corporation to a foreign eligible entity becomes effective, the converted entity is deemed to:

> **(1)** appoint the secretary of state as its agent for service of process in a proceeding to enforce the rights of shareholders who exercise appraisal rights in connection with the conversion; and

> **(2)** agree that it will promptly pay the amount, if any, to which such shareholders are entitled under chapter 13.

(c) Except as otherwise provided in the articles of incorporation of a domestic corporation or the organic law or organic rules of a foreign corporation or a domestic or foreign eligible entity, a shareholder or eligible interest holder who becomes subject to interest holder liability in respect of a domestic corporation or eligible entity as a result of the conversion shall have such interest holder liability only in respect of interest holder liabilities that arise after the conversion becomes effective.

(d) Except as otherwise provided in the organic law or the organic rules of the eligible entity, the interest holder liability of an interest holder in a converting eligible entity that converts to a domestic corporation who had interest holder liability in respect of such converting eligible entity before the conversion becomes effective shall be as follows:

(1) The conversion does not discharge that prior interest holder liability with respect to any interest holder liabilities that arose before the conversion became effective.

(2) The provisions of the organic law of the eligible entity shall continue to apply to the collection or discharge of any interest holder liabilities preserved by subsection (d)(1), as if the conversion had not occurred.

(3) The eligible interest holder shall have such rights of contribution from other persons as are provided by the organic law of the eligible entity with respect to any interest holder liabilities preserved by subsection (d)(1), as if the conversion had not occurred.

(4) The eligible interest holder shall not, by reason of such prior interest holder liability, have interest holder liability with respect to any interest holder liabilities that arise after the conversion becomes effective.

(e) A conversion does not require the converting entity to wind up its affairs and does not constitute or cause the dissolution or termination of the entity.

(f) Property held for charitable purposes under the laws of this state by a corporation or a domestic or foreign eligible entity immediately before a conversion shall not, as a result of the transaction, be diverted from the objects for which it was donated, granted, devised, or otherwise transferred except and to the extent permitted by or pursuant to the laws of this state addressing cy près or dealing with nondiversion of charitable assets.

(g) A bequest, devise, gift, grant, or promise contained in a will or other instrument of donation, subscription, or conveyance which is made to the converting entity and which takes effect or remains payable after the conversion inures to the converted entity.

(h) A trust obligation that would govern property if transferred to the converting entity applies to property that is transferred to the converted entity after the conversion takes effect.

Chapter 10. Amendment of Articles of Incorporation and Bylaws

Subchapter A. Amendment of Articles of Incorporation

§ 10.01. Authority to Amend

(a) A corporation may amend its articles of incorporation at any time to add or change a provision that is required or permitted in the articles of incorporation as of the effective date of the amendment or to delete a provision that is not required to be contained in the articles of incorporation.

(b) A shareholder of the corporation does not have a vested property right resulting from any provision in the articles of incorporation, including provisions relating to management, control, capital structure, dividend entitlement, or purpose or duration of the corporation.

§ 10.02. Amendment Before Issuance of Shares

If a corporation has not yet issued shares, its board of directors, or its incorporators if it has no board of directors, may adopt one or more amendments to the corporation's articles of incorporation.

§ 10.03. Amendment by Board of Directors and Shareholders

If a corporation has issued shares, an amendment to the articles of incorporation shall be adopted in the following manner:

(a) The proposed amendment shall first be adopted by the board of directors.

(b) Except as provided in sections 10.05, 10.07, and 10.08, the amendment shall then be approved by the shareholders. In submitting the proposed amendment to the shareholders for approval, the board of directors shall recommend that the shareholders approve the amendment, unless (i) the board of directors makes a determination that because of conflicts of interest or other special circumstances it should not make such a recommendation, or (ii) § 8.26 applies. If either (i) or (ii) applies, the board must inform the shareholders of the basis for its so proceeding.

(c) The board of directors may set conditions for the approval of the amendment by the shareholders or the effectiveness of the amendment.

(d) If the amendment is required to be approved by the shareholders, and the approval is to be given at a meeting, the corporation shall notify each shareholder, regardless of whether entitled to vote, of the meeting of shareholders at which the amendment is to be submitted for approval. The notice must state that the purpose, or one of the purposes, of the meeting is to consider the amendment. The notice must contain or be accompanied by a copy of the amendment.

(e) Unless the articles of incorporation, or the board of directors acting pursuant to subsection (c), require a greater vote or a greater quorum, approval of the amendment requires the approval of the shareholders at a meeting at which a quorum consisting of a majority of the votes entitled to be cast on the amendment exists, and, if any class or series of shares is entitled to vote as a separate group on the amendment, except as provided in § 10.04(c), the approval of each such separate voting group at a meeting at which a quorum of the voting group exists consisting of a majority of the votes entitled to be cast on the amendment by that voting group.

(f) If as a result of an amendment of the articles of incorporation one or more shareholders of a domestic corporation would become subject to new interest holder liability, approval of the amendment requires the signing in connection with the amendment, by each such shareholder, of a separate written consent to become subject to such new interest holder liability, unless in the case of a shareholder that already has interest holder liability the terms and conditions of the new interest holder liability (i) are substantially identical to those of the existing interest holder liability, or (ii)

are substantially identical to those of the existing interest holder liability (other than changes that eliminate or reduce such interest holder liability).

(g) For purposes of subsection (f) and § 10.09, "new interest holder liability" means interest holder liability of a person resulting from an amendment of the articles of incorporation if (i) the person did not have interest holder liability before the amendment becomes effective, or (ii) the person had interest holder liability before the amendment becomes effective, the terms and conditions of which are changed when the amendment becomes effective.

§ 10.04. Voting on Amendments by Voting Groups

(a) The holders of the outstanding shares of a class are entitled to vote as a separate voting group (if shareholder voting is otherwise required by this Act) on a proposed amendment to the articles of incorporation if the amendment would:

> **(1)** effect an exchange or reclassification of all or part of the shares of the class into shares of another class;

> **(2)** effect an exchange or reclassification, or create the right of exchange, of all or part of the shares of another class into shares of the class;

> **(3)** change the rights, preferences, or limitations of all or part of the shares of the class;

> **(4)** change the shares of all or part of the class into a different number of shares of the same class;

> **(5)** create a new class of shares having rights or preferences with respect to distributions that are prior or superior to the shares of the class;

> **(6)** increase the rights, preferences, or number of authorized shares of any class that, after giving effect to the amendment, have rights or preferences with respect to distributions that are prior or superior to the shares of the class;

> **(7)** limit or deny an existing preemptive right of all or part of the shares of the class; or

> **(8)** cancel or otherwise affect rights to distributions that have accumulated but not yet been

authorized on all or part of the shares of the class.

(b) If a proposed amendment would affect a series of a class of shares in one or more of the ways described in subsection (a), the holders of shares of that series are entitled to vote as a separate voting group on the proposed amendment.

(c) If a proposed amendment that entitles the holders of two or more classes or series of shares to vote as separate voting groups under this section would affect those two or more classes or series in the same or a substantially similar way, the holders of shares of all the classes or series so affected shall vote together as a single voting group on the proposed amendment, unless otherwise provided in the articles of incorporation or added as a condition by the board of directors pursuant to § 10.03(c).

(d) A class or series of shares is entitled to the voting rights granted by this section even if the articles of incorporation provide that the shares are nonvoting shares.

§ 10.05. Amendment by Board of Directors

Unless the articles of incorporation provide otherwise, a corporation's board of directors may adopt amendments to the corporation's articles of incorporation without shareholder approval:

(a) to extend the duration of the corporation if it was incorporated at a time when limited duration was required by law;

(b) to delete the names and addresses of the initial directors;

(c) to delete the name and address of the initial registered agent or registered office, if a statement of change is on file with the secretary of state;

(d) if the corporation has only one class of shares outstanding:

> **(1)** to change each issued and unissued authorized share of the class into a greater number of whole shares of that class; or

> **(2)** to increase the number of authorized shares of the class to the extent necessary to permit the issuance of shares as a share dividend;

(e) to change the corporate name by substituting the word "corporation," "incorporated," "company," "limited," or the abbreviation "corp.," "inc.," "co.," or "ltd.," for a similar word or abbreviation in the name, or by adding, deleting, or changing a geographical attribution for the name;

(f) to reflect a reduction in authorized shares, as a result of the operation of § 6.31(b), when the corporation has acquired its own shares and the articles of incorporation prohibit the reissue of the acquired shares;

(g) to delete a class of shares from the articles of incorporation, as a result of the operation of § 6.31(b), when there are no remaining shares of the class because the corporation has acquired all shares of the class and the articles of incorporation prohibit the reissue of the acquired shares; or

(h) to make any change expressly permitted by § 6.02(a) or (b) to be made without shareholder approval.

§ 10.06. Articles of Amendment

(a) After an amendment to the articles of incorporation has been adopted and approved in the manner required by this Act and by the articles of incorporation, the corporation shall deliver to the secretary of state for filing articles of amendment, which must set forth:

> **(1)** the name of the corporation;

> **(2)** the text of each amendment adopted, or the information required by § 1.20(k)(5);

> **(3)** if an amendment provides for an exchange, reclassification, or cancellation of issued shares, provisions for implementing the amendment if not contained in the amendment itself, (which may be made dependent upon facts objectively ascertainable outside the articles of amendment in accordance with § 1.20(k)(5);

> **(4)** the date of each amendment's adoption; and

> **(5)** if an amendment:

>> **(i)** was adopted by the incorporators or board of directors without shareholder approval, a statement that the amendment was

duly adopted by the incorporators or by the board of directors, as the case may be, and that shareholder approval was not required;

(ii) required approval by the shareholders, a statement that the amendment was duly approved by the shareholders in the manner required by this Act and by the articles of incorporation; or

(iii) is being filed pursuant to § 1.20(k)(5), a statement to that effect.

(b) Articles of amendment shall take effect at the effective date determined in accordance with § 1.23.

§ 10.07. Restated Articles of Incorporation

(a) A corporation's board of directors may restate its articles of incorporation at any time, without shareholder approval, to consolidate all amendments into a single document.

(b) If the restated articles include one or more new amendments that require shareholder approval, the amendments shall be adopted and approved as provided in § 10.03.

(c) A corporation that restates its articles of incorporation shall deliver to the secretary of state for filing articles of restatement setting forth:

(1) the name of the corporation;

(2) the text of the restated articles of incorporation;

(3) a statement that the restated articles consolidate all amendments into a single document; and

(4) if a new amendment is included in the restated articles, the statements required under § 10.06 with respect to the new amendment.

(d) Duly adopted restated articles of incorporation supersede the original articles of incorporation and all amendments to the articles of incorporation.

(e) The secretary of state may certify restated articles of incorporation as the articles of incorporation currently in effect, without including the statements required by subsection (c)(4).

§ 10.08. Amendment Pursuant to Reorganization

(a) A corporation's articles of incorporation may be amended without action by the board of directors or shareholders to carry out a plan of reorganization ordered or decreed by a court of competent jurisdiction under the authority of a law of the United States.

(b) The individual or individuals designated by the court shall deliver to the secretary of state for filing articles of amendment setting forth:

(1) the name of the corporation;

(2) the text of each amendment approved by the court;

(3) the date of the court's order or decree approving the articles of amendment;

(4) the title of the reorganization proceeding in which the order or decree was entered; and

(5) a statement that the court had jurisdiction of the proceeding under federal statute.

(c) This section does not apply after entry of a final decree in the reorganization proceeding even though the court retains jurisdiction of the proceeding for limited purposes unrelated to consummation of the reorganization plan.

§ 10.09. Effect of Amendment

(a) An amendment to the articles of incorporation does not affect a cause of action existing against or in favor of the corporation, a proceeding to which the corporation is a party, or the existing rights of persons other than the shareholders. An amendment changing a corporation's name does not affect a proceeding brought by or against the corporation in its former name.

(b) A shareholder who becomes subject to new interest holder liability in respect of the corporation as a result of an amendment to the articles of incorporation shall have that new interest holder liability only in respect of interest holder liabilities that arise after the amendment becomes effective.

(c) Except as otherwise provided in the articles of incorporation of the corporation, the interest holder liability of a shareholder who had interest holder liability in respect of the corporation before the amendment becomes effective and has new interest holder liability after the amendment becomes effective shall be as follows:

(1) The amendment does not discharge that prior interest holder liability with respect to any interest holder liabilities that arose before the amendment becomes effective.

(2) The provisions of the articles of incorporation of the corporation relating to interest holder liability as in effect immediately prior to the amendment shall continue to apply to the collection or discharge of any interest holder liabilities preserved by subsection (c)(1), as if the amendment had not occurred.

(3) The shareholder shall have such rights of contribution from other persons as are provided by the articles of incorporation relating to interest holder liability as in effect immediately prior to the amendment with respect to any interest holder liabilities preserved by subsection (c)(1), as if the amendment had not occurred.

(4) The shareholder shall not, by reason of such prior interest holder liability, have interest holder liability with respect to any interest holder liabilities that arise after the amendment becomes effective.

Subchapter B. Amendment of Bylaws

§ 10.20. Authority to Amend

(a) A corporation's shareholders may amend or repeal the corporation's bylaws.

(b) A corporation's board of directors may amend or repeal the corporation's bylaws, unless:

(1) the articles of incorporation, § 10.21 or, if applicable, § 10.22 reserve that power exclusively to the shareholders in whole or part; or

(2) except as provided in § 2.06(d), the shareholders in amending, repealing, or adopting a bylaw expressly provide that the board of directors may not amend, repeal, or adopt that bylaw.

(c) A shareholder of the corporation does not have a vested property right resulting from any provision in the bylaws.

§ 10.21. Bylaw Increasing Quorum or Voting Requirement for Directors

(a) A bylaw that increases a quorum or voting requirement for the board of directors or that requires a meeting of shareholders to be held at a place may be amended or repealed:

(1) if originally adopted by the shareholders, only by the shareholders, unless the bylaw otherwise provides; or

(2) if adopted by the board of directors, either by the shareholders or by the board of directors.

(b) A bylaw adopted or amended by the shareholders that increases a quorum or voting requirement for the board of directors may provide that it can be amended or repealed only by a specified vote of either the shareholders or the board of directors.

(c) Action by the board of directors under subsection (a) to amend or repeal a bylaw that changes a quorum or voting requirement for the board of directors shall meet the same quorum requirement and be adopted by the same vote required to take action under the quorum and voting requirement then in effect or proposed to be adopted, whichever is greater.

§ 10.22. Bylaw Provisions Relating to the Election of Directors

(a) Unless the articles of incorporation (i) specifically prohibit the adoption of a bylaw pursuant to this section, (ii) alter the vote specified in § 7.28(a), or (iii) provide for cumulative voting, a corporation may elect in its bylaws to be governed in the election of directors as follows:

(1) each vote entitled to be cast may be voted for or against up to that number of candidates that is equal to the number of directors to be elected, or a shareholder may indicate an abstention, but without cumulating the votes;

(2) to be elected, a nominee shall have received a plurality of the votes cast by holders of shares entitled to vote in the election at a meeting at which a quorum is present, provided that a

nominee who is elected but receives more votes against than for election shall serve as a director for a term that shall terminate on the date that is the earlier of (i) 90 days from the date on which the voting results are determined pursuant to § 7.29(b)(5) or (ii) the date on which an individual is selected by the board of directors to fill the office held by such director, which selection shall be deemed to constitute the filling of a vacancy by the board to which § 8.10 applies. Subject to subsection (a)(3), a nominee who is elected but receives more votes against than for election shall not serve as a director beyond the 90-day period referenced above; and

(3) the board of directors may select any qualified individual to fill the office held by a director who received more votes against than for election.

(b) Subsection (a) does not apply to an election of directors by a voting group if (i) at the expiration of the time fixed under a provision requiring advance notification of director candidates, or (ii) absent such a provision, at a time fixed by the board of directors which is not more than 14 days before notice is given of the meeting at which the election is to occur, there are more candidates for election by the voting group than the number of directors to be elected, one or more of whom are properly proposed by shareholders. An individual shall not be considered a candidate for purposes of this subsection if the board of directors determines before the notice of meeting is given that such individual's candidacy does not create a bona fide election contest.

(c) A bylaw electing to be governed by this section may be repealed:

(1) if originally adopted by the shareholders, only by the shareholders, unless the bylaw otherwise provides;

(2) if adopted by the board of directors, by the board of directors or the shareholders.

Chapter 11. Mergers and Share Exchanges

§ 11.01. Definitions

As used in this chapter:

"Acquired entity" means the domestic or foreign corporation or eligible entity that will have all of one or more classes or series of its shares or eligible interests acquired in a share exchange.

"Acquiring entity" means the domestic or foreign corporation or eligible entity that will acquire all of one or more classes or series of shares or eligible interests of the acquired entity in a share exchange.

"New interest holder liability" means interest holder liability of a person, resulting from a merger or share exchange, that is (i) in respect of an entity which is different from the entity in which the person held shares or eligible interests immediately before the merger or share exchange became effective; or (ii) in respect of the same entity as the one in which the person held shares or eligible interests immediately before the merger or share exchange became effective if (A) the person did not have interest holder liability immediately before the merger or share exchange became effective, or (B) the person had interest holder liability immediately before the merger or share exchange became effective, the terms and conditions of which were changed when the merger or share exchange became effective.

"Party to a merger" means any domestic or foreign corporation or eligible entity that will merge under a plan of merger but does not include a survivor created by the merger.

"Survivor" in a merger means the domestic or foreign corporation or eligible entity into which one or more other corporations or eligible entities are merged.

§ 11.02. Merger

(a) By complying with this chapter:

(1) one or more domestic business corporations may merge with one or more domestic or foreign business corporations or eligible entities pursuant to a plan of merger, resulting in a survivor; and

(2) two or more foreign business corporations or domestic or foreign eligible entities may merge, resulting in a survivor that is a domestic business corporation created in the merger.

(b) By complying with the provisions of this chapter applicable to foreign entities, a foreign business corporation or a foreign eligible entity may be a party to a merger with a domestic business corporation, or may be created as the survivor in a merger in which a domestic business corporation is a party, but only if the merger is permitted by the organic law of the foreign business corporation or eligible entity.

(c) If the organic law or organic rules of a domestic eligible entity do not provide procedures for the approval of a merger, a plan of merger may nonetheless be adopted and approved by the unanimous consent of all of the interest holders of such eligible entity, and the merger may thereafter by effected as provided in the other provisions of this chapter; and for the purposes of applying this chapter in such a case:

(1) the eligible entity, its members or interest holders, eligible interests and articles of incorporation or other organic rules taken together shall be deemed to be a domestic business corporation, shareholders, shares and articles of incorporation, respectively and vice versa as the context may require; and

(2) if the business and affairs of the eligible entity are managed by a person or persons that are not identical to the members or interest holders, that group shall be deemed to be the board of directors.

(d) The plan of merger must include:

(1) as to each party to the merger, its name, jurisdiction of formation, and type of entity;

(2) the survivor's name, jurisdiction of formation, and type of entity, and, if the survivor is to be created in the merger, a statement to that effect;

(3) the terms and conditions of the merger;

(4) the manner and basis of converting the shares of each merging domestic or foreign business corporation and eligible interests of each merging domestic or foreign eligible entity into shares or other securities, eligible interests, obligations, rights to acquire shares, other securities or eligible interests, cash, other property, or any combination of the foregoing;

(5) the articles of incorporation of any domestic or foreign business or nonprofit corporation, or the public organic record of any domestic or foreign unincorporated entity, to be created by the merger, or if a new domestic or foreign business or nonprofit corporation or unincorporated entity is not to be created by the merger, any amendments to the survivor's articles of incorporation or other public organic record; and

(6) any other provisions required by the laws under which any party to the merger is organized or by which it is governed, or by the articles of incorporation or organic rules of any such party.

(e) In addition to the requirements of subsection (d), a plan of merger may contain any other provision not prohibited by law.

(f) Terms of a plan of merger may be made dependent on facts objectively ascertainable outside the plan in accordance with § 1.20(k).

(g) A plan of merger may be amended only with the consent of each party to the merger, except as provided in the plan. A domestic party to a merger may approve an amendment to a plan:

(1) in the same manner as the plan was approved, if the plan does not provide for the manner in which it may be amended; or

(2) in the manner provided in the plan, except that shareholders, members, or interest holders that were entitled to vote on or consent to approval of the plan are entitled to vote on or consent to any amendment of the plan that will change:

(i) the amount or kind of shares or other securities, eligible interests, obligations, rights to acquire shares, other securities or eligible interests, cash, or other property to be received under the plan by the shareholders, members, or interest holders of any party to the merger;

(ii) the articles of incorporation of any domestic or foreign business or nonprofit corporation, or the organic rules of any unincorporated entity, that will be the survivor of the merger, except for changes permitted by § 10.05 or by comparable provisions of the organic law of any such foreign corporation or domestic or foreign nonprofit corporation or unincorporated entity; or

(iii) any of the other terms or conditions of the plan if the change would adversely affect such shareholders, members, or interest holders in any material respect.

§ 11.03. Share Exchange

(a) By complying with this chapter:

(1) a domestic corporation may acquire all of the shares of one or more classes or series of shares of another domestic or foreign corporation, or all of the eligible interests of one or more classes or series of interests of a domestic or foreign eligible entity, in exchange for shares or other securities, eligible interests, obligations, rights to acquire shares or other securities or eligible interests, cash, other property, or any combination of the foregoing, pursuant to a plan of share exchange; or

(2) all of the shares of one or more classes or series of shares of a domestic corporation may be acquired by another domestic or foreign corporation or eligible entity, in exchange for shares or other securities, eligible interests, obligations, rights to acquire shares or other securities or eligible interests, cash, other property, or any combination of the foregoing, pursuant to a plan of share exchange.

(b) A foreign corporation or eligible entity may be the acquired entity in a share exchange only if the share exchange is permitted by the organic law of that corporation or other entity.

(c) If the organic law or organic rules of a domestic eligible entity do not provide procedures for the approval of a share exchange, a plan of share exchange may be adopted and approved, and the share exchange effected, in accordance with the procedures, if any, for a merger. If the organic law or organic rules of a domestic eligible entity do not provide procedures for the approval of either a share exchange or a merger, a plan of share exchange may nonetheless be adopted and approved by the unanimous consent of all of the interest holders of such eligible entity whose interests will be exchanged under the plan of share exchange, and the share exchange may thereafter be effected as provided in the other provisions of this chapter; and for purposes of applying this chapter in such a case:

(1) the eligible entity, its interest holders, interests and articles of incorporation or other organic rules taken together shall be deemed to be a domestic business corporation, shareholders, shares and articles of incorporation, respectively and vice versa as the context may require; and

(2) if the business and affairs of the eligible entity are managed by a person or persons that are not identical to the members or interest holders, that person or those persons shall be deemed to be the board of directors.

(d) The plan of share exchange must include:

(1) the name of each domestic or foreign corporation or other eligible entity the shares or eligible interests of which will be acquired and the name of the domestic or foreign corporation or eligible entity that will acquire those shares or eligible interests;

(2) the terms and conditions of the share exchange;

(3) the manner and basis of exchanging shares of a domestic or foreign corporation or eligible interests in a domestic or foreign eligible entity the shares or eligible interests of which will be acquired under the share exchange for shares or other securities, eligible interests, obligations, rights to acquire shares, other securities, or eligible interests, cash, other property, or any combination of the foregoing; and

(4) any other provisions required by the organic law governing the acquired entity or its articles of incorporation or organic rules.

(e) Terms of a plan of share exchange may be made dependent on facts objectively ascertainable outside the plan in accordance with § 1.20(k).

(f) A plan of share exchange may be amended only with the consent of each party to the share exchange, except as provided in the plan. A domestic entity may approve an amendment to a plan:

(1) in the same manner as the plan was approved, if the plan does not provide for the manner in which it may be amended; or

(2) in the manner provided in the plan, except that shareholders, members, or interest holders that were entitled to vote on or consent to approval of the plan are entitled to vote on or consent to any amendment of the plan that will change:

(i) the amount or kind of shares or other securities, eligible interests, obligations, rights to acquire shares, other securities or eligible interests, cash, or other property to be received under the plan by the shareholders, members or interest holders of the acquired entity; or

(ii) any of the other terms or conditions of the plan if the change would adversely affect such shareholders, members or interest holders in any material respect.

§ 11.04. Action on a Plan of Merger or Share Exchange

In the case of a domestic corporation that is a party to a merger or the acquired entity in a share exchange, the plan of merger or share exchange shall be adopted in the following manner:

(a) The plan of merger or share exchange shall first be adopted by the board of directors.

(b) Except as provided in subsections (h), (j) and (l) and in § 11.05, the plan of merger or share exchange shall then be approved by the shareholders. In submitting the plan of merger or share exchange to the shareholders for approval, the board of directors shall recommend that the shareholders approve the plan or, in the case of an offer referred to in subsection (j)(2), that the shareholders tender their shares to the offeror in response to the offer, unless (i) the board of directors makes a determination that because of conflicts of interest or other special circumstances it should not make such a recommendation or (ii) § 8.26 applies. If either (i) or (ii) applies, the board shall inform the shareholders of the basis for its so proceeding.

(c) The board of directors may set conditions for the approval of the plan of merger or share exchange by the shareholders or the effectiveness of the plan of merger or share exchange.

(d) If the plan of merger or share exchange is required to be approved by the shareholders, and if the approval is to be given at a meeting, the corporation shall notify each shareholder, regardless of whether entitled to vote, of the meeting of shareholders at which the plan is to be submitted for approval. The notice must state that the purpose, or one of the purposes, of the meeting is to consider the plan and must contain or be accompanied by a copy or summary of the plan. If the corporation is to be merged into an existing foreign or domestic corporation or eligible entity, the notice must also include or be accompanied by a copy or summary of the articles of incorporation and bylaws or the organic rules of that corporation or eligible entity. If the corporation is to be merged with a domestic or foreign corporation or eligible entity and a new domestic or foreign corporation or eligible entity is to be created pursuant to the merger, the notice must include or be accompanied by a copy or a summary of the articles of incorporation and bylaws or the organic rules of the new corporation or eligible entity.

(e) Unless the articles of incorporation, or the board of directors acting pursuant to subsection (c), require a greater vote or a greater quorum, approval of the plan of merger or share exchange requires the approval of the shareholders at a meeting at which a quorum exists consisting of a majority of the votes entitled to be cast on the plan, and, if any class or series of shares is entitled to vote as a separate group on the plan of merger or share exchange, the approval of each such separate voting group at a meeting at which a quorum of the voting group is present consisting of a majority of the votes entitled to be cast on the merger or share exchange by that voting group.

(f) Subject to subsection (g), separate voting by voting groups is required:

(1) on a plan of merger, by each class or series of shares that:

(i) are to be converted under the plan of merger into shares, other securities, eligible interests, obligations, rights to acquire shares, other securities or eligible interests, cash, other property, or any combination of the foregoing; or

(ii) are entitled to vote as a separate group on a provision in the plan that constitutes a proposed amendment to the articles of incorporation of a surviving corporation that requires action by separate voting groups under § 10.04;

(2) on a plan of share exchange, by each class or series of shares included in the exchange, with each class or series constituting a separate voting group; and

(3) on a plan of merger or share exchange, if the voting group is entitled under the articles of incorporation to vote as a voting group to approve a plan of merger or share exchange, respectively.

(g) The articles of incorporation may expressly limit or eliminate the separate voting rights provided in subsections (f)(1)(i) and (f)(2) as to any class or series of shares, except when the plan of merger or share exchange (i) includes what is or

would be in effect an amendment subject to subsection (f)(1)(ii), and (ii) will not effect a substantive business combination.

(h) Unless the articles of incorporation otherwise provide, approval by the corporation's shareholders of a plan of merger is not required if:

(1) the corporation will survive the merger;

(2) except for amendments permitted by § 10.05, its articles of incorporation will not be changed;

(3) each shareholder of the corporation whose shares were outstanding immediately before the effective date of the merger or share exchange will hold the same number of shares, with identical preferences, rights and limitations, immediately after the effective date of the merger; and

(4) the issuance in the merger of shares or other securities convertible into or rights exercisable for shares does not require a vote under § 6.21(f).

(i) If as a result of a merger or share exchange one or more shareholders of a domestic corporation would become subject to new interest holder liability, approval of the plan of merger or share exchange requires the signing in connection with the transaction, by each such shareholder, of a separate written consent to become subject to such new interest holder liability, unless in the case of a shareholder that already has interest holder liability with respect to such domestic corporation, (i) the new interest holder liability is with respect to a domestic or foreign corporation (which may be a different or the same domestic corporation in which the person is a shareholder), and (ii) the terms and conditions of the new interest holder liability are substantially identical to those of the existing interest holder liability (other than for changes that eliminate or reduce such interest holder liability).

(j) Unless the articles of incorporation otherwise provide, approval by the shareholders of a plan of merger or share exchange is not required if:

(1) the plan of merger or share exchange expressly (i) permits or requires the merger or share exchange to be effected under this subsection and (ii) provides that, if the merger or share exchange is to be effected under this subsection, the merger or share exchange will be effected as soon as practicable following the satisfaction of the requirement set forth in subsection (j)(6);

(2) another party to the merger, the acquiring entity in the share exchange, or a parent of another party to the merger or the acquiring entity in the share exchange, makes an offer to purchase, on the terms provided in the plan of merger or share exchange, any and all of the outstanding shares of the corporation that, absent this subsection, would be entitled to vote on the plan of merger or share exchange, except that the offer may exclude shares of the corporation that are owned at the commencement of the offer by the corporation, the offeror, or any parent of the offeror, or by any wholly owned subsidiary of any of the foregoing;

(3) the offer discloses that the plan of merger or share exchange provides that the merger or share exchange will be effected as soon as practicable following the satisfaction of the requirement set forth in subsection (j)(6) and that the shares of the corporation that are not tendered in response to the offer will be treated as set forth in subsection (j)(8);

(4) the offer remains open for at least 10 days;

(5) the offeror purchases all shares properly tendered in response to the offer and not properly withdrawn;

(6) the shares listed below are collectively entitled to cast at least the minimum number of votes on the merger or share exchange that, absent this subsection, would be required by this chapter and by the articles of incorporation for the approval of the merger or share exchange by the shareholders and by any other voting group entitled to vote on the merger or share exchange at a meeting at which all shares entitled to vote on the approval were present and voted:

> **(i)** shares purchased by the offeror in accordance with the offer;

> **(ii)** shares otherwise owned by the offeror or by any parent of the offeror or any wholly owned subsidiary of any of the foregoing; and

> **(iii)** shares subject to an agreement that they are to be transferred, contributed or delivered to the offeror, any parent of the offeror, or any wholly owned subsidiary of any of the foregoing in exchange for shares or eligible interests in such offeror, parent or subsidiary;

(7) the offeror or a wholly owned subsidiary of the offeror merges with or into, or effects a share exchange in which it acquires shares of, the corporation; and

(8) each outstanding share of each class or series of shares of the corporation that the offeror is offering to purchase in accordance with the offer, and that is not purchased in accordance with the offer, is to be converted in the merger into, or into the right to receive, or is to be exchanged in the share exchange for, or for the right to receive, the same amount and kind of securities, eligible interests, obligations, rights, cash, or other property to be paid or exchanged in accordance with the offer for each share of that class or series of shares that is tendered in response to the offer, except that shares of the corporation that are owned by the corporation or that are described in clause (ii) or (iii) of subsection (j)(6) need not be converted into or exchanged for the consideration described in this subsection (j)(8).

(k) As used in subsection (j):

(1) "offer" means the offer referred to in subsection (j)(2);

(2) "offeror" means the person making the offer;

(3) "parent" of an entity means a person that owns, directly or indirectly (through one or more wholly owned subsidiaries), all of the outstanding shares of or eligible interests in that entity;

(4) shares tendered in response to the offer shall be deemed to have been "purchased" in accordance with the offer at the earliest time as of which (i) the offeror has irrevocably accepted those shares for payment and (ii) either (A) in the case of shares represented by certificates, the offeror, or the offeror's designated depository or other agent, has physically received the certificates representing those shares or (B) in the case of shares without certificates, those shares have been transferred into the account of the offeror or its designated depository or other agent, or an agent's message relating to those shares has been received by the offeror or its designated depository or other agent; and

(5) "wholly owned subsidiary" of a person means an entity of or in which that person owns, directly or indirectly (through one or more wholly owned subsidiaries), all of the outstanding shares or eligible interests.

(l) Unless the articles of incorporation otherwise provide,

(1) approval of a plan of share exchange by the shareholders of a domestic corporation is not required if the corporation is the acquiring entity in the share exchange; and

(2) shares not to be exchanged under the plan of share exchange are not entitled to vote on the plan.

§ 11.05. Merger Between Parent and Subsidiary or Between Subsidiaries

(a) A domestic or foreign parent entity that owns shares of a domestic corporation which carry at least 90% of the voting power of each class and series of the outstanding shares of the subsidiary that has voting power may (i) merge the subsidiary into itself (if it is a domestic or foreign corporation or eligible entity) or into another domestic or foreign corporation or eligible entity in which the parent entity owns at least 90% of the voting power

of each class and series of the outstanding shares or eligible interests which have voting power, or (ii) merge itself (if it is a domestic or foreign corporation or eligible entity) into such subsidiary, in either case without the approval of the board of directors or shareholders of the subsidiary, unless the articles of incorporation or organic rules of the parent entity or the articles of incorporation of the subsidiary corporation otherwise provide. Section 11.04(i) applies to a merger under this section. The articles of merger relating to a merger under this section do not need to be signed by the subsidiary.

(b) A parent entity shall, within 10 days after the effective date of a merger approved under subsection (a), notify each of the subsidiary's shareholders that the merger has become effective.

(c) Except as provided in subsections (a) and (b), a merger between a parent entity and a domestic subsidiary corporation shall be governed by the provisions of chapter 11 applicable to mergers generally.

§ 11.06. Articles of Merger or Share Exchange

(a) After (i) a plan of merger has been adopted and approved as required by this Act, or (ii) if the merger is being effected under § 11.02(a)(2), the merger has been approved as required by the organic law governing the parties to the merger, then articles of merger shall be signed by each party to the merger except as provided in § 11.05(a). The articles must set forth:

(1) the name, jurisdiction of formation, and type of entity of each party to the merger;

(2) the name, jurisdiction of formation, and type of entity of the survivor;

(3) if the survivor of the merger is a domestic corporation and its articles of incorporation are amended, or if a new domestic corporation is created as a result of the merger:

(i) the amendments to the survivor's articles of incorporation; or

(ii) the articles of incorporation of the new corporation;

(4) if the survivor of the merger is a domestic eligible entity and its public organic record is amended, or if a new domestic eligible entity is created as a result of the merger:

    (i) the amendments to the public organic record of the survivor; or

    (ii) the public organic record of the new eligible entity;

(5) if the plan of merger required approval by the shareholders of a domestic corporation that is a party to the merger, a statement that the plan was duly approved by the shareholders and, if voting by any separate voting group was required, by each such separate voting group, in the manner required by this Act and the articles of incorporation;

(6) if the plan of merger or share exchange did not require approval by the shareholders of a domestic corporation that is a party to the merger, a statement to that effect;

(7) as to each foreign corporation that is a party to the merger, a statement that the participation of the foreign corporation was duly authorized as required by its organic law;

(8) as to each domestic or foreign eligible entity that is a party to the merger, a statement that the merger was approved in accordance with its organic law or § 11.02(c); and

(9) if the survivor is created by the merger and is a domestic limited liability partnership, the filing required to become a limited liability partnership, as an attachment.

(b) After a plan of share exchange in which the acquired entity is a domestic corporation or eligible entity has been adopted and approved as required by this Act, articles of share exchange shall be signed by the acquired entity and the acquiring entity. The articles shall set forth:

(1) the name of the acquired entity;

(2) the name, jurisdiction of formation, and type of entity of the domestic or foreign corporation or eligible entity that is the acquiring entity; and

(3) a statement that the plan of share exchange was duly approved by the acquired entity by:

    (i) the required vote or consent of each class or series of shares or eligible interests included in the exchange; and

    (ii) the required vote or consent of each other class or series of shares or eligible interests entitled to vote on approval of the exchange by the articles of incorporation or organic rules of the acquired entity or § 11.03(c).

(c) In addition to the requirements of subsection (a) or (b), articles of merger or share exchange may contain any other provision not prohibited by law.

(d) The articles of merger or share exchange shall be delivered to the secretary of state for filing and, subject to subsection (e), the merger or share exchange shall take effect at the effective date determined in accordance with § 1.23.

(e) With respect to a merger in which one or more foreign entities is a party or a foreign entity created by the merger is the survivor, the merger itself shall become effective at the later of:

(1) when all documents required to be filed in foreign jurisdictions to effect the merger have become effective, or

(2) when the articles of merger take effect.

(f) Articles of merger filed under this section may be combined with any filing required under the organic law governing any domestic eligible entity involved in the transaction if the combined filing satisfies the requirements of both this section and the other organic law.

§ 11.07. Effect of Merger or Share Exchange

(a) When a merger becomes effective:

(1) the domestic or foreign corporation or eligible entity that is designated in the plan of merger as the survivor continues or comes into existence, as the case may be;

(2) the separate existence of every domestic or foreign corporation or eligible entity that is a party to the merger, other than the survivor, ceases;

(3) all property owned by, and every contract right possessed by, each domestic or foreign corporation or eligible entity that is a party to the merger, other than the survivor, are the property and contract rights of the survivor without transfer, reversion or impairment;

(4) all debts, obligations and other liabilities of each domestic or foreign corporation or eligible entity that is a party to the merger, other than the survivor, are debts, obligations or liabilities of the survivor;

(5) the name of the survivor may, but need not be, substituted in any pending proceeding for the name of any party to the merger whose separate existence ceased in the merger;

(6) if the survivor is a domestic entity, the articles of incorporation and bylaws or the organic rules of the survivor are amended to the extent provided in the plan of merger;

(7) the articles of incorporation and bylaws or the organic rules of a survivor that is a domestic entity and is created by the merger become effective;

(8) the shares of each domestic or foreign corporation that is a party to the merger, and the eligible interests in an eligible entity that is a party to a merger, that are to be converted in accordance with the terms of the merger into shares or other securities, eligible interests, obligations, rights to acquire shares, other securities, or eligible interests, cash, other property, or any combination of the foregoing, are converted, and the former holders of such shares or eligible interests are entitled only to the rights provided to them by those terms or to any rights they may have under chapter 13 or the organic law governing the eligible entity or foreign corporation;

(9) except as provided by law or the terms of the merger, all the rights, privileges, franchises, and immunities of each entity that is a party to the merger, other than the survivor, are the rights, privileges, franchises, and immunities of the survivor; and

(10) if the survivor exists before the merger:

(i) all the property and contract rights of the survivor remain its property and contract rights without transfer, reversion, or impairment;

(ii) the survivor remains subject to all its debts, obligations, and other liabilities; and

(iii) except as provided by law or the plan of merger, the survivor continues to hold all of its rights, privileges, franchises, and immunities.

(b) When a share exchange becomes effective, the shares or eligible interests in the acquired entity that are to be exchanged for shares or other securities, eligible interests, obligations, rights to acquire shares, other securities or eligible interests, cash, other property, or any combination of the foregoing, are entitled only to the rights provided to them in the plan of share exchange or to any rights they may have under chapter 13 or under the organic law governing the acquired entity.

(c) Except as otherwise provided in the articles of incorporation of a domestic corporation or the organic law governing or organic rules of a foreign corporation or a domestic or foreign eligible entity, the effect of a merger or share exchange on interest holder liability is as follows:

(1) A person who becomes subject to new interest holder liability in respect of an entity as a result of a merger or share exchange shall have that new interest holder liability only in respect of interest holder liabilities that arise after the merger or share exchange becomes effective.

(2) If a person had interest holder liability with respect to a party to the merger or the acquired entity before the merger or share exchange becomes effective with respect to shares or eligible interests of such party or acquired entity which were (i) exchanged in the merger or share exchange, (ii) were cancelled in the merger or (iii) the terms and conditions of which relating to interest holder liability were amended pursuant to the merger:

(i) The merger or share exchange does not discharge that prior interest holder liability with respect to any interest holder liabilities that arose before the merger or share exchange becomes effective.

(ii) The provisions of the organic law governing any entity for which the person had that prior interest holder liability shall continue to apply to the collection or discharge of any interest holder liabilities preserved by subsection (c)(2)(i), as if the merger or share exchange had not occurred.

(iii) The person shall have such rights of contribution from other persons as are provided by the organic law governing the entity for which the person had that prior interest holder liability with respect to any interest holder liabilities preserved by subsection (c)(2)(i), as if the merger or share exchange had not occurred.

(iv) The person shall not, by reason of such prior interest holder liability, have interest holder liability with respect to any interest holder liabilities that arise after the merger or share exchange becomes effective.

(3) If a person has interest holder liability both before and after a merger becomes effective with unchanged terms and conditions with respect to the entity that is the survivor by reason of owning the same shares or eligible interests before and after the merger becomes effective, the merger has no effect on such interest holder liability.

(4) A share exchange has no effect on interest holder liability related to shares or eligible interests of the acquired entity that were not exchanged in the share exchange.

(d) Upon a merger becoming effective, a foreign corporation, or a foreign eligible entity, that is the survivor of the merger is deemed to:

(1) appoint the secretary of state as its agent for service of process in a proceeding to enforce the rights of shareholders of each domestic corporation that is a party to the merger who exercise appraisal rights; and

(2) agree that it will promptly pay the amount, if any, to which such shareholders are entitled under chapter 13.

(e) Except as provided in the organic law governing a party to a merger or in its articles of incorporation or organic rules, the merger does not give rise to any rights that an interest holder, governor, or third party would have upon a dissolution, liquidation, or winding up of that party. The merger does not require a party to the merger to wind up its affairs and does not constitute or cause its dissolution or termination.

(f) Property held for a charitable purpose under the law of this state by a domestic or foreign corporation or eligible entity immediately before a merger becomes effective may not, as a result of the transaction, be diverted from the objects for which it was donated, granted, devised, or otherwise transferred except and to the extent permitted by or pursuant to the laws of this state addressing cy près or dealing with nondiversion of charitable assets.

(g) A bequest, devise, gift, grant, or promise contained in a will or other instrument of donation, subscription, or conveyance which is made to an entity that is a party to a merger that is not the survivor and which takes effect or remains payable after the merger inures to the survivor.

(h) A trust obligation that would govern property if transferred to a nonsurviving entity applies to property that is transferred to the survivor after a merger becomes effective.

§ 11.08. Abandonment of a Merger or Share Exchange

(a) After a plan of merger or share exchange has been adopted and approved as required by this chapter, and before articles of merger or share exchange have become effective, the plan may be abandoned by a domestic business corporation that is a party to the plan without action by its shareholders in accordance with any procedures set forth in the plan of merger or share exchange or, if no such procedures are set forth in the plan, in the manner determined by the board of directors.

(b) If a merger or share exchange is abandoned under subsection (a) after articles of merger or share exchange have been delivered to the secretary of state for filing but before the merger or share exchange has become effective, a statement of abandonment signed by all the parties that signed the articles of merger or share exchange shall be delivered to the secretary of state for filing before the articles of merger or share exchange become effective. The statement shall take effect on filing and the merger or share exchange shall be deemed abandoned and shall not become effective. The statement of abandonment must contain:

(1) the name of each party to the merger or the names of the acquiring and acquired entities in a share exchange;

(2) the date on which the articles of merger or share exchange were filed by the secretary of state; and

(3) a statement that the merger or share exchange has been abandoned in accordance with this section.

Chapter 12. Disposition of Assets

§ 12.01. Disposition of Assets Not Requiring Shareholder Approval

No approval of the shareholders is required, unless the articles of incorporation otherwise provide:

(a) to sell, lease, exchange, or otherwise dispose of any or all of the corporation's assets in the usual and regular course of business;

(b) to mortgage, pledge, dedicate to the repayment of indebtedness (whether with or without recourse), or otherwise encumber any or all of the corporation's assets, regardless of whether in the usual and regular course of business;

(c) to transfer any or all of the corporation's assets to one or more domestic or foreign corporations or other entities all of the shares or interests of which are owned by the corporation; or

(d) to distribute assets pro rata to the holders of one or more classes or series of the corporation's shares.

§ 12.02. Shareholder Approval of Certain Dispositions

(a) A sale, lease, exchange, or other disposition of assets, other than a disposition described in § 12.01, requires approval of the corporation's shareholders if the disposition would leave the corporation without a significant continuing business activity. A corporation will conclusively be deemed to have retained a significant continuing business activity if it retains a business activity that represented, for the corporation and its subsidiaries on a consolidated basis, at least (i) 25% of total assets at the end of the most recently completed fiscal year, and (ii) either 25% of either income from continuing operations before taxes or 25% of revenues from continuing operations, in each case for the most recently completed fiscal year.

(b) To obtain the approval of the shareholders under subsection (a) the board of directors shall first adopt a resolution authorizing the disposition. The disposition shall then be approved by the shareholders. In submitting the disposition to the shareholders for approval, the board of directors shall recommend that the shareholders approve the disposition, unless (i) the board of directors makes a determination that because of conflicts of interest or other special circumstances it should not make such a recommendation, or (ii) § 8.26 applies. If either (i) or (ii) applies, the board shall inform the shareholders of the basis for its so proceeding.

(c) The board of directors may set conditions for the approval by the shareholders of a disposition or the effectiveness of the disposition.

(d) If a disposition is required to be approved by the shareholders under subsection (a), and if the approval is to be given at a meeting, the corporation shall notify each shareholder, regardless of whether entitled to vote, of the meeting of shareholders at which the disposition is to be submitted for approval. The notice must state that the purpose, or one of the purposes, of the meeting is to consider the disposition and must contain a description of the disposition, including the terms and conditions of the disposition and the consideration to be received by the corporation.

(e) Unless the articles of incorporation or the board of directors acting pursuant to subsection (c) require a greater vote or a greater quorum, the approval of a disposition by the shareholders shall require the approval of the shareholders at a meeting at which a quorum exists consisting of a majority of the votes entitled to be cast on the disposition.

(f) After a disposition has been approved by the shareholders under this chapter, and at any time before the disposition has been consummated, it may be abandoned by the corporation without action by the shareholders, subject to any contractual rights of other parties to the disposition.

(g) A disposition of assets in the course of dissolution under chapter 14 is not governed by this section.

(h) The assets of a direct or indirect consolidated subsidiary shall be deemed to be the assets of the parent corporation for the purposes of this section.

Chapter 13. Appraisal Rights

Subchapter A. Right to Appraisal and Payment for Shares

§ 13.01. Definitions

In this chapter:

"Affiliate" means a person that directly or indirectly through one or more intermediaries controls, is controlled by, or is under common control with another person or is a senior executive of such person. For purposes of § 13.02(b)(4), a person is deemed to be an affiliate of its senior executives.

"Corporation" means the domestic corporation that is the issuer of the shares held by a shareholder demanding appraisal and, for matters covered in sections 13.22 through 13.31, includes the survivor of a merger.

"Fair value" means the value of the corporation's shares determined:

(i) immediately before the effectiveness of the corporate action to which the shareholder objects;

(ii) using customary and current valuation concepts and techniques generally employed for similar businesses in the context of the transaction requiring appraisal; and

(iii) without discounting for lack of marketability or minority status except, if appropriate, for amendments to the articles of incorporation pursuant to § 13.02(a)(4).

"Interest" means interest from the date the corporate action becomes effective until the date of payment, at the rate of interest on judgments in this state on the effective date of the corporate action.

"Interested transaction" means a corporate action described in § 13.02(a), other than a merger pursuant to § 11.05, involving an interested person in which any of the shares or assets of the corporation are being acquired or converted. As used in this definition:

(i) "Interested person" means a person, or an affiliate of a person, who at any time during the one-year period immediately preceding approval by the board of directors of the corporate action:

(A) was the beneficial owner of 20% or more of the voting power of the corporation, other than as owner of excluded shares;

(B) had the power, contractually or otherwise, other than as owner of excluded shares, to cause the appointment or election of 25% or more of the directors to the board of directors of the corporation; or

(C) was a senior executive or director of the corporation or a senior executive of any affiliate of the corporation, and that senior executive or director will receive, as a result of the corporate action, a financial benefit not generally available to other shareholders as such, other than:

(I) employment, consulting, retirement, or similar benefits established separately and not as part of or in contemplation of the corporate action;

(II) employment, consulting, retirement, or similar benefits established in contemplation of, or as part of, the corporate action that are not more favorable than those existing before the corporate action or, if more favorable, that have been approved on behalf of the corporation in the same manner as is provided in § 8.62; or

(III) in the case of a director of the corporation who will, in the corporate action, become a director or governor of the acquiror or any of its affiliates, rights and benefits as a director or governor that are provided on the same basis as those afforded by the acquiror generally to other directors or governors of such entity or such affiliate.

(ii) "Beneficial owner" means any person who, directly or indirectly, through any contract, arrangement, or understanding, other than a revocable proxy, has or shares the power to vote, or to direct the voting of, shares; except that a member of a national securities exchange is not deemed to be a beneficial owner of securities held directly or indirectly by it on behalf of another person if the member is precluded by the rules of the exchange from voting without instruction on contested matters or matters that may affect substantially the rights or privileges of the holders of the securities to be voted. When two or more persons agree to act together for the purpose of voting their shares of the corporation, each member of the group formed thereby is deemed to have acquired beneficial ownership, as of the date of the agreement, of all shares having voting power of the corporation beneficially owned by any member of the group.

(iii) "Excluded shares" means shares acquired pursuant to an offer for all shares having voting power if the offer was made within one year before the corporate action for consideration of the same kind and of a value equal to or less than that paid in connection with the corporate action.

"Preferred shares" means a class or series of shares whose holders have preference over any other class or series of shares with respect to distributions.

"Senior executive" means the chief executive officer, chief operating officer, chief financial officer, and any individual in charge of a principal business unit or function.

"Shareholder" means a record shareholder, a beneficial shareholder, and a voting trust beneficial owner.

§ 13.02. Right to Appraisal

(a) A shareholder is entitled to appraisal rights, and to obtain payment of the fair value of that shareholder's shares, in the event of any of the following corporate actions:

(1) consummation of a merger to which the corporation is a party (i) if shareholder approval is required for the merger by § 11.04, or would be required but for the provisions of § 11.04(j), except that appraisal rights shall not be available to any shareholder of the corporation with respect to shares of any class or series that remain outstanding after consummation of the merger, or (ii) if the corporation is a subsidiary and the merger is governed by § 11.05;

(2) consummation of a share exchange to which the corporation is a party the shares of which will be acquired, except that appraisal rights shall not be available to any shareholder of the corporation with respect to any class or series of shares of the corporation that is not acquired in the share exchange;

(3) consummation of a disposition of assets pursuant to § 12.02 if the shareholder is entitled to vote on the disposition, except that appraisal rights shall not be available to any shareholder of the corporation with respect to shares of any class or series if (i) under the terms of the corporate action approved by the shareholders there is to be distributed to shareholders in cash the corporation's net assets, in excess of a reasonable amount reserved to meet claims of the type described in sections 14.06 and 14.07, (A) within one year after the shareholders' approval of the action and (B) in accordance with their respective interests determined at the time of distribution, and (ii) the disposition of assets is not an interested transaction;

(4) an amendment of the articles of incorporation with respect to a class or series of shares that reduces the number of shares of a class or series owned by the shareholder to a fraction of a share if the corporation has the obligation or right to repurchase the fractional share so created;

(5) any other merger, share exchange, disposition of assets or amendment to the articles of incorporation, in each case to the extent provided by the articles of incorporation, bylaws or a resolution of the board of directors;

(6) consummation of a domestication pursuant to § 9.20 if the shareholder does not receive shares in the foreign corporation resulting from the domestication that have terms as favorable to the shareholder in all material respects, and represent at least the same percentage interest of the total voting rights of the outstanding shares of the foreign corporation, as the shares held by the shareholder before the domestication;

(7) consummation of a conversion of the corporation to a nonprofit corporation pursuant to § 9.30; or

(8) consummation of a conversion of the corporation to an unincorporated entity pursuant to § 9.30.

(b) Notwithstanding subsection (a), the availability of appraisal rights under subsections (a)(1), (2), (3), (4), (6) and (8) shall be limited in accordance with the following provisions:

(1) Appraisal rights shall not be available for the holders of shares of any class or series of shares which is:

(i) a covered security under § 18(b)(1)(A) or (B) of the Securities Act of 1933;

(ii) traded in an organized market and has at least 2,000 shareholders and a market value of at least $20 million (exclusive of the value of such shares held by the corporation's subsidiaries, senior executives and directors and by any beneficial shareholder and any voting trust beneficial owner owning more than 10% of such shares); or

(iii) issued by an open end management investment company registered with the Securities and Exchange Commission under the Investment Company Act of 1940 and which may be redeemed at the option of the holder at net asset value.

(2) The applicability of subsection (b)(1) shall be determined as of:

(i) the record date fixed to determine the shareholders entitled to receive notice of the meeting of shareholders to act upon the corporate action requiring appraisal rights or, in the case of an offer made pursuant to § 11.04(j), the date of such offer; or

(ii) if there is no meeting of shareholders and no offer made pursuant to § 11.04(j), the day before the consummation of the corporate action or effective date of the amendment of the articles of incorporation, as applicable.

(3) Subsection (b)(1) shall not be applicable and appraisal rights shall be available pursuant to subsection (a) for the holders of any class or series of shares (i) who are required by the terms of the corporate action requiring appraisal rights to accept for such shares anything other than cash or shares of any class or any series of shares of any corporation, or any other proprietary interest of any other entity, that satisfies the standards set forth in subsection (b)(1) at the time the corporate action becomes effective, or (ii) in the case of the consummation of a disposition of assets pursuant to § 12.02, unless the cash, shares, or proprietary interests received in the disposition are, under the terms of the corporate action approved by the shareholders, to be distributed to the shareholders, as part of a distribution to shareholders of the net assets of the corporation in excess of a reasonable amount to meet claims of the type described in sections 14.06 and 14.07, (A) within one year after the shareholders' approval of the action, and (B) in accordance with their respective interests determined at the time of the distribution.

(4) Subsection (b)(1) shall not be applicable and appraisal rights shall be available pursuant to subsection (a) for the holders of any class or series of shares where the corporate action is an interested transaction.

(c) Notwithstanding any other provision of § 13.02, the articles of incorporation as originally filed or any amendment to the articles of incorporation may limit or eliminate appraisal rights for any class or series of preferred shares, except that (i) no such limitation or elimination shall be effective if the class or series does not have the right to vote separately as a voting group (alone or as part of a group) on the action or if the action is a conversion under § 9.30, or a merger having a similar effect as a conversion in which the converted entity is an eligible entity, and (ii) any such limitation or elimination contained in an amendment to the articles of incorporation that limits or eliminates appraisal rights for any of such shares that are outstanding immediately before the effective date of such amendment or that the corporation is or may be required to issue or sell thereafter pursuant to any conversion, exchange or other right existing immediately before the effective date of such amendment shall not apply to any corporate action that becomes effective within one year after the effective date of such amendment if such action would otherwise afford appraisal rights.

§ 13.03. Assertion of Rights by Nominees and Beneficial Shareholders

(a) A record shareholder may assert appraisal rights as to fewer than all the shares registered in the record shareholder's name but owned by a beneficial shareholder or a voting trust beneficial owner only if the record shareholder objects with respect to all shares of a class or series owned by the beneficial shareholder or the voting trust beneficial owner and notifies the corporation in writing of the name and address of each beneficial shareholder or voting trust beneficial owner on whose behalf appraisal rights are being asserted. The rights of a record shareholder who asserts appraisal rights for only part of the shares held of record in the record shareholder's name under this subsection shall be determined as if the shares as to which the record shareholder objects and the record shareholder's other shares were registered in the names of different record shareholders.

(b) A beneficial shareholder and a voting trust beneficial owner may assert appraisal rights as to shares of any class or series held on behalf of the shareholder only if such shareholder:

(1) submits to the corporation the record shareholder's written consent to the assertion of such rights no later than the date referred to in § 13.22(b)(2)(ii); and

(2) does so with respect to all shares of the class or series that are beneficially owned by the beneficial shareholder or the voting trust beneficial owner.

Subchapter B. Procedure for Exercise of Appraisal Rights

§ 13.20. Notice of Appraisal Rights

(a) Where any corporate action specified in § 13.02(a) is to be submitted to a vote at a shareholders' meeting, the meeting notice (or where no approval of such action is required pursuant to § 11.04(j), the offer made pursuant to § 11.04(j)), must state that the corporation has concluded that appraisal rights are, are not or may be available under this chapter. If the corporation concludes that appraisal rights are or may be available, a copy of this chapter must accompany the meeting notice or offer sent to those record shareholders entitled to exercise appraisal rights.

(b) In a merger pursuant to § 11.05, the parent entity shall notify in writing all record shareholders of the subsidiary who are entitled to assert appraisal rights that the corporate action became effective. Such notice shall be sent within 10 days after the corporate action became effective and include the materials described in § 13.22.

(c) Where any corporate action specified in § 13.02(a) is to be approved by written consent of the shareholders pursuant to § 7.04:

> **(1)** written notice that appraisal rights are, are not or may be available shall be sent to each record shareholder from whom a consent is solicited at the time consent of such shareholder is first solicited and, if the corporation has concluded that appraisal rights are or may be available, the notice must be accompanied by a copy of this chapter; and

> **(2)** written notice that appraisal rights are, are not or may be available must be delivered together with the notice to nonconsenting and nonvoting shareholders required by sections 7.04(e) and (f), may include the materials described in § 13.22 and, if the corporation has concluded that appraisal rights are or may be available, must be accompanied by a copy of this chapter.

(d) Where corporate action described in § 13.02(a) is proposed, or a merger pursuant to § 11.05 is effected, the notice referred to in subsection (a) or (c), if the corporation concludes that appraisal rights are or may be available, and in subsection (b) must be accompanied by:

> **(1)** financial statements of the corporation that issued the shares that may be subject to appraisal, consisting of a balance sheet as of the end of a fiscal year ending not more than 16 months before the date of the notice, an income statement for that year, and a cash flow statement for that year; provided that, if such financial statements are not reasonably available, the corporation shall provide reasonably equivalent financial information; and

> **(2)** the latest interim financial statements of such corporation, if any.

(e) The right to receive the information described in subsection (d) may be waived in writing by a shareholder before or after the corporate action.

§ 13.21. Notice of Intent to Demand Payment and Consequences of Voting or Consenting

(a) If a corporate action specified in § 13.02(a) is submitted to a vote at a shareholders' meeting, a shareholder who wishes to assert appraisal rights with respect to any class or series of shares:

> **(1)** shall deliver to the corporation, before the vote is taken, written notice of the shareholder's intent to demand payment if the proposed action is effectuated; and

> **(2)** shall not vote, or cause or permit to be voted, any shares of such class or series in favor of the proposed action.

(b) If a corporate action specified in § 13.02(a) is to be approved by written consent, a shareholder who wishes to assert appraisal rights with respect to any class or series of shares shall not sign a consent in favor of the proposed action with respect to that class or series of shares.

(c) If a corporate action specified in § 13.02(a) does not require shareholder approval pursuant to § 11.04(j), a shareholder who wishes to assert appraisal rights with respect to any class or series of shares (i) shall deliver to the corporation before the shares are purchased pursuant to the offer written notice of the shareholder's intent to demand payment if the proposed action is effected; and (ii) shall not tender, or cause or permit to be tendered, any shares of such class or series in response to such offer.

(d) A shareholder who fails to satisfy the requirements of subsection (a), (b) or (c) is not entitled to payment under this chapter.

§ 13.22. Appraisal Notice and Form

(a) If a corporate action requiring appraisal rights under § 13.02(a) becomes effective, the corporation shall deliver a written appraisal notice and form required by subsection (b) to all shareholders who satisfy the requirements of sections 13.21(a), (b) or (c). In the case of a merger under § 11.05, the parent shall deliver an appraisal notice and form to all record shareholders who may be entitled to assert appraisal rights.

(b) The appraisal notice shall be delivered no earlier than the date the corporate action specified in § 13.02(a) became effective, and no later than 10 days after such date, and must:

(1) supply a form that (i) specifies the first date of any announcement to shareholders made before the date the corporate action became effective of the principal terms of the proposed corporate action, and (ii) if such announcement was made, requires the shareholder asserting appraisal rights to certify whether beneficial ownership of those shares for which appraisal rights are asserted was acquired before that date, and (iii) requires the shareholder asserting appraisal rights to certify that such shareholder did not vote for or consent to the transaction as to the class or series of shares for which appraisal is sought;

(2) state:

(i) where the form shall be sent and where certificates for certificated shares shall be deposited and the date by which those certificates must be deposited, which date may not be earlier than the date by which the corporation must receive the required form under subsection (b)(2)(ii);

(ii) a date by which the corporation shall receive the form, which date may not be fewer than 40 nor more than 60 days after the date the subsection (a) appraisal notice is sent, and state that the shareholder shall have waived the right to demand appraisal with respect to the shares unless the form is received by the corporation by such specified date;

(iii) the corporation's estimate of the fair value of the shares;

(iv) that, if requested in writing, the corporation will provide, to the shareholder so requesting, within 10 days after the date specified in subsection (b)(2)(ii) the number of shareholders who return the forms by the specified date and the total number of shares owned by them; and

(v) the date by which the notice to withdraw under § 13.23 shall be received, which date shall be within 20 days after the date specified in subsection (b)(2)(ii); and

(3) be accompanied by a copy of this chapter.

§ 13.23. Perfection of Rights; Right to Withdraw

(a) A shareholder who receives notice pursuant to § 13.22 and who wishes to exercise appraisal rights shall sign and return the form sent by the corporation and, in the case of certificated shares, deposit the shareholder's certificates in accordance with the terms of the notice by the date referred to in the notice pursuant to § 13.22(b)(2)(ii). In addition, if applicable, the shareholder shall certify on the form whether the beneficial owner of such shares acquired beneficial ownership of the shares before the date required to be set forth in the notice pursuant to § 13.22(b)(1)(i). If a shareholder fails to make this certification, the corporation may elect to treat the shareholder's shares as after-acquired shares under § 13.25. Once a shareholder deposits that shareholder's certificates or, in the case of uncertificated shares, returns the signed forms, that shareholder loses all rights as a shareholder, unless the shareholder withdraws pursuant to subsection (b).

(b) A shareholder who has complied with subsection (a) may nevertheless decline to exercise appraisal rights and withdraw from the appraisal process by so notifying the corporation in writing by the date set forth in the appraisal notice pursuant to § 13.22(b)(2)(v). A shareholder who fails to so withdraw from the appraisal process may not thereafter withdraw without the corporation's written consent.

(c) A shareholder who does not sign and return the form and, in the case of certificated shares, deposit that shareholder's share certificates where required, each by the date set forth in the notice described in § 13.22(b), shall not be entitled to payment under this chapter.

§ 13.24. Payment

(a) Except as provided in § 13.25, within 30 days after the form required by § 13.22(b)(2)(ii) is due, the corporation shall pay in cash to those shareholders who complied with § 13.23(a) the amount the corporation estimates to be the fair value of their shares, plus interest.

(b) The payment to each shareholder pursuant to subsection (a) must be accompanied by:

(1) (i) financial statements of the corporation that issued the shares to be appraised, consisting of a balance sheet as of the end of a fiscal year ending not more than 16 months before the date of payment, an income statement for that year, and a cash flow statement for that year; provided that, if such annual financial statements are not reasonably available, the corporation shall provide reasonably equivalent financial information, and (ii) the latest interim financial statements of such corporation, if any;

(2) a statement of the corporation's estimate of the fair value of the shares, which estimate shall equal or exceed the corporation's estimate given pursuant to section 13.22(b)(2)(iii); and

(3) a statement that shareholders described in subsection (a) have the right to demand further payment under § 13.26 and that if any such shareholder does not do so within the time period specified in § 13.26(b), such shareholder shall be deemed to have accepted the payment under subsection (a) in full satisfaction of the corporation's obligations under this chapter.

§ 13.25. After-Acquired Shares

(a) A corporation may elect to withhold payment required by § 13.24 from any shareholder who was required to, but did not certify that beneficial ownership of all of the shareholder's shares for which appraisal rights are asserted was acquired before the date set forth in the appraisal notice sent pursuant to § 13.22(b)(1).

(b) If the corporation elected to withhold payment under subsection (a), it shall, within 30 days after the form required by § 13.22(b)(2)(ii) is due, notify all shareholders who are described in subsection (a):

(1) of the information required by § 13.24(b)(1);

(2) of the corporation's estimate of fair value pursuant to § 13.24(b)(2);

(3) that they may accept the corporation's estimate of fair value, plus interest, in full satisfaction of their demands or demand appraisal under § 13.26;

(4) that those shareholders who wish to accept such offer shall so notify the corporation of their acceptance of the corporation's offer within 30 days after receiving the offer; and

(5) that those shareholders who do not satisfy the requirements for demanding appraisal under § 13.26 shall be deemed to have accepted the corporation's offer.

(c) Within 10 days after receiving the shareholder's acceptance pursuant to subsection (b)(4), the corporation shall pay in cash the amount it offered under subsection (b)(2) plus interest to each shareholder who agreed to accept the corporation's offer in full satisfaction of the shareholder's demand.

(d) Within 40 days after delivering the notice described in subsection (b), the corporation shall pay in cash the amount it offered to pay under subsection (b)(2) plus interest to each shareholder described in subsection (b)(5).

§ 13.26. Procedure If Shareholder Dissatisfied with Payment or Offer

(a) A shareholder paid pursuant to § 13.24 who is dissatisfied with the amount of the payment shall notify the corporation in writing of that shareholder's estimate of the fair value of the shares and demand payment of that estimate (less any payment under § 13.24) plus interest. A shareholder offered payment under § 13.25 who is dissatisfied with that offer shall reject the offer and demand payment of the shareholder's stated estimate of the fair value of the shares plus interest.

(b) A shareholder who fails to notify the corporation in writing of that shareholder's demand to be paid the shareholder's stated estimate of the fair value plus interest under subsection (a) within 30 days after receiving the corporation's payment or offer of payment under § 13.24 or § 13.25, respectively, waives the right to demand payment under this section and shall be entitled only to the payment made or offered pursuant to those respective sections.

Subchapter C. Judicial Appraisal of Shares

§ 13.30. Court Action

(a) If a shareholder makes demand for payment under § 13.26 which remains unsettled, the corporation shall commence a proceeding within 60 days after receiving the payment demand and petition the court to determine the fair value of the shares and accrued interest. If the corporation does not commence the proceeding within the 60-day period, it shall pay in cash to each shareholder the amount the shareholder demanded pursuant to § 13.26 plus interest.

(b) The corporation shall commence the proceeding in the [name or describe court].

(c) The corporation shall make all shareholders (regardless of whether they are residents of this state) whose demands remain unsettled parties to the proceeding as in an action against their shares, and all parties shall be served with a copy of the petition. Nonresidents may be served by registered or certified mail or by publication as provided by law.

(d) The jurisdiction of the court in which the proceeding is commenced under subsection (b) is plenary and exclusive. The court may appoint one or more persons as appraisers to receive evidence and recommend a decision on the question of fair value. The appraisers shall have the powers described in the order appointing them, or in any amendment to it. The shareholders demanding appraisal rights are entitled to the same discovery rights as parties in other civil proceedings. There shall be no right to a jury trial.

(e) Each shareholder made a party to the proceeding is entitled to judgment (i) for the amount, if any, by which the court finds the fair value of the shareholder's shares exceeds the amount paid by the corporation to the shareholder for such shares, plus interest, or (ii) for the fair value, plus interest, of the shareholder's shares for which the corporation elected to withhold payment under § 13.25.

§ 13.31. Court Costs and Expenses

(a) The court in an appraisal proceeding commenced under § 13.30 shall determine all court costs of the proceeding, including the reasonable compensation and expenses of appraisers appointed by the court. The court shall assess the court costs against the corporation, except that the court may assess court costs against all or some of the shareholders demanding appraisal, in amounts which the court finds equitable, to the extent the court finds such shareholders acted arbitrarily, vexatiously, or not in good faith with respect to the rights provided by this chapter.

(b) The court in an appraisal proceeding may also assess the expenses of the respective parties in amounts the court finds equitable:

> **(1)** against the corporation and in favor of any or all shareholders demanding appraisal if the court finds the corporation did not substantially comply with the requirements of sections 13.20, 13.22, 13.24, or 13.25; or

> **(2)** against either the corporation or a shareholder demanding appraisal, in favor of any other party, if the court finds the party against whom expenses are assessed acted arbitrarily, vexatiously, or not in good faith with respect to the rights provided by this chapter.

(c) If the court in an appraisal proceeding finds that the expenses incurred by any shareholder were of substantial benefit to other shareholders similarly situated and that such expenses should not be assessed against the corporation, the court may direct that such expenses be paid out of the amounts awarded the shareholders who were benefited.

(d) To the extent the corporation fails to make a required payment pursuant to sections 13.24, 13.25, or 13.26, the shareholder may sue directly for the amount owed, and to the extent successful, shall be entitled to recover from the corporation all expenses of the suit.

Subchapter D. Other Remedies

§ 13.40. Other Remedies Limited

(a) The legality of a proposed or completed corporate action described in § 13.02(a) may not be contested, nor may the corporate action be enjoined, set aside or rescinded, in a legal or equitable proceeding by a shareholder after the shareholders have approved the corporate action.

(b) Subsection (a) does not apply to a corporate action that:

    (1) was not authorized and approved in accordance with the applicable provisions of:

        (i) chapter 9, 10, 11, or 12;

        (ii) the articles of incorporation or bylaws; or

        (iii) the resolution of the board of directors authorizing the corporate action;

    (2) was procured as a result of fraud, a material misrepresentation, or an omission of a material fact necessary to make statements made, in light of the circumstances in which they were made, not misleading;

    (3) is an interested transaction, unless it has been recommended by the board of directors in the same manner as is provided in § 8.62 and has been approved by the shareholders in the same manner as is provided in § 8.63 as if the interested transaction were a director's conflicting interest transaction; or

    (4) is approved by less than unanimous consent of the voting shareholders pursuant to § 7.04 if:

        (i) the challenge to the corporate action is brought by a shareholder who did not consent and as to whom notice of the approval of the corporate action was not effective at least 10 days before the corporate action was effected; and

        (ii) the proceeding challenging the corporate action is commenced within 10 days after notice of the approval of the corporate action is effective as to the shareholder bringing the proceeding.

Chapter 14. Dissolution

Subchapter A. Voluntary Dissolution

§ 14.01. Dissolution by Incorporators or Initial Directors

A majority of the incorporators or initial directors of a corporation that has not issued shares or has not commenced business may dissolve the corporation by delivering to the secretary of state for filing articles of dissolution that set forth:

(a) the name of the corporation;

(b) the date of its incorporation;

(c) either (i) that none of the corporation's shares has been issued or (ii) that the corporation has not commenced business;

(d) that no debt of the corporation remains unpaid;

(e) that the net assets of the corporation remaining after winding up have been distributed to the shareholders, if shares were issued; and

(f) that a majority of the incorporators or initial directors authorized the dissolution.

§ 14.02. Dissolution by Board of Directors and Shareholders

(a) The board of directors may propose dissolution for submission to the shareholders by first adopting a resolution authorizing the dissolution.

(b) For a proposal to dissolve to be adopted, it shall then be approved by the shareholders. In submitting the proposal to dissolve to the shareholders for approval, the board of directors shall recommend that the shareholders approve the dissolution, unless (i) the board of directors determines that because of conflict of interest or other special circumstances it should make no recommendation or (ii) § 8.26 applies. If either (i) or (ii) applies, the board shall inform the shareholders of the basis for its so proceeding.

(c) The board of directors may set conditions for the approval of the proposal for dissolution by shareholders or the effectiveness of the dissolution.

(d) If the approval of the shareholders is to be given at a meeting, the corporation shall notify each shareholder, regardless of whether entitled to vote, of the meeting of shareholders at which the dissolution is to be submitted for approval. The notice must state that the purpose, or one of the purposes, of the meeting is to consider dissolving the corporation.

(e) Unless the articles of incorporation or the board of directors acting pursuant to subsection (c) require a greater vote, a greater quorum, or a vote by voting groups, adoption of the proposal to dissolve shall require the approval of the shareholders at a meeting at which a quorum exists consisting of a majority of the votes entitled to be cast on the proposal to dissolve.

§ 14.03. Articles of Dissolution

(a) At any time after dissolution is authorized, the corporation may dissolve by delivering to the secretary of state for filing articles of dissolution setting forth:

(1) the name of the corporation;

(2) the date that dissolution was authorized; and

(3) if dissolution was approved by the shareholders, a statement that the proposal to dissolve was duly approved by the shareholders in the manner required by this Act and by the articles of incorporation.

(b) The articles of dissolution shall take effect at the effective date determined in accordance with

§ 1.23. A corporation is dissolved upon the effective date of its articles of dissolution.

(c) For purposes of this subchapter, "dissolved corporation" means a corporation whose articles of dissolution have become effective and includes a successor entity to which the remaining assets of the corporation are transferred subject to its liabilities for purposes of liquidation.

§ 14.04. Revocation of Dissolution

(a) A corporation may revoke its dissolution within 120 days after its effective date.

(b) Revocation of dissolution shall be authorized in the same manner as the dissolution was authorized unless that authorization permitted revocation by action of the board of directors alone, in which event the board of directors may revoke the dissolution without shareholder action.

(c) After the revocation of dissolution is authorized, the corporation may revoke the dissolution by delivering to the secretary of state for filing articles of revocation of dissolution, together with a copy of its articles of dissolution, that set forth:

(1) the name of the corporation;

(2) the effective date of the dissolution that was revoked;

(3) the date that the revocation of dissolution was authorized;

(4) if the corporation's board of directors (or incorporators) revoked the dissolution, a statement to that effect;

(5) if the corporation's board of directors revoked a dissolution as authorized by the shareholders, a statement that revocation was permitted by action by the board of directors alone pursuant to that authorization; and

(6) if shareholder action was required to revoke the dissolution, a statement that the revocation was duly approved by the shareholders in the manner required by this Act and by the articles of incorporation.

(d) The articles of revocation of dissolution shall take effect at the effective date determined in accordance with § 1.23. Revocation of dissolution is effective upon the effective date of the articles of revocation of dissolution.

(e) When the revocation of dissolution is effective, it relates back to and takes effect as of the effective date of the dissolution and the corporation resumes carrying on its business as if dissolution had never occurred.

§ 14.05. Effect of Dissolution

(a) A corporation that has dissolved continues its corporate existence but the dissolved corporation may not carry on any business except that appropriate to wind up and liquidate its business and affairs, including:

    (1) collecting its assets;

    (2) disposing of its properties that will not be distributed in kind to its shareholders;

    (3) discharging or making provision for discharging its liabilities;

    (4) making distributions of its remaining assets among its shareholders according to their interests; and

    (5) doing every other act necessary to wind up and liquidate its business and affairs.

(b) Dissolution of a corporation does not:

    (1) transfer title to the corporation's property;

    (2) prevent transfer of its shares or securities;

    (3) subject its directors or officers to standards of conduct different from those prescribed in chapter 8;

    (4) change (i) quorum or voting requirements for its board of directors or shareholders; (ii) provisions for selection, resignation, or removal of its directors or officers or both; or (iii) provisions for amending its bylaws;

    (5) prevent commencement of a proceeding by or against the corporation in its corporate name;

    (6) abate or suspend a proceeding pending by or against the corporation on the effective date of dissolution; or

    (7) terminate the authority of the registered agent of the corporation.

(c) A distribution in liquidation under this section may only be made by a dissolved corporation. For purposes of determining the shareholders entitled to receive a distribution in liquidation, the board of directors may fix a record date for determining shareholders entitled to a distribution in liquidation, which date may not be retroactive. If the board of directors does not fix a record date for determining shareholders entitled to a distribution in liquidation, the record date is the date the board of directors authorizes the distribution in liquidation.

§ 14.06. Known Claims Against Dissolved Corporation

(a) A dissolved corporation may dispose of the known claims against it by notifying its known claimants in writing of the dissolution at any time after its effective date.

(b) The written notice must:

    (1) describe information that must be included in a claim;

    (2) provide a mailing address where a claim may be sent;

    (3) state the deadline, which may not be fewer than 120 days after the written notice is effective, by which the dissolved corporation shall receive the claim; and

    (4) state that the claim will be barred if not received by the deadline.

(c) A claim against the dissolved corporation is barred:

    (1) if a claimant who was given written notice under subsection (b) does not deliver the claim to the dissolved corporation by the deadline; or

    (2) if a claimant whose claim was rejected by the dissolved corporation does not commence a proceeding to enforce the claim within 90 days after the rejection notice is effective.

(d) For purposes of this section, "claim" does not include a contingent liability or a claim based on an event occurring after the effective date of dissolution.

§ 14.07. Other Claims Against Dissolved Corporation

(a) A dissolved corporation may publish notice of its dissolution and request that persons with claims against the dissolved corporation present them in accordance with the notice.

(b) The notice must:

(1) be published (i) one time in a newspaper of general circulation in the county where the dissolved corporation's principal office (or, if none in this state, its registered office) is or was last located or (ii) be posted conspicuously for at least 30 days on the dissolved corporation's website;

(2) describe the information that must be included in a claim and provide a mailing address where the claim may be sent; and

(3) state that a claim against the dissolved corporation will be barred unless a proceeding to enforce the claim is commenced within three years after the publication of the notice.

(c) If the dissolved corporation publishes a notice in accordance with subsection (b), the claim of each of the following claimants is barred unless the claimant commences a proceeding to enforce the claim against the dissolved corporation within three years after the publication date of the notice:

(1) a claimant who was not given written notice under § 14.06;

(2) a claimant whose claim was timely sent to the dissolved corporation but not acted on by the corporation;

(3) a claimant whose claim is contingent or based on an event occurring after the effective date of dissolution.

(d) A claim that is not barred by § 14.06(c) or § 14.07(c) may be enforced:

(1) against the dissolved corporation, to the extent of its undistributed assets; or

(2) except as provided in § 14.08(d), if the assets have been distributed in liquidation, against a shareholder of the dissolved corporation to the extent of the shareholder's pro rata share of the claim or the corporate assets distributed to the shareholder in liquidation, whichever is less, but a shareholder's total liability for all claims under this section may not exceed the total amount of assets distributed to the shareholder.

§ 14.08. Court Proceedings

(a) A dissolved corporation that has published a notice under § 14.07 may file an application with the [name or describe court] for a determination of the amount and form of security to be provided for payment of claims that are contingent or have not been made known to the dissolved corporation or that are based on an event occurring after the effective date of dissolution but that, based on the facts known to the dissolved corporation, are reasonably estimated to arise after the effective date of dissolution. Provision need not be made for any claim that is or is reasonably anticipated to be barred under § 14.07(c).

(b) Within 10 days after the filing of the application, notice of the proceeding shall be given by the dissolved corporation to each claimant holding a contingent claim whose contingent claim is shown on the records of the dissolved corporation.

(c) The court may appoint a guardian ad litem to represent all claimants whose identities are unknown in any proceeding brought under this section. The reasonable fees and expenses of such guardian, including all reasonable expert witness fees, shall be paid by the dissolved corporation.

(d) Provision by the dissolved corporation for security in the amount and the form ordered by the court under § 14.08(a) shall satisfy the dissolved corporation's obligations with respect to claims that are contingent, have not been made known to the dissolved corporation or are based on an event occurring after the effective date of dissolution, and such claims may not be enforced against a shareholder who received assets in liquidation.

§ 14.09. Director Duties

(a) Directors shall cause the dissolved corporation to discharge or make reasonable provision for the payment of claims and make distributions in liquidation of assets to shareholders after payment or provision for claims.

(b) Directors of a dissolved corporation which has disposed of claims under § 14.06, 14.07, or 14.08 shall not be liable for breach of § 14.09(a) with respect to claims against the dissolved corporation that are barred or satisfied under § 14.06, 14.07 or 14.08.

Subchapter B. Administrative Dissolution

§ 14.20. Grounds for Administrative Dissolution

The secretary of state may commence a proceeding under § 14.21 to dissolve a corporation administratively if:

(a) the corporation does not pay within 60 days after they are due any fees, taxes, interest or penalties imposed by this Act or other laws of this state;

(b) the corporation does not deliver its annual report to the secretary of state within 60 days after it is due;

(c) the corporation is without a registered agent or registered office in this state for 60 days or more;

(d) the secretary of state has not been notified within 60 days that the corporation's registered agent or registered office has been changed, that its registered agent has resigned, or that its registered office has been discontinued; or

(e) the corporation's period of duration stated in its articles of incorporation expires.

§ 14.21. Procedure for and Effect of Administrative Dissolution

(a) If the secretary of state determines that one or more grounds exist under § 14.20 for dissolving a corporation, the secretary of state shall serve the corporation with written notice of such determination under § 5.04.

(b) If the corporation does not correct each ground for dissolution or demonstrate to the reasonable satisfaction of the secretary of state that each

ground determined by the secretary of state does not exist within 60 days after service of the notice under § 5.04, the secretary of state shall administratively dissolve the corporation by signing a certificate of dissolution that recites the ground or grounds for dissolution and its effective date. The secretary of state shall file the original of the certificate and serve a copy on the corporation under § 5.04.

(c) A corporation administratively dissolved continues its corporate existence but may not carry on any business except that necessary to wind up and liquidate its business and affairs under § 14.05 and notify claimants under sections 14.06 and 14.07.

(d) The administrative dissolution of a corporation does not terminate the authority of its registered agent.

§ 14.22. Reinstatement Following Administrative Dissolution

(a) A corporation administratively dissolved under § 14.21 may apply to the secretary of state for reinstatement within two years after the effective date of dissolution. The application must:

> **(1)** state the name of the corporation and the effective date of its administrative dissolution;

> **(2)** state that the ground or grounds for dissolution either did not exist or have been eliminated;

> **(3)** state that the corporation's name satisfies the requirements of § 4.01; and

> **(4)** contain a certificate from the [taxing authority] reciting that all taxes owed by the corporation have been paid.

(b) If the secretary of state determines that the application contains the information required by subsection (a) and that the information is correct, the secretary of state shall cancel the certificate of dissolution and prepare a certificate of reinstatement that recites such determination and the effective date of reinstatement, file the original of the certificate, and serve a copy on the corporation under § 5.04.

(c) When the reinstatement is effective, it relates back to and takes effect as of the effective date of the administrative dissolution and the corporation resumes carrying on its business as if the administrative dissolution had never occurred.

§ 14.23. Appeal from Denial of Reinstatement

(a) If the secretary of state denies a corporation's application for reinstatement following administrative dissolution, the secretary of state shall serve the corporation under § 5.04 with a written notice that explains the reason or reasons for denial.

(b) The corporation may appeal the denial of reinstatement to the [name or describe court] within 30 days after service of the notice of denial is effected. The corporation appeals by petitioning the court to set aside the dissolution and attaching to the petition copies of the secretary of state's certificate of dissolution, the corporation's application for reinstatement, and the secretary of state's notice of denial.

(c) The court may summarily order the secretary of state to reinstate the dissolved corporation or may take other action the court considers appropriate.

(d) The court's final decision may be appealed as in other civil proceedings.

Subchapter C. Judicial Dissolution

§ 14.30. Grounds for Judicial Dissolution

(a) The [name or describe court or courts] may dissolve a corporation:

(1) in a proceeding by the attorney general if it is established that:

    (i) the corporation obtained its articles of incorporation through fraud; or

    (ii) the corporation has continued to exceed or abuse the authority conferred upon it by law;

(2) in a proceeding by a shareholder if it is established that:

    (i) the directors are deadlocked in the management of the corporate affairs, the shareholders are unable to break the deadlock, and irreparable injury to the corporation is threatened or being suffered, or the business and affairs of the corporation can no longer be conducted to the advantage of the shareholders generally, because of the deadlock;

    (ii) the directors or those in control of the corporation have acted, are acting, or will act in a manner that is illegal, oppressive, or fraudulent;

    (iii) the shareholders are deadlocked in voting power and have failed, for a period that includes at least two consecutive annual meeting dates, to elect successors to directors whose terms have expired; or

    (iv) the corporate assets are being misapplied or wasted;

(3) in a proceeding by a creditor if it is established that:

    (i) the creditor's claim has been reduced to judgment, the execution on the judgment returned unsatisfied, and the corporation is insolvent; or

    (ii) the corporation has admitted in writing that the creditor's claim is due and owing and the corporation is insolvent;

(4) in a proceeding by the corporation to have its voluntary dissolution continued under court supervision; or

(5) in a proceeding by a shareholder if the corporation has abandoned its business and has failed within a reasonable time to liquidate and distribute its assets and dissolve.

(b) Subsection (a)(2) shall not apply in the case of a corporation that, on the date of the filing of the proceeding, has a class or series of shares which is:

(1) a covered security under § 18(b)(1)(A) or (B) of the Securities Act of 1933; or

(2) not a covered security, but is held by at least 300 shareholders and the shares outstanding have a market value of at least $20 million (exclusive of the value of such shares held by the corporation's subsidiaries, senior executives, directors and beneficial shareholders and voting trust beneficial owners owning more than 10% of such shares).

(c) In subsection (a), "shareholder" means a record shareholder, a beneficial shareholder, and an unrestricted voting trust beneficial owner, and in subsection (b), "shareholder" means a record shareholder, a beneficial shareholder, and a voting trust beneficial owner.

§ 14.31. Procedure for Judicial Dissolution

(a) Venue for a proceeding by the attorney general to dissolve a corporation lies in [name or describe court]. Venue for a proceeding brought by any other party named in § 14.30(a) lies in [name or describe court].

(b) It is not necessary to make shareholders parties to a proceeding to dissolve a corporation unless relief is sought against them individually.

(c) A court in a proceeding brought to dissolve a corporation may issue injunctions, appoint a receiver or custodian during the proceeding with all powers and duties the court directs, take other action required to preserve the corporate assets wherever located, and carry on the business of the corporation until a full hearing can be held.

(d) Within 10 days of the commencement of a proceeding to dissolve a corporation under section 14.30(a)(2), the corporation shall deliver to all shareholders, other than the petitioner, a notice stating that the shareholders are entitled to avoid the dissolution of the corporation by electing to purchase the petitioner's shares under § 14.34 and accompanied by a copy of § 14.34.

§ 14.32. Receivership or Custodianship

(a) Unless an election to purchase has been filed under § 14.34, a court in a judicial proceeding brought to dissolve a corporation may appoint one or more receivers to wind up and liquidate, or one or more custodians to manage, the business and affairs of the corporation. The court shall hold a hearing, after notifying all parties to the proceeding and any interested persons designated by the court, before appointing a receiver or custodian.

The court appointing a receiver or custodian has jurisdiction over the corporation and all of its property wherever located.

(b) The court may appoint an individual or a domestic or foreign corporation or eligible entity as a receiver or custodian, which, if a foreign corporation or foreign eligible entity, must be registered to do business in this state. The court may require the receiver or custodian to post bond, with or without sureties, in an amount the court directs.

(c) The court shall describe the powers and duties of the receiver or custodian in its appointing order, which may be amended from time to time. Among other powers:

> **(1)** the receiver (i) may dispose of all or any part of the assets of the corporation wherever located, at a public or private sale; and (ii) may sue and defend in the receiver's own name as receiver of the corporation in all courts of this state;

> **(2)** the custodian may exercise all of the powers of the corporation, through or in place of its board of directors, to the extent necessary to manage the affairs of the corporation in the best interests of its shareholders and creditors.

The receiver or custodian shall have such other powers and duties as the court may provide in the appointing order, which may be amended from time to time.

(d) The court during a receivership may redesignate the receiver a custodian and during a custodianship may redesignate the custodian a receiver.

(e) The court from time to time during the receivership or custodianship may order compensation paid and expenses paid or reimbursed to the receiver or custodian from the assets of the corporation or proceeds from the sale of the assets.

§ 14.33. Decree of Dissolution

(a) If after a hearing the court determines that one or more grounds for judicial dissolution described in § 14.30 exist, it may enter a decree dissolving the corporation and specifying the effective date of the dissolution, and the clerk of the court shall deliver a certified copy of the decree to the secretary of state for filing.

(b) After entering the decree of dissolution, the court shall direct the winding-up and liquidation of the corporation's business and affairs in accordance with § 14.05 and the notification of claimants in accordance with sections 14.06 and 14.07.

§ 14.34. Election to Purchase in Lieu of Dissolution

(a) In a proceeding under § 14.30(a)(2) to dissolve a corporation, the corporation may elect or, if it fails to elect, one or more shareholders may elect to purchase all shares owned by the petitioning shareholder at the fair value of the shares. An election pursuant to this section shall be irrevocable unless the court determines that it is equitable to set aside or modify the election.

(b) An election to purchase pursuant to this section may be filed with the court at any time within 90 days after the filing of the petition under § 14.30(a)(2) or at such later time as the court in its discretion may allow. If the election to purchase is filed by one or more shareholders, the corporation shall, within 10 days thereafter, give written notice to all shareholders, other than the petitioner. The notice must state the name and number of shares owned by the petitioner and the name and number of shares owned by each electing shareholder and must advise the recipients of their right to join in the election to purchase shares in accordance with this section. Shareholders who wish to participate shall file notice of their intention to join in the purchase no later than 30 days after the effectiveness of the notice to them. All shareholders who have filed an election or notice of their intention to participate in the election to purchase thereby become parties to the proceeding and shall participate in the purchase in proportion to their ownership of shares as of the date the first election was filed, unless they otherwise agree or the court otherwise directs. After an election has been filed by the corporation or one or more shareholders, the proceeding under § 14.30(a)(2) may not be discontinued or settled, nor may the petitioning shareholder sell or otherwise dispose of his or her shares, unless the court determines that it would be equitable to the corporation and the shareholders, other than the petitioner, to permit such discontinuance, settlement, sale, or other disposition.

(c) If, within 60 days of the filing of the first election, the parties reach agreement as to the fair value and terms of purchase of the petitioner's shares, the court shall enter an order directing the purchase of the petitioner's shares upon the terms and conditions agreed to by the parties.

(d) If the parties are unable to reach an agreement as provided for in subsection (c), the court, upon application of any party, shall stay the proceedings under § 14.30(a)(2) and determine the fair value of the petitioner's shares as of the day before the date on which the petition under § 14.30(a)(2) was filed or as of such other date as the court deems appropriate under the circumstances.

(e) Upon determining the fair value of the shares, the court shall enter an order directing the purchase upon such terms and conditions as the court deems appropriate, which may include payment of the purchase price in installments, where necessary in the interests of equity, provision for security to assure payment of the purchase price and any additional expenses as may have been awarded, and, if the shares are to be purchased by shareholders, the allocation of shares among them. In allocating the petitioner's shares among holders of different classes or series of shares, the court should attempt to preserve the existing distribution of voting rights among holders of different classes or series insofar as practicable and may direct that holders of a specific class or classes or series shall not participate in the purchase. Interest may be allowed at the rate and from the date determined by the court to be equitable, but if the court finds that the refusal of the petitioning shareholder to accept an offer of payment was arbitrary or otherwise not in good faith, no interest shall be allowed. If the court finds that the petitioning shareholder had probable grounds for relief under sections

14.30(a)(2)(ii) or (iv), it may award expenses to the petitioning shareholder.

(f) Upon entry of an order under subsections (c) or (e), the court shall dismiss the petition to dissolve the corporation under § 14.30(a)(2), and the petitioning shareholder shall no longer have any rights or status as a shareholder of the corporation, except the right to receive the amounts awarded by the order of the court which shall be enforceable in the same manner as any other judgment.

(g) The purchase ordered pursuant to subsection (e) shall be made within 10 days after the date the order becomes final.

(h) Any payment by the corporation pursuant to an order under subsections (c) or (e), other than an award of expenses pursuant to subsection (e), is subject to the provisions of § 6.40.

Subchapter D. Miscellaneous

§ 14.40. Deposit with State Treasurer

Assets of a dissolved corporation that should be transferred to a creditor, claimant, or shareholder of the corporation who cannot be found or who is not competent to receive them shall be reduced to cash and deposited with the state treasurer or other appropriate state official for safekeeping. When the creditor, claimant, or shareholder furnishes satisfactory proof of entitlement to the amount deposited, the state treasurer or other appropriate state official shall pay such person or his or her representative that amount.

Chapter 15. Foreign Corporations

§ 15.01. Governing Law

(a) The law of the jurisdiction of formation of a foreign corporation governs:

> **(1)** the internal affairs of the foreign corporation; and

> **(2)** the interest holder liability of its shareholders.

(b) A foreign corporation is not precluded from registering to do business in this state because of any difference between the law of the foreign corporation's jurisdiction of formation and the law of this state.

(c) Registration of a foreign corporation to do business in this state does not permit the foreign corporation to engage in any business or affairs or exercise any power that a domestic corporation may not engage in or exercise in this state.

§ 15.02. Registration to Do Business in This State

(a) A foreign corporation may not do business in this state until it registers with the secretary of state under this chapter.

(b) A foreign corporation doing business in this state may not maintain a proceeding in any court of this state until it is registered to do business in this state.

(c) The failure of a foreign corporation to register to do business in this state does not impair the validity of a contract or act of the foreign corporation or preclude it from defending a proceeding in this state.

(d) A limitation on the liability of a shareholder or director of a foreign corporation is not waived solely because the foreign corporation does business in this state without registering.

(e) Section 15.01(a) applies even if a foreign corporation fails to register under this chapter.

§ 15.03. Foreign Registration Statement

To register to do business in this state, a foreign corporation shall deliver a foreign registration statement to the secretary of state for filing. The registration statement must be signed by the foreign corporation and state:

(a) the corporate name of the foreign corporation and, if the name does not comply with § 4.01, an alternate name as required by § 15.06;

(b) the foreign corporation's jurisdiction of formation;

(c) the street and mailing addresses of the foreign corporation's principal office and, if the law of the foreign corporation's jurisdiction of formation requires the foreign corporation to maintain an office in that jurisdiction, the street and mailing addresses of that office;

(d) the street and mailing addresses of the foreign corporation's registered office in this state and the name of its registered agent at that office;

(e) the names and business addresses of its directors and principal officers; and (f) a brief description of the nature of its business to be conducted in this state.

§ 15.04. Amendment of Foreign Registration Statement

A registered foreign corporation shall sign and deliver to the secretary of state for filing an amendment to its foreign registration statement if there is a change in:

(a) its name or alternate name;

(b) its jurisdiction of formation, unless its registration is deemed to have been withdrawn under § 15.08 or transferred under § 15.10; or (c) an address required by § 15.03(c).

§ 15.05. Activities Not Constituting Doing Business

(a) Activities of a foreign corporation that do not constitute doing business in this state for purposes of this chapter include:

(1) maintaining, defending, mediating, arbitrating, or settling a proceeding;

(2) carrying on any activity concerning the internal affairs of the foreign corporation, including holding meetings of its shareholders or board of directors;

(3) maintaining accounts in financial institutions;

(4) maintaining offices or agencies for the transfer, exchange, and registration of securities of the foreign corporation or maintaining trustees or depositories with respect to those securities;

(5) selling through independent contractors;

(6) soliciting or obtaining orders by any means if the orders require acceptance outside this state before they become contracts;

(7) creating or acquiring indebtedness, mortgages, or security interests in property;

(8) securing or collecting debts or enforcing mortgages or security interests in property securing the debts, and holding, protecting, or maintaining property so acquired;

(9) conducting an isolated transaction that is not in the course of similar transactions;

(10) owning, protecting and maintaining property; and

(11) doing business in interstate commerce.

(b) This section does not apply in determining the contacts or activities that may subject a foreign corporation to service of process, taxation, or regulation under the laws of this state other than this Act.

§ 15.06. Noncomplying Name of Foreign Corporation

(a) A foreign corporation whose name does not comply with § 4.01 may not register to do business in this state until it adopts, for the purpose of doing business in this state, an alternate name that complies with § 4.01 by filing a foreign registration statement under § 15.03, or if applicable, a transfer of registration statement under § 15.10, setting forth that alternate name. A foreign corporation adopting an alternate name as provided in this subsection need not file under this state's assumed or fictitious name statute with respect that alternate name. After registering to do business in this state with an alternate name, a foreign corporation shall do business in this state under:

(1) the alternate name;

(2) the foreign corporation's name, with the addition of its jurisdiction of formation; or

(3) a name the foreign corporation is authorized to use under the assumed or fictitious name statute of this state.

(b) If a registered foreign corporation changes its name after registration to a name that does not comply with § 4.01, it may not do business in this state until it complies with subsection (a) by amending its registration statement to adopt an alternate name that complies with § 4.01.

§ 15.07. Withdrawal of Registration of Registered Foreign Corporation

(a) A registered foreign corporation may withdraw its registration by delivering a statement of withdrawal to the secretary of state for filing. The statement of withdrawal must be signed by the foreign corporation and state:

> **(1)** the name of the foreign corporation and its jurisdiction of formation;

> **(2)** that the foreign corporation is not doing business in this state and that it withdraws its registration to do business in this state;

> **(3)** that the foreign corporation revokes the authority of its registered agent in this state; and

> **(4)** an address to which process on the foreign corporation may be sent by the secretary of state under § 5.04(c).

(b) After the withdrawal of the registration of a foreign corporation, service of process in any proceeding based on a cause of action arising during the time the entity was registered to do business in this state may be made as provided in § 5.04.

§ 15.08. Deemed Withdrawal Upon Domestication or Conversion to Certain Domestic Entities

A registered foreign corporation that domesticates to a domestic business corporation or converts to a domestic nonprofit corporation or any type of domestic filing entity or to a domestic limited liability partnership is deemed to have withdrawn its registration on the effectiveness of such event.

§ 15.09. Withdrawal Upon Dissolution or Conversion to Certain Nonfiling Entities

(a) A registered foreign corporation that has dissolved and completed winding up or has converted to a domestic or foreign nonfiling entity other than a limited liability partnership shall deliver to the secretary of state for filing a statement of with-

drawal. The statement must be signed by the dissolved corporation or the converted domestic or foreign nonfiling entity and state:

> **(1)** in the case of a foreign corporation that has completed winding up:

>> **(i)** its name and jurisdiction of formation;

>> **(ii)** that the foreign corporation withdraws its registration to do business in this state and revokes the authority of its registered agent to accept service on its behalf; and

>> **(iii)** an address to which process on the foreign corporation may be sent by the secretary of state under § 5.04(c); or

> **(2)** in the case of a foreign corporation that has converted to a domestic or foreign nonfiling entity other than a limited liability partnership:

>> **(i)** the name of the converting foreign corporation and its jurisdiction of formation;

>> **(ii)** the type of the nonfiling entity to which it has converted and its name and jurisdiction of formation;

>> **(iii)** that it withdraws its registration to do business in this state and revokes the authority of its registered agent to accept service on its behalf; and

>> **(iv)** an address to which process on the foreign corporation may be sent by the secretary of state under 5.04(c).

(b) After the withdrawal of the registration of a foreign corporation, service of process in any proceeding based on a cause of action arising during the time the entity was registered to do business in this state may be made as provided in § 5.04.

§ 15.10. Transfer of Registration

(a) If a registered foreign corporation merges into a nonregistered foreign corporation or converts to a foreign corporation required to register with the secretary of state to do business in this state, the foreign corporation shall deliver to the secretary of state for filing a transfer of registration statement. The transfer of registration statement must be signed by the surviving or converted foreign corporation and state:

(1) the name of the registered foreign corporation and its jurisdiction of formation before the merger or conversion;

(2) the name of the surviving or converted foreign corporation and its jurisdiction of formation after the merger or conversion and, if the name does not comply with § 4.01, an alternate name adopted pursuant to § 15.06; and

(3) the following information regarding the surviving or converted foreign corporation after the merger or conversion:

> **(i)** the street and mailing addresses of the principal office of the foreign corporation and, if the law of the foreign corporation's jurisdiction of formation requires it to maintain an office in that jurisdiction, the street and mailing addresses of that office; and

> **(ii)** the street and mailing addresses of the foreign corporation's registered office in this state and the name of its registered agent at that office.

(b) On the effective date of a transfer of registration statement as determined in accordance with § 1.23, the registration of the registered foreign corporation to do business in this state is transferred without interruption to the foreign corporation into which it has merged or to which it has been converted.

§ 15.11. Administrative Termination of Registration

(a) The secretary of state may terminate the registration of a registered foreign corporation in the manner provided in subsections (b) and (c) if:

(1) the foreign corporation does not pay within 60 days after they are due any fees, taxes, interest or penalties imposed by this Act or other laws of this state;

(2) the foreign corporation does not deliver its annual report to the secretary of state within 60 days after it is due;

(3) the foreign corporation is without a registered agent or registered office in this state for 60 days or more; or

(4) the secretary of state has not been notified within 60 days that the foreign corporation's registered agent or registered office has been changed, that its registered agent has resigned, or that its registered office has been discontinued.

(b) The secretary of state may terminate the registration of a registered foreign corporation by:

(1) filing a certificate of termination; and

(2) delivering a copy of the certificate of termination to the foreign corporation's registered agent or, if the foreign corporation does not have a registered agent, to the foreign corporation's principal office.

(c) The certificate of termination must state:

(1) the effective date of the termination, which must be not less than 60 days after the secretary of state delivers the copy of the certificate of termination as prescribed in subsection (b)(2); and

(2) the grounds for termination under subsection (a).

(d) The registration of a registered foreign corporation to do business in this state ceases on the effective date of the termination as set forth in the certificate of termination, unless before that date the foreign corporation cures each ground for termination stated in the certificate of termination. If the foreign corporation cures each ground, the secretary of state shall file a statement that the certificate of termination is withdrawn.

(e) After the effective date of the termination as set forth in the certificate of termination, service of process in any proceeding based on a cause of action arising during the time the entity was registered to do business in this state may be made as provided in § 5.04.

§ 15.12. Action by [Attorney General]

The [attorney general] may maintain an action to enjoin a foreign corporation from doing business in this state in violation of this Act.

Chapter 16. Records and Reports

Subchapter A. Records

§ 16.01. Corporate Records

(a) A corporation shall maintain the following records:

> **(1)** its articles of incorporation as currently in effect;

> **(2)** any notices to shareholders referred to in § 1.20(k)(5) specifying facts on which a filed document is dependent if those facts are not included in the articles of incorporation or otherwise available as specified in § 1.20(k)(5);

> **(3)** its bylaws as currently in effect;

> **(4)** all written communications within the past three years to shareholders generally;

> **(5)** minutes of all meetings of, and records of all actions taken without a meeting by, its shareholders, its board of directors, and board committees established under section 8.25;

> **(6)** a list of the names and business addresses of its current directors and officers; and

> **(7)** its most recent annual report delivered to the secretary of state under § 16.21.

(b) A corporation shall maintain all annual financial statements prepared for the corporation for its last three fiscal years (or such shorter period of existence) and any audit or other reports with respect to such financial statements.

(c) A corporation shall maintain accounting records in a form that permits preparation of its financial statements.

(d) A corporation shall maintain a record of its current shareholders in alphabetical order by class or series of shares showing the address of, and the number and class or series of shares held by, each shareholder. Nothing contained in this subsection shall require the corporation to include in such record the electronic mail address or other electronic contact information of a shareholder.

(e) A corporation shall maintain the records specified in this section in a manner so that they may be made available for inspection within a reasonable time.

§ 16.02. Inspection Rights of Shareholders

(a) A shareholder of a corporation is entitled to inspect and copy, during regular business hours at the corporation's principal office, any of the records of the corporation described in § 16.01(a), excluding minutes of meetings of, and records of actions taken without a meeting by, the corporation's board of directors and board committees established under § 8.25, if the shareholder gives the corporation a signed written notice of the shareholder's demand at least five business days before the date on which the shareholder wishes to inspect and copy.

(b) A shareholder of a corporation is entitled to inspect and copy, during regular business hours at a reasonable location specified by the corporation, any of the following records of the corporation if the shareholder meets the requirements of subsection (c) and gives the corporation a signed written notice of the shareholder's demand at least five business days before the date on which the shareholder wishes to inspect and copy:

> **(1)** the financial statements of the corporation maintained in accordance with § 16.01(b);

> **(2)** accounting records of the corporation;

> **(3)** excerpts from minutes of any meeting of, or records of any actions taken without a meeting by, the corporation's board of directors and board committees maintained in accordance with § 16.01(a); and

> **(4)** the record of shareholders maintained in accordance with § 16.01(d).

(c) A shareholder may inspect and copy the records described in subsection (b) only if:

> **(1)** the shareholder's demand is made in good faith and for a proper purpose;

> **(2)** the shareholder's demand describes with reasonable particularity the shareholder's purpose and the records the shareholder desires to inspect; and

(3) the records are directly connected with the shareholder's purpose.

(d) The corporation may impose reasonable restrictions on the confidentiality, use or distribution of records described in subsection (b).

(e) For any meeting of shareholders for which the record date for determining shareholders entitled to vote at the meeting is different than the record date for notice of the meeting, any person who becomes a shareholder subsequent to the record date for notice of the meeting and is entitled to vote at the meeting is entitled to obtain from the corporation upon request the notice and any other information provided by the corporation to shareholders in connection with the meeting, unless the corporation has made such information generally available to shareholders by posting it on its website or by other generally recognized means. Failure of a corporation to provide such information does not affect the validity of action taken at the meeting.

(f) The right of inspection granted by this section may not be abolished or limited by a corporation's articles of incorporation or bylaws.

(g) This section does not affect:

(1) the right of a shareholder to inspect records under § 7.20 or, if the shareholder is in litigation with the corporation, to the same extent as any other litigant; or

(2) the power of a court, independently of this Act, to compel the production of corporate records for examination and to impose reasonable restrictions as provided in § 16.04(c), provided that, in the case of production of records described in subsection (b) of this section at the request of a shareholder, the shareholder has met the requirements of subsection (c).

(h) For purposes of this section, "shareholder" means a record shareholder, a beneficial shareholder, and an unrestricted voting trust beneficial owner.

§ 16.03. Scope of Inspection Right

(a) A shareholder may appoint an agent or attorney to exercise the shareholder's inspection and copying rights under § 16.02.

(b) The corporation may, if reasonable, satisfy the right of a shareholder to copy records under § 16.02 by furnishing to the shareholder copies by photocopy or other means chosen by the corporation, including furnishing copies through an electronic transmission.

(c) The corporation may comply at its expense with a shareholder's demand to inspect the record of shareholders under § 16.02(b)(4) by providing the shareholder with a list of shareholders that was compiled no earlier than the date of the shareholder's demand.

(d) The corporation may impose a reasonable charge to cover the costs of providing copies of documents to the shareholder, which may be based on an estimate of such costs.

§ 16.04. Court-Ordered Inspection

(a) If a corporation does not allow a shareholder who complies with § 16.02(a) to inspect and copy any records required by that section to be available for inspection, the [name or describe court] may summarily order inspection and copying of the records demanded at the corporation's expense upon application of the shareholder.

(b) If a corporation does not within a reasonable time allow a shareholder who complies with § 16.02(b) to inspect and copy the records required by that section, the shareholder who complies with § 16.02(c) may apply to the [name or describe court] for an order to permit inspection and copying of the records demanded. The court shall dispose of an application under this subsection on an expedited basis.

(c) If the court orders inspection and copying of the records demanded under § 16.02(b), it may impose reasonable restrictions on their confidentiality, use or distribution by the demanding shareholder and it shall also order the corporation to pay the shareholder's expenses incurred to obtain the order unless the corporation establishes that it refused inspection in good faith because the corporation had:

> **(1)** a reasonable basis for doubt about the right of the shareholder to inspect the records demanded; or

> **(2)** required reasonable restrictions on the confidentiality, use or distribution of the records demanded to which the demanding shareholder had been unwilling to agree.

§ 16.05. Inspection Rights of Directors

(a) A director of a corporation is entitled to inspect and copy the books, records and documents of the corporation at any reasonable time to the extent reasonably related to the performance of the director's duties as a director, including duties as a member of a board committee, but not for any other purpose or in any manner that would violate any duty to the corporation.

(b) The [name or describe court] may order inspection and copying of the books, records and documents at the corporation's expense, upon application of a director who has been refused such inspection rights, unless the corporation establishes that the director is not entitled to such inspection rights. The court shall dispose of an application under this subsection on an expedited basis.

(c) If an order is issued, the court may include provisions protecting the corporation from undue burden or expense, and prohibiting the director from using information obtained upon exercise of the inspection rights in a manner that would violate a duty to the corporation, and may also order the corporation to reimburse the director for the director's expenses incurred in connection with the application.

Subchapter B. Reports

§ 16.20. Financial Statements for Shareholders

(a) Upon the written request of a shareholder, a corporation shall deliver or make available to such requesting shareholder by posting on its website or by other generally recognized means annual financial statements for the most recent fiscal year of the corporation for which annual financial statements have been prepared for the corporation. If financial statements have been prepared for the corporation on the basis of generally accepted accounting principles for such specified period, the corporation shall deliver or make available such financial statements to the requesting shareholder. If the annual financial statements to be delivered or made available to the requesting shareholder are audited or otherwise reported upon by a public accountant, the report shall also be delivered or made available to the requesting shareholder.

(b) A corporation shall deliver, or make available and provide written notice of availability of, the financial statements required under subsection (a) to the requesting shareholder within five business days of delivery of such written request to the corporation.

(c) A corporation may fulfill its responsibilities under this section by delivering the specified financial statements, or otherwise making them available, in any manner permitted by the applicable rules and regulations of the United States Securities and Exchange Commission.

(d) Notwithstanding the provisions of subsections (a), (b) and (c) of this section:

> **(1)** as a condition to delivering or making available financial statements to a requesting shareholder, the corporation may require the requesting shareholder to agree to reasonable restrictions on the confidentiality, use and distribution of such financial statements; and

> **(2)** the corporation may, if it reasonably determines that the shareholder's request is not made in good faith or for a proper purpose, decline to deliver or make available such financial statements to that shareholder.

(e) If a corporation does not respond to a shareholder's request for annual financial statements pursuant to this section in accordance with subsection (b) within five business days of delivery of such request to the corporation:

(1) The requesting shareholder may apply to the [name or describe court] for an order requiring delivery of or access to the requested financial statements. The court shall dispose of an application under this subsection on an expedited basis.

(2) If the court orders delivery or access to the requested financial statements, it may impose reasonable restrictions on their confidentiality, use or distribution.

(3) In such proceeding, if the corporation has declined to deliver or make available such financial statements because the shareholder had been unwilling to agree to restrictions proposed by the corporation on the confidentiality, use and distribution of such financials statements, the corporation shall have the burden of demonstrating that the restrictions proposed by the corporation were reasonable.

(4) In such proceeding, if the corporation has declined to deliver or make available such financial statements pursuant to § 16.20(d)(2), the corporation shall have the burden of demonstrating that it had reasonably determined that the shareholder's request was not made in good faith or for a proper purpose.

(5) If the court orders delivery or access to the requested financial statements it shall order the corporation to pay the shareholder's expenses incurred to obtain such order unless the corporation establishes that it had refused delivery or access to the requested financial statements because the shareholder had refused to agree to reasonable restrictions on the confidentiality, use or distribution of the financial statements or that the corporation had reasonably determined that the shareholder's request was not made in good faith or for a proper purpose.

§ 16.21. Annual Report for Secretary of State

(a) Each domestic corporation shall deliver to the secretary of state for filing an annual report that sets forth:

(1) the name of the corporation;

(2) the street and mailing address of its registered office and the name of its registered agent at that office in this state;

(3) the street and mailing address of its principal office;

(4) the names and business addresses of its directors and principal officers;

(5) a brief description of the nature of its business;

(6) the total number of authorized shares, itemized by class and series, if any, within each class; and

(7) the total number of issued and outstanding shares, itemized by class and series, if any, within each class.

(b) Each foreign corporation registered to do business in this state shall deliver to the secretary of state for filing an annual report that sets forth:

(1) the name of the foreign corporation and, if the name does not comply with § 4.01, an alternate name as required by § 15.06;

(2) the foreign corporation's jurisdiction of formation;

(3) the street and mailing addresses of the foreign corporation's principal office and, if the law of the foreign corporation's jurisdiction of formation requires the foreign corporation to maintain an office in that jurisdiction, the street and mailing addresses of that office;

(4) the street and mailing addresses of the foreign corporation's registered office in this state and the name of its registered agent at that office;

(5) the names and business addresses of its directors and principal officers; and

(6) a brief description of the nature of its business conducted in this state.

(c) Information in the annual report must be current as of the date the annual report is signed on behalf of the corporation.

(d) The first annual report shall be delivered to the secretary of state between January 1 and April 1 of the year following the calendar year in which a domestic corporation was incorporated or a foreign corporation was registered to do business. Subsequent annual reports shall be delivered to the secretary of state between January 1 and April 1 of the following calendar years.

(e) If an annual report does not contain the information required by this section, the secretary of state shall promptly notify the reporting domestic or foreign corporation in writing and return the report to it for correction. If the report is corrected to contain the information required by this section and delivered to the secretary of state within 30 days after the notice from the secretary of state becomes effective as determined in accordance with § 1.41, it is deemed to be timely filed.

Chapter 17. Transition Provisions

§ 17.01. Application to Existing Domestic Corporations

This Act applies to all domestic corporations in existence on its effective date that were incorporated under any general statute of this state providing for incorporation of corporations for profit if power to amend or repeal the statute under which the corporation was incorporated was reserved.

§ 17.02. Application to Existing Foreign Corporations

A foreign corporation registered or authorized to do business in this state on the effective date of this Act is subject to this Act, is deemed to be registered to do business in this state, and is not required to file a foreign registration statement under this Act.

§ 17.03. Saving Provisions

(a) Except as to procedural provisions, this Act does not affect a pending action or proceeding or a right accrued before the effective date of this Act, and a pending civil action or proceeding may be completed, and a right accrued may be enforced, as if this Act had not become effective.

(b) If a penalty or punishment for violation of a statute or rule is reduced by this Act, the penalty,

if not already imposed, shall be imposed in accordance with this Act.

§ 17.04. Severability

If any provision of this Act or its application to any person or circumstance is held invalid by a court of competent jurisdiction, the invalidity does not affect other provisions or applications of this Act that can be given effect without the invalid provision or application.

§ 17.05. Repeal

The following laws and parts of laws are repealed: [to be inserted by the adopting state].

Securities Exchange Act and Rules (2021)

Table of Contents

Securities Exchange Act

15 U.S.C. § 78m(d) Reports by Persons Acquiring More Than Five Per Centum of Certain Classes of Securities

(1) Any person who, after acquiring directly or indirectly the beneficial ownership of any equity security of a class which is registered pursuant to § 78*l* of this title, or any equity security of an insurance company which would have been required to be so registered except for the exemption contained in § 78*l*(g)(2)(G) of this title, or any equity security issued by a closed-end investment company registered under the Investment Company Act of 1940 or any equity security issued by a Native Corporation pursuant to § 1629c(d)(6) of Title 43, or otherwise becomes or is deemed to become a beneficial owner of any of the foregoing upon the purchase or sale of a security-based swap that the Commission may define by rule, and is directly or indirectly the beneficial owner of more than 5 per centum of such class shall, within ten days after such acquisition or within such shorter time as the Commission may establish by rule, file with the Commission, a statement containing such of the following information, and such additional information, as the Commission may by rules and regulations, prescribe as necessary or appropriate in the public interest or for the protection of investors--

(A) the background, and identity, residence, and citizenship of, and the nature of such beneficial ownership by, such person and all other persons by whom or on whose behalf the purchases have been or are to be effected;

(B) the source and amount of the funds or other consideration used or to be used in making the purchases, and if any part of the purchase price is represented or is to be represented by funds or other consideration borrowed or otherwise obtained for the purpose of acquiring, holding, or trading such security, a description of the transaction and the names of the parties thereto, except that where a source of funds is a loan made in the ordinary course of business by a bank, as defined in § 78c(a)(6) of this title, if the person filing such statement so requests, the name of the bank shall not be made available to the public;

(C) if the purpose of the purchases or prospective purchases is to acquire control of the business of the issuer of the securities, any plans or proposals which such persons may have to liquidate such issuer, to sell its assets to or merge it with any other persons, or to make any other major change in its business or corporate structure;

(D) the number of shares of such security which are beneficially owned, and the number of shares concerning which there is a right to acquire, directly or indirectly, by (i) such person, and (ii) by each associate of such person, giving the background, identity, residence, and citizenship of each such associate; and

(E) information as to any contracts, arrangements, or understandings with any person with respect to any securities of the issuer, including but not limited to transfer of any of the securities, joint ventures, loan or option arrangements, puts or calls, guaranties of loans, guaranties against loss or guaranties of profits, division of losses or profits, or the giving or withholding of proxies, naming the persons with whom such contracts, arrangements, or understandings have been entered into, and giving the details thereof.

(2) If any material change occurs in the facts set forth in the statement filed with the Commission, an amendment shall be filed with the Commission, in accordance with such rules and regulations as the Commission may prescribe as necessary or appropriate in the public interest or for the protection of investors.

(3) When two or more persons act as a partnership, limited partnership, syndicate, or other group for the purpose of acquiring, holding, or disposing of securities of an issuer, such syndicate or group shall be deemed a "person" for the purposes of this subsection.

(4) In determining, for purposes of this subsection, any percentage of a class of any security, such class shall be deemed to consist of the amount of the outstanding securities of such class, exclusive of any securities of such class held by or for the account of the issuer or a subsidiary of the issuer.

(5) The Commission, by rule or regulation or by order, may permit any person to file in lieu of the statement required by paragraph (1) of this subsection or the rules and regulations thereunder, a notice stating the name of such person, the number of shares of any equity securities subject to paragraph (1) which are owned by him, the date of their acquisition and such other information as the Commission may specify, if it appears to the Commission that such securities were acquired by such person in the ordinary course of his business and were not acquired for the purpose of and do not

have the effect of changing or influencing the control of the issuer nor in connection with or as a participant in any transaction having such purpose or effect.

(6) The provisions of this subsection shall not apply to--

(A) any acquisition or offer to acquire securities made or proposed to be made by means of a registration statement under the Securities Act of 1933;

(B) any acquisition of the beneficial ownership of a security which, together with all other acquisitions by the same person of securities of the same class during the preceding twelve months, does not exceed 2 per centum of that class;

(C) any acquisition of an equity security by the issuer of such security;

(D) any acquisition or proposed acquisition of a security which the Commission, by rules or regulations or by order, shall exempt from the provisions of this subsection as not entered into for the purpose of, and not having the effect of, changing or influencing the control of the issuer or otherwise as not comprehended within the purposes of this subsection.

15 U.S.C. § 78n(d) Tender Offer by Owner of More Than Five Per Centum of Class of Securities; Exceptions

(1) It shall be unlawful for any person, directly or indirectly, by use of the mails or by any means or instrumentality of interstate commerce or of any facility of a national securities exchange or otherwise, to make a tender offer for, or a request or invitation for tenders of, any class of any equity security which is registered pursuant to § 78*l* of this title, or any equity security of an insurance company which would have been required to be so registered except for the exemption contained in § 78*l*(g)(2)(G) of this title, or any equity security issued by a closed-end investment company registered under the Investment Company Act of 1940, if, after consummation thereof, such person would, directly or indirectly, be the beneficial owner of more than 5 per centum of such class, unless at the time copies of the offer or request or invitation are first published or sent or given to security holders such person has filed with the Commission a statement containing such of the information specified in § 78m(d) of this title, and such additional information as the Commission may by rules and regulations prescribe as necessary or appropriate in the public interest or for the protection of investors. All requests or invitations for tenders or advertisements making a tender offer or requesting or inviting tenders of such a security shall be filed as a part of such statement and shall contain such of the information contained in such statement as the Commission may by rules and regulations prescribe. Copies of any additional material soliciting or requesting such tender offers subsequent to the initial solicitation or request shall contain such information as the Commission may by rules and regulations prescribe as necessary or appropriate in the public interest or for the protection of investors, and shall be filed with the Commission not later than the time copies of such material are first published or sent or given to security holders. Copies of all statements, in the form in which such material is furnished to security holders and the Commission, shall be sent to the issuer not later than the date such material is first published or sent or given to any security holders.

(2) When two or more persons act as a partnership, limited partnership, syndicate, or other group for the purpose of acquiring, holding, or disposing of securities of an issuer, such syndicate or group shall be deemed a "person" for purposes of this subsection.

(3) In determining, for purposes of this subsection, any percentage of a class of any security, such class shall be deemed to consist of the amount of the outstanding securities of such class, exclusive of any securities of such class held by or for the account of the issuer or a subsidiary of the issuer.

(4) Any solicitation or recommendation to the holders of such a security to accept or reject a tender offer or request or invitation for tenders shall be made in accordance with such rules and regula-

tions as the Commission may prescribe as necessary or appropriate in the public interest or for the protection of investors.

(5) Securities deposited pursuant to a tender offer or request or invitation for tenders may be withdrawn by or on behalf of the depositor at any time until the expiration of seven days after the time definitive copies of the offer or request or invitation are first published or sent or given to security holders, and at any time after sixty days from the date of the original tender offer or request or invitation, except as the Commission may otherwise prescribe by rules, regulations, or order as necessary or appropriate in the public interest or for the protection of investors.

(6) Where any person makes a tender offer, or request or invitation for tenders, for less than all the outstanding equity securities of a class, and where a greater number of securities is deposited pursuant thereto within ten days after copies of the offer or request or invitation are first published or sent or given to security holders than such person is bound or willing to take up and pay for, the securities taken up shall be taken up as nearly as may be pro rata, disregarding fractions, according to the number of securities deposited by each depositor. The provisions of this subsection shall also apply to securities deposited within ten days after notice of an increase in the consideration offered to security holders, as described in paragraph (7), is first published or sent or given to security holders.

(7) Where any person varies the terms of a tender offer or request or invitation for tenders before the expiration thereof by increasing the consideration offered to holders of such securities, such person shall pay the increased consideration to each security holder whose securities are taken up and paid for pursuant to the tender offer or request or invitation for tenders whether or not such securities have been taken up by such person before the variation of the tender offer or request or invitation.

(8) The provisions of this subsection shall not apply to any offer for, or request or invitation for tenders of, any security--

(A) if the acquisition of such security, together with all other acquisitions by the same person of securities of the same class during the preceding twelve months, would not exceed 2 per centum of that class;

(B) by the issuer of such security; or

(C) which the Commission, by rules or regulations or by order, shall exempt from the provisions of this subsection as not entered into for the purpose of, and not having the effect of, changing or influencing the control of the issuer or otherwise as not comprehended within the purposes of this subsection.

Securities Exchange Act Rules

§ 240.14a-8   Shareholder Proposals.

This section addresses when a company must include a shareholder's proposal in its proxy statement and identify the proposal in its form of proxy when the company holds an annual or special meeting of shareholders. In summary, in order to have your shareholder proposal included on a company's proxy card, and included along with any supporting statement in its proxy statement, you must be eligible and follow certain procedures. Under a few specific circumstances, the company is permitted to exclude your proposal, but only after submitting its reasons to the Commission. We structured this section in a question-and-answer format so that it is easier to understand. The references to "you" are to a shareholder seeking to submit the proposal.

(a) *Question 1:* What is a proposal? A shareholder proposal is your recommendation or requirement that the company and/or its board of directors take action, which you intend to present at a meeting of the company's shareholders. Your proposal should state as clearly as possible the course of action that you believe the company should follow. If your proposal is placed on the company's proxy card, the company must also provide in the form of proxy means for shareholders to specify by boxes a choice between approval or disapproval, or abstention. Unless otherwise indicated, the word "proposal" as used in this section refers both to your proposal, and to your corresponding statement in support of your proposal (if any).

(b) *Question 2:* Who is eligible to submit a proposal, and how do I demonstrate to the company that I am eligible?

(1) To be eligible to submit a proposal, you must satisfy the following requirements:

(i) You must have continuously held:

(A) At least $2,000 in market value of the company's securities entitled to vote on the proposal for at least three years; or

(B) At least $15,000 in market value of the company's securities entitled to vote on the proposal for at least two years; or

(C) At least $25,000 in market value of the company's securities entitled to vote on the proposal for at least one year; or

(D) The amounts specified in paragraph (b)(3) of this section. This paragraph (b)(1)(i)(D) will expire on the same date that § 240.14a-8(b)(3) expires; and

(ii) You must provide the company with a written statement that you intend to continue to hold the requisite amount of securities, determined in accordance with paragraph (b)(1)(i)(A) through (C) of this section, through the date of the shareholders' meeting for which the proposal is submitted; and

(iii) You must provide the company with a written statement that you are able to meet with the company in person or via teleconference no less than 10 calendar days, nor more than 30 calendar days, after submission of the shareholder proposal. You must include your contact information as well as business days and specific times that you are available to discuss the proposal with the company. You must identify times that are within the regular business hours of the company's principal executive offices. If these hours are not disclosed in the company's proxy statement for the prior year's annual meeting, you must identify times that are between 9 a.m. and 5:30 p.m. in the time zone of the company's principal executive offices. If you elect to co-file a proposal, all co-filers must either:

(A) Agree to the same dates and times of availability, or

(B) Identify a single lead filer who will provide dates and times of the lead filer's availability to engage on behalf of all co-filers; and

(iv) If you use a representative to submit a shareholder proposal on your behalf, you must provide the company with written documentation that:

(A) Identifies the company to which the proposal is directed;

(B) Identifies the annual or special meeting for which the proposal is submitted;

(C) Identifies you as the proponent and identifies the person acting on your behalf as your representative;

(D) Includes your statement authorizing the designated representative to submit the proposal and otherwise act on your behalf;

(E) Identifies the specific topic of the proposal to be submitted;

(F) Includes your statement supporting the proposal; and

(G) Is signed and dated by you.

(v) The requirements of paragraph (b)(1)(iv) of this section shall not apply to shareholders that are entities so long as the representative's authority to act on the shareholder's behalf is apparent and self-evident such that a reasonable person would understand that the agent has authority to submit the proposal and otherwise act on the shareholder's behalf.

(vi) For purposes of paragraph (b)(1)(i) of this section, you may not aggregate your holdings with those of another shareholder or group of shareholders to meet the requisite amount of securities necessary to be eligible to submit a proposal.

(2) One of the following methods must be used to demonstrate your eligibility to submit a proposal:

(i) If you are the registered holder of your securities, which means that your name appears in the company's records as a shareholder, the company can verify your eligibility on its own, although you will still have to provide the company with a written statement that you intend to continue to hold the requisite amount of securities, determined in accordance with paragraph (b)(1)(i)(A) through (C) of this section, through the date of the meeting of shareholders.

(ii) If, like many shareholders, you are not a registered holder, the company likely does not *know* that you are a shareholder, or how many shares you own. In this case, at the time you submit your proposal, you must prove your eligibility to the company in one of two ways:

(A) The first way is to submit to the company a written statement from the "record" holder of your securities (usually a broker or bank) verifying that, at the time you submitted your proposal, you continuously held at least $2,000, $15,000, or $25,000 in market value of the company's securities entitled to vote on the proposal for at least three years, two years, or one year, respectively. You must also include your own written statement that you intend to continue to hold the requisite amount of securities, determined in accordance with paragraph (b)(1)(i)(A) through (C) of this section, through the date of the shareholders' meeting for which the proposal is submitted; or

(B) The second way to prove ownership applies only if you were required to file, and filed, a Schedule 13D (§ 240.13d-101), Schedule 13G (§ 240.13d-102), Form 3 (§ 249.103 of this chapter), Form 4 (§ 249.104 of this chapter), and/or Form 5 (§ 249.105 of this chapter), or amendments to those documents or updated forms, demonstrating that you meet at least one of the share ownership requirements under paragraph (b)(1)(i)(A) through (C) of this section. If you have filed one or more of these documents with the SEC, you may demonstrate your eligibility to submit a proposal by submitting to the company:

(1) A copy of the schedule(s) and/or form(s), and any subsequent amendments reporting a change in your ownership level;

(2) Your written statement that you continuously held at least $2,000, $15,000, or $25,000 in market value of the company's securities entitled to vote on the proposal for at least three years, two years, or one year, respectively; and

(3) Your written statement that you intend to continue to hold the requisite amount of securities, determined in accordance with paragraph (b)(1)(i)(A) through (C) of this section, through the date of the company's annual or special meeting.

(3) If you continuously held at least $2,000 of a company's securities entitled to vote on the proposal for at least one year as of January 4, 2021, and you have continuously maintained a minimum investment of at least $2,000 of such securities from January 4, 2021 through the date the proposal is submitted to the company, you will be eligible to submit a proposal to such company for an annual or special meeting to be held prior to January 1, 2023. If you rely on this provision, you must provide the company with your written statement that you intend to continue to hold at least $2,000 of such securities through the date of the shareholders' meeting for which the proposal is submitted. You must also follow the procedures set forth in paragraph (b)(2) of this section to demonstrate that:

(i) You continuously held at least $2,000 of the company's securities entitled to vote on the proposal for at least one year as of January 4, 2021; and

(ii) You have continuously maintained a minimum investment of at least $2,000 of such securities from January 4, 2021 through the date the proposal is submitted to the company.

(iii) This paragraph (b)(3) will expire on January 1, 2023

(c) *Question 3:* How many proposals may I submit? Each person may submit no more than one proposal, directly or indirectly, to a company for a particular shareholders' meeting. A person may not rely on the securities holdings of another person for the purpose of meeting the eligibility requirements and submitting multiple proposals for a particular shareholders' meeting.

(d) *Question 4:* How long can my proposal be? The proposal, including any accompanying supporting statement, may not exceed 500 words.

(e) *Question 5:* What is the deadline for submitting a proposal?

(1) If you are submitting your proposal for the company's annual meeting, you can in most cases find the deadline in last year's proxy statement. However, if the company did not hold an annual meeting last year, or has changed the date of its meeting for this year more than 30 days from last year's meeting, you can usually find the deadline in one of the company's quarterly reports on Form 10-Q (§ 249.308a of this chapter), or in shareholder reports of investment companies under § 270.30d-1 of this chapter of the Investment Company Act of 1940. In order to avoid controversy, shareholders should submit their proposals by means, including electronic means, that permit them to prove the date of delivery.

(2) The deadline is calculated in the following manner if the proposal is submitted for a regularly scheduled annual meeting. The proposal must be received at the company's principal executive offices not less than 120 calendar days before the date of the company's proxy statement released to shareholders in connection with the previous year's annual meeting. However, if the company did not hold an annual meeting the previous year, or if the date of this year's annual meeting has been changed by more than 30 days from the date of the previous year's meeting, then the deadline is a reasonable time before the company begins to print and send its proxy materials.

(3) If you are submitting your proposal for a meeting of shareholders other than a regularly scheduled annual meeting, the deadline is a reasonable time before the company begins to print and send its proxy materials.

(f) *Question 6:* What if I fail to follow one of the eligibility or procedural requirements explained in answers to Questions 1 through 4 of this section?

(1) The company may exclude your proposal, but only after it has notified you of the problem, and you have failed adequately to correct it. Within 14 calendar days of receiving your proposal, the company must notify you in writing of any procedural or eligibility deficiencies, as well as of the time frame for your response. Your response must be postmarked, or transmitted electronically, no later than 14 days from the date you received the company's notification. A company need not provide you such notice of a deficiency if the deficiency cannot be remedied, such as if you fail to submit a proposal by the company's properly determined deadline. If the company intends to exclude the proposal, it will later have to make a submission under § 240.14a-8 and provide you with a copy under Question 10 below, § 240.14a-8(j).

(2) If you fail in your promise to hold the required number of securities through the date of the meeting of shareholders, then the company will be permitted to exclude all of your proposals from its proxy materials for any meeting held in the following two calendar years.

(g) *Question 7:* Who has the burden of persuading the Commission or its staff that my proposal can be excluded? Except as otherwise noted, the burden is on the company to demonstrate that it is entitled to exclude a proposal.

(h) *Question 8:* Must I appear personally at the shareholders' meeting to present the proposal?

(1) Either you, or your representative who is qualified under state law to present the proposal on your behalf, must attend the meeting to present the proposal. Whether you attend the meeting yourself or send a qualified representative to the meeting in your place, you should make sure that you, or your representative, follow the proper state law procedures for attending the meeting and/or presenting your proposal.

(2) If the company holds its shareholder meeting in whole or in part via electronic media, and the company permits you or your representative to present your proposal via such media, then you may appear through electronic media rather than traveling to the meeting to appear in person.

(3) If you or your qualified representative fail to appear and present the proposal, without good cause, the company will be permitted to exclude all of your proposals from its proxy materials for any meetings held in the following two calendar years.

(i) *Question 9:* If I have complied with the procedural requirements, on what other bases may a company rely to exclude my proposal?

(1) Improper under state law: If the proposal is not a proper subject for action by shareholders under the laws of the jurisdiction of the company's organization;

Note to paragraph (i)(1):

Depending on the subject matter, some proposals are not considered proper under state law if they would be binding on the company if approved by shareholders. In our experience, most proposals that are cast as recommendations or requests that the board of directors take specified action are proper under state law. Accordingly, we will assume that a proposal drafted as a recommendation or suggestion is proper unless the company demonstrates otherwise.

(2) *Violation of law:* If the proposal would, if implemented, cause the company to violate any state, federal, or foreign law to which it is subject;

Note to paragraph (i)(2):

We will not apply this basis for exclusion to permit exclusion of a proposal on grounds that it would violate foreign law if compliance with the foreign law would result in a violation of any state or federal law. ·

(3) *Violation of proxy rules:* If the proposal or supporting statement is contrary to any of the Commission's proxy rules, including § 240.14a-9, which prohibits materially false or misleading statements in proxy soliciting materials;

(4) *Personal grievance; special interest:* If the proposal relates to the redress of a personal claim or grievance against the company or any other person, or if it is designed to result in a benefit to you, or to further a personal interest, which is not shared by the other shareholders at large;

(5) *Relevance:* If the proposal relates to operations which account for less than 5 percent of the company's total assets at the end of its most recent fiscal year, and for less than 5 percent of its net earnings and gross sales for its most recent fiscal year, and is not otherwise significantly related to the company's business;

(6) *Absence of power/authority:* If the company would lack the power or authority to implement the proposal;

(7) *Management functions:* If the proposal deals with a matter relating to the company's ordinary business operations;

(8) *Director elections:* If the proposal:

(i) Would disqualify a nominee who is standing for election;

(ii) Would remove a director from office before his or her term expired;

(iii) Questions the competence, business judgment, or character of one or more nominees or directors;

(iv) Seeks to include a specific individual in the company's proxy materials for election to the board of directors; or

(v) Otherwise could affect the outcome of the upcoming election of directors.

(9) *Conflicts with company's proposal:* If the proposal directly conflicts with one of the company's own proposals to be submitted to shareholders at the same meeting;

Note to paragraph (i)(9):

A company's submission to the Commission under this section should specify the points of conflict with the company's proposal.

(10) *Substantially implemented:* If the company has already substantially implemented the proposal;

Note to paragraph (i)(10):

A company may exclude a shareholder proposal that would provide an advisory vote or seek future advisory votes to approve the compensation of executives as disclosed pursuant to Item 402 of Regulation S-K (§ 229.402 of this chapter) or any successor to Item 402 (a "say-on-pay vote") or that relates to the frequency of say-on-pay votes, provided that in the most recent shareholder vote required by § 240.14a-21(b) of this chapter a single year (i.e., one, two, or three years) received approval of a majority of votes cast on the matter and the company has adopted a policy on the frequency of say-on-pay votes that is consistent with the choice of the majority of votes cast in the most recent shareholder vote required by § 240.14a-21(b) of this chapter.

(11) *Duplication:* If the proposal substantially duplicates another proposal previously submitted to the company by another proponent that will be included in the company's proxy materials for the same meeting;

(12) *Resubmissions:* If the proposal addresses substantially the same subject matter as a proposal, or proposals, previously included in the company's proxy materials within the preceding five calendar years if the most recent vote occurred within the preceding three calendar years and the most recent vote was:

    (i) Less than 5 percent of the votes cast if previously voted on once;

    (ii) Less than 15 percent of the votes cast if previously voted on twice; or

    (iii) Less than 25 percent of the votes cast if previously voted on three or more times.

(13) *Specific amount of dividends:* If the proposal relates to specific amounts of cash or stock dividends.

(j) *Question 10:* What procedures must the company follow if it intends to exclude my proposal?

(1) If the company intends to exclude a proposal from its proxy materials, it must file its reasons with the Commission no later than 80 calendar days before it files its definitive proxy statement and form of proxy with the Commission. The company must simultaneously provide you with a copy of its submission. The Commission staff may permit the company to make its submission later than 80 days before the company files its definitive proxy statement and form of proxy, if the company demonstrates good cause for missing the deadline.

(2) The company must file six paper copies of the following:

    (i) The proposal;

    (ii) An explanation of why the company believes that it may exclude the proposal, which should, if possible, refer to the most recent applicable authority, such as prior Division letters issued under the rule; and

    (iii) A supporting opinion of counsel when such reasons are based on matters of state or foreign law.

(k) *Question 11:* May I submit my own statement to the Commission responding to the company's arguments? Yes, you may submit a response, but it is not required. You should try to submit any response to us, with a copy to the company, as soon as possible after the company makes its submission. This way, the Commission staff will have time to consider fully your submission before it issues its response. You should submit six paper copies of your response.

(l) *Question 12:* If the company includes my shareholder proposal in its proxy materials, what information about me must it include along with the proposal itself?

(1) The company's proxy statement must include your name and address, as well as the number of the company's voting securities that you hold. However, instead of providing that information, the company may instead include a statement that it will provide the information to shareholders promptly upon receiving an oral or written request.

(2) The company is not responsible for the contents of your proposal or supporting statement.

(m) *Question 13:* What can I do if the company includes in its proxy statement reasons why it believes shareholders should not vote in favor of my proposal, and I disagree with some of its statements?

(1) The company may elect to include in its proxy statement reasons why it believes shareholders should vote against your proposal. The company is allowed to make arguments reflecting its own point of view, just as you may express your own point of view in your proposal's supporting statement.

(2) However, if you believe that the company's opposition to your proposal contains materially false or misleading statements that may violate our anti-fraud rule, § 240.14a-9, you should promptly send to the Commission staff and the company a letter explaining the reasons for your view, along with a copy of the company's statements opposing your proposal. To the extent possible, your letter should include specific factual information demonstrating the inaccuracy of the company's claims. Time permitting, you may wish to try to work out your differences with the company by yourself before contacting the Commission staff.

(3) We require the company to send you a copy of its statements opposing your proposal before it sends its proxy materials, so that you may bring to our attention any materially false or misleading statements, under the following timeframes:

(i) If our no-action response requires that you make revisions to your proposal or supporting statement as a condition to requiring the company to include it in its proxy materials, then the company must provide you with a copy of its opposition statements no later than 5 calendar days after the company receives a copy of your revised proposal; or

(ii) In all other cases, the company must provide you with a copy of its opposition statements no later than 30 calendar days before its files definitive copies of its proxy statement and form of proxy under § 240.14a-6.

§ 240.14d-3   Filing and Transmission of Tender Offer Statement.

(a) Filing and transmittal. No bidder shall make a tender offer if, after consummation thereof, such bidder would be the beneficial owner of more than 5 percent of the class of the subject company's securities for which the tender offer is made, unless as soon as practicable on the date of the commencement of the tender offer such bidder:

(1) Files with the Commission a Tender Offer Statement on Schedule TO (§ 240.14d-100), including all exhibits thereto;

(2) Delivers a copy of such Schedule TO, including all exhibits thereto:

(i) To the subject company at its principal executive office; and

(ii) To any other bidder, which has filed a Schedule TO with the Commission relating to a tender offer which has not yet terminated for the same class of securities of the subject company, at such bidder's principal executive office or at the address of the person authorized to receive notices and communications (which is disclosed on the cover sheet of such other bidder's Schedule TO);

(3) Gives telephonic notice of the information required by Rule 14d-6(d)(2)(i) and (ii) (§ 240.14d-6(d)(2)(i) and (ii)) and mails by means of first class mail a copy of such Schedule TO, including all exhibits thereto:

(i) To each national securities exchange where such class of the subject company's securities is registered and listed for trading (which may be based upon information contained in the subject company's most recent Annual Report on Form 10-K (§ 249.310 of this chapter) filed with the Commission unless the bidder has reason to believe that such information is not current), which telephonic notice shall be made when practicable before the opening of each such exchange; and

(ii) To the National Association of Securities Dealers, Inc. ("NASD") if such class of the subject company's securities is authorized for quotation in the NASDAQ interdealer quotation system.

(b) Post-commencement amendments and additional materials. The bidder making the tender offer must file with the Commission:

(1) An amendment to Schedule TO (§ 240.14d-100) reporting promptly any material changes in the information set forth in the schedule previously filed and including copies of any additional tender offer materials as exhibits; and

(2) A final amendment to Schedule TO (§ 240.14d-100) reporting promptly the results of the tender offer.

Instruction to paragraph (b):

A copy of any additional tender offer materials or amendment filed under this section must be sent promptly to the subject company and to any exchange and/or NASD, as required by paragraph (a) of this section, but in no event later than the date the materials are first published, sent or given to security holders.

(c) Certain announcements. Notwithstanding the provisions of paragraph (b) of this section, if the additional tender offer material or an amendment to Schedule TO discloses only the number of shares deposited to date, and/or announces an extension of the time during which shares may be tendered, then the bidder may file such tender offer material or amendment and send a copy of such tender offer material or amendment to the subject company, any exchange and/or the NASD, as required by paragraph (a) of this section, promptly after the date such tender offer material is first published or sent or given to security holders.

§ 240.14e-1 Unlawful Tender Offer Practices.

As a means reasonably designed to prevent fraudulent, deceptive or manipulative acts or practices within the meaning of § 14(e) of the Act, no person who makes a tender offer shall:

(a) Hold such tender offer open for less than twenty business days from the date such tender offer is first published or sent to security holders; provided, however, that if the tender offer involves a roll-up transaction as defined in Item 901(c) of Regulation S-K (17 CFR 229.901(c)) and the securities being offered are registered (or authorized to be registered) on Form S-4 (17 CFR 229.25) or Form F-4 (17 CFR 229.34), the offer shall not be open for less than sixty calendar days from the date the tender offer is first published or sent to security holders;

(b) Increase or decrease the percentage of the class of securities being sought or the consideration offered or the dealer's soliciting fee to be given in a tender offer unless such tender offer remains open for at least ten business days from the date that notice of such increase or decrease is first published or sent or given to security holders.

Provided, however, That, for purposes of this paragraph, the acceptance for payment of an additional amount of securities not to exceed two percent of the class of securities that is the subject of the tender offer shall not be deemed to be an increase. For purposes of this paragraph, the percentage of a class of securities shall be calculated in accordance with § 14(d)(3) of the Act.

(c) Fail to pay the consideration offered or return the securities deposited by or on behalf of security holders promptly after the termination or withdrawal of a tender offer. This paragraph does not prohibit a bidder electing to offer a subsequent offering period under § 240.14d-11 from paying for securities during the subsequent offering period in accordance with that section.

(d) Extend the length of a tender offer without issuing a notice of such extension by press release or other public announcement, which notice shall include disclosure of the approximate number of securities deposited to date and shall be issued no later than the earlier of: (i) 9:00 a.m. Eastern time, on the next business day after the scheduled expiration date of the offer or (ii), if the class of securities which is the subject of the tender offer is registered on one or more national securities exchanges, the first opening of any one of such exchanges on the next business day after the scheduled expiration date of the offer.

(e) The periods of time required by par~ and (b) of this section sh~ll ~ during wh~~~

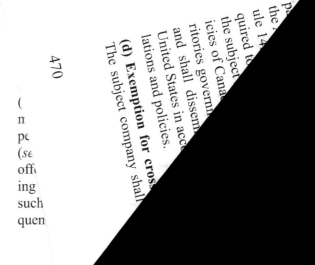

470

§ 240.14e-2   Position of Subject Company with Respect to a Tender Offer.

(a) *Position of subject company.* As a means reasonably designed to prevent fraudulent, deceptive or manipulative acts or practices within the meaning of § 14(e) of the Act, the subject company, no later than 10 business days from the date the tender offer is first published or sent or given, shall publish, send or give to security holders a statement disclosing that the subject company:

    (1) Recommends acceptance or rejection of the bidder's tender offer;

    (2) Expresses no opinion and is remaining neutral toward the bidder's tender offer; or

    (3) Is unable to take a position with respect to the bidder's tender offer. Such statement shall also include the reason(s) for the position (including the inability to take a position) disclosed therein.

(b) *Material change.* If any material change occurs in the disclosure required by paragraph (a) of this section, the subject company shall promptly publish or send or give a statement disclosing such material change to security holders.

(c) Any issuer, a class of the securities of which is the subject of a tender offer filed with the Commission on Schedule 14D-1F and conducted in reliance upon and in conformity with Rule 14d-1(b) under the Act, and any director or officer of such issuer where so required by the laws, regulations and policies of Canada and/or any of its provinces or territories, in lieu of the statements called for by paragraph (a) of this section and Rule 14d-9 under the Act, shall file with the Commission on Schedule 14D-9F the entire disclosure document(s) required to be furnished to holders of securities of the issuer by the laws, regulations and policies of Canada and/or any of its provinces or territories governing the conduct of the tender offer, and disseminate such document(s) in the manner and in accordance with such laws, regulations and policies.

(d) *Cross-border tender offers.* [A bidder or subject company shall] be exempt from this section with respect to a tender offer conducted under § 240.14d-1(c).

UCC Article 8 - Investment Securities (1994)

Table of Contents

Part 1. Short Title and General Matters

§ 8-101. Short Title.

This Article may be cited as Uniform Commercial Code--Investment Securities.

§ 8-102. Definitions.

(a) In this Article:

(1) "**Adverse claim**" means a claim that a claimant has a property interest in a financial asset and that it is a violation of the rights of the claimant for another person to hold, transfer, or deal with the financial asset.

(2) "**Bearer form,**" as applied to a certificated security, means a form in which the security is payable to the bearer of the security certificate according to its terms but not by reason of an indorsement.

(3) "**Broker**" means a person defined as a broker or dealer under the federal securities laws,

but without excluding a bank acting in that capacity.

(4) "**Certificated security**" means a security that is represented by a certificate.

(5) "**Clearing corporation**" means:

(i) a person that is registered as a "clearing agency" under the federal securities laws;

(ii) a federal reserve bank; or

(iii) any other person that provides clearance or settlement services with respect to financial assets that would require it to register as a clearing agency under the federal securities laws but for an exclusion or exemption from the registration requirement, if its activities as a clearing corporation, including promulgation of rules, are subject to regulation by a federal or state governmental authority.

(6) "**Communicate**" means to:

(i) send a signed writing; or

(ii) transmit information by any mechanism agreed upon by the persons transmitting and receiving the information.

(7) "**Entitlement holder**" means a person identified in the records of a securities intermediary as the person having a security entitlement against the securities intermediary. If a person acquires a security entitlement by virtue of § 8-501(b)(2) or (3), that person is the entitlement holder.

(8) "**Entitlement order**" means a notification communicated to a securities intermediary directing transfer or redemption of a financial asset to which the entitlement holder has a security entitlement.

(9) "**Financial asset,**" except as otherwise provided in § 8-103, means:

(i) a security;

(ii) an obligation of a person or a share, participation, or other interest in a person or in property or an enterprise of a person, which is, or is of a type, dealt in or traded on financial markets, or which is recognized in any area in which it is issued or dealt in as a medium for investment; or

(iii) any property that is held by a securities intermediary for another person in a securities account if the securities intermediary has expressly agreed with the other person that the property is to be treated as a financial asset under this Article.

As context requires, the term means either the interest itself or the means by which a person's claim to it is evidenced, including a certificated or uncertificated security, a security certificate, or a security entitlement.

(10) [reserved]

(11) "**Indorsement**" means a signature that alone or accompanied by other words is made on a security certificate in registered form or on a separate document for the purpose of assigning, transferring, or redeeming the security or granting a power to assign, transfer, or redeem it.

(12) "**Instruction**" means a notification communicated to the issuer of an uncertificated security which directs that the transfer of the security be registered or that the security be redeemed.

(13) "**Registered form,**" as applied to a certificated security, means a form in which:

(i) the security certificate specifies a person entitled to the security; and

(ii) a transfer of the security may be registered upon books maintained for that purpose by or on behalf of the issuer, or the security certificate so states.

(14) "Securities intermediary" means:

(i) a clearing corporation; or

(ii) a person, including a bank or broker, that in the ordinary course of its business maintains securities accounts for others and is acting in that capacity.

(15) "**Security,**" except as otherwise provided in § 8-103, means an obligation of an issuer or a share, participation, or other interest in an issuer or in property or an enterprise of an issuer:

(i) which is represented by a security certificate in bearer or registered form, or the transfer of which may be registered upon books maintained for that purpose by or on behalf of the issuer;

(ii) which is one of a class or series or by its terms is divisible into a class or series of shares, participations, interests, or obligations; and

(iii) which:

(A) is, or is of a type, dealt in or traded on securities exchanges or securities markets; or

(B) is a medium for investment and by its terms expressly provides that it is a security governed by this Article.

(16) "**Security certificate**" means a certificate representing a security.

(17) "**Security entitlement**" means the rights and property interest of an entitlement holder

473

with respect to a financial asset specified in Part 5.

(18) "**Uncertificated security**" means a security that is not represented by a certificate.

(b) Other definitions applying to this Article and the sections in which they appear are:

Appropriate person § 8-107

Control § 8-106

Delivery § 8-301

Investment company security § 8-103

Issuer § 8-201

Overissue § 8-210

Protected purchaser § 8-303

Securities account § 8-501

(c) In addition, Article 1 contains general definitions and principles of construction and interpretation applicable throughout this Article.

(d) The characterization of a person, business, or transaction for purposes of this Article does not determine the characterization of the person, business, or transaction for purposes of any other law, regulation, or rule.

§ 8-103. Rules for Determining Whether Certain Obligations and Interests Are Securities or Financial Assets.

(a) A share or similar equity interest issued by a corporation, business trust, joint stock company, or similar entity is a security.

(b) An "**investment company security**" is a security. "Investment company security" means a share or similar equity interest issued by an entity that is registered as an investment company under the federal investment company laws, an interest in a unit investment trust that is so registered, or a face-amount certificate issued by a face-amount certificate company that is so registered. Investment company security does not include an insurance policy or endowment policy or annuity contract issued by an insurance company.

(c) An interest in a partnership or limited liability company is not a security unless it is dealt in or traded on securities exchanges or in securities markets, its terms expressly provide that it is a security governed by this Article, or it is an investment company security. However, an interest in a partnership or limited liability company is a financial asset if it is held in a securities account.

(d) A writing that is a security certificate is governed by this Article and not by Article 3, even though it also meets the requirements of that Article. However, a negotiable instrument governed by Article 3 is a financial asset if it is held in a securities account.

(e) An option or similar obligation issued by a clearing corporation to its participants is not a security, but is a financial asset.

(f) A commodity contract, as defined in Section 9-102(a)(15), is not a security or a financial asset.

(g) A document of title is not a financial asset unless § 8-102(a)(9)(iii) applies.

§ 8-104. Acquisition of Security or Financial Asset or Interest Therein.

(a) A person acquires a security or an interest therein, under this Article, if:

(1) the person is a purchaser to whom a security is delivered pursuant to § 8-301; or

(2) the person acquires a security entitlement to the security pursuant to § 8-501.

(b) A person acquires a financial asset, other than a security, or an interest therein, under this Article, if the person acquires a security entitlement to the financial asset.

(c) A person who acquires a security entitlement to a security or other financial asset has the rights specified in Part 5, but is a purchaser of any security, security entitlement, or other financial asset held by the securities intermediary only to the extent provided in § 8-503.

(d) Unless the context shows that a different meaning is intended, a person who is required by other law, regulation, rule, or agreement to transfer, deliver, present, surrender, exchange, or otherwise put in the possession of another person a security or financial asset satisfies that requirement by causing the other person to acquire an interest in the security or financial asset pursuant to subsection (a) or (b).

§ 8-105. Notice of Adverse Claim.

(a) A person has notice of an adverse claim if:

(1) the person knows of the adverse claim;

(2) the person is aware of facts sufficient to indicate that there is a significant probability that the adverse claim exists and deliberately avoids information that would establish the existence of the adverse claim; or

(3) the person has a duty, imposed by statute or regulation, to investigate whether an adverse claim exists, and the investigation so required would establish the existence of the adverse claim.

(b) Having knowledge that a financial asset or interest therein is or has been transferred by a representative imposes no duty of inquiry into the rightfulness of a transaction and is not notice of an adverse claim. However, a person who knows that a representative has transferred a financial asset or interest therein in a transaction that is, or whose proceeds are being used, for the individual benefit of the representative or otherwise in breach of duty has notice of an adverse claim.

(c) An act or event that creates a right to immediate performance of the principal obligation represented by a security certificate or sets a date on or after which the certificate is to be presented or surrendered for redemption or exchange does not itself constitute notice of an adverse claim except in the case of a transfer more than:

(1) one year after a date set for presentment or surrender for redemption or exchange; or

(2) six months after a date set for payment of money against presentation or surrender of the certificate, if money was available for payment on that date.

(d) A purchaser of a certificated security has notice of an adverse claim if the security certificate:

(1) whether in bearer or registered form, has been indorsed "for collection" or "for surrender" or for some other purpose not involving transfer; or

(2) is in bearer form and has on it an unambiguous statement that it is the property of a person other than the transferor, but the mere writing of a name on the certificate is not such a statement.

(e) Filing of a financing statement under Article 9 is not notice of an adverse claim to a financial asset.

§ 8-106. Control.

(a) A purchaser has "**control**" of a certificated security in bearer form if the certificated security is delivered to the purchaser.

(b) A purchaser has "control" of a certificated security in registered form if the certificated security is delivered to the purchaser, and:

(1) the certificate is indorsed to the purchaser or in blank by an effective indorsement; or

(2) the certificate is registered in the name of the purchaser, upon original issue or registration of transfer by the issuer.

(c) A purchaser has "control" of an uncertificated security if:

(1) the uncertificated security is delivered to the purchaser; or

(2) the issuer has agreed that it will comply with instructions originated by the purchaser without further consent by the registered owner.

(d) A purchaser has "control" of a security entitlement if:

(1) the purchaser becomes the entitlement holder; or

(2) the securities intermediary has agreed that it will comply with entitlement orders originated by the purchaser without further consent by the entitlement holder, or

(3) another person has control of the security entitlement on behalf of the purchaser or, having previously acquired control of the security entitlement, acknowledges that it has control on behalf of the purchaser.

(e) If an interest in a security entitlement is granted by the entitlement holder to the entitlement holder's own securities intermediary, the securities intermediary has control.

(f) A purchaser who has satisfied the requirements of subsection (c) or (d) has control even if the registered owner in the case of subsection (c) or the entitlement holder in the case of subsection (d) retains the right to make substitutions for the uncertificated security or security entitlement, to originate instructions or entitlement orders to the issuer or securities intermediary, or otherwise to deal with the uncertificated security or security entitlement.

(g) An issuer or a securities intermediary may not enter into an agreement of the kind described in subsection (c)(2) or (d)(2) without the consent of the registered owner or entitlement holder, but an issuer or a securities intermediary is not required to enter into such an agreement even though the registered owner or entitlement holder so directs. An issuer or securities intermediary that has entered into such an agreement is not required to confirm the existence of the agreement to another party unless requested to do so by the registered owner or entitlement holder.

§ 8-107. Whether Indorsement, Instruction, Or Entitlement Order Is Effective.

(a) "Appropriate person" means:

(1) with respect to an indorsement, the person specified by a security certificate or by an effective special indorsement to be entitled to the security;

(2) with respect to an instruction, the registered owner of an uncertificated security;

(3) with respect to an entitlement order, the entitlement holder;

(4) if the person designated in paragraph (1), (2), or (3) is deceased, the designated person's successor taking under other law or the designated person's personal representative acting for the estate of the decedent; or

(5) if the person designated in paragraph (1), (2), or (3) lacks capacity, the designated person's guardian, conservator, or other similar representative who has power under other law to transfer the security or financial asset.

(b) An indorsement, instruction, or entitlement order is **effective** if:

(1) it is made by the appropriate person;

(2) it is made by a person who has power under the law of agency to transfer the security or financial asset on behalf of the appropriate person, including, in the case of an instruction or entitlement order, a person who has control under § 8-106(c)(2) or (d)(2); or

(3) the appropriate person has ratified it or is otherwise precluded from asserting its ineffectiveness.

(c) An indorsement, instruction, or entitlement order made by a representative is effective even if:

(1) the representative has failed to comply with a controlling instrument or with the law of the State having jurisdiction of the representative relationship, including any law requiring the representative to obtain court approval of the transaction; or

(2) the representative's action in making the indorsement, instruction, or entitlement order or using the proceeds of the transaction is otherwise a breach of duty.

(d) If a security is registered in the name of or specially indorsed to a person described as a representative, or if a securities account is maintained in the name of a person described as a representative, an indorsement, instruction, or entitlement order made by the person is effective even though the person is no longer serving in the described capacity.

(e) Effectiveness of an indorsement, instruction, or entitlement order is determined as of the date the indorsement, instruction, or entitlement order is made, and an indorsement, instruction, or entitlement order does not become ineffective by reason of any later change of circumstances.

§ 8-108. Warranties in Direct Holding.

(a) A person who transfers a certificated security to a purchaser for value warrants to the purchaser, and an indorser, if the transfer is by indorsement, warrants to any subsequent purchaser, that:

> **(1)** the certificate is genuine and has not been materially altered;

> **(2)** the transferor or indorser does not know of any fact that might impair the validity of the security;

> **(3)** there is no adverse claim to the security;

> **(4)** the transfer does not violate any restriction on transfer;

> **(5)** if the transfer is by indorsement, the indorsement is made by an appropriate person, or if the indorsement is by an agent, the agent has actual authority to act on behalf of the appropriate person; and

> **(6)** the transfer is otherwise effective and rightful.

(b) A person who originates an instruction for registration of transfer of an uncertificated security to a purchaser for value warrants to the purchaser that:

> **(1)** the instruction is made by an appropriate person, or if the instruction is by an agent, the agent has actual authority to act on behalf of the appropriate person;

> **(2)** the security is valid;

> **(3)** there is no adverse claim to the security; and

> **(4)** at the time the instruction is presented to the issuer:

>> **(i)** the purchaser will be entitled to the registration of transfer;

>> **(ii)** the transfer will be registered by the issuer free from all liens, security interests, restrictions, and claims other than those specified in the instruction;

>> **(iii)** the transfer will not violate any restriction on transfer; and

>> **(iv)** the requested transfer will otherwise be effective and rightful.

(c) A person who transfers an uncertificated security to a purchaser for value and does not originate an instruction in connection with the transfer warrants that:

> **(1)** the uncertificated security is valid;

> **(2)** there is no adverse claim to the security;

> **(3)** the transfer does not violate any restriction on transfer; and

> **(4)** the transfer is otherwise effective and rightful.

(d) A person who indorses a security certificate warrants to the issuer that:

> **(1)** there is no adverse claim to the security; and

> **(2)** the indorsement is effective.

(e) A person who originates an instruction for registration of transfer of an uncertificated security warrants to the issuer that:

> **(1)** the instruction is effective; and

> **(2)** at the time the instruction is presented to the issuer the purchaser will be entitled to the registration of transfer.

(f) A person who presents a certificated security for registration of transfer or for payment or exchange warrants to the issuer that the person is entitled to the registration, payment, or exchange, but a purchaser for value and without notice of adverse claims to whom transfer is registered warrants only that the person has no knowledge of any unauthorized signature in a necessary indorsement.

(g) If a person acts as agent of another in delivering a certificated security to a purchaser, the identity of the principal was known to the person to whom the certificate was delivered, and the certificate delivered by the agent was received by the agent from the principal or received by the agent from another person at the direction of the principal, the person delivering the security certificate warrants only that the delivering person has authority to act for the principal and does not know of any adverse claim to the certificated security.

(h) A secured party who redelivers a security certificate received, or after payment and on order of the debtor delivers the security certificate to another person, makes only the warranties of an agent under subsection (g).

(i) Except as otherwise provided in subsection (g), a broker acting for a customer makes to the issuer and a purchaser the warranties provided in subsections (a) through (f). A broker that delivers a security certificate to its customer, or causes its customer to be registered as the owner of an uncertificated security, makes to the customer the warranties provided in subsection (a) or (b), and has the rights and privileges of a purchaser under this section. The warranties of and in favor of the broker acting as an agent are in addition to applicable warranties given by and in favor of the customer.

§ 8-109. Warranties in Indirect Holding.

(a) A person who originates an entitlement order to a securities intermediary warrants to the securities intermediary that:

> **(1)** the entitlement order is made by an appropriate person, or if the entitlement order is by an agent, the agent has actual authority to act on behalf of the appropriate person; and

> **(2)** there is no adverse claim to the security entitlement.

(b) A person who delivers a security certificate to a securities intermediary for credit to a securities account or originates an instruction with respect to an uncertificated security directing that the uncertificated security be credited to a securities account makes to the securities intermediary the warranties specified in § 8-108(a) or (b).

(c) If a securities intermediary delivers a security certificate to its entitlement holder or causes its entitlement holder to be registered as the owner of an uncertificated security, the securities intermediary makes to the entitlement holder the warranties specified in § 8-108**(a)** or (b).

§ 8-110. Applicability; Choice of Law.

(a) The local law of the issuer's jurisdiction, as specified in subsection (d), governs:

> **(1)** the validity of a security;

> **(2)** the rights and duties of the issuer with respect to registration of transfer;

> **(3)** the effectiveness of registration of transfer by the issuer;

> **(4)** whether the issuer owes any duties to an adverse claimant to a security; and

> **(5)** whether an adverse claim can be asserted against a person to whom transfer of a certificated or uncertificated security is registered or a person who obtains control of an uncertificated security.

(b) The local law of the securities intermediary's jurisdiction, as specified in subsection (e), governs:

> **(1)** acquisition of a security entitlement from the securities intermediary;

> **(2)** the rights and duties of the securities intermediary and entitlement holder arising out of a security entitlement;

> **(3)** whether the securities intermediary owes any duties to an adverse claimant to a security entitlement; and

> **(4)** whether an adverse claim can be asserted against a person who acquires a security entitlement from the securities intermediary or a person who purchases a security entitlement or interest therein from an entitlement holder.

(c) The local law of the jurisdiction in which a security certificate is located at the time of delivery governs whether an adverse claim can be asserted against a person to whom the security certificate is delivered.

(d) "Issuer's jurisdiction" means the jurisdiction under which the issuer of the security is organized or, if permitted by the law of that jurisdiction, the law of another jurisdiction specified by the issuer. An issuer organized under the law of this State may specify the law of another jurisdiction as the law governing the matters specified in subsection (a)(2) through (5).

(e) The following rules determine a "securities intermediary's jurisdiction" for purposes of this section:

(1) If an agreement between the securities intermediary and its entitlement holder governing the securities account expressly provides that a particular jurisdiction is the securities intermediary's jurisdiction for purposes of this part, this article, or this act, that jurisdiction is the securities intermediary's jurisdiction.

(2) If paragraph (1) does not apply and an agreement between the securities intermediary and its entitlement holder expressly provides that the agreement is governed by the law of a particular jurisdiction, that jurisdiction is the securities intermediary's jurisdiction.

(3) If neither paragraph (i) nor paragraph (ii) applies and an agreement between the securities intermediary and its entitlement holder governing the securities account expressly provides that the securities account is maintained at an office in a particular jurisdiction, that jurisdiction is the securities intermediary's jurisdiction.

(4) If none of the preceding paragraphs applies, the securities intermediary's jurisdiction is the jurisdiction in which the office identified in an account statement as the office serving the entitlement holder's account is located.

(5) If none of the preceding paragraphs applies, the securities intermediary's jurisdiction is the jurisdiction in which the chief executive office of the securities intermediary is located.

(f) A securities intermediary's jurisdiction is not determined by the physical location of certificates representing financial assets, or by the jurisdiction in which is organized the issuer of the financial asset with respect to which an entitlement holder has a security entitlement, or by the location of facilities for data processing or other record keeping concerning the account.

§ 8-111. Clearing Corporation Rules.

A rule adopted by a clearing corporation governing rights and obligations among the clearing corporation and its participants in the clearing corporation is effective even if the rule conflicts with this [Act] and affects another party who does not consent to the rule.

§ 8-112. Creditor's Legal Process.

(a) The interest of a debtor in a certificated security may be reached by a creditor only by actual seizure of the security certificate by the officer making the attachment or levy, except as otherwise provided in subsection (d). However, a certificated security for which the certificate has been surrendered to the issuer may be reached by a creditor by legal process upon the issuer.

(b) The interest of a debtor in an uncertificated security may be reached by a creditor only by legal process upon the issuer at its chief executive office in the United States, except as otherwise provided in subsection (d).

(c) The interest of a debtor in a security entitlement may be reached by a creditor only by legal process upon the securities intermediary with whom the debtor's securities account is maintained, except as otherwise provided in subsection (d).

(d) The interest of a debtor in a certificated security for which the certificate is in the possession of a secured party, or in an uncertificated security registered in the name of a secured party, or a security entitlement maintained in the name of a secured party, may be reached by a creditor by legal process upon the secured party.

(e) A creditor whose debtor is the owner of a certificated security, uncertificated security, or security entitlement is entitled to aid from a court of competent jurisdiction, by injunction or otherwise, in reaching the certificated security, uncertificated security, or security entitlement or in satisfying the claim by means allowed at law or in equity in regard to property that cannot readily be reached by other legal process.

§ 8-113. Statute of Frauds Inapplicable.

A contract or modification of a contract for the sale or purchase of a security is enforceable whether or not there is a writing signed or record authenticated by a party against whom enforcement is sought, even if the contract or modification is not capable of performance within one year of its making.

§ 8-114. Evidentiary Rules Concerning Certificated Securities.

The following rules apply in an action on a certificated security against the issuer:

(1) Unless specifically denied in the pleadings, each signature on a security certificate or in a necessary indorsement is admitted.

(2) If the effectiveness of a signature is put in issue, the burden of establishing effectiveness is on the party claiming under the signature, but the signature is presumed to be genuine or authorized.

(3) If signatures on a security certificate are admitted or established, production of the certificate entitles a holder to recover on it unless the defendant establishes a defense or a defect going to the validity of the security.

(4) If it is shown that a defense or defect exists, the plaintiff has the burden of establishing that the plaintiff or some person under whom the plaintiff claims is a person against whom the defense or defect cannot be asserted.

§ 8-115. Securities Intermediary and Others Not Liable to Adverse Claimant.

A securities intermediary that has transferred a financial asset pursuant to an effective entitlement order, or a broker or other agent or bailee that has dealt with a financial asset at the direction of its customer or principal, is not liable to a person having an adverse claim to the financial asset, unless the securities intermediary, or broker or other agent or bailee:

(1) took the action after it had been served with an injunction, restraining order, or other legal process enjoining it from doing so, issued by a court of competent jurisdiction, and had a reasonable opportunity to act on the injunction, restraining order, or other legal process; or

(2) acted in collusion with the wrongdoer in violating the rights of the adverse claimant; or

(3) in the case of a security certificate that has been stolen, acted with notice of the adverse claim.

§ 8-116. Securities Intermediary as Purchaser for Value.

A securities intermediary that receives a financial asset and establishes a security entitlement to the financial asset in favor of an entitlement holder is a purchaser for value of the financial asset. A securities intermediary that acquires a security entitlement to a financial asset from another securities intermediary acquires the security entitlement for value if the securities intermediary acquiring the security entitlement establishes a security entitlement to the financial asset in favor of an entitlement holder.

Part 2. Issue and Issuer

§ 8-201. Issuer.

(a) With respect to an obligation on or a defense to a security, an **"issuer"** includes a person that:

(1) places or authorizes the placing of its name on a security certificate, other than as authenticating trustee, registrar, transfer agent, or the like, to evidence a share, participation, or other interest in its property or in an enterprise, or to evidence its duty to perform an obligation represented by the certificate;

(2) creates a share, participation, or other interest in its property or in an enterprise, or undertakes an obligation, that is an uncertificated security;

(3) directly or indirectly creates a fractional interest in its rights or property, if the fractional interest is represented by a security certificate; or

(4) becomes responsible for, or in place of, another person described as an issuer in this section.

(b) With respect to an obligation on or defense to a security, a guarantor is an issuer to the extent of its guaranty, whether or not its obligation is noted on a security certificate.

(c) With respect to a registration of a transfer, issuer means a person on whose behalf transfer books are maintained.

§ 8-202. Issuer's Responsibility and Defenses; Notice of Defect or Defense.

(a) Even against a purchaser for value and without notice, the terms of a certificated security include terms stated on the certificate and terms made part of the security by reference on the certificate to another instrument, indenture, or document or to a constitution, statute, ordinance, rule, regulation, order, or the like, to the extent the terms referred to do not conflict with terms stated on the certificate. A reference under this subsection does not of itself charge a purchaser for value with notice of a defect going to the validity of the security, even if the certificate expressly states that a person accepting it admits notice. The terms of an uncertificated security include those stated in any instrument, indenture, or document or in a constitution, statute, ordinance, rule, regulation, order, or the like, pursuant to which the security is issued.

(b) The following rules apply if an issuer asserts that a security is not valid:

(1) A security other than one issued by a government or governmental subdivision, agency, or instrumentality, even though issued with a defect going to its validity, is valid in the hands of a purchaser for value and without notice of the particular defect unless the defect involves a violation of a constitutional provision. In that case, the security is valid in the hands of a purchaser for value and without notice of the defect, other than one who takes by original issue.

(2) Paragraph (1) applies to an issuer that is a government or governmental subdivision, agency, or instrumentality only if there has been substantial compliance with the legal requirements governing the issue or the issuer has received a substantial consideration for the issue as a whole or for the particular security and a stated purpose of the issue is one for which the issuer has power to borrow money or issue the security.

(c) Except as otherwise provided in -205, lack of genuineness of a certificated security is a complete defense, even against a purchaser for value and without notice.

(d) All other defenses of the issuer of a security, including nondelivery and conditional delivery of a certificated security, are ineffective against a purchaser for value who has taken the certificated security without notice of the particular defense.

(e) This section does not affect the right of a party to cancel a contract for a security "when, as and if issued" or "when distributed" in the event of a material change in the character of the security that is the subject of the contract or in the plan or arrangement pursuant to which the security is to be issued or distributed.

(f) If a security is held by a securities intermediary against whom an entitlement holder has a security entitlement with respect to the security, the issuer may not assert any defense that the issuer could not assert if the entitlement holder held the security directly.

§ 8-203. Staleness as Notice of Defect or Defense.

After an act or event, other than a call that has been revoked, creating a right to immediate performance of the principal obligation represented by a certificated security or setting a date on or after which the security is to be presented or surrendered for redemption or exchange, a purchaser is charged with notice of any defect in its issue or defense of the issuer, if the act or event:

(1) requires the payment of money, the delivery of a certificated security, the registration of transfer of an uncertificated security, or any of them on presentation or surrender of the security certificate, the money or security is available on the date set for payment or exchange, and the purchaser takes the security more than one year after that date; or

(2) is not covered by paragraph (1) and the purchaser takes the security more than two years after the date set for surrender or presentation or the date on which performance became due.

§ 8-204. Effect of Issuer's Restriction on Transfer.

A restriction on transfer of a security imposed by the issuer, even if otherwise lawful, is ineffective against a person without knowledge of the restriction unless:

    (1) the security is certificated and the restriction is noted conspicuously on the security certificate; or

    (2) the security is uncertificated and the registered owner has been notified of the restriction.

§ 8-205. Effect of Unauthorized Signature on Security Certificate.

An unauthorized signature placed on a security certificate before or in the course of issue is ineffective, but the signature is effective in favor of a purchaser for value of the certificated security if the purchaser is without notice of the lack of authority and the signing has been done by:

    (1) an authenticating trustee, registrar, transfer agent, or other person entrusted by the issuer with the signing of the security certificate or of similar security certificates, or the immediate preparation for signing of any of them; or

    (2) an employee of the issuer, or of any of the persons listed in paragraph (1), entrusted with responsible handling of the security certificate.

§ 8-206. Completion or Alteration of Security Certificate.

(a) If a security certificate contains the signatures necessary to its issue or transfer but is incomplete in any other respect:

    (1) any person may complete it by filling in the blanks as authorized; and

    (2) even if the blanks are incorrectly filled in, the security certificate as completed is enforceable by a purchaser who took it for value and without notice of the incorrectness.

(b) A complete security certificate that has been improperly altered, even if fraudulently, remains enforceable, but only according to its original terms.

§ 8-207. Rights and Duties of Issuer with Respect to Registered Owners.

(a) Before due presentment for registration of transfer of a certificated security in registered form or of an instruction requesting registration of transfer of an uncertificated security, the issuer or indenture trustee may treat the registered owner as the person exclusively entitled to vote, receive notifications, and otherwise exercise all the rights and powers of an owner.

(b) This Article does not affect the liability of the registered owner of a security for a call, assessment, or the like.

§ 8-208. Effect of Signature of Authenticating Trustee, Registrar, or Transfer Agent.

(a) A person signing a security certificate as authenticating trustee, registrar, transfer agent, or the like, warrants to a purchaser for value of the certificated security, if the purchaser is without notice of a particular defect, that:

    (1) the certificate is genuine;

    (2) the person's own participation in the issue of the security is within the person's capacity and within the scope of the authority received by the person from the issuer; and

    (3) the person has reasonable grounds to believe that the certificated security is in the form and within the amount the issuer is authorized to issue.

(b) Unless otherwise agreed, a person signing under subsection (a) does not assume responsibility for the validity of the security in other respects.

§ 8-209. Issuer's Lien.

A lien in favor of an issuer upon a certificated security is valid against a purchaser only if the right of the issuer to the lien is noted conspicuously on the security certificate.

§ 8-210. Overissue.

(a) In this section, "**overissue**" means the issue of securities in excess of the amount the issuer has corporate power to issue, but an overissue does not occur if appropriate action has cured the overissue.

(b) Except as otherwise provided in subsections (c) and (d), the provisions of this Article which validate a security or compel its issue or reissue do not apply to the extent that validation, issue, or reissue would result in overissue.

(c) If an identical security not constituting an over-issue is reasonably available for purchase, a person entitled to issue or validation may compel the issuer to purchase the security and deliver it if certificated or register its transfer if uncertificated, against surrender of any security certificate the person holds.

(d) If a security is not reasonably available for purchase, a person entitled to issue or validation may recover from the issuer the price the person or the last purchaser for value paid for it with interest from the date of the person's demand.

Part 3. Transfer of Certificated and Uncertificated Securities

§ 8-301. Delivery.

(a) **Delivery** of a certificated security to a purchaser occurs when:

> **(1)** the purchaser acquires possession of the security certificate;

> **(2)** another person, other than a securities intermediary, either acquires possession of the security certificate on behalf of the purchaser or, having previously acquired possession of the certificate, acknowledges that it holds for the purchaser; or

> **(3)** a securities intermediary acting on behalf of the purchaser acquires possession of the security certificate, only if the certificate is in registered form and is (i) registered in the name of the purchaser, (ii) payable to the order of the purchaser, or (iii) specially indorsed to the purchaser by an effective indorsement and has not been indorsed to the securities intermediary or in blank.

(b) Delivery of an uncertificated security to a purchaser occurs when:

> **(1)** the issuer registers the purchaser as the registered owner, upon original issue or registration of transfer; or

> **(2)** another person, other than a securities intermediary, either becomes the registered owner of the uncertificated security on behalf of the purchaser or, having previously become the registered owner, acknowledges that it holds for the purchaser.

§ 8-302. Rights of Purchaser.

(a) Except as otherwise provided in subsections (b) and (c), a purchaser of a certificated or uncertificated security acquires all rights in the security that the transferor had or had power to transfer.

(b) A purchaser of a limited interest acquires rights only to the extent of the interest purchased.

(c) A purchaser of a certificated security who as a previous holder had notice of an adverse claim does not improve its position by taking from a protected purchaser.

§ 8-303. Protected Purchaser.

(a) **"Protected purchaser"** means a purchaser of a certificated or uncertificated security, or of an interest therein, who:

> **(1)** gives value;

> **(2)** does not have notice of any adverse claim to the security; and

> **(3)** obtains control of the certificated or uncertificated security.

(b) In addition to acquiring the rights of a purchaser, a protected purchaser also acquires its interest in the security free of any adverse claim.

§ 8-304. Indorsement.

(a) An indorsement may be in blank or special. An indorsement in blank includes an indorsement to bearer. A **special indorsement** specifies to whom a security is to be transferred or who has power to transfer it. A holder may convert a blank indorsement to a special indorsement.

(b) An indorsement purporting to be only of part of a security certificate representing units intended by the issuer to be separately transferable is effective to the extent of the indorsement.

(c) An indorsement, whether special or in blank, does not constitute a transfer until delivery of the certificate on which it appears or, if the indorsement is on a separate document, until delivery of both the document and the certificate.

483

(d) If a security certificate in registered form has been delivered to a purchaser without a necessary indorsement, the purchaser may become a protected purchaser only when the indorsement is supplied. However, against a transferor, a transfer is complete upon delivery and the purchaser has a specifically enforceable right to have any necessary indorsement supplied.

(e) An indorsement of a security certificate in bearer form may give notice of an adverse claim to the certificate, but it does not otherwise affect a right to registration that the holder possesses.

(f) Unless otherwise agreed, a person making an indorsement assumes only the obligations provided in § 8-108 and not an obligation that the security will be honored by the issuer.

§ 8-305. Instruction.

(a) If an instruction has been originated by an appropriate person but is incomplete in any other respect, any person may complete it as authorized and the issuer may rely on it as completed, even though it has been completed incorrectly.

(b) Unless otherwise agreed, a person initiating an instruction assumes only the obligations imposed by § 8-108 and not an obligation that the security will be honored by the issuer.

§ 8-306. Effect of Guaranteeing Signature, Indorsement, or Instruction.

(a) A person who guarantees a signature of an indorser of a security certificate warrants that at the time of signing:

    (1) the signature was genuine;

    (2) the signer was an appropriate person to indorse, or if the signature is by an agent, the agent had actual authority to act on behalf of the appropriate person; and

    (3) the signer had legal capacity to sign.

(b) A person who guarantees a signature of the originator of an instruction warrants that at the time of signing:

    (1) the signature was genuine;

    (2) the signer was an appropriate person to originate the instruction, or if the signature is

by an agent, the agent had actual authority to act on behalf of the appropriate person, if the person specified in the instruction as the registered owner was, in fact, the registered owner, as to which fact the signature guarantor does not make a warranty; and

    (3) the signer had legal capacity to sign.

(c) A person who specially guarantees the signature of an originator of an instruction makes the warranties of a signature guarantor under subsection (b) and also warrants that at the time the instruction is presented to the issuer:

    (1) the person specified in the instruction as the registered owner of the uncertificated security will be the registered owner; and

    (2) the transfer of the uncertificated security requested in the instruction will be registered by the issuer free from all liens, security interests, restrictions, and claims other than those specified in the instruction.

(d) A guarantor under subsections (a) and (b) or a special guarantor under subsection (c) does not otherwise warrant the rightfulness of the transfer.

(e) A person who guarantees an indorsement of a security certificate makes the warranties of a signature guarantor under subsection (a) and also warrants the rightfulness of the transfer in all respects.

(f) A person who guarantees an instruction requesting the transfer of an uncertificated security makes the warranties of a special signature guarantor under subsection (c) and also warrants the rightfulness of the transfer in all respects.

(g) An issuer may not require a special guaranty of signature, a guaranty of indorsement, or a guaranty of instruction as a condition to registration of transfer.

(h) The warranties under this section are made to a person taking or dealing with the security in reliance on the guaranty, and the guarantor is liable to the person for loss resulting from their breach. An indorser or originator of an instruction whose signature, indorsement, or instruction has been guaranteed is liable to a guarantor for any loss suffered by the guarantor as a result of breach of the warranties of the guarantor.

§ 8-307. Purchaser's Right to Requisites for Registration of Transfer.

Unless otherwise agreed, the transferor of a security on due demand shall supply the purchaser with proof of authority to transfer or with any other requisite necessary to obtain registration of the transfer of the security, but if the transfer is not for value, a transferor need not comply unless the purchaser pays the necessary expenses. If the transferor fails within a reasonable time to comply with the demand, the purchaser may reject or rescind the transfer.

Part 4. Registration

§ 8-401. Duty of Issuer to Register Transfer.

(a) If a certificated security in registered form is presented to an issuer with a request to register transfer or an instruction is presented to an issuer with a request to register transfer of an uncertificated security, the issuer shall register the transfer as requested if:

(1) under the terms of the security the person seeking registration of transfer is eligible to have the security registered in its name;

(2) the indorsement or instruction is made by the appropriate person or by an agent who has actual authority to act on behalf of the appropriate person;

(3) reasonable assurance is given that the indorsement or instruction is genuine and authorized (§ 8-402);

(4) any applicable law relating to the collection of taxes has been complied with;

(5) the transfer does not violate any restriction on transfer imposed by the issuer in accordance with § 8-204;

(6) a demand that the issuer not register transfer has not become effective under § 8-403, or the issuer has complied with § 8-403(b) but no legal process or indemnity bond is obtained as provided in § 8-403(d); and

(7) the transfer is in fact rightful or is to a protected purchaser.

(b) If an issuer is under a duty to register a transfer of a security, the issuer is liable to a person presenting a certificated security or an instruction for registration or to the person's principal for loss resulting from unreasonable delay in registration or failure or refusal to register the transfer.

§ 8-402. Assurance That Indorsement or Instruction Is Effective.

(a) An issuer may require the following assurance that each necessary indorsement or each instruction is genuine and authorized:

(1) in all cases, a guaranty of the signature of the person making an indorsement or originating an instruction including, in the case of an instruction, reasonable assurance of identity;

(2) if the indorsement is made or the instruction is originated by an agent, appropriate assurance of actual authority to sign;

(3) if the indorsement is made or the instruction is originated by a fiduciary pursuant to § 8-107(a)(4) or (a)(5), appropriate evidence of appointment or incumbency;

(4) if there is more than one fiduciary, reasonable assurance that all who are required to sign have done so; and

(5) if the indorsement is made or the instruction is originated by a person not covered by another provision of this subsection, assurance appropriate to the case corresponding as nearly as may be to the provisions of this subsection.

(b) An issuer may elect to require reasonable assurance beyond that specified in this section.

(c) In this section:

(1) "Guaranty of the signature" means a guaranty signed by or on behalf of a person reasonably believed by the issuer to be responsible. An issuer may adopt standards with respect to responsibility if they are not manifestly unreasonable.

(2) "Appropriate evidence of appointment or incumbency" means:

    (i) in the case of a fiduciary appointed or qualified by a court, a certificate issued by or under the direction or supervision of the court or an officer thereof and dated within 60 days before the date of presentation for transfer; or

    (ii) in any other case, a copy of a document showing the appointment or a certificate issued by or on behalf of a person reasonably believed by an issuer to be responsible or, in the absence of that document or certificate, other evidence the issuer reasonably considers appropriate.

§ 8-403. Demand That Issuer Not Register Transfer.

(a) A person who is an appropriate person to make an indorsement or originate an instruction may demand that the issuer not register transfer of a security by communicating to the issuer a notification that identifies the registered owner and the issue of which the security is a part and provides an address for communications directed to the person making the demand. The demand is effective only if it is received by the issuer at a time and in a manner affording the issuer reasonable opportunity to act on it.

(b) If a certificated security in registered form is presented to an issuer with a request to register transfer or an instruction is presented to an issuer with a request to register transfer of an uncertificated security after a demand that the issuer not register transfer has become effective, the issuer shall promptly communicate to (i) the person who initiated the demand at the address provided in the demand and (ii) the person who presented the security for registration of transfer or initiated the instruction requesting registration of transfer a notification stating that:

    (1) the certificated security has been presented for registration of transfer or the instruction for registration of transfer of the uncertificated security has been received;

    (2) a demand that the issuer not register transfer had previously been received; and

    (3) the issuer will withhold registration of transfer for a period of time stated in the notification in order to provide the person who initiated the demand an opportunity to obtain legal process or an indemnity bond.

(c) The period described in subsection (b)(3) may not exceed 30 days after the date of communication of the notification. A shorter period may be specified by the issuer if it is not manifestly unreasonable.

(d) An issuer is not liable to a person who initiated a demand that the issuer not register transfer for any loss the person suffers as a result of registration of a transfer pursuant to an effective indorsement or instruction if the person who initiated the demand does not, within the time stated in the issuer's communication, either:

    (1) obtain an appropriate restraining order, injunction, or other process from a court of competent jurisdiction enjoining the issuer from registering the transfer; or

    (2) file with the issuer an indemnity bond, sufficient in the issuer's judgment to protect the issuer and any transfer agent, registrar, or other agent of the issuer involved from any loss it or they may suffer by refusing to register the transfer.

(e) This section does not relieve an issuer from liability for registering transfer pursuant to an indorsement or instruction that was not effective.

§ 8-404. Wrongful Registration.

(a) Except as otherwise provided in § 8-406, an issuer is liable for wrongful registration of transfer if the issuer has registered a transfer of a security to a person not entitled to it, and the transfer was registered:

    (1) pursuant to an ineffective indorsement or instruction;

(2) after a demand that the issuer not register transfer became effective under § 8-403(a) and the issuer did not comply with § 8-403(b);

(3) after the issuer had been served with an injunction, restraining order, or other legal process enjoining it from registering the transfer, issued by a court of competent jurisdiction, and the issuer had a reasonable opportunity to act on the injunction, restraining order, or other legal process; or

(4) by an issuer acting in collusion with the wrongdoer.

(b) An issuer that is liable for wrongful registration of transfer under subsection (a) on demand shall provide the person entitled to the security with a like certificated or uncertificated security, and any payments or distributions that the person did not receive as a result of the wrongful registration. If an overissue would result, the issuer's liability to provide the person with a like security is governed by § 8-210.

(c) Except as otherwise provided in subsection (a) or in a law relating to the collection of taxes, an issuer is not liable to an owner or other person suffering loss as a result of the registration of a transfer of a security if registration was made pursuant to an effective indorsement or instruction.

§ 8-405. Replacement of Lost, Destroyed, or Wrongfully Taken Security Certificate.

(a) If an owner of a certificated security, whether in registered or bearer form, claims that the certificate has been lost, destroyed, or wrongfully taken, the issuer shall issue a new certificate if the owner:

(1) so requests before the issuer has notice that the certificate has been acquired by a protected purchaser;

(2) files with the issuer a sufficient indemnity bond; and

(3) satisfies other reasonable requirements imposed by the issuer.

(b) If, after the issue of a new security certificate, a protected purchaser of the original certificate presents it for registration of transfer, the issuer shall register the transfer unless an overissue would result. In that case, the issuer's liability is governed by § 8-210. In addition to any rights on the indemnity bond, an issuer may recover the new certificate from a person to whom it was issued or any person taking under that person, except a protected purchaser.

§ 8-406. Obligation to Notify Issuer of Lost, Destroyed, or Wrongfully Taken Security Certificate.

If a security certificate has been lost, apparently destroyed, or wrongfully taken, and the owner fails to notify the issuer of that fact within a reasonable time after the owner has notice of it and the issuer registers a transfer of the security before receiving notification, the owner may not assert against the issuer a claim for registering the transfer under § 8-404 or a claim to a new security certificate under § 8-405.

§ 8-407. Authenticating Trustee, Transfer Agent, and Registrar.

A person acting as authenticating trustee, transfer agent, registrar, or other agent for an issuer in the registration of a transfer of its securities, in the issue of new security certificates or uncertificated securities, or in the cancellation of surrendered security certificates has the same obligation to the holder or owner of a certificated or uncertificated security with regard to the particular functions performed as the issuer has in regard to those functions.

Part 5. Security Entitlements

§ 8-501. Securities Account; Acquisition of Security Entitlement from Securities Intermediary.

(a) "Securities account" means an account to which a financial asset is or may be credited in accordance with an agreement under which the person maintaining the account undertakes to treat the person for whom the account is maintained as entitled to exercise the rights that comprise the financial asset.

(b) Except as otherwise provided in subsections (d) and (e), a person acquires a security entitlement if a securities intermediary:

    (1) indicates by book entry that a financial asset has been credited to the person's securities account;

    (2) receives a financial asset from the person or acquires a financial asset for the person and, in either case, accepts it for credit to the person's securities account; or

    (3) becomes obligated under other law, regulation, or rule to credit a financial asset to the person's securities account.

(c) If a condition of subsection (b) has been met, a person has a security entitlement even though the securities intermediary does not itself hold the financial asset.

(d) If a securities intermediary holds a financial asset for another person, and the financial asset is registered in the name of, payable to the order of, or specially indorsed to the other person, and has not been indorsed to the securities intermediary or in blank, the other person is treated as holding the financial asset directly rather than as having a security entitlement with respect to the financial asset.

(e) Issuance of a security is not establishment of a security entitlement.

§ 8-502. Assertion of Adverse Claim Against Entitlement Holder.

An action based on an adverse claim to a financial asset, whether framed in conversion, replevin, constructive trust, equitable lien, or other theory, may not be asserted against a person who acquires a security entitlement under § 8-501 for value and without notice of the adverse claim.

§ 8-503. Property Interest of Entitlement Holder in Financial Asset Held by Securities Intermediary.

(a) To the extent necessary for a securities intermediary to satisfy all security entitlements with respect to a particular financial asset, all interests in that financial asset held by the securities intermediary are held by the securities intermediary for the entitlement holders, are not property of the securities intermediary, and are not subject to claims of creditors of the securities intermediary, except as otherwise provided in § 8-511.

(b) An entitlement holder's property interest with respect to a particular financial asset under subsection (a) is a pro rata property interest in all interests in that financial asset held by the securities intermediary, without regard to the time the entitlement holder acquired the security entitlement or the time the securities intermediary acquired the interest in that financial asset.

(c) An entitlement holder's property interest with respect to a particular financial asset under subsection (a) may be enforced against the securities intermediary only by exercise of the entitlement holder's rights under Sections 8-505 through 8-508.

(d) An entitlement holder's property interest with respect to a particular financial asset under subsection (a) may be enforced against a purchaser of the financial asset or interest therein only if:

    (1) insolvency proceedings have been initiated by or against the securities intermediary;

    (2) the securities intermediary does not have sufficient interests in the financial asset to satisfy the security entitlements of all of its entitlement holders to that financial asset;

    (3) the securities intermediary violated its obligations under § 8-504 by transferring the financial asset or interest therein to the purchaser; and

    (4) the purchaser is not protected under subsection (e).

The trustee or other liquidator, acting on behalf of all entitlement holders having security entitlements with respect to a particular financial asset, may recover the financial asset, or interest therein, from the purchaser. If the trustee or other liquidator elects not to pursue that right, an entitlement holder whose security entitlement remains unsatisfied has the right to recover its interest in the financial asset from the purchaser.

(e) An action based on the entitlement holder's property interest with respect to a particular financial asset under subsection (a), whether framed in conversion, replevin, constructive trust, equitable lien, or other theory, may not be asserted against any purchaser of a financial asset or interest therein who gives value, obtains control, and does not act in collusion with the securities intermediary in violating the securities intermediary's obligations under § 8-504.

§ 8-504. Duty of Securities Intermediary to Maintain Financial Asset.

(a) A securities intermediary shall promptly obtain and thereafter maintain a financial asset in a quantity corresponding to the aggregate of all security entitlements it has established in favor of its entitlement holders with respect to that financial asset. The securities intermediary may maintain those financial assets directly or through one or more other securities intermediaries.

(b) Except to the extent otherwise agreed by its entitlement holder, a securities intermediary may not grant any security interests in a financial asset it is obligated to maintain pursuant to subsection (a).

(c) A securities intermediary satisfies the duty in subsection (a) if:

(1) the securities intermediary acts with respect to the duty as agreed upon by the entitlement holder and the securities intermediary; or

(2) in the absence of agreement, the securities intermediary exercises due care in accordance with reasonable commercial standards to obtain and maintain the financial asset.

(d) This section does not apply to a clearing corporation that is itself the obligor of an option or similar obligation to which its entitlement holders have security entitlements.

§ 8-505. Duty of Securities Intermediary with Respect to Payments and Distributions.

(a) A securities intermediary shall take action to obtain a payment or distribution made by the issuer of a financial asset. A securities intermediary satisfies the duty if:

(1) the securities intermediary acts with respect to the duty as agreed upon by the entitlement holder and the securities intermediary; or

(2) in the absence of agreement, the securities intermediary exercises due care in accordance with reasonable commercial standards to attempt to obtain the payment or distribution.

(b) A securities intermediary is obligated to its entitlement holder for a payment or distribution made by the issuer of a financial asset if the payment or distribution is received by the securities intermediary.

§ 8-506. Duty of Securities Intermediary to Exercise Rights as Directed by Entitlement Holder.

A securities intermediary shall exercise rights with respect to a financial asset if directed to do so by an entitlement holder. A securities intermediary satisfies the duty if:

(1) the securities intermediary acts with respect to the duty as agreed upon by the entitlement holder and the securities intermediary; or

(2) in the absence of agreement, the securities intermediary either places the entitlement holder in a position to exercise the rights directly or exercises due care in accordance with reasonable commercial standards to follow the direction of the entitlement holder.

§ 8-507. Duty of Securities Intermediary to Comply with Entitlement Order.

(a) A securities intermediary shall comply with an entitlement order if the entitlement order is originated by the appropriate person, the securities intermediary has had reasonable opportunity to assure itself that the entitlement order is genuine and authorized, and the securities intermediary has had reasonable opportunity to comply with the entitlement order. A securities intermediary satisfies the duty if:

(1) the securities intermediary acts with respect to the duty as agreed upon by the entitlement holder and the securities intermediary; or

(2) in the absence of agreement, the securities intermediary exercises due care in accordance with reasonable commercial standards to comply with the entitlement order.

(b) If a securities intermediary transfers a financial asset pursuant to an ineffective entitlement order, the securities intermediary shall reestablish a security entitlement in favor of the person entitled to it, and pay or credit any payments or distributions that the person did not receive as a result of the wrongful transfer. If the securities intermediary does not reestablish a security entitlement, the securities intermediary is liable to the entitlement holder for damages.

§ 8-508. Duty of Securities Intermediary to Change Entitlement Holder's Position to Other Form of Security Holding.

A securities intermediary shall act at the direction of an entitlement holder to change a security entitlement into another available form of holding for which the entitlement holder is eligible, or to cause the financial asset to be transferred to a securities account of the entitlement holder with another securities intermediary. A securities intermediary satisfies the duty if:

(1) the securities intermediary acts as agreed upon by the entitlement holder and the securities intermediary; or

(2) in the absence of agreement, the securities intermediary exercises due care in accordance with reasonable commercial standards to follow the direction of the entitlement holder.

§ 8-509. Specification of Duties of Securities Intermediary by Other Statute or Regulation; Manner of Performance of Duties of Securities Intermediary and Exercise of Rights of Entitlement Holder.

(a) If the substance of a duty imposed upon a securities intermediary by Sections 8-504 through 8-508 is the subject of other statute, regulation, or rule, compliance with that statute, regulation, or rule satisfies the duty.

(b) To the extent that specific standards for the performance of the duties of a securities intermediary or the exercise of the rights of an entitlement

holder are not specified by other statute, regulation, or rule or by agreement between the securities intermediary and entitlement holder, the securities intermediary shall perform its duties and the entitlement holder shall exercise its rights in a commercially reasonable manner.

(c) The obligation of a securities intermediary to perform the duties imposed by Sections 8-504 through 8-508 is subject to:

(1) rights of the securities intermediary arising out of a security interest under a security agreement with the entitlement holder or otherwise; and

(2) rights of the securities intermediary under other law, regulation, rule, or agreement to withhold performance of its duties as a result of unfulfilled obligations of the entitlement holder to the securities intermediary.

(d) Sections 8-504 through 8-508 do not require a securities intermediary to take any action that is prohibited by other statute, regulation, or rule.

§ 8-510. Rights of Purchaser of Security Entitlement from Entitlement Holder.

(a) In a case not covered by the priority rules in Article 9 or the rules stated in subsection (c), an action based on an adverse claim to a financial asset or security entitlement, whether framed in conversion, replevin, constructive trust, equitable lien, or other theory, may not be asserted against a person who purchases a security entitlement, or an interest therein, from an entitlement holder if the purchaser gives value, does not have notice of the adverse claim, and obtains control.

(b) If an adverse claim could not have been asserted against an entitlement holder under § 8-502, the adverse claim cannot be asserted against a person who purchases a security entitlement, or an interest therein, from the entitlement holder.

(c) In a case not covered by the priority rules in Article 9, a purchaser for value of a security entitlement, or an interest therein, who obtains control has priority over a purchaser of a security entitlement, or an interest therein, who does not obtain control. Except as otherwise provided in subsection (d), purchasers who have control rank according to priority in time of:

(1) the purchaser's becoming the person for whom the securities account, in which the security entitlement is carried, is maintained, if the purchaser obtained control under § 8-106(d)(1);

(2) the securities intermediary's agreement to comply with the purchaser's entitlement orders with respect to security entitlements carried or to be carried in the securities account in which the security entitlement is carried, if the purchaser obtained control under § 8-106(d)(2); or

(3) if the purchaser obtained control through another person under § 8-106(d)(3), the time on which priority would be based under this subsection if the other person were the secured party.

(d) A securities intermediary as purchaser has priority over a conflicting purchaser who has control unless otherwise agreed by the securities intermediary.

§ 8-511. Priority Among Security Interests and Entitlement Holders.

(a) Except as otherwise provided in subsections (b) and (c), if a securities intermediary does not have sufficient interests in a particular financial asset to satisfy both its obligations to entitlement holders who have security entitlements to that financial asset and its obligation to a creditor of the securities intermediary who has a security interest in that financial asset, the claims of entitlement holders, other than the creditor, have priority over the claim of the creditor.

(b) A claim of a creditor of a securities intermediary who has a security interest in a financial asset held by a securities intermediary has priority over claims of the securities intermediary's entitlement holders who have security entitlements with respect to that financial asset if the creditor has control over the financial asset.

(c) If a clearing corporation does not have sufficient financial assets to satisfy both its obligations to entitlement holders who have security entitlements with respect to a financial asset and its obligation to a creditor of the clearing corporation who has a security interest in that financial asset, the claim of the creditor has priority over the claims of entitlement holders.

Part 6. Transition Provisions for Revised Article 8 and Conforming Amendments to Articles 1, 4, 5, 9, And 10

§ 8-601. Effective Date.

This [Act] takes effect ... .

§ 8-602. Repeals.

This [Act] repeals ... .

§ 8-603. Savings Clause.

(a) This [Act] does not affect an action or proceeding commenced before this [Act] takes effect.

(b) If a security interest in a security is perfected at the date this [Act] takes effect, and the action by which the security interest was perfected would suffice to perfect a security interest under this [Act], no further action is required to continue perfection. If a security interest in a security is perfected at the date this [Act] takes effect but the action by which the security interest was perfected would not suffice to perfect a security interest under this [Act], the security interest remains perfected for a period of four months after the effective date and continues perfected thereafter if appropriate action to perfect under this [Act] is taken within that period. If a security interest is perfected at the date this [Act] takes effect and the security interest can be perfected by filing under this [Act], a financing statement signed by the secured party instead of the debtor may be filed within that period to continue perfection or thereafter to perfect.

Uniform Voidable Transactions Act (2014)

Copyright © 2014 by National Conference of Commissioners on Uniform State Laws

Table of Contents

Uniform Voidable Transactions Act (2014)

§ 1. Definitions.

As used in this [Act]:

(1) "Affiliate" means:

(i) a person that directly or indirectly owns, controls, or holds with power to vote, 20 percent or more of the outstanding voting securities of the debtor, other than a person that holds the securities:

(A) as a fiduciary or agent without sole discretionary power to vote the securities; or

(B) solely to secure a debt, if the person has not in fact exercised the power to vote;

(ii) a corporation 20 percent or more of whose outstanding voting securities are directly or indirectly owned, controlled, or held with power to vote, by the debtor or a person that directly or indirectly owns, controls, or holds, with power to vote, 20 percent or more of the outstanding voting securities of the debtor, other than a person that holds the securities:

(A) as a fiduciary or agent without sole discretionary power to vote the securities; or

(B) solely to secure a debt, if the person has not in fact exercised the power to vote;

(iii) a person whose business is operated by the debtor under a lease or other agreement, or a person substantially all of whose assets are controlled by the debtor; or

(iv) a person that operates the debtor's business under a lease or other agreement or controls substantially all of the debtor's assets.

(2) "Asset" means property of a debtor, but the term does not include:

(i) property to the extent it is encumbered by a valid lien;

(ii) property to the extent it is generally exempt under nonbankruptcy law; or

(iii) an interest in property held in tenancy by the entireties to the extent it is not subject to process by a creditor holding a claim against only one tenant.

(3) "Claim", except as used in "claim for relief", means a right to payment, whether or not the right is reduced to judgment, liquidated, unliquidated, fixed, contingent, matured, unmatured, disputed, undisputed, legal, equitable, secured, or unsecured.

(4) "Creditor" means a person that has a claim.

(5) "Debt" means liability on a claim.

(6) "Debtor" means a person that is liable on a claim.

(7) "Electronic" means relating to technology having electrical, digital, magnetic, wireless, optical, electromagnetic, or similar capabilities.

(8) "Insider" includes:

   (i) if the debtor is an individual:

      (A) a relative of the debtor or of a general partner of the debtor;

      (B) a partnership in which the debtor is a general partner;

      (C) a general partner in a partnership described in clause (B); or

      (D) a corporation of which the debtor is a director, officer, or person in control;

   (ii) if the debtor is a corporation:

      (A) a director of the debtor;

      (B) an officer of the debtor;

      (C) a person in control of the debtor;

      (D) a partnership in which the debtor is a general partner;

      (E) a general partner in a partnership described in clause (D); or

      (F) a relative of a general partner, director, officer, or person in control of the debtor;

   (iii) if the debtor is a partnership:

      (A) a general partner in the debtor;

      (B) a relative of a general partner in, a general partner of, or a person in control of the debtor;

      (C) another partnership in which the debtor is a general partner;

      (D) a general partner in a partnership described in clause (C); or

      (E) a person in control of the debtor;

   (iv) an affiliate, or an insider of an affiliate as if the affiliate were the debtor; and

   (v) a managing agent of the debtor.

(9) "Lien" means a charge against or an interest in property to secure payment of a debt or performance of an obligation, and includes a security interest created by agreement, a judicial lien obtained by legal or equitable process or proceedings, a common-law lien, or a statutory lien.

(10) "Organization" means a person other than an individual.

(11) "Person" means an individual, estate, partnership, association, trust, business or nonprofit entity, public corporation, government or governmental subdivision, agency, or instrumentality, or other legal or commercial entity.

(12) "Property" means anything that may be the subject of ownership.

(13) "Record" means information that is inscribed on a tangible medium or that is stored in an electronic or other medium and is retrievable in perceivable form.

(14) "Relative" means an individual related by consanguinity within the third degree as determined by the common law, a spouse, or an individual related to a spouse within the third degree as so determined, and includes an individual in an adoptive relationship within the third degree.

(15) "Sign" means, with present intent to authenticate or adopt a record:

   (i) to execute or adopt a tangible symbol; or

   (ii) to attach to or logically associate with the record an electronic symbol, sound, or process.

(16) "Transfer" means every mode, direct or indirect, absolute or conditional, voluntary or involuntary, of disposing of or parting with an asset or an interest in an asset, and includes payment of money, release, lease, license, and creation of a lien or other encumbrance.

(17) "Valid lien" means a lien that is effective against the holder of a judicial lien subsequently obtained by legal or equitable process or proceedings.

§ 2. Insolvency.

(a) A debtor is insolvent if, at a fair valuation, the sum of the debtor's debts is greater than the sum of the debtor's assets.

(b) A debtor that is generally not paying the debtor's debts as they become due other than as a result of a bona fide dispute is presumed to be insolvent. The presumption imposes on the party against which the presumption is directed the burden of proving that the nonexistence of insolvency is more probable than its existence.

(c) Assets under this section do not include property that has been transferred, concealed, or removed with intent to hinder, delay, or defraud creditors or that has been transferred in a manner making the transfer voidable under this [Act].

(d) Debts under this section do not include an obligation to the extent it is secured by a valid lien on property of the debtor not included as an asset.

§ 3. Value.

(a) Value is given for a transfer or an obligation if, in exchange for the transfer or obligation, property is transferred or an antecedent debt is secured or satisfied, but value does not include an unperformed promise made otherwise than in the ordinary course of the promisor's business to furnish support to the debtor or another person.

(b) For the purposes of § 4(a)(2) and § 5, a person gives a reasonably equivalent value if the person acquires an interest of the debtor in an asset pursuant to a regularly conducted, noncollusive foreclosure sale or execution of a power of sale for the acquisition or disposition of the interest of the debtor upon default under a mortgage, deed of trust, or security agreement.

(c) A transfer is made for present value if the exchange between the debtor and the transferee is intended by them to be contemporaneous and is in fact substantially contemporaneous.

§ 4. Transfer or Obligation Voidable as to Present or Future Creditor.

(a) A transfer made or obligation incurred by a debtor is voidable as to a creditor, whether the creditor's claim arose before or after the transfer was made or the obligation was incurred, if the debtor made the transfer or incurred the obligation:

(1) with actual intent to hinder, delay, or defraud any creditor of the debtor; or

(2) without receiving a reasonably equivalent value in exchange for the transfer or obligation, and the debtor:

(i) was engaged or was about to engage in a business or a transaction for which the remaining assets of the debtor were unreasonably small in relation to the business or transaction; or

(ii) intended to incur, or believed or reasonably should have believed that the debtor would incur, debts beyond the debtor's ability to pay as they became due.

(b) In determining actual intent under subsection (a)(1), consideration may be given, among other factors, to whether:

(1) the transfer or obligation was to an insider;

(2) the debtor retained possession or control of the property transferred after the transfer;

(3) the transfer or obligation was disclosed or concealed;

(4) before the transfer was made or obligation was incurred, the debtor had been sued or threatened with suit;

(5) the transfer was of substantially all the debtor's assets;

(6) the debtor absconded;

(7) the debtor removed or concealed assets;

(8) the value of the consideration received by the debtor was reasonably equivalent to the value of the asset transferred or the amount of the obligation incurred;

(9) the debtor was insolvent or became insolvent shortly after the transfer was made or the obligation was incurred;

(10) the transfer occurred shortly before or shortly after a substantial debt was incurred; and

(11) the debtor transferred the essential assets of the business to a lienor that transferred the assets to an insider of the debtor.

(c) A creditor making a claim for relief under subsection (a) has the burden of proving the elements of the claim for relief by a preponderance of the evidence.

§ 5. Transfer or Obligation Voidable as to Present Creditor.

(a) A transfer made or obligation incurred by a debtor is voidable as to a creditor whose claim arose before the transfer was made or the obligation was incurred if the debtor made the transfer or incurred the obligation without receiving a reasonably equivalent value in exchange for the transfer or obligation and the debtor was insolvent at that time or the debtor became insolvent as a result of the transfer or obligation.

(b) A transfer made by a debtor is voidable as to a creditor whose claim arose before the transfer was made if the transfer was made to an insider for an antecedent debt, the debtor was insolvent at that time, and the insider had reasonable cause to believe that the debtor was insolvent.

(c) Subject to § 2(b), a creditor making a claim for relief under subsection (a) or (b) has the burden of proving the elements of the claim for relief by a preponderance of the evidence.

§ 6. When Transfer Is Made or Obligation Is Incurred.

For the purposes of this [Act]:

(1) a transfer is made:

(i) with respect to an asset that is real property other than a fixture, but including the interest of a seller or purchaser under a contract for the sale of the asset, when the transfer is so far perfected that a good-faith purchaser of the asset from the debtor against which applicable law permits the transfer to be perfected cannot acquire an interest in the asset that is superior to the interest of the transferee; and

(ii) with respect to an asset that is not real property or that is a fixture, when the transfer is so far perfected that a creditor on a simple contract cannot acquire a judicial lien otherwise than under this [Act] that is superior to the interest of the transferee;

(2) if applicable law permits the transfer to be perfected as provided in paragraph (1) and the transfer is not so perfected before the commencement of an action for relief under this [Act], the transfer is deemed made immediately before the commencement of the action;

(3) if applicable law does not permit the transfer to be perfected as provided in paragraph (1), the transfer is made when it becomes effective between the debtor and the transferee;

(4) a transfer is not made until the debtor has acquired rights in the asset transferred; and

(5) an obligation is incurred:

(i) if oral, when it becomes effective between the parties; or

(ii) if evidenced by a record, when the record signed by the obligor is delivered to or for the benefit of the obligee.

§ 7. Remedies of Creditor.

(a) In an action for relief against a transfer or obligation under this [Act], a creditor, subject to the limitations in § 8, may obtain:

(1) avoidance of the transfer or obligation to the extent necessary to satisfy the creditor's claim;

(2) an attachment or other provisional remedy against the asset transferred or other property of the transferee if available under applicable law; and

(3) subject to applicable principles of equity and in accordance with applicable rules of civil procedure:

(i) an injunction against further disposition by the debtor or a transferee, or both, of the asset transferred or of other property;

(ii) appointment of a receiver to take charge of the asset transferred or of other property of the transferee; or

(iii) any other relief the circumstances may require.

(b) If a creditor has obtained a judgment on a claim against the debtor, the creditor, if the court so orders, may levy execution on the asset transferred or its proceeds.

§ 8. Defenses, Liability, and Protection of Transferee or Obligee.

(a) A transfer or obligation is not voidable under § 4(a)(1) against a person that took in good faith and for a reasonably equivalent value given the debtor or against any subsequent transferee or obligee.

(b) To the extent a transfer is avoidable in an action by a creditor under § 7(a)(1), the following rules apply:

(1) Except as otherwise provided in this section, the creditor may recover judgment for the value of the asset transferred, as adjusted under subsection (c), or the amount necessary to satisfy the creditor's claim, whichever is less. The judgment may be entered against:

(i) the first transferee of the asset or the person for whose benefit the transfer was made; or

(ii) an immediate or mediate transferee of the first transferee, other than:

(A) a good-faith transferee that took for value; or

(B) an immediate or mediate good-faith transferee of a person described in clause (A).

(2) Recovery pursuant to § 7(a)(1) or (b) of or from the asset transferred or its proceeds, by levy or otherwise, is available only against a person described in paragraph (1)(i) or (ii).

(c) If the judgment under subsection (b) is based upon the value of the asset transferred, the judgment must be for an amount equal to the value of the asset at the time of the transfer, subject to adjustment as the equities may require.

(d) Notwithstanding voidability of a transfer or an obligation under this [Act], a good-faith transferee or obligee is entitled, to the extent of the value given the debtor for the transfer or obligation, to:

(1) a lien on or a right to retain an interest in the asset transferred;

(2) enforcement of an obligation incurred; or

(3) a reduction in the amount of the liability on the judgment.

(e) A transfer is not voidable under § 4(a)(2) or § 5 if the transfer results from:

(1) termination of a lease upon default by the debtor when the termination is pursuant to the lease and applicable law; or

(2) enforcement of a security interest in compliance with Article 9 of the Uniform Commercial Code, other than acceptance of collateral in full or partial satisfaction of the obligation it secures.

(f) A transfer is not voidable under § 5(b):

(1) to the extent the insider gave new value to or for the benefit of the debtor after the transfer was made, except to the extent the new value was secured by a valid lien;

(2) if made in the ordinary course of business or financial affairs of the debtor and the insider; or

(3) if made pursuant to a good-faith effort to rehabilitate the debtor and the transfer secured present value given for that purpose as well as an antecedent debt of the debtor.

(g) The following rules determine the burden of proving matters referred to in this section:

(1) A party that seeks to invoke subsection (a), (d), (e), or (f) has the burden of proving the applicability of that subsection.

(2) Except as otherwise provided in paragraphs (3) and (4), the creditor has the burden of proving each applicable element of subsection (b) or (c).

(3) The transferee has the burden of proving the applicability to the transferee of subsection (b)(1)(ii)(A) or (B).

(4) A party that seeks adjustment under subsection (c) has the burden of proving the adjustment.

(h) The standard of proof required to establish matters referred to in this section is preponderance of the evidence.

§ 9. Extinguishment of Claim for Relief.

A claim for relief with respect to a transfer or obligation under this [Act] is extinguished unless action is brought:

(a) under § 4(a)(1), not later than four years after the transfer was made or the obligation was incurred or, if later, not later than one year after the transfer or obligation was or could reasonably have been discovered by the claimant;

(b) under § 4(a)(2) or 5(a), not later than four years after the transfer was made or the obligation was incurred; or

(c) under § 5(b), not later than one year after the transfer was made.

§ 10. Governing Law.

(a) In this section, the following rules determine a debtor's location:

(1) A debtor who is an individual is located at the individual's principal residence.

(2) A debtor that is an organization and has only one place of business is located at its place of business.

(3) A debtor that is an organization and has more than one place of business is located at its chief executive office.

(b) A claim for relief in the nature of a claim for relief under this [Act] is governed by the local law of the jurisdiction in which the debtor is located when the transfer is made or the obligation is incurred.

§ 11. Application to Series Organization.

(a) In this section:

(1) "Protected series" means an arrangement, however denominated, created by a series organization that, pursuant to the law under which the series organization is organized, has the characteristics set forth in paragraph (2).

(2) "Series organization" means an organization that, pursuant to the law under which it is organized, has the following characteristics:

(i) The organic record of the organization provides for creation by the organization of one or more protected series, however denominated, with respect to specified property of the organization, and for records to be maintained for each protected series that identify the property of or associated with the protected series.

(ii) Debt incurred or existing with respect to the activities of, or property of or associated with, a particular protected series is enforceable against the property of or associated with the protected series only, and not against the property of or associated with the organization or other protected series of the organization.

(iii) Debt incurred or existing with respect to the activities or property of the organization is enforceable against the property of the organization only, and not against the property of or associated with a protected series of the organization.

(b) A series organization and each protected series of the organization is a separate person for purposes of this [Act], even if for other purposes a protected series is not a person separate from the organization or other protected series of the organization.

Legislative Note: *This section should be enacted even if the enacting jurisdiction does not itself have legislation enabling the creation of protected series. For example, in such an enacting jurisdiction this section will apply if a protected series of a series organization organized under the law of a different jurisdiction makes a transfer to another protected series of that organization and, under applicable choice of law rules, the voidability of the transfer is governed by the law of the enacting jurisdiction.*

§ 12. Supplementary Provisions.

Unless displaced by the provisions of this [Act], the principles of law and equity, including the law merchant and the law relating to principal and agent, estoppel, laches, fraud, misrepresentation, duress, coercion, mistake, insolvency, or other validating or invalidating cause, supplement its provisions.

§ 13. Uniformity of Application and Construction.

This [Act] shall be applied and construed to effectuate its general purpose to make uniform the law with respect to the subject of this [Act] among states enacting it.

§ 14. Relation to Electronic Signatures in Global and National Commerce Act.

This [Act] modifies, limits, or supersedes the Electronic Signatures in Global and National Commerce Act, 15 U.S.C. § 7001 et seq., but does not modify, limit, or supersede § 101(c) of that act, 15 U.S.C. § 7001(c), or authorize electronic delivery of any of the notices described in § 103(b) of that act, 15 U.S.C. § 7003(b).

§ 15. Short Title.

This [Act], which was formerly cited as the Uniform Fraudulent Transfer Act, may be cited as the Uniform Voidable Transactions Act.

§ 16. Repeals; Conforming Amendments.

(a) . . . .

(b) . . . .

(c) . . . .

Legislative Note: The legislation enacting the 2014 amendments in a jurisdiction in which the act is already in force should provide as follows: (i) the amendments apply to a transfer made or obligation incurred on or after the effective date of the enacting legislation, (ii) the amendments do not apply to a transfer made or obligation incurred before the effective date of the enacting legislation, (iii) the amendments do not apply to a right of action that has accrued before the effective date of the enacting legislation, and (iv) for the foregoing purposes a transfer is made and an obligation is incurred at the time provided in Section 6 of the act. In addition, the enacting legislation should revise any reference to the act by its former title in other permanent legislation of the enacting jurisdiction.

Made in the USA
Middletown, DE
08 September 2021